BEST SELLER

For 2025 Exam

OSWAAL BOOKS®
LEARNING MADE SIMPLE

UPDATED AS PER
RELEASED ON 22ND MAR 2024
LATEST CBSE SYLLABUS

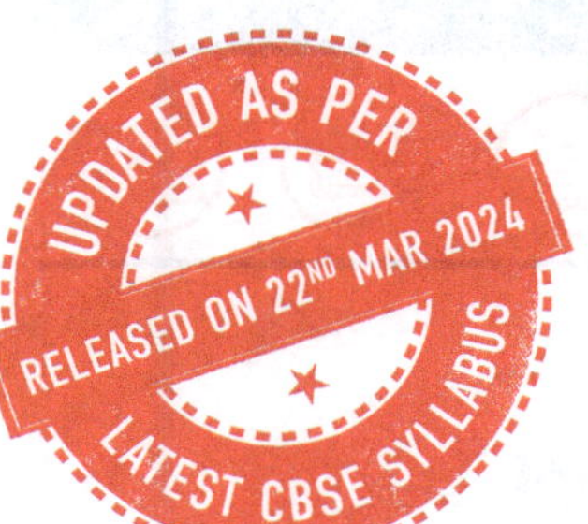

CBSE QUESTION BANK

Chapterwise & Topicwise

SOLVED PAPERS

CLASS 12

BUSINESS STUDIES

Strictly as per the Latest CBSE Circulars & Syllabus released on 22nd March and 3rd April 2024 (CBSE Cir. No. Acad-29/2024; 30/2024)

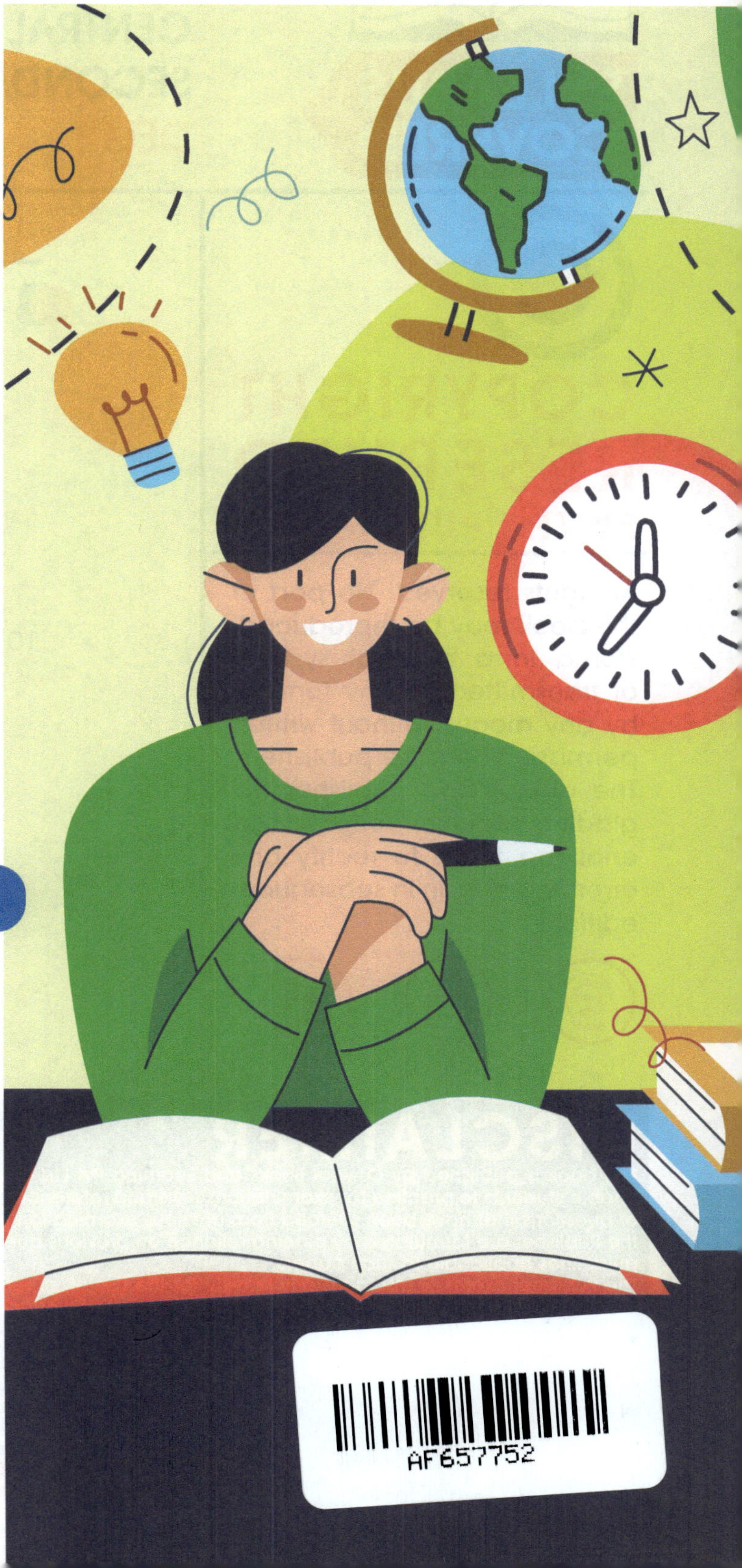

Get the #OswaalEdge

1. **100% Updated** with Latest Syllabus, Additional Practice Papers & Fully Solved Papers issued by Board
2. **Timed Revision** with Crisp Revision Notes, Smart Mind Maps & Mnemonics
3. **Extensive Practice** with Practice Papers, 3000+ Questions & Board Marking Scheme Answers **(2015-2024)**
4. **Concept Clarity** with 1000+ Concepts & 50+ Concept Videos
5. **100% as per NEP 2020** with Art Integration & Competency Based Questions

AF657752

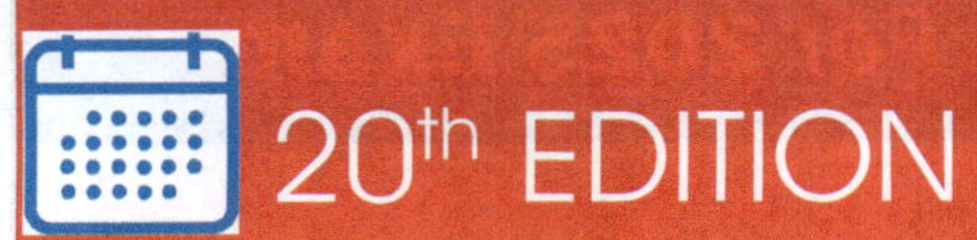

20th EDITION

YEAR 2024-25

ISBN "9789359584560"

SYLLABUS COVERED

CENTRAL BOARD OF SECONDARY EDUCATION

DELHI

PUBLISHED BY

OSWAAL BOOKS & LEARNING PVT. LTD.

1/11, Sahitya Kunj, M.G. Road,
Agra - 282002, (UP) India

1010, Cambourne Business Centre
Cambridge, Cambridgeshire
CB 236DP, United Kingdom

0562-2857671

contact@oswaalbooks.com

www.OswaalBooks.com

Printed at Repro India Ltd.

Contents

In each chapter, for better comprehension, questions have been categorized according to the typology issued by CBSE as follows : **R** - Remembering, **U** - Understanding, **Ap** - Applying, **AE** - Analyzing & Evaluating, **C** - Creating.

Abbreviations used - **[AI]** Academic Intelligence
[OEB] Oswaal Editorial Board

UNIT-I: PRINCIPLES AND FUNCTIONS OF MANAGEMENT

UNIT-II: BUSINESS FINANCE AND MARKETING

How to use this Book

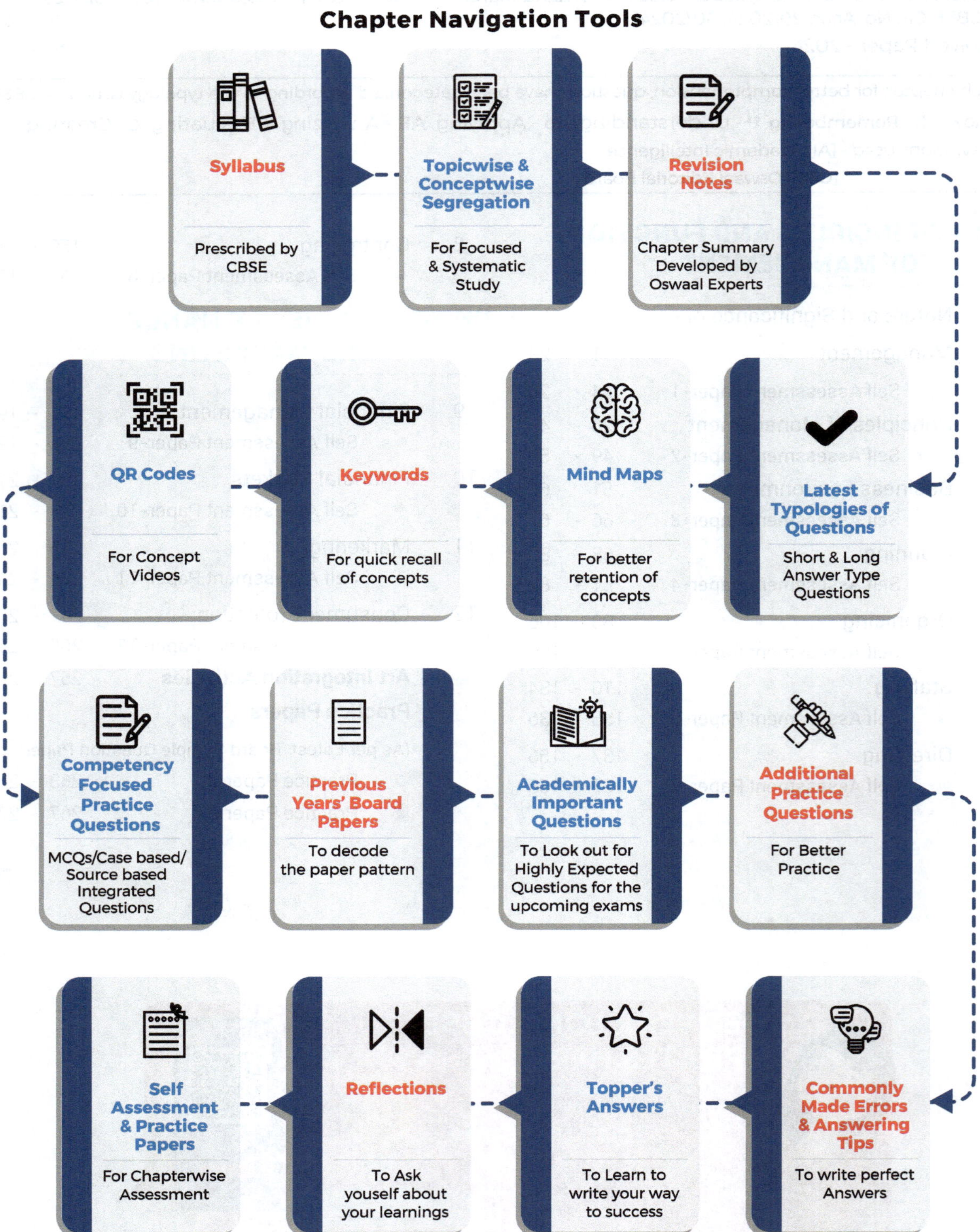

Preface

Elevate Your Performance, Surpassing the Past

Get ready for another epic journey through the academic wonders of the academic year 2024-2025 with your trustworthy companion—Oswaal Books! Remember last year's triumphs? Well, buckle up because we are about to make this year even more awesome!

As the legendary dancer Martha Graham once said, **"Practice means to perform, repeatedly in the face of all obstacles, some act of vision, of faith, of desire."** We have taken this wisdom to heart and packed it into our brand-new Question Banks for 2024-2025. They are a magical mix of CBSE Board Updates, cool questions from the past, and specially crafted ones tailored to the Latest Typologies. Oh, and did we mention the fantastic Learning Resources that come with them?

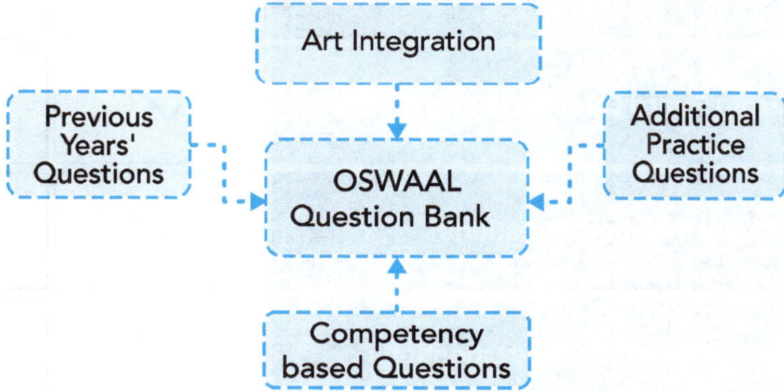

What makes these Question Banks truly exceptional?

- **100% Updated Syllabus & Fully Solved Board Papers:** We have got you covered with the latest and 100% updated curriculum
- **Crisp Revision with Topic-wise Revision Notes, Smart Mind Maps & Mnemonics:** Study smart, not hard!
- **Extensive Practice with 1050+ Questions & Board Marking Scheme Answers:** To give you 1050+ chances to become a champ!
- **Concept Clarity with 550+ Concepts & 50+ Concept Videos:** For you to learn the cool way—with videos and mind-blowing concepts
- **NEP 2020 Compliance with Art Integration & Competency-Based Questions:** For you to be on the cutting edge of the coolest educational trends.

If you are looking to conquer every study challenge, these Question Banks are your secret weapon. It is like having a superhero ally for your exams! So, let's kick off this exciting journey, fill those learning gaps, and rock the year with ease and confidence.

Big shoutout to our superhero team—the Oswaal Editorial Board! They're the brains behind this incredible resource, working day and night just for you. And a massive thank you to you, our fellow Students, Parents & Teachers for your awesome inputs that make this book one-of-a-kind.

Wishing you all the best, superheroes-in-the-making! Strive for greatness! Team Oswaal Books

Why Oswaal Question Bank is your Ultimate Board Companion?

Exam Oriented Content	Oswaal Books	CBSE
Previous Years' Exam Questions	✓	✓
Previous Years' Board Sample Questions	✓	✓
Questions from Board Question Bank	✓	✓
Board Additional Practice Questions	✓	✓
Competency Focused Practice Questions	✓	✓
Question from Curriculum Aligned Competency based Test Items	✓	✓
Board Marking Scheme Answers	✓	✓
Answering Tips & Commonly Made Errors	✓	X
Mnemonics, Key Terms & Concept Applied	✓	X

केन्द्रीय माध्यमिक शिक्षा बोर्ड
(शिक्षा मंत्रालय भारत सरकार के अधीन एक स्वायत्त संगठन)

CENTRAL BOARD OF SECONDARY EDUCATION
(An Autonomous Organisation Under the Ministry of Education, Govt. of India)

CBSE/ACADEMIC/JS(SG)/2024/ — **3rd April, 2024**

Circular No. Acad-30/2024

All the Heads of Schools affiliated to CBSE

Subject : Assessment and Evaluation Practices of the Board for the Session 2024-25.

- The Board in accordance with National Education Policy, 2020 has taken multiple steps towards implementation of Competency Based Education in schools, ranging from aligning assessment to competencies, development of exemplar resources for teachers and students as well as continuous capacity building of the teachers etc. The main emphasis of the Board was to create an educational ecosystem that would move away from rote memorization and towards learning that is focused on developing the creative, critical and systems thinking capacities of students to meet the challenges of the 21st century.

- The Board has released guidelines vide Circular No. Acad- 05/2019 dated 18.01.2019; Circular No. Acad-11/2019 dated 06.03.2019; Circular No. Acad-18/2020 dated 16.03.2020; and Circular No. Acad-57/2022 dated 20.05.2022 to progressively align assessment to the vision of the NEP by including more competency-based questions in the Classes X and XII Board examinations.

- Appropriately, the Board is continuing with aligning of the assessments and evaluation practices with NEP- 2020 for the academic session 2024-2025. Consequently, in the forthcoming session, the percentage of Competency Based Questions that assess application of concepts in real-life situations included in the question papers of the Board is given as under:

(Dr. Joseph Emmanuel)
Director (Academics)

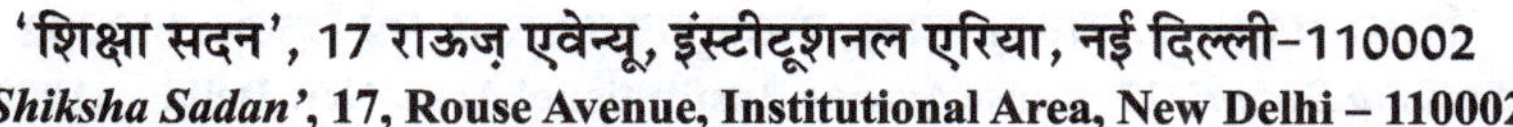

'शिक्षा सदन', 17 राऊज़ एवेन्यू, इंस्टीटूशनल एरिया, नई दिल्ली-110002
'Shiksha Sadan', 17, Rouse Avenue, Institutional Area, New Delhi – 110002
फोन/Telephone: 011-23212603 वेबसाइट/Website:http://cbseacademic.nic.in मेल/e-mail: directoracad.cbse@nic.in.

CBSE CIRCULAR 2024-25

केन्द्रीय माध्यमिक शिक्षा बोर्ड
(शिक्षा मंत्रालय भारत सरकार के अधीन एक स्वायत्त संगठन)

CENTRAL BOARD OF SECONDARY EDUCATION
(An Autonomous Organisation Under the Ministry of Education, Govt. of India)

The changes for classes IX-XII year-end Board Examinations (2024-25)

(Classes IX-X)		
Particulars	**Academic Session 2023-24**	**Academic Session 2024-25** **(No change from previous academic session)**
Composition of question paper for year-end examination/ Board Examination (Theory)	• Competency Focused Questions in the form of MCQs/ Case Based Questions, Source-based Integrated Questions or any other type = 50% • Select response type questions (MCQ) = 20% • Constructed response questions (Short Answer/Long Answer Type Questions, as per existing pattern) = 30%	• Competency Focused Questions in the form of MCQs/Case Based Questions, Source-based Integrated Questions or any other type = 50% • Select response type questions (MCQ) = 20% • Constructed response questions (Short Answer/Long Answer Type Questions, as per existing pattern) = 30%
(Classes IX-XII)		
Particulars	**Academic Session 2023-24**	**Academic Session 2024-25**
Composition of question paper for year-end examination/ Board Examination (Theory)	• Competency Focused Questions in the form of MCQs/ Case Based Questions, Source-based Integrated Questions or any other type = 40% • Select response type questions (MCQ) = 20% • Constructed response questions (Short Answer Questions/Long Answer type Questions, as per existing pattern) = 40%	• Competency Focused Questions in the form of MCQs/ Case Based Questions, Source-based Integrated Questions or any other type = 50% • Select response type questions (MCQ) = 20% • Constructed response questions (Short Answer Questions/Long Answer type Questions, as per existing pattern) = 30%

Curriculum document released by the Board for the Academic Session 2024-25 and the Sample Question Papers may also be referred to for details of the QP design of individual subjects. Learning frameworks for various subjects for classes IX-XII are available at the link https://cbseacademic.nic.in for reference.

(Dr. Joseph Emmanuel)
Director (Academics)

'शिक्षा सदन', 17 राऊज़ एवेन्यू, इंस्टीटूशनल एरिया, नई दिल्ली–110002
'Shiksha Sadan', 17, Rouse Avenue, Institutional Area, New Delhi – 110002

फोन/Telephone: 011-23212603 वेबसाइट/Website:http://cbseacademic.nic.in मेल/e-mail: directoracad.cbse@nic.in.

CBSE Circular 2024-25

केन्द्रीय माध्यमिक शिक्षा बोर्ड

(शिक्षा मंत्रालय भारत सरकार के अधीन एक स्वायत्त संगठन)

CENTRAL BOARD OF SECONDARY EDUCATION

(An Autonomous Organisation Under the Ministry of Education, Govt. of India)

F.1001/CBSE-Acad/Curriculum/2024 **March 22, 2024**

Cir No: Acad-29/2024

All Heads of Institutions affiliated to CBSE

Subject : Secondary and Senior School Curriculum for the session 2024-25 and new textbooks to be published by NCERT for classes III and VI.

1. CBSE provides the annual curriculum for classes IX to XII containing academic content, syllabus for examinations with learning outcomes, pedagogical practices, and assessment guidelines.
2. It is imperative for schools to ensure adherence to the curriculum directives outlined in the initial pages of the curriculum document. Subjects should be taught in accordance with the prescribed curriculum, incorporating methodologies such as Multilingualism, Art-Integrated Education, Experiential Learning, and Pedagogical Plans, wherever feasible.
3. With the adoption of the National Curriculum Framework for School Education - 2023 by CBSE, schools are advised to align their practices with the recommendations delineated in NCF-SE-2023. This includes adherence to guidelines concerning content, pedagogical strategies, assessment methodologies, and other pertinent areas as communicated by the Board from time to time.
4. The National Council of Educational Research and Training (NCERT) has informed CBSE through a letter dated 18.03.2024 that new syllabi and textbooks for Grades 3 and 6 are currently under development and will soon be released. Consequently, Schools are advised to follow these new syllabi and textbooks for classes 3 and 6 in place of textbooks published by NCERT till the year 2023. Additionally, a bridge course for class 6, and concise guidelines for class 3 are being developed by NCERT for facilitating a seamless transition for students to new pedagogical practices and areas of study aligned with NCF-SE 2023. These resources will be disseminated to all the schools online once they are received from NCERT. The Board will also organize capacity building programs for School Heads and Teachers to orient them with the new teaching learning perspectives as envisioned in NEP-2020.
5. There will be no change in the Curriculum and textbooks for other classes for the academic year 2024-25 commencing from 1st April 2024.
6. Schools are requested to share the Curriculum 2024-25 available on Boards website www. cbseacademic.nic.in with all students and teachers. CBSE Curriculum for classes IX-XII 2024-25 can be accessed at the link-Secondary & Senior Secondary School Curriculum https://cbseacademic.nic.in/curriculum_2025.html .

(Dr. Joseph Emmanuel)
Director (Academics)

'शिक्षा सदन', 17 राऊज़ एवेन्यू, इंस्टीटूशनल एरिया, नई दिल्ली-110002
'Shiksha Sadan', 17, Rouse Avenue, Institutional Area, New Delhi – 110002

फोन/Telephone: 011-23212603 वेबसाइट/Website:http://cbseacademic.nic.in मेल/e-mail: directoracad.cbse@nic.in.

Syllabus 2024-25

BUSINESS STUDIES (Code No. 054)
CLASS–XII

Theory : 80 Marks **Time : 3 Hours**
Project : 20 Marks

Units		Periods	Marks
Part A	**PRINCIPLES AND FUNCTIONS OF MANAGEMENT**		
1.	Nature and Significance of Management	12	16
2.	Principles of Management	14	
3.	Business Environment	12	
4.	Planning	14	14
5.	Organising	15	
6.	Staffing	16	20
7.	Directing	15	
8.	Controlling	12	
	Total	**110**	**50**
Part B	**BUSINESS FINANCE AND MARKETING**		
9.	Financial Management	20	15
10.	Financial Markets	18	
11.	Marketing Management	30	15
12.	Consumer Protection	12	
	Total	**80**	**30**
Part C	**PROJECT WORK (ONE)**	**30**	**20**

Part A: Principles and Functions of Management

Unit 1 : Nature and Significance of Management

Concept	After going through this unit, the student/ learner would be able to :
Management-concept, objectives and importance	• Understand the concept of management. • Explain the meaning of 'Effectiveness and Efficiency'. • Discuss the objectives of management. • Describe the importance of management.
Management as Science, Art and Profession	• Examine the nature of management as a science, art and profession.
Levels of Management	• Understand the role of top, middle and lower levels of management.
Management functions - planning, organizing, staffing, directing and controlling	• Explain the functions of management.
Coordination- concept and importance	• Discuss the concept and characteristics of coordination. • Explain the importance of coordination.

Unit 2 : Principles of Management

Principles of Management- concept and significance.	• Understand the concept of principles of management. • Explain the significance of management principles.
Fayol's principles of management	• Discuss the principles of management developed by Fayol.

Taylor's Scientific Management - principles and techniques	• Explain the principles and techniques of 'Scientific Management'. • Compare the contributions of Fayol and Taylor.

Unit 3 : Business Environment

Business Environment- concept and importance	• Understand the concept of 'Business Environment'. • Describe the importance of Business environment.
Dimensions of Business Environment- Economic, Social, Technological, Political and Legal Demonetization - concept and features	• Describe the various dimensions of 'Business Environment'. • Understand the concept of demonetization.

Unit 4: Planning

Planning: Concept, importance and limitation	• Understand the concept of planning. • Describe the importance of planning. • Understand the limitations of planning.
Planning process	• Describe the steps in the process of planning.
Single use and Standing Plans. Objectives, Strategy, Policy, Procedure, Method, Rule, Budget and Programme	• Develop an understanding of single use and standing plans. • Describe objectives, policies, strategy, procedure, method, rule, budget and programme as types of plans.

Unit 5 : Organising

Organising: Concept and importance	• Understand the concept of organizing as a structure and as a process. • Explain the importance of organising.
Organising Process	• Describe the steps in the process of organising.
Structure of organisation- functional and divisional concept. Formal and informal organization - concept	• Describe functional and divisional structures of organisation. • Explain the advantages, disadvantages and suitability of functional and divisional structure. • Understand the concept of formal and informal organisation. • Discuss the advantages and disadvantages of formal and informal organisation.
Delegation : concept, elements and importance	• Understand the concept of delegation. • Describe the elements of delegation. • Appreciate the importance of Delegation.
Decentralisation: concept and importance	• Understand the concept of decentralisation. • Explain the importance of decentralisation. • Differentiate between delegation and decentralisation.

Unit 6 : Staffing

Staffing: Concept and importance of staffing	• Understand the concept of staffing. • Explain the importance of staffing.
Staffing as a part of Human Resource Management concept	• Understand the specialized duties and activities performed by Human Resource Management.
Staffing process	• Describe the steps in the process of staffing.

Recruitment Process	• Understand the meaning of recruitment. • Discuss the sources of recruitment. • Explain the merits and demerits of internal and external sources of recruitment.
Selection – process	• Understand the meaning of selection. • Describe the steps involved in the process of selection.
Training and Development- concept and importance, methods of training- on the job and off the job - vestibule training, apprenticeship training and internship training	• Understand the concept of training and development. • Appreciate the importance of training to the organisation and to the employees. • Discuss the meaning of induction training, vestibule training, apprenticeship training and internship training. • Differentiate between training and development. • Discuss on the job and off the job methods of training.

Unit 7 : Directing

Directing: Concept and importance	• Describe the concept of directing. • Discuss the importance of directing.
Elements of Directing	• Describe the various elements of directing.
Motivation - concept, Maslow's hierarchy of needs, financial and non-financial incentives	• Understand the concept of motivation. • Develop an understanding of Maslow's hierarchy of needs. • Discuss the various financial and non-financial incentives.
Leadership- concept, styles- authoritative, democratic and laissez faire	• Understand the concept of leadership. • Understand the various styles of leadership.
Communication- concept, formal and informal communication; barriers to effective communication, how to overcome the barriers	• Understand the concept of communication. • Understand the elements of the communication process. • Discuss the concept of formal and informal communication. • Discuss the various barriers to effective communication. • Suggest measures to overcome barriers to communication.

Unit 8 : Controlling

Controlling - concept and importance	• Understand the concept of controlling. • Explain the importance of controlling.
Relationship between planning and controlling	• Describe the relationship between planning and controlling.
Steps in process of control	• Discuss the steps in the process of controlling.

Part B: Business Finance and Marketing

Unit 9 : Financial Management

Financial Management: Concept, role and objectives	• Understand the concept of financial management. • Explain the role of financial management in an organisation. • Discuss the objectives of financial management.
Financial decisions: investment, financing and dividend - meaning and factors affecting	• Discuss the three financial decisions and the factors affecting them.

Financial Planning- concept and importance	• Describe the concept of financial planning and its objectives. • Explain the importance of financial planning.
Capital Structure – concept and factors affecting capital structure	• Understand the concept of capital structure. • Describe the factors determining the choice of an appropriate capital structure of a company.
Fixed and Working Capital - concept and factors affecting their requirements	• Understand the concept of fixed and working capital. • Describe the factors determining the requirements of fixed and working capital.

Unit 10 : Financial Markets

Financial Markets: Concept	• Understand the concept of financial market.
Money Market: Concept	• Understand the concept of money market.
Capital market and its types (primary and secondary)	• Discuss the concept of capital market. • Explain primary and secondary markets as types of capital market. • Differentiate between capital market and money market. • Distinguish between primary and secondary markets.
Stock Exchange - functions and trading procedure	• Give the meaning of a stock exchange. • Explain the functions of a stock exchange. • Discuss the trading procedure in a stock exchange. • Give the meaning of depository services and demat account as used in the trading procedure of securities.
Securities and Exchange Board of India (SEBI)-objectives and functions	• State the objectives of SEBI. • Explain the functions of SEBI.

Unit 11 : Marketing

Marketing – Concept, functions and philosophies	• Understand the concept of marketing. • Explain the features of marketing. • Discuss the functions of marketing. • Explain the marketing philosophies.
Marketing Mix – Concept and elements	• Understand the concept of marketing mix. • Describe the elements of marketing mix.
Product - branding, labelling and packaging – Concept	• Understand the concept of product as an element of marketing mix. • Understand the concept of branding, labelling and packaging.
Price - Concept, factors determining price	• Understand the concept of price as an element of marketing mix. • Describe the factors determining price of a product.
Physical Distribution – Concept, components and channels of distribution	• Understand the concept of physical distribution. • Explain the components of physical distribution. • Describe the various channels of distribution.

Promotion – Concept and elements; Advertising, Personal Selling, Sales Promotion and Public Relations	• Understand the concept of promotion as an element of marketing mix. • Describe the elements of promotion mix. • Understand the concept of advertising. • Understand the concept of sales promotion. • Discuss the concept of public relations.

Unit 12 : Consumer Protection

Consumer Protection: Concept and importance	• Understand the concept of consumer protection. • Describe the importance of consumer protection. • Discuss the scope of Consumer Protection Act, 2019.
The Consumer Protection Act, 2019: *Source:* http://egazette.nic.in/WriteReadData/2019/210422.pdf Meaning of consumer Rights and responsibilities of consumers Who can file a complaint? Redressal machinery Remedies available	• Understand the concept of a consumer according to the Consumer Protection Act, 2019. • Explain the consumer rights. • Understand the responsibilities of consumers. • Understand who can file a complaint and against whom? • Discuss the legal redressal machinery under Consumer Protection Act, 2019. • Examine the remedies available to the consumer under Consumer Protection Act, 2019.
Consumer awareness - Role of consumer organizations and Non-Governmental Organizations (NGOs)	• Describe the role of consumer organizations and NGOs in protecting consumers' interests.

Unit 13 : Project Work

PROJECT WORK IN BUSINESS STUDIES FOR CLASS XI AND XII

Introduction

The course in Business Studies is introduced at Senior School level to provide students with a sound understanding of the principles and practices bearing in business (trade and industry) as well as their relationship with the society. Business is a dynamic process that brings together technology, natural resources and human initiative in a constantly changing global environment. With the purpose to help them understand the framework within which a business operates, and its interaction with the social, economic, technological and legal environment, the CBSE has introduced Project Work in the Business Studies Syllabus for Classes XI and XII. The projects have been designed to allow students to appreciate that business is an integral component of society and help them develop an understanding of the social and ethical issues concerning them.

The project work also aims to empower the teacher to relate all the concepts with what is happening around the world and the student's surroundings, making them appear more clear and contextual. This will enable the student to enjoy studies and use his free time effectively in observing what's happening around.

By means of Project Work the students are exposed to life beyond textbooks giving them opportunities to refer materials, gather information, analyze it further to obtain relevant information and decide what matter to keep.

Objectives

After doing the Project Work in Business Studies, the students will be able to do the following:

- develop a practical approach by using modern technologies in the field of business and management;
- get an opportunity for exposure to the operational environment in the field of business management and related services;
- inculcate important skills of team work, problem solving, time management, information collection, processing, analysing and synthesizing relevant information to derive meaningful conclusions
- get involved in the process of research work; demonstrate his or her capabilities while working independently and
- make studies an enjoyable experience to cherish.

CLASS XII : GUIDELINES FOR TEACHERS

Syllabus 2024-25

Students are supposed to select one unit out of four and are required to make only ONE project from the selected unit. (Consist of one project of 20 marks)

1. Help students to select any ONE Topic for the entire year.
2. The topic should be assigned after discussion with the students in the class and should then be discussed at every stage of the submission of the project.

The teacher should play the role of a facilitator and should closely supervise the process of project completion. The teachers must ensure that the project work assigned to the students whether individually or in group are discussed at different stages right from assignment to drafts review and finalization. Students should be facilitated in terms of providing relevant materials or suggesting websites, or obtaining required permissions from business houses, malls etc for their project. The periods assigned to the Project Work should be suitably spaced throughout the academic session. The teachers MUST ensure that the student actually go through the rigors and enjoy the process of doing the project rather than depending on any readymade material available outside.

3. The students must make a presentation of the project before the class.
4. The teachers must ensure that the student's self-esteem and creativity is enhanced and both the teacher and the student enjoy this process.
5. The teachers should feel pride in the fact that they have explored the different dimensions of the project in an innovative way and their students have put in genuine work.

I. Project One: Elements of Business Environment

The teachers should help the students in selecting any one element of the following:

1. Changes witnessed over the last few years on mode of packaging and its economic impact. The teacher may guide the students to identify the following changes:
   (a) The changes in transportation of fruits and vegetables such as cardboard crates being used in place of wooden crates, etc. Reasons for above changes.
   (b) Milk being supplied in glass bottles, later in plastic bags and now in tetra-pack and through vending machines.
   (c) Plastic furniture [doors and stools] gaining preference over wooden furniture.
   (d) The origin of cardboard and the various stages of changes and growth.
   (e) Brown paper bags packing to recycled paper bags to plastic bags and cloth bags.
   (f) Re use of packaging [bottles, jars and tins] to attract customers for their products.
   (g) The concept of pyramid packaging for milk.
   (h) Cost being borne by the consumer/ manufacturer.
   (i) Packaging used as means of advertisements.
2. The reasons behind changes in the following: Coca – Cola and Fanta in the seventies to Thums up and Campa Cola in the eighties to Pepsi and Coke in nineties.
   The teacher may guide the students to the times when India sold Coca Cola and Fanta which were being manufactured in India by the foreign companies.
   The students may be asked to enquire about :
   (a) Reasons of stopping the manufacturing of the above mentioned drinks in India THEN.
   (b) The introduction of Thums up and Campa Cola range.
   (c) Re entry of Coke and introduction of Pepsi in the Indian market.
   (d) Factors responsible for the change.
   (e) Other linkages with the above.
   (f) Leading brands and the company having the highest market share.
   (g) Different local brands venturing in the Indian market.
   (h) The rating of the above brands in the market.
   (i) The survival and reasons of failure in competition with the international brands.
   (j) Other observations made by the students

The teacher may develop the following on the above lines :

3. Changing role of the women in the past 25 years relating to joint families, nuclear families, women as a bread earner of the family, changes in the requirement trend of mixers, washing machines, micro wave and standard of living.
4. The changes in the pattern of import and export of different products.
5. The trend in the changing interest rates and their effect on savings.
6. A study on child labour laws, its implementation and consequences.
7. The state of 'anti plastic campaign,' the law, its effects and implementation.
8. The laws of mining /setting up of industries, rules and regulations, licences required for running that business.
9. Social factors affecting acceptance and rejection of an identified product. (Dish washer, Atta maker, etc)

10. What has the effect of change in environment on the types of goods and services?

The students can take examples like:

(a) Washing machines, micro waves, mixers and grinders.

(b) Need for crèche, day care centre for young and old.

(c) Ready to eat food, eating food outside and tiffin centres.

11. Change in the man-machine ratio with technological advances resulting in change of cost structure.

12. Effect of changes in technological environment on the behaviour of employees.

II. Project Two: Principles of Management

Students are required to visit any one of the following:

1. A departmental store.
2. An Industrial unit.
3. A fast food outlet.
4. Any other organisation approved by the teacher.

They are required to observe the application of the general principles of management advocated by Fayol.

Fayol's principles :

1. Division of work
2. Unity of command
3. Unity of direction
4. Scalar chain
5. Espirit de corps
6. Fair remuneration to all
7. Order
8. Equity
9. Discipline
10. Subordination of individual interest to general interest
11. Initiative
12. Centralisation and decentralisation
13. Stability of tenure
14. Authority and Responsibility

OR

They may enquire into the application of scientific management techniques by F.W. Taylor in the unit visited.

Scientific techniques of management :

1. Functional foremanship
2. Standardisation and simplification of work
3. Method study
4. Motion Study
5. Time Study
6. Fatigue Study
7. Differential piece rate plan

Tips to teacher

(i) The teacher may organize this visit.

(ii) The teacher should facilitate the students to identify any unit of their choice and guide them to identify the principles that are being followed.

(iii) Similarly they should guide the students to identify the techniques of scientific management implemented in the organisation.

(iv) It may be done as a group activity.

(v) The observations could be on the basis of :

- The different stages of division of work resulting to specialisation.
- Following instructions and accountability of subordinates to higher authorities.
- Visibility of order and equity in the unit.
- Balance of authority and responsibility.
- Communication levels and pattern in the organisation.
- Methods and techniques followed by the organisation for unity of direction and coordination amongst all.
- Methods of wage payments followed. The arrangements of fatigue study.
- Derivation of time study.
- Derivation and advantages of method study.
- Organisational chart of functional foremanship.
- Any other identified in the organisation.

(vi) It is advised that students should be motivated to pick up different areas of visit. As presentations of different areas in the class would help in better understanding to the other students.

(vii) The students may be encouraged to develop worksheets. Teachers should help students to prepare observation tools to be used for undertaking the project.

Examples: worksheets, questionnaire, interviews and organisational chart etc.

III. Project Three: Stock Exchange

The purpose of this project is to teach school students the values of investing and utilising the stock market. This project also teaches important lessons about the economy, mathematics and financial responsibility.

The basis of this project is to learn about the stock market while investing a specified amount of fake money in certain stocks. Students then study the results and buy and sell as they see fit.

This project will also guide the students and provide them with the supplies necessary to successfully monitor stock market trends and will teach students how to calculate profit and loss on stock.

The project work will enable the students to:

- understand the topics like sources of business finance and capital market.
- understand the concepts used in stock exchange.
- inculcate the habit of watching business channels, reading business journals/ newspapers and seeking information from their elders.

The students are expected to:

- Develop a brief report on History of Stock Exchanges in India. (your country)
- Prepare a list of at least 25 companies listed on a Stock Exchange.
- To make an imaginary portfolio totalling a sum of ₹ 50,000 equally in any of the 5 companies of their choice listed above over a period of twenty working days.

The students may be required to report the prices of the stocks on daily basis and present it diagrammatically on the graph paper.

- They will understand the weekly holidays and the holidays under the Negotiable Instruments Act.
- They will also come across with terms like closing prices, opening prices, etc.
- During this period of recording students are supposed to distinctively record the daily and starting and closing prices of the week other days under the negotiable instrument act so that they acquire knowledge about closing and opening prices.
- The students may conclude by identifying the causes in the fluctuations of prices. Normally it would be related to the front page news of a business journal, for example,
  - Change of seasons
  - Festivals
  - Spread of epidemic
  - Strikes and accidents
  - Natural and human disasters
  - Political environment
  - Lack of faith in the government policies
  - Impact of changes in government policies for specific industry
  - International events
  - Contract and treaties at the international scene.
  - Relations with the neighbouring countries
  - Crisis in developed countries, etc.

The students are expected to find the value of their investments and accordingly rearrange their portfolio. The project work should cover the following aspects:

1. Graphical presentation of the share prices of different companies on different dates.
2. Change in market value of shares due to change of seasons, festivals, natural and human disasters.
3. Change in market value of shares due to change in political environment/ policies of various countries/crisis in developed countries or any other reasons
4. Identify the top ten companies out of the 25 selected on the basis of their market value of shares.

It does not matter if they have made profits or losses.

IV. Project Four: Marketing

1. Adhesives	2. Air conditioners
3. Baby diapers	4. Bathing Soap
5. Bathroom cleaner	6. Bike
7. Blanket	8. Body Spray
9. Bread	10. Breakfast cereal
11. Butter	12. Camera
13. Car	14. Cheese spreads
15. Chocolate	16. Coffee
17. Cosmetology product	18. Crayons
19. Crockery	20. Cutlery
21. Cycle	22. DTH
23. Eraser	24. e-wash
25. Fairness cream	26. Fans
27. Fruit candy	28. Furniture

29. Hair Dye
30. Hair Oil
31. Infant dress
32. Inverter
33. Jams
34. Jeans
35. Jewellery
36. Kurti
37. Ladies bag
38. Ladies footwear
39. Learning Toys
40. Lipstick
41. Microwave oven
42. Mixers
43. Mobile
44. Moisturizer
45. Music player
46. Nail polish
47. Newspaper
48. Noodles
49. Pen
50. Pen drive
51. Pencil
52. Pickles
53. Razor
54. Ready Soups
55. Refrigerator
56. RO system
57. Roasted snacks
58. Salt
59. Sarees
60. Sauces/ Ketchup
61. Shampoo
62. Shaving cream
63. Shoe polish
64. Shoes
65. Squashes
66. Suitcase/ airbag
67. Sunglasses
68. Tea
69. Tiffin Wallah
70. Toothpaste
71. Wallet
72. Washing detergent
73. Washing machine
74. Washing powder
75. Water bottle
76. Water storage tank
77. Wipes

Any more as suggested by the teacher.

The teacher must ensure that the identified product should not be items whose consumption/use is discouraged by the society and government like alcohol products/pan masala and tobacco products, etc.

Identify one product/service from the above which the students may like to manufacture/provide [pre-assumption].

Now the students are required to make a project on the identified product/service keeping in mind the following:

1. Why have they selected this product/service?
2. Find out '5' competitive brands that exist in the market.
3. What permission and licences would be required to make the product?
4. What are your competitors Unique Selling Proposition. [U.S.P.]?
5. Does your product have any range give details?
6. What is the name of your product?
7. Enlist its features.
8. Draw the 'Label' of your product.
9. Draw a logo for your product.
10. Draft a tag line.
11. What is the selling price of your competitor's product?
    (i) Selling price to consumer
    (ii) Selling price to retailer
    (iii) Selling price to wholesaler
    What is the profit margin in percentage to the:
    (i) Manufacturer.
    (ii) Wholesaler.
    (iii) Retailer.
12. How will your product be packaged?
13. Which channel of distribution are you going to use? Give reasons for selection?
14. Decisions related to warehousing, state reasons.
15. What is going to be your selling price?
    (i) To consumer
    (ii) To retailer

(iii) To wholesaler

16. List 5 ways of promoting your product.
17. Any schemes for:
    (i) The wholesaler
    (ii) The retailer
    (iii) The consumer
18. What is going to be your U.S.P?
19. What means of transport you will use and why?
20. Draft a social message for your label.
21. What cost effective techniques will you follow for your product.
22. What cost effective techniques will you follow for your promotion plan.

At this stage the students will realise the importance of the concept of marketing mix and the necessary decisions regarding the four P's of marketing.

(i) Product
(ii) Place
(iii) Price
(iv) Promotion

On the basis of the work done by the students the project report should include the following:

1. Type of product /service identified and the (consumer/industries) process involve there in.
2. Brand name and the product.
3. Range of the product.
4. Identification mark or logo.
5. Tagline.
6. Labelling and packaging.
7. Price of the product and basis of price fixation.
8. Selected channels of distribution and reasons thereof.
9. Decisions related to transportation and warehousing. State reasons.
10. Promotional techniques used and starting reasons for deciding the particular technique.
11. Grading and standardization.

Presentation and Submission of Project Report

At the end of the stipulated term, each student will prepare and submit his/her project report.
Following essentials are required to be fulfilled for its preparation and submission.

1. The total length of the project will be of 25 to 30 pages.
2. The project should be handwritten.
3. The project should be presented in a neat folder.
4. The project report should be developed in the following sequence :
    - Cover page should include the title of the Project, student information, school and year.
    - List of contents.
    - Acknowledgements and preface (acknowledging the institution, the places visited and the persons who have helped).
    - Introduction.
    - Topic with suitable heading.
    - Planning and activities done during the project, if any.
    - Observations and findings of the visit.
    - Conclusions (summarized suggestions or findings, future scope of study).
    - Photographs (if any).
    - Appendix
    - Teacher's observation.
    - Signatures of the teachers.
    - At the completion of the evaluation of the project, it should be punched in the centre so that the report may not be reused but is available for reference only.
    - The project will be returned after evaluation. The school may keep the best projects.

ASSESSMENT

Allocation of Marks **20 Marks**

The marks will be allocated under the following heads :

1.	Initiative, cooperativeness and participation	2 Mark
2.	Creativity in presentation	2 Mark
3.	Content, observation and research work	4 Marks
4.	Analysis of situations	4 Marks
5.	Viva	8 Marks
	Total	**20 Marks**

❑❑

SUGGESTED QUESTION PAPER DESIGN

Business Studies (Code No. 054)

Class XII

Duration: 3 Hours			Max. Marks: 80
S.No.	**Typology of Questions**	**Marks**	**Percentage**
1.	**Remembering and Understanding:** Exhibit memory of previously learned material by recalling facts, terms, basic concepts, and answers. Demonstrate understanding of facts and ideas by organizing, comparing, translating, interpreting, giving descriptions, and stating main ideas	44	55%
2.	**Applying :** Solve problems to new situations by applying acquired knowledge, facts, techniques and rules in a different way	19	23.75%
3.	**Analysing, Evaluating and Creating:** Examine and break information into parts by identifying motives or causes. Make inferences and find evidence to support generalizations. Present and defend opinions by making judgments about information, validity of ideas, or quality of work based on a set of criteria. Compile information together in a different way by combining elements in a new pattern or proposing alternative solutions..	17	21.25%
	Total	**80**	**100%**

How to Use Scratch Code?

Welcome to Oswaal Books innovative learning experience! With your scratch code, located on the back inner cover of your book, you can unlock access to comprehensive solutions by scanning the QR code provided at the end of each self-assessment paper & Practice Paper. Follow the step-by-step instructions outlined in the flowchart below, from accessing detailed explanations to reinforcing your understanding.

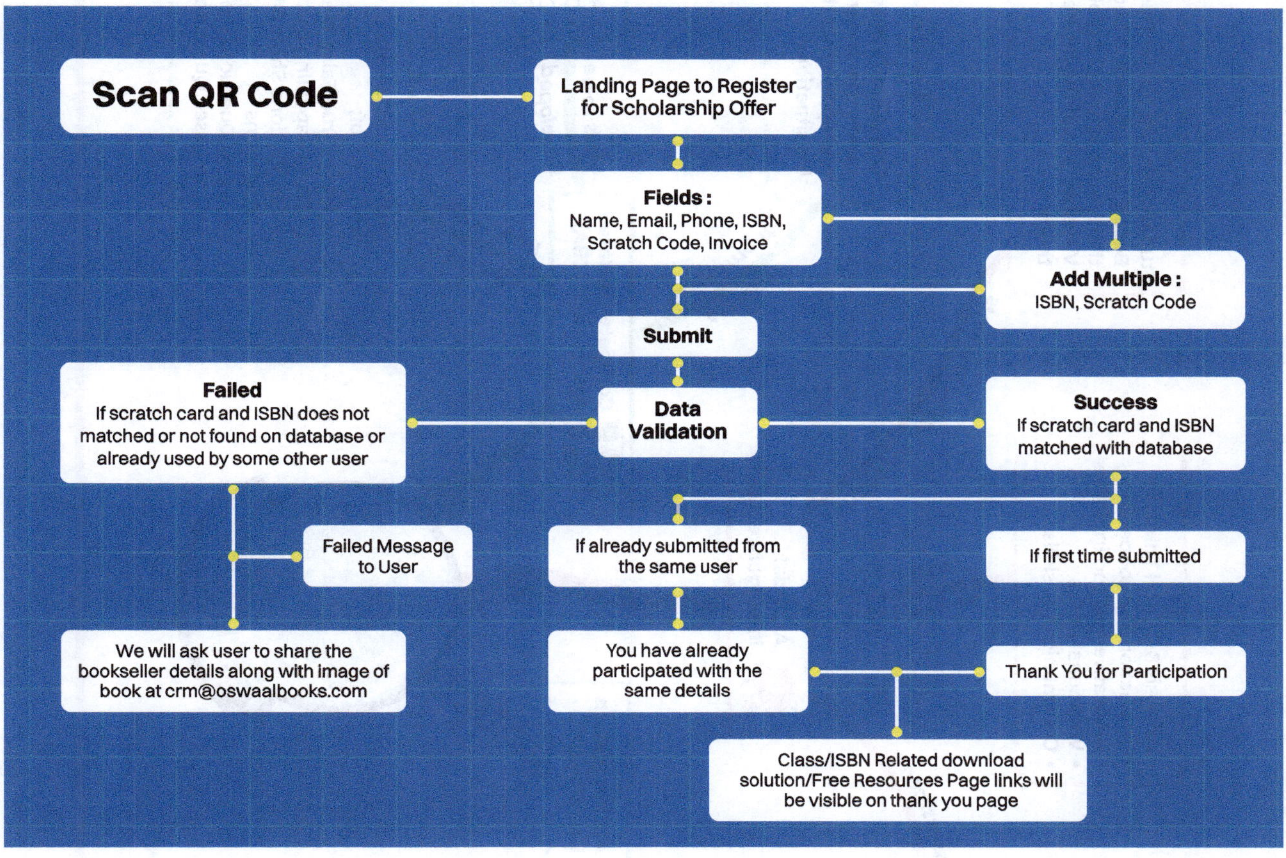

❑❑

NEP Derived Learning Resources Prescribed by CBSE for Year 2024-25

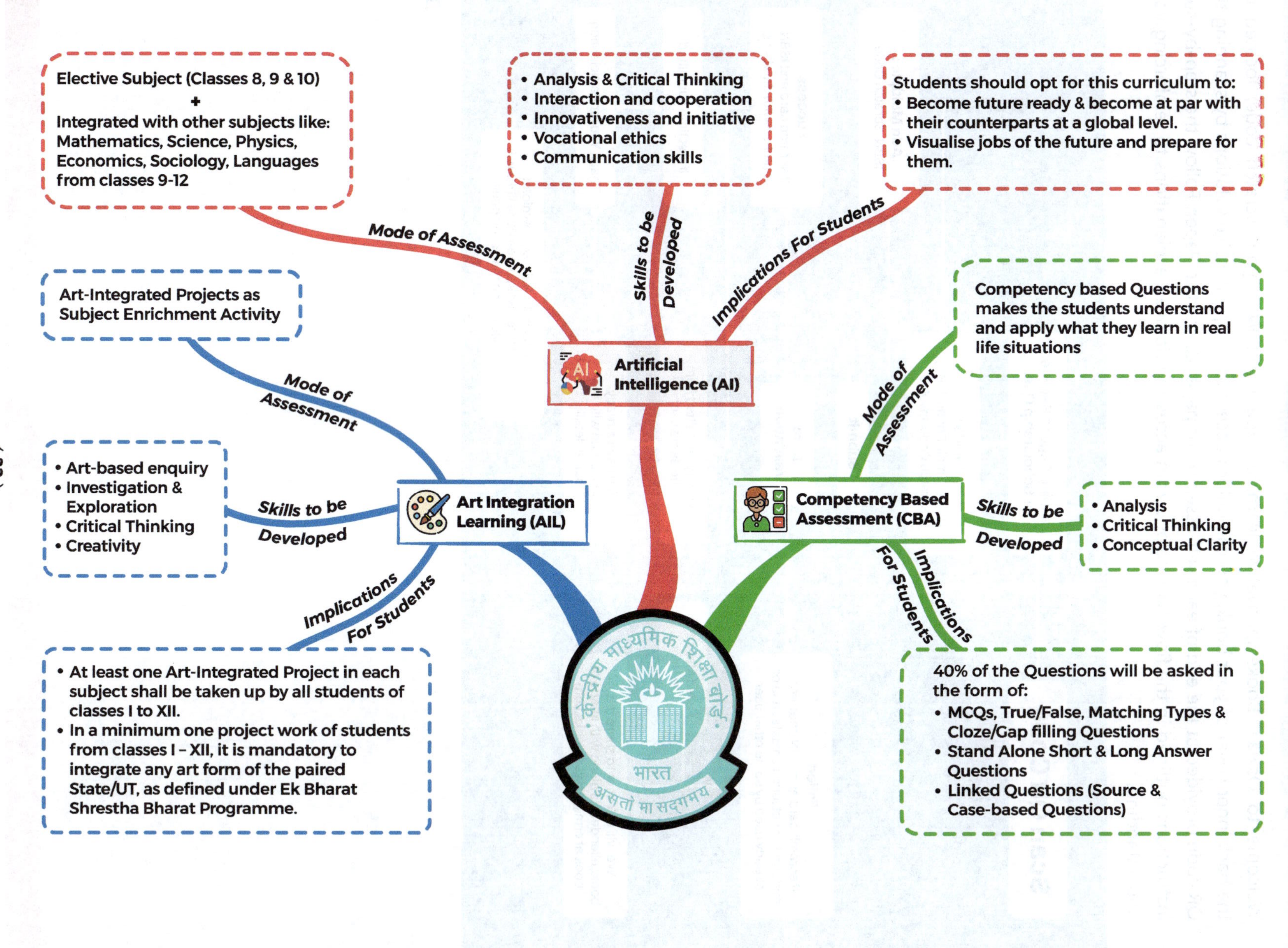

Exclusive School Books Suppliers

ANDHRA PRADESH
VIJAYAWADA Sri Vikas Book Centre, 9848571114, 9440715700,

ASSAM
WEST KAMENG Dutta Book Stall, 8729948473

GUJRAT
RAJKOT Royal Stationers, 9824207514

KARNATAKA
BANGLORE Satish Agencies, 8861630123

MAHARASHTRA
JALNA Anil Paper Mart, 9422722522, (02482) 230733
PUNE Madhusheela Books & Stationery, 7875899892

TAMIL NADU
CHENNAI Bookmark-IT, 7305151653

TELANGANA
HYDERABAD Sri Balaji Book Depot , 9676996199, (040) 27613300

WEST BENGAL
KOLKATA United Book House, 9831344622

Our Distributors

ANDHRA PRADESH
TIRUPATI Shree Aditya Book Centre, 7013300914, 8332972720
VISAKHAPATHAM JBD Educational, 9246632691, 9246633693, Sri Rajeshwari Book Link, 9848036014
VIJAYAWADA Akshaya Books Corner, 9666155555

ANDAMAN & NICOBAR ISLAND
PORTBLAIR Krishna Book Centre, 9474205570, Kumar Book Depot, 9932082455

ARUNACHAL PRADESH
NAHARLAGUN New Pothi Ghar, 8731832947

ASSAM
GUWAHATI Book Emporium, 9675972993, 6000763186, Ashok Publication, 7896141127, Kayaan Enterprises, (0361) 2630443, Orchid Book house, 9864624209, Newco, 9864178188

BIHAR
PATNA Nova Publisher & Distributors, (0612) 2666404, Shri Durga Pustak Mandir, 9334477386, Sharda Pustak Bhandar, 9334259293, Vikas Book Depot, 9504780402, Alka Book Agency, 9835655005, Metro Book(E&C), Ishu Pustak Bhandar, 8294576789, Gyan Ganga Limited, 9304826651,
MUZAFFARPUR Pustak Bhandar, 7870834225

CHATTISGARH
AMBIKAPUR Saini Brothers, 9425582561, M.P Department Stores, 9425254264
BOKARO Bokaro Student Friends Pvt. Ltd, Bokaro, 7277931285
BHILAI Anil Book Depot, 9425234260
DURG Bhagwati Bhawani Book Depot, 0788-2327620, 9827473100
KORBA Kitab Ghar, Korba (E & C), 9425226528
RAIPUR Shri Ramdev Traders, 9981761797, Gupta Pustak Mandir, 7974220323, Anil Publication, 9691618258/7999078802
RAIGARH Sindhu Book Deopt, 9981935763

DELHI
DELHI Mittal Books, (011) 23288887, 9899037390, Singhania Book & Stationer, 9212028238, Aone Books, New Delhi, 8800497047, Radhey Book Depot, 9818314141, Batheja Super Store, 9871833924, Lov Dev & Sons, Delhi (E & C), 9811182352, Zombozone, 9871274082, LDS Marketing, 9811182352/9999353491

GUJARAT
AHMEDABAD Patel Book Agencies, 9898184248, 9824386112, 9825900335, Zaveri Agency, 9979897312, 9979890330, Hardik Book Agency, (ISC) 9898618613
BHAVNAGAR Samir Book Stall, Bhavnagar (ISC) 9586305305, 7825658466
DAHOD Collegian Book Corner, 9925501981
VAPI Goutam Book Sellers, 9081790813
VALSAD Mahavir Stationers, 9429474177
NAVSARI College Store, (ISC) NO CALL 02637-258642, 9825099121,8141913750
SURAT Shopping Point, 9824108663
VADODARA Umakant Book Sellers & Stationer, 6359396370

HARYANA
ROHTAK Manish Traders, 9812556687, Swami Kitab Ghar, 9355611088, Babu Ram Pradeep Kumar, 9813214692
REWARI Sanjay book depot, 9255447231
BALLABGARH Kashi Ram Kishan lal, 9289504004, 8920567245
HISAR Natraj Book Distributors, 7988917452
BHUNA Khurana Book Store, 9896572520

JAMMU
Sahitya Sangam, 9419190177

JHARKHAND
BOKARO Bokaro Student Friends Pvt. Ltd. (0654) 2233094, 7360021503, Bharati Bhawan Agencies, 06542-265302, 9431740797
RANCHI Crown Book Distributor & Publishers, (0651) 2213735, 9431173904, Pustak Mandir, 9431115138,
DUMKA Vidyarthi Pustak Bhandar, 9431310228

KARNATAKA
HUBLI Renuka Book Distributor, (0836) 2244124, Vidyamandir Book Distributors, 9980773976
BANGLORE Krishna book house, 9739847334, Hema Book Stores, 9986767000, Sapna Book House Pvt. Ltd., 9980513242,
BELLERI Hema Book World, (Chamrajpet) (ISC) 080-40905110, 9945731121

KERALA
ERNAKULAM Academic Book House, (0484) 2376613, H & C Store, 9864196344, Surya Book House, 9847124217, 9847238314, Asad Book Centere
KOTTAYAM Book Centre, (0481) 2566992
TRIVANDRUM Academic Book House, (0471) 2333349, 9447063349, Ponni Book Stall, 9037591721
CALICUT Aman Book Stall, (0495) 2721282,

MADHYA PRADESH
CHHINDWARA Pustak Bhawan, (E & C), 8982150100
GWALIOR Agarwal Book Depot, 9425116210
INDORE Bhaiya Industries, 9893326853, Sushil Prakashan,(0731) 2503333, 2535892, 9425322330, Bhaiya Store, 9425318103, Arun Prakashan, 9424890785, Bhaiya Book Centre, 9424081874, Seva Suppliers, 9826451052
JABALPUR Vinay Pustak Sadan, 8962362667, Anand Books and Stationers, 9425323508
SAGAR Princi Book Depot, Sagar, 9977277011
KATNI Shri Mahavir Agency, 9425363412
UJJAIN Shreenath Book Depot, 9827544045
BHOPAL Gupta Brother, 9644482444

MAHARASHTRA
PUNE Natraj Book Depot, (020) 24485054, 9890054092, Vikas Book House, 9921331187, Pravin Sales, 9890683475, New Saraswati Granth Bhandar, 9422323859, Akshar Books & Stationary, 7385089789, Vardhaman Educational, 9860574354, Yash Book Centre, 9890156763, Pragati Book Centre, (ISC), 9850039311, Praveen Sales, Pragati Book Centre, Pune (E & C), 9850039311
AURANGABAD Shree Sainath Agencies, 7350294089, Maya Book Centre, (ISC), 9372360150
BECD Adarsh Book Depot, 9860374645
MUMBAI Vidyarthi Sales Agencies, 9819776110, New Student Agencies, 7045065799, Shivam Books & Stationery, 8619805332
JALGAON Sharma Book Depot & Stat. (ISC), 9421393040
LATUR Yash Book House, 9637936999, Shri Ganesh Pustakalay, 9730172188
KOLHAPUR Granth the Book World, 9922295522
NAGPUR Laxmi Pustakalay and Stationers, (0712) 2727354, Vijay Book Depot, 9860122094
Renuka Book distributor, 9765406133, Novelty Book Depot, 9657690220, Karamveer Book Depot, 9923966466, Arun Book & Stationers, 9423110953, Shree Mahalaxmi Pustakalaya, 7507099360
NANDED Abhang Pustakalaya, 9823470756/9175940756
NASHIK Rahul Book Centre, 9970849681, New India Book House, 9623123458
DHULE Navjeevan Book Stall, 7020525561
YAVATMAL Shri Ganesh Pustkalaya, 9423131275
VASAI Prime Book Centre, Vasai, 9890293662

ODISHA
CUTTACK A. K. Mishra Agencies, 9437025991, 9437081319
BHUBANESHWAR M/s Pragnya, 8847888616, 9437943777, Padmalaya, 9437026922, Bidyashree, 9937017070, Books Godown, 7894281110
BARIPADA Trimurti Book World, 9437034735
KEONJHAR Students corner, 7008435418

PUNJAB
AMBALA Bharat Book Depot, 7988455354
PATIALA Goel Sons, 9463619978, Adarsh Enterprises, 9814347613
JALANDHAR Cheap Book Store, 9872223458, 9878258592, City Book Shop, 9417440753, Subhash Book Depot, 9876453625, Paramvir Enterprises, 9878626248, Gaurav Book world, 9478821183
FEROZPUR Sita Ram book Depot, 9463039199, 7696141911
LUDHIANA Amit Book, 9815807871, Gupta Brothers, 9888200206, Bhatia Book Centre, 9815277131
CHANDIGARH Mohindra Book Depot, 9814920226

RAJASTHAN
AJMER Laxmi General Store, Ajmer, 0145- 2428942 9460652197
KOTA Vardhman Book Depot, 9571365020, 8003221190 Raj Traders, 9309232829
BHILWARA Nakoda Book Depot, (01482) 243653, 9214983594,
BHIWADI Alankar Book Depot, 9414707462
JAIPUR Ravi Enterprises, 9829060694, Saraswati Book House, (0141) 2610823, 9829811155, Goyal Book Distt., 9460983939, 9414782130
UDAIPUR Sunil Book Store, 9828682260
JODHPUR Second Hand Book Stall, 9460004745

TRIPURA
AGARTALA BookS Corner, 8794894165, 8984657146, Book Emporium, 9089230412

TAMIL NADU
COIMBATORE Majestic Book House, (0422) 2384333, CBSC Book Shop, 9585979752
CHENNAI Arraba Book Traders, (044) 25387868, 9841459105, M.R. Book Store (044) 25364596, Kalaimagal Store, (044) 5544072, 9940619404, Vijaya Stores, 9381037417, Bookmark It-Books & Stat. Store, 7305151653, M.K. Stores, 9840030099, Tiger Books Pvt. Ltd., 9710447000, New Mylai Stationers, 9841313062, Prince Book House, Chennai, 0444-2053926, 9952068491, S K Publishers & Distributors, 9789865544, Dharma Book Shop, 8667227171
PUDUCHERRY Sri Lakshmi Book Seller, 7871555145
SALEM Pattu book centre, 9894816280, Selem Book House, 9487724584
TRICHY P.R.Sons Book Seller, 9443370597, Rasi Publication, 9894816280
THENI Maya Book Centre, 9443929274
MADURAI Selvi Book Shoppe, 9843057435, Jayam Book Centre, 9894658036
VELLORE G.K book centre and collections, 9894517994

3003

Exclusive School Books Suppliers

City	Suppliers
	TELANGANA
HYDERABAD	Sri Balaji Book Depot, (040) 27613300, 9866355473, Shah Book House, 9849564564
	Vishal Book Distributors, 9246333166, Himalaya Book World, 7032578527
	UTTARAKHAND
DEHRADUN	Inder Book Agencies, 9634045280, Amar Book Depot , 8130491477, Goyal Book Store, 9897318047, New National Book House, 9897830283/9720590054
MUSSORIE	Ram Saran Dass Chanda kiran, 0135-2632785, 9761344588
	UTTAR PRADESH
AGRA	Sparsh Book Agency, 9412257817, Om Pustak Mandir, (0562) 2464014, 9319117771,
	Sanjay Publication, 8126699922 Arti book centre, 8630128856, Panchsheel Books, 9412257962, Bhagwati Book Store, (E & C), 9149081912
ALLAHABAD	Mehrotra Book Agency, (0532) 2266865, 9415636890
AZAMGARH	Sasta Sahitya Bhandar, 9450029674
ALIGARH	K.B.C.L. Agarwal, 9897124960, Shaligram Agencies, 9412317800,
	New Vimal Books, 9997398868, T.I.C Book centre, 9808039570
BULANDSHAHAR	Rastogi Book Depot, 9837053462/9368978202
BALRAMPUR	Universal Book Center, 8933826726
BAREILLY	Siksha Prakashan, 9837829284, Deepak Book Depot 9837027416
HARDOI	Mittal Pustak Kendra, 9838201466
DEORIA	Kanodia Book Depot, 9415277835
VARANASI	Gupta Books, 8707225564, Bookman & Company,9935194495/7668899901
MATHURA	Sapra Traders, 9410076716, Vijay Book House , 9897254292
FARRUKHABAD	Anurag Book Agencies, 8844007575
NAJIBABAD	Gupta News Agency, 8868932500, Gupta News Agency, (E & C), 8868932500
DHAMPUR	Ramkumar Mahaveer Prasad, 9411942550
GORAKHPUR	Central Book House, 9935454590, Friends & Co., 9450277154, Dinesh book depot, 9125818274, Friends & Co., 9450277154, Dwivedi Brothers, 8299684731
JHANSI	Bhanu Book Depot, 9415031340
KANPUR	Radha News Agency, 8957247427, Raj Book Dist., 9235616506, H K Book Distributors, 9506033137/9935146730
LUCKNOW	Vyapar Sadan, 7607102462, Om Book Depot, 7705871398, Azad Book Depot Pvt. Ltd., 7317000250, Book Sadan, 9839487327, Rama Book Depot(Retail), 7355078254,
	Ashirwad Book Depot, 9235501197, Book.com, 7458922755, Universal Books, 9450302161, Sheetla Book Agency, 9235832418, Vidyarthi Kendra Publisher &
	Distributor Pvt Ltd, (Gold), 9554967415, Tripathi Book House, 9415425943, Navyoug Book Agencies, 8073564410
MEERUT	Ideal Book Depot, (0121) 4059252, 9837066307
NOIDA	Prozo (Global Edu4 Share Pvt. Ltd), 9318395520, Goyal Books Overseas Pvt.Ltd., 1204655555 9873387003
PRAYAGRAJ	Kanhaiya Pustak Bhawan, 9415317109
MAWANA	Subhash Book Depot, 9760262264
RENUKOOT	Om Stationers, 7007326732
SHAHJAHANPUR	New Rastogi Book Seller, 9935395062
	WEST BENGAL
KOLKATA	Oriental Publishers & Distributor (033) 40628367, Katha 'O' Kahini, (033) 22196313, 22419071, Saha Book House, (033), 22193671, 9333416484,
	United Book House, 9831344622, Bijay Pustak Bhandar, 8961260603, Shawan Books Distributors, 8336820363, Krishna Book House, 9123083874
COOCH BEHAR	S.B. Book Distributor, Cooch behar, 9002670771
KHARAGPUR	Subhani Book Store, 9046891334
SILIGURI	Agarwal Book House, 9832038727, Modern Book Agency, 8145578772
DINAJPUR	Krishna Book House, 9434394212
MURSHIDABAD	New Book House, 8944876176, 9434013126

Entrance & Competition Distributors

City	Distributors
	BIHAR
PATNA	Metro Books Corner, 9431647013, Alka Book Agency, 9835655005, Vikas Book Depot, 9504780402, Ishu Pustak Bhandar, 9334186300, 8294576789
	CHATTISGARH
KORBA	Kitab Ghar, 9425226528,
RAIPUR	Shri Ramdev Traders, 9981761797
	DELHI
DELHI	Singhania Book & Stationer, 9212028238, Radhey Book depot, 9818314141, The Book Shop, 9310262701, Mittal Books, 9899037390, Lov Dev & Sons, 9999353491
NEW DELHI	Anupam Sales, 9560504617, A ONE BOOKS, 8800497047
	HARYANA
AMBALA	Bharat Book Depot, 7988455354
	JHARKHAND
BOKARO	Bokaro Student Friends Pvt. Ltd, 7360021503
	MADHYA PRADESH
INDORE	Bhaiya Industries, 9109120101
CHHINDWARA	Pustak Bhawan, 9827255997
	MAHARASHTRA
NAGPUR	Laxmi Pustakalay and Stationers, (0712) 2727354
PUNE	Pragati Book Centre, 9850039311
MUMBAI	New Student Agencies LLP, 7045065799
	ODISHA
BARIPADA	Trimurti Book World, 9437034735
CUTTAK	A.K.Mishra Agencies, 9437025991
BHUBANESHWAR	M/s Pragnya, 9437943777
	PUNJAB
JALANDHAR	Cheap Book Store, 9872223458, 9878258592
	RAJASTHAN
KOTA	Vardhman Book Depot, 9571365020, Raj Traders, 9309232829
JAIPUR	Goyal Book Distributors, 9414782130
	UTTAR PRADESH
AGRA	BHAGWATI BOOK STORE, 9149081912, Sparsh Book Agency, 9412257817, Sanjay Publication, 8126699922
ALIGARH	New Vimal Books, 9997398868
ALLAHABAD	Mehrotra Book Agency, (532) 2266865, 9415636890
GORAKHPUR	Central Book House, 9935454590
KANPUR	Raj Book Dist, 9235616506 H K Book Distributors (E & C)
LUCKNOW	Azad Book Depot PVT LTD, 7317000250, Rama Book Depot(Retail), 7355078254 Ashirwad Book Depot , 9235501197, Book Sadan, 8318643277, Book.com , 7458922755, Sheetla Book Agency, 9235832418
NAJIBABAD	Gupta News Agency, (E & C), 8868932500
PRAYAGRAJ	Format Center, 9335115561, Garg Brothers Trading & Services Pvt. Ltd., 7388100499
	UTTARAKHAND
DEHRADUN	Inder Book Agancies, 9634045280
	WEST BENGAL
KOLKATA	Bijay Pustak Bhandar Pvt. Ltd., 8961260603, Saha Book House, 9674827254 United Book House, 9831344622, Techno World, 9830168159

3003

CBSE Board Examination – 2024
BUSINESS STUDIES
Class-12th
(Solved)
(Delhi & Outside Delhi Sets)

Time : 3 Hours **Max. Marks : 80**

General Instructions:

Read the following instructions carefully and follow them:

(i) This question paper contains 34 questions. All questions are compulsory.
(ii) Marks are indicated against each question.
(iii) Answer should be brief and to the point.
(iv) Answer to the questions carrying 3 marks may be from 50 to 75 words.
(v) Answer to the questions carrying 4 marks may be in about 150 words.
(vi) Answer to the questions carrying 6 marks may be in about 200 words.
(vii) Attempt all parts of a question together.

Delhi Set-1 **66/5/1**

1. 'Vanguard Inc', a company manufacturing footwear for men, women and children has been earning consistent profits for the last many years. It has a democratic style of working. Workers are encouraged to develop and carry out plans for improvement in the organisation. Varun who is working in the production department gave a suggestion which resulted in 10% '- reduction in the cost of production of shoes. He was rewarded for his suggestion. Identify the principle of management followed by 'Vanguard . Inc.' in the above case: **1**

(A) Esprit De Corps
(B) Subordination of Individual Interest to General Interest
(C) Initiative
(D) Equity

2. 'Child-O' is a garment manufacturing company which makes clothes with unique and stylish designs for children. Naisha was working as the Human Resource Manager with 'Child-O'. Inspite of good pay and many other benefits offered, the company is facing problem of high turnover of its employees. Naisha tried to find out the reason but could not. She appointed a person with the permission of the Chief Executive Officer to find out the reason. It was found that other organisations were giving more autonomy and authority to their employees which made them feel that their jobs were important. This was attracting the employees of 'Child-O' to other organisations. The incentive which attracted the employees Of 'Child-O' to other organisations is: **1**

(A) Employee Recognition Programmes
(B) Employee Participation
(C) Career Advancement Opportunity
(D) Employee Empowerment

3. 'Since business environment consists of numerous interrelated and dynamic conditions or forces which -arise from different sources, it becomes difficult to comprehend at once what exactly constitutes a given environment'. Thus it is relatively easier to understand the environment in parts but difficult to grasp in its totality. Identify the feature of business environment highlighted above : **1**

(A) Uncertainty **(B)** Complexity
(C) Relativity **(D)** Dynamic nature

4. Naman and Vineet were childhood friends and both were working in : 'Sunshine Crockery.' Naman was working as the Chief Executive Officer - while Vineet was the Production Manager. They would generally discuss company related issues over lunch-time or while travelling together. The company had recently received an order for supply of 5,000 dinner sets from Shaurya Hotel. It was an unexpected order and would increase the revenue of the company. This order was communicated by Naman to Vineet over intercom. Vineet executed the order within the given time period. For this, he was appreciated by Naman.

The type of communication used by Naman to communicate the order to Vineet was : **1**

(A) Formal Communication
(B) Informal Communication
(C) Online Communication
(D) Visual Communication

5. Statement-I : The basic function of a Stock Exchange is the creation of a continuous market where securities are bought and sold.

Statement-II : The Stock Exchange provides both liquidity and easy marketability to already existing securities in the market.

Choose the correct option from the following : 1

(A) Statement-I is true and Statement-II is false.

(B) Statement-II is true and Statement-I is false.

(C) Both the Statements are true.

(D) Both the Statements are false.

6. As per Plastic Waste: Management Rule 2022, single use plastic items were prohibited in Delhi from 1st July, 2022. The dimension of business environment referred to here is 1

(A) Economic environment

(B) Legal environment

(C) Technological environment

(D) Political environment

7. Statement-I : Motivation can be either positive or negative

Statement-II : Motivation is a complex process as the-individuals are heterogeneous in their expectations, perceptions and reactions.

Choose the correct option from the following : 1

(A) Statement-I is true and Statement-II is false

(B) Statement-II' is true and Statement-I is false

(C) Both the Statements are true.

(D) Both the Statements are false

8. Navya went to a supermarket for grocery shopping. She bought one kg of bajra flour from the supermarket. On reaching home when she opened the packet she found worms inside it. She was disappointed and told her son about the same. Her son asked her to check the label. When she checked the label of the packet, she found that bajra flour was stale and beyond the expiry date. She approached the sales-person at the supermarket who replaced the bajra flour immediately. When she thanked the sales-person, she was told that it was the policy of the supermarket to satisfy the customers. He further told that satisfied customers not only lead to repeat sales but they also provide good feedback to prospective customers which helps in increasing the customer base of business. Identify the point of importance of consumer protection from the point of view of the supermarket which is helping them to increase the customer base: 1

(A) Long term interest of the business

(B) Moral justification

(C) Social responsibility

(D) Government intervention

9. Which of the following is not an element of social environment ? 1

(A) Composition of family

(B) Consumption habits

(C) Rates of saving and investment

(D) Educational system and literacy rates

10. Read the following statements :

Assertion'(A) and Reason (R). Choose the correct alternative from those given below :

Assertion (A) : Availability of leasing facilities may reduce the funds required to be invested in fixed assets thereby reducing the fixed capital requirements.

Reason (R) : When an asset is taken on lease, the firm pays lease rentals to use it and avoids to invest huge sums required to purchase it. 1

(A) Both Assertion (A) and Reason (R) are true and Reason (R) is the correct explanation of Assertion (A).

(B) Both Assertion (A) and Reason (R) are true but Reason (R) is not the correct explanation of Assertion (A).

(C) Assertion (A) is true but Reason (R) is false.

(D) Assertion (A) is false but Reason (R) is true.

11. Match the terms given in Column-I with their meaning in Column-II.

	Column-I		Column-II
a.	Trademark	(i)	A name, term, sign, symbol, design or some combination of them used to identify the products and differentiate them from the competitors
b.	Brand name	(ii)	A brand or a part of the brand that is given legal protection.
c.	Brand	(iii)	That part of the brand which can be recognised but which is not utterable.
d.	Brand mark	(iv)	That part of the brand which can be spoken.

Choose the correct option from the following : 1

	a	b	c	d
(A)	(i)	(ii)	(iii)	(iv)
(B)	(ii)	(iii)	(i)	(iv)
(C)	(ii)	(iv)	(i)	(iii)
(D)	(ii)	(i)	(iv)	(iii)

12. 'Kanand Lad.' is an Automobile manufacturing company started in 2014 under 'Make in India' initiative of the Government of India. Expecting higher growth in future, it developed higher capacity in the current year taking advantage of the subsidies provided by the government. This would enable 'Kanand Ltd.' to meet anticipated higher demand quickly. For this, 'Kanand Ltd.' invested large amounts in fixed assets leading to higher requirements of fixed capita] Identify the factor affecting fixed capital requirements which 'Kanand Ltd.' kept in mind to meet higher anticipated demand quicker. 1

(A) Scale of operations **(B)** Nature of business

(C) Diversification **(D)** Growth prospects

13. Many reputed business organisations keep a database of unsolicited applicants in their offices. Such job seekers can be a valuable source of manpower. A list of such job seekers can be prepared and can be screened to fill the vacancies as they arise.

The source of recruitment discussed above is : 1

(A) Direct recruitment (B) Casual callers

(C) Labour contractors (D) Campus recruitment

14. Identify from the following — what is shown in the picture of refrigerator given below ? 1

(A) Brand name (B) Brand mark

(C) Trademark (D) Label

15. Which of the following is NOT a factor affecting 'financing decision' ? 1

(A) Fixed operating costs

(B) Cash flow position

(C) Control considerations

(D) Diversification

16. For holding securities in an electronic form, the investor has to open a demat account with an organisation called............ 1

(A) Depository

(B) Securities and Exchange Board of India

(C) Stock Exchange

(D) Mutual Fund

17. .... means doing the task correctly and with minimum cost. 1

(A) Efficiency (B) Effectiveness

(C) Management (D) Coordination

18. Which of the following is the function of Top level management? 1

(A) They ensure that their department has the necessary personnel.

(B) They interact with the actual work force and pass on instructions of the middle management to the workers

(C) They co-operate with other departments for smooth functioning of the organisation.

(D) They analyse the business environment and its implications or the survival of the firm.

19. The activities involved in managing the enterprise are common to all organisations whether economic, political or social. Identify the feature of management: 1

(A) Management is multidimensional.

(B) Management is all pervasive.

(C) Management is a continuous process

(D) Management is a dynamic function

20. Choose the incorrect statement about 'Money market': 1

(A) The main instruments traded in this market are Treasury bills, Trade bills, Commercial paper and Certificates of deposit.

(B) In this market, transactions entail huge sums of money as the instruments are quite expensive.

(C) Participation in this market is by and large undertaken by institutional participants such as the Reserve Bank of India, banks, financial institutions and finance companies.

(D) It deals in medium and long term securities.

21. 'Cortico Fabrics' was started by Ashish in 2001 to sell bed sheets, towels, comforters, pillows, cushions, bath mats etc. It is now a famous name and its branches are across India. To manage the work all over India, it has eight teams-two each for North, South, East and West India. Ashish spends a considerable amount of time to develop an orderly pattern of group efforts among different teams and to secure unity of action in pursuit of a common purpose.

To ensure suitable allocation of tasks to the various members of the teams and to see that the tasks are performed with harmony among the members, he tries to balance the different teams at different locations.

(a) Identify and explain the concept of management discussed in the above para.

(b) Also, explain any one point of importance of the concept identified in (a) above. 3

22. State any three points of importance of staffing function of management. 3

23. 'Caro', a car manufacturing company was manufacturing high cost, good quality luxury cars. For the last few years, the company was not earning good profits as the demand for the cars was very low.

Chief Executive Officer of the company, Piyush had a meeting with the Production and Sales Managers to discuss how to increase the revenue of the company. They found that nowadays instead of purchasing luxury cars people prefer to have such cars on rental basis. So they decided to start 'Car rental service'. The Production Manager also suggested that as these cars were sophisticated and each spare part was very costly it would be better to provide these cars for rental service along with trained drivers so that there would be less wear and tear. Piyush agreed and a training unit was started. Two of the available cars were used for training the drivers. People were very happy as they were getting these cars on rental basis with trained drivers. The idea was a big hit and the company was able to surpass its profit targets of the last 20 years

(a) Identify and explain the method of training given by 'Caro' to its drivers.

(a) Also, state any two advantages the drivers will get after this training. 3

24. State any three protective functions of 'Securities and Exchange Board of India'. 3

25. Kewalram started a Pri shop 'Karamati Sweets' in 1950. The sweets were famous all over India for their good quality and people would come from far and wide to purchase sweets from him. As he grew old, he could no longer run the shop. So, he sold the shop to one of his neighbours 'Bholaram'. After a few months, to further increase the revenue, 'Bholaram' started engaging in unfair trade practices like using adulterated khoya and paneer. He thought that no one would know about it as 'Karamati Sweets' had a good image in the eyes of the people.

Slowly, people started falling sick after consuming sweets purchased from 'Karamati Sweets' but they did not know where to go and to whom to complain. Raghav, a resident of the village had recently completed his studies. He was also a member of a non-governmental organisation. 'Meri Voice'. He felt that the villagers should be made aware about the rights and reliefs available to them. He started creating awareness about consumer rights among the villagers to protect their interest through a series of talks and presentations in the village.

(a) Identify and explain the consumer right discussed in the above para.

(b) Also, identify and explain the consumer right violated by 'Bholaram' in the above case. 4

26. A Business Process Outsourcing centre, 'Chromosome' which deals in conversion of voice reports dictated by physicians and other healthcare providers into text format has 40 employees. They ensure that their employees are well versed in at least one foreign language one Indian language. The employees are given the required training to ensure that the reports are processed correctly as they are the backbone of the patients' medical history. On frequent complaints about some of its employees, it was observed that they were facing problems in decoding the message as they were not very proficient with the language in which the voice message was received. As a result, they would make mistakes causing different meaning to the message. Not only this, sometimes there were technical words used in voice reports, the actual meaning of which was also not understood by the employees. Due to this, 'Chromosome' was slowly losing its business to competitors.

The above case highlights two communication barriers. Identify and explain these barriers. 4

27. (a) State any four limitations of planning. 4

OR

(b) Explain the following types of plans :

(i) Strategy

(ii) Procedure 4

28. Differentiate between 'Production concept' and 'Marketing concept' of marketing management philosophies on the basis of : 4

(a) Meaning **(b)** Main focus

(c) Means **(d)** Ends

29. Inspired by the success of Chandrayaan-3, the Chief Scientist at 'Space B Rover' a private research group, decided to send some innovative ideas regarding the mission to the Chief Scientist of Chandrayaan-8

The Chief Scientist at 'Space Rover' formed four groups for the same. As it was an intellectual activity of thinking rather than doing, these four groups started interacting with each other and friendships developed. On the basis of their interaction and friendship, some members from each group formed 'Entertainment Through Reading' group which showed conformity in terms of their interest. 'Entertainment Through Reading' group had no written rules, was unstable in form and scope and had no fixed lines of communication. The members of this group enhanced the morale of each other, enjoyed drinking coffee together, read books, served different issues of their work areas and provided support to each other. Ultimately this group developed some innovative ideas which were sent by 'Space Rover' to the Chief Scientist of Chandrayaan-3. Though this group was formed for recreation but it contributed towards fulfillment of organisational objectives. 4

(a) Identify and explain the type of organization which emerged as 'Entertainment Through Reading'.

(b) State any three advantages of the type of organisation identified in (a) above.

30. (a) Explain the following functions of marketing :

(i) Product Designing and Development.

(ii) Standardisation and grading 4

OR

(b) Explain the four important elements of marketing mix. 4

31. (a) Explain the following characteristics of Principles of Management :

(i) General guidelines

(ii) Flexible

(iii) Cause and effect relationship 6

OR

(b) Explain the following techniques of Scientific Management :

(i) Method Study

(ii) Differential Piece Wage System

(iii) Fatigue Study 6

32. (a) Explain the following factors affecting the working capital requirements of a business :

(i) Operating efficiency

(ii) Credit availed

(iii) Level of competition 6

OR

(b) Explain the following factors the dividend decision of a company : 6

(i) Stability of dividends

(ii) Contractual constraints

(iii) Stock market

33. The G20 Summit was organised in India. The government left no stone unturned to make G20 summit a success.

At the higher level, the work to be performed was identified and grouped to enable people to work most effectively together for accomplishing objectives. This involved building infrastructure, beautification of the city, hospitality, security arrangements etc. Duties were assigned to different job positions which led to establishment of clear relationships. This helped . in creating a hierarchical structure and in co-ordination amongst all working for the summit

(a) Identify and explain the function of management discussed in the above para.

(b) Explain any four points of importance of the function identified in (a) above. **6**

34. 'Memo Builders' was constructing a five star hotel for a leading hotel chain. The hotel had to be given possession by next year but the construction of the hotel was running six months behind schedule. The Chief Executive Officer of 'Memo Builders' was concerned as Memo Builders was known for its quality and timely completion of projects. He asked Nitin, the senior of the Project Head for a thorough investigation. Nitin investigated and reported to the Chief Executive Officer that inspite of huge absenteeism of workers, additional workers were not called. Nitin also reported to the Chief Executive Officer that three of the ten machines being used by the workers were defective. Nitin ordered for repair of the machines and asked the Project Head to appoint additional workers with attractive wages to ensure that the deadline is met. **6**

(a) Identify the function of management. Quoting the lines from the above para, explain the steps of the process of the function of management discussed.

(b) Also explain any two points of importance of the function of management identified in (a) above.

Delhi Set-2 66/5/2

Note: *Except these, all other questions have been given in Delhi Set-1*

27. **(b)** Explain the following types of plans :

(i) Objective

(ii) Programme **4**

28. Differentiate between 'Product Concept' and 'Societal Marketing Concept' of marketing management philosophies on the basis of : **4**

(a) Meaning

(b) Main focus

(c) Means

(d) Ends

30. **(a)** Explain the following functions of marketing :

(i) Customer support services

(ii) Physical distribution **4**

OR

(b) State any four factors which affect the fixation of price of a product. **4**

31. **(a)** Explain the following characteristics of principles of management :

(i) Universal applicability

(ii) Formed by practice and experimentation

(iii) Contingent **6**

OR

(b) Explain the following principles of management:

(i) Division of work

(ii) Order

(iii) Unity of command **6**

32. **(a)** Explain the following factors affecting the working capital requirements of a business :

(i) Inflation

(ii) Business cycle

(iii) Nature of business **6**

OR

(b) Explain the following factors affecting the dividend decision of a company :

(i) Access to capital market

(ii) Legal constraints

(iii) Taxation policy **6**

Delhi Set-3 66/5/3

Note: *Except these, all other questions have been given in Delhi Set-1&2*

27. **(a)** State any four characteristics of planning. **4**

OR

(b) Explain the following types of plans:

(i) Policy

(ii) Budget **4**

28. Differentiate between 'Selling Concept' and 'Production Concept' of marketing management philosophies on the basis of: **4**

(a) Meaning

(b) Main focus

(c) Means

(d) Ends

30. **(a)** Explain the following functions of marketing:

(i) Gathering and Analysing Market Information

(ii) Marketing Planning **4**

OR

(b) State the four major components of physical distribution. **4**

31. **(a)** Explain the following points of significance of principles of management:

(i) Providing managers with useful insights into reality.

(ii) Meeting changing environment requirements.

(iii) Scientific decisions **6**

OR

(b) Explain the following principles of management:

(i) Unity of direction

(ii) Remuneration to employees

(iii) Equity 6

32. (a) Explain the following factors affecting the working capital requirements of a business:

(i) Credit allowed

(ii) Production cycle

(iii) Availability of raw material 6

OR

(b) Explain the following factors affecting the dividend decision of a company:

(i) Growth opportunities

(ii) Cash flow position

(iii) Shareholders' preference 6

Outside Delhi Set-1 66/4/1

1. A multinational sweets and snacks company had been into catering business for the last many years. To add to its prospects and to grow in the long run. it wants to increase its sales volume, the number of products and capital investment.

The organisational objective of management it seeks to achieve is: 1

(A) Survival

(B) Profit

(C) Growth

(D) Corporate Social responsibility

2. With respect to levels of management choose the incorrect statement from the following: 1

(A) Operational level management is responsible for maintaining safety standards in the organisations.

(B) At middle level management, managers ensure that their department has the necessary personnel.

(C) Chief Executive officer at Top Level management is responsible for all activities of first line mangers.

(D) Top level management is responsible for all the activities of the business and for its impact on the society.

3. 'Merely allocating work is not enough. Each individual should also know who be has to take orders from and to whom he is accountable'.

The above statement is related to one of the steps of organising process. Identify the step from the following: 1

(A) Identification and division of work

(B) Departmentalisation

(C) Assignment of duties

(D) Establishing authority and reporting relationship

4. .... is the step in the controlling process where standards may have to be revised in case the deviation can not be corrected through managerial action. 1

(A) Setting Performance Standards

(B) Measurement of Actual performance

(C) Comparing Actual Performance with standards and analysing deviations

(D) Taking corrective action

5. Read the following statements Assertion (A) and Reason (R). Choose the correct option from the given options. 1

Assertion (A): Amount of Earnings is a major determinant of the decision about dividend.

Reason (R): Dividends are paid out of current and past earnings.

(A) Both Assertion (A) and Reason (R) are true and Reason (R) is correct explanation of Assertion (A).

(B) Both Assertion (A) and Reason (R) are true but Reason (R) is not the correct explanation of Assertion (A).

(C) Assertion (A) is true but Reason (R) is false.

(D) Assertion (A) is false but Reason (R) is true.

6. 'It is a process that allocates or directs funds available for investment into their most productive instrument opportunity'. 1

This is known as:

(A) Financial planning

(B) Financial Intermediation

(C) Allocative function

(D) Capital budgeting

7. Which of the following is NOT a feature of 'Directing' function of management? 1

(A) Direction initiates Action.

(B) Directing takes place at every level of management.

(C) Directing ensures that activities are performed as per plans.

(D) Directing flows from top to bottom.

8. Which of the following is an advantage of Informal organisation? 1

(A) It provides stability to the organisation because behaviour of employees can be fairly predicted since there are specific rules to guide them.

(B) It leads to effective accomplishment of goals by providing a framework for the operations to be performed.

(C) It enhances the employee's job satisfaction since it gives them a sense of belongings in the organisation and allows them to find like minded people.

(D) It helps in avoiding duplication of efforts as there is no ambiguity in the role that each member has to play.

9. 'Marbury biscuits' launched its new range of oat cookies in three varieties. They decided to distribute free samples of their biscuits in schools as a part of their promotional campaign.

Identify the tool of promotion used by 'Marbury Biscuits': 1

(A) Advertising
(B) Personal Selling
(C) Sales Promotion
(D) Public Relations

10. .... is the process by which a manager synchronises the activities of different departments.
(A) Management 1
(B) Planning
(C) Co-ordinaltion
(D) Directing

11. Match the functions of Securities and Exchange board of India given in Column-I with their headings given in Column-II:

	Column-I		Column-II
A.	Training of intermediaries of securities markets	(i)	Regulatory function
B.	Regulation of takeover bids by companies	(ii)	Protective function
C.	Controlling insider trading and imposing penalties for such practices	(iii)	Development function

1

Choose the correct alternative: 1
(A) A(ii); B(iii); C(i)
(B) A(i); B(ii); C(iii)
(C) A(iii); B(i); C(ii)
(D) A(iii); B(ii); C(i)

12. Lyka Ltd. launched its new range of herbal shampoos at the beginning of the year. As per legal framework, Lyka Ltd. provided the name and address of the manufacturer, the weight, manufacturing date, expiry date, maximum retail price etc. on the package and label of the herbal shampoo. 1
The consumer right highlighted above is:
(A) Right to choose
(B) Right to be informed
(C) Right to consumer education
(D) Right to safety

13. **Statement-I:** Business Environment is dynamic as it differs from country to country.
Statement-II: Business Environment is largely uncertain as it is very difficult to predict future happenings. 1
Choose the correct option from the following.
(A) Statement I is true and Statement II is false.
(B) Statement II is true and Statement I is false.
(C) Both the statements are true.
(D) Both the statements are false.

14. Which of the following is NOT a feature of demonetization? 1
(A) It leads to creation of a less-cash or cash-less (free) economy i.e. channelling more savings through the formal financial system and improving tax compliance.
(B) It is interpreted as a shift on the part of the government indicating that tax evasion will no longer be tolerated or accepted.
(C) It is viewed as a tax administration measure.
(D) It led to tax administration channelising savings away from the formal financial system.

15. Samaira and her friend, Sana wanted to watch a movie over the weekend. They booked the movie tickets online and chose the seats as per their preference at the click of a button at the desired movie hall. Now going to theatre for booking of tickets is no longer required.
The dimension of business environment reflected in the above para is: 1
(A) Political environment
(B) Social environment
(C) Legal environment
(D) Technological environment

16. Payal was working in a Multinational company. Her father gifted her a smart phone worth ₹40,500 on her birthday. The mobile phone was purchased by her father from his friend's shop. After few months, the mobile phone started creating problems. Payal tried to contact the manufacturer many times but he did not respond. Ultimately Payal decided to file a complaint against the manufacturer. The appropriate grievance redressal machinery where Payal can file a complaints is: 1
(A) District Forum/Commission
(B) State Commission
(C) National Commission
(D) Supreme Court

17. .... is the process of holding securities in electronic form. 1
(A) Financial Intermediation
(B) Dematerialisation
(C) Allocative function
(D) Mobilisation of securities

18. Rajat was carrying on a business of manufacturing plastic disposable like plastic plates, plastic cups and plastic straws. He heard about the upcoming ban on single use plastics. He was able to identify this external environmental trend which could hinder his firm's performance. So he took action and shifted to manufacturing the plates, cups and straws from bamboo and palm leaves. As a result, his business not only survived but was able to generate profit.
The point of importance of Business Environment highlighted above is: 1
(A) It enables the firm to identify opportunities and getting the first mover advantage.
(B) It helps the firm to identify threats and early warning signals.
(C) It helps in tapping useful resources.
(D) It helps in assisting in planning and policy formulation

19. **Statement I:** That part of a brand which can be spoken is called a brand name.

Statement II: That part of the brand which is given legal protection is called Trademark.

Choose the correct option form the following: 1

(A) Statement I is true and Statement II is false.
(B) Statement II IS true and Statement I is false.
(C) Both the statement are true.
(D) Both the statements are false.

20. The picture given below is the package of a perfume bottle:

Identify the level of packaging of the box shown above: 1

(A) Primary package
(B) Secondary packaging
(C) Transportation packaging
(D) Both (A) and (B)

21. Three friends, Aman, Ashish and Ashi after completing their MBA from a reputed management institute, formed a start up named 'Solutions'. The goal of the start up was to make a social and environmental impact through its services. 'Solutions' supports social business ideas to improve living conditions in slums of Mumbai. As all the three friends are specialised in social work, they adopted three different slums of Mumbai and started education the slum dwellers in their own creative manner. Aman used 'playway method', Ashish used 'music' as a method of learning while Ashi used 'activity based method of learning,. They used basic knowledge in their unique manner and were able to educate the slum dwellers.

It implies that skillful and personal application of acquired knowledge varies from individual to individual in achieving desired results. 3

(a) Identify and state the nature of management discussed in the above case.

(b) Quoting lines from the above para, state any two features of nature of management identified in (a) above.

22. (a) Explain the following as factors affecting 'Financing Decision': 3

(i) Fixed operating costs and

(ii) Cash flow position of the company

OR

(b) State any three points of difference between 'Primary Market' and 'Secondary Market'. 3

23. The rapid changes having taken place in the society have created pressure on organisations to readapt its products, type of jobs required and type of skills necessary to complete these jobs. To keep up pace with the rapid changes in the business environment, 'Suzon cars', a company manufacturing automobiles for the last thirty years decided to start manufacturing electric cars with Artificial Intelligence technology. With the introduction of Artificial Intelligence, the company had to improve the knowledge and skills of its employees. The wanted that all their employees improve their performance on the current job and are prepared for any intended job in future. This way they would not only be able to increase their knowledge and skills but would also improve their performance. By doing this, the organisation too would get various benefits. 3

(a) Identify the concept discussed above which would help the employees to do the job in a better way using Artificial Intelligence Technology.

(b) State any five benefits of the concept identified in (a) above to the organisation.

24. (a) 'Planning and controlling are inseparable twins of management'. Explain with the help of any three points. 3

OR

(b) Explain 'Critical point control' and 'Management by exception' as discussed in the controlling process. 3

25. (a) State any four features of directing function of management. 4

OR

(b) Explain the following 'Semantic barriers' to communication: 4

(i) Technical jargon

(ii) Body language and gesture decoding

26. (a) Explain the following steps of the selection process: 4

(i) Selection Tests

(ii) Employment Interview

OR

(b) State any four points of importance of 'Staffing' function of management. 4

27. 'Shanta Enterprises' was in the business of manufacturing solar panels for the last fifteen years. With their expertise now they were able to manufacture good quality solar panels at lower cost. As a result 'Shanta Enterprises' was flooded with orders and was able to generate a good profit margin.

To motivate the employees the company decided to compensate some of them for their hard work. Arvind and Yogesh, who were working on contract basis, were absorbed permanently in the company. Both were happy as now there was stability about their future income. Ekta, a regular employee of the company, working as Research and Development Head, was awarded the 'Best Employee of the year Award'. 4

(a) Identify and explain the incentives given by Shanta Enterprises to its employees.

(b) State the needs of the employees being met by such incentives as per Maslaw's Need Hierarchy Theory.

28. Explain the following factors affecting the working capital requirements of a company: 4

(a) Level of competition

(b) Inflation

29. Nishi had gone to a grocery store to make routine purchases. On reaching home, as she took out Binx tomato chips packet from the bag to give it to her son, she felt that it was underweight. She checked its weight on the kitchen weighing scale and found that it weighed 60 grams whereas the label on the chips packet mentioned the weight of the packet as 100 grams. She approached the manufacturer and complained about it. The manufacturer offered her a gift hamper and requested her not to disclose this to anyone. Nishi refused to accept the gift hamper and took the issue to a redressal agency. 4

(a) State two responsibilities discharged by Nishi, as a consumer, in the above case.

(b) State any two reliefs which can be granted to Nishi, if the consumer court is satisfied with the genuineness of the complaint.

30. Kaysons Ltd. was a reputed company manufacturing automotive parts for electric vehicles. As the demand for the electric vehicles grew, Kayaons Ltd. needed more capital to keep up with the demand for automotive parts. Atul, the Finance Manager of Kaysons Ltd. suggested that the company should raise funds through a public issue of shares as the stock market was bullish. The chief Executive Officer fully understood that this process of raising funds would not only reduce the managements' holding in the company but would also require considerable expenditure. Even then he agreed with the Finance Manager and the public issue of shares was made complying with the guidelines of Securities and Exchange Board of India.

Identify and state four factors affecting choice of capital structure being discussed above. 4

31. (a) Explain the following types of plans:

(i) Strategy

(ii) Method

(i) Budget 6

OR

(b) Explain the following limitations of planning function of management:

(i) Planning may not work in a dynamic environment

(ii) Planning leads to rigidity

(i) Planning is time consuming. 6

32. Ankur Sachdeva did his MBA from ITB University. He decided to apply his knowledge of scientific management in the fast food restaurant chain Coffee Bean' set up by him. This restaurant was providing burgers, fries, shakes etc. as a part of its menu.

Now a days people are quality conscious, so he was using standardised raw materials, processes, methods, working conditions, machinery etc. The objective was not only able to reduce the cost but was also able to provide new varieties of burgers, fries and shakes leading to increased turnover.

Ankur Sachdeva also believed that there was only one best method to maximise efficiency. As a result be developed best way of grilling burgers, cooking fries and preparing shakes. His main objective was to maximise the satisfaction of customers, which he was able to achieve.

Not only to learn the best way of doing a job, but to perform their tasks efficiently, 'Coffee Bean' regularly invests in training and development programmes to equip employees with the necessary skill and knowledge. 'Coffee Bean' believed that efficient employees will produce more and earn more. This will ensure their greatest efficiency and prosperity for both company and workers. 6

The above case highlights the use of Scientific principles and techniques by 'Coffee Bean'. Explain any one such principle and two techniques.

33. (a) Explain the following functions of marketing:

(i) Marketing Planning

(ii) Branding

(i) Pricing 6

OR

(b) Explain 'Advertising', 'Sales Promotion' and 'Public Relations' as elements of promotion mix. 6

34. Preeti started her own cooking channel on Youtube 'Mood Art'. As her subscribers increased, she was not in a position to manage everything on her own. She hired Rahul and Riya to help her with filming, editing, lighting and content research. She granted authority to them to operate wihtin prescribed limits. She was thus, able to use her time on high priority activities like developing new recipes and content development etc. As a result, Rahul and Riya were given opportunities to develop and exercise initiative. Preeti was now able to focus on objectives and meet the target of achieving a subscriber base of one million in six months. 6

(a) Identify the concept of management used by Preeti to focus on objectives of her business and meet her targets.

(b) Explain any five point of importance of the concept identified in (a) above.

Outside Delhi Set-2 66/4/2

Note: *Except these, all other questions have been given in Outside Delhi Set-1*

2. Choose the incorrect statement with respect to levels of management from the following: 1

(A) Operational level management is responsible for maintaining quality of output.

(B) At middle level management, managers carry out the plans formulated by the top level managers.

(C) At top level management, the managers are responsible for all the activities of the business and its impact on the society.

(D) At top level management, the managers co-operate with other departments for smooth functioning of the organisation.

22. (a) Distinguish between 'Capital Market' and 'Money Market' on the basis of: 3

(i) Participants

(ii) Investment Outlay

(iii) Expected Return

OR

(b) Explain the following as factors affecting Long-Term Investment decision: 3

(i) Cash flows of the project and

(ii) The investment criteria involved

25. (a) State any four pints that highlight the importance of directing function of management. 4

OR

(b) Explain the following as 'Semantic barriers to communication': 4

(i) Badly Expressed message

(ii) Symbols with different meanings

28. Explain the following factors affecting the working capital requirements of a company: 4

(a) Production cycle

(b) Seasonal factors

31. (a) Explain the following as types of plans: 6

(i) Objectives

(ii) Policy

(iii) Programme

OR

(b) Explain the following limitations of planning function of management: 6

(i) Planning reduces creativity.

(ii) Planning involves huge costs.

(iii) Planning does not guarantee success.

33. (a) Explain the following as functions of marketing: 6

(i) Gathering and Analysing Market Information

(ii) Standardisation and Grading

(iii) Consumer Support Service

OR

(b) Explain the components of Physical distribution. 6

Outside Delhi Set-3 66/4/3

Note: *Except these, all other questions have been given in Outside Delhi Set-1&2*

2. Choose the incorrect statement with respect to levels of management from the following: 1

(A) Operational level management is responsible for implementing and controlling plans and strategies developed by top management.

(B) At middle level management, managers interpret the policies framed by top management.

(C) At operational level management with the efforts supervisors wastage of materials is minimised.

(D) Employee Empowerment

22. (a) Distinguish between 'Capital Market' and 'Money Market' on the basis of: 3

(i) Instruments

(ii) Liquidity

(ii) Safety

OR

(b) Explain the following as factors affecting financing decision: 3

(i) Fixed operating costs

(ii) State of Capital Market

25. (a) Give the meaning of 'Leadership' and 'Communication' as elements of directing function of management. 4

OR

(b) Explain the following as 'semantic barriers to communication': 4

(i) Faulty translation

(ii) Unclarified assumptions

28. Explain the following factors affecting the working capital requirements of a company: 4

(a) Operating Efficiency

(b) Availability of Raw material

31. (a) Explain the following as features of planning function of management: 6

(i) Planning focuses on achieving objectives.

(ii) Planning is futuristic.

(ii) Planning involves decision making.

OR

(b) Explain the following steps in the process of planning: 6

(i) Setting objectives

(ii) Developing Premises

(ii) Identifying alternative courses of action

■■

ANSWERS

Delhi Set-1 66/5/1

1. **Option (C) is correct.**
Explanation: Varun, an employee in the production department, was encouraged to develop and implement a plan for improvement in the organisation, which resulted in a significant reduction in production costs. Additionally, he was rewarded for his suggestion, which further reflects the company's support for employee initiatives and innovative ideas.

2. **Option (D) is correct.**
Explanation: The incentive that attracted employees of 'Child-O' to other organisations is Employee Empowerment, which involves giving employees more autonomy and authority over their work, making them feel their jobs are important.

3. **Option (B) is correct.**
Explanation: The feature of the business environment highlighted in the statement is Complexity, which refers to the difficult and interconnected nature of various factors, making it challenging to understand the environment in its entirety at once.

4. **Option (B) is correct.**
Explanation: The communication used by Naman to communicate the order to Vineet was Informal Communication, indicated by the casual and spontaneous nature of their interaction over the intercom during non-official times.

5. **Option (C) is correct.**
Explanation: In Statement-I highlights the basic function of a stock exchange as creating a continuous market for buying and selling securities, while Statement-II emphasizes how stock exchanges provide liquidity and marketability to existing securities.

6. **Option (B) is correct.**
Explanation: The dimension of the business environment being discussed in this context is the legal environment, which includes laws, regulations, and policies that impact businesses and their operations.

7. **Option (C) is correct.**
Explanation: Motivation may come from rewards, recognition, and opportunities for growth, as well as negative factors like fear of failure, consequences, or punishment. Motivation can be complex since people have varied expectations, perceptions, and responses to the same factors. Different people are motivated by different things.

8. **Option (A) is correct.**
Explanation: Consumer protection for the supermarket, helping them increase the customer base, is the long-term interest of the business. This is achieved by satisfying customers, ensuring repeat sales, and receiving positive feedback that attracts new customers.

9. **Option (C) is correct.**
Explanation: The rate of saving and investment is more related to the economic environment rather than the social environment, which typically includes aspects like family composition, consumption habits, and educational system.

10. **Option (A) is correct.**
Explanation: Leasing facilities can reduce the funds required for fixed assets because instead of purchasing the asset outright, a firm can use leasing arrangements to pay lease rentals, which can be more manageable than the initial investment needed for ownership.

11. **Option (C) is correct.**
Explanation: Trademark refers to a brand or a part of the brand that is given legal protection. Brand name involves that part of the brand which can be spoken. Brand means a name, term, sign, symbol, design or some combination of them used to identify the products and differentiate them from the competitors. Brand mark includes that part of the brand which can be recognised but which is not utterable.

12. **Option (D) is correct.**
Explanation: Kanand Ltd. invested in the capacity to fulfil expected demand quickly, showing a prospective for growth. Future company development forecasts affect fixed asset investment choices to enable increasing production capacity and fulfil future demand.

13. **Option (B) is correct.**
Explanation: Casual callers are unsolicited candidates seeking job possibilities at a company's office. Casual callers may be used as a source of personnel by maintaining a database and screening them for employment openings.

14. **Option (D) is correct.**
Explanation: Labels on refrigerators provide information that helps consumers make informed decisions, use the appliance safely, and comply with regulations.

15. **Option (D) is correct.**
Explanation: A stronger cash flow position makes debt financing more viable than funding through equity.
If a business has high fixed operating costs, for example: rent, insurance premium, etc., it should opt for less fixed financing cost (interest) by using less debt financing. Similarly, if fixed operating cost is less, more debt financing can be done.
Issue of more equity may lead to dilution of management control over the business. Companies which may be afraid of a takeover bid may prefer debt to equity.

16. Option (A) is correct.
Explanation: A depository is an institution that, at the investors' request and via a registered depository participant, maintains securities in electronic format.

17. Option (A) is correct.
Explanation: Efficiency emphasises resource utilization and job completion at a low cost. It's different from effectiveness, which seeks objectives at any cost, and management, which plans and organises resources.

18. Option (D) is correct.
Explanation: Top management makes strategic decisions and directs the company. Top management must assess the business climate and its effects on the firm's survival and performance.

19. Option (B) is correct.
Explanation: Management activities are common and applicable to all types of organizations, regardless of their economic, political, or social nature. Any company, regardless of kind or goal, needs management concepts and practices to perform well.

20. Option (D) is correct.
Explanation: Short-term debt instruments and securities like Treasury bills, Trade bills, Commercial paper, Certificates of deposit, etc. dominate the money market. Money market transactions are usually short-term lending and borrowing using short-term instruments.

21. (a) The concept of management discussed in the paragraph is "coordination." Coordination involves organizing and synchronizing the activities of different individuals or groups within an organization to achieve a common goal effectively and efficiently.

(b) One point of importance of the concept of coordination is: Coordination improves management productivity and efficiency. When team members are assigned jobs and perform in unity, it lowers duplication, disagreements, and resource waste. Smoother operations, higher productivity, and better organization performance result.

22. The following three points emphasise its importance:

1. **Talent Acquisition:** Staffing entails finding, recruiting, and employing qualified candidates for company positions. This boosts the company's success and competitiveness.
2. **Skill Development:** Staffing comprises staff training and development. This boosts productivity, creativity, and company agility.
3. **Employee Engagement and Retention:** Good staffing methods prioritize create a happy work atmosphere, create development opportunities, and recognize employee efforts to retain top talent, decrease turnover, and establish a strong, cohesive team.

23. (a) Vestibule Training: Vestibule Training is a method of training which is conducted on the equipments and machines employees will be using, away from the actual place of work. It is generally used where the employees are required to handle sophisticated machinery.

(b) Two advantages the drivers will get after this training are:

1. Employees can concentrate solely on learning without worrying about errors affecting the manufacturing process.
2. Employees can overcome nervousness about working in the real environment by familiarizing themselves with the simulated work environment during training.

24. SEBI is vital to investor protection and securities market integrity. SEBI has three protective functions:

1. **Investor Protection:** SEBI protects investors' interests. It governs brokers, stock exchanges, and listed firms to promote securities market openness, fairness, and integrity. SEBI facilitates investor education and awareness to inform investors of their rights, dangers, and duties.
2. **Market surveillance:** SEBI monitors trade to identify market manipulation, insider trading, and other misconduct. SEBI detects fraudulent transactions and takes immediate regulatory action to protect investors and market efficiency.
3. **Regulation Enforcement:** SEBI enforces industry ethics and securities law compliance. It punishes regulatory violators with fines and disciplinary actions to deter misconduct and ensure securities market accountability.

25. (a) Right to Consumer Education: The consumer has a right to acquire knowledge and to be a well informed consumer throughout life. He should be aware about his rights and the reliefs available to him in case of a product or service falling short of his expectations. Many consumer organisations and some enlightened businesses are taking an active part in educating consumers in this respect.

(b) The consumer right violated by 'Bholaram' in the above case is the right to safety. This right protects consumers against damaging goods and services. In 'Karamati Sweets,' 'Bholaram' used contaminated khoya and paneer, which made customers ill. This right-to-safety breach shows the significance of product quality and safety to safeguard customers' health and well-being.

26. The case of 'Chromosome' highlights two significant communication barriers in their business process outsourcing (BPO) centre:

1. **Faulty Translations:** One of the communication barriers is related to the employees' proficiency in different languages. The organisation requires its staff to speak at least one foreign and one Indian language, however, some may not be fluent. Lack of expertise might make it difficult to decode audio messages in multiple languages, leading to interpretation errors.
2. **Technical Jargons:** The second barrier is the employees' understanding of technical vocabulary used in the voice reports. Technical language in

medical reports requires expertise to comprehend. Lack of training or familiarity with technical vocabulary may cause staff to misinterpret words or phrases, resulting in report transcription mistakes.

27. (a) Here are four planning limitations:

1. **Change and Uncertainty:** Current facts and future assumptions influence plans. However, market dynamics, technology advances, and legislative changes make the future unpredictable. It might be hard to develop proper preparations with this uncertainty.
2. **Time and Cost:** Planning takes time, resources, and effort to acquire, evaluate, and develop plans. This may be time-consuming and expensive for intricate or long-term strategies. Unexpected delays or financial restrictions might also affect planning and execution.
3. **Change Resistance:** Organisational stakeholders may reject planned changes owing to fear of the unknown, job security concerns, or disagreement with recommended tactics. This resistance might hamper plan execution and take more work to overcome.
4. **Planning is overemphasized:** Plan-focused businesses might suffer from analysis paralysis or bureaucracy. Too much preparation without execution and adaptability may lead to lost opportunities, inefficiencies, and inability to change rapidly.

OR

(b) (i) Strategy: Strategies are high-level plans to accomplish an organisation's long-term aims. This entails studying the competitive environment, finding opportunities and challenges, and creating a strategy to acquire an edge. Top management develops strategies for directing the organisation's direction and resource allocation. They are forward-looking and focus on positioning the organisation for success in the future.

(ii) Procedure: A procedure is a detailed step-by-step sequence of activities or actions that individuals or teams must follow to accomplish a specific task or achieve a particular goal. Procedures are often documented in manuals, guides, or standard operating procedures to ensure consistency, efficiency, and compliance with organisational standards and policies.

28.

Basis	**Production Concept**	**Marketing Concept**
Meaning	Focuses on mass production and efficiency in manufacturing.	Emphasises identifying and satisfying customer needs and wants.
Main Focus	Production efficiency and cost reduction.	Customer satisfaction and creating customer value.
Means	Efficient production processes, and economies of scale.	Market research, customer segmentation, and product differentiation.
Ends	Selling what is produced (product-centric).	Meeting customer demands (customer-centric).

29. (a) The type of organisation that emerged as "Entertainment Through Reading" can be identified as an informal organisation. An informal organisation spontaneously forms inside a formal organisation via social contacts, similar interests, and personal ties. Here, 'Space Rover' members from various groups met informally because they liked reading and playing.

(b) Three advantages of the informal organisation identified in (a) above are:

1. **Improved Morale and Engagement:** Informal gatherings like 'Entertainment Through Reading' may enhance morale and engagement. Social connections, shared activities, and mutual support help members feel more connected to each other.
2. **Creativity and Innovation:** Informal groupings encourages creativity and innovation. In the instance of 'Entertainment Through Reading,' individuals from varied backgrounds and experience discussed, shared ideas, and developed unique solutions or proposals that helped the organisation's goals.
3. **Flexibility and Adaptability:** Informal groups adapt to changing conditions. They can quickly form, evolve, or dissolve based on members' interests and needs. This flexibility promotes spontaneous cooperation, problem-solving, and information exchange.

30. (a) (i) Product Designing and Development: Marketing creates and improves goods and services to fulfil client demands. Using market research and customer input, product designers develop concepts and features. It comprises aesthetics, utility, usefulness, and innovation to set the product apart and attract customers. However, development involves prototyping, testing, and improving the planned product.

(ii) Standardization and Grading: This marketing strategy ensures product and service quality and specifications across markets and manufacturing batches. Standardizing goods, processes, and services ensures uniformity in performance, appearance, safety, and other aspects. This boosts brand recognition, lowers manufacturing costs, and simplifies market entry. However, grading classifies things by quality, size, colour, or performance. Pricing differences and informed client choice are possible with it.

OR

(b) The marketing mix consists of four important elements, also known as the 4Ps:

1. **Product:** This element refers to the goods or services offered by a company to meet customer needs and wants. It covers product characteristics, quality, design, branding, packaging, and after-sales assistance.
2. **Price:** The price customers pay for the product or service. Pricing tactics, discounts, payment conditions, and competitive and perceived value pricing structures are involved.
3. **Place:** Place, also known as distribution, involves the channels and methods used to make the product or service available to customers. Distribution, logistics, warehousing, transportation, and retail choices are included.
4. **Promotion:** Promotion involves communicating and promoting the product or service to the target market. It includes advertising, sales promotions, PR, direct marketing, social media marketing, and personal selling.

31. (a) (i) General Guidelines: Principles of management provide general guidelines or fundamental rules that guide managerial decision-making and actions within an organisation. Observations, experiences, and research on managing behaviours across sectors and situations influence these concepts. They help managers use planning, organising, leading, and regulating ideas.

(ii) Flexible: The principle of management is flexible. The situation, objectives, and operational environment may affect these concepts. This allows managers to creatively adapt principles to business culture, industry developments, technology, and market dynamics. When managers adapt while following management principles, the company may be creative, agile, and responsive.

(iii) Cause and Effect Relationship: Principles of management often describe cause-and-effect relationships between managerial actions and organisational outcomes. They assist managers in understanding how actions and behaviours affect employee motivation, productivity, job satisfaction, and performance. Management improves with rigorous and analytical problem-solving and decision-making under this cause-and-effect relationship.

OR

(b) (i) Method Study: Method Study is a systematic approach used to analyse and improve work methods and processes within an organisation. It includes dividing jobs into smaller parts and examining their sequencing, time, and resources. By identifying process inefficiencies, redundancies, and bottlenecks, method study standardizes, simplifies, and optimizes work processes to boost productivity, decrease waste, and improve organisational performance.

(ii) Differential Piece Wage System: The Differential Piece Wage System pays workers differently per unit of output based on performance. Productivity increases earnings, whereas lesser productivity decreases them. The approach encourages workers to work harder, increasing production and lowering expenses.

(iii) Fatigue Study: The Fatigue Study focuses on understanding and mitigating the physical and mental fatigue experienced by workers during their tasks. Organisations may enhance worker well-being, safety, and performance by understanding and managing tiredness.

32. (a) (i) Operating Efficiency: Operating efficiency refers to how effectively a company manages its resources and processes to generate revenue and control costs. It affects inventories, receivables, and payables management, which affects working capital. A firm with great operational efficiency may manage inventory levels, reduce stockouts and inventory expenses, increase sales cash flow, and negotiate advantageous supplier credit terms.

(ii) Credit Availed: The credit availed by a business, including short-term loans, lines of credit, and trade credit from suppliers, affects its working capital requirements significantly. Credit can fund everyday operations, cash flow volatility, and corporate development. However, excessive credit use increases interest and debt service costs, increasing working capital demands. Effective credit management, prompt repayment, and smart credit use may maximise working capital use and alleviate the financial burden on the organisation.

(iii) Level of Competition: The level of competition in the industry or market where a business operates influences its working capital requirements. Competitive pricing, lengthier receivables collection times, and aggressive marketing and promotional costs might occur. These characteristics may boost working capital for sales growth, inventory management, and customer satisfaction.

OR

(b) (i) **Stability of dividends:** This refers to the consistency and predictability of dividend payments over time. Companies often aim for a stable dividend policy to signal financial strength and attract investors who prefer regular income. Income stability, cash flow predictability, and future investment possibilities affect the company's dividend payout ratio.

(ii) **Contractual constraints:** Companies may have contractual obligations, such as loan covenants or agreements with preferred shareholders, that dictate dividend payments. The company's payout amount and frequency may be limited by these factors. Legal or financial consequences might result from dividend non-payment.

(iii) **Stock market reaction:** The stock market's reaction to dividend announcements or changes can influence a company's dividend decisions. Investor confidence and support for the company's dividend policy may be shown by a stock price gain following larger distributions. Conversely, negative market reactions may prompt a re-evaluation of dividend policies to align with investor expectations and market sentiment.

33. (a) The function of management discussed in the paragraph is "Organising." Organising involves arranging resources, tasks, and people in a structured manner to achieve organisational goals efficiently.

(b) The importance of organising in the context of the G20 Summit preparations includes:

1. **Efficiency:** Organising ensures that resources are allocated effectively, tasks are streamlined, and responsibilities are clearly defined. This boosts summit infrastructure, beautification, hospitality, and security efficiency.
2. **Coordinating:** Organising clarifies relationships and hierarchies, making summit preparations easier for departments, teams, and individuals. The coordination promotes easy communication, cooperation, and integration of activities toward shared goals.
3. **Resource Optimisation:** Sorting activities and responsibilities helps management maximise people, materials, and cash. This avoids duplication, and waste, and optimizes production from limited resources, making it cost-effective.
4. **Goal Alignment:** Organising helps match tasks and responsibilities to G20 Summit goals. This helps team members understand their roles in the bigger picture, gives them purpose and direction, and boosts motivation and commitment.

34. (a) The function of management identified in the scenario is controlling. Controlling is monitoring performance, comparing it to goals, and correcting as needed to meet goals efficiently.

1. **Comparing Actual Performance with Standards: Line:** 'The hotel had to be given possession by next year but the construction of the hotel was running six months behind schedule.'

   This step involves comparison of actual performance with the standard. Such comparison will reveal the deviation between actual and desired results.
2. **AnalysingDeviations:Line:**'Nitininvestigated and reported to the Chief Executive Officer that inspite of huge absenteeism of workers, additional workers were not called. Nitin also reported to the Chief Executive Officer that three of the ten machines being used by the workers were defective.'

   After identifying the deviations that demand managerial attention, these deviations need to be analysed for their causes. Deviations may have multiple
3. **Taking Corrective Action: Line:** 'Nitin ordered for repair of the machines and asked the Project Head to appoint additional workers with . attractive wages to ensure that the deadline is met.'

   This is the last step of Controlling process. By comparing actual performance with established standards, deviations are revealed. The remedial or corrective action is to be taken to remove deficiencies. Here, it involves change in working methods, material, machines, policies and procedures.

(b) Importance of controlling:

(i) Accomplishing organisational goals: The controlling function measures progress towards the organisational goals and brings to light the deviations, if any, and indicates corrective action.

(ii) Judging accuracy of standards: A good control system enables management to verify whether the standards set are accurate and objective.

(iii) Making efficient use of resources: By exercising control, a manager seeks to reduce wastage and spoilage of resources. Each activity is performed in accordance with predetermined standards and norms.

(iv) Improving employee motivation: A good control system ensures that employees know well in advance what they are expected to do and what are the standards of performance on the basis of which they are appraised. (Any two)

1. **On-Time Completion:** Effective control assures project completion. Identifying and fixing absenteeism and malfunctioning machinery helps the hotel fulfill its possession deadline.
2. **Maintaining Quality Standards:** Controlling is essential to quality. Despite project problems, Memo Builders can maintain its excellent building reputation by repairing broken machinery and guaranteeing adequate staff.

Delhi Set-2 **66/5/2**

Note: *Except these, all other questions have been given in Delhi Set-1*

27. (b) (i) Objectives: Objectives are the desired outcomes or targets,an organisation aims to achieve within a limited time frame. These are the guiding principles which provide direction, purpose, and a sense of focus to the organisation's activities. Objectives serve as a roadmap for decision-making and resource allocation, guiding individuals and departments towards the desired goals. Objectives can be categorized on various criteria, such as time frame, scope, and nature. Examples of objectives include increasing market share, improving customer satisfaction, enhancing product quality, and maximising profitability.

(ii) Programme: Programmes are detailed action plans or sequences of activities designed to achieve specific objectives or goals. They provide a structured framework for implementing strategies, coordinating resources, and monitoring progress toward desired outcomes. Programmes break down objectives into manageable tasks, allocate responsibilities, set timelines, and define performance metrics to track results. They help oragnisations translate strategic intent into actionable steps, ensuring alignment between planning and execution. Programmes often involve multiple projects or initiatives coordinated to achieve a common objective. They may include various elements, such as project plans, budgets, resource allocations, milestones, and risk management strategies. Examples of programmes include marketing campaigns, product launches, process improvement initiatives, and organisational development projects.

28. (a) Meaning:

Product Concept: It revolves around the belief that consumers will favour those products that offer the most in quality, performance, and features.

Societal Marketing Concept: It focus on meeting the needs and wants of consumers in a way that also benefits society as a whole.

(b) Main focus:

Product Concept: The main focus of the product concept is on the product itself. It helps on developing and offering high-quality products with superior features and attributes.

Societal Marketing Concept: The societal marketing concept's main focus is on simultaneously meeting customer needs and societal welfare. Organisations following this concept aim to create value for customers while also contributing to the well-being of society and the environment.

(c) Means:

Product Concept: The means of implementing the product concept involve continuous product development, innovation, and improvement. Organisations invest in research and development (R&D).

Societal Marketing Concept: The means of implementing the societal marketing concept involve integrating social and environmental considerations into business practices and marketing strategies. Organisations adopt ethical business practices, environmental sustainability initiatives, and Corporate Social Responsibility (CSR) programmes.

(d) Ends:

Product Concept: The ends or objectives of the product concept are to achieve market success and profitability by offering superior products that meet or exceed customer expectations.

Societal Marketing Concept: The ends or objectives of the societal marketing concept are two folded: first to meet customer needs and wants effectively and other to contribute to the overall well-being of society and the environment.

30. (a) (i) Customer Support Services: Customer support services involve providing assistance, guidance, and solutions to customers before, during, and after the purchase process to enhance customer satisfaction, loyalty, and retention. These services play a crucial role in facilitating post-purchase interactions with the customers and focus on building a strong relationship and addressing their needs and concerns effectively.

(ii) Physical Distribution: Physical distribution, also known as logistics or distribution management, involves the planning, implementation, and control of the flow of goods and services from the point of production to the point of consumption. It encompasses various activities and functions aimed at efficiently and effectively managing the movement and storage of products throughout the supply chain. The key components of physical distribution include order processing , inventory management and warehousing and storage.

OR

(b) The following are the factors that affect the fixation of the price of a product:

Cost of Production: The cost of production, including raw materials, labour, overhead expenses, and manufacturing costs, influences the pricing decisions of a product.

Competition: The level of competition in the market affects the pricing strategy of a product. Companies need to consider the prices charged by competitors for similar products and adjust their prices accordingly to remain competitive and attract maximum customers.

Demand and Supply: The demand and supply dynamics in the market influence pricing decisions. Higher demand relative to supply allows companies to charge higher prices, while lower demand may require companies to lower prices to stimulate sales. Pricing decisions need to balance demand and supply to maximize revenue and profitability.

Market Conditions: Companies need to assess market conditions and adjust their prices accordingly to reflect changes in consumer behaviour and market trends.

31. (a) The following characteristics of principles of management are explained below:

(i) Universal Applicability: Universal applicability refers to the idea that principles of management are applicable in all types of organisations, at all levels and at all time. It means that these principles are relevant and can be applied in various organisational settings, regardless of industry, size, location, or cultural context. They are based on fundamental truths about human behaviour, organisational dynamics, and effective management practices, which transcend specific circumstances or environments. For example, principles such as unity of direction, equity, and division of work are universally applicable concepts.

(ii) Formed by Practice and Experimentation: Principles of management are developed through practice, observation, and experimentation over time. They emerge from the experiences, insights, and lessons learned by managers and theorists as they navigate through the challenges and complexities of managing organisations. These principles are not static or immutable but evolve and adapt in response to changing business environments, technological advancements, and societal trends. For example, Henry Fayol's principles of management, derived from his observations and experiences as a manager in a mining company, emphasizse concepts such as division of work, scalar chain, and discipline.

(iii) Contingent: The contingency perspective suggests that principles of management are contingent upon various factors such as organizational context, goals, objectives, external environment, and internal capabilities. Different situations may require different approaches or principles to be effective. Managers must assess the specific circumstances and adapt their management practices accordingly to achieve desired outcomes. For example, the principle of delegation may be effective in empowering employees and fostering decision-making autonomy in certain organisations with a flat organisational structure.

OR

(b) The following principles of management are explained below:

(i) Division of Work: The principle of division of work, also known as specialisation, states that total task should be divided into smaller jobs or activities and assigned to different individuals based on their skills, abilities, and expertise so they concentrate on only one type of work. By dividing work into specialized tasks, organisations can increase efficiency, productivity, and quality of output. Specialisation allows individuals to focus on specific tasks, develop expertise and perform their work more efficiently, leading to economies of scale and improved overall performance.

(ii) Order: The principle of order emphasises the importance of arranging resources, materials, equipment, and personnel in a systematic and orderly manner to achieve organisational objectives efficiently. Orderliness involves organising resources in such a way that facilitates smooth workflow, minimizes waste, and maximizes productivity. By maintaining order, organisations can streamline operations, reduce errors and delays, and optimise resource utilization. For example, implementing standardised procedures for inventory management and workflow processes helps maintain orderliness in manufacturing operations.

(iii) Unity of Command: The principle of unity of command states that each employee should receive instructions and guidance from only one superior or manager., and must be accountable to them only. This principle helps avoid confusion, conflicts, and set priorities by ensuring clear lines of authority and accountability within the organisation. When employees report to multiple supervisors or managers, it can lead to ambiguity, inconsistency, and inefficiency in decision-making and coordination. For example, in a military organisation, soldiers report to their immediate superior officer, ensuring unity of command and coordination of operations on the battlefield.

32. (a) The following are the factors affecting the working capital requirements of a business:

(i) Inflation: Inflation refers to the general and persistent rise in prices of goods and services over time. Inflation affects the working capital requirements of a business in several ways:

(a) Inflation leads to higher costs of raw materials, labour, and other inputs required for production. As a result, businesses need to invest more working capital to maintain adequate inventory levels and cover the increased production costs.

(b) Inflation leads to delays in receiving payments from customers as they seek extended credit terms to cope with the increased prices. This delay in cash inflows can strain working capital and increase the need for short-term financing to cover operating expenses.

(ii) **Business Cycle:** The business cycle refers to the recurring pattern of expansion and contraction in economic activities over time. It consists of four phases: expansion, peak, contraction (recession), and trough. The business cycle influences the working capital requirements of a business as follows:

(a) **During Expansion:** In the expansion phase of the business cycle, economic activities grow, and demand for goods and services is high. Businesses may need to increase their working capital to finance higher levels of production.

(b) **During Contraction:** In the contraction phase, economic activities slow down, and the demand for goods and services declines. Businesses may experience reduced sales, excess inventory, and liquidity challenges. To cope with reduced cash flows and tighter credit conditions, businesses may need to reduce their working capital requirements.

(iii) **Nature of Business:** The nature of the business, including its industry, size, operating cycle, and seasonality, influences its working capital requirements:

(a) **Industry Characteristics:** Different industries have varying working capital requirements based on their business models, production processes, and sales cycles.

(b) **Seasonality:** Seasonal businesses experience fluctuations in demand and cash flows throughout the year based on seasonal trends or consumer preferences. These businesses may require higher working capital during peak seasons to finance increased production, inventory build-up, and marketing efforts to capitalize on seasonal demand.

OR

(b) The following are the factors affecting the dividend decision of the company:

(i) **Access to Capital Market:** The availability and cost of external financing options influence the dividend decision of a company. Companies with easy access to capital markets, such as equity and debt markets may be more inclined to retain earnings and reinvest them in growth opportunities rather than distributing dividends to shareholders. On the other hand, companies facing limited access to capital markets or higher financing costs may prioritize dividend payments to attract and retain investors and maintain shareholder confidence.

(ii) **Legal Constraints:** Legal constraints, including corporate laws, regulations, and contractual obligations, may restrict a company's ability to pay dividends. Companies must comply with legal requirements and restrictions regarding dividend payments, including solvency tests, capital maintenance rules, and restrictions on dividend payouts specified in loan agreements or bond covenants. Failure to comply with legal constraints can lead to legal liabilities, financial penalties, and reputational damage.

(iii) **Taxation Policy:** Taxation policies, including corporate tax rates, dividend tax rates, and tax treatment of dividends, influence the dividend decision of a company. Higher corporate tax rates may incentivise companies to retain earnings rather than distribute dividends to shareholders to minimise tax liabilities. Similarly, tax policies that favour dividend income over capital gains may encourage companies to distribute dividends to shareholders. Companies must consider the tax implications of dividend payments for both the company and its shareholders when making dividend.

Delhi Set-3 66/5/3

Note: *Except these, all other questions have been given in Delhi Set-1 & 2.*

27. (a) The following are the characteristics of planning:

(i) **Goal-oriented:** Planning involves setting specific goals, objectives, and targets that the organisation aims to achieve within a defined time frame. Planning predetermines the goals of a business organisation and provide a clear direction and purpose for the organisation's activities.

(ii) **Forward-looking:** Planning is future-oriented as it is carried out to achieve some objectives in the future. It focuses on anticipating and preparing for future opportunities, challenges, and uncertainties.

(iii) Flexible: Planning should be flexible and adaptable to changes in the internal and external environment. As conditions evolve and new information becomes available, plans may need to be revised, adjusted, or realigned to remain relevant and effective.

(iv) Continuous: Planning is a never-ending process as it is an ongoing and iterative process that evolves over time. After the plan is made, the organisation has to be in touch with the changing environment and must constantly adapt to the changing internal and external conditions.

OR

(b) (i) Policy: A policy is a general guideline or principle that provides a framework for decision-making and action within an organisation.

Characteristics of policies include:

Broad Scope: Policies address broad areas of organisational activities and apply to multiple situations or scenarios.

Long-term Orientation: Policies are formulated with a long-term perspective and are intended to provide consistent guidance over time.

(ii) Budget: A budget is a quantitative financial plan that allocates resources, such as funds, time, and manpower, to specific activities, projects, or departments within an organisation.

Characteristics of budgets include:

Quantitative: Budgets involve numerical estimates and allocations of resources, such as revenues, expenses, and expenditures, expressed in monetary terms.

Time-bound: Budgets cover a specific period, such as a fiscal year, quarter, or month, and outline the planned inflows and outflows of financial resources over that period.

28. The following are the differences between the Selling Concept and Production Concept of Marketing Management Philosophies:

(a) Meaning:

Selling Concept: It emphasies aggressive selling and promotional efforts to persuade customers to buy a company's products or services.

Production Concept: The production concept of marketing management philosophy focuses on maximizing production efficiency and output.

(b) Main Focus:

Selling Concept: The main focus of the selling concept is on maximsing sales transactions and persuading customers to buy existing products, regardless of their actual needs or wants.

Production Concept: The main focus of the production concept is on production efficiency and maximising output. Companies prioritize increasing production capacity, reducing production costs, and achieving economies of scale.

(c) Means:

Selling Concept: The means employed under the selling concept include aggressive sales and promotional strategies such as personal selling, advertising, sales promotions, and direct marketing.

Production Concept: The means employed under the production concept include investments in production technology, process optimisation, and supply chain management to maximise production efficiency and output.

(d) Ends:

Selling Concept: The end goal of the selling concept is to generate sales revenue by persuading customers to buy existing products through aggressive selling and promotional efforts.

Production Concept: The end goal of the production concept is to maximise production efficiency and output to meet existing demand for standardised products.

30. (a) The following are the functions of marketing:

(i) Gathering and Analysing Market Information: This involves collecting, processing, and interpreting data related to market trends, customer preferences, competitor activities, and other relevant factors. This function serves several purposes such as:

(1) Understanding customer needs

(2) Monitoring competitor strategies

(ii) Marketing Planning: Marketing planning is the process of developing comprehensive marketing strategies and action plans to achieve organisational objectives and goals. This function involves several key activities:

- **Setting Objectives:** Marketing planning begins with setting clear and measurable marketing objectives. Like increasing market share, launching new products, expanding into new markets, or enhancing brand awareness and reputation.
- **Market Research:** It involves a systematic gathering, analysis, and interpretation of data. It provides insights into market dynamics, customer behaviour and other factors that influence business decisions.

OR

(b) The following are the major components of the physical distribution:

(i) **Order Processing:** Order processing involves receiving, recording, and processing customer orders, as well as coordinating order fulfillment and delivery. This component includes activities such as order entry, order verification, order picking, packing, and invoicing.

(ii) **Inventory Management:** Inventory management focuses on planning, controlling, and optimising inventory levels to meet customer demand while minimising holding costs and stockouts. This component includes inventory planning, replenishment, stock-keeping, inventory tracking, and inventory control measures.

(iii) **Warehousing and Storage:** Warehousing and storage involve the storage, handling, and management of goods within distribution centers or warehouses. This component includes activities such as receiving incoming shipments, storing inventory, managing warehouse layouts, organising stock, and facilitating order picking and packing.

(iv) **Transportation:** Transportation refers to the movement of goods from production facilities to distribution centers and ultimately to customers using various modes of transportation such as road, rail, air, and sea.

31. (a) The following are the points of significance of principles of management:

(i) **Providing Managers with Useful Insights into Reality:** Principles of management provide managers with valuable insights into the realities of organisational dynamics, human behaviour, and effective management practices. By studying and understanding these principles, managers gain deeper insights into how organisations function, how people behave within the organisations and what managerial approaches are most effective in achieving organisational goals. Principles such as division of work, unity of command, and scalar chain offer practical guidelines for managers to structure organisations, assign responsibilities, and coordinate activities effectively.

(ii) **Meeting Changing Environmental Requirements:** Principles of management serve as flexible guidelines that can be adapted to meet changing environmental requirements and challenges. In today's dynamic and uncertain business environment, organisations face constant changes in technology, market conditions, competitive landscapes, regulatory frameworks, and societal expectations. Principles such as flexibility, adaptation, and contingency planning help managers anticipate and respond to these changes effectively.

(iii) **Scientific Decision-making:** Principles of management promote scientific decision-making by providing a systematic and rational framework for analysing problems, evaluating alternatives, and making informed choices. Management principles such as unity of command, discipline, and orderliness emphasise the importance of logical reasoning, evidence-based analysis, and data-driven decision-making. By applying these principles, managers can assess the costs and benefits of different courses of action, weigh trade-offs, and select the most effective solutions to organizational challenges.

OR

(b) (i) Unity of Direction: Unity of direction is a principle of management that emphasises the importance of aligning organisational activities and efforts toward common objectives and goals. Each group of activities should be under the control of one superior only. Unity of direction helps avoid conflicting priorities, duplication of efforts, and wastage of resources by ensuring that everyone works towards shared organizational goals.

(ii) **Remuneration to Employees:** The principle of Remuneration to Employees highlights the importance of providing fair and equitable compensation to employees,reasonable and satisfactory to both employees and employers. . According to this principle, employees should receive compensation and rewards commensurate with their skills, efforts, and performance to motivate and retain them. Remuneration includes various forms of financial and non-financial rewards such as wages, salaries, bonuses, incentives, benefits, and recognition. By aligning employee rewards with organizational goals and performance expectations, managers can incentivise desired behaviours, foster a positive work culture, and drive employee engagement and performance.

(iii) **Equity:** The principle of equity emphasizes fairness, justice, and impartiality in the treatment of employees within the organization. According to this principle, managers should treat their employees with justice and kindness. They must ensure that policies, practices, and decisions are applied fairly and consistently to all employees, without discrimination or favouritism.. By promoting equity, managers create a supportive and inclusive work environment where employees feel valued, respected, and treated fairly. Equity fosters trust, collaboration, and teamwork among employees, leading to higher levels of satisfaction, commitment, and performance.

32. (a) The factors affecting the working capital requirements of a business are:

(i) Credit Allowed: The credit allowed by suppliers and the credit terms negotiated with creditors significantly impact the working capital requirements of a business. When suppliers offer favourable credit terms, such as extended payment periods or trade credit, it reduces the immediate cash outflow required to purchase raw materials or inventory. This allows the business to conserve its cash reserves and use them for other operational needs.

(ii) Production Cycle: The production cycle, which encompasses the time required to convert raw materials into finished goods and sell them to customers, influences the working capital requirements of a business. Longer production cycles typically require higher levels of working capital to finance inventory holding costs, labor expenses, and overheads during the production process. Businesses with extended production cycles may need to maintain larger inventories to ensure uninterrupted production and meet customer demand.

(iii) Availability of Raw Material: The availability and accessibility of raw materials necessary for production affect the working capital requirements of a business. If raw materials are readily available from reliable suppliers at competitive prices, it reduces the need for excess inventory and working capital tied up in stockpiling materials. Conversely, if raw materials are scarce, subject to price volatility, or sourced from distant suppliers, it may necessitate higher inventory levels and working capital to ensure uninterrupted production and mitigate supply chain risks.

OR

(b) The following are the factors affecting the dividend decision of a company:

(i) Growth Opportunities: The availability of growth opportunities influences the dividend decision of a company. If the company has promising investment opportunities that offer potential for profitable growth and expansion, management may choose to retain earnings rather than distribute them as dividends. Retaining earnings allows the company to reinvest capital into new projects, research and development, acquisitions, or market expansion initiatives that can generate higher returns and enhance shareholder value over the long term.

(ii) Cash Flow Position: Companies with strong cash flow generation and liquidity reserves may have greater flexibility to pay dividends to shareholders without jeopardising their operational and investment needs. Management evaluates the company's cash flow position, projected cash needs, and financial obligations when determining the amount and timing of dividend payments to shareholders.

(iii) Shareholders' Preference: The preferences and expectations of shareholders regarding dividend payments influence the dividend decision of a company. Some shareholders, such as income-oriented investors or retirees, may prioritize receiving regular dividend income as a source of passive income and capital preservation. In contrast, other shareholders, such as growth-oriented investors or institutional investors, may prioritize capital appreciation and reinvestment of earnings to maximise long-term returns. Management considers shareholders' preferences, communication channels, and feedback mechanisms to strike a balance between dividend payouts and retained earnings that align with shareholder interests and expectations.

Outside Delhi Set-1 66/4/1

1. Option (C) is correct.

Explanation: Growth is an organisational objective which involves the increase in work and prospects of the business.

2. Option (C) is correct.

Explanation: The middle level management is responsible for the activities of the first line managers.

3. Option (D) is correct.

Explanation: Merely allocation of work is not enough. The establishment of reporting relationships is important to establish hierarchal structure and create coordination.

4. Option (D) is correct.

Explanation: By comparing actual performance with established standards, deviations are revealed. The remedial or corrective action is to be taken to remove deficiencies. Here, it involves change in working methods, material, machines, policies and procedures. It may also require improvement in the motivation, supervision and modifications in the business plans.

5. **Option (A) is correct.**
Explanation: The dividends are declared by the companies based on the earnings- past or present.
6. **Option (C) is correct.**
Explanation: A financial market helps to link the savers and the investors by mobilizing funds between them. In doing so it performs what is known as an allocative function.
7. **Option (C) is correct.**
Explanation: Directing focuses on guiding and motivating employees to achieve organizational goals, but it does not directly ensure that activities are performed as per plans. That responsibility typically falls under the planning function of management
8. **Option (C) is correct.**
Explanation: Interaction among people at work gives rise to a 'network of social relationships among employees' called the informal organisation. It provides them a sense of belongings.
9. **Option (C) is correct.**
Explanation: Sales promotion refers to short-term incentives, offered to encourage immediate sale of the product.
10. **Option (C) is correct.**
Explanation: Coordination is a process by which a manager synchronises the activities of different departments to achieve the common organisational goals. It is the force that binds all the other functions of management.
11. **Option (C) is correct.**
Explanation: The protective function deals with protecting the interest of investors and other financial entities. The regulatory function of SEBI includes making rules and regulations for financial entities, including intermediaries and corporates. The development function of the SEBI deals with the steps taken by SEBI to provide the knowledge of the trading and the market functions to the investors.
12. **Option (B) is correct.**
Explanation: The consumer has a right to have complete information about the product he intends to buy including its ingredients, date of manufacture, price, quantity, directions for use, etc.
13. **Option (B) is correct.**
Explanation: Business environment is relative because it varies from country to country. It is dynamic because it keeps on changing.
14. **Option (D) is correct.**
Explanation: Demonetisation leads to channelising the savings into formal system.
15. **Option (D) is correct.**
Explanation: Technological Environment of business includes forces relating to scientific improvements and innovations which provide new ways of producing goods and services and new methods and techniques of operating a business.
16. **Option (A) is correct.**
Explanation: For complaints below ₹1 crore, consumers can go to district commission.
17. **Option (B) is correct.**
Explanation: The process where securities held by the investor in the physical form are cancelled and the investor is given an electronic entry or number so that she/he can hold it as an electronic balance in an account. This process of holding securities in an electronic form is called dematerialisation.
18. **Option (B) is correct.**
Explanation: Threats refer to the external environment trends and changes that will hinder a firm's performance. Besides opportunities, environment happens to be the source of many threats. Environmental awareness can help managers to identify various threats on time and serve as an early warning signal.
19. **Option (C) is correct.**
Explanation: Brand name is the verbal component of the brand. A brand or part of a brand that is given legal protection is called trademark.
20. **Option (B) is correct.**
Explanation: Secondary packaging refers to additional layers of protection that are kept till the product is ready for use
21. **(a)** Management as an art
(b) The nature of management as an art is:
- Personalised application: The use of knowledge is different for different people. Art is a personalised concept. He studies critical situations and formulates his own theories for use in a given situation.
Lines "They used basic knowledge in their unique manner."
- Based on practice and creativity: Art is practical and involves the creative practice of the existing theoretical knowledge. Managers apply the principles based on how creative they are.
Lines "As all the friends are specialised in social work, they adopted three different slums of Mumbai and started educating the slum dwellers in their own creative manner."

22. **(a)** (i) Fixed operating costs: Costs like building rent, insurance premium, salaries, etc. which have to be incurred irrespective of the production level are called fixed operating costs. If a business has high fixed operating costs, it should opt for less fixed financing cost (interest) by using less debt financing. Similarly, if fixed operating cost is less, more debt financing can be done.
(ii) Cash flow position of the company: A stronger cash flow position makes debt financing more viable than funding through equity according to marks. Could add A company's cash flow position is its cash inflows and outflows over a period. This shows how suc-

cessfully an organization manages its cash to handle its financial obligations and encourage activities. Positive cash flow indicates healthy financial management, while negative cash flow may signal potential challenges

(b) The difference between primary market and secondary market is:

Basis	Primary Market	Secondary Market
Securities traded	There is sale of securities by new companies for further (new) issues of securities by existing companies to investors.	There is trading of existing securities only.
Instruments	Securities are sold by the company to the investor directly (or through an intermediary)	Ownership of existing securities is exchanged between investors. The company is not involved at all.
Capital formation	The flow of funds is from savers to investors, i.e. the primary market directly promotes capital formation.	Enhances encashability (liquidity) of securities, i.e., the secondary market indirectly promotes capital formation.
Buying/Selling	Only buying of securities takes place in the primary market. Securities cannot be sold by the investors.	Both the buying and the selling of securities can take place on the stock exchange.
Price determination	Prices are determined and decided by the management of the company.	Prices are determined by demand and supply of the securities.
Location	There is no fixed geographical location.	Located at specified places.

[Any three]

23. (a) Training and Development

(b) Five benefits of training and development to Suzon Cars are:

- Systematic learning prevents wastage of efforts and money of the organisation.
- Enhances employee's productivity leading to higher profits for the firm.
- Enables employee to become managers in future.
- Increases employee morale and reduces employee turnover.
- Obtains better response to the dynamic environment.

24. (a) Planning and controlling are inseparable twins of management. Planning provides the basis for controlling. The desired standards are set in the process of planning in clear and specific terms. In the process of controlling the actual performance is measured and compared with these standards and the deviations if any are identified and appropriate corrective action is taken. Thus, planning without controlling is meaningless and controlling without planning is blind.

(b) Planning is prescriptive whereas controlling is evaluative. Planning is an intellectual activity which is concerned with thinking, articulating and analysing various alternative course of actions and prescribing the best possible alternative in order to achieve the desired goals efficiently and effectively. Controlling on the other hand is concerned with ensuring that events conform to plans.

(c) Planning is looking ahead while controlling is looking back. Plans are prepared for future and are based on forecasts about future conditions.

OR

(b) (i) Critical Point Control: It is neither economical nor easy to keep a check on each and every activity in an organisation. Control should, therefore, focus on key result areas (KRAs) which are critical to the success of an organisation. These KRAs are set as the critical points. If anything goes wrong at the critical points, the entire organisation suffers. For instance, in a manufacturing organisation, an increase of 5 per cent in the labour cost may be more troublesome than a 15 per cent increase in postal charges.

(ii) Management by Exception: Management by exception, which is often referred to as control by exception, is based on the belief that an attempt to control everything results in controlling nothing. Thus, only significant deviations which go beyond the permissible limit should be brought to the notice of management.

25. (a) The features of directing are:

(i) Directing initiates action: Directing is a key managerial function. A manager has to perform this function along with planning, organising, staffing and controlling while discharging his duties in the organisation. While other functions prepare a setting for action, directing initiates action in the organisation.

(ii) Directing takes place at every level of management: Every manager, from top executive to supervisor performs the function of directing. The directing takes place wherever superior – subordinate relations exist.

(iii) **Directing is a continuous process:** Directing is a continuous activity. It takes place throughout the life of the organisation irrespective of people occupying managerial positions. Organisations like Infosys, Tata, BHEL, HLL and the managers may change but the directing process continues because without direction the organisational activities cannot continue further.

(iv) **Directing flows from top to bottom:** Directing is first initiated at top level and flows to the bottom through organisational hierarchy. It means that every manager can direct his immediate subordinate and take instructions from his immediate boss.

OR

(b) The semantic barriers are:

(i) **Technical Jargon:** Many specialists like doctor, engineer, scientist etc. use technical words in their communication which may not be understood by the listeners. This leads to poor communication like patients do not understand the words used by doctors.

(ii) **Body language and gesture decoding:** The information communicated can be misinterpreted if the sender's body movements do not match the verbal communication. If there is no match between what is said and what is expressed in body movements, communications may be wrongly perceived.

26. (a) The steps in the process of selection are:

(i) **Selection tests:** Selection tests measure the aptitude, intelligence, personality etc. of the candidates who have applied for the vacant jobs. They are intended to measure certain characteristics of the individuals.

(ii) **Employment Interview:** It is a formal interaction between the employer and job candidate. It is an in-depth conversation which is conducted to evaluate an applicant's suitability for the position. The interviewer seeks information and the interviewee provides the same. Part b is missing the importance of staffing as management function.

(b) Importance of staffing function of management:

(i) **Competent personnel:** Staffing helps in discovering and obtaining competent personnel for various jobs. To prevent the shortage of technically skilled personnel, staffing is necessary.

(ii) **Better performance:** Staffing ensures better performance by putting right person in the right job. The efficiency of the people increases.

(iii) **Optimum utilisation of the resources:** Efficient human resource is one of the requirements for optimum utilisation of the resources. Staffing ensures optimum amount of workforce in the organisation by indicating shortage of the personnel in advance and avoiding over manning. Thus, it also avoids disruption of work and high labour costs.

(iv) **Improves job satisfaction:** Staffing involves objective assessment, thus result in fair rewarding for employees' contribution. This ultimately improves job satisfaction and morale of the employees.

27. (a) **Non-financial incentives:** It refers to the incentives which are related to psychological, social and emotional factors. Some of the incentives referred in the above case are:

- Job Security, refers to providing stability to the employees about future income and work so that they do not feel worried on these aspects and work with a greater zeal.
- Employee Recognition, which means acknowledgement with a show of appreciation.

(b) **Security or safety needs:** These refer to the needs for physical safety, protection and economic security which include safety of person and property and come into picture only when physiological needs are satisfied.

Esteem needs: These needs refer to factors such as self-respect, independence, status, recognition, appreciation and attention and their satisfaction leads to increased confidence.

28. The factors affecting working capital requirements are:

(a) **Level of competition:** The level of competition affects the working capital requirement of the organisation. When the level of competition is high, the firms require larger stocks to meet urgent orders from customers and thus, higher working capital is required. At times, due to competition, the firms have to extend the credit terms as well.

(b) **Inflation:** Inflation increases the prices of the product in the market. Larger amounts are required even to maintain the constant volume of production and sales. As the rate of inflation rises, the working capital requirement of the business increases even at the same level of inventory.

29. (a) **Two responsibilities discharged by Nishi are:**

- Read the labels carefully to get information about the prices, net weight, manufacturing and expiry date of the product.

- File a case in the consumer court in case of deficient services or defective product. Do not fail to take an action even if the amount involved is small.

(b) Two reliefs which can be granted to Nishi are:
- Refund of price and payment of punitive damages.
- Discontinue unfair trade practices.

30. The factors affecting choice of capital structure discussed over here are:
- **Floatation cost:** The cost of raising the funds is known as floatation cost. They affect the choice of capital structure as higher the floatation cost, less attractive the source of finance.
- **Control:** The issue of debt does not lead to a dilution of management's control over the business but, the issue of equity reduces the management's holding in the company.
- **Stock market conditions:** The stock market conditions affect the capital structure. During the boom period, equity shares can be easily issued even at a higher price. During recession, the company may find it difficult to issue equity capital.
- **Regulatory framework:** Every company has to operate according to the regulatory framework given by the law. Raising funds require fulfilment of certain norms and regulations laid down by SEBI.

31. (a) (i) Strategy: A strategy provides the broad contours of an organisation's business. It will also refer to future decisions defining the organisations direction and scope in the long run. Thus, we can say a strategy is a comprehensive plan for accomplishing an organisation's objectives.

(ii) Method: Methods provide the prescribed ways or manner in which a task has to be performed considering the objective. The selection of proper method saves time, money and effort which increases the efficiency.

(iii) Budget: A budget is a statement of expected results expressed in numerical terms. It is a plan which quantifies future facts and figures. A budget is a useful tool for planning and controlling. Making a budget involves forecasting.

OR

(b) The limitations of planning are:

(i) Planning may not work in dynamic environment: The business environment is dynamic, nothing is constant. It becomes difficult to accurately assess future trends in the environment if economic policies are modified or political conditions in the country are not stable or there is a natural calamity. In such situations, the plans can fail.

(ii) Planning leads to rigidity: In an organisation, a well-defined plan is drawn up with specific goals to be achieved within a specific time frame. These plans then decide the future course of action and managers may not be in a position to change it. This kind of rigidity in plans may create difficulty. Managers need to be given some flexibility to be able to cope with the changed circumstances. Following a pre-decided plan, when circumstances have changed, may not turn out to be in the organisations interest.

(iii) Planning is time consuming: Sometimes plans to be drawn up take so much of time that there is not much time left for their implementation. Planning is a lengthy process which might lead to delay. The collection, analysis and interpretation of data takes a lot of time. It can also lead to delay in decisions and action.

32. The techniques used are:

(a) Standardisation and simplification: Standardisation refers to the process of setting standards for every business activity. Simplification refers to eliminating unnecessary diversity of the products.

(b) Method Study: Method study refers to finding out the one best way of doing the job. The objective is to minimise the cost of production and maximise the quality and satisfaction of the customer. To determine the best way there are several parameters. Right from procurement of raw materials till the final product is delivered to the customer every activity is part of method study. Taylor devised the concept of assembly line by using method study.

The principle used here is:

Development of each and every person to his or her greatest efficiency and prosperity: Worker training is essential to learn the 'best method' developed as a consequence of the scientific approach. Taylor was of the view that the concern for efficiency could be built in right from the process of employee selection. Each person should be scientifically selected. Then, work assigned should suit her/his physical, mental and intellectual capabilities. To increase efficiency, they should be given required training. Efficient employees would produce more and earn more.

33. (a) The functions of marketing are:

(i) Marketing planning: The goal of marketer is to develop appropriate marketing plan so that the marketing objectives of the organisation could be achieved. A complete marketing plan will include important aspects like increasing the level of production, promotion of the products, etc.

(ii) Branding: It is the process of creating a name or symbol or combination of both to differentiate the product of the company from the competitors. A marketer has to decide whether to sell the product under the generic name or with a brand name. Brand name helps in creating product differentiation, i.e., providing basis for distinguishing the product of a firm with that of the competitor, which in turn, helps in building customer's loyalty and in promoting its sale.

(iii) Pricing: Price of product refers to the amount of money customers have to pay to obtain a product. Price is an important factor affecting the success or failure of a product in the market. The demand for the product is related to its price. The lower the price, higher will be the demand for the product and vice-versa.

OR

Promotion mix refers to a combination of tools used to communicate with potential customers to inform them about a product and persuading them to buy it.

Advertising: It is an impersonal form of communication which is paid by the marketers to promote goods or services. Advertising is a medium through which a large number of people can be reached over a vast geographical area. For example, an advertisement message placed in a national daily reaches lakh of its subscribers. Advertising is less flexible as the message is standardised and is not tailor made to the requirements of the different customer groups.

Sales Promotion: It refers to short-term incentives, offered to encourage immediate sale of the product. The companies use the sales promotion techniques for tradesmen and middlemen also. The various sales promotion techniques are rebates, discount, refunds etc.

Public Relations: It involves activities required to promote and protect the image of a company or its product. Public relations programmes help in building corporate image that affects favourably on the products.

34. (a) Preeti has used 'Delegation'. The delegation of authority refers to the division of labour and decision-making responsibility to an individual that reports to a manager.

(b) Importance of delegation:

(i) Effective management: By empowering the employees, the managers are able to function more efficiently as they get more time to concentrate on important matters.

(ii) Employee development: Delegation empowers the employees by providing them with the chance to use their skills, gain experience and develop themselves for higher positions.

(iii) Motivation of employees: Superior's trust improves employee's self-esteem and confidence . When a superior entrusts a subordinate with a task, it is not merely the sharing of work but involves trust on the superior's part and commitment on the part of the subordinate.

(iv) Facilitation of growth: Delegation helps in the expansion of an organisation by providing a ready workforce to take up leading positions in new ventures.

(v) Basis of management hierarchy: Delegation of authority establishes superior-subordinate relationships, which are the basis of hierarchy of management.

(vi) Better co-ordination: Clarity in reporting relationships help in developing and maintaining effective coordination amongst the departments, levels and functions of management. **(Any five)**

Outside Delhi Set-2 66/4/2

Note: *Except these, all other questions have been given in Outside Delhi Set-1.*

2. Option (C) is correct.

***Explanation*:** This statement is incorrect. While top-level managers are responsible for overseeing the overall direction and strategy of the business, they typically do not handle all activities of the business directly. They are responsible for setting the over all-dirction of the organisation and make sure that the desired goals are achieved Additionally, while they may consider the societal impact of their decisions, it's not solely their responsibility. Societal impact is often a concern across all levels of management.

22. (a) The following are the differences between the capital market and money market based on following:

(i) Participants:

Capital Market: Participants in the capital market include individuals, institutional investors, corporations, governments, and other entities that seek to raise long-term funds or invest in long-term securities.

Money Market: Participants in the money market primarily consist of financial institutions, such as commercial banks, central banks, investment banks, and corporations that deal with short-term money requirements.

(ii) Investment Outlay:

Capital Market: Investment outlay refers to the funds required for long-term investments in assets.

Money Market: The investment outlay in the money market is focused on short-term financial instruments that mature within one year or less.

(iii) Expected Return:

Capital Market: Investors in the capital market typically expect higher returns compared to the money market due to the longer investment horizon and higher risk associated with long-term investments.

Money Market: Investments in the money market generally offer lower returns compared to the capital market due to their short-term nature and lower risk.

OR

(b) The following are the factors affecting long-term investment decision:

(i) Cash flows of the project: Investors and companies analyse the projected cash inflows and outflows associated with an investment project to assess its profitability and viability over the long term. Positive cash flows indicate that the project is generating sufficient revenue to cover expenses and provide a return on investment. Conversely, negative cash flows may signal financial difficulties and indicate a potential lack of profitability. Evaluating the timing and magnitude of cash flows helps investors make informed decisions about allocating capital to long-term investment opportunities.

(ii) The investment criteria involved: Long-term investment decisions are influenced by various investment criteria, including Return on Investment (ROI), Net Present Value (NPV), Internal Rate of Return (IRR), payback period, and risk considerations. These criteria help investors assess the potential profitability, risk, and feasibility of investment opportunities over the long term. Risk considerations involve evaluating factors such as market volatility, economic conditions, regulatory changes, and industry-specific risks to assess the likelihood of achieving the desired investment outcomes. By considering these investment criteria, investors can make informed decisions about allocating capital to long-term investment projects that align with their financial objectives and risk tolerance.

25. (a) The following are the points that highlight the importance of directing as a function of management:

(i) Alignment of Efforts: The directing function ensures that all employees understand their roles, responsibilities, and objectives within the organisation. By providing clear direction and guidance, managers can align individual efforts with organisational goals, fostering synergy and coordination across departments.

(ii) Motivation and Engagement: Effective directing involves motivating and inspiring employees to perform at their best. Managers can use various motivational techniques, such as recognition, rewards, and feedback, to boost employee morale, commitment, and job satisfaction. Engaged employees are more likely to demonstrate higher levels of productivity, creativity, and initiative.

(iii) Clarity and Communication: Directing facilitates clear communication channels within the organisation. Managers communicate goals, expectations, and performance standards to employees, ensuring that everyone understands what is expected of them. Clear communication helps minimise misunderstandings, conflicts, and errors, promoting smooth workflow and collaboration.

(iv) Adaptation and Flexibility: In dynamic and uncertain environments, the directing function helps organisations adapt to changes effectively. By facilitating flexibility and agility, directing enables organisations to stay competitive and responsive to market demands.

OR

(b) The following are the semantic barriers to the communication:

(i) Badly Expressed Message:

A badly expressed message refers to communication that is unclear, ambiguous, or poorly articulated, leading to misunderstandings and misinterpretations. This barrier can arise due to various factors, such as vague language, technical jargon, or lack of clarity in conveying ideas. To overcome this barrier, communicators should strive to use clear and concise language, provide context or examples where necessary, and encourage feedback to ensure mutual understanding.

(ii) Symbols with Different Meanings:

Symbols with different meanings refer to non-verbal or visual cues that may carry different interpretations across individuals or cultures. This barrier can occur when symbols, gestures, or expressions are used without considering their cultural, contextual, or personal significance. When symbols with different meanings are used in communication, it can lead to misunderstandings, miscommunication, or even conflict. To address this barrier, communicators should be mindful of cultural differences, use symbols judiciously, and seek clarification or provide context when necessary to ensure that messages are interpreted accurately and respectfully across diverse audiences.

28. The following are the ways in which below mentioned factors affect the working capital requirements of a company:

(a) **Production cycle.** The production cycle directly influences the working capital requirements of a company due to its impact on the cash conversion cycle.

(i) **Procurement of Raw Materials:** At the beginning of the production cycle, the company needs to purchase raw materials to initiate the manufacturing process. This requires funds to be allocated for inventory procurement, which raises the working capital needs in the company.

(ii) **Manufacturing Processes:** During the production process, raw materials are transformed into work-in-progress and eventually finished goods. This stage may require significant investment in labor, machinery, utilities, and overhead costs. These expenses contribute to the working capital requirements.

(b) **Seasonal factors.**

(i) **Fluctuating Sales:** Seasonal businesses experience peaks and troughs in sales volume throughout the year. During peak seasons, higher sales may necessitate increased production, inventory build-up, and the need for additional working capital to support higher levels of activity. Conversely, during off-peak seasons, sales may decline, leading to excess inventory, reduced cash inflows, and increased working capital needs to cover operating expenses.

(ii) **Inventory Management:** Seasonal fluctuations often require companies to adjust their inventory levels to meet changing demand patterns. During peak seasons, companies may need to build up inventory levels to ensure product availability and meet customer demand. This requires additional investment in inventory, tying up working capital. Conversely, during off-peak seasons, excess inventory may need to be managed to avoid carrying costs and obsolescence, impacting working capital requirements.

31. (a) The following are the explanations for the types of plans:

(i) **Objectives:**

Objectives are the desired outcomes or targets an organisation aims to achieve within a limited time frame. These are the guiding principles which provide direction, purpose, and a sense of focus to the organisation's activities. Objectives serve as a road map for decision-making and resource allocation, guiding individuals and departments towards the desired goals. Objectives can be categorized on various criteria, such as time frame, scope, and nature.

Examples of objectives include increasing market share, improving customer satisfaction, enhancing product quality, and maximizing profitability.

(ii) **Policy:**

Policies are guidelines or principles that provide a framework for decision-making and action within an organisation. They outline the organisation's overall direction, values, and standards, guiding behaviour and decisions at all levels. Policies serve s broad directives that define acceptable behaviour, establish boundaries and provide a framework for standardised actions in the organisation. They help clarify expectations, reduce ambiguity, and promote uniformity in decision-making across different functions and departments.

Examples of policies include employee code of conduct, financial reporting procedures, quality assurance standards, and environmental sustainability guidelines. Policies are typically formulated by top management and communicated to employees.

(iii) **Programme:**

Programmes are detailed action plans or sequences of activities designed to achieve specific objectives or goals. They provide a structured framework for implementing strategies, coordinating resources, and monitoring progress toward desired outcomes. Programmes break down objectives into manageable tasks, allocate responsibilities, set timelines, and define performance metrics to track results. They help organisations translate strategic intent into actionable steps, ensuring alignment between planning and execution. Programmes often involve multiple project.

Examples of programmes include marketing campaigns, product launches, process improvement initiatives, and organisational development projects.

OR

(b) The following are the limitations of functions of management:

(i) **Planning reduces creativity:**

One limitation of planning is that it can stifle creativity and innovation by imposing rigid structures, procedures, and standards. Overemphasis on detailed planning may discourage experimentation, risk-taking, and thinking outside the box. Employees may feel constrained by predefined goals and strategies, limiting their ability to explore new ideas or adapt to changing circumstances. To mitigate this limitation, managers should balance structured planning with opportunities for creativity and flexibility, fostering a culture that encourages innovation, experimentation, and continuous improvement.

(ii) Planning involves huge costs:

Planning can be resource-intensive, requiring significant time, effort, and financial investment to develop, implement, and maintain plans effectively. The process of gathering information, analyzing data, forecasting trends, and formulating strategies can be complex and time-consuming, consuming valuable organisational resources. To address this limitation, managers should prioritize planning activities based on their potential impact on organisational performance and allocate resources efficiently to maximize value.

(iii) Planning does not guarantee success:

Despite careful planning and thorough analysis, there is no guarantee that plans will always succeed or achieve desired outcomes. Planning is based on assumptions, forecasts, and projections about future events, which are inherently uncertain and subject to change. External factors, such as market dynamics, competitive pressures, technological advancements, and regulatory changes, can disrupt plans and undermine their effectiveness. While planning provides a roadmap for action, it cannot eliminate risk or guarantee success. Instead, managers should adopt a proactive and adaptive approach to planning, continuously monitoring performance, identifying emerging trends, and adjusting strategies accordingly to enhance resilience and agility.

33. (a) (i) Gathering and Analysing Market Information:

Gathering and analysing market information is a critical function of marketing aimed at understanding the needs, preferences, behaviours, and trends of consumers and the overall market environment. This function involves systematic collection, processing, and interpretation of data related to customers, competitors, products, pricing, distribution channels, and macroeconomic factors.

(ii) Standardisation and Grading:

Standardisation: Standardisation involves establishing uniform guidelines, specifications and features, for products or services across different markets or segments. This simplifies production, distribution, and marketing processes, reduces costs, and enhances efficiency.

Grading: Grading involves classifying products or services into different categories based on predetermined criteria. Grading systems help consumers make informed purchase decisions by providing clear standards for comparison and evaluation. For example, agricultural products like fruits, vegetables, and grains are graded based on factors such as size, colour, ripeness, and freshness.

(iii) Consumer Support Services:

Consumer support services are one of the key functions of marketing aimed at providing assistance, guidance, and solutions to consumers before, during, and after the purchase process to enhance customer satisfaction, loyalty, and retention. It helps to build a strong customer relationship by facilitating customer interactions.

OR

(b) The following are the components of the physical distribution:

(i) Order Processing:

Order processing involves the activities associated with receiving, recording, and fulfilling customer orders. This component includes order entry, order confirmation, order picking, packing, and order verification.

(ii) Inventory Management:

Inventory management entails the control and optimisation of inventory levels to meet customer demand while minimising holding costs and stock outs. This component involves inventory planning, replenishment, storage, and tracking.

(iii) Warehousing and Storage:

Warehousing and storage involve the physical facilities and infrastructure for storing, handling, and managing inventory. This component includes warehouse layout design, storage systems, material handling equipment, and inventory control processes. Warehousing operations aim to optimise space utilisation, facilitate efficient product flow, ensure inventory accuracy, and provide value-added services.

(iv) Transportation:

Transportation encompasses the movement of goods from one location to another within the supply chain. This component includes various modes of transportation such as road, rail, air, sea, and intermodal transportation. Transportation activities involve route planning, carrier selection, freight consolidation, shipment tracking, and delivery scheduling. Efficient transportation management helps minimise transit times, reduce shipping costs, improve service levels, and enhance supply chain visibility and responsiveness.

(v) Packaging:

Packaging involves the design, development, and utilisation of containers, materials, and protective packaging to safeguard products during transportation, storage, and handling. This component includes packaging design, labelling, marking, and compliance with regulatory requirements.

(vi) Materials Handling:

Materials handling encompasses the movement, loading, unloading, and storage of goods within warehouses, distribution centres, and vehicles. This component includes the use of equipment and technologies such as forklifts, conveyors, pallet jacks, and automated systems. Materials handling activities aim to streamline operations, reduce labor costs, improve efficiency, and enhance safety and ergonomics in handling operations.

Outside Delhi Set-3 — 66/4/3

Note: *Except these, all other questions have been given in Outside Delhi Set-1 & 2.*

2. Option (C) is correct.

***Explanation*:** The statement is incorrect because while minimising wastage of materials is an important aspect of operational management, it is not solely the responsibility of supervisors. It involves coordination among various levels of management, including operational, middle, and top management, as well as the involvement of employees at all levels.

22. (a) The following are the differences between the capital market and money market:

(i) Instruments:

Capital Market: The Capital market deals with long-term securities, with maturities exceeding one year.

Money Market: The money market deals with short-term debt instruments with maturities typically ranging from overnight to one year.

(ii) Liquidity:

Capital Market: Liquidity in the capital market tends to be lower compared to the money market

Money Market: Money market instruments are highly liquid, with low transaction costs and high trading volumes.

(iii) Safety:

Capital Market: Investments in the capital market carry varying degrees of risk depending on the type of security and issuer.

Money Market: Money market instruments are generally considered safe investments due to their short maturities and high credit quality. (3)

OR

(b) The following are the factors affecting financial decision:

(i) Fixed Operating Costs:

Fixed operating costs affect the financing decision in several ways:

(a) Impact on Break-Even Point: Fixed operating costs contribute to a company's break-even point, the level of sales at which total revenue equals total costs. Higher fixed costs increase the break-even point, requiring the company to generate higher sales volumes to cover its fixed expenses and achieve profitability.

(b) Risk Assessment: Fixed operating costs represent a financial commitment that must be met regardless of business performance. High fixed costs increase the financial risk associated with the business, especially during periods of low sales or economic downturns.

(ii) State of Capital Market:

The state of the capital market can significantly impact a company's financing decision in several ways:

(a) Cost of Capital: The cost of capital, including interest rates, equity valuations, and investor sentiment, is influenced by market conditions. A favourable capital market environment characterized by low-interest rates, high investor confidence, and strong demand for securities may reduce the cost of debt and equity financing for companies. Conversely, adverse market conditions, such as economic uncertainty, market volatility, or credit market disruptions, may increase financing costs and limit access to capital.

(b) Availability of Financing: The state of the capital market affects the availability of financing options for businesses. In a buoyant capital market, companies may have easier access to various sources of funding, including bank loans, bond issuances, initial public offerings (IPOs), and venture capital investments. However, during periods of market turmoil or credit tightening, financing options may become limited.

25. (a) In the directing function of management, leadership and communication play crucial roles:

(i) Leadership: Leadership refers to the ability of an individual or a group of individuals to influence and guide others towards the accomplishment of organisational goals. It involves providing direction, inspiring others, making decisions, and coordinating efforts to achieve organizational objectives. Leadership, as an element of directing, plays a crucial role in inspiring, coordinating and empowering the individuals to perform their roles efficiently. In the directing function, leadership ensures that organisational resources are effectively utilised, employees are motivated, and tasks are completed efficiently.

(ii) Communication: Communication is the process of exchanging information, ideas, thoughts, and feelings between individuals or groups. It involves sending and receiving messages through various channels such as verbal communication, written communication, non-verbal cues, and visual aids. Effective communication is essential for the directing function of management as it facilitates the transmission of instructions, feedback, goals, and expectations among managers, employees, and other stakeholders.

OR

(b) Semantic barriers to communication refer to obstacles that arise due to misunderstandings or misinterpretations of the meaning of words, phrases, or symbols. Two common examples of semantic barriers are:

(i) Faulty translations: This occurs when the meaning of a message is inaccurately conveyed during translation from one language to another. Cultural nuances, idiomatic expressions, and linguistic differences can lead to misinterpretations, resulting in confusion and misunderstanding among individuals or groups communicating in different languages.

(ii) Unclarified assumptions: Unclarified assumptions occur when individuals make assumptions about the meaning of words or concepts without verifying or seeking clarification. These assumptions may be based on personal beliefs, past experiences, or cultural biases, leading to misunderstandings and miscommunication. When assumptions are left unclarified, it can result in incomplete or inaccurate information being exchanged, affecting decision-making, problem-solving, and collaboration within an organisation.

28. The following are the factors affecting the working capital requirements of a company:

(a) Operating Efficiency:

Operating efficiency impacts the working capital requirements in several ways:

(i) Inventory Management: Efficient inventory management ensures that the company maintains optimal levels of inventory to meet customer demand while minimising carrying costs. A company with better operating efficiency can effectively manage its inventory turnover, reducing the need for excess working capital tied up in stock.

(ii) Accounts Receivable Management: Timely collection of accounts receivable improves cash flow and reduces the need for additional working capital to cover operational expenses. Companies with strong operating efficiency typically have streamlined credit policies, effective invoicing systems, and rigorous follow-up procedures to accelerate cash inflows.

(b) Availability of Raw Material: Availability of raw material affects the working capital requirement in the following ways:

(i) Lead Times: Longer lead times for raw material procurement necessitate higher inventory levels to buffer against supply chain disruptions. Companies may need to maintain larger inventories of raw materials to ensure uninterrupted production, increasing their working capital requirements.

(ii) Supplier Relationships: Strong relationships with reliable suppliers can mitigate the risk of raw material shortages and enable more favourable payment terms. Companies with secure and efficient supply chains can manage their working capital more effectively by optimizing inventory levels and negotiating favourable pricing and payment terms.

31. (a) The following are the features of planning function of management:

(i) Planning Focuses on Achieving Objectives:

Planning is primarily concerned with setting objectives and determining the most effective means of achieving them. Objectives provide a clear direction for the organisation and serve as benchmarks for evaluating performance. A key feature of planning is its emphasis on aligning all activities and resources towards the attainment of organisational goals.

(ii) Planning is Futuristic:

Planning is future oriented as it is carried out to achieve some objectives in the future. Planning involves forecasting future conditions, anticipating potential opportunities and threats, and developing strategies to address them proactively. This forward-looking perspective allows managers to anticipate challenges, capitalize on emerging trends, and position the organization for long-term success.

(iii) Planning Involves Decision Making:

Planning requires making decisions about the allocation of resources, the selection of strategies, and the identification of action steps to achieve objectives. Managers must analyse available information, evaluate alternative courses of action, and make informed choices based on their assessment of risks, benefits, and resource constraints.

OR

(b) The following are the explanations for the steps in the process of planning:

(i) Setting Objectives:

The first step in the planning process is to establish clear and specific objectives which define the desired outcomes or results to be achieved. Objectives provide a systematic framework for decision-making, guide resource allocation, and serve as criteria for evaluating performance. Effective objectives are SMART (Specific, Measurable, Achievable, Relevant, Time-bound) and aligned with the organisation's mission, vision, and strategic priorities.

(ii) Developing Premises:

Developing premises involves identifying and analysing the assumptions, forecasts, and factors that may influence the planning process. This step requires gathering relevant data, conducting market research, and assessing internal and external conditions that could impact the organisation's operations. By identifying key premises, such as market trends, technological advancements, regulatory changes, and competitive dynamics, planners can make more informed decisions and develop realistic plans that account for potential uncertainties.

(iii) Identifying Alternative Courses of Action:

Once the objectives are established and premises are developed, planners identify alternative courses of action or strategies for achieving the desired objectives. This step involves brainstorming creative solutions, evaluating different approaches, and considering the potential risks and benefits associated with each option. The goal is to develop flexible and adaptable plans that can accommodate changing circumstances and support the organisation's long-term success.

■■■

CHAPTER 1 NATURE AND SIGNIFICANCE OF MANAGEMENT

LEARNING OBJECTIVES

After going through this unit, the student/learner would be able to:

- Understand the concept of management.
- Explain the meaning of 'Effectiveness and Efficiency.
- Discuss the objectives of management.
- Describe the importance of management.
- Examine the nature of management as a science, art and profession.
- Understand the role of top, middle and lower levels of management.
- Explain the functions of management.
- Discuss the concept and characteristics of coordination.
- Explain the importance of coordination.

Study Plan
Maximum Time = 3.45 Hrs
Maximum Questions = 82

LIST OF TOPICS

TOPIC-1 Introduction to Management

Concepts Covered:
- Concept of management • Meaning of effectiveness and efficiency • Objectives of management • Importance of management

Revision Notes

- **Management:** Management is a process of planning, organising, staffing, directing, and controlling the resources of an enterprise efficiently and effectively for achieving the organisational goals.
- **Effectiveness v/s Efficiency:** Effectiveness is doing the right things whereas efficiency is doing things the right way. Effectiveness is concerned with the end result whereas efficiency means doing the task correctly and with minimum cost. [Board, 2019]

Characteristics of Management:

(i) **Goal-Oriented Process:** Management integrates the efforts of different individuals to achieve organisational goals.
(ii) **Dynamic:** Management has to adapt itself and its goals according to the changing needs of the business environment.
(iii) **Intangible:** Management cannot be seen but its presence can be felt in the way an organisation functions.
(iv) **Group Activity:** Diverse members of management work towards fulfilling the common organisational goals.
(v) **All Pervasive:** Managerial activities are performed in all types of organisations, across all departments and at all the levels of management.
(vi) **Multi-dimensional:** It has three dimensions *viz.* management of work, people and operations.
(vii) **Continuous Process:** The process of management consists of a series of continuous, composite, but separate functions (planning, organising, directing, staffing and controlling).

Objectives of Management:

(i) **Social Objectives:** To create economic value consistently for various constituents of a society.
(ii) **Organisational Objectives:** Utilising human and material resources to the maximum possible advantage, which is to fulfill economic objectives of a business i.e., survival, profit and growth.
(iii) **Personal Objectives:** Reconcile personal goals with organisational objectives so as to maintain harmony in the organisation. [Board, 2016]

Importance of Management:

(i) **Helps in achieving group goals:** Gives a common direction to diverse individual efforts.
(ii) **Increases efficiency:** Reduces cost and increases productivity.
(iii) **Creates a dynamic organisation:** Helps people to adjust with the changing environment.
(iv) **Helps in achieving personal objectives:** Helps individuals to achieve personal goals along with overall organisational goals.
(v) **Helps in the development of the society:** Provides good quality products, generates employment, etc. [Board, 2023]

AMAZING FACT
Management is 10% work and 90% people.

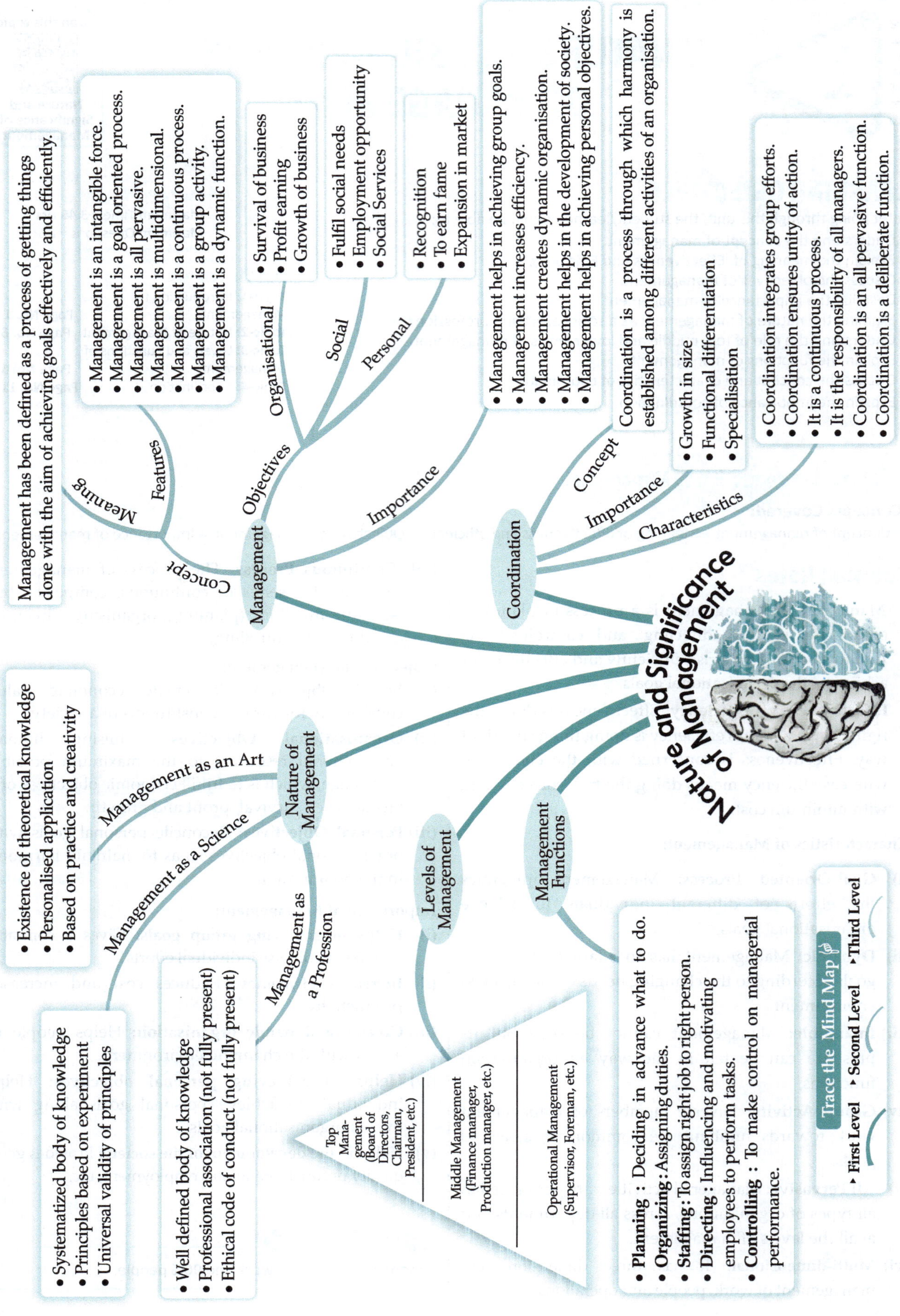

Nature and Significance of Management

Management

Concept

Meaning

Management has been defined as a process of getting things done with the aim of achieving goals effectively and efficiently.

Features

- Management is an intangible force.
- Management is a goal oriented process.
- Management is all pervasive.
- Management is multidimensional.
- Management is a continuous process.
- Management is a group activity.
- Management is a dynamic function.

Objectives

Organisational

- Survival of business
- Profit earning
- Growth of business

Social

- Fulfil social needs
- Employment opportunity
- Social Services

Personal

- Recognition
- To earn fame
- Expansion in market

Importance

- Management helps in achieving group goals.
- Management increases efficiency.
- Management creates dynamic organisation.
- Management helps in the development of society.
- Management helps in achieving personal objectives.

Coordination

Concept

Coordination is a process through which harmony is established among different activities of an organisation.

Importance

- Growth in size
- Functional differentiation
- Specialisation

Characteristics

- Coordination integrates group efforts.
- Coordination ensures unity of action.
- It is a continuous process.
- It is the responsibility of all managers.
- Coordination is an all pervasive function.
- Coordination is a deliberate function.

Nature of Management

Management as a Science

- Systematized body of knowledge
- Principles based on experiment
- Universal validity of principles

Management as an Art

- Existence of theoretical knowledge
- Personalised application
- Based on practice and creativity

Management as a Profession

- Well defined body of knowledge
- Professional association (not fully present)
- Ethical code of conduct (not fully present)

Levels of Management

- Top Management (Board of Directors, Chairman, President, etc.)
- Middle Management (Finance manager, Production manager, etc.)
- Operational Management (Supervisor, Foreman, etc.)

Management Functions

- **Planning** : Deciding in advance what to do.
- **Organizing** : Assigning duties.
- **Staffing** : To assign right job to right person.
- **Directing** : Influencing and motivating employees to perform tasks.
- **Controlling** : To make control on managerial performance.

Trace the Mind Map

First Level · Second Level · Third Level

MNEMONICS

Concept: Features of Management
Go Get Important Data from Computer
Interpretations:
G: Group Activity G: Goal-Oriented I: Intangible M: Multidimensional
P: Pervasive D: Dynamic C: Continuous
Concept: Objectives of Management
Please Open the Shop
Interpretations:
P: Personal O: Organisational S: Social
Concept: Importance of Management
Do Eat Grapes and Drink Pure water
Interpretations:
D: Dynamic organisation E: Efficient organisation G: Goal achievement
D: Development of society P: Personal objective achievement

Scan this

Importance of Management

Scan this

Objectives of Management

SUBJECTIVE TYPE QUESTIONS

Short Answer Type Questions-I (3 marks each)

1. **Captcha Ltd. is a construction company where all the employees learn various ways of dealing with diverse situations from their seniors. The company provides financial as well as non-financial incentives. This helps the employees to grow and develop their abilities. The organisation is a responsible constituent of society and always creates good quality products. It has a positive image in the market. The training modules are excellent and the employees always try to find unique ways of providing solutions in the rapidly changing business environment. This has helped the organisation to adjust smoothly.**
Identify and state three points of importance of management being highlighted here.
A [SQP 2023-24]

Ans. The importance of management highlighted:

(i) Helps in achieving personal objectives: A manager motivates and leads his team in such a manner that individual members can achieve personal goals while contributing to the overall organisational goals. **[1]**

(ii) Helps in the development of society: The organisation tries to behave as a responsible constituent of society and always creates good quality products. **[1]**

(iii) Creates a dynamic organisation: Organisations have to function in a constantly changing environment. Management helps people adapt to the changes so that the organisation can maintain a competitive edge. [Marking Scheme SQP 2023-24) **[1]**

2. **Explain any three points that highlight the importance of 'Management'.** U [Delhi Set-1, 2023]

Ans.

Topper Answer, 2023

a) Following are the Importance of management→

1) Management increases efficiency→ The aim of a manager is to reduce costs & increase productivity through better planning, organising, staffing, directing & controlling the activities of the organisation.

2) Leads to optimum utilisation of Resources→ A good management brings together human material resources in the right proportion.
Human resources may prove to be ineffective without sound management.

3) Management helps in the development of society→ In the process of fulfilling the multiple objectives of a business, management also helps in the development of the society by providing good quality products & services, generating employment opportunities, adoption of new technology which leads to growth & development of society as a whole.

3. **Mita has a successful ice cream business in Bikaner, namely 'Smart Flavours'. Her ice creams are utterly delicious. She makes ice creams from fresh milk and the same are available in a wide range of flavours and packs. She sets viable business objectives and works with the same in mind in order to ensure that the customers will come back for purchasing. Having the first mover advantage, her business was doing well. To earn higher profits, she started cutting down costs. This would sometimes lead to delay in delivery and the ice cream was not reaching the market in time. Over a period of time,the demand for her ice cream declined and because of it the competitors entered the market. She lost some of her market share to competitors. At the beginning of summer season, she got back to back orders for supply of 4,000 ice cream packs of different flavours for special occasions. To ensure that the task was completed and orders delivered in time she hired additional workers. She was, thus, able to produce and deliver the ice cream packs but at a high production cost. While completing activities and finishing the given task for achieving goals, Mita realised that she was ignoring one of the important aspects of management.**

Identify the aspect of management that has been ignored by Mita. Also explain the same with the help of an example. C [Delhi Set 1, 2, 3, 2019]

Ans. Efficiency: Efficiency means doing the task correctly **and** with minimum cost. **[1]**

Example: Say, a company's target production is 5,000 units in a year. The manager wants to achieve the production target by cutting down costs. He was able to cut down costs but could not achieve the target production. In this case, the manager was efficient but not effective. **[2]**

(or any other correct example)

OR

Effectiveness means doing the right task, completing activities and achieving goals. **[1]**

Example: Say, a company's target production is 5,000 units in a year. To achieve this target the manager has to operate on double shifts due to power failure most of the time. The manager is able to produce 5,000 units but at a higher production cost. In this case, the manager was effective but not so efficient. **[2]**

(or any other correct example)

[Marking Scheme, Delhi, 2019]

4. **Management is a complex activity that has three main dimensions. State these dimensions.**
U [Delhi Set-1, 2019]

5. **Briefly describe the organisational objectives of Management.**
U [Outside Delhi Comptt. Set-3, 2016]

Ans. Following are the economic objectives/ organisational objectives of Management:

(i) **Survival:** Management must strive to ensure the survival of the organisation by earning adequate revenues **to cover its costs**, produce or sell standardised goods or services, keeping the motivation level of the employees high.

(ii) **Profit:** Management should make every effort to minimise the cost and maximise profits and production. Profit provides a vital incentive for the continuous successful operations of the enterprise.

(iii) **Growth:** To grow in the industry, the management of an organisation must optimally utilise all its scarce resources. [Marking Scheme, OD, 2016]

Commonly Made Error

Students get confused and explain the objectives of management viz. organisational, personal and social instead of the specific organisational objectives of management.

Answering Tip

Students should have conceptual clarity regarding the organisational, social and personal objectives and should give specific answer to what is being asked.

Short Answer Type Questions-II (4 marks each)

1. **What is meant by 'Management' ? State any three objectives of Management.**
R [Outside Delhi Set 1, 2, 3, 2015]

Ans. Management is a process of getting things done through and with the people in an effective and efficient manner.

Objectives:

(i) **Organisational Objectives:** An organisation has to achieve its different objectives like—(a) Survival (b) Profit (c) Growth.

(ii) **Social Objectives:** An organisation has social objectives towards different groups of society like providing quality products at fair prices, generating employment opportunities, etc.

(iii) **Personal Objectives:** An organisation strives to fulfill personal objectives of its employees and also to reconcile their objectives with the organisational objectives, e.g., competitive salaries, personal growth, etc. **[1 + 1 + 1 + 1 = 4]**

[Marking Scheme, Delhi, 2015]

2. **'Success of every organisation depends upon its management.' Justify.** A&I U [OEB]

Concept Applied: Importance of Management

Ans. Success of every organisation depends upon its management because:

(i) **Management helps in achieving group goals:** Management is required not for itself but for achieving the goals of an organisation. The task of a manager is to give a common directions to the individual effort in achieving the overall goal of an organisation.

(ii) **Management increases efficiency:** The aim of a manager is to reduce costs and increase productivity through better planning, organising, staffing, directing and controlling the activities of an organisation.

(iii) **Management creates a dynamic organisation:** All organisations have to function in an environment which is constantly changing. It is generally seen that individuals in an organisation resist change. Management helps people to adapt to these changes so that the organisation is able to maintain its competitive edge.

(iv) **Management helps in achieving personal objectives:** A manager motivates and leads his team in such a manner that individual members are able to achieve personal goals while contributing to the overall organisational objective. Through motivation and leadership, management helps individuals to develop team spirit, co-operation and commitment to the group success.

(v) **Management helps in the development of society:** An organisation has multiple objectives to serve the purpose of different groups that constitute it. In the process of fulfilling all these, management helps in the development of the organisation and society. It helps to provide good quality products and services, create employment opportunities, adopt new technology and lead the path towards growth and development. **(Any four) [1×4=4]**

This Question is for practice and its solution is given at the end of the chapter.

Long Answer Type Questions (6 marks each)

1. Both Apple Inc. and Samsung Ltd. require management, although difference lies in the way they are managed. Identify the feature of management stated above. Explain briefly other four features of 'Management'. A [OEB]

Concept Applied | Features of Management

Ans. Management is all pervasive: Management is a universal management. The activities involved in managing an enterprise are common to all the organisations whether economic, social or political. [1½]

Other Features of Management:

(i) Management is a goal-oriented process: An organisation has a set of basic goals which are the reason for its existence. These should be simple and clearly stated. Different organisations have different goals. For example, the goal of a retail store may be to increase sales, but the goal of the Spastics Society of India is to impart education to children with special needs. Management unites the efforts of different individuals in the organisation towards achieving these goals.

(ii) Management is multidimensional: Management is a complex activity that has three main dimensions. These are:

(a) Management of work: All organisations exist for the performance of some work. Management translates this work in terms of goals to be achieved and assigns the means to achieve it. This is done in terms of problems to be solved, decisions to be made, plans to be established, budgets to be prepared, responsibilities to be assigned and authority to be delegated.

(b) Management of people: Human resources of people are the organisation's greatest asset. Managing people has two dimensions viz. dealing with employees as individuals with diverse needs and behaviour and dealing with individuals as a group or people. The task of management is to make people work towards achieving the organisation's goals, by making their strength effective and their weaknesses irrelevant.

(c) Management of operations: No matter which type of organisation it is, it has some basic products or services to provide in order to survive. This requires a production process which entails the flow of input material and the technology for transforming this input into the desired output for consumption. This is interlinked with both the management of work and the management of people. [1½]

(iii) Management is a continuous process: The process of management is a series of continuous, composite but separate functions. These functions are simultaneously performed by all managers all the time. The task of a manager consists of an ongoing series of functions. [1½]

(iv) Management is a group activity: An organisation is a collection of diverse individuals with different needs. Every member of the group has a different purpose for joining the organisation but as members of the organisation, they work towards fulfilling the common organisational goal. This requires team work and coordination of individual efforts in a common direction. At the same time, management should enable all its members to grow and develop as needs and opportunities change. [1½]

(v) Management is a dynamic function: Management is a dynamic function and has to adapt itself to the changing environment. An organisation interacts with its external environment which consists of various social, economic, political and legal factors. In order to be successful, an organisation must change itself and its goals according to the needs of the environment. **[1½] (Any four)**

2. XYZ Power Ltd. set up a factory for manufacturing solar lanterns in a remote village as there was no reliable supply of electricity in rural areas. The revenue earned by the company was sufficient to cover the costs and the risks. As the demand of lanterns was increasing day- by-day, the company decided to increase production to generate higher sales. For this they decided to employ people from a nearby village as very few job opportunities were available in that area. The company also decided to open schools and creches for the children of its employees. Identify and explain the objectives of management discussed above. A [OEB]

Concept Applied | Objectives of Management

Ans. The objectives of management discussed above are:

(i) Organisational objectives: Management is responsible for setting and achieving objectives for the organisation. It has to achieve a variety of objectives in all areas considering the interest of all stakeholders including, shareholders, employees, customers and the government. The main objective of any organisation should be to utilise human and material resources to the maximum possible advantage, i.e., to fulfill the economic objectives of a business. These are survival, profit and growth.

(ii) Social Objectives: It involves the creation of benefit for society. As a part of society, every organisation whether it is business or non-business, has a social obligation to fulfill. This refers to consistently creating economic value for various constituents of society. This includes using environment friendly methods of production, giving employment opportunities to the underprivileged sections of society and providing basic amenities like schools and healthcare, etc., for community. **[3+3=6]**

TOPIC-2 Nature of Management

Concepts Covered:

- Management as a Science • Management as an Art • Management as a Profession

Revision Notes

- **Management as an Art:** Art is the skillful and personal application of existing knowledge to achieve desired results. It can be acquired through study, observation and experience. Since art is concerned with personal application of knowledge, some kind of ingenuity and creativity is required to practice the basic principles learnt.

  Features of Management as an Art: [Board, 2019]

  (i) Personalised application

  (ii) Based on practice and creativity

  (iii) Existence of theoretical knowledge

  Management is an art as it satisfies all the features for being an art.

- **Management as a Science:** Science is a systematised body of knowledge that explains certain general truths or the operation of general laws.

  Features of Management as a Science: [Board, 2015]

  (i) Systematised body of knowledge

  (ii) Principles based on experiments

  (iii) Universal validity

  Management is an inexact science as its principles have to be modified according to a given situation.

  It is a social science as it deals with human beings.

- **Management as a Profession:** Profession is an occupation which is regulated by a legally recognised body and requires specific and formal qualification. Entry is limited in case of profession. [Board, 2019]

  Features of Management as a Profession:

  (i) Well-defined body of knowledge

  (ii) Professional association

  (iii) Restricted entry

  (iv) Ethical code of conduct

  (v) Service motive

  Management is on the path of becoming a profession but not a full-fledged profession.

SUBJECTIVE TYPE QUESTIONS

Short Answer Type Questions-I (3 marks each)

1. "Art is concerned with personal application of knowledge." In the light of this statement compare all the features of management with art and prove that it is an art. U [Delhi Set-3, 2019]

OR

'Art is the skillful and personalised application of existing knowledge to achieve desired results and some kind of ingenuity and creativity is required to practice its basic principles learnt.' Pick up points from the statements and explain the same to prove that management is an art.

U [Outside Delhi Comptt. Set-2, 2016]

Concept Applied Management as an art.

Ans. "Art is concerned with personal application of knowledge". **Management is an art because of the following reasons:**

(i) Existence of theoretical knowledge: As in art, in management too, there is a lot of literature available in various areas of management which the manager has to specialise in.

(ii) Personalised application: Like in any art, in management too, a manager applies his acquired knowledge in a personalised and unique manner. This gives rise to different styles of management.

(iii) Based on practice and creativity: Management satisfies this criteria as a manager gains experience through regular practice and becomes more effective. Like any other art, a manager after studying various situations, formulates his own theories for use in a given situation. This gives rise to different styles of management.

As all the criteria of art are satisfied by management, it qualifies as an art. [1×3=3]

[Marking Scheme, Delhi, 2019]

2. Identify and explain the nature of management when it is said to be a systematised body of knowledge that explains certain general truths. U [OEB]

Ans. Management as a science: Science is a systematised body of knowledge that explains certain general truths or the operation of general laws. Its principles are based on a cause and effect relationship.

Like science, management has a systematised body of knowledge which has its own theory and principles that have developed over a period of time. Since it is drawn from repeated experimentation and observation in different types of organisations, it explains some general truth. 1+2=3

3. Explain why management is considered to be both an Art and a Science. A [OEB]

Short Answer Type Questions-II (3 marks each)

1. Monika, Rashmi, and Garima are school friends. After completing their education, Monika joined a school as a teacher. Rashmi joined a firm as a Chartered Accountant and Garima as a General Manager in a Multinational Company. After a

This Question is for practice and its solution is given at the end of the chapter.

long time at a reunion function at the school, they met each other. Rashmi said that they were all professionals now. Garima told Rashmi that she could say this about Monika and herself but not about her since manager is not considered a full-fledged professional. Why did Garima say that she is not a professional? State any three points in support of your answer. AI Ap [SQP 2023-24]

OR

Explain the features of management that do not establish it as a profession.

U [Outside Delhi Set-2, 2016]

Ans. The features of management that do not establish it as a profession are:

(i) Restricted entry: The entry to a profession is restricted through a prescribed qualification. But there is no restriction on anyone being appointed as a manager in any business enterprise.

(ii) Professional association: All professions are affiliated with a professional association that regulates entry and grants certificates of practice. There is no compulsion for managers to be members of such associations.

(iii) Ethical code of conduct: All professions are bound by a code of conduct that guides the behaviour of its members. AIMA has devised a code of conduct for Indian managers but there is no statutory backing for this code.

(iv) Service motive: The motive of a profession is to serve their client's interests by rendering dedicated and committed service. The basic purpose of management is to help the organisation to achieve its stated goal which may be profit maximisation. However, profit maximisation as the objective of management does not hold and is fast changing. So, presently this feature of the profession is not fully present in management.

[Marking Scheme SQP 2023-24]

2. Define Management. Explain the features that establish it as a Social Science.

U [Outside Delhi Set-2, 2016]

Ans. Management is the process of getting things done with the aim of achieving goals effectively and efficiently.

The features that establish management as a social science are:

(i) Principles based on observation and experimentation: Like science, management principles are derived through observations and repeated experimentations.

However, since management deals with human beings, the outcome of these experiments are not capable of being accurately predicted.

(ii) Universal validity: Principles of management like principles of pure science, provide managers with certain standardised techniques that can be used in different situations.

Since they have to be modified according to a given situation, their application and use is not universal. So, this feature of science is not fully present in management.

Therefore, management is considered as a social science. **[1 + 1½ + 1½ = 4]**

[Marking Scheme, 2016]

Long Answer Type Questions-I (6 marks each)

1. 'Management is regarded as an art by some, as science or as inexact science by others. The truth seems to be somewhere in between.'

In the light of this statement, explain the true nature of management. A [OEB]

Ans. Management is an art as well as a science or an inexact science.

(i) Management as an Art: Management may be regarded as an art because of the following reasons:

(a) Existence of theoretical knowledge: A successful manager practices the art of management in the day-to-day job of managing an enterprise based on study, observation and experience.

(b) Personalised application: The use of basic knowledge varies from individual to individual; therefore, it is a personalised concept, e.g. two dancers, two speakers will always differ in demonstrating their art.

(c) Based on practice and creativity: A good manager works through a combination of practice, creativity, imagination, initiative and innovation. He uses tact and creativity to develop his own style. Thus, management is an art because it satisfies all the characteristics of an art. **[3]**

(ii) Management as a Science: Management may be regarded as a science because it fulfils the following characteristics of science:

(a) Systematised body of knowledge: As science, management has a systematised body of knowledge. It has its own theories and principles that have been developed over a period of time. It also **draws some principles from other disciplines such as economics, sociology, psychology and mathematics.**

(b) Principles based on scientific observation and experiments: Like science, management principles are based on scientific enquiry and observations.

(c) Universal validity and application: Like science, principles of management are universally applicable. Thus, we can say that management is also a science.

However, the principles of management are not as exact as the principles of Physics or Chemistry. Management principles are flexible and can be modified to suit different situations. Thus, management can be called as an inexact science also.

In the light of both the above statement, the true nature of management can be defined as, management is both an art and a science. Principles of management constitute the science of management and the practice of management principles is the art of management. **[3]**

2. Explain Management as a Profession.

U [Outside Delhi Set-3, 2019]

This Question is for practice and its solution is given at the end of the chapter.

3. Kamal, Khan and David are partners in a firm engaged in the distribution of dairy products in Madhya Pradesh. Kamal is a holder of Senior Secondary School Certificate from Central Board of Secondary Education with Business Studies as one of his elective subjects. Khan had done his post-graduation in Hindi Literature and David in Dairy Farming. One day there was a serious discussion between Khan and David regarding the nature of 'Management as a Science'. Khan argued that Management was not a science whereas David was of the opinion that Management was a science. Kamal intervened and corrected both Khan and David about the nature of Management as a Science with the help of his knowledge of Business Studies. Explain, how Kamal would have been able to satisfy both Khan and David.

A I C [Outside Delhi Comptt. Set 1, 2, 3, 2015]

Ans. Kamal would have been able to satisfy both Khan and David by explaining the following features of Management as a Science:

(i) Systematised body of knowledge: Like science, management is a **systematic body of knowledge with its own theories and principles** that have been developed over a period of time. So, this feature of science is present in the management.

(ii) Principles based on observation and experimentation: Like science, management principles are derived through observation and repeated experimentation. So, this feature of science is present in management. However, since management deals with human beings, the outcome of these experiments cannot be accurately predicted.

(iii) Universal validity: Principles of Management like principles of pure science, provide managers with certain standardised techniques that can be used in different situations. Since they have to be modified according to a given situation, their application and use is not universal. So, this feature of **science is not fully present in management.**

Through the above discussion Kamal would have been able to satisfy both Khan and David by making them understand that management is a science but not an exact science. **[2 × 3 = 6]**

[Marking Scheme, OD 2015]

4. James joins an IT firm as a system analyst after completing his masters in Computer Science. As the nature of his work demands he has to work in very close coordination with all the departmental heads in the firm. Very soon James realises that each departmental head has own individual style of working. They differ greatly in their day-to-day approach to work. They tend to deal with a given situation, an issue or a problem through a combination of their own experience, creativity, imagination, initiative and innovation. Identify and explain the nature of management highlighted in the above case. A [OEB]

TOPIC-3 LEVELS AND FUNCTIONS OF MANAGEMENT

Concepts Covered:

- Different levels of Management and their roles, • Management functions-POSDCo.

Revision Notes

- **Levels of management** means different categories of managers, the lowest to the highest on the basis of their responsibilities, authority, and status.

Levels of Management:

(i) Top-Level Management: Consists of Board of Directors, Chairman, Managing Directors, Chief Executives, etc. These top level managers are responsible for the welfare and survival of the organisation. [Board, 2017]

Example-1

Consider an international CEO. The CEO sets corporate strategy, makes merger and acquisition choices, and represents the firm globally. Long-term objectives, performance, and industry position are their priorities.

Tips & Tricks

Level of management have function to perform do not use term as feature of level of management.

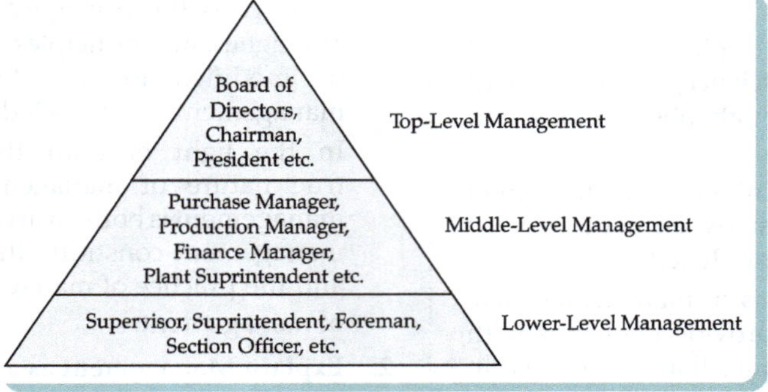

This Question is for practice and its solution is given at the end of the chapter.

(ii) **Middle-Level Management:** Consists of Departmental Heads, e.g., Finance Manager, Production Manager, etc. Middle Management is the link between top and lower level managers. They are subordinate to top managers and superior to the first line managers.

[Board, 2017]

Example-2

Imagine a retail regional sales manager. This manager coordinates regional sales. They set regional sales objectives, supervise several store managers, and assure regional sales strategy implementation.

(iii) **Lower/Supervisory/Operational-Level Management:** Consists of Foremen, Supervisors, Superintendents, etc. Lower level managers directly oversee the efforts of the work force, their authority and responsibility is limited according to the plans of management.

Example-3

Imagine a factory front-line supervisor. This supervisor oversees shop floor activities daily. They oversee workers, meet production objectives, resolve urgent concerns, and update middle-level supervisors on daily operations. They prioritise task efficiency and operational issues.

Functions of Management:

(i) **Planning:** Planning is the function of deciding in advance what to do, when do to, how to do and who should do it.

(ii) **Organising:** Organising is the management function of assigning duties, grouping tasks, establishing authority and allocating resources required to carry out a specific plan.

(iii) **Staffing:** This function is concerned with finding the right person for the right job.

(iv) **Directing:** Directing is the process of supervising, motivating, leading and communicating with the subordinates to achieve the organisational objectives.

(v) **Controlling:** The task of controlling involves establishing standards of performance, measuring current performance, comparing it with established standards and taking corrective actions.

Tips & Tricks

Function of Management always starts with planning function followed by organising, staffing, directing and controlling.

MNEMONICS

(i) **Concept: Levels of Management:**
Interpretations: Mummy Loves Tea
M: Middle level L: Lower level T: Top level

(ii) **Concept: Functions of Management:**
Interpretations: Do Save Plants or Creatures
D: Directing S: Staffing P: Planning
O: Organising C: Controlling

KEY TERMS

Board of Directors: The governing body elected by a group of individuals that represent shareholders.
Foreman: A trained worker who is person-in-charge of a group of workers.
Hierarchy: A system ranking the members according to relative status or authority.

FUNDAMENTAL FACT

Planning is about preparing for the future, not predicting it.

SUBJECTIVE TYPE QUESTIONS

Short Answer Type Questions-I (3 marks each)

1. Identify the level of management whose basic task is to integrate diverse elements and coordinate the activities of different departments according to the overall objectives of the organisation. State any two functions of the level of management identified.

R [SQP 2021-22]

Ans. Top-level management
Functions of top-level management:
(i) The top-level managers are responsible for the welfare and survival of the organisation.
(ii) They analyse the business environment and its implications for the survival of the firm.
(iii) They formulate overall organisational goals and strategies for their achievement.
(iv) They are responsible for all the activities of the business and for its impact on society.

(Any two) [1 + 2 = 3]
[Marking Scheme, SQP 2021-22]

2. Explain the three levels of management ?

U [OEB]

3. Ritu is the manager of the northern division of a large corporate house. At what level does she work in the organisation? What are her basic functions? U [OEB]

Ans. Ritu is working at the middle level of management.
The functions that she will have to perform at this level are stated below:
(i) She has to ensure that his department has the necessary staff.
(ii) She has to assign duties and responsibilities to the people in his department.
(iii) She has to motivate the people in his department to achieve the desired objectives.
(iv) She has to co-operate with the other departments for ensuring smooth functioning of the organisation.

(Any three) [1×3=3]

Short Answer Type Questions-II (4 marks each)

1. Chandrika Bhattacharya is working in Olax Ltd., a company manufacturing room heaters. She is responsible for all the activities of the business and for its impact on the society. Her job demands long hours and commitment to the organisation.
(i) Identify the level at which Chandrika Bhattacharya is working.
(ii) State three more functions required to be performed by Chandrika Bhattacharya at this level. A [OEB]

This Question is for practice and its solution is given at the end of the chapter.

OR

Ashutosh Goenka was working in 'Axe Ltd.' a company manufacturing air purifiers. He found that the profits had started declining from the last six months. Profit has an implication on the survival of the firm, so he analysed the business environment to find out the reasons for this decline.

(i) Identify the level of management at which Ashutosh Goenka was working.

(ii) State three other functions being performed by Ashutosh Goenka. A [Delhi Set-1, 2017]

Concept Applied Top level management and its functions

Ans. (i) Top level

(ii) Functions of the top level of management:

(a) To coordinate the activities of different departments.

(b) To be responsible for welfare and survival of the organisation.

(c) To formulate overall organisational goals and strategies.

(d) To be responsible for all the activities of the business and for its impact on the society.

(Any three) [1+3=4]

2. Rishitosh Mukerjee has recently joined AMV Ltd., a company manufacturing refrigerators. He found that his department was under staffed and other departments were not cooperating with his department for smooth functioning of the organisation. Therefore, he ensured that his department has the required number of employees and its cooperation with other departments is improved.

(i) Identify the level at which Rishitosh Mukerjee was working.

(ii) Also, state three more functions required to be performed by Rishitosh Mukerjee at this level.

A [Outside Delhi Set-1, 2, 3, 2017]

Concept Applied Middle Level Management and its Function.

Ans.

Topper Answer, 2017

(a) Rishitosh works at MIDDLE LEVEL of management.

(b) Functions

① Interpret the policies framed by top management.

② Assign necessary duties & responsibilities to subordinates.

③ Motivate them (subordinates) to achieve the desired objectives.

Main task of middle management is to carry out plans developed by top management.

Long Answer Type Questions (6 marks each)

1. Gayatri is working in a private sector bank. One of her key function relates to the formulation of the overall organisational goals and strategies of the bank. Identify and explain the level of management at which she is working? Also, state the other functions that she has to perform at this level.

U [OEB]

Ans. Gayatri is working at the top level of management in the private sector bank. Top management consists of the senior-most executives of the organisation. They are usually referred to as the chairman, the chief executive officer, chief operating officer, president and vice-president. Top management is a team consisting of managers from different functional levels, heading finance, marketing, etc. For example, chief finance officer, vice president (marketing), etc. **[1]**

Functions of the top-level management:

(i) Their basic task is to integrate diverse elements and coordinate the activities of different departments according to the overall objectives of the organisation.

(ii) These top-level managers are responsible for the welfare and survival of the organisation.

(iii) They analyse the business environment and its implications for the survival of the firm.

(iv) They formulate overall organisational goals and strategies for their achievement. They are responsible for all the activities of the business and for its impact on society.

(v) The job of the top manager is complex and stressful, demanding long hours and commitment to the organisation. **[1×5=5]**

2. Give the meaning of middle-level management. State any five functions performed by the manager who is working at the middle level of management.

R [OEB]

Ans. Middle management is the link between top and lower level managers. They are subordinate to top managers and superior to the first line managers.

They are usually known as division heads, e.g., production manager.

Following are the functions performed by a middle level managers:

(i) Interpreting policies: At this level, policies framed by top-level managers are interpreted. Like the marketing manager introduces his salesman to the sales policy of the company.

(ii) Ensures the availability of personnel in departments: Manager working under middle level management has to ensure that this department has the necessary personnel to perform the task.

(iii) Assigns duties and responsibilities: Superior manager assigns the duties and responsibilities to various workers working under him/her.

(iv) Motivating employees: Middle-level managers motivate their employees by various means so that they work most efficiently to achieve organisational objectives.

(v) Creating cooperation : Cooperation among different divisions is required to successfully achieve company's objectives and this is done by middle-level managers. **[1 + 1 × 5 = 6]**

3. Distinguish between top-level, middle-level, and lower-level of Management. U [OEB]

This Question is for practice and its solution is given at the end of the chapter.

TOPIC-4 COORDINATION

Concepts Covered:
• Concept of Coordination, • Importance of Coordination, • Coordination as the Essence of Management.

Revision Notes

- **Meaning:** Coordination is a process by which a manager synchronises the activities of different departments to achieve the common organisational goals. It is the force that binds all the other functions of management.
- **Nature/Features of Coordination:** [Board, 2016]

(i) All pervasive
(ii) Integrates group efforts
(iii) Continuous process
(iv) Ensures unity of action
(v) Responsibility of all managers
(vi) Deliberate function

- **Importance of Coordination:**

(i) **Functional differentiation:** Ensures unity of action among different departments which have independent functioning by linking their activities.
(ii) **Growth in size:** Integrates individual goals with organisational goals to achieve organisational efficiency as organisations grow in size.
(iii) **Specialisation:** Integrates efforts of various specialists in the organisation which avoids conflict.

- **Coordination is the essence of Management** [Board, 2019]

(i) **Needed in all management functions:**
(a) **Planning:** Coordination between organisational plan and departmental plan.
(b) **Organising:** Required between authority, responsibility and accountability.
(c) **Staffing:** To achieve balance between job requirement and qualities of personnel.
(d) **Directing:** Required between supervision, motivation and leadership.
(e) **Controlling:** Ensure actual result conform to expected results.
(ii) **Needed at all levels of management:**
(a) **Top level:** Coordination to integrate activities of the organisation for accomplishing the organisational goals.
(b) **Middle level:** Coordination of the efforts of different sections and sub-sections.
(c) **Lower level:** Coordination of the activities of workers to ensure the progress of work.

Scan this

Nature of Coordination

MNEMONICS

(i) **Concept: Features of Coordination:**
Interpretations: Draw UR PIC
D: Deliberate
U: Unity of action
R: Manager's responsibility
P: Pervasive
I: Integrates efforts
C: Continuous
(ii) **Concept: Importance of Coordination:**
Interpretations: Grab Some Food
G: Growth in size
S: Specialisation
F: Functional differentiation

SUBJECTIVE TYPE QUESTIONS

Short Answer Type Questions-I (3 marks each)

1. **Top management plans for the entire organisation. According to these plans the organisational structure is developed and staffed.**
In order to ensure that these plans are executed according to plans, directing is required.
Any discrepancies between actual and realised activities are then taken care of at the stage of controlling. Name and explain the process highlighted above which started at the planning stage itself and is implicit and inherent in all the functions of management in an organisation.
AE [SQP 2023-24]

Concept Applied | Coordination and its features

Ans. Coordination [1]
The process by which a manager harmonise and synchronises the activities of different departments is known as coordination.
Coordination is the force that binds all the other functions of management. It is the common thread that runs through all activities. It is implicit and inherent in all functions of an organisation. [2]

2. **'Coordination is the essence of management.' Explain.**
U [Delhi Set-3, 2019]

3. **Coordination is needed at all levels of management, and is the responsibility of all managers. Explain.**
U [Delhi Set-2, 2019]

Ans. Coordination is needed at all levels of management:
(i) Coordination is required at all levels of management due to the interdependent nature of activities of various departments.
(ii) It integrates the efforts of different departments and different levels.

Coordination is the responsibility of all managers:
(i) Coordination is the function of every manager in the organisation.
(ii) Top level managers need to coordinate with their subordinates to ensure that the overall policies for the organisation are duly carried out.
(iii) Middle-level management coordinates with both the top level and first line managers.
(iv) Operational-level management coordinates the activities of its workers to ensure that work proceeds according to plans. [1½ + 1½ = 3]
[Marking Scheme, Delhi, 2019]

This Question is for practice and its solution is given at the end of the chapter.

Short Answer Type Questions-II (4 marks each)

1. Explain how coordination 'integrates group efforts' and 'ensures unity of actions'? U [OEB]

Concept Applied | Features of coordination

Ans. (i) Integrates group effort: Coordination is not required when the entire job is performed by an individual. Coordination is instead needed when many individuals are working together, have different backgrounds and methods of working. Coordination unifies their diverse activities and gives a common focus to the group efforts to ensure that performance is as it was planned and scheduled.

(ii) Ensures unity of actions: The purpose of coordination is to secure unity of action in the realisation of a common purpose. It acts as the binding force between departments and ensures that all action is aimed at achieving the goals of the organisation. Thus, all departmental goals of purchase, sales, finance departments, etc. are streamlined to focus towards the achievement of the common organisational objective. **[2 + 2 = 4]**

2. "The process of linking the activities of various departments is accomplished by coordination." Justify the statement. U [OEB]

Ans. In an organisation there may be separate departments of finance, production, marketing or human resources. All these departments may have their own objectives, policies and their own style of working. For example, the marketing department's objective may be to increase sales by 10 per cent by offering discounts. But, the finance department may not approve of such discounts as it means loss of revenue. These kinds of conflict arise in organisations because each unit/department is performing activities in isolation from others and barriers between departments are becoming more rigid. However, all departments and individuals are interdependent and they have to depend on each other for information to perform their activities. The activity of each department needs to be focused on attainment of common organisational goals. The process of linking the activities of various departments is accomplished by coordination. **[4]**

Long Answer Type Questions (6 marks each)

1. Interdependence between departments and individuals and harmonisation of individual goals with organisational goals makes coordination necessary. In the light of this statement, discuss why coordination is important. AI AE [OEB]

Concept Applied | Coordination and its importance

Ans. Coordination is important as it integrates the efforts of individuals, departments and specialists and harmonises their goals.

Its importance is as follows:

(i) Growth in size: As organisations grow in size, the number of people employed by the organisation also increases. Thus, it becomes difficult to integrate their efforts and activities. All individuals differ in their habits of work, background, approaches to situations and relationships with others. It becomes necessary to ensure that all individuals work towards achieving the common goals of the organisation. But employees may have their own individual goals also. Therefore, for organisational efficiency, it is important to harmonise individual goals and organisational goals through coordination.

(ii) Functional differentiation: Functions of an organisation are divided into departments, divisions and sections. In an organisation there may be separate departments of finance, production, marketing or human resources. All these departments may have their own objectives, policies and their own style of working. For example, the marketing department's objective may be to increase sales by 10 percent by offering discounts. Coordination ensures unity of action among these different departments.

(iii) Specialisation: Complexity of modern business requires various functions to be performed by specialists. Specialisation, in turn, brings out the need for greater coordination because of the diversity of activities of different specialists otherwise it often leads to a conflict among them because they do not take advice or suggestions from others in matters pertaining to their area of specialisation. Thus, coordination is required to reconcile the differences in approach, interest or opinion of the specialists.

[2 + 2 + 2 = 6]

2. CareTech is a company which deals with providing car service at home and on road. There are different departments in this company like Human Resources, Marketing, Finance, Research and Development and Operations. The top management of the company tries its level best to synchronise the activities of different departments in the best possible manner. The result is the increased efficiency and attainment of goals. However, with the passing of time the size of the company has grown and now there are many branches of this company. The synchronisation has turned more important with the increase in the size of the company and the number of employees. The Departmental Heads of the company are specialists in their respective areas and the top management tries to work with them not with authority but by respecting their views on the subject. Their ego clashes are avoided to ensure smooth functioning of the organisation.

Identify the concept of management highlighted above. Also give the benefits highlighted in the above paragraph of this concept. A

3. Describe any four characteristics of 'Coordination'. AI R [Outside Delhi Set-1, 2, 3, 2016]

These Questions are for practice and their solutions are given at the end of the chapter.

COMPETENCY BASED QUESTIONS

Objective Type Questions

[A] Multiple Choice Questions

1. Management is an integral part of all organisations and it consists of a series of interrelated functions that are performed by all the managers. What is the role of middle management in an organisation?

(A) To interact with the actual workforce and oversee their work.

(B) To lay down the overall goals and strategies of the organisation.

(C) To implement the plans and strategies developed for the organisation.

(D) To ensure the welfare and survival of the organisation. AI U [CFPQ, 2023]

Ans. Option (C) is correct.

Explanation: Middle management plays a crucial role in translating the overall goals and strategies set by top management into actionable plans and activities. They are responsible for implementing and overseeing the day-to-day operations to ensure that organisational objectives are met.

2. Over the past five years, there has been an exponential increase in the number of people practising healthier lifestyles in India. Doctors and nutritionists are advising people to reduce the daily intake of soft drinks as they are aerated, which can lead to obesity and other health issues. To cope with the setback in the demand from the consumers, "ENERGISE', a soft drink giant decided to introduce a tea brand named 'SFUR-TEA' and a wellness drink named 'FORTY PLUS' for women. The company received a hearty response from the consumers.

Identify the feature of management reflected in the above paragraph.

(A) Management is intangible.

(B) Management is a dynamic function.

(C) Management is a group activity.

(D) Management is multi-dimensional.

AI [APQ, 2023-24]

Ans. Option (B) is correct.

Explanation: The scenario showcases how 'ENERGISE,' the soft drink giant, responded to the changing consumer demand and market trends by introducing new products like 'SFUR-TEA' and 'FORTY PLUS.' This action highlights the dynamic nature of management, where companies need to adapt and make strategic changes to address evolving market conditions and consumer preferences. Management as a dynamic function involves constant assessment, adaptation, and innovation to stay relevant and meet the needs of the market and consumers.

[Marking Scheme, APQ, 2023]

3.

Identify the feature of Coordination illustrated in the picture.

(A) Pervasive function **(B)** Deliberate function

(C) Continuous process **(D)** Integrates group efforts

R [APQ, 2023-24]

Ans. Option (D) is correct.

Explanation: Coordination acts as the glue that binds individual efforts, ensures a harmonious flow of activities, and maximises the effectiveness and productivity of the entire group or organisation.

[Marking Scheme APQ, 2023]

4. Light and Sound Pvt. Ltd. manufactures custom in-ear monitors for musicians. Although it has been in the business for the last five years and has a considerable market share, on conducting an analysis, it found that the company was spending almost 10% of the total cost on packaging. The company decided to outsource the packaging function to a professional packaging company. The decision helped the firm to achieve its goals through greater customer satisfaction through timely delivery of orders and also helped the company in reducing the cost of packaging by 5%. After the implementation of the decision for outsourcing, the company has become.

(A) Effective

(B) Efficient

(C) Both efficient and effective

(D) Neither efficient nor effective

AI A [APQ, 2023-24]

Ans. Option (C) is correct.

Explanation: Outsourcing the packaging function resulted in cost reduction and improved customer satisfaction through timely order deliveries. The cost of packaging decreased by 5%, indicating increased efficiency in cost management. Moreover, achieving greater customer satisfaction demonstrates effectiveness in meeting customer needs and expectations. Therefore, the company became both efficient (in cost reduction) and effective (in meeting customer satisfaction goals) after outsourcing the packaging function.

[Marking Scheme APQ, 2023]

5. Mr. Anand Niketan has been successfully running a chain of restaurants in Delhi and Gurgaon for the past 15 years. Aadhavan, his son, returned to India after acquiring a Master's degree in Social

Work. He suggested to his father that they should enter into a new line of business of Coffee Bars and provide employment opportunities to differently-abled people and, in the process, create greater economic value for different sections. After a lot of deliberation, Aadhavan opened his first Coffee Bar under the name of 'SPESH' near the college campus. The idea of taking orders was unique. The staff gave a pen and a pad and had codes on the menu in front of the dishes. On pressing the bell, the light would pop and the staff would come to assist customers. The users loved the concept and very soon 'SPESH' expanded its outlets to other parts of the city. Aadhavan hired an additional 70 employees to manage the new outlets. Identify the objective(s) that SPESH seeks to achieve through its new venture.

(A) Organisational and personnel objective
(B) Organisational and social objective
(C) Social and personnel objective
(D) Social objective **U [APQ, 2023]**

Ans. Option (B) is correct.

Explanation: The venture aims not only to expand the business (organisational objective) but also to create social impact by providing employment opportunities to differently-abled individuals (social objective).

[Marking Scheme APQ, 2023]

6. Identify the reason which makes management important in the light of the fact that it is generally seen that individuals in an organisation resist change, as a change often means moving from a familiar, secure environment into a newer and a more challenging one.

(A) Management helps in achieving group goals
(B) Management creates a dynamic organisation
(C) Management increases efficiency
(D) Management helps in the development of society. **U [SQP 2023-24]**

Ans. Option (B) is correct.

Explanation: Management creates a dynamic organisation as it includes goal, objectives, and other activities which keeps on changing according to the changes taking place in the business environment.

7. Also a mobility platform is in the process of laying off 400-500 employees in a move aimed at driving cost efficiency.

Which objective of management will the firm not be able to achieve by carrying out this process?

(A) Efficiency **(B)** Social
(C) Profit **(D)** Survival

U [SQP 2023-24]

Ans. Option (B) is correct.

Explanation: Social objectives of a business includes production and supply of quality and standard goods and services, adoption of fair-trade practices and contribution to the general welfare of society and provision of welfare amenities.

8. Raman and Vasudev were two employees who were embessling an import-export company in Varanasi where they were working. The finance manager of the company Sampat Singh became suspicious of the two employees when he realised that their activities were not being performed as per the plans. He installed a software program that could secretly log every single stroke of the suspects' computer keys and send an encrypted email report to the Cyber police. The police were able to catch the two dishonest employees red handed and arrest them. Identify the function of management being discussed above.

(A) Staffing **(B)** Coordination
(C) Controlling **(D)** Organising

U [SQP 2023-24]

Concept Applied: Function of management.

Ans. Option (C) is correct.

Explanation: The controlling function helps in measuring the progress towards the organisational goals and brings any deviations and indicates corrective action.

9. 'SORT- IT Ltd.' is a leading software development company. The company is satisfying the diverse needs of its employees. Its employees are given competitive salaries and perks. They have been given chance for their personal growth and development. For harmony in the organisation, management has to reconcile personal goals with organisational objectives.

Identify the objective of management being met by 'SORT-IT Ltd.'

(A) Social **(B)** Personnel
(C) Organisational
(D) Both social and personnel

A [SQP Term-1, Exam 2022]

Ans. Option (B) is correct

Explanation: Organisations are made up of people who have **different personalities, backgrounds, experiences and objectives**. They all become part of the organisation to satisfy their diverse needs. Management has to reconcile personal goals with organisational objectives to establish harmony in the organisation.

10. At times, a business may concentrate on producing goods with fewer resources but cannot achieve the targeted production. In such a case, the business is said to be:

(A) Effective but not efficient
(B) Efficient but not effective
(C) Both effective and efficient
(D) Neither effective nor efficient

U [SQP Term-1, Exam 2022]

Ans. Option (B) is correct.

Explanation: There is efficiency in this case because the business can make things with fewer resources. However, it fails to meet the output goals, which suggests that it may not be meeting its goals or meeting customer needs effectively. So, the company is efficient (it makes good use of its resources) but not effective (it achieves its goals).

11. Identify the dimension of the characteristic of management- "it is multidimensional", which specifies that the task of management is to make the strengths of human resources effective and their weaknesses irrelevant towards achieving the organisation's objectives.

(A) Management of work
(B) Management of people
(C) Management of operations
(D) Management of goals

U [SQP Term-1, Exam 2022]

Ans. Option (B) is correct.

Explanation: Human resources or people are the organisation's greatest asset. Despite all developments in technology "getting work done through people" is still a major task for the manager. The task of management is to make people work towards achieving the organisational goals, by making their strengths effective and their weaknesses irrelevant.

12. "The management gives a common direction to the individual effort in achieving the overall goal of the organisation."
Which point of importance of management is highlighted in this statement?

(A) Helps in achieving personal objectives.
(B) Helps in achieving group goals.
(C) Helps to increase efficiency.
(D) Helps to create a dynamic organisation.

U [SQP Term-1, Exam 2022]

Ans. Option (B) is correct.

Explanation: Management is required not for itself but for achieving the goals of the organisation. The task of a manager is to give a common direction to the individual effort in achieving the overall goal of the organisation.

13. Ram Murty, a professor of Management conducted a class on 'Management Principles' and explained to his students the significance of management principles. In the next class, the professor asked his students to play roles of different managers. He gave them various situations and asked them to think like managers and provide solutions to the problems given in these situations. Each student applied the principles of management to the given situation in his own personalised manner, depending upon his creativity.
The nature of management highlighted in the above case is:

(A) Management as a science
(B) Management as an art
(C) Management both as an art and as a science
(D) Management as a profession

A [SQP Term-1, Exam 2022]

Ans. Option (B) is correct.

Explanation: Since art is concerned with personal application of knowledge, some kind of ingenuity and creativity is required to practice the basic principles learnt. The use of this basic knowledge varies from individual to individual. Art, therefore, is a very personalised concept. For example, two dancers, two speakers, two actors, or two writers will always differ in demonstrating their art.

14. Which of the following feature of a profession is fully satisfied by management?

(A) Service motive
(B) Well defined body of knowledge
(C) Restricted entry
(D) Ethical code of conduct

U [SQP Term-1, Exam 2022]

Ans. Option (B) is correct.

Explanation: All professions are based on a well-defined body of knowledge that can be acquired through instructions. All over the world there is marked growth in management as a discipline. It is based on a systematic body of knowledge comprising well-defined business situations. This knowledge can be acquired at different colleges and professional institutes and through a number of books and journals. Thus, Management has a systematised body of knowledge.

15. Which level of management is responsible for coordinating the activities of different departments according to overall objectives of the organisation?

(A) Top level
(B) Middle level
(C) Supervisory level
(D) Both middle and supervisory level.

U [SQP Term-1, Exam 2022]

Ans. Option (A) is correct.

Explanation: Top Level Management's basic task is to integrate diverse elements and coordinate the activities of different departments according to the overall objectives of the organisation. These top level managers are responsible for the welfare and survival of the organisation. They analyse the business environment and its implications for the survival of the firm. They formulate overall organisational goals and strategies for their achievement.

16. IND Dyechem Ltd. is a chemical manufacturing company producing dyes and pigments both for domestic and international markets. It has enjoyed a considerable market share but lately, it has been facing problems in terms of target sales and customer satisfaction. This is due to the reason that new entrants have emerged with better technology and competitive pricing. The Chairman of the company addressed this issue in the departmental meeting. The production head, Mr. Kamble, advised the Chairman to revamp the system and take immediate necessary actions to rectify the problem so that sales are achieved as per the plans.
Identify the relevant function of management being discussed here. AI AE [SQP, 2023-24]

(A) Organising (B) Staffing
(C) Controlling (D) Planning

Ans. Option (C) is correct.

Explanation: Controlling is the comparison of actual performance with the planned performance to find out deviations and correct them.

[Marking Scheme, SQP, 2023-24]

17. Different organisations have different goals. 'Zeepo' is an upcoming retail chain for providing consumer goods door-to-door, the objective of this organisation is to increase sales. 'Allie' is an educational organisation working to provide education to underprivileged children of the society. Management of each of these organisations unites the efforts of their employees toward achieving organisational goals.

The characteristic of management discussed above is : [SQP, 2023-24]

(A) Management is goal-oriented.
(B) Management is a continuous process.
(C) Management is a dynamic function.
(D) Management is an intangible force.

Ans. Option (A) is correct.

Explanation: Management is the process of reaching organisational goals by working with and through people and other organisational resources.

[Marking Scheme, SQP, 2023-24]

18. Himanshu is working as a 'Marketing Manager at 'Suvidit-Air-Conditioners, a well-known brand in the field of air-conditioners. Till last month the company was able to achieve its sales targets. But this month Himanshu observed that targets were not being met and the number of air-conditioners sold was decreasing. He analysed the situation and found that the new salesman appointed last month was not good and for this, he took necessary action. Which of the following functions of management helped Himanshu to identify the decrease in sales?

(A) Planning (B) Organising
(C) Directing (D) Controlling

[SQP, 2023-24]

Ans. Option (D) is correct.

Explanation: Controlling, conversely, checks whether decisions have been translated into desired action. Planning is thus, prescriptive whereas, controlling is evaluative. It is often said that planning is looking ahead while controlling is looking back. [Marking Scheme, SQP, 2023-24]

19. Akash works as a production manager in 'Elite Enterprises' manufacturing LED lights. Due to the festive season, there is a lot of demand for their lights. Akash was given the task of producing 100 units of LED lights @ ₹ 200 per unit within 5 days for an urgent order. Akash was able to achieve the target of 100 units of LED lights within 5 days @ ₹ 220 per unit.

Identify from the following whether Akash is:

AI [Outside Delhi Set-1, 2023]

(A) Efficient only
(B) Effective only
(C) Both efficient and effective
(D) Neither efficient nor effective

Ans. Option (B) is correct.

Explanation: Akash even though completed the task within the required time frame but was not within the cost limit, he is only effective and not efficient

20. The management of a bag manufacturing company has recently changed. Due to this, an improvement can be felt in how the company functions. Now, targets are met according to plans, whereas, earlier deadlines were never given importance. Now there is orderliness, instead of chaos in the organisation and the employees are happy and satisfied. From the following identify the characteristic of management that is highlighted in the above case:

(A) Management is dynamic.
(B) Management is a continuous process.
(C) Management is a group activity.
(D) Management is an intangible force.

[SQP, 2023-24]

Ans. Option (A) is correct.

Explanation: Management is a dynamic function and has to adapt itself to the changing environment. An organisation interacts with its external environment which consists of various social, economic, political, and legal factors. To be successful, an organisation must change itself and its goals according to the needs of the environment.

21. 'It acts as a binding force between departments and ensures that all action are aimed at achieving the goals of the organisation'. The statement highlights the following characteristic of co- ordination:

(A) Co-ordination is an all-pervasive function.
(B) Co-ordination is the responsibility of all managers.
(C) Co-ordination is a continuous process.
(D) Co-ordination ensures unity of action.

U [SQP Term-1, Exam 2022]

Ans. Option (D) is correct.

Explanation: The purpose of coordination is to secure unity of action in the realisation of a common purpose. It acts as the binding force between departments and ensures that all action is aimed at achieving the goals of the organisation.

22. The Topper group is looking to make a foray into manufacturing of semiconductors and it has set up a business to seize the business opportunity and add to its prospects in the long run. The company has already pivoted into a number of new projects like electronics, 5G network equipment, as well as semiconductors. Which economic objective of management does the business seek to fulfil?

(A) Survival (B) Growth
(C) Profit (D) Efficiency

A [SQP Term-1, 2022-23]

Ans. Option (B) is correct.

Explanation: A business needs to add to its prospects in the long run. For this, it is important for the business to grow. To remain in the industry, management must exploit fully the growth potential of the organisation. Growth of a business can be measured in terms of sales volume, increase in the number of employees, the number of products or the increase in capital investment, etc.

23. Ravi joined a marketing firm as a sales manager. On his first day in the company, during the orientation programme, the CEO of the company told Ravi

that he will have to simultaneously perform the functions of management (planning, organising, staffing, directing, controlling) all the time. Which characteristic of management was the CEO referring to?

(A) Management is a continuous process.
(B) Management is all pervasive.
(C) Management is multidimensional.
(D) Management is goal oriented.

A [SQP Term-1, 2022-23]

Concept Applied | Characteristics of Management

Ans. Option (A) is correct.

Explanation: The process of management consist of a series of continuous, composite, but separate functions (planning, organising, staffing, directing, and controlling). These functions are simultaneously performed by all managers all the time. The task of a manager consists of an ongoing series of functions.

24. "What distinguishes a successful manager from a less successful one is the ability to put the principles into practice." Which aspect of the nature of management is highlighted in the above statement?

(A) Management as a science.
(B) Management as an art.
(C) Management as a profession.
(D) Management is an intangible force.

A [SQP Term-1, 2022-23]

Ans. Option (B) is correct.

Explanation: Art involves the creative practice of existing theoretical knowledge. A successful manager practices the art of management in the day-to-day job of managing an enterprise based on study, observation and experience.

25. Silico Ltd. has appointed the former Consulting Executive of Shri Shakti Ltd. Rajan Bahl as its Vice President. What will be his basic task?

(A) To integrate diverse elements and coordinate activities of different departments.
(B) To carry out plans formulated by top managers.
(C) To oversee the efforts of the workforce.
(D) Help to maintain quality of output.

A [SQP Term-1, 2022-23]

Ans. Option (A) is correct.

Explanation: Top Management consists of the senior-most executives of the organisation. They are usually referred to as the chairman, the chief executive officer, chief operating officer, president and vice-president. Top management is a team consisting of managers from different functional levels, heading finance, marketing, etc. For example chief finance officer, vice president (marketing). Their basic task is to integrate diverse elements and coordinate the activities of different departments according to the overall objectives of the organisation.

26. The production department at Karishmaa Ltd., a firm manufacturing ready-made garments for men has an objective to increase production by 10% but the Sales department does not approve of the increase in production, till changes are brought about in the product to incorporate latest fashion. These kinds of conflicts bring to light the following importance of the force that can help to accomplish the linking of activities of various departments:

(A) Growth in size
(B) Functional differentiation.
(C) Specialisation
(D) Efficiency

A [SQP Term-1, 2022-23]

Ans. Option (B) is correct.

Explanation: Functions of an organisation are divided into departments, divisions and sections. In an organisation there may be separate departments of finance, production, marketing or human resources. All these departments may have their own objectives, policies and their own style of working.

27. "A manager in a conscious manner has to ensure that even where members of a department willingly cooperate, coordination gives direction to the willing spirit."

The characteristic of coordination being highlighted above is:

(A) Coordination is the responsibility of all managers.
(B) Coordination is a deliberate function.
(C) Coordination integrates group efforts.
(D) Coordination is a continuous process

U [SQP Term-1, 2022-23]

Ans. Option (B) is correct.

Explanation: A manager has to coordinate the efforts of different people in a conscious and deliberate manner. Even where members of a department willingly cooperate and work, coordination gives a direction to that willing spirit. Cooperation in the absence of coordination may lead to waste effort and coordination without cooperation may lead to dissatisfaction among employees.

28. Name the process of working with and through others to effectively achieve organisational objectives by efficiently using limited resources in a changing environment.

(A) Management (B) Planning
(C) Organising (D) Controlling

U [SQP 2021-22]

29. "Anyone can be called a manager irrespective of the educational qualification possessed." Identify the characteristic of the profession that Management does not fulfil in the statement being discussed above:

(A) Ethical code of conduct
(B) Professional association
(C) Restricted entry
(D) Service motive

U [SQP 2021-22]

Ans. Option (C) is correct.

Explanation: The entry to a profession is restricted through an examination or through acquiring an educational degree. Whereas there is no legal restriction on appointment of a manager, anyone can become a manager irrespective of the educational qualification.

30. .... is the process by which the manager brings order out of chaos, removes conflict among people

This Question is for practice and its solution is given at the end of the chapter.

over allotted work or responsibility-sharing and creates an environment suitable for teamwork.

(A) Planning (B) Organising
(C) Staffing (D) Controlling

U [SQP 2021-22]

Ans. Option (B) is correct.

Explanation: Proper organisational techniques help in the accomplishment of work and promote both the efficiency of operations and the effectiveness of results.

31. The festive season was about to come. Mrs. Rubi, Head of Production department, called for a meeting of all the subordinates and communicated the objectives. Now she is establishing authority-responsibility relationship between superior and subordinates to avoid any delay.

.... function of management is stated in the above case.

(A) Organising (B) Controlling
(C) Directing (D) Planning

AI U [SQP 2021-22]

32. Name the function of management which helps in the formulation of future plans, in the light of the problems that were identified and thus, helps in better planning in the future period.

(A) Planning (B) Organising
(C) Directing (D) Controlling

U [SQP 2021-22]

Concept Applied Functions of Management

Ans. Option (D) is correct.

33. Statement-I: Management consists of a series of functions.

Statement-II: Management is a group activity.

Choose the correct option from the options given below:

(A) Statement I is true and II is false.
(B) Statement II is true and I is false.
(C) Both the statements are true.
(D) Both the statements are false.

U [OEB]

Ans. Option (C) is correct.

Explanation: Management involves a series of interrelated functions like planning, organising, staffing, directing, and controlling, which makes it a process. Management is a group activity since it involves managing and coordinating activities of different people as a team to attain the desired objectives of the organisation.

34. Match the columns on the basis of importance of management:

Column I	Column II
(1) Creates dynamic organisation	(a) The task of managers is to reduce the cost and to increase the productivity.
(2) Increases efficiency	(b) Job of the manager is to give common direction to individual efforts.
(3) Achieves group goals	(c) Organisations have to work in an environment which is constantly changing.
(4) Development of Society	(d) Provides good quality products, generates employment, etc.

(A) 1-b, 2-c, 3-a, 4-d (B) 1-c, 2-a, 3-b, 4-d
(C) 1-a, 2-c, 3-b, 4-d (D) 1-b, 2-a, 3-c, 4-d

U [OEB]

Ans. Option (B) is correct.

35. Statement-I: Top management is a team consisting of managers from different functional levels, heading finance, marketing, etc.

Statement-II: Middle management is responsible for implementing and controlling plans and strategies developed by top management.

Choose the correct option from the options given below:

(A) Statement I is true and II is false.
(B) Statement II is true and I is false.
(C) Both the statements are true.
(D) Both the statements are false.

U [OEB]

Ans. Option (C) is correct.

36. Match the column on the basis of the functions of management:

Column I	Column II
(1) Planning	(a) Assigning duties, grouping tasks, and establishing authority.
(2) Organising	(b) Leading, influencing and motivating employees
(3) Directing	(c) Setting goals in advance
(4) Staffing	(d) This function is concerned with finding the right person for the right job.

(A) 1-b, 2-c, 3-a, 4-d (B) 1-c, 2-a, 3-b, 4-d
(C) 1-a, 2-c, 3-b, 4-d (D) 1-b, 2-a, 3-c, 4-d

U [OEB]

Ans. Option (B) is correct.

37.

This Question is for practice and its solution is given at the end of the chapter.

Which of the following concept of management is absent in the given image.

(A) Management (B) Coordination

(C) Planning (D) Directing A [OEB]

Ans. Option (B) is correct.

Explanation: Coordination is a process by which a manager synchronises the activities of different departments to achieve the common organisational goals. In the absence of coordination, there will be chaos and conflicts in the organisation.

[B] Assertion & Reason

Directions: In the following questions, a statement of assertion (A) is followed by a statement of reason (R). Mark the correct choice as:

(A) Both assertion (A) and reason (R) are true and reason (R) is the correct explanation of assertion (A).

(B) Both assertion (A) and reason (R) are true but reason (R) is not the correct explanation of assertion (A).

(C) Assertion (A) is true but reason (R) is false.

(D) Assertion (A) is false but reason (R) is true.

1. **Assertion (A):** Management is concerned with the efficient use of resources.

   Reason (R): For management, efficiency and effectiveness must be balanced. U [SQP, 2023-24]

Ans. Option (B) is correct.

Explanation: Efficiency and effectiveness help to get maximum product in quantity and quality.

[Marking Scheme, SQP, 2023-24]

2. **Assertion (A):** Management is a dynamic function and has to adapt itself to the changing environment.

   Reason (R): The effect of management is noticeable in an organisation where targets are met according to plans. U [OEB]

Ans. Option (B) is correct.

Explanation: An organisation interacts with its external environment which consists of various social, economic and political factors. In order to be successful, an organisation must change itself and its goals according to the needs of the environment.

3. **Assertion (A):** Management is a goal-oriented process.

   Reason (R): An organisation has a set of basic goals which are the basic reasons for its existence. R [OEB]

Ans. Option (A) is correct.

Explanation: Different organisations have different goals. Management unites the efforts of different individuals in the organisation towards achieving these goals.

4. **Assertion (A):** Management is responsible for setting and achieving objectives for the organisation.

   Reason (R): The basic objective of any business is survival. U [OEB]

Ans. Option (A) is correct.

Explanation: Management has to achieve a variety of objectives in all areas considering the interest of all stakeholders. The main objective of any organisation should be to utilise human and material resources to the maximum possible advantage, i.e., to fulfil the economic objectives of a business. These are survival, profit and growth.

5. **Assertion (A):** Management increases efficiency.

   Reason (R): An organisation has a single objective to serve the purpose of different groups that constitute it. U [OEB]

Concept Applied Objectives of Management

6. **Assertion (A):** Management helps in achieving personal objectives.

   Reason (R): Through motivation and leadership the management helps individuals to develop team spirit, cooperation and commitment to group success. R [OEB]

Ans. Option (A) is correct.

Explanation: A manager motivates and leads his team in such a manner that individual members are able to achieve personal goals while contributing to the overall organisational objective.

7. **Assertion (A):** Management is a systematic body of knowledge.

   Reason (R): Management has its own theory and principles that have developed over a period of time. R [OEB]

8. **Assertion (A):** All professions are bound by a code of conduct which guides the behaviour of its members.

   Reason (R): There are several associations of practicing managers in India, that have laid down a code of conduct to follow. AI U [OEB]

Ans. Option (A) is correct.

Explanation: Every profession has a certain code of conduct to follow. There are several associations of practicing managers in India, like the AIMA (All India Management Association) that have laid down a code of conduct to regulate the activities of their members.

9. **Assertion (A):** Middle management is the link between top and lower level managers.

   Reason (R): Middle management is subordinate to top managers and superior to the first line managers. U [OEB]

10. **Assertion (A):** Coordination begins at the planning stage and continues till controlling.

    Reason (R): Coordination is a one-time process. U [OEB]

Ans. Option (C) is correct.

Explanation: Coordination is a continuous process. It is not a one-time function but a continuous process. It begins at the planning stage and continues till controlling.

[C] Case Based MCQs

I. Read the below case and answer the questions that follow:

Sana is the branch manager of ABC Handicrafts Pvt. Ltd. The company's objective is to promote the sales of Indian handloom and handicraft products. It sells fabrics, furnishings, ready-mades and household items made out of traditional Indian fabrics. Sana decides quantities,

These Questions are for practice and their solutions are given at the end of the chapter.

varieties, colours and textures of all the above items and then allocates resources for their purchase from different suppliers. She appointed a team of designers and crafts people in the company, who developed some prints for bed covers in bright colour on silk. Although the products looked very attractive and impressive, they were relatively expensive on the front of affordability for an average customer. Sana suggested that they should keep the silk bed covers for special festive occasions and offer the cotton bed covers on a regular basis to keep costs under control. U [OEB]

1. **"She appointed a team of designers and crafts people in the company, who developed some prints for bed covers in bright colour on silk." Which function of management is highlighted in this context ?**

   (A) Controlling **(B)** Staffing
   (C) Planning **(D)** Directing

Ans. Option (B) is correct.

Explanation: Staffing is a very important aspect of management so as to make sure that right people with right qualifications are available at the right places and at right times to accomplish the goals of the organisation.

2. **In the above case "company's objective is to promote the sales of Indian handloom and handicraft products." The above line focuses on which feature of management?**

   (A) Management is an intangible force.
   (B) Management is a goal oriented process.
   (C) Management is pervasive in nature.
   (D) Management is a continuous process.

Ans. Option (B) is correct.

Explanation: An organisation has a set of basic goals which are the basic reason for its existence. Management unites the efforts of different individuals in the organisation towards achieving these goals.

3. **With reference to the above case, at which level of management Sana is working?**

   (A) Lower level **(B)** Top level
   (C) Middle level **(D)** Shop floor

Ans. Option (C) is correct.

Explanation: Middle Management is the link between top and lower level managers. They are subordinate to top managers and superior to the first line managers. They are usually known as division heads.

4. **"Sana suggested that they should keep the silk bed covers for special festive occasions and offer the cotton bed covers on a regular basis to keep costs under control." Which function of management is highlighted in this context?**

   (A) Controlling **(B)** Staffing
   (C) Organising **(D)** Planning

Ans. Option (A) is correct.

Explanation: Controlling is the management function of monitoring organisational performance towards the attainment of organisational goals. The task of controlling involves establishing standards of performance, measuring current performance, comparing this with established standards and taking corrective action where any deviation is found.

II. Read the below case and answer the questions that follow: U [OEB]

Best Textiles Ltd. is a big company. Managing many employees at the same moment is a challenge which this company always faces. Since the company has many departments it is necessary for the company to ensure unity of action among various departments. The various departments are human resources, marketing, finance, operations and sales. The top-level managers coordinate with all middle-level managers. The middle-level managers coordinate simultaneously with top as well as lower-level managers. The lower-level managers coordinate with middle-level managers and the workers. The employees are always concerned about the company and are a useful resource to their organisation. Though they have diverse interests and have to perform different activities, the management ensures that the efforts of the employees should be given a focus so as to achieve the organisational goals.

The different departments have their own interests but due to proper coordination, conflict of interest between departments is minimised to zero. When it comes to the employees, the organisation shows its concern. The career of employees is shown a developmental path through proper training modules and job enrichment. Sanjeev is a manager who takes care of all the duties and responsibilities to be assigned to his employees in the department. He uses all sources to develop a proper communication with them and leaves no attempt to motivate them. This year the company has decided to give the best manager award to Sanjeev for his contribution to the organisation.

1. **Which characteristic of coordination has been highlighted in the above case?**

   (A) Unity of action
   (B) Responsibility of all managers
   (C) Integration of group efforts
   (D) All of the above

Ans. Option (D) is correct.

Explanation: The significant role of coordination within an organisation, emphasising aspects such as unity of action, the responsibility of all managers at different levels, and the integration of group efforts to achieve common organisational goals.

2. **Which importance of management has been highlighted above?**

   (A) Functional differentiation
   (B) Growth in size
   (C) Specialisation
   (D) All of the above

Ans. Option (A) is correct.

Explanation: Functions of an organisation are divided into departments, divisions and sections. In an organisation there may be separate departments of finance, production, marketing or human resources. The activity of each department needs to be focused on attainment of common organisational goals.

The process of linking the activities of various departments is accomplished by coordination.

3. Which type of objective is fulfilled here?

(A) Personal **(B)** Social
(C) Organisational **(D)** None of these

Ans. Option (A) is correct.

Explanation: Organisations are made up of people who have different personalities, backgrounds, experiences and objectives. Management has to reconcile personal goals with organisational objectives for harmony in the organisation.

4. At which level of management does Sanjeev work?

(A) Top **(B)** Middle
(C) Lower **(D)** None of these

Ans. Option (B) is correct.

SOLUTIONS FOR PRACTICE QUESTIONS (TOPIC-1)

SATQs-I

Ans 4. Management is a complex activity that has three main dimensions. These dimensions are:

(i) Management of work
(ii) Management of people
(iii) Management of operations

[Marking Scheme, Delhi, 2019] 1×3=3

SOLUTIONS FOR PRACTICE QUESTIONS (TOPIC-2)

SATQs-I

Ans 3. Management is an art as well as a science though an inexact science.

(i) Art is the skillful and personal application of existing knowledge to achieve desired results.

Management is an art because like any other art, it has existence of theoretical knowledge and personalised application based on continuous practice.

(ii) Science is a systematised body of knowledge that explains certain general truths. Like science, management principles are derived through observation and repeated experiments. Since management deals with human beings, the outcome of these experiments cannot be accurately predicted.

Moreover, they have to be modified according to the given situation. Hence, it is an inexact science.

[1½ × 2 = 3]

LATQs-I

Ans 2. Management as a Profession:

(i) Well-defined body of knowledge: All professions are based on a well-defined body of knowledge that can be acquired through instruction. In management also, there is a systematic body of knowledge comprising well-defined principles based on a variety of business situations that is taught at different institutions. This feature of profession is present in management.

(ii) Restricted entry: The entry to profession is restricted through a prescribed qualification. But there is no restriction on anyone being appointed as a manager in any business enterprise. So, presently this feature of profession is not present in management.

(iii) Professional association: Legal and medical professions are affiliated to a professional association like bar council and medical council which regulates entry, grants certificate of practice and formulates and enforces a code of conduct. There are several associations of practicing managers in India, like AIMA that has laid down a code.

Ans 4. In the above case, management is being considered as an art.

Art is the skillful and personal application of existing knowledge to achieve desired results. The evaluation of management as an art is given below:

(i) Existence of theoretical knowledge: Art presupposes the existence of certain knowledge. Management fulfills this criterion as there exist a number of theories and principles on management which have been formulated by various management experts.

(ii) Personalised applications: Art is a personalised concept. Management fulfills this criterion as a good manager works through a combination of his own experience, creativity, imagination, initiative and innovation to carry out the assigned work.

(iii) Based on practice and creativity: All art is practical. Management fulfills this criterion as a person becomes a better manager with constant practice and experience. This also leads to emergence of different styles of management. **[3+3=6]**

SOLUTIONS FOR PRACTICE QUESTIONS (TOPIC-3)

SATQs-I

Ans 2. Organisational structure possesses three levels of management which are as follows:

(i) Top-level management: It consists of the Board of Directors, Chief Executive Officers, Chief Operational Officers and many more.

This level of management frames policies for overall attainment of management objectives.

(ii) Middle-level management : It consists of departmental heads, section officers, etc. This level interprets and explains the policies framed by the top-level management.

They are involved more in collecting and reporting feedbacks to the top level.

(iii) Operational-level management : It is the lowest level of management. It consists of plant superintendents, clerks, supervisors, etc. They are concerned with technical and routine work on a day-to-day basis.

[1 × 3 = 3]

LATQs-I

Ans. 3. Difference between top-level, middle-level, and lower-or supervisory-level of management:

S. No.	Basis	Top-Level	Middle-Level	Lower-Level
(i)	**Time range**	It covers a long span of period.	It covers a moderate range of period.	It is concerned with short period.
(ii)	**Skills**	It requires creative skills.	It needs persuasive skills.	It is concerned with operative skills.
(iii)	**Evaluation**	It is difficult to evaluate their achievement.	It is less difficult to evaluate their performance.	It is easy to evaluate their performance.
(iv)	**Number of Persons**	It involves few persons.	It involves moderate number of persons.	It is concerned with large number of persons.
(v)	**Policy Formulation**	It is concerned with the formulation of policies to a great extent.	It is moderately concerned with policy formulation.	It is least concerned with policy formation.
(vi)	**Nature**	It is determinative.	It is more administrative than determinative.	It is more executory and managerial than administrative.

[1 × 6 = 6]

SOLUTIONS FOR PRACTICE QUESTIONS (TOPIC-4)

SATQs-I

Ans. 2. Coordination is not a separate function of management. It is the force that binds all other functions and thus called the essence of management.

(i) The process of coordinating the activities begins at the planning stage in which the top management plans for the entire organization.

(ii) At the organising stage, the organisational structure is developed as per plans.

(iii) The staffing function is performed thereafter as per the structure developed in the organisation.

(iv) Directing is then required to ensure that these plans are executed accordingly.

(v) Controlling function ensures that the discrepancies between actual and planned activities are taken care of. Coordination, therefore, synchronises the efforts through all functions of management and ensures that the organizational objectives are achieved with a minimum of conflict.

[Marking Scheme, Delhi, 2019]

(Any three) [1 × 3 = 3]

LATQs

Ans 3. Characteristics of Coordination:

(i) Coordination integrates group efforts: Coordination unifies unrelated or diverse interests into purposeful work activity. It gives a common focus to the group efforts to ensure that performance is same as it was planned and scheduled.

(ii) Coordination ensures unity of action: The purpose of Coordination is to secure unity of action in the realisation of a common purpose. It acts as the binding force between different departments and ensures that all actions are aimed at achieving the goals of the organisation.

(iii) Coordination is a continuous process: Coordination is not a one-time function but a continuous process. It begins at the planning stage and continues till controlling.

(iv) Coordination is an all pervasive function: Coordination is required at all levels of management due to the interdependent nature of activities of various departments. It integrates the efforts of different departments and different levels. **[½×4=6]**

Ans 2. The concept of management highlighted above is that of Coordination.

Importance of coordination:

(i) Growth in size: As organisations grow in size, the number of people employed by the organisation also increases. At times, it may become difficult to integrate their efforts and activities. All individuals differ in their habits of work, background, approaches to situations and relationships with others. It becomes necessary to ensure that all individuals work towards the common goals of the organisation. But employees may have their own individual goals also. Therefore, for organisational efficiency, it is important to harmonise individual goals and organisational goals through coordination.

(ii) Functional differentiation: Functions of an organisation are divided into departments, divisions and sections. In an organisation there may be separate departments of finance, production, marketing or human resources. All these departments may have their own objectives, policies and their own style of working. However, all departments and individuals are interdependent and they have to depend on each other for information to perform their activities.

The activity of each department needs to be focused on attainment of common organisational goals. The process of linking the activities of various departments is accomplished by coordination.

(iii) Specialisation: Modern organisations are characterised by a high degree of specialisation. Specialisation arises out of the complexities of modern technology and the diversity of tasks to be performed. Organisations, therefore,need to employ a number of specialists. Specialists usually think that they only are qualified to evaluate, judge and decide according to their professional criteria. They do not take advice or suggestions from others in matters pertaining to their area of specialisation. This often leads to conflict amongst different specialists as well as others in the organisation. Therefore, some coordination is required by an independent person to reconcile the differences in approach, interest or opinion of the specialists. **[6]**

SOLUTIONS FOR OBJECTIVE PRACTICE QUESTIONS

[A] MCQs

Ans 31. Option (D) is correct.

Explanation: Controlling is the management function of monitoring organisational performance towards the attainment of organisational goals.

Ans 28. Option (A) is correct.

Explanation: Management as a process means to carry out primary functions or activities that management performs to get things done using limited resources. These functions are planning, organising, staffing, directing and controlling.

Ans 30. Option (A) is correct.

Explanation: Organising is the management function of assigning duties, grouping tasks establishing authority and allocating resources required to carry out a specific plan.

[B] A & R

Ans 5. Option (C) is correct.

Explanation: The aim of a manager is to reduce costs and increase productivity through better planning, organising, directing, staffing and controlling activities of the organisation.

An organisation has multiple objectives to serve the purpose of different groups that constitute it. In the process of fulfilling all these, management helps in the development of the organisation and through that it helps in the development of society.

Ans 7. Option (A) is correct.

Explanation: Management has a systematised body of knowledge. Like all other organised activities, management has its own theory, principles, vocabulary of terms and concepts.

Ans 9. Option (A) is correct.

Explanation: Middle management is responsible for implementing and controlling plans and strategies developed by top management. At the same time, they are responsible for all the activities of first line managers.

REFLECTION

(a) Were you able to identity the level of management concerned with developing cooperation with other departments for smooth functioning of organisation?

(b) Did you know which objective of management is fulfilled by a business manufacturing biscuits by using environmental friendly methods of production?

(c) Were you able to explain coordination as an essence of management?

(d) Could you identify and explain the feature of profession stated below:

"In order to become a lawyer one has to register himself as a member of Bar Council of India."

(e) Were you able to identify function of management involved in determining in advance what is to be done in future?

SELF ASSESSMENT PAPER - 1

Maximum Time: 1 hour **MM: 30**

General Instructions:

(i) All the questions are compulsory
(ii) Q.1 to Q.10 are 1 mark questions
(3) Q.11 to Q.12 are 3 mark questions
(iv) Q.13 to Q.14 are 4 marks questions
(v) Q.15 is a 6 marks question

Objective Type Questions [1 Mark]

1. Sunlent Power Ltd. set up a factory for manufacturing solar lanterns in a remote village as there was no reliable supply of electricity in rural areas. Company decided to employ people from the nearby villages as very few job opportunities were available in that area. The company also decided to open schools and creches for the children of its employees. Identify the objectives of management discussed above.

(A) Organisational **(B)** Social
(C) Personnel **(D)** All of these [1]

2.

Identify the level of workers illustrated in the picture above.

(A) Top level **(B)** Middle level
(C) Lower level **(D)** None of these [1]

3. "The task of management is to make people work towards achieving the organisation's goals, by making their strengths effective and their weaknesses irrelevant." The above statement highlights which of the following dimension of management:

(A) Management of work
(B) Management of people
(C) Management of operations
(D) All of these [1]

4. Match the column on the basis of the functions of management:

Column I		Column II	
(1)	Planning	(a)	Assigning duties, grouping tasks and establishing authority.
(2)	Organising	(b)	Leading, influencing and motivating employees
(3)	Directing	(c)	Setting goals in advance
(4)	Controlling	(c)	Establishing standards of performance, measuring current performance in column II

(A) 1-b, 2-c, 3-a, 4-d **(B)** 1-c, 2-a, 3-b, 4-d
(C) 1-a, 2-c, 3-b, 4-d **(D)** 1-b, 2-a, 3-c, 4-d
[1]

5. For the following two statements choose the correct option:

Statement I: An organisation has a set of basic goals.

Statement II: Different organisations have different goals.

Choose the correct option from the options given below:

(A) Statement I is correct and II is wrong.
(B) Statement II is correct and I is wrong.
(C) Both the statements are correct.
(D) Both the statements are incorrect. [1]

6. Assertion (A): Coordination integrates group efforts.

Reason (R): Coordination unifies unrelated or diverse interests into purposeful work activity.

(A) Both assertion (A) and reason (R) are true and reason (R) is the correct explanation of assertion (A).
(B) Both assertion (A) and reason (R) are true but reason (R) is not the correct explanation of assertion (A).
(C) Assertion (A) is true but reason (R) is false.
(D) Assertion (A) is false but reason (R) is true.

Read following case and answer Q. 7-10 on the basis of the same.

Ronan Corporation, a multinational technology company, faced challenges in its operations due to a lack of effective management practices. Recognising the need for improved management, the company embarked on a journey to understand the nature and significance of management. Ronan Corporation operates in a highly competitive industry and has been experiencing inefficiencies in its workflow, communication gaps, and a decline in employee morale. To address these issues, the management decided to reevaluate its approach to better understand the nature and significance of management. The management team at Ronan Corporation initiated training programs, conducted workshops, and sought external expertise to enhance their understanding of the principles and significance of effective management.

Based on the above case answer the following question:

7. What is the primary objective of understanding the nature of management at Ronan Corporation? [1]

(A) To increase shareholder value
(B) To improve operational efficiency
(C) To reduce employee turnover
(D) To launch new products

8. Which aspect of management is crucial for coordinating diverse activities within the organisation? **[1]**
   (A) Planning **(B)** Organising
   (C) Directing **(D)** Controlling

9. How does an understanding of the nature of management benefit employees at Ronan Corporation? **[1]**
   (A) It reduces their workload
   (B) It enhances job satisfaction
   (C) It eliminates the need for training
   (D) It increases competition among employees

10. What is the fundamental role of management in achieving organisational goals at Ronan Corporation? **[1]**
   (A) To minimise costs
   (B) To maximise profits
   (C) To coordinate and align efforts
   (D) To eliminate employees

Short Answer Type Questions - I [3 Marks]

11. Management is skillful and personal application of existing knowledge to achieve desired results. Explain.

12. Rahul has retired from an organisation in which he was responsible for implementing the plans developed by the top management. At which level of management was he working? State two more function performed at this level.

Short Answer Type Questions - II [4 Marks]

13. Coordination is needed at all levels of management and is the responsibility of all managers. Explain how?

14. What is meant by management as a science? Explain with the help of any two features.

Long Answer Type Questions - II [6 Marks]

15. John and Vipul are good friends. After completing their MBA, both of them take up a job at managerial level in different organisations as per their individual areas of interest considering the fact that the activities involved in managing an enterprise are common to all organisations. John takes up a marketing job in a retail company and strives to increase sales whereas Vipul joins a garment factory as a plant supervisor in Mumbai. His goal is to produce 2000 garments a day. Both of them have to perform a series of continuous, composite, but separate functions. On some days, John may spend more time in planning a future display layout and on another day, he may spend time in sorting out an employee's problem. Both John and Vipul make conscious efforts to build a feeling of team spirit and coordination among diverse individuals with different needs who work under them. The effect of their management is noticeable in their respective departments as the targets are met according to plans, employees are happy and satisfied, and there is orderliness in its functioning rather than chaos.

    In context of the above case, identify any four features of management highlighted in the above paragraph by quoting lines from it.

CHAPTER 2 PRINCIPLES OF MANAGEMENT

LEARNING OBJECTIVES

After going through this unit, the student/learner would be able to:

- Understand the concept of principles of management.
- Explain the significance of management principles.
- Discuss the principles of management developed by Fayol.
- Explain the principles and techniques of 'Scientific Management'.
- Compare the contributions of Fayol and Taylor.

Study Plan
Maximum Time = 3.00 Hrs
Maximum Questions = 68

LIST OF TOPICS

TOPIC-1 Principles of Management: Concept and Significance

Concepts Covered:
- Concept of Principles of Management
- Significance of Principles of Management

Revision Notes

- **Principles of Management:**

(i) Principles are guidelines to take decisions or actions while practicing techniques.

(ii) A managerial principle is a broad and general guideline for decision making and behaviour.

- **Nature or Features of Management Principles:** [Board, 2019]

(i) **Universal applicability:** Applicable in all types of organisations, irrespective of size, nature and objectives.

(ii) **Formed by practice and experience:** Formed by experimentation, experience and collective wisdom of the managers.

(iii) **General guidelines:** Guidelines to actions are available but they do not provide ready-made straitjacket solutions to all managerial problems.

(iv) **Flexible:** Can be modified by a manager according to the situation, they are not rigid prescriptions.

(v) **Mainly behavioural:** Aim at influencing behaviour of human beings.

(vi) **Cause and effect relationship:** Establish cause and effect relationship i.e., if a particular principle is applied in a particular situation, what would be its likely effect.

(vii) **Contingent:** The use of management principles is contingent or dependent upon the prevailing situation at a particular point of time.

- **Significance of Principles of Management:**

(i) **Provide useful insights into reality to the managers:** Use of these principles increases managerial efficiency by adding to their knowledge and ability to understand various real world situations more accurately.

(ii) **Optimum utilisation of resources and effective administration:** Principles of management help the managers to foresee the cause and effect relationships of their decisions and reduce wastage associated with trial and error approach.

Scan this
Significance of Management Principles

(iii) **Scientific decisions:** Principles of management help in taking decisions scientifically based on logic and objective assessment of situations rather than blind faith and personal prejudices.

(iv) **Meeting requirements of changing environment:** Principles of management are modified to help the managers to meet the requirements of changing environment.

(v) **Fulfilling social responsibility:** The management principles have been developed in such a way that they help in fulfilling social responsibilities of an organisation.

(vi) **Management training, education and research:** Principles of management are the basis of management theories, which are used in training, motivation, research and development.

MNEMONICS

Concept: Nature of Management Principles
Interpretations: U Can Group Chat with FB Friends

U: Universal
C: Contingent
G: General guidelines
C: Cause and effect relationship
F: Flexible
B: Behavioural
F: Formed by practice

KEY TERMS

Social Responsibility: Obligation to work for the benefit of the society at large.
Trial and Error Approach: Problem solving method in which multiple attempts are made to reach a solution.
Contingent: Dependent on or conditioned by something else.

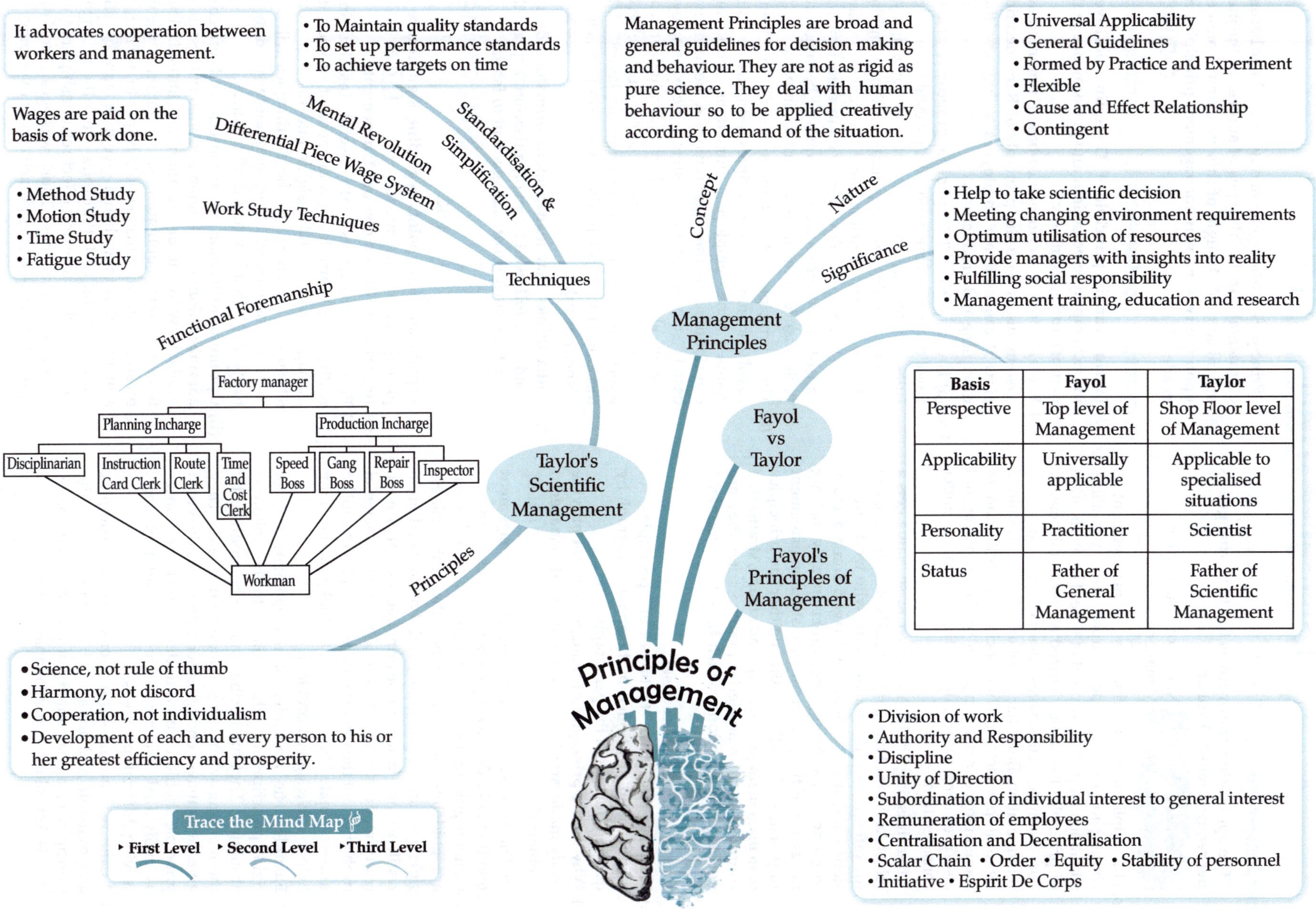

Principles of Management

Management Principles

Concept

Management Principles are broad and general guidelines for decision making and behaviour. They are not as rigid as pure science. They deal with human behaviour so to be applied creatively according to demand of the situation.

Nature

- Universal Applicability
- General Guidelines
- Formed by Practice and Experiment
- Flexible
- Cause and Effect Relationship
- Contingent

Significance

- Help to take scientific decision
- Meeting changing environment requirements
- Optimum utilisation of resources
- Provide managers with insights into reality
- Fulfilling social responsibility
- Management training, education and research

Fayol vs Taylor

Basis	Fayol	Taylor
Perspective	Top level of Management	Shop Floor level of Management
Applicability	Universally applicable	Applicable to specialised situations
Personality	Practitioner	Scientist
Status	Father of General Management	Father of Scientific Management

Fayol's Principles of Management

- Division of work
- Authority and Responsibility
- Discipline
- Unity of Direction
- Subordination of individual interest to general interest
- Remuneration of employees
- Centralisation and Decentralisation
- Scalar Chain • Order • Equity • Stability of personnel
- Initiative • Espirit De Corps

Taylor's Scientific Management

Principles

- Science, not rule of thumb
- Harmony, not discord
- Cooperation, not individualism
- Development of each and every person to his or her greatest efficiency and prosperity.

Techniques

Standardisation & Simplification

- To Maintain quality standards
- To set up performance standards
- To achieve targets on time

Mental Revolution

It advocates cooperation between workers and management.

Differential Piece Wage System

Wages are paid on the basis of work done.

Work Study Techniques

- Method Study
- Motion Study
- Time Study
- Fatigue Study

Functional Foremanship

Factory manager
- Planning Incharge: Disciplinarian, Instruction Card Clerk, Route Clerk, Time and Cost Clerk
- Production Incharge: Speed Boss, Gang Boss, Repair Boss, Inspector

All → Workman

Trace the Mind Map
- First Level
- Second Level
- Third Level

SUBJECTIVE TYPE QUESTIONS

Short Answer Type Questions-I (3 marks each)

1. "The application of principles has to be changed as per requirements". Explain. A [OEB]

Concept Applied	Nature of Principles of Management

Ans. The application of principles of management is contingent or dependent upon the prevailing situation at a particular point of time. The application of principles has to be changed as per requirements. For example, employees deserve fair and just remuneration. But what is just and fair is determined by multiple factors. They include contribution of the employee, paying capacity of the employer and also prevailing wage rate for the occupation under consideration.

2. After finishing her BBA degree course, Sania gets a job of Assistant Manager in a retail company through the reference of her cousin Sonia, who works in the same company as a Senior Manager. Sonia decides to guide Sania through her experience by making her aware of the important facts about management in practice. She tells her that neither the principles of management provide any ready made, straitjacket solutions to all managerial problems nor they are not rigid prescriptions, which have to be followed absolutely.

In context of the above case:

(i) Identify the two features of principles of management mentioned in the above paragraph by quoting lines from the paragraph.

(ii) Why do the principles of management not provide ready made, straitjacket solutions to all managerial problems? A [OEB]

Ans. (i) The two features of principles of management mentioned in the above paragraph are as follows:

(a) General guidelines: The principles of management are guidelines to action. Since the real business situations are very complex and dynamic and are a result of many factors, these principles do not provide ready made, straitjacket solutions to all managerial problems. But the importance of principles cannot be underestimated because even a small guideline may help to solve a given problem.

(b) Flexible: The principles of management are not rigid prescriptions which have to be followed absolutely. They are flexible and can be modified by the manager when the situation so demands. They give the manager enough discretion to decide which principle should be used under what circumstances as individual principles are like different tools serving different purposes.

(ii) As the **real business situations are very complex and dynamic** and are a result of many factors, the principles of management not provide ready made, straitjacket solutions to all managerial problems.

(2+1=3)

3. "Principles of Management now a days have become an integral part for all types of successful business organisations". In light of this statement, comment upon the reasons why management principles are needed ? U [OEB]

Short Answer Type Questions-II (4 marks each)

1. (a) How can the principle of "Discipline" positively impact employee behaviour and performance in the manufacturing company?

(b) Explain how a performance-based remuneration system aligns with the principle of Remuneration. How it can motivate employees to improve their discipline and productivity? U [APQ 2023-24]

Ans. (a) The principle of "Discipline" as proposed by Henry Fayol emphasises the importance of establishing clear rules, guidelines, and consequences for employee conduct within the organisation. When applied effectively, this principle can have several positive impacts accountability, reduced absenteeism, and consistent performance on employee behavior and performance in the manufacturing company.

(b) The principle of "Remuneration" in Henry Fayol's management principles pertains to fairly compensating employees for their work and contributions to the organisation. A performance-based remuneration system ties employee compensation directly to their individual or team performance. This creates a direct link between efforts and rewards, motivating employees to be disciplined and put in their best effort to achieve higher rewards. **[2+2=4]**

2. Ishita thinks that management principles do not need to be followed by an organisation. Explain the need for principles of management to Ishita.

U [SQP 2023-24]

OR

Explain any four points regarding significance of principles of management. AI U [OEB]

Ans. Importance of Principles of Management:

(i) Providing managers with useful insights into reality: The Principles of Management provide the managers with useful insights into the real world situations. Adherence to these principles will add to their knowledge, ability and understanding of managerial situations and circumstances.

(ii) Optimum utilisation of resources and effective administration: Both human and material resources available with an organisation are limited. They have to be put to optimum use. By optimum use we mean that the resources should be put to use in such a manner that they should give maximum benefits with minimum cost. Principles equip the managers to foresee the cause and effect relationships of their decisions and actions. Thus, wastages associated with a trial-and-error approach can be overcome.

This Question is for practice and its solution is given at the end of the chapter.

(iii) Scientific decisions: Decisions must be based on facts, thoughtful and justifiable in terms of the intended purposes. They must be timely, realistic and subjected to measurement and evaluation. Management principles help in thoughtful decision-making. They emphasise logic rather than blind faith. Management decisions are taken on the basis of principles which are free from bias and prejudice. They are based on the objective assessment of the situation.

(iv) Meeting changing environment requirements : Although the principles are in the nature of general guidelines but they are modified and help managers to meet changing requirements of the environment. Management principles are flexible to adapt to a dynamic business environment.

(v) Fulfilling Social Responsibility: The principles of management increase the efficiency of the managers and enable them to fulfill their social responsibility. More efficient managers can make good quality products at reasonable prices available all the times.

(vi) Management Training, Education and Research: The advantages of the principles of management encourage the researchers to bring in more improvement in them. The attitude of the managers has molded itself in such a fashion that they are doing, consciously or unconsciously, something new.

(Any four) (1×4=4)

3. "Excellence Academy" is a disciplined organisation. However, it lacks well defined rules and regulations. With the passage of time, management of the organisation finds out that if there are proper rules and regulations for the students and the teachers the result of the school improves.

Identify and explain the nature of principles of management highlighted here? U [OEB]

Ans. The nature of principle of management which is highlighted here is 'Principles of management are formed by practice and experimentation'. The **principles of management are formed by** experience and collective wisdom **of managers as well as experimentation**. For example, it is a matter of common experience that discipline is indispensable for accomplishing any purpose. This principle finds mention in management theory. On the other hand, in order to remedy the problem of fatigue of workers in the factory, an experiment may be conducted to see the effect of improvement of physical conditions to reduce stress. **4**

Long Answer Type Questions (6 marks each)

1. The manager of a retail store has a team of ten sales associates. To improve their efficiency, she decides to implement the principle of "Division of Work" and delegate specific tasks to each team member. However, one sales associate is unhappy with their assigned responsibilities and believes they should have more authority in decision-making.

(a) How can the principle of "Division of Work" help improve the store's efficiency and productivity?

(b) How can the manager balance the delegation of tasks while ensuring appropriate authority is given to each team member? Explain in three points.

U [APQ 2023-24]

Ans. (a) The principle of "Division of Work," as proposed by Henry Fayol, advocates dividing the overall work into specialised tasks and assigning them to individuals based on their skills and expertise. Implementing this principle in the retail store can lead to several benefits that improve efficiency and productivity.

(b) As a manager, follow these steps to achieve a balanced approach:

1. **Assess Individual Capabilities:** Before task delegation, assess each team member's strengths, weaknesses, skills, and preferences. Understanding their capabilities enables the manager to allocate tasks that align with their expertise, ensuring a better fit between the individual and the assigned responsibility.
2. **Encourage Input and Involvement:** Involve team members in the decision-making process. Allow them to provide suggestions, express preferences, and contribute ideas regarding the tasks they are assigned. This involvement fosters a sense of ownership and encourages proactive engagement.
3. **Set Clear Expectations:** Communicate the expectations associated with each task. Define objectives, timelines, and desired outcomes. Additionally, outline the boundaries of authority for each role to avoid confusion and ensure everyone understands their level of decision-making autonomy.
4. **Foster a Collaborative Culture:** Promote an environment where collaboration and teamwork are encouraged. Even with specialised tasks, encourage communication and cooperation among team members. This promotes knowledge sharing and support, enhancing overall efficiency.
5. **Provide Feedback and Recognition:** Regularly provide constructive feedback to team members about their performance. Recognise their efforts and accomplishments, and acknowledge their contributions. This feedback loop helps in continuous improvement and boosts morale.

(Any three) [1×3=3]

2. Explain any four points that summarise the nature of principles of management. U [APQ 2023-24]

OR

Explain any two of the following features of principles of management:

(i) Flexible

(ii) Mainly behavioral

(iii) Cause and effect relationships U [SQP 2023-24]

OR

Explain any six features of Principles of Management. R [Delhi Set-2, 2019]

OR

Explain any six characteristics of principles of management. R [Outside Delhi Set-2, 2019]

Ans. Characteristics/Nature of Principles of Management:

(i) Universal applicability: The principles of management are intended to apply to all types of organisations, business as well as non-business, small as well as large, public sector as well as private sector, manufacturing as well as the service sectors.

However, the extent of their applicability would vary with the nature of the organisation, business activity, scale of operations, etc.

(ii) General guidelines: The principles of management are guidelines to action but do not provide ready-made and to the point solutions to all managerial problems. This is so because real business situations are very complex and dynamic and are a result of many factors. However, the importance of principles cannot be underestimated because even a small guideline helps to solve a given problem.

(iii) Formed by practice and experimentation: The **principles of management are formed by** experience and collective wisdom of managers as well as experimentation. For example, it is a matter of common experience that discipline is indispensable for accomplishing any purpose. This principle is mentioned in the management theory. On the other hand, in order to remedy the problem of fatigue of workers in the factory, an experiment may be conducted to see the effect of improvement of physical conditions to reduce the stress.

(iv) Flexible: The principles of management are not rigid prescriptions, which have to be followed absolutely. They are flexible and can be modified by the managers when the situation so demands. They give the manager enough discretion to do so.

(v) Mainly behavioural: Management principles aim at influencing behaviour of human beings. Therefore, principles of management are mainly behavioural in nature. It is not that these principles do not pertain to things and phenomenon at all; it is just a matter of emphasis. Moreover, principles enable a better understanding of the relationship between human and material resources in accomplishing organisational purposes.

(vi) Cause and effect relationships: The principles of management are intended to establish relationship between cause and effect so that they can be used in similar situations in a large number of cases. Thus, they tell us if a particular principle if applied in a particular situation, what would be its likely effect. The principles of management are less than perfect since they mainly apply to human behaviour. In real life, situations are not identical. Therefore, accurate cause and effect relationships may be difficult to establish.

(vii) Contingent: The application of principles of management is contingent or dependent upon the prevailing situation at a particular point of time. The application of principles has to be changed as per requirements. **(Any six) (1×6=6)**

3. In a huge manufacturing company, there was a constant training programme running for the workers throughout the year. The workers were trained about the machines as the management realised that management is all about the relationship among workers and their proper handling of the machines. As the size of the organisation increased, the management decided to release their hold on day to day activities of the organisation. A more decentralised approach was adopted where the workers could decide about the machines and the amount of raw material required instead of the traditional centralised approach as per the needs. The management knew that the external environment is dynamic. In order to meet stiff competition, they clarified to the workers that their instructions should not be taken strictly and should be moulded as per the requirements of the organisation at the level where actual action takes place.

Identify and explain the nature of principles of management that have been highlighted in the above case? A [OEB]

Concept Applied	Characteristics of Principles of Management

4. Pink Steps is a very innovative footwear organisation. The company has the policy of paying proper attention to the training of the managers. The organisation teaches various management principles to the managers whenever required so that they can apply them and understand the practical aspects of business through them. Year by year the organisation is able to increase its revenue. This is because the managers are able to economically use the funds of the organisation and increase the output of the workers through various principles like discipline and science, not rule of thumb. This year, the company will be opening its 14th branch in India. The firm has decided to start the campaign for adopting poor children. This year the target is 500 poor children due to be adopted. This will help the organisation put noticeable example in front of others who can learn a lot from this initiative of the company.

Identify and explain the importance of principles of management that are highlighted in the above case? A [OEB]

Ans. The points of importance of principles of management highlighted above are:

(i) Providing managers with useful insight into reality: The principles of management provide the managers with useful insights into real world situations. Adherence to these principles will add to their knowledge, ability and understanding of managerial situations and circumstances. It will also enable managers to learn from past mistakes and conserve time by solving recurring problems quickly. As such management principles increase managerial efficiency. For example, a manager can leave routine decision-making to his subordinates and deal with exceptional situations which require her/his expertise by following the principles of delegation.

(ii) Optimum utilisation of resources and effective administration: Resources both human and material available with the company are limited. They have to be put to optimum use. By optimum use we mean that the resources should be put to use in such a manner that they should give maximum benefit with minimum cost. Principles equip the managers to foresee the cause and effect relationships of their decisions and actions. As such the wastages associated with a trial-and-error approach can be

This Question is for practice and its solution is given at the end of the chapter.

overcome. Effective administration necessitates impersonalisation of managerial conduct so that managerial power is used with due discretion. Principles of management limit the boundary of managerial discretion so that their decisions may be free from personal prejudices and biases.

(iii) Fulfilling social responsibility: The increased awareness of the public forces businesses, especially limited companies, to fulfill their social responsibilities. Management theory and management principles have also evolved in response to these demands. Moreover, the interpretation of the principles also assumes newer and contemporary meanings with the change in time. So, if one were to talk of 'equity' today, it does not apply to wages alone. Value to the customer, care for the environment, dealings with business associates would all come under the purview of this principle. **(2 × 3 = 6)**

5. (i) Explain any two of the following importance of principles of management:

(a) Meeting changing environment requirements

(b) Fulfilling social responsibility

(c) Management training, education and research

(ii) "The application of principles of management has to be changed as per requirements". Explain.

AI R [SQP, 2023-24]

Ans. (i) (a) Meeting changing environment requirements: Although the principles are like general guidelines they are modified and help managers to meet changing requirements of the environment. Management principles are flexible to adapt to a dynamic business environment. **[1½]**

(b) Fulfilling Social Responsibility: The principles of management increase the efficiency of the managers and enable them to fulfill their social responsibility. More efficient managers can make good quality products at reasonable prices available all the time.

(c) Management Training, Education, and Research: The advantages of the principles of management encourage the researchers to bring in more improvements in them. The attitude of the managers has molded itself in such a fashion that they are doing, consciously or unconsciously, something new.

(ii) The application of principles of management is contingent or dependent upon the prevailing situation at a particular point in time. The application of principles has to be changed as per requirements. For example, employees deserve fair and just remuneration. But what is just and fair is determined by multiple factors. They include the contribution of the employee, the paying capacity of the employer, and also prevailing wage rate for the occupation under consideration. **[3+3=6]**

TOPIC-2 Fayol's Principles of Management

Concepts Covered:

- Principles of management developed by Fayol.

Revision Notes

Scan this

Henry Fayol's 14 Principles of Management

- **Fayol's Principles of Management**

(i) Division of Work: Work is to be divided into small tasks and it should be completed by a specialised worker only. [Board, 2019]

Example-1

In the manufacturing sector, workers are assigned jobs by skill. Efficiency and specialisation increases when assembly line workers concentrate on particular components.

(ii) Authority and Responsibility: Authority is the right to give orders and obtain obedience, and responsibility is the corollary of authority. There should be a balance between authority and responsibility. [Board, 2019]

(iii) Discipline: Discipline is the obedience to organisational rules and employment agreement which are necessary for the working of the organisation. [Board, 2019]

(iv) Unity of Command: Each employee should receive orders in a hierarchy and should be responsible to only one superior. There should be one and only one boss for every individual employee. [Board, 2019]

Example-2

Construction workers report to one supervisor. This streamlines the workflow by avoiding misunderstanding and contradicting directions.

(v) Unity of Direction: Each group of activities having the same objective must have one head and one plan. [Board, 2019]

(vi) Subordination of Individual Interest to General Interest: Organisational interest should supercede individual interest. The interests of an organisation should take priority over the interests of any one individual employee. [Board, 2017]

(vii) Remuneration of Employees: Pay and compensation should be fair to both the employees and the organisation. [Board, 2023]

(viii) Centralisation and Decentralisation: There is a need to balance subordinate involvement through decentralisation with managers' retention of final authority through centralisation.

(ix) Scalar Chain: Organisations should have a chain of authority and communication that runs from top to bottom and should be followed by managers and the subordinates. This chain should not be violated in the normal course of formal communication. However, if there is an emergency then through 'Gang Plank' communication can be done smoothly without any delay. [Board, 2017]

Example-3

To ensure proper communication, hospital nurses communicate patient updates from the nurse to the head nurse to the department head.

(x) Order: People and resources should be in suitable places at the appropriate time for maximum efficiency. [Board, 2017]

Example-4

A warehouse organises inventory systematically. Employees can find and manage goods more easily since each item has a location.

(xi) **Equity:** Kind and just behaviour with all employees without discrimination.

(xii) **Stability of Personnel:** Minimise employee turnover to maintain organisational efficiency.

(xiii) **Initiative:** Encourage employees to take initiative in thinking and executing plans. [Board 2019]

(xiv) **Esprit de Corps:** Promote a team spirit of unity and harmony among employees. [Board 2019]

MNEMONICS

Concept: Henry Fayol's 14 principles of management

Interpretations: I C DRESSES and DO U2?

I: Initiative

C: Centralisation and Decentralisation

D: Discipline

R: Remuneration of personnel

E: Equity

S: Subordination of individual interest to general interest

S: Scalar chain

E: Esprit de Corps

S: Stability in the tenure of personnel

A: Authority and Responsibility

D: Division of work

O: Order

U: Unity of command

U: Unity of direction

SUBJECTIVE TYPE QUESTIONS

Short Answer Type Questions-I (3 marks each)

1. Explain briefly 'Initiative' and 'Esprit de Corps' as principles of general management.

U [Outside Delhi Set-2, 2019]

Ans. Initiative: It states that the workers should be encouraged to develop and carry out their plans for improvement in the organisation.

It does not mean going against the established practices of the company for the sake of being different.

Esprit de Corps: It states that management should promote a team spirit of unity and harmony among employees to realise organisational objectives.

The manager should replace 'I' with 'We' to foster team spirit. This will give rise to a spirit of mutual trust and belongingness among team members. It will also minimise the need for using penalties.

[Marking Scheme, OD 2017] **1½+1½=3**

2. Explain 'order' and 'initiative' as principles of general management. U [Delhi Set-3, 2017]

Ans. Order: It states that there should be a place for everything and everyone in an organisation and that thing or person should be found in its allotted place.

People and materials must be in suitable places at appropriate time for maximum efficiency. **1½**

Initiative: It states that the workers should be encouraged to develop and carry out their plans for improvement in the organisation.

It does not mean going against the established practices of the company for the sake of being different. [Marking Scheme, Delhi, 2017] **1½**

3. Explain briefly 'Unity of Direction' and 'Order' as principles of general management.

R [Outside Delhi Set-1, 2017]

Ans.

Topper Answer, 2017

Principles of Management → Unity of Direction; Order

① UNITY OF DIRECTION

· There should be one head & one plan for a group of activities having same objectives.

· Efforts of all the members should be directed towards the common goal.

· Merits:
→ ensures unity of action & coordination
→ helps in achievement of group goals

Eg. If a company manufactures both cars & motorcycles, it should have separate divisions for both. Each division should have its own
· incharge
· plan
· execution resources.

On no account, working of the two divisions should overlap.

② ORDER:

· According to Fayol, there should be material & social order.

· Material order:
Place for everything & everything in its right place

· Social Order:
Place for everyone & everyone in his/her right place.

· According to Fayol, people & materials must be in suitable places at appropriate time for maximum efficiency.

· Merits:
→ ensures optimum utilisation of human &

Topper Answer, 2017

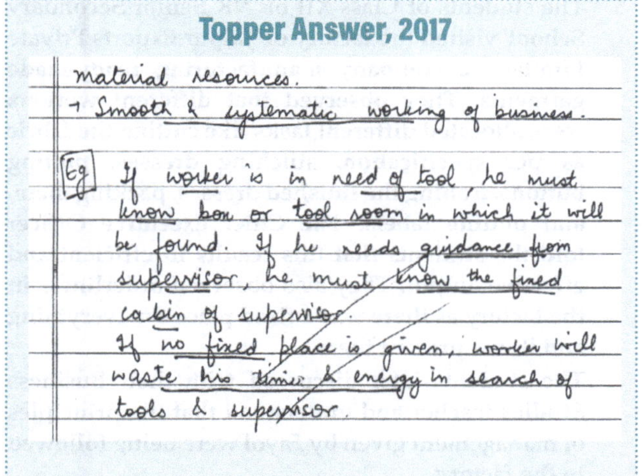

4. **Explain briefly 'Remuneration of Employees' and 'Scalar Chain' as general principles of management.** U [Outside Delhi Set-3, 2017]

Long Answer Type Questions-I (6 marks each)

1. **Briefly explain any three of the following principles of management given by Henry Fayol:**
   (i) Unity of command
   (ii) Equity
   (iii) Remuneration
   (iv) Initiative U [SQP 2023-24]

Ans. Principles of Management given by Henry Fayol:

(i) Unity of Command: According to Fayol, there should be one and only one boss for every individual employee. Fayol gave a lot of importance to this principle. He felt that if this principle is violated "authority is undermined; discipline is in jeopardy, order disturbed and stability threatened". Suppose a sales person is asked to clinch a deal with a buyer and is allowed to give a 10% discount by the marketing manager. But the finance department tells her/ him not to offer more than 5% discount. Now there is no unity of command.

(ii) Equity: "Good sense and experience are needed to ensure fairness to all employees, who should be treated as fairly as possible," according to Fayol. This principle emphasises kindliness and justice in the behaviour of managers towards workers. This will ensure loyalty and devotion. Fayol does not rule out use of force sometimes. Rather he says that lazy personnel should be dealt with sternly to send the message that everyone is equal in the eyes of the management. There should be no discrimination against anyone on account of sex, religion, language, caste, belief or nationality etc. In practice we can observe that now a days in multinational corporations people of various nationalities work together in a discrimination free environment. Equal opportunities are available for everyone in such companies to rise.

(iii) Remuneration of Employees: The overall pay and compensation should be fair to both employees and the organisation. The employees should be paid fair wages, which should give them at least a reasonable standard of living. At the same time it should be within the paying capacity of the company. In other words, remuneration should be just and equitable. This will ensure a congenial atmosphere and good relations between workers and management. Consequently, the working of the company would be smooth.

(iv) Initiative: Workers should be encouraged to develop and carry out their plans for improvements according to Fayol. Initiative means taking the first step with self-motivation. It is thinking out and executing the plan. It is one of the traits of an intelligent person. Initiative should be encouraged. But it does not mean going against the established practices of the company for the sake of being different. A good company should have an employee suggestion system whereby initiative/suggestions would result in substantial cost/time reduction. [2×3=6]

2. **Amaira Lunch Box service was started in Mumbai by the Mumbai Dabbawalas. The Dabbawalas who are the soul of entire Mumbai aim to provide prompt and efficient services by providing tasty homemade tiffin to all office goes at the right time and place. The service is uninterrupted even on the days of bad weather, political unrest and social disturbances. Recently, they have started online booking system through their website 'mydabbawala.com'. Owing to their tremendous popularity amongst the happy and satisfied customers and members, the Dabbawalas were invited as guest lecturer by top business schools. The Dabbawalas operate in a group of 25-30 people along with a group leader. Each group teams up with other groups in order to deliver the tiffins on time. They are not transferred on frequent basis as they have to remember the addresses of their customers. They follow certain rules while doing trade—no alcohol during working hours; no leaves without permission; wearing white caps and carrying ID cards during business hours.**
   Recently, on the suggestion of a few self-motivated fellow men, the dabbawalas thought out and executed a plan of providing food left in tiffins by customers to slum children. They have instructed their customers to place red sticker if food is left in the tiffin, to be fed to poor children later. Identify and explain the principle of management given by Fayol mentioned in the above case. A [OEB]

Concept Applied	Principles of management by Fayol

3. **Sahil works as a plant superintendent in a carpet making factory. In order to complete the export orders on time, the production manager asks him to make the workers work over time whereas the finance manager is strictly against this practice because it will increase the cost of production. Moreover, Sahil feels that since the company is manufacturing handmade carpets as well as machine made carpets there is a lot of overlapping of activities. Therefore, there should be two separate divisions for both of them wherein each division**

should have its own incharge, plans and execution resources. In context of the above case:

(i) Identify and explain the principle of management which is being violated.

(ii) Also identify the principle of management that Sahil feels should be implemented in the factory.

A [OEB]

Ans. (i) The principle of management which is being violated is Unity of Command. According to Fayol, there should be one and only one boss for every individual employee. If an employee gets orders from two superiors at the same time the principle of unity of command is violated. The principle of unity of command states that each participant in a formal organisation should receive orders from and be responsible to only one superior. Fayol gave a lot of importance to this principle. He felt that if this principle is violated "authority is undermined, discipline is in jeopardy, order disturbed and stability threatened".

(ii) Unity of Direction: All the units of an organisation should be moving towards the same objectives through coordinated and focussed efforts. Each group of activities having the same objective must have one head and one plan. This ensures unity of action and coordination. For example, if a company is manufacturing motorcycles as well as cars then it should have two separate divisions for both of them. Each division should have its own incharge, plans and execution resources. On no account should the working of two divisions overlap. **2×3=6**

4. Explain the following principles of general management:

(i) Division of Work;

(ii) Authority and Responsibility; and

(iii) Discipline. U [Outside Delhi Set-1, 2019]

Ans. (i) Division of Work:

(a) The principle of division of work suggests that work can be performed more efficiently if it is divided into specialised tasks.

(b) A trained specialist who is competent, is required to perform each job leading to specialisation which results in efficient and effective output.

(ii) Authority and Responsibility:

(a) Authority is the right to give orders and obtain obedience, and responsibility is the corollary of authority.

(b) The principle of authority and responsibility suggests that managers require authority commensurate with their responsibility.

(c) An organisation should build safeguards against abuse of managerial power. At the same time, a manager should have necessary authority to carry out his responsibility.

(iii) Discipline:

(a) It is the obedience to organisational rules and employment agreement which are necessary for the working of the organisation.

(b) It requires good superiors at all levels, clear and fair agreement and judicious application of penalties.

(or any other suitable explanation) **2 + 2 + 2 = 6**

[Marking Scheme, OD, 2019]

5. The students of Class XII of 'NK Senior Secondary School' visited the factory of 'Jaipur Exports Private Limited', a company manufacturing ready-made garments. They observed that different workers were allocated different tasks like cutting the fabric as per specification, stitching dresses, putting buttons, ironing the finished dresses, packing them, and putting labels. The Chief Executive Officer told the students that this results in efficient and effective output. They also observed orderliness in the factory as there was a fixed place for everything and it was present there.

The students later discussed with their Business Studies teacher and understood that the principles of management given by Fayol were being followed in the factory.

Identify and explain the two principles of management that have been discussed in the above case. AI AE [Outside Delhi Set-1]

Ans. The two principles of management that have been discussed here are:

(i) Division of Work: According to this principle, the whole work must be divided into small units and instead of assigning the whole work to one person, one unit of work should be assigned to one person according to the capability, qualification, and experience of the person.

(ii) Order: There must be a material and social order in an enterprise. Material order implies "a proper place for everything and everything in its right place." Similarly, social order means "a place for everyone and everyone in his appointed place". The right man in the right job is very important for the successful functioning of an organisation.

[Marking Scheme, OD 2023]

6. (a) Explain the following principles of management given by Fayol :

(i) Discipline

(ii) Remuneration to employees

(iii) Unity of Command

AI R [Outside Delhi Set-1, 2023]

Ans. The principles given by Fayol are:

(i) Discipline: Discipline refers to general rules and regulations for systematic working in an organisation. Discipline does not mean only rules and regulations but it also means developing commitment in the employees towards the organisation as well as towards each other. Fayol insists that discipline is required at the superior as well as the subordinate level.

(ii) Remuneration of Persons: According to this principle, employees in the organisation must be paid fairly or adequately to give them maximum satisfaction. The employees should be paid fair wages and salaries, which would give them at least a reasonable standard of living.

(iii) **Unity of Command:** According to this principle, an employee should receive orders from one boss only because if he is receiving orders from more than one boss then he will get confused and will not be able to understand whose orders must be executed first. [Marking Scheme, OD 2023]

7. Explain 'Unity of Command', 'Remuneration', and 'Initiative' as principles of General Management given by Henry Fayol. U [SQP, 2023-24]

Ans. Unity of Command: According to Fayol, there should be one and only one boss for every individual employee. Fayol gave a lot of importance to this principle. He felt that if this principle is violated "authority is undermined; discipline is in jeopardy, order disturbed and stability threatened". The principle resembles military organisation. Dual subordination should be avoided. This is to prevent confusion regarding tasks to be done. Suppose a salesperson is asked to clinch a deal with a buyer and is allowed to give a 10% discount by the marketing manager. But the finance department tells her/ him not to offer more than 5% discount. Now there is no unity of command.

Remuneration of Employees: The overall pay and compensation should be fair to both employees and the organisation. The employees should be paid fair wages, which should give them at least a reasonable standard of living. At the same time, it should be within the paying capacity of the company. In other words, remuneration should be just and equitable. This will ensure a congenial atmosphere and good relations between workers and management. Consequently, the working of the company would be smooth.

Initiative: Workers should be encouraged to develop and carry out their plans for improvements according to Fayol. Initiative means taking the first step with self-motivation. It is thinking out and executing the plan. It is one of the traits of an intelligent person. The initiative should be encouraged. But it does not mean going against the established practices of the company for the sake of being different. A good company should have an employee suggestion system whereby initiative/ suggestions would result in substantial cost/time reduction. **2×3=6**

[Marking Scheme, SQP 2023-24]

TOPIC-3 Taylor's Scientific Management: Principles and Techniques

Concepts Covered:

- Principles and Techniques of 'Scientific Management'.

Revision Notes

Principles of Scientific Management:

(i) **Science, not rule of thumb:** Decisions on the basis of scientific study and analysis rather than traditional methods of trial and error. [Board 2018]

(ii) **Harmony, not discord:** Eliminate class-conflict and develop harmony between the management and workers. Both should realise that each one is important. To achieve this state, Taylor called for complete mental revolution on the part of both management and workers.

(iii) **Co-operation, not individualism:** Competition should be replaced by co-operation. Management and workers should realise that they need each other.

(iv) **Development of each and every person to his/ her greatest efficiency and prosperity:** Personnel competencies should be developed by scientific selection, and training should be given for worker development and maximum organisational progress. [Board 2023]

Mental Revolution

- In Frederick Taylor's Scientific Management, the term "mental revolution" describes a shift in thinking that places an emphasis on communication and cooperation between employees and supervisors. In order to cultivate a new culture in the workplace, one must follow procedures including training, feedback, recognition, communication, and setting clear expectations. A shift in perspective like this boosts morale, which in turn increases output.
- Manufacturing plant workers once saw management as remote and authoritative. A mental revolution encouraged free communication between management and workers, boosting cooperation. Everyone accepted their responsibilities as valuable contributors to the company's success, which promoted trust, shared objectives, and efficiency.

Techniques of Scientific Management: [Board 2017]

(i) **Functional Foremanship:** Separation of planning and execution function.

(ii) **Standardisation and Simplification:** Establish standards for every business activity and eliminating unnecessary diversity of products.

(iii) **Method Study:** Identify one best way to do a job.

(iv) **Motion Study:** Eliminate wasteful and unnecessary movements.

(v) **Time Study:** Determine standard time required to perform a well-defined job.

(vi) **Fatigue Study:** Determine the amount and frequency of rest intervals in completing a task.

(vii) **Differential Piece Wage System:** Determine different wage rates for efficient and inefficient workers.

Tips & Tricks

- Do not confuse with the principles of scientific management and techniques of scientific management.
- The principles provide the guiding philosophy, when it comes to improving workplace efficiency and productivity, where as the techniques are the actual procedures that are generated from those ideas.

MNEMONICS

Concept: Principles of Scientific Management:
Interpretations: Hearts Diamonds Clubs Spades
H: Harmony, not discord
D: Development of each person to her/his greatest efficiency and prosperity
C: Cooperation, not individualism
S: Science, not the rule of thumb
Concept: Techniques of Scientific Management
Interpretations: To Make My Face Smile Do something Funny
T: Time study M: Method study
M: Motion study F: Fatigue study
S: Standardisation and simplification of work
D: Differential piece wage system
F: Functional foremanship

KEY TERMS

Mental Revolution: Change in the attitude of workers and management towards one another from competition to cooperation. It means that management and workers should transform their thinking.

Foremanship: Position or office of being a foreman or supervisor.

Standardisation: It refers to the process of setting standards for every business activity; it can be standardisation of process, raw material, time, product, machinery, methods or working conditions.

Principles of Management offer broader guidance, while Techniques of Scientific Management focus on specific methodologies for improving operational efficiency.

SUBJECTIVE TYPE QUESTIONS

Short Answer Type Questions-I (3 marks each)

1. Explain any three of the following Concepts by F. W. Taylor:
(a) Differential Piece Wage Rate System
(b) Mental Revolution
(c) Harmony, not Discord
(d) Functional Foremanship R [APQ, 2023-24]

Ans. (a) Differential Piece Wage Rate System: It is a method of F.W. Taylor to incentivise workers and increase productivity. Under this system, workers are paid different rates for each unit of output they produce. The idea behind this approach is to reward higher productivity with higher wages. Taylor believed that by offering financial incentives, workers would be motivated to work more efficiently and increase their output, leading to greater overall productivity for the organisation. This concept laid the foundation for modern performance-based pay systems and piece-rate systems that are still in use today in some industries.

(b) Mental Revolution: The term "Mental Revolution" coined by F.W. Taylor refers to a fundamental change in the mindset and attitudes of both workers and management towards work. Taylor observed that there was often a significant divide between workers and management, with both sides viewing each other with suspicion and distrust. He advocated for a mental revolution that involved workers acknowledging that their interests were aligned with those of management, and vice versa. Taylor believed that through cooperation and understanding, both parties could work together to achieve common goals, such as increased efficiency and productivity. This mental revolution was seen as a prerequisite for successfully implementing scientific management principles in an organisation.

(c) Harmony, not Discord: F.W. Taylor emphasised the importance of achieving harmony rather than discord in the workplace. He believed that conflicts and antagonism between workers and management were detrimental to productivity and hindered organisational success. To achieve harmony, Taylor proposed the application of scientific management principles, which involved careful planning, standardisation of work processes, and clear communication between workers and management. By removing unnecessary frictions and creating an environment of mutual trust and cooperation, Taylor aimed to establish a harmonious relationship between employees and management, ultimately leading to increased productivity and efficiency.

(d) Functional Foremanship: Functional Foremanship is a concept developed by F.W. Taylor as part of his scientific management system. Under this approach, the traditional role of a single foreman overseeing a group of workers is divided into multiple specialised foremen, each responsible for a specific aspect of the production process. Taylor identified eight distinct functions that were crucial for efficient production, such as route clerk, instruction card clerk, time and cost clerk, etc. [Marking Scheme, APQ 2023-24]

2. If you are the production manager in an organisation, setting a standard task, which study will you conduct first time study or motion study, and why ? C [OEB]

Concept Applied	Techniques of Scientific Management.

Ans. Time Study: Its basic purpose is to determine the standard time for performing a job. Time measuring devices are used for each element of task to fix the standard time.

Motion Study: Its basic purpose is to eliminate unnecessary movements or motions. The idea is to determine the least possible time required to complete the job efficiently.

Hence, motion study should precede time study because the time standards so determined will be free from the time spent on wasteful activities.

(1½×2=3)

3. Ramajun is a scientist. He works in a factory for the betterment of the operational aspect and to study all the steps involved in the manufacturing of the product. He, very attentively noticed all sorts of movements to arrive at a simpler way of doing all the activities possible. With his hard work he was

able to bring down the number of activities for the manufacturing of the final product from 54 to 40. This work was able to bring down the labour charges and decrease the total time of production. Thus, he gave the organisation an added advantage. Identify and explain the type of scientific technique is discussed here? U [OEB]

Ans. The type of study refers over here is motion study. Motion study refers to the study of movements like lifting, putting objects, sitting and changing positions etc., which are undertaken while doing a typical job. Unnecessary movements are sought to be eliminated so that it takes less time to complete the job efficiently. **3**

Short Answer Type Questions-II (4 marks each)

1. **Sanket, after completing his entrepreneurship course from U.S.A. returned to India and started a coffee shop 'Fioma Coffee' in a famous mall in Mumbai. The speciality of the coffee shop was the special aroma of coffee and a wide variety of flavours to choose from. Somehow, the business was neither profitable nor popular. Sanket was keen to find out the reason. He appointed Riya, an MBA from a reputed management institute as a manager to find out the causes of the business not doing well. Riya, took a feedback from the clients and found out that though they loved the special unique aroma of coffee but were not happy with the long waiting time being taken to process the order. She analysed and found out that there were many unnecessary obstructions which could be eliminated. She fixed a standard time for processing the order. She also realised that there were many flavours whose demand was not enough. So, she also decided to discontinue the sale of such flavours. As a result, within a short period Riya was able to attract the customers.**

   Identify and explain any two techniques of scientific management used by Riya to solve the problem.

   A [Outside Delhi Set-1, 2017]

Ans. Techniques of Scientific Management used by Riya to solve the problem were:

(i) Motion Study

(a) Meaning: It is a technique to study the movements that are necessary for doing a well- defined job.

(b) It seeks to eliminate unnecessary and wasteful movements so that it takes less time to complete a job efficiently.

(ii) Time Study

(a) Meaning: It is a technique to determine the standard time taken by a worker of reasonable skill and efficiency to perform a well-defined job.

(b) It helps in deciding the number of workers to be employed, frame suitable incentive schemes and determine labour costs.

(iii) Simplification of Work

(a) Meaning: It is a technique to eliminate superfluous varieties, sizes and dimensions of products.

(b) It leads to reduced inventories, fuller utilisation of equipment and increased turnover to reduce costs.

(Any two) 2+2

[Marking Scheme, OD, 2017]

2. **'Chennai Leather Ltd.' is the manufacturer of leather products. It is producing on large scale and its organisational structure is functional. In the production department, various foremen have been employed. Each foreman has been made responsible for production planning, implementation and control. This has led to a situation of confusion and uncertainty. Suggest a technique of 'Scientific Management' to Chennai Leather Ltd. which may help it to effectively organise planning and its execution.** A [OEB]

Concept Applied	Coordination and its features

Ans. Technique of Scientific Management which may help Chennai Leather Ltd. to effectively organise planning and its execution is Functional Foremanship.

(i) Functional foremanship is a technique which aims to improve the quality of supervision at shop floor.

(ii) Taylor identified a list of qualities of a good foreman or a supervisor. Since all the qualities could not be found in a single person, Taylor proposed eight specialists.

(iii) In this technique, planning is separated from execution. Taylor suggested four foremen for planning under planning incharge and four foremen for execution under production incharge.

(iv) It is an extension of the principle of division of work and specialisation.

(v) The four foremen for planning were route clerk, instruction card clerk, time and cost clerk and disciplinarian. They would draft instructions for the workers, specify the route of production, prepare time and cost sheet and ensure discipline respectively.

(vi) The four foremen for execution were speed boss, gang boss, repair boss and inspector. These were responsible for timely and accurate completion of the job, keeping machines and tools ready for operation by the workers, ensuring proper working conditions of machines and tools and checking the quality of work. **1 + 3 = 4**

3. **Explain 'Cooperation, Not Individualism' as a principle and 'Fatigue Study' as a technique of scientific management.** [Delhi Set-3, 2023]

Ans. Cooperation, Not Individualism: This principle is an extension of the principle of 'Harmony, not discord' and lays stress on cooperation between workers and the management.

Cooperation, confidence, sense of goodwill should prevail among both, managers as well as workers.

Fatigue study refers to the long working hours with sufficient breaks which results in stress, which is also known as fatigue. This hurts the health of the employees. Through the study of fatigue, one can reduce the level of stress and maintain optimum operational efficiency.

[Marking Scheme, Delhi, 2023]

Long Answer Type Questions (6 marks each)

1. **Briefly explain any three of the following techniques of Scientific Management as given by F.W. Taylor:**

(i) Method study
(ii) Functional foremanship
(iii) Standardisation
(iv) Differential piece wage system R [SQP 2023-24]

Ans. Techniques of Scientific Management given by F.W. Taylor:

(i) Method Study: The objective of method study is to find out one best way of doing the job. There are various methods of doing the job. To determine the best way there are several parameters. Right from procurement of raw materials till the final product is delivered to the customer every activity is part of method study. Taylor devised the concept of assembly line by using method study. Ford Motor Company used this concept very successfully. Even now auto companies are using it. The objective of the whole exercise is to minimise the cost of production and maximise the quality and satisfaction of the customer. For this purpose many techniques like process charts and operations research, etc. are used. For designing a car, the assembly line production would entail deciding the sequence of operations, place for men, machines and raw materials, etc. All this is part of method study.

(ii) Functional Foremanship: Functional foremanship is an extension of the principle of division of work and specialisation to the shop floor. Each worker will have to take orders from these eight foremen in the related process or function of production. Foremen should have intelligence, education, tact, grit, judgment, special knowledge, manual dexterity, and energy, honesty and good health. Since all these qualities could not be found in a single person, Taylor proposed eight specialists. Each specialist is to be assigned work according to her/his qualities. For example, those with technical mastery, intelligence and grit may be given planning work, those with energy and good health may be assigned execution work.

(iii) Standardisation: Standardisation refers to the process of setting standards for every business activity; it can be standardisation of process, raw material, time, product, machinery, methods or working conditions. These standards are the benchmarks, which must be adhered to during production. The objectives of standardisation are (a) To reduce a given line or product to fixed types, sizes and characteristics. (b) To establish interchangeability of manufactured parts and products. (c) To establish standards of excellence and quality in materials. (d) To establish standards of performance of men and machines.

(iv) Piece Wage System: Taylor was a strong advocate of a piece wage system. He wanted to differentiate between efficient and inefficient workers. The standard time and other parameters should be determined on the basis of the work- study discussed above. The workers can then be classified as efficient or inefficient on the basis of these standards. He wanted to reward efficient workers. So he introduced different rates of wage payment for those who performed above standard and for those who performed below standard. [3 × 2 = 6]

2. Explain 'Science, not rule of thumb', 'Harmony, not discord', and 'Development of each and every person to his or her greatest efficiency and prosperity' as Principles of Scientific Management given by F.W. Taylor. U [SQP 2021-22]

Ans. Science, not rule of thumb: Taylor pioneered the introduction of the method of scientific inquiry into the domain of management practice. We have already referred to the limitations of the rule of thumb approach of management.

As different managers would follow their indigenous rules of thumb, it is but a statement of the obvious that all would not be equally effective. Taylor believed that there was only one best method to maximise efficiency. This method can be developed through study and analysis. The method so developed should substitute 'Rule of Thumb' throughout the organisation. Scientific method involved investigation of traditional methods through work-study, unifying the best practices and developing a standard method.

Harmony, not discord: Factory system of production implied that managers served as a link between the owners and the workers. Since as managers they had the mandate to 'get work done' from the workers. Taylor recognised that this conflict helped none, the workers, the managers or the factory owners. He emphasised that there should be complete harmony between the management and workers. Both should realise that each one is important. To achieve this state, Taylor called for a complete Mental Revolution on part of both management and workers. It means that management and workers should transform their thinking. Management should share the gains of the company with the workers. At the same time, workers should work hard and be willing to embrace change for the good of the company.

Development of each and every person to his or her greatest efficiency and prosperity: As such, scientific management also stood for worker development. Worker training was essential also to learn the 'best method' developed as a consequence of the scientific approach. Taylor was of the view that the concern for efficiency could be built in right from the process of employee selection. Each person should be scientifically selected. Then, work assigned should suit her/his physical, mental and intellectual capabilities. To increase efficiency, they should be given required training. Efficient employees would produce more and earn more. This will ensure their greatest efficiency and prosperity for both company and workers. **3×2=6**

[Marking Scheme, SQP 2021-22]

3. Karan Nath took over 'D'north Motor Company' from his ailing father three months ago. In the past, the company was not performing well. Karan was determined to improve the company's performance. He observed that the methods of production as well as selection of employees in the company were not scientific.

He believed that there was only one best method to maximise efficiency. He also felt that once the method is developed, the workers of the company should be trained to learn that 'best method'.

He asked the Production Manager to develop the best method and carry out the necessary training. The Production Manager developed this method using several parameters right from deciding the sequence of operations, place for men, machines and raw materials till the delivery of the product to the customers. This method was implemented throughout the organisation. It helped in increasing the output, improving the quality and reducing the cost and wastage.

Identify and explain the principles and the technique of scientific management followed by the Production Manager in the above case.

A [Delhi & Outside Delhi, 2018]

Ans. Principles of Management followed in the above case:

(i) Science, not rule of thumb:

(a) It states that there was only one best method to maximise efficiency.

(b) This method can be developed through scientific study and analysis of each element of a job and should substitute 'Rule of Thumb'.

(c) This standard method then should be followed throughout the organisation.

(ii) Development of each and every person to his greatest efficiency and prosperity:

(a) This principle is concerned with efficiency of employees which could be built in right from the process of employee selection.

(b) The work assigned to employees should suit their capabilities. They should be given the required training to increase their efficiency.

(c) Efficient employees would produce more and earn more. This will ensure their greatest efficiency and prosperity for both the company and the workers.

Technique of Scientific Management followed in the above case:

Method Study:

(a) It is a study to find out one best way of doing the job.

(b) It helps to minimise the cost of production, improve the quality and maximise satisfaction of the customer.

(c) It includes all activities from procurement of raw materials till the final product is delivered to the customer. **[2 + 2 + 2 = 6]**

[Marking Scheme, Delhi and OD 2018]

4. (i) Explain any two techniques of Scientific Management from the following:

(a) Method study (b) Motion study (c) Time study

(ii) Differentiate between Unity of Command and Unity of Direction on any three basis.

R [APQ 2023-24]

Ans. (i) (a) Method Study: The objective of a method study is to find out the best way of doing the job. There are various methods of doing the job. To determine the best way there are several parameters. Right from procurement of raw materials till the final product is delivered to the customer every activity is part of the method study. The objective of the whole exercise is to minimise the cost of production and maximise the quality and satisfaction of the customer. For this purpose, many techniques like process charts and operations research etc., are used.

(b) Motion Study: Motion study refers to the study of movements like lifting, putting objects, sitting and changing positions, etc., which are undertaken while doing a typical job. Unnecessary movements are sought to be eliminated so that it takes less time to complete the job efficiently. On close examination of body motions, for example, it is possible to find out:

- Motions which are productive
- Motions which are incidental (e.g., going to stores)
- Motions which are unproductive.

(c) Time Study: It determines the standard time taken to perform a well-defined job. Time measuring devices are used for each element of the task. The standard time is fixed for the whole of the task by taking several readings. The method of time study will depend upon the volume and frequency of the task, the cycle time of the operation, and time measurement costs. The objective of the time study is to determine the number of workers to be employed; frame suitable incentive schemes and determine labor costs. **(Any two) [1½×2=3]**

(ii)

Basis of Difference	Unity of Command	Unity of Direction
Meaning	One subordinate should receive orders from and should be responsible to only one superior.	Each group of activities having same objective must have one head and one plan.
Aim	It prevents dual subordination.	It prevents overlapping of activities.
Implication	It affects an individual employee.	It affects the entire organisation.

[1×3=3]

5. (i) Explain any two principles of Fayol from the following:

(a) Discipline (b) Order (c) Initiative

(ii) Differentiate between contributions made by F.W. Taylor and Henry Fayol on any three basis.

R [APQ 2023-24]

Ans. (i) (a) Discipline: Discipline is the obedience to organisational rules and employment agreements which are necessary for the working of the organisation. According to Fayol, discipline requires good superiors at all levels, clear and fair agreements, and judicious application of penalties.

(b) Order: According to Fayol, "People and materials must be in suitable places at appropriate times for maximum efficiency." The principle of the order states that 'a place for everything (everyone) and everything (everyone) in its (her/his) place'. If there is a fixed place for everything and it is present there, then there will be no hindrance in the activities of the business/ factory. This will lead to increased productivity and efficiency.

(c) Initiative: Workers should be encouraged to develop and carry out their plans for improvements, according to Fayol. Initiative means taking the first step with self-motivation. It is thinking out and executing the plan. The initiative should be encouraged. But it does not mean going against the established practices of the company for the sake of being different. A good company should have an employee suggestion system whereby initiatives/ suggestions that result in substantial cost/time reduction should be rewarded.

(Any two) [1½ × 2 = 3]

(ii)

Basis of Difference	Henri Fayol	F.W Taylor
Perspective	Top-level of Management	The shop floor level of a factory.
Unity of Command	Staunch Proponent	Did not feel that it is important as under functional foremanship a worker receives orders from eight specialists
Applicability	Applicable Universally	Applicable to specialised situations

[Marking Scheme, APQ 2023-24]

6. (a) Explain : (i) Science not Rule of Thumb' as a principle of management and (ii) Method Study' and Time Study' as techniques of Scientific Management.

A I AE [Delhi Set-1, 2023]

Ans. (a) (i) Science, not the Rule of Thumb: This rule focuses on increasing the efficiency of an organization through scientific analysis of work and not with the 'Rule of Thumb' method. Taylor believed that even a small activity like loading paper sheets into boxcars can be planned scientifically. This will save time and also human energy. This decision should be based on scientific analysis and cause and effect relationships rather than the 'Rule of Thumb' where the decision is taken according to the manager's judgment.

(ii) Time study: It determines the standard time taken to perform a well-defined job. Time-measuring devices were used to conduct this study. This type of study helps decide the time required to perform a job.

(iii) Method study: This technique of scientific management is conducted to find out the 'one best method or way' of performing a particular task. The objective of this study is to minimise the cost of production and maximise the quality and satisfaction of the customer. **[2×3=6]**

[Marking Scheme, Delhi, 2023]

7. (a) Explain 'Harmony'. Not Discord' as a principle and 'Motion-Study' as a technique of scientific management. **A I R [Delhi Set-2, 2023]**

Ans. (a) Harmony, not discord: According to this principle, there should be complete harmony between management and workers and there should be a transformation in the thinking of both parties, called mental revolution. For example, if a worker is having a problem with the working hours, he should talk to the manager about it, instead of letting it affect production (by going on a strike). Similarly, managers should listen to the worker's suggestions and demands rather than ignoring them.

Motion study: It refers to the study of movements like lifting, putting objects, sitting and changing positions, etc., which are undertaken while doing a typical job. Unnecessary movements are sought to be eliminated so that it takes less time to complete the job efficiently. **[1×3=6]**

[Marking Scheme, Delhi, 2023]

8. F.W. Taylor gave the scientific management principles. He explained 'Science, not rule of thumb', 'Harmony, not discord', and 'Development of every person to his or her greatest efficiency and prosperity' as the principles of Scientific Management. Bhawan had problems understanding the concept. His friend explains the three principles as given by Taylor. **C [SQP, 2023-24]**

Ans. Science, not rule of thumb: Taylor pioneered the introduction of the method of scientific inquiry into the domain of management practice. As different managers would follow their indigenous rules of thumb, it is but a statement of the obvious that all would not be equally effective. Taylor believed that there was only one best method to maximise efficiency. This method can be developed through study and analysis. The method so developed should substitute the 'Rule of Thumb' throughout the organisation. The scientific method involves the investigation of traditional methods through work-study, unifying the best practices, and developing a standard method.

Harmony, not discord: The factory system of production implied that managers served as a link between the owners and the workers. Since as managers they had the mandate to 'get work done' from the workers, Taylor recognised that this conflict helped none, the workers, the managers, or the factory owners. He emphasised that there should be complete harmony between the management and workers. Both should realise that each one is important. To achieve this state, Taylor called for a complete Mental Revolution on the part of both management and workers. It means that management and workers should transform their thinking. Management should share the gains of the company with the workers. At the same time, workers should work hard and be willing to embrace change for the good of the company.

Development of every person to his or her greatest efficiency and prosperity: As such, scientific management also stood for worker development. Worker training was essential also to learn the 'best method' developed as a consequence of the scientific approach. Taylor was of the view that the concern for efficiency could be built in right from the process of employee selection. Each person should be scientifically selected. Then, the work assigned should suit her/his physical, mental, and intellectual capabilities. To increase efficiency, they should be given the required training. Efficient employees would produce more and earn more. This will ensure the greatest efficiency and prosperity for both the company and its workers. **[2×3=6]**

[Marking Scheme, SQP 2023-24]

9. F.W. Taylor is known as the father of scientific management. Explain the principles of management as given by him. U [SQP 2023-24]

Ans. (i) Division of Work: According to this principle the whole work must be divided into small units and instead of assigning the whole work to one person, one unit of work should be assigned to one person according to the capability, qualification, and experience of the person.

(ii) Authority and Responsibility: Authority means the power to make decisions. Responsibility means an obligation to complete the job assigned on time. According to this principle, authority without matching responsibility may bring negative results, and excess of responsibility without matching authority will not allow the worker to complete his job on time. There is a need to bring parity between both for best results.

(iii) Discipline: Discipline refers to general rules and regulations for systematic working in an organisation. Discipline does not mean only rules and regulations but it also means developing commitment in the employees towards the organisation as well as towards each other. Fayol insists that discipline is required at the superior as well as subordinate level.

(iv) Unity of Command: According to this principle, an employee should receive orders from one boss only because if he is receiving orders from more than one boss then he will get confused and will not be able to understand whose orders must be executed first.

(v) Unity of direction: There should be one head and one plan for a group of activities having the same objective. In other words, each group of activities with the same objective must have one plan of action and must be under the control of one superior. Without unity of direction unity of action and coordination of efforts are not possible.

(vi) Subordination of Individual Interest to General Interest: The business enterprise is superior to its employees. The interests of the business organisation must prevail over the personal interests of the individuals. This principle calls for the reconciliation of the goals of individuals with those of the organisation.

(vii) Remuneration of Persons: According to this principle, employees in the organisation must be paid fairly or adequately to give them maximum satisfaction. The employees should be paid fair wages and salaries, which would give them at least a reasonable standard of living.

(viii) Centralisation and Decentralisation: Centralisation refers to the concentration of authority power in a few hands at the top level. Decentralisation means even distribution of power at every level of management. According to Fayol a company must not be completely centralised or completely decentralised but there must be a combination of both depending upon the nature and size of the organisation.

(ix) Principle of Scalar Chain: Scalar chain means a line of authority of chain of superiors from highest to lowest rank. Fayol insists that this chain must be followed strictly in the organisation. Every piece of information must pass through every key of this chain, no skipping of any one key should be allowed. **(Any six) [1×6=6]**

[Marking Scheme, SQP 2023-24)

COMPETENCY BASED QUESTIONS

Objective Type Questions

[A] Multiple Choice Questions

1. Management has its own set of principles, which are broad and general guidelines about management, decision-making, and behaviour.

Which of the following techniques of scientific management relates efficiency to remuneration?

(A) Differential Piece Wage System

(B) Time Study

(C) Standardisation and Simplification of Work

(D) Motion Study R [CFPQ, 2023]

Ans. Option (A) is correct.

Explanation: The technique of scientific management that relates efficiency to remuneration is the Differential Piece Wage System. In this system, workers are paid at different piece rates based on their level of performance or efficiency. The idea is to provide higher wages to those who demonstrate higher levels of productivity, creating a direct link between individual performance and compensation. [Marking Scheme, CFPQ, 2023]

2. 'Management principles help in thoughtful decision-making. They emphasise logic rather than

blind faith'. This statement describes the following point of significance of principles of management:

(A) Fulfilling social responsibility
(B) Scientific decisions
(C) Meeting changing environment requirements.
(D) Optimum utilisation of resources and effective administration. U [SQP, Term-1, Exam 2021-22]

Ans. Option (B) is correct.

Explanation: Management principles help in thoughtful decision-making. They emphasise logic rather than blind faith. Management decisions taken on the basis of principles are free from bias and prejudice. They are based on the objective assessment of the situation.

3. **"The application of principles of management is dependent upon the prevailing situation at a particular point of time". The above statement highlights that principles of management are:**

(A) Flexible (B) Contingent
(C) Behavioral (D) Universal

U [SQP Term-1, Exam 2021-22]

Ans. Option (B) is correct.

Explanation: The application of principles of management is contingent or dependent upon the prevailing situation at a particular point of time. The application of principles has to be changed as per requirements.

4. **'The principle will give rise to a spirit of mutual trust and belongingness among team members. Which principle of management stated by Fayol is highlighted by this statement?**

(A) Initiative
(B) Esprit de corps
(C) Equity
(D) Remuneration of employees

U [SQP Term-1, Exam 2021-22]

Ans. Option (B) is correct.

Explanation: Management should promote teamwork especially in large organisations otherwise objectives would be difficult to achieve. A manager should replace 'I' with 'We' in all his conversations with workers to foster team spirit. This will give rise to a spirit of mutual trust and belongingness among team members.

5. **'Organisations should have a chain of authority and communication that runs from top to bottom and should be followed by managers and the subordinates. Which principle of management given by Fayol is highlighted in the above statement?**

(A) Authority and responsibility
(B) Discipline
(C) Scalar chain
(D) Centralisation and decentralisation

U [SQP Term-1, Exam 2021-22]

Ans. Option (C) is correct.

Explanation: The formal lines of authority from highest to lowest ranks is known as scalar chain. According to Fayol, "Organisations should have a chain of authority and communication that runs from top to bottom and should be followed by managers and the subordinates."

6. **Pioneer Ltd. is dealing in fruit juices and hair oils. To ensure unity of action and coordination, it has made two separate divisions for each product. Each division has its own incharge, plans and execution resources. Thus, both the divisions are moving towards the same objectives through focused efforts. Identify the principle of management followed by Pioneer Ltd. in the above case.**

(A) Esprit de corps
(B) Equity
(C) Unity of direction
(D) Authority and responsibility

U [SQP Term-1, Exam 2023-24]

Ans. Option (C) is correct.

Explanation: Unity of Direction means all the units of an organisation should be moving towards the same objectives through coordinated and focussed efforts. Each group of activities having the same objective must have one head and one plan. This ensures unity of action and coordination.

7. **Fayol's principle of ________ emphasises on kindliness and justice in the behaviour of managers towards workers.**

(A) Equity (B) Discipline
(C) Esprit de corps (D) Scalar chain

R [SQP Term-1, Exam 2023-24]

8. **Vidhya Public School is a renowned school in Nagpur. The management recently appointed a new Business Studies teacher, Shweta, to teach classes XI and XII and gave her a monthly salary of ₹ 50,000. Shweta is not satisfied with it and said "the salary is not just and equitable as per the amount of work required to be done by a Business Studies teacher. Other schools in the city are paying ₹ 70,000 to their teachers teaching classes XI and XII". Name the principle of management that has been violated by Vidhya Public School in the above case:**

(A) Discipline
(B) Remuneration of employees
(C) Equity
(D) Esprit de corps A [SQP Term-1, Exam 2021-22]

Ans. Option (B) is correct.

Explanation: The overall pay and compensation should be fair to both employees and the organisation. Remuneration should be just and equitable. This will ensure congenial atmosphere and good relations between workers and management. Consequently, the working of the company would be smooth.

9. **The ________ technique proposed by Taylor aims at eliminating unnecessary diversity of products.**

(A) Motion study
(B) Standardisation and simplification of work
(C) Differential piece wage system
(D) Functional foremanship

U [SQP Term-1, Exam 2023-24]

Ans. Option (B) is correct.

This Question is for practice and its solution is given at the end of the chapter.

10. **Somesh works as a foreman in 'Lakshmi Automotive Ltd.', a company manufacturing car. He is subordinate to Ramesh, who is the production incharge in the factory. Somesh is incharge of timely and accurate completion of job by workers working in the production department. There are three other foremen who work under the production incharge, while four other foremen work under Naresh, the planning incharge in the factory. Each of the eight foremen are specialist in their areas and give orders to the workers relating to it.**

    The technique of scientific management highlighted in the above case is:

    (A) Method study
    (B) Differential piece wage system
    (C) Functional foremanship
    (D) Standardisation and simplification of work

    A [SQP Term-1, Exam 2023-24]

Ans. Option (C) is correct.

Explanation: Functional foremanship is an extension of the principle of division of work and specialisation to the shop floor. Taylor advocated separation of planning and execution functions. Each worker will have to take orders from eight foremen (4 from Production and 4 from Planning) in the related process or function of production.

11. **'Flavours of South' is a famous chain of South Indian restaurants. It believes in complete co-operation between the labour and management. It's management encourages the employees for their constructive suggestions. They take their employees into confidence for all important decisions.**

    Which principle of scientific management has been followed by 'Flavours of South'?

    (A) Science, not rule of thumb
    (B) Harmony, not discord
    (C) Co-operation, not individualism
    (D) Development of each and every person to his or her greatest efficiency and prosperity

    A [SQP Term-1, Exam 2023-24]

Ans. Option (C) is correct.

Explanation: According to this principle, there should be complete cooperation between the labour and the management instead of individualism. For this, management should not close its ears to any constructive suggestions made by the employees. They should be rewarded for their suggestions which results in substantial reduction in costs. They should be part of management and, if any important decisions are taken, workers should be taken into confidence.

12. **In 'Delight Ice Creams Ltd.', decision making authority is concentrated at the top level and no authority has been delegated among the subordinates. On the other hand, in "Tasty Ice Creams Ltd.", a big organisation as compared to 'Delight Ice Creams Ltd.', decision making authority is always delegated among more than one person.**

    Identify the principle of management discussed above.

    (A) Stability of personnel
    (B) Centralisation and decentralisation
    (C) Authority and responsibility
    (D) Scalar chain

    A [SQP 2021-22]

Ans. Option (B) is correct.

Explanation: The concentration of decision-making authority is called centralisation whereas its dispersal among more than one person is known as decentralisation. The degree of centralisation will depend upon the circumstances in which the company is working. In general, large organisations have more decentralisation than small organisations.

13. **The CEO of Radhe Cycles Pvt. Ltd. Mr. Kumar wants to get maximum output from the employees at a competitive cost. On the other hand, Ramakaant, an employee of the company wants to get the maximum salary while working the least. The Principle of management given by Fayol being violated by Ramakaant is ___________.**

    (A) Remuneration
    (B) Equity
    (C) Discipline
    (D) Subordination of individual interest to general interest.

    A [SQP 2021-22]

Ans. Option (D) is correct.

Explanation: The interests of an organisation should take priority over the interests of any one individual employee according to Fayol. Every worker has some individual interest for working in a company. The company has its own objectives. For example,the company would want to get maximum output from its employees at a competitive cost (salary). On the other hand, an employee may want to get maximum salary while working the least.

14. **Name the principle of management given by Fayol which when applied would mean that the workers and management both honour their commitments without any prejudice towards one another.**

    (A) Discipline
    (B) Mental revolution
    (C) Remuneration of employees
    (D) Scalar chain

    U [SQP 2021-22]

15. **The objective of which of the following techniques of scientific management is to determine the number of workers to be employed in an organisation?**

    (A) Method study
    (B) Motion study
    (C) Time study
    (D) Differential piece wage system

    R [SQP 2021-22]

Concept Applied	Techniques of scientific management.

Ans. Option (C) is correct.

Explanation: The objective of time study is to determine the standard time taken for performing a specified job to ascertain the number of workers to be employed, incentive schemes and determine labour costs.

This Question is for practice and its solution is given at the end of the chapter.

16. According to the technique of Scientific Management "Differential Piece Wage System", how much more will a worker making 60 units earn as compared to a worker making 49 units, if the standard output per day is 50 units and those who make standard output or more than standard get ₹ 75 per unit and those below get ₹ 65 per unit.

(A) ₹ 4,500 (B) ₹ 3,185
(C) ₹ 1,315 (D) ₹ 3,250

A [SQP 2021-22]

Ans. Option (C) is correct.

Explanation: It is determined that standard output per worker per day is 50 units and those who made standard or more than standard will get ₹ 75 per unit and those below will get ₹ 65 per unit. Now an efficient worker making 60 units will get 60 × ₹ 75 = ₹ 4,500 per day whereas a worker who makes 49 units will get 49 × ₹ 65 = ₹ 3,185 per day. According to Taylor, the difference of ₹ 1,315 should be enough for the inefficient worker to be motivated to perform better.

17. Taylor proposed eight specialists from whom each worker will have to take orders as part of the technique of Functional Foremanship specified by him. Those with technical, mastery, intelligence and grit may be given ___________ work. Those with energy and good health may be assigned___________ work.

(A) Planning, Execution
(B) Execution, Planning
(C) Production, Planning
(D) Implementation, Production A [SQP 2021-22]

Concept Applied	Techniques of Scientific Management

Ans. Option (A) is correct.

Explanation: In the factory system, the foreman represents the managerial figure with whom the workers are in face-to-face contact on a daily basis. Taylor advocated separation of planning and execution functions. This concept was extended to the lowest level of the shop floor. It was known as functional foremanship. Those with technical mastery, intelligence and grit may be given planning work. Those with energy and good health may be assigned execution work.

18. The concept of 'mental revolution', as prescribed by Taylor, involves, a change in the mind set of:

(A) Workers towards the management.
(B) Management towards the workers.
(C) Workers and management towards one another from competition to cooperation.
(D) Customers towards the management of the organisation. U [SQP Term-1, Exam 2021-22]

Concept Applied	Principles of Scientific Management

Ans. Option (C) is correct.

Explanation: Mental revolution involves a change in the attitude of workers and management towards one another from competition to cooperation. Both should realise that they require one another.

19. For the following two statements, choose the correct option:

Statement I: Management principles aim at influencing behaviour of human beings.

Statement II: Principles enable a better understanding of the relationship between human and material resources in accomplishing organisational purposes.

U [OEB]

Choose the correct option from options given below:

(A) Statement I is correct and statement II is wrong.
(B) Statement II is correct and statement I is wrong.
(C) Both the statements are correct.
(D) Both the statements are wrong.

Ans. Option (C) is correct.

20. For the following two statements, choose the correct option:

Statement I: The principles of management provide the managers with useful insights into real world situations.

Statement II: Management principles help in thoughtful decision-making.

Choose the correct option from options given below: U [OEB]

(A) Statement I is correct and statement II is wrong.
(B) Statement II is correct and statement I is wrong.
(C) Both the statements are correct.
(D) Both the statements are wrong.

Ans. Option (C) is correct.

21. Identify Fayol's principles of management illustrated in the image given below.

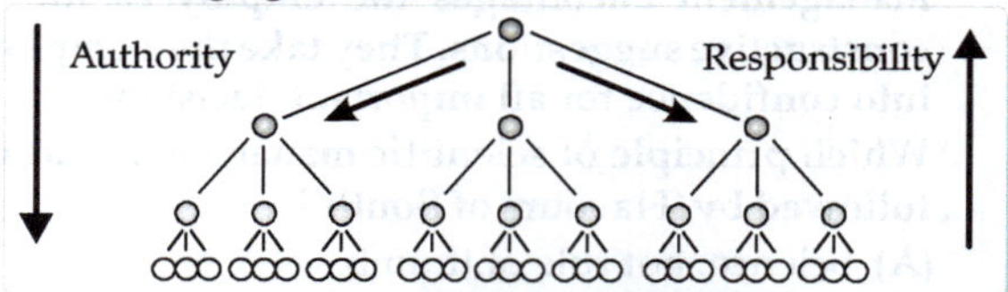

(A) Stability of Tenure
(B) Remuneration to the employee
(C) Unity of command
(D) Equity A [OEB]

Ans. Option (C) is correct.

Explanation: Each employee should receive orders in a hierarchy and should be responsible to only one superior. There should be one and only one boss for every individual employee.

22. Match the principle with their respective statements:

Column I	Column II
(1) Initiatives	(a) To ensure fairness to all employees.
(2) Remuneration	(b) To implement good suggestion system.
(3) Equity	(c) Clear and fair agreements.
(4) Discipline	(d) Fair wages.

(A) 1-a, 2-d, 3-c, 4-b (B) 1-a, 2-d, 3-b, 4-c
(C) 1-b, 2-d, 3-a, 4-c (D) 1-b, 2-d, 3-c, 4-a

U [OEB]

Ans. Option (C) is correct.

[B] Assertion & Reason

Directions: In the following questions, a statement of assertion (A) is followed by a statement of reason (R). Mark the correct choice as:

(A) Both assertion (A) and reason (R) are true and reason (R) is the correct explanation of assertion (A).

(B) Both assertion (A) and reason (R) are true but reason (R) is not the correct explanation of assertion (A).

(C) Assertion (A) is true but reason (R) is false.

(D) Assertion (A) is false but reason (R) is true.

1. **Assertion (A):** The application of principles of management is contingent.

   Reason (R): The principles of management are not rigid prescriptions, which have to be followed absolutely. A [OEB]

Ans. Option (B) is correct.

Explanation: The application of principles of management is dependent upon the prevailing situation at a particular point of time. It has to be changed as per the requirements. Principles of management are flexible and can be modified by the manager when the situation so demands.

2. **Assertion (A):** Managerial principles help the management to come out with the methods that help in reducing wastages.

   Reason (R): Principles of management cannot be modified. U [OEB]

Concept Applied	Features of management principles.

Ans. Option (C) is correct.

Explanation: As the principles of management can be modified, they help the managers to meet the changing environment requirements.

3. **Assertion (A):** Segregating work in the workforce amongst the workers will enhance the quality of the product.

   Reason (R): Division of work leads to specialisation. U [OEB]

Ans. Option (A) is correct.

Explanation: Division of work leads to specialisation, and specialisation helps to increase efficiency, which results in improvement in the productivity and profitability of the organisation.

4. **Assertion (A):** In an organisation, there should be a chain of superiors ranging from the ultimate authority to the lowest.

   Reason (R): Managers require authority commensurate with their responsibility. U [OEB]

Ans. Option (B) is correct.

Explanation: There should be a balance between Authority and Responsibility. Authority facilitates the management to work efficiently, and responsibility makes them responsible for the work done under their guidance or leadership.

5. **Assertion (A):** There should be one and only one boss for every individual employee.

   Reason (R): If an employee has to follow more than one boss, there begins a conflict of interest and can create confusion. U [OEB]

Concept Applied	Principle of unity of command

Ans. Option (A) is correct.

Explanation: According to Fayol, there should be one and only one boss for every individual employee. If an employee gets orders from two superiors at the same time the principle of unity of command is violated. He felt that if this principle is violated "authority is undermined, discipline is in jeopardy, order disturbed and stability threatened".

6. **Assertion (A):** Time study helps in deciding the number of workers to be employed, frame suitable incentive schemes and determine labour costs.

   Reason (R): It is a technique to determine the standard time taken by a worker of reasonable skill and efficiency to perform a well-defined job. U [OEB]

[C] Case Based MCQs

I. Read the following text and answer the following questions on the basis of the same:

After completing her Bachelors in Fashion Designing from a well-known college in France, Aditi has opened a boutique in a posh market in Kolkata. She has divided the work in smaller units and each employee is well trained to perform his/her task efficiently. The sales persons are allowed to close a deal with a buyer by giving a maximum of 5 percent discount, whereas the decision to give any further discount rests with Aditi as the final authority. In the earlier period of her business venture, employees were asked to put in extra hours of work. In return she had promised to give them a special incentive within a year. Therefore, when the business was doing well, she honours her commitment by giving bonus to her employees. She also instructed her employees that communication from top to bottom should follow the official lines of command. However, she tends to be more biased towards her female employees, when it comes to solve the conflicts among employees. [OEB]

1. **Aditi has divided the work in smaller units and each employee is well trained to perform his/ her task efficiently. Which principle of management is being followed here?**

   (A) Centralisation and Decentralisation
   (B) Division of work
   (C) Discipline
   (D) Order

Ans. Option (B) is correct.

Explanation: Henry Fayol has stressed on the specialisation of jobs. He recommended that work of all kinds must be divided and subdivided and allotted to various persons according to their expertise in a particular area. Subdivision of work makes it simpler and results in efficiency.

2. **"The sales persons are allowed to close a deal with a buyer by giving a maximum of 5 percent discount, whereas the decision to give any further discount rests with Aditi as the final authority." Identify the principle of Management being followed here:**

   (A) Centralisation and Decentralisation
   (B) Authority and Responsibility
   (C) Unity of Command
   (D) Unity of Direction

This Question is for practice and its solution is given at the end of the chapter.

Ans. Option (A) is correct.

Explanation: Centralisation means concentration of authority at the top level. In other words, centralisation is a situation in which top management retains most of the decision making authority.

Decentralisation means disposal of decision making authority to all the levels of the organisation. In other words, sharing authority downwards is decentralisation.

3. "Therefore, when the business was doing well, she honoured her commitment by giving bonus to her employees." Which principle of management is being highlighted here?

(A) Discipline (B) Order
(C) Remuneration to Employees
(D) Unity of Direction

Ans. Option (A) is correct.

Explanation: This principle applies that subordinate should respect their superiors and obey their order.

Discipline is an important requisite for smooth running of the enterprise.

4. Aditi tends to be more biased towards her female employees, when it comes to solve the conflicts among employees. Which principle is being violated here?

(A) Discipline (B) Order
(C) Equity (D) None of these

Ans. Option (C) is correct.

Explanation: Equity means combination of fairness, kindness and justice. The employees should be treated with kindness and equity if devotion is expected of them. It implies that managers should be fair and impartial while dealing with the subordinates.

II. Read the following text and answer the questions given below: **[OEB]**

Shruti, a student of management at MDI, Gurgaon, likes to relate what she has learnt in her classes during study to real life situations around her. She observed many situations while watching educational programmes on television that remind her of concepts of Scientific Management. In one such programme, factories manufacturing parts for products like automobiles, computers and mobile phones were being telecast. These factories had defined benchmarks during production and were continuously aiming at eliminating unnecessary diversity of products. Thus, they aimed at eliminating superfluous varieties, sizes and dimensions and devising new varieties instead of the existing ones. While watching the programme, Shruti realised that these companies could adopt one best way of doing the job in order to be more productive. She also felt that the employees of these companies were working for long hours continuously and needed to adopt certain strategies in order to improve their efficiency. The programme also showed a few interviews where some workers were found to be highly efficient as compared with a few others.

1. Name the technique of Scientific Management that these factories are adhering to while manufacturing parts for such products.

(A) Method Study (B) Motion Study
(C) Standardisation and simplification of work
(D) Time Study

Ans. Option (C) is correct.

2. Which Scientific Management technique would Shruti recommend for these factories if they have to find out one best way of doing the job?

(A) Motion Study (B) Time Study
(C) Method Study (D) Fatigue Study

Ans. Option (C) is correct.

Explanation: The objective of method study is to find out one best way of doing the job. There are various methods of doing the job.

3. Which Scientific Management technique would Shruti suggest for these factories if they have to help the workers regain their stamina and enable them to work again with the same capacity?

(A) Motion Study (B) Time Study
(C) Method Study (D) Fatigue Study

Ans. Option (D) is correct.

Explanation: Fatigue study seeks to determine the amount and frequency of rest intervals in completing a task.

4. Which Scientific Management technique would Shruti advise these factories to implement in order to motivate the inefficient workers to perform better?

(A) Functional Foremanship
(B) Method Study
(C) Time Study
(D) Differential Piece Wage System

Ans. Option (D) is correct.

Explanation: This technique of wage payment is based on efficiency of workers. The efficient workers are paid more wages than inefficient one. On the other hand, those workers who produce less than standard number of pieces are paid wages at lower rate than prevailing rate i.e. worker is penalised for his inefficiency.

SOLUTIONS FOR PRACTICE QUESTIONS (TOPIC-1)

SATQs-I

Ans 3. Importance of Principles of Management:

(i) Provide managers with useful insights into reality.
(ii) Optimum utilisation of resources and effective administration.
(iii) Scientific decisions.
(iv) Meeting changing environment requirements.
(v) Fulfilling social responsibility.
(vi) Used as a basis for management training, education and research. **(Any three) [1 × 3 = 3]**

For detail, refer to Q. 2 of Short Answer Type Questions–II of Topic-I.

LATQs

Ans 3. The nature of principles of management highlighted above are as follows:

(i) Mainly Behavioural: Management principles aim at influencing behaviour of human beings. Therefore, principles of management are mainly behavioural in nature. It is not that these principles do not pertain to things and phenomenon at all, it is just a matter of emphasis. Moreover, principles enable a better understanding of the relationship between human and material resources in accomplishing organisational purposes.

(ii) Flexible: The principles of management are not rigid prescriptions, which have to be followed absolutely. They are flexible and can be modified by the manager when the situation so demands. They give the manager enough discretion to do so. For example, the degree of concentration of authority(centralisation) or its dispersal (decentralisation) will depend upon the situations and circumstances of each enterprise.

(iii) General Guidelines: The principles are guidelines to action but do not provide ready-made, straitjacket solutions to all managerial problems. This is so because real business situations are very complex and dynamic and are a result of many factors. However, the importance of principles cannot be underestimated because even a small guideline helps to solve a given problem. For example,in dealing with a situation of conflict between two departments, a manager may emphasise the primacy of the overall goals of the organisation. **[2 × 3 = 6]**

SOLUTIONS FOR PRACTICE QUESTIONS (TOPIC-2)

SATQs-I

Ans 4. (i) Remuneration of employees: It states that the remuneration of employees should be justifiable and equitable. Employees should be paid fair wages, which should give them at least a reasonable standard of living. At the same time, it should be within the paying capacity of the company.

(ii) Scalar chain: It refers to the chain of authority and communication that runs from top to bottom and should be followed by the managers and subordinates.

For example: There is one head A who has two lines of authority under him, B-C-D and L-M-N. If D has to communicate with N who is at the same level of authority, then he has to transverse the route D-C-B-A-L-M-N due to the principle of scalar chain. However, if there is an emergency, then D can directly contact N through gang plank.

Gang Plank: It is a shorter route and has been provided so that communication is not delayed.

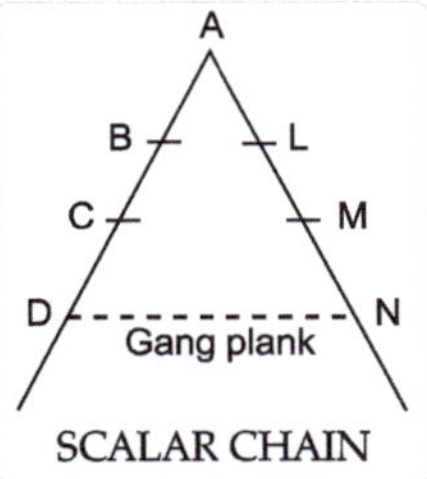

SCALAR CHAIN

[1½ × 2 = 3]

LATQs

Ans 2. The following principles of management are highlighted in the above case:

(i) Discipline: Discipline is the obedience to organisational rules and employment agreement which are necessary for the working of the organisation. According to Fayol, discipline requires good superiors at all levels, clear and fair agreements and judicious application of penalties.

(ii) Stability of Personnel: "Employee turnover should be minimised to maintain organisational efficiency", according to Fayol. Personnel should be selected and appointed after due and rigorous procedure. But once selected they should be kept at their post/ position for a minimum fixed tenure. They should have stability of tenure. They should be given reasonable time to show results. Any adhocism in this regard will create instability/insecurity among employees. They would tend to leave the organisation. Recruitment, selection and training cost will be high. So, stability in tenure of personnel is good for the business.

(iii) Initiative: Workers should be encouraged to develop and carry out their plans for improvements according to Fayol. Initiative means taking the first step with self-motivation. It is thinking out and executing the plan. It is one of the traits of an intelligent person. Initiative should be encouraged. But it does not mean going against the established practices of the company for the sake of being different. A good company should have an employee suggestion system whereby initiative/ suggestions which result in substantial cost/time reduction should be rewarded.

(iv) Esprit De Corps: Management should promote a team spirit of unity and harmony among employees, according to Fayol. Management should promote teamwork especially in large organisations because otherwise objectives would be difficult to realise. It will also result in a loss of coordination. A manager should replace 'I' with 'We' in all his conversations with workers to foster team spirit. This will give rise to a spirit of mutual trust and belongingness among team members. It will also minimise the need for using penalties. **[1½×4=6]**

Commonly Made Error

⚠ Most of the students make mistakes in identifying the correct principles of management given in the passage.

Answering Tip

Practice more case-based questions and learn the content of principles of management given by Fayol by heart so that mistakes can be avoided while identifying the correct principle.

SOLUTIONS FOR OBJECTIVE PRACTICE QUESTIONS

[A] MCQs

Ans. 7. Option (A) is correct.

Explanation: This principle emphasises kindliness and justice in the behaviour of managers towards workers. "Good sense and experience are needed to ensure fairness to all employees, who should be treated as fairly as possible," according to Fayol.

Ans. 14. Option (A) is correct.

Explanation: Discipline is the obedience to organisational rules and employment agreement which are necessary for the smooth functioning of the organisation. According to Fayol, discipline requires good superiors at all levels, clear and fair agreements and judicious application of penalties.

[B] A & R

Ans. 6. Option (A) is correct.

Explanation: Time study determines the standard time taken to perform a well-defined job. Time measuring devices are used for each element of task. The standard time is fixed for the whole of the task by taking several readings. The method of time study will depend upon volume and frequency of the task, the cycle time of the operation and time measurement costs. The objective of time study is to determine the number of workers to be employed; frame suitable incentive schemes and determine labour costs.

REFLECTION

(a) Were you able to differentiate between unity of command and unity of direction?

(b) Were you able to explain Fayol's principles of management with examples?

(c) Were you able to explain the principles and techniques of 'Scientific Management'?

(d) Did you understand the importance of principles of management?

(e) Were you able to identify the principle of management in the below mentioned line:
"People and materials must be in suitable places at appropriate time for maximum efficiency."

(f) Were you able to identify the technique of scientific management in the below mentioned line:
"Unnecessary movements are sought to be eliminated so that it takes less time to complete the job efficiently."

SELF ASSESSMENT PAPER - 2

Maximum Time: 1 hour **MM: 30**

General Instructions:

(i) All the questions are compulsory
(ii) Q.1 to Q.10 are 1 mark questions
(3) Q.11 to Q.12 are 3 mark questions
(iv) Q.13 to Q.14 are 4 marks questions
(v) Q.15 is a 6 marks question

Objective Type Questions [1 Mark]

1.

Identify the principle of Fayol illustrated in the picture above.

(A) Equity
(B) Authority and Responsibility
(C) Division of Work
(D) Unity of Direction **[1]**

2. Which of the following technique of scientific management is an extension of the principle of division of work and specialisation to the shop floor?

(A) Functional foremanship
(B) Standardisation and Simplification of Work
(C) Time study
(D) Fatigue study **[1]**

3. Match the techniques of scientific management with their respective statements:

Column I		Column II	
(1)	Method study	**(a)**	Standard time taken to perform a well-defined job.
(2)	Motion Study	**(b)**	Find out one best way of doing the job
(3)	Time Study	**(c)**	To determine the amount and frequency of rest intervals
(4)	Fatigue Study	**(d)**	Study of movements

(A) 1-a, 2-d, 3-c, 4-b **(B)** 1-a, 2-d, 3-b, 4-c
(C) 1-b, 2-d, 3-a, 4-c **(D)** 1-b, 2-d, 3-c, 4-a **[1]**

4. Which of the following principle of management replaces 'I' with 'We' in all his conversation with workers?

(A) Order **(B)** Initiative
(C) Discipline **(D)** Esprit De Corps **[1]**

5. For the following two statements, choose the correct option:

Statement I: The overall pay and compensation should be fair to both employees and the organisation.

Statement II: The employees should be paid fair wages, which should give them at least a reasonable standard of living.

Choose the correct option from options given below:

(A) Statement I is correct and statement II is wrong.
(B) Statement II is correct and statement I is wrong.
(C) Both the statements are correct.
(D) Both the statements are wrong. **[1]**

6. Assertion (A): The application of principles has to be changed as per requirements.

Reason (R): The application of principles of management is dependent upon the prevailing situation at a particular point of time.

(A) Both assertion (A) and reason (R) are true and reason (R) is the correct explanation of assertion (A).
(B) Both assertion (A) and reason (R) are true but reason (R) is not the correct explanation of assertion (A).
(C) Assertion (A) is true but reason (R) is false.
(D) Assertion (A) is false but reason (R) is true.

Read the Case Study and answer the following question 7-10:

XYZ Manufacturing, a large production facility, faced challenges related to low productivity, high employee turnover, and inefficient processes. The management decided to implement Frederick Taylor's principles of scientific management to address these issues.

The company identified key areas for improvement, such as the need for systematic workflow, standardised procedures, and a scientific approach to employee management. The management aimed to apply Taylor's principles to enhance efficiency and productivity.

The recommendation is to discuss various methods to improve productivity in a production process. Time and motion studies were conducted to analyse tasks and find ways to reduce time and effort. Standardised work methods were developed based on these studies to ensure consistency. A piece-rate system was introduced to motivate employees by paying them based on their production output. Scientific selection and training methods were used to match individuals with suitable jobs and enhance their skills. Functional foremanship was implemented to assign specific supervisors for different aspects of the production process, aiming to improve efficiency and accountability.

Based on the above case answer the following question:

7. What is the primary goal of conducting Time and

Motion Studies in scientific management? **[1]**
(A) Increase employee salaries
(B) Analyse the production process for efficiency
(C) Encourage multitasking
(D) Implement a flexible work schedule

8. Why were Standardised Work Methods introduced at XYZ Manufacturing? **[1]**
(A) To create confusion among employees
(B) To discourage consistency in work processes
(C) To reduce variability in task execution
(D) To promote individual creativity in work methods

9. What is the purpose of the Piece-Rate System in scientific management? **[1]**
(A) To discourage employees from increasing their output
(B) To reduce overall productivity
(C) To motivate employees by linking pay to production
(D) To promote a fixed salary structure

10. How does Scientific Selection and Training contribute to efficiency at XYZ Manufacturing? **[1]**
(a) By randomly selecting employees for different tasks
(B) By matching individuals with jobs based on abilities
(C) By ignoring the skills of employees
(D) By discouraging training programs

Short Answer Type Questions - I [3 Marks]

11. Neelam is a commerce student in a reputed school in Delhi. Navya is her elder sister who is doing her MBA from Mumbai. During vacations when Navya comes home, Neelam shows her the business studies project that she is preparing on the topic 'Principles of Management'. Navya tells her that these principles are also a part of MBA course curriculum at the beginner's level as they form the core of management in practice. But she finds these principles different from those of pure science. In context of the above case outline the concept of principles of management.

12. Name and explain the technique of scientific management which helps in establishing interchangeability of manufactured parts and products.

Short Answer Type Questions - II [4 Marks]

13. After finishing her diploma in management course, Vaishali gets a job of a Manager in a company through the reference of her friend Swapna who works in the same company as a Senior Manager. Swapna decides to guide Vaishali through her experience by making her aware of the important facts about management in practice. She tells her that neither the principles of management provide any ready-made, straitjacket solutions to all managerial problems nor they are not rigid prescriptions, which have to be followed absolutely.

In context of the above case:
(i) Identify the two features of principles of management mentioned in the above paragraph by quoting lines from the paragraph.
(ii) Why do the principles of management not provide ready-made, straitjacket solutions to all managerial problems?

14. The principles of Taylor and Fayol are mutually complementary. One believed that management should share the gains with the workers while the other suggested that employees' compensation should depend on the earning capacity of the company and should give them a reasonable standard of living.

Identify and explain the principles of Fayol and Taylor referred to in the above paragraph.

Long Answer Type Questions [6 Marks]

15. Manju opens a showroom in Delhi after completing a course in fashion designing. She has employed 12 persons in her showroom. For greater productivity, she divides the work into small tasks and each employee is trained to perform his/her specialised job. The sales persons are allowed to close a deal with a buyer by giving a maximum of 15% discount, whereas the decision to give any further discount rests with Manju as the final authority. In the earlier days of starting of the business, six of her employees were asked to put in extra hours of work. In return she had promised to give them a special incentive within a year. Therefore, after eight months when the business was doing well, she awarded a cash bonus to each of these employees to honour her commitment. However, when it comes to settling the conflicts among her employees, she tends to be more biased towards her female employees. In context of the above case:
(i) Identify and explain the various principles of management that are being applied by Manju by quoting lines from the paragraph.
(ii) Identify and explain the principle of management which is being violated by Manju by quoting lines from the paragraph.
(iii) State any one effect of the violation of the principle of management by Manju as identified in part(ii) of the question.

BUSINESS ENVIRONMENT

LEARNING OBJECTIVES

After going through this unit, the student/learner would be able to:

- Understand the concept of 'Business Environment'.
- Describe the importance of business environment.
- Describe the various dimensions of 'Business Environment'.
- Understand the concept of demonetization.

Study Plan
Maximum Time = 3.30 Hrs
Maximum Questions = 56

LIST OF TOPICS

TOPIC-1 Business Environment: Concept and Importance

Concepts Covered

- Concept of Business Environment
- Features and Importance.

Revision Notes

- **Business Environment:** The term 'business environment' means the sum total of all individuals, institutions and other forces that are outside the control of a business enterprise but that may affect its performance.

Features of Business Environment: [Board, 2019]

(i) **Totality of external forces:** Business environment is the sum total of all things external to business firms and, as such, is aggregative in nature.

(ii) **Specific and general forces:** Specific forces (such as investors, customers, competitors and suppliers) affect individual enterprises directly and immediately in their day-to-day working. General forces (such as social, political, legal and technological conditions) have impact on all business enterprises and thus may affect an individual firm only indirectly.

(iii) **Inter-relatedness:** Different elements of business environment are closely inter-related.

(iv) **Dynamic nature:** It keeps on changing due to changes in its various components.

(v) **Uncertainty:** It is very difficult to predict future happenings in business environment with accuracy.

(vi) **Complexity:** It is relatively easier to understand in parts but difficult to grasp in totality.

(vii) **Relativity:** It differs from country to country and region to region.

Importance of Business Environment: [Board, 2019]

(i) Enables the firm to identify opportunities and getting the first mover advantage.

(ii) Helps the firm to identify threats and early warning signals.

(iii) Helps in tapping useful resources.

(iv) Helps in coping with rapid changes.

(v) Helps in assisting in planning and policy formulation.

(vi) Helps in improving performance.

MNEMONICS

Concept: Characteristics of Business Environment:
Interpretations: Did U SIT in a Racing Car?
D : Dynamic nature
U : Uncertainty
S : Specific and general forces
I : Inter-relatedness
T : Totality of external forces
R : Relativity
C : Complexity

KEY TERMS

Environment: Everything that surrounds us.
Dynamic: Continuously changing or developing.
Uncertainty: A situation in which something is not known.
Opportunity: Positive external trends that helps a firm to improve its performance.
Threat: External environmental trends that hinder a firm's performance.

SUBJECTIVE TYPE QUESTIONS

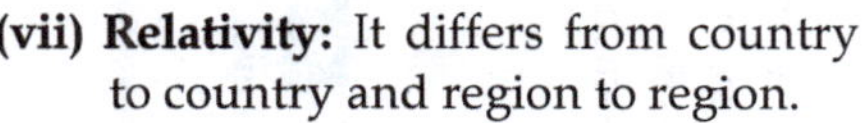

Short Answer Type Questions-II (4 marks each)

1. Explain any four features of business environment.
U [Outside Delhi Set-1, 2019]

OR

Explain any four characteristics of business environment.
U [Delhi Compt. Set-1, 2019]

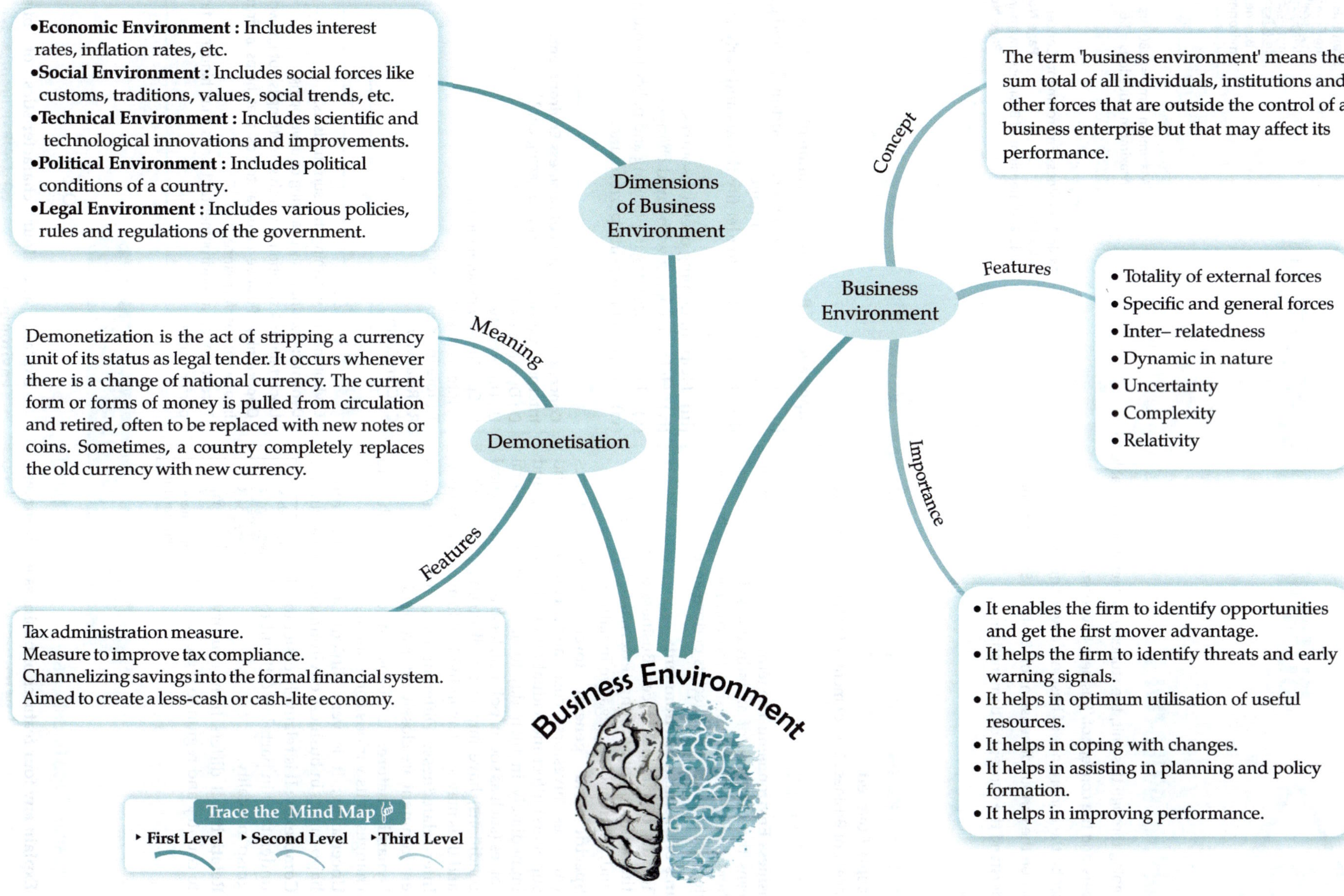
Business Environment
Business Environment
Concept
The term 'business environment' means the sum total of all individuals, institutions and other forces that are outside the control of a business enterprise but that may affect its performance.
Features
• Totality of external forces
• Specific and general forces
• Inter– relatedness
• Dynamic in nature
• Uncertainty
• Complexity
• Relativity
Importance
• It enables the firm to identify opportunities and get the first mover advantage.
• It helps the firm to identify threats and early warning signals.
• It helps in optimum utilisation of useful resources.
• It helps in coping with changes.
• It helps in assisting in planning and policy formation.
• It helps in improving performance.
Dimensions of Business Environment
•Economic Environment : Includes interest rates, inflation rates, etc.
•Social Environment : Includes social forces like customs, traditions, values, social trends, etc.
•Technical Environment : Includes scientific and technological innovations and improvements.
•Political Environment : Includes political conditions of a country.
•Legal Environment : Includes various policies, rules and regulations of the government.
Demonetisation
Meaning
Demonetization is the act of stripping a currency unit of its status as legal tender. It occurs whenever there is a change of national currency. The current form or forms of money is pulled from circulation and retired, often to be replaced with new notes or coins. Sometimes, a country completely replaces the old currency with new currency.
Features
Tax administration measure.
Measure to improve tax compliance.
Channelizing savings into the formal financial system.
Aimed to create a less-cash or cash-lite economy.
Trace the Mind Map
First Level
Second Level
Third Level

Ans.

Topper Answer, 2019

The four features of business environment are–

Totality of External Forces → Specific & General Forces

BUSINESS ENVIRONMENT

Uncertain   Dynamic

→ Totality of External Forces– Business environment consists of all those things that are external to business firm and as such aggregative in nature.

→ Specific and General Forces– Business Environment includes both, specific and general forces. Specific forces (competitors, customers, investors, suppliers) affect individual firms directly in their day to day activities. General forces (social, political, technical, legal condition) affect business firms indirectly.

→ Dynamic– Business Environment is dynamic which keeps on changing with time whether in terms of technological improvements, shift in consumer preferences or entry of a new competitor in the market.

→ Uncertain– Business Environment is uncertain as it is difficult to predict future environmental changes and their impact with full accuracy.

Commonly Made Error

⚠ Generally, students get confused between importance and features and write same points.

Answering Tip

While learning, give special emphasis on the features and importance separately.

2. **Explain any four points of importance of business environment.** A [Outside Delhi Set 2, 2019]

3. **Explain, how does the understanding of business environment help the management in the following:**

(i) **Tapping useful resources; and**

(ii) **Coping with rapid changes.** A [OEB]

Ans. (i) Understanding of business environment helps in **tapping useful resources by designing the policies** that allow it to get the resources it needs, so that, it can convert those resources into outputs that the environment desires.

(ii) Understanding of business environment **helps in coping with rapid changes by developing suitable courses of action** to deal with changes taking place in the environment as well as with the pace of change. **2 + 2 = 4**

Long Answer Type Questions (6 marks each)

1. **'Flora beauty' is one of the leading cosmetic industries. Recently, the company's board of directors had a meeting in which all the reasons which were outside the control of the organisation were discussed. The organisation wanted to maintain its supremacy in the market. They decided to break the meeting into two parts. In the first part customers, competitors, suppliers, etc. were discussed where as in the second part the political, economic, social conditions in the country were discussed. It was concluded that company was doing extremely well in the domestic market and the client base was expanding. However, when the company's performance in foreign markets was evaluated it was found that conditions were different in different countries so the strategies adopted would have to be different. After the meeting the company was looking forward to making new gains. Identify with the lines and explain the features of business environment that have been highlighted in the above case.** A [OEB]

Ans. The features of business environment which have been highlighted are:

(i) **Totality of external forces:** Business environment is the sum total of all things external to business firms and, as such, is aggregative in nature.

(ii) **Specific and general forces:** Business environment includes both specific and general forces. **Specific forces (such as** investors, customers, competitors and suppliers**)** affect individual enterprises directly and immediately in their day-to-day working. General forces (such as social, political, legal and technological conditions) have impact on all business enterprises and thus may affect an individual firm only indirectly.

(iii) **Relativity:** Business environment is a relative concept since it differs from country to country and even region to region. Political conditions in the USA, for instance, differ from those in China or Pakistan. Similarly, demand for sarees may be fairly high in India whereas it may be almost non-existent in France. **2 × 3 = 6**

2. **'Konark Ltd.' is electronic goods manufacturing enterprise situated in Shivpuri, Madhya Pradesh. It is earning very low revenue in comparison to competing electronic goods manufacturing enterprise, 'Nova Ltd.' situated in Mumbai. Both Konark's and Nova's operations are affected directly by the investors, customers, competitors, and suppliers, which are unique to their respective locations. In addition to this, individual firms of this field are affected indirectly by the factors like**

This Question is for practice and its solution is given at the end of the chapter.

the money supply in the economy, composition of the families, the technological changes, etc.

(i) Identify and state the feature of the concept discussed in the above paragraph.

(ii) Also, state any five points of importance of this concept. A [Delhi Set-1, 2018]

Concept Applied	Importance of Business Environment

3. Parul and Sapna after finishing their diploma in management decided to start their own travel agency which will book Rail Tickets and Air Tickets on commission basis. They also thought of providing tickets within ten minutes through the use of internet. They discussed the idea with their friends Rahul and Sohan who were having experience of running business of 15 years. Rahul and Sohan liked the idea and suggested them to first analyse the business environment which consists of investors', competitors and other forces like social, political etc. that may affect their business directly or indirectly. They further told them about the technological improvements and shifts in consumer preferences that were taking place and hence they should be aware of the environmental trends and changes which may hinder their business performance. They emphasised on making plans keeping in mind the threat posed by the competitors, so that they can deal with the situation effectively. This alignment of business operations with the business environment will result in better performance. Identify any two features of business environment and any two points of importance of business environment discussed in the above situation. A [OEB]

Concept Applied	Features and Importance of Business Environment.

Ans. (i) The two features of business environment as discussed are as follows:

(a) **Dynamic nature:** Business environment is dynamic in that it keeps on changing whether in terms of technological improvement, shifts in consumer preferences or entry of new competition in the market.

(b) **Inter-relatedness:** Different elements or parts of business environment are closely interrelated. For example, increased life expectancy of people and increased awareness for health care have increased the demand for many health products and services like soft drinks, fat-free cooking oil, and health resorts. New health products and services have, in turn, changed people's life styles.

(ii) The two points of importance of business environment are:

(a) **It enables the firm to identify opportunities and getting the first mover advantage:** Opportunities refer to the positive external trends or changes that will help a firm to improve its performance. Environment provides numerous opportunities for business success. Early identification of opportunities helps an enterprise to be the first to exploit them instead of losing them to competitors. For example, Maruti Udyog became the leader in the small car market because it was the first to recognise the need for small cars in an environment of rising petroleum prices and a large middle class population in India.

(b) **It helps the firm to identify threats and early warning signals:** Threats refer to the external environment trends and changes that will hinder a firm's performance. Besides opportunities, environment happens to be the source of many threats. Environmental awareness can **help managers to** identify various threats on time and serve as an early warning signal. For example, if an Indian firm finds that a foreign multinational is entering the Indian market with new substitutes, it should act as a warning signal. On the basis of this information, the Indian firms can prepare themselves to meet the threat by adopting such measures as improving the quality of the product, reducing cost of production, engaging in aggressive advertising, and so on.

(3 + 3 = 6)

TOPIC-2 Dimensions of Business Environment

Concepts Covered:

- Dimensions of Business Environment-Economic, Social, Technological, Political and Legal.
- Demonetisation - concept and features.

Revision Notes

(i) **Social Environment:** It includes forces such as customs, traditions, social expectations, literacy rate, etc. [Board, 2019]

Example-1

Social Environment as a shift towards healthier lifestyles may create opportunities for companies producing organic or health-focused products.

(ii) **Economic Environment:** It includes factors such as inflation rates, interest rates, stock market indices, etc.

Example-2

A company operating in a country experiencing inflation and economic downturns might face challenges in pricing its products and managing costs.

This Question is for practice and its solution is given at the end of the chapter.

(iii) Technological Environment: It includes forces related to scientific improvements and innovations in the methods of production and techniques of operating a business. [Board, 2023]

Scan this
Dimensions of Business Environment

Example-3

The rise of e-commerce has transformed the retail industry, requiring traditional brick-and-mortar stores to adapt or face challenges.

(iv) Political Environment: It includes political conditions such as general stability of the ruling party, government ideologies, values and practices of the ruling party, etc.

(v) Legal Environment: It includes various legislations passed by the Government, administrative orders, court judgments, etc. [Board, 2023]

Example-4

Industries heavily regulated by specific laws, such as healthcare or finance, require businesses to ensure compliance. Changes in regulations can necessitate adjustments in business practices.

- **Demonetisation:** Demonetisation is the act of stripping a currency unit of its status as legal tender. It occurs whenever there is a change of national currency. The current form or forms of money is pulled from circulation and retired, often to be replaced with new notes or coins. Sometimes, a country completely replaces the old currency with new currency.
- **Features of demonetisation:**

(i) Demonetisation is viewed as a tax administration measure.

(ii) Demonetisation is also interpreted as a measure to improve tax compliance.

(iii) Demonetisation also lead to channelising savings into the formal financial system.

(iv) Demonetisation is aimed to create a less-cash or cash-lite economy.

AMAZING FACTS

Demonetisation across the world

(i) In 1873, USA: Silver coins were demonetised resulting in 5 years economic depression. As a result, silver was demonetised in 1878.

(ii) In 2002, Europe: German Marc, French Franc, and Italian Lira were demonetised in favour of Euro issued by European Union to facilitate trade.

(iii) In 2015, Zimbabwe: Zimbabwean Dollar were demonetised in favour of US Dollar, Botswana Pula and South African Rand.

History of Demonetisation in India.

(i) On 12/01/1946: All notes of denominations of ₹ 500 and ₹ 1,000 were demonetised with a time limit of 10 days to exchange demonetised notes. Its purpose was to catch tax evaders.

(ii) On 16/01/1978: All notes of denominations of ₹ 1,000, ₹ 5,000 and ₹ 10,000 were demonetised with a time limit of 3 days to exchange demonetised notes. Its purpose was to catch corrupt leaders and officials in predecessor governments.

(iii) On 08/11/2016: All notes of denominations of ₹ 500 and ₹ 1,000 were demonetised with a time limit of 50 days to exchange demonetised notes from banks and settle payments against utility services.

KEY TERMS

Inflation: Decline in the purchasing power of a currency over a period of time.

Stock Market: Stock market refers to public markets that exist for issuing, buying and selling stocks that trade on a stock exchange or over the counter.

SUBJECTIVE TYPE QUESTIONS

Short Answer Type Questions-I (3 marks each)

1. Define Demonetisation. R [OEB]

Ans. Demonetisation is the process of detaching a currency unit from its status as legal tender in the country. This process results in total or partial change in the existing national currency where the present currency unit in circulation is pulled off and new currency unit is circulated. 3

2. Advertisements of cold drinks must inform the potential buyer that the product if taken beyond a particular limit can be harmful to the diabetics. Identify and explain the dimension of business environment highlighted in the above case? U [OEB]

Ans. The dimension of business environment which is highlighted here is the "Legal Environment" as it comes under the legal laws to clearly state the necessary information as directed by the government. Legal environment includes various legislations passed by the Government administrative orders issued by government authorities, court judgments as well as the decisions rendered by various commissions and agencies at every level of the government— centre, state or local. It is imperative for the management of every enterprise to obey the law of the land. 3

3. Acro Ltd. is a leading car manufacturing company. It claims that it can create a fuel in its laboratory which can run the newly designed car. The company is ready to provide this fuel to its customers for free for one year provided they buy the car. Identify and explain the dimension of business environment which is highlighted in the above case. A [OEB]

Concept Applied: Dimension of Business Environment

This Question is for practice and its solution is given at the end of the chapter.

Short Answer Type Questions-II (4 marks each)

1. Mahinder Agro Ltd. started a new venture for distribution of harmless and chemical-free fertiliser vegetables. They conducted a survey to find out consumer preferences for such vegetables. They found that most of the consumers were concerned about the harmful chemicals being used in growing the vegetables. They found out that 90% of the households were searching for alternatives. The company contacted a group of agricultural experts to lay down the procedure for growing the vegetables by the farmers. They decided to train the farmers in new technology to grow chemical-free vegetables according to new innovative methods. The experts also suggested soil management techniques through which farmers would be able to create an abundant and lasting harvest.

Identify and explain the two dimensions of business environment highlighted in the above para.

A [Delhi Set-1, 2, 3, 2019]

OR

With change in the consumption habits of people, Neelesh, who was running a sweets shop shifted to chocolate business. On the eve of Diwali, he offered chocolates in attractive packages at reasonable prices. He anticipated huge demand and created a website "chocolove.com" for taking orders online. He got a lot of orders online and earned huge profit by selling chocolates.

Identify and explain any two the dimensions of business environment discussed in the above case.

A [OEB]

Ans. Dimensions of business environment highlighted above are:

(i) Social Dimension: Social Environment includes social forces like customs and traditions, values, social trends and society's expectation from business.

(ii) Technological Dimension: Technological Environment of business includes forces relating to scientific improvements and innovations which provide new ways of producing goods and services and new methods and techniques of operating a business.

[Marking Scheme, Delhi, 2019] 2 + 2 = 4

2. A recent rate cut in the interest on loans announced by the banks encouraged Amit, a science student of Progressive School, to take a loan from State Bank of India to experiment and develop cars to be powered by fuel produced from garbage. He developed such a car and exhibited it in the Science Fair organised by the Directorate of Education. He was awarded first prize for his invention.

Identify and explain the dimensions of business environment discussed in the above case. A [OEB]

Ans. Dimensions of Business Environment:

(i) Economic environment: Economic environment refers to factors and forces concerning means of production and distribution of wealth.

OR

Economic environment refers to factors like interest rates, inflation rates and changes in disposable income of people, etc. which have an impact on business enterprise.

(ii) Technological environment: Technological environment of business includes forces relating to scientific improvements and innovations which provide new ways of producing goods and services and new methods and techniques of operating a business.

2 + 2 = 4

Long Answer Type Questions-I (6 marks each)

1. With rapid advancements in the field of replacing manual work with machines, a robot named 'Sujan' has been invented and developed and is likely to get the citizenship of the country of its origin.

It has led to a stage where machines are being used in place of human beings. 'Sujan' is doing all types of work whether routine or hazardous and even answering the queries of people. However, this issue has to be carefully looked into keeping in mind the consumer attitude towards product innovations, problem of unemployment and its impact on the quality of life. Through the orders and decisions of various commissions and agencies at Centre, State or local level, the Indian Government is playing a very significant role in balancing the use of human and machine power.

Various dimensions of business environment are being discussed in the above para. By quoting the lines from the above identify and explain any three dimensions. A [Comptt. Delhi Set-1, 2, 3, 2018]

Ans. (i) Technological Environment

'With rapid advancements in the field of replacing manual work with machines, a robot named 'Sujan' has been invented and developed'.

Technological Environment includes forces relating to scientific improvements and innovations which provide new ways of producing goods and services and new methods and techniques of operating a business.

(ii) Social Environment

'However, this issue has to be carefully looked into keeping in mind the consumer attitude towards product innovations, problem of unemployment and its impact on the quality of life'.

Social Environment includes social forces like customs and traditions, values, social trends and society's expectation from business.

(iii) Legal environment

'Through the orders and decisions of various commissions and agencies at Centre, State or local level the Indian Government is playing a very significant role in balancing the use of human and machine power.'

Legal environment includes various legislations passed by the Government, administrative orders issued by government authorities, court judgments as well as the decisions rendered by various commissions and agencies at every level of the government; Centre, State or Local.

2×3=6 [Marking Scheme, Delhi, 2018]

2. The State Government of Gujarat in 2012 had made it mandatory for hostels and canteens in

educational institutions to secure the Food Safety and Standards Authority of India (FSSAI) licence to ensure food safety. As the educational institutions also get categorised as food business operators in the event of the annual turnover of the hostels, they run exceeding ₹ 15 lakh per annum. Identify and explain the various dimensions of business environment being referred to here. A [OEB]

Ans. (i) Political: Political environment includes political conditions such as general stability and peace in the country and specific attitudes that elected government representatives hold towards business.

The significance of political conditions in business success lies in the predictability of business activities under stable political conditions.

(ii) Legal: Legal environment includes various legislations passed by the Government administrative orders issued by government authorities, court judgments as well as the decisions rendered by various commissions and agencies at every level of the government—centre, state or local. **3+3=6**

COMPETENCY BASED QUESTIONS

Objective Type Questions

[A] Multiple Choice Questions

1. A few years ago, people had to go to the railway station in order to book train tickets for their travel. Now, they can sit at home and get information about all the trains running between two stations, check the availability of seats, and book the tickets. This is an example of change in which of the following dimensions of business environment?

(A) Technological environment
(B) Social environment
(C) Political environment
(D) Economic environment R [CFPQ 2023]

Ans. Option (A) is correct.

Explanation: The shift from physically visiting the railway station to book train tickets to the convenience of online booking and information retrieval reflects a change in the technological environment. This change is driven by advancements in technology, particularly the internet, making the process more efficient and accessible.

[Marking Scheme, CFPQ 2023]

2. Startup 20 India Chairperson Chintan Vaishnav the G20 startup group's goal of pushing for a $1 trillion investment in the global startup ecosystem. Which of the following dimensions of the business environment will this goal most likely influence?

(A) Fiscal policy of the government
(B) Foreign policy of the government
(C) Foreign trade policy of the government
(D) Foreign exchange policy of the government

[APQ 2023-24]

Ans. Option (B) is correct.

Explanation: If the goal of pushing for a $1 trillion investment in the global startup ecosystem is more likely to influence the foreign policy of the government, it suggests that governments might align their diplomatic strategies to attract foreign investments in startups. This can involve creating favorable favourable diplomatic relationships, trade agreements, or policies that attract global investors to the country's startup ecosystem.

[Marking Scheme, APQ 2023-24]

3. With the advent of 'Talk GPT, the Information Technology industry, companies have started investing in Artificial Intelligence to fulfil the expectations of the customers. Largely the customers are showing a positive attitude to the new Artificial Intelligence-based Talkbot'. Identify the dimensions of the business environment being referred to here.

(A) Social and economic environment
(B) Technological and social environment
(C) Economic and technological environment
(D) Legal and social environment [APQ 2023-24]

Ans. Option (B) is correct.

Explanation: The scenario highlights the integration of Artificial Intelligence (AI) technology, specifically a Talkbot, into the Information Technology industry. This represents the technological aspect, referring to advancements and innovations in AI. Additionally, it mentions customers showing a positive attitude toward the AI-based Talkbot, which reflects the social aspect, indicating customer attitudes, preferences, and behaviors behaviours toward technological advancements.

[Marking Scheme, APQ 2023-24]

4. Business environment is said to be uncertain as:

(A) Different elements or parts of the business environment are closely interrelated.
(B) It differs from country to country.
(C) It consists of interrelated forces that arise from different sources.
(D) It is very difficult to predict future happenings especially when environmental changes are taking place too frequently. U [APQ 2023-24]

Ans. Option (D) is correct.

Explanation: The uncertainty in the business environment arises from the dynamic and unpredictable nature of changes that occur, making it challenging for businesses to foresee and plan for every change effectively. Rapid and frequent environmental changes, whether they're technological, economic, social, or regulatory, contribute to this uncertainty, making it difficult to predict future developments accurately.

[Marking Scheme, APQ 2023-24]

5. Demonetisation has shown a major impact on all major sectors of the economy. Choose the incorrect statement about the impact of demonetisation.

(A) Decline in cash transactions
(B) Increase in bank deposits
(C) Increase in real estate prices
(D) Increase in financial savings

A I U [APQ 2023-24]

Ans. Option (C) is correct.

Explanation: During the period of demonetisation, the real estate sector experienced a decline or stagnation in prices due to reduced liquidity in the market and a slowdown in transactions. This was primarily because real estate deals often involved significant cash transactions, which were affected by the shortage of cash in circulation.

[Marking Scheme, APQ 2023-24]

6. **With the presence of women in the workforce, there has been a shift towards formal wear, increased demand for electronic gadgets, and an increase in demand for cosmetics. The related dimension of the business environment referred to in the above lines is:**

(A) Technological environment
(B) Social environment
(C) Political environment
(D) Economic environment [SQP 2023-24]

Ans. Option (B) is correct.

Explanation: The Social Environment consists of the customs and traditions of the society in which business exists. It includes the standards of living, tastes, preferences, and education level of the people living in the society where business exists.

[Marking Scheme, SQP 2023-24]

7. **Mr. Vivek is working as the General Manager of Oshin Hotels Ltd. Mr. Vivek observed that the Government was taking a special interest in the Tourism industry as this sector is an important source of foreign exchange and employment promotion. Based on this news, the company decided to set up hotels at several tourist places. Oshin Hotels Ltd., established 50 hotels before other companies considered this issue. Very soon, this brand, Oshin Hotels Ltd., became well known in the market. Identify the importance of the business environment described here.**

(A) It enables the firm to identify opportunities and get the first-mover advantage.
(B) It helps the firm to identify threats and early warning signals.
(C) It helps in tapping useful resources.
(D) It helps in improving performance.

AE [SQP 2023-24]

Ans. Option (A) is correct.

Explanation: By analysing the business environment, the firm can get first mover advantage and can analyse the opportunities and threats before it affects the business working in the long run.

[Marking Scheme, SQP 2023-24]

8. **'Pace.' is a reputed Chartered Accountant firm that renders services to big MNCs. The Chartered Accountants of the firm are required to travel to Delhi and NCR for which they use the company's cars. The firm decided to convert its Petrol cars to Electric cars to improve the quality of life of people. Identify the dimensions of the business environment.**

(A) Political and Legal environment
(B) Legal and Social environment
(C) Technological and Political environment
(D) Social and Technological Environment

A [SQP, 2023-24]

Ans. Option (D) is correct.

Explanation: The Social environment consists of the customs and traditions of the society in which business exists. Technological environment refers to the state of technology in the areas of manufacturing, mining, construction, transportation, etc.

[Marking Scheme, SQP 2023-24]

9. **"Cartoony Planet' is a well-known indoor playground for organising parties for children in Noida. It has many play-stations and it organises various activities for the kids to enjoy. Looking at the increasing number of children visiting 'Cartoony Planet', a new indoor playground in the name of 'Tiny Tots House' came up with advanced swings, play stations, and entertainment activities near 'Cartoony Planet'. To compete with the newly opened indoor playground, 'Cartoony Planet' also added some advanced swings and entertainment activities to attract more children.**

The above information highlights one of the features of Business Environment'. Identify the feature from the following:

(A) Uncertainty **(B)** Dynamic Nature
(C) Relativity **(D)** Interrelatedness

A I A [SQP 2023-24]

Ans. Option (B) is correct.

Explanation: The business environment is highly flexible and keeps changing. It is not static or rigid which is why it is essential to monitor and scan the business environment continuously.

[Marking Scheme, SQP 2023-24]

10. **Dolma' and 'Una' were gardeners with decades of hands-on experience. They were the first ones to recognise the need for indoor gardens especially for plant-lovers living in apartments. They took advantage of this opportunity and decided to offer beautiful design ideas for indoor gardening through their innovative venture 'My Space'. 'My Space' offered creative ideas like a garden wall', 'Hanging Garden', Window Garden', 'Book-shelf garden', and many more. Since there were no competitors, they soon became the market leaders in the field.**

From the following points, identify the importance of Business- Environment highlighted above:

(A) Business Environment helps the firm to identify threats and early warning signals.
(B) Business Environment helps in tapping useful resources.
(C) Business Environment enables the firm to identify opportunities and get the first mover advantage.

(D) Business Environment helps in assisting in planning and policy formulation.

AI A [SQP 2023-24]

Ans. Option (C) is correct.

Explanation: The study of the business environment enables us to know about the opportunities available. A company that is more conscious about the changes taking place in the business environment is the first mover. It takes advantage of it by becoming the first supplier.

[Marking Scheme, 2023-24]

11. Which characteristic of the business environment is highlighted when changes are taking place too frequently and it becomes difficult to predict the future?

(A) Uncertainty (B) Complexity
(C) Inter-relatedness (D) Relativity

U [SQP 2023-24]

Ans. Option (A) is correct.

Explanation: Business environment is very uncertain as one cannot predict what will happen in the future, especially in the case of the fashion industry, film industry, and information technology. Its dynamic nature makes it all more challenging to handle uncertainty.

12. Airlines will be able to offer the benefit of lower pricing to customers on sectors/routes due to the decision of the civil aviation ministry to remove price caps from August 31, 2022. This can help an airline to do better performance if they take early decisions regarding future courses of action after understanding and doing analysis. Which importance of business environment and its understanding by managers is not highlighted above?

(A) It helps in improving performance.
(B) It helps in assisting in planning and policy formulation.
(C) It helps in tapping useful resources.
(D) It enables a firm to identify opportunities and get first mover advantage. A [SQP 2023-24]

Ans. Option (C) is correct.

Explanation: Understanding of business environment helps in tapping useful resources by designing the policies that allow it to get the resources it needs so that it can convert those resources into outputs that the environment desires.

13.

Identify the dimensions of the business environment illustrated by the picture given above in which Sapna who has joined the workforce recently is working on an accounting software.

(A) Technological and social environment
(B) Technological and political environment
(C) Political and economic environment
(D) Social and legal environment A [SQP 2023-24]

Ans. Option (A) is correct.

Explanation: The social environment includes factors like lifestyle, consumer trends, and working in the community. The technological environment includes factors like using software and machine learning.

14. The government of India made an announcement regarding demonetisation of the Indian economy on November 8, 2016 with profound implications for it. The process which put restrictions on convertibility of domestic money and bank deposits was meant to create a less-cash economy. One argument against the cash-lite economy is that:

(A) Internet connectivity is a prerequisite.
(B) More people will be introduced into the formal economy.
(C) Financial saving will increase.
(D) Tax evasion will be reduced. AE [SQP 2023-24]

Ans. Option (A) is correct.

Explanation: Cashless economy cannot function without the internet as the payments cannot be done or processed without the internet.

15. Which of the following is an element of political environment?

(A) Existing structure of the economy in terms of relative role of private and public sectors.
(B) Rise in the disposable income of people due to increase in the gross domestic product of a country.
(C) Legislations passed by the government authorities.
(D) Attitude of the elected government representatives towards business. R [SQP Term-I Exam, 2021-22]

Ans. Option (D) is correct.

Explanation: Political environment includes political conditions such as general stability and peace in the country and specific attitudes that elected government representatives hold towards business. The significance of political conditions in business success lies in the predictability of business activities under stable political conditions.

16. Business environment is said to be uncertain as:

(A) Different elements or parts of business environment are closely interrelated.
(B) It differs from country to country.
(C) It is difficult to predict future happenings especially when environment changes are taking place too frequently.
(D) It consists of numerous interrelated forces which arise from different sources.

U [SQP Term-1 Exam, 2021-22]

17. The sum total of all individuals, institutions and other forces that are outside the control of a business enterprise but that may affect its performance is known as _________ .

(A) Business environment
(B) Social environment
(C) Political environment
(D) Economic environment U [SQP 2021-22]

Ans. Option (A) is correct.

This Question is for practice and its solution is given at the end of the chapter.

Explanation: The term 'business environment' means the sum total of all individuals, institutions and other forces that are outside the control of a business enterprise but that may affect its performance. Thus, the economic, social, political, technological and other forces which operate outside a business enterprise are part of its environment. So also, the individual consumers or competing enterprises as well as the governments, consumer groups, competitors, courts, media and other institutions working outside an enterprise constitute its environment.

18. Even though the political conditions vary from country to country, they impact the sentiment of an investor in the business, if the instability of the political conditions cause uncertainty and make it difficult for him to predict the future. Which feature of the business environment is being highlighted in the above statement?

(A) Specific and general forces
(B) Dynamic nature
(C) Relativity
(D) All of the above A [SQP 2021-22]

Ans. Option (D) is correct.

Explanation: Business environment includes both specific and general forces. Business environment is dynamic, *i.e.*, it keeps on changing whether in terms of technological improvement, shifts in consumer preferences or entry of new competition in the market. Business environment is a relative concept since it differs from country to country and even region to region.

19. "The increase in the demand for many Ayurvedic medicines, health products and services in the past few months, is related to the need for building immunity and an increased awareness for health care due to the spread of Coronavirus." Identify the feature of business environment being described above.

(A) Specific and general forces
(B) Inter-relatedness
(C) Relativity
(D) None of the above A [SQP 2021-22]

Ans. Option (B) is correct.

Explanation: Different forces of business environment are interrelated to each other. One component of the business environment affects the functioning of other components.

20. For the following two statements, choose the correct option:

Statement I: Environmental awareness can help managers to identify various threats on time and serve as an early warning signal.

Statement II: A good understanding of environment by business managers enables them not only to identify and evaluate, but also to react to the forces external to their firms.

Choose the correct option from options given below:

(A) Statement I is correct and statement II is wrong.
(B) Statement II is correct and statement I is wrong.
(C) Both the statements are correct.
(D) Both the statements are wrong.

U [SQP 2021-22]

Ans. Option (C) is correct.

21. Mohammad Kanjiwal, a beekeeper since April 2021 is now part of the growing tribe of at least 50 urban dwellers across Maharashtra raising bees and harvesting honey in their balconies, rooftops and backgardens. As he had been focussed on eating right the thought of domesticating honey bees to promote healthy consumption habits and seeing honey being cultivated right before his eyes was mesmerising for him. Identify the factor constituting the general environment being discussed above.

(A) Economic environment
(B) Social environment
(C) Technological environment
(D) Political environment A [SQP 2021-22]

Ans. Option (B) is correct.

Explanation: The social environment of business includes the social forces like customs and traditions, values, social trends, society's expectations from business, etc. Social trends present various opportunities and threats to business enterprises.

22. Several initiatives have been undertaken by the government of India to encourage domestic manufacturing and export of defence equipment. 'Make in India' in defence, was one such scheme launched by the government to encourage companies across the world to manufacture defence products in India.

To which dimension of business environment does the above case relates to?

(A) Economic environment
(B) Legal environment
(C) Political environment
(D) Social environment A [SQP 2021-22]

Ans. Option (C) is correct.

Explanation: The "Make in India" initiative in defence, launched by the government of India, signifies a strategic decision taken at the political level to encourage domestic manufacturing and export of defence equipment. This strategy uses government policies, legislation, and diplomacy to entice foreign businesses to invest in Indian defence product manufacture.

23. "The nature of the relationship of our country with foreign countries", is a major element of which of the following components of business environment?

(A) Social Environment
(B) Legal Environment
(C) Political Environment
(D) Economic Environment U [SQP 2021-22]

Ans. Option (C) is correct.

24. As part of regulations to be followed by advertisers, the advertisement for a new brand of baby food for infants provides important information for potential buyers that it is "Not recommended for infants under the age of four months". Which dimension of the business environment is highlighted in the above statement?

(A) Social Environment
(B) Legal Environment
(C) Political Environment
(D) Economic Environment A [SQP 2021-22]

Ans. Option (B) is correct.

Explanation: Legal environment includes various legislations passed by the Government administrative orders issued by government authorities, court judgments as well as the decisions rendered by various commissions and agencies at every level of the government— centre, state or local. Impact of legal environment can be illustrated with the help of government regulations to protect consumer's interests.

25. India has launched its most advanced Geo-imaging satellite which will allow better monitoring of the subcontinent, including its borders with neighbouring countries, by imaging the country 4-5 times a day. The satellite is capable of near real time monitoring of floods and cyclones. The factor constituting the business environment being discussed above is:

(A) Social environment
(B) Economic environment
(C) Technological environment
(D) Political environment U [SQP 2021-22]

Ans. Option (C) is correct.

Explanation: Technological environment includes forces relating to scientific improvements and innovations which provide new ways of producing goods and services and new methods and techniques of operating a business.

26. Aiming to revive Jammu and Kashmir's attraction as a top location for film shooting the J&K film policy, 2021 offers a host of incentives to the filmmakers, such as subsidies and low long term interest rates, for films with patriotic and certain other themes shot in J&K, for giving work opportunities to local artistes, etc. This will have an impact on business enterprises in the state. Which component of business environment is highlighted above?

(A) Specific and general forces
(B) Technological environment
(C) Economic environment
(D) Totality of external forces A [SQP 2021-22]

Ans. Option (C) is correct.

Explanation: Interest rates, inflation rates, changes in disposable income of people, stock market indices and the value of rupee are some of the economic factors that can affect management practices in a business enterprise.

27. "Even after opening up of the Indian economy in 1991 foreign companies found it extremely difficult to cut through the bureaucratic red tape to get permits for doing business in India, which created a negative impact on business."

Identify the dimension of the business environment which led to creation of the negative impact on business.

(A) Social Environment
(B) Technological Environment
(C) Political Environment
(D) Legal Environment  A [SQP 2021]

28. Match the following.

Column I	Column II
(1) Payment through e-wallets	(a) Economic environment
(2) Rise in inflation	(b) Political environment
(3) Attitude of government towards business	(c) Legal environment
(4) Statutory warning on advertisement	(d) Technological environment

(A) a, b, c, d (B) b, d, c, a
(C) d, a, b, c (D) c, a, b, d U [OEB]

Ans. Option (C) is correct.

29. Statement I: Gross domestic product of an economy is an example of economic environment.

Statement II: Attitude of government towards different groups of societies is an example of political environment.

Choose the correct option from options given below:

(A) Statement I is correct and statement II is wrong.
(B) Statement II is correct and statement I is wrong.
(C) Both the statements are correct.
(D) Both the statements are wrong. [OEB]

Ans. Option (C) is correct.

30. 'Digilocker' is a flagship initiative of 'Ministry of Electronics and IT,' Government of India. It aims at digital empowerment of the citizens by providing access to authentic digital documents such as academic certificates issued by different Examination Boards, Driving Licenses, Vehicle registrations, etc. in a digital format. The above paragraph discusses a few dimensions of the Business Environment. Identify the correct dimensions from the following:

(A) Economic Environment and Technological Environment
(B) Social Environment and Economic Environment
(C) Social Environment and Political Environment
(D) Political Environment and Technological Environment. AI AE [SQP 2023-24]

Ans. Option (D) is correct.

Explanation: The political environment comprises those elements that are related to government affairs in the type of government in power. The technological environment refers to external factors in technology that impact business operations. Changes in technology affect how a company will do business. A business may have to dramatically change its operating strategy as a result of changes in the technological environment.

[Marking Scheme, SQP 2023-24]

31. Which of the following items is a component of the economic environment?

(A) Expansion of transportation and communication services in Delhi.
(B) Facility of booking train tickets, through mobile apps.

This Question is for practice and its solution is given at the end of the chapter.

(C) Restriction on 15-year-old petrol vehicles plying on roads in Delhi.
(D) The Haryana Government's announcement of free bus rides for females on the occasion of Rakshabandhan.

A I R [Outside Delhi Set-1, 2023]

Ans. Option (A) is correct.

Explanation: The facility to book train tickets through mobile apps is a technological environment component. So, option B is incorrect. Option C is incorrect, as Restriction on a 15-year-old petrol vehicle is an ecological environment component. Option D is incorrect, as the Haryana Government's announcement is a political environment component.

[Marking Scheme, OD 2023]

32. With a revolution taking place in the manufacturing of mobile phones with super-class cameras, the business of cameras in the consumer market has taken a hit. Studies show that mobile phone photography has devastated the camera industry. The dimension of the business environment highlighted in the above case is:

(A) Economic Environment
(B) Technological Environment
(C) Social Environment
(D) Political Environment

[Outside Delhi Set-1, 2023]

Ans. Option (B) is correct.

Explanation: The technological Environment of business includes forces relating to scientific improvements and innovations that provide new ways of producing goods and services and new methods and techniques of operating a business.

[Marking Scheme, OD 2023]

33. Bhrama & Co. has come up with special offers for its customers for Diwali. Their marketing and graphics team has designed a pamphlet to be shared with the customers on social media. Which dimension of the business environment does this situation cover?

(A) Legal and social environment
(B) Political and social environment
(C) Technological and legal environment
(D) Technological and social environment

[SQP 2023-24]

Ans. Option (D) is correct.

Explanation: As the religious festival is targeted, the aspect of the business environment is Social. As the graphics team is involved as well as the target is through social media, the technological dimension of the business environment is targeted here.

[Marking Scheme, SQP 2023-24]

34. "Global stock indices have fallen on account of the pandemic."
The above statement DIRECTLY falls under which dimension of the business environment?

(A) Legal environment
(B) Social environment
(C) Economic environment
(D) Technological environment

U [SQP 2023-24]

Ans. Option (C) is correct.

Explanation: Economic environment refers to factors like interest rates, inflation rates, and changes in disposable income of people, etc. which have an impact on business enterprise.

[Marking Scheme, SQP 2023-24]

35. Which characteristic of the business environment is highlighted when changes are taking place too frequently and it becomes difficult to predict the future?

(A) Uncertainty (B) Complexity
(C) Inter-relatedness (D) Relativity

U [SQP 2023-24]

Ans. Option (A) is correct.

Explanation: The business environment is very uncertain as one cannot predict what will happen in the future, especially in the case of the fashion industry, film industry, and information technology. Its dynamic nature makes it all more challenging to handle uncertainty.

[Marking Scheme, SQP 2023-24]

36.

Identify the dimensions of the business environment illustrated by the picture given above. [OEB]

(A) Technological (B) Social
(C) Political (D) Legal

Ans. Option (A) is correct.

Explanation: Technological environment includes forces related to scientific improvements and innovations in the methods of production and techniques of operating a business.

[B] Assertion & Reason

Directions: In the following questions, a statement of assertion (A) is followed by a statement of reason (R). Mark the correct choice as:

(A) Both assertion (A) and reason (R) are true and reason (R) is the correct explanation of assertion (A).
(B) Both assertion (A) and reason (R) are true but reason (R) is not the correct explanation of assertion (A).
(C) Assertion (A) is true but reason (R) is false.
(D) Assertion (A) is false but reason (R) is true.

1. Assertion (A): Changes in fashions and tastes of consumers may shift demand in the market from existing products to new ones.
Reason (R): Business environment is dynamic, *i.e.*, it keeps on changing in consumer preferences. A [OEB]

Ans. Option (A) is correct.

Explanation: Business environment is dynamic, *i.e.*, it keeps on changing whether in terms of technological improvement, shifts in consumer preferences or entry of new competition in the market.

2. **Assertion (A):** Business environment includes both specific and general forces.

Reason (R): General forces such as investors, customers, competitors and suppliers affect individual enterprises directly and immediately in their day-to-day working. R [OEB]

Concept Applied	Features of Business Environment

Ans. Option (C) is correct.

Explanation: General forces such as social, political, legal and technological conditions have an impact on all business enterprises and thus, may affect an individual firm only indirectly.

3. **Assertion (A):** Interest rates, taxes, inflation, stock market indices, value of rupee, personal disposable income, unemployment rate, etc. are the factors which affect the economic environment.

Reason (R): The economic environment consists of an economic system, economic policies and economic conditions prevailing in a country. A [OEB]

Ans. Option (A) is correct.

Explanation: Economic Environment consists of factors like inflation rates, interest rates, consumers' incomes, economic policies, market conditions, etc. which affect the performance of a business firm.

4. **Assertion (A):** Understanding of legal knowledge is a prerequisite for the smooth functioning of business and industry.

Reason (R): Legal environment includes various legislations passed by the Government, administrative orders issued by government authorities, court judgments as well as the decisions rendered by various commissions and agencies at every level of the government; Centre, State or Local. U [OEB]

Ans. Option (B) is correct.

Explanation: Non-compliance with the laws of the land can put business firms into legal problems.

5. **Assertion (A):** Shift in demand from propeller airplanes to jets and from typewriters to computer based word processors have all been responsible and creating new business.

Reason (R): The impact of changes in technological environment on business is a significant factor for the success or failure of that business. A [OEB]

[C] Case Based MCQs

I. Read the below case and answer the questions that follow:

The name and taste of Coca-Cola is known to almost each and every individual in India as well as throughout the world. This carbonated soft drink holds the most market share in the soft drink market and got itself a special seat in each and every gathering. The Coca-Cola Company has on occasion introduced other cola drinks under the Coke name. The most common of these are Diet Coke, along with others including Caffeine free Coca-Cola, Diet Coke Caffeine free, Coca-Cola Zero Sugar, Coca Cola Cherry, Coca-Cola Vanilla and the list goes on. It has capitalised on each and every opportunity to market itself effectively and place itself in the middle of every gathering. The main reason for such an outstanding placement of product goes to the way they have established the connection between every occasion and the need for Coke to be present there, product design and creative advertising. [OEB]

1. **In the context of the above given case, identify one valid importance of business environment.**

(A) Enables a firm to identify opportunities and getting first mover advantage
(B) Uncertainty
(C) Delay in action
(D) Pervasive function

Ans. Option (A) is correct.

Explanation: Environment provides numerous opportunities for business success. Early identification of opportunities helps an enterprise to be the first to exploit them instead of losing them to competitors.

2. **Identify the feature of business environment which the Coca-Cola Company managed to get in their favour.**

(A) Complex
(B) Specific and general forces
(C) Futuristic
(D) Mental Exercise

Ans. Option (B) is correct.

Explanation: Business environment includes both specific and general forces. Specific forces (such as investors, customers, competitors and suppliers) affect individual enterprises directly and immediately in their day-to-day working. General forces (such as social, political, legal and technological conditions) have an impact on all business enterprises and thus, may affect an individual firm only indirectly.

3. **Which business environment did Coca-Cola majorily tap into ?**

(A) Technological Environment
(B) Social Environment
(C) Political Environment
(D) Economic Environment

Ans. Option (B) is correct.

Explanation: The social environment of business includes the social forces like customs and traditions, values, social trends, society's expectations from business, etc.

4. **Which dimension of the business environment does Coca-Cola's emphasis on creative advertising and effective marketing primarily correspond to?**

(A) Economic environment
(B) Technological environment
(C) Cultural environment
(D) Political environment

Ans. Option (C) is correct

Explanation: Coca-Cola prioritises innovative advertising and successful marketing to align with the cultural environment of the company. Coca-Cola's marketing methods typically reflect cultural themes, customs, and beliefs, helping customers feel connected. Coca-Cola efficiently conveys its brand message and strengthens its social presence by knowing and using local subtleties.

This Question is for practice and its solution is given at the end of the chapter.

II. Read the below case and answer the questions that follow: **[OEB]**

As the government has opened up its economy to Multinational Corporations, it has encouraged foreign companies to invest in some sectors of retailing. It has also put in place new rules and regulations for FDI (Foreign Direct Investment) in the retail sector. The FDI policy allows foreign investment through two modes. It may be either under the 'automatic route' or under the 'approval route' where prior approval of the Indian Government is required for any foreign investment in an Indian company which is carrying on retailing business in India. Moreover, the policy also talks about 'Single brand retailing' like Nike or 'Multi- brand retailing' like Walmart. The argument is that customers can afford to purchase the products of these companies as their income is rising gradually. It will increase research and innovations in the retail sector which will provide new ways of producing goods as well as increase the variety of goods in the market. This will eventually improve the quality of life.

1. **"As the government has opened up its economy to Multinational Corporations, it has encouraged foreign companies to invest in some sectors of retailing." Identify which dimension of business environment is depicted here.**

   (A) Political environment
   (B) Legal environment
   (C) Technological environment
   (D) Economic environment

Ans. Option (A) is correct.

Explanation: Political environment includes political conditions such as general stability and peace in the country and specific attitudes that elected government representatives hold towards business.

2. **"Customers can afford to purchase the products of these companies as their income is rising gradually." Identify which dimension of business environment is depicted here.**

   (A) Social environment
   (B) Legal environment
   (C) Technological environment
   (D) Economic environment

Ans. Option (D) is correct.

Explanation: Economic environment refers to factors like interest rates, inflation rates and changes in disposable income of people, etc. which have an impact on business enterprise.

3. **"It will increase research and innovations in the retail sector..." Identify which dimension of business environment is depicted here.**

   (A) Social environment
   (B) Political environment
   (C) Technological environment
   (D) Economic environment

Ans. Option (C) is correct.

Explanation: Technological environment includes forces relating to scientific improvements and innovations which provide new ways of producing goods and services and new methods and techniques of operating a business.

4. **"This will eventually improve the quality of life." Identify which dimension of business environment is depicted here.**

   (A) Social environment
   (B) Legal environment
   (C) Technological environment
   (D) Economic environment

Ans. Option (A) is correct.

Explanation: The social environment of business includes the social forces like customs and traditions, values, social trends, society's expectations from business, etc.

SOLUTIONS FOR PRACTICE QUESTIONS (TOPIC-1)

SATQs-II

Ans. 2. Importance of Business Environment:

(i) It enables the firm to identify opportunities and getting the first mover advantages: Analysis of business environment helps to identify opportunities *i.e.,* positive external changes to be exploited first instead of losing them to competitors.

(ii) It helps the firms to identify threats and early warning signals: A study of business environment helps an enterprise to identify threats *i.e.,* negative signals that hinders business performance and take appropriate preventive measures on time.

(iii) It helps in tapping useful resources: A business enterprise depends on environment as a source of input like raw materials, labour, etc. and as an outlet for output *i.e.,* goods, services, taxes, etc. Analysis of environment helps to get resources that it needs to be converted into outputs which an environment desires.

(iv) It helps in coping with rapid changes: It helps the management to become more sensitive to ever changing needs of the customers. As a result, they are able to respond to such changes effectively.

(v) It helps in assisting in planning and policy formulation: Environmental scanning provides the basis for deciding future course of action (planning) and guidelines for decision making (policy).

(vi) It helps in improving performance: The continuous monitoring of environment and adopting suitable business practices not only improve their present performance but also help them continue to succeed in the market for a longer period. **(Any four) 1×4=4**

LATQs

Ans. 2. (i) Specific and General Forces: Business environment includes both specific and general forces. Specific forces affect individual enterprises directly and immediately in their day-to-day working. General forces have impact on all business enterprises and thus may affect an individual firm only indirectly.

(ii) Importance of business environment: (Any five)

(a) It helps to identify opportunities and getting the first mover advantage instead of losing them to the competitors.

(b) It helps to identify threats on time which serves as an early warning signal.

(c) It helps in tapping useful resources so that it can convert them into output that the environment desires.

(d) It helps in coping with rapid changes in an increasingly dynamic environment.

(e) It helps in assisting in planning and policy formulation.

(f) It helps in improving performance by continuously monitoring the environment and adopting suitable practices.

(If an examinee has given only the headings, ½ mark for each heading should be awarded).

(1+5=6) [Marking Scheme, Delhi 2018]

SOLUTIONS FOR PRACTICE QUESTIONS (TOPIC-2)

SATQs-I

Ans. 3. The dimension of business which is affected here by the company's innovation is the "Technological" environment. Technological environment includes forces relating to scientific improvements and innovations which provide new ways of producing goods and services and new methods and techniques of operating a business. **3**

SOLUTIONS FOR OBJECTIVE PRACTICE QUESTIONS

[A] MCQs

Ans. 16. Option (C) is correct.

Explanation: Business environment is largely uncertain as it is very difficult to predict future happenings, especially when environment changes are taking place too frequently as in the case of information technology or fashion industries.

Ans. 27. Option (C) is correct.

Explanation: Political Environment means that the actions were taken by the government, which potentially affect the routine activities of any business or company on a domestic or at the global level.

[B] A & R

Ans. 5. Option (A) is correct.

Explanation: Technological environment includes the discovery of new methods and techniques for the production of goods and services. Technological changes make available better methods of production and that makes the optimum use of the raw material possible.

REFLECTION

(a) Were you able to understand the concept and importance of business environment?

(b) Were you able to describe the various dimensions of business environment?

(c) Have you understood the concept of demonetisation?

(d) Were you able to identify the dimension of business environment in the below mentioned line:
"Short and long term interest rates significantly affect the demand for product and services."

(e) Did you know which dimension of business environment includes forces relating to scientific improvements?

SELF ASSESSMENT PAPER - 3

Maximum Time: 1 hour **MM: 30**

General Instructions:

(i) All the questions are compulsory
(ii) Q.1 to Q.10 are 1 mark questions
(3) Q.11 to Q.12 are 3 mark questions
(iv) Q.13 to Q.14 are 4 marks questions
(v) Q.15 is a 6 marks question

Objective Type Questions [1 Mark]

1. Business environment is called dynamic because:
   (A) It keeps on changing.
   (B) It is not static.
   (C) Its components are highly flexible.
   (D) All of these. [1]

2. 

   Identify the dimension of the business environment illustrated by the picture given above.
   (A) Technological (B) Political
   (C) Economic (D) Legal [1]

3. Texo Ltd. has recently shifted their resources in manufacturing transistors from vacuum tubes as the demand of transistors has started rising. Identify the dimension of business environment highlighted here.
   (A) Technological (B) Social
   (C) Political (D) Economic [1]

4. Match the following

Column I	Column II
(1) Totality of external forces	(a) Difficult to predict future happenings
(2) Uncertainty	(b) Numerous interrelated and dynamic conditions
(3) Complexity	(c) Differs from country to country
(4) Relativity	(d) Sum total of all things external to business

   (A) a, b, c, d (B) b, d, c, a
   (C) d, a, b, c (D) c, b, d, a [1]

5. For the following two statements, choose the correct option:
   Statement I: The significance of political conditions in business success lies in the predictability of business activities under stable political conditions.
   Statement II: There may be uncertainty of business activities due to political unrest and threats to law and order.
   Choose the correct option from options given below:
   (A) Statement I is correct and statement II is wrong.
   (B) Statement II is correct and statement I is wrong.
   (C) Both the statements are correct.
   (D) Both the statements are wrong. [1]

6. For the following two statements, choose the correct option:
   Statement I: It is imperative for the management of every enterprise to obey the law of the land.
   Statement II: Adequate knowledge of rules and regulations framed by the Government is a prerequisite for better business performance.
   Choose the correct option from options given below:
   (A) Statement I is correct and statement II is wrong.
   (B) Statement II is correct and statement I is wrong.
   (C) Both the statements are correct.
   (D) Both the statements are wrong. [1]

Read the text given below and answer Q. 7-10 on the basis of the same.

ABC Corporation, a well-established multinational company, operates in a highly dynamic business environment. The business environment is influenced by various dimensions that impact ABC's operations and strategic decisions.

ABC Corporation operates in the technology sector, producing and selling electronic devices globally. In recent years, the company has faced challenges due to changes in the dimensions of its business environment. ABC Corporation faces fluctuations in exchange rates and global economic downturns. This affects production costs, pricing strategies, and overall profitability. Changes in consumer preferences, cultural trends, and societal values impact ABC's product development and marketing strategies. The company must stay attuned to these changes to remain competitive.

ABC Corporation operates in multiple countries with varying political climates and legal systems. Changes in government policies, trade regulations, and intellectual property laws can significantly affect the company's operations. Rapid advancements in technology pose both opportunities and challenges for ABC. Staying ahead in innovation is crucial, but it also requires continuous investment in research and development.

Based on the above case answer the following question:

7. Which dimension of the business environment involves changes in consumer preferences, cultural trends, and societal values? [1]

(A) Economic Dimension
(B) Social and Cultural Dimension
(C) Political and Legal Dimension
(D) Technological Dimension

8. How does the economic dimension impact ABC Corporation? [1]
(A) Affects political climates
(B) Influences cultural trends
(C) Impacts production costs and profitability
(D) Drives technological advancements

9. In which dimension does ABC Corporation navigate changes in government policies and trade regulations? [1]
(A) Social and Cultural Dimension
(B) Technological Dimension
(C) Political and Legal Dimension
(D) Economic Dimension

10. Why is staying ahead in innovation crucial for ABC Corporation? [1]
(A) To influence cultural trends
(B) To navigate political climates
(C) To meet changing consumer preferences
(D) To impact exchange rates

Short Answer Type Questions - I [3 Marks]

11. How business environment helps the firm to identify threats and early warning signals?

12. What are the economic factors that can affect management practices in a business enterprise?

Short Answer Type Questions - II [4 Marks]

13. There is a recent cut in the rate of interest on loans announced by the Banks. This has encouraged Sahil, a science student of class 12 from Global Education to take a loan from ICICI bank to experiment and develop cars to be powered by fuel produced from garbage. He developed such a car and exhibited it in the Science Fair organized by Directorate of Education. He was awarded first prize for his invention. Identify and explain the dimensions of business environment discussed in the above case.

14. Blue Bird Ltd. has recently entered the market and has opened a customised Jackets business. The company has done a lot of research on the nature of business environment in which it is doing business. The market has fragmented as there are many players, brand loyalties of the customers keep on changing, customers are more demanding and there is intense competition in the market. The board of directors very frequently have meeting and decides the future course of action. They rely on their surveys and past performances of other companies to achieve policy making and deciding future course of action. The company devotes its lot of time in understanding the external environment. With all the research the company has realised that the business environment does tend to have a lot of impact on the company so it is necessary to continuously monitor it. Identify and explain any two importance of business environment highlighted above?

Long Answer Type Questions [6 Marks]

15. "Everycard Ltd." is a greeting card making company which is flourishing well. There is a card for everyone and for every occasion. During the time of Christmas and New Year, the production and selling of cards reaches a new high as the company originates from Europe. The company exists in an environment which is democratic and there are rules for every business firm. Outside the company there are customers, competitors, government authority and almost everything one can think of. The company appears to have a promising future. However, the firm will have to understand the close relationship between various elements of the business environment around it. In the context of the case:
(i) Identify and explain the dimension of business environment.
(ii) Explain the features of business environment which are mentioned here.

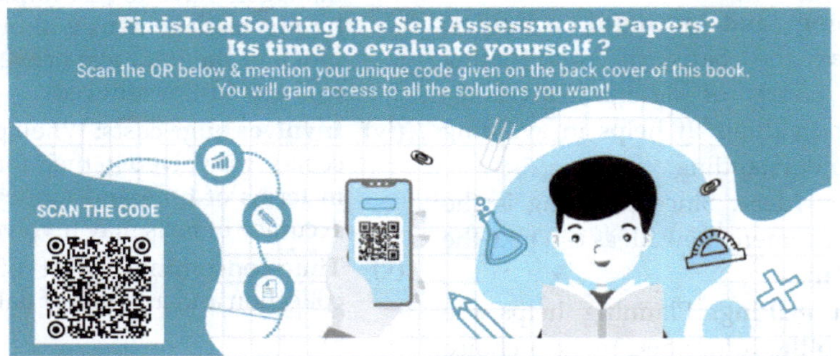

PLANNING

LEARNING OUTCOMES

After going through this unit, the student/learner would be able to:

- Understand the concept of planning.
- Describe the importance of planning.
- Understand the limitations of planning.
- Describe the steps in the process of planning.
- Develop an understanding of single use and standing plans
- Describe objectives, policies, strategy, procedure, method, rule, budget and programme as types of plans.

Study Plan
Maximum Time = 2.30 Hrs
Maximum Questions = 42

LIST OF TOPICS

TOPIC-1 Planning: Concept, Importance and Limitations

Concepts Covered:
- Concept • Importance and Limitations of planning

Revision Notes

- **Planning:** It means setting objectives and formulating an action plan to achieve them. It includes deciding in advance what to do, how to do, when to do and who is going to do it.

Importance of Planning: [Board, 2019]

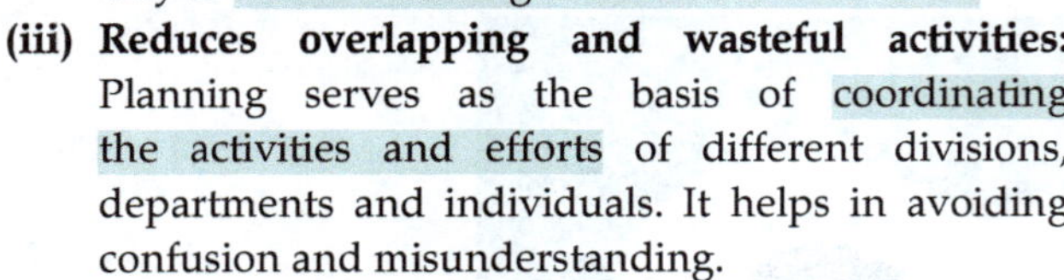

(i) Provides directions: By stating in advance how the work is to be done planning provides direction for action.

(ii) Reduces the risks of uncertainty: By deciding in advance the tasks to be performed, planning shows the way to deal with changes and uncertain events.

(iii) Reduces overlapping and wasteful activities: Planning serves as the basis of coordinating the activities and efforts of different divisions, departments and individuals. It helps in avoiding confusion and misunderstanding.

(iv) Promotes innovative ideas: Since planning is the first function of management, new ideas can take the shape of concrete plans.

(v) Facilitates decision making: Planning helps the manager to look into the future and make a choice from amongst various alternative courses of action.

(vi) Establishes standards for controlling: Planning provides the goals or standards against which actual performance is measured.

Limitations of Planning [Board, 2019]

(i) Leads to rigidity: Once a plan is drawn, managers may not be in a position to change it.

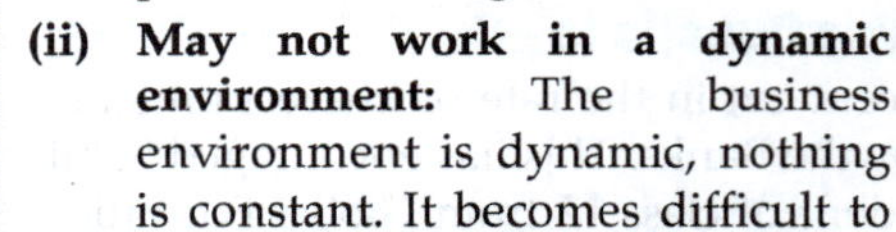

(ii) May not work in a dynamic environment: The business environment is dynamic, nothing is constant. It becomes difficult to accurately assess future trends in the environment if economic policies are modified or political conditions in the country are not stable or there is a natural calamity.

(iii) Reduces creativity: Middle level and lower level managers have to just implement the plans framed by top management without any deviations. Thus, much of the initiative or creativity inherent in them also gets lost or reduced.

(iv) Involves huge costs: When plans are drawn up huge costs are involved in their formulation. These may be in terms of time and money for example, checking accuracy of facts may involve lot of time.

(v) Time-consuming: A lot of time is consumed in collection and analysis of data, choice of alternatives, etc.

(vi) Planning does not guarantee success: Previous successful plans may not work again in the future. It is not a solution to all the problems.

SUBJECTIVE TYPE QUESTIONS

Short Answer Type Questions-I (3 marks each)

1. **Explain how planning**
   (a) Provides the basis of control
   (b) Helps in taking rational decisions U [APQ 2023-24]

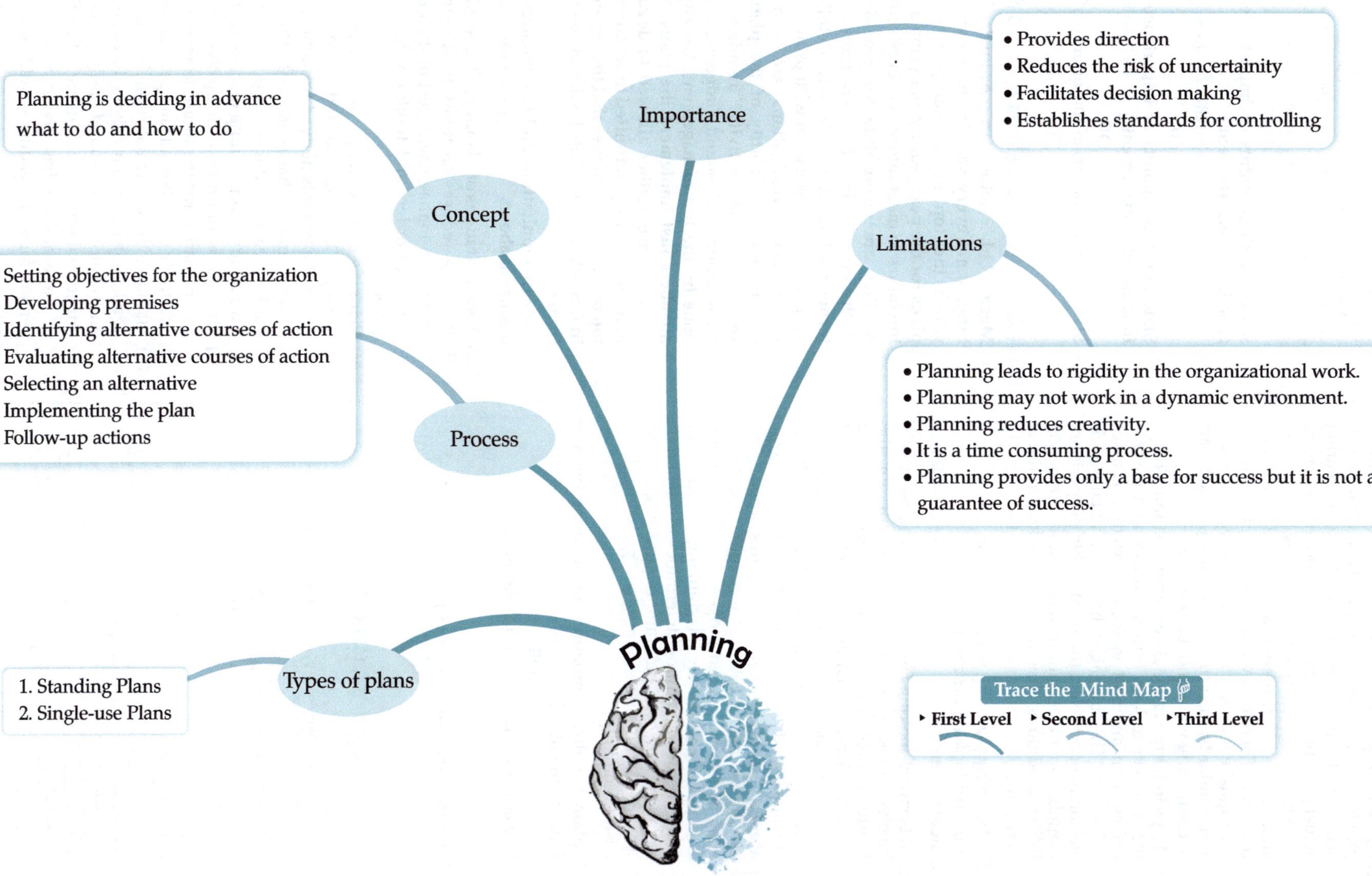
Planning
Concept
Planning is deciding in advance what to do and how to do
Importance
• Provides direction
• Reduces the risk of uncertainity
• Facilitates decision making
• Establishes standards for controlling
Limitations
• Planning leads to rigidity in the organizational work.
• Planning may not work in a dynamic environment.
• Planning reduces creativity.
• It is a time consuming process.
• Planning provides only a base for success but it is not a guarantee of success.
Process
• Setting objectives for the organization
• Developing premises
• Identifying alternative courses of action
• Evaluating alternative courses of action
• Selecting an alternative
• Implementing the plan
• Follow-up actions
Types of plans
1. Standing Plans
2. Single-use Plans
Trace the Mind Map
First Level
Second Level
Third Level

Ans. (a) Planning provides the basis of control: Planning provides the goals or standards against which actual performance is measured. By comparing actual performance with some standard, managers can know whether they have actually been able to attain the goals. If there is any deviation it can be corrected. Therefore, we can say that planning is a prerequisite for controlling. If there were no goals and standards, then finding deviations which part of controlling would not be possible.

(b) Helps in taking rational decisions: Planning helps the manager to look into the future and make a choice from amongst various alternative courses of action. The manager has to evaluate each alternative and select the most viable proposition. Planning involves setting targets and predicting future conditions, thus helping in taking rational decisions. [Marking Scheme APQ 2023-24]

2. Explain why planning is regarded as:
(a) a forward looking function
(b) a mental exercise [APQ 2023-24]

Ans. (a) Forward-looking Function: Planning essentially involves looking ahead and preparing for the future. It implies peeping into the future, analysing it and predicting it. Planning is, therefore, regarded as a forward looking function based on forecasting. Through forecasting, future events and conditions are anticipated and plans are drawn accordingly.

(b) Mental Exercise: Planning requires application of the mind involving foresight, intelligent imagination and sound judgement. It is basically an intellectual activity of thinking rather than doing, because planning determines the action to be taken. However, planning requires logical and systematic thinking rather than guess work or wishful thinking. [Marking Scheme APQ 2023–24]

3. Explain any three limitations of planning function of management. R [Outside Delhi Set-1, 2, 3, 2019]

OR

State any three limitations of planning. R [Delhi Set-2, 2017]

OR

State any three limitations of planning. R [Outside Delhi Set-3, 2017]

Ans.

Topper's Answer, 2019

Ans 9 - The three limitations of planning function of management are–

i - Planning may not work in a ~~dy~~ dynamic environment – This is so because the environment in which a business operates keeps on changing and planning may not foresee everything. Changes in social, political, technical and legal conditions take place so rapidly that planning premises of managers may turn wrong and their plans may fail.

ii - Planning reduces creativity – Planning is generally done by the top management. Lower hierarchy manager's (middle management and other decision makers) only implement the plan. They have no right either to deviate from plans or take action on their own. Thus, much of the creativity and talent inherent in them gets lost.

Ex - I've already produced 100 pens, the target. Should I produce more? – Worker 1.
CREATIVITY REDUCED!!
Are you mad?? Why to exceed target?? – Worker-2.

iii - Planning does not guarantee success – This is so because managers have a tendency to rely on previously tried and tested successful plans which may create a false sense of security and leads to failure because it is not sure that a plan which has worked before will work effectively again.

4. State any three points of importance of planning function of management. R [Outside Delhi Set-1, 2, 3, 2019]

OR

State any three points of importance of planning function of management. R [Delhi Set-1, 2017]

OR

State any three points of importance of planning. R [Outside Delhi Set-2, 2017]

Short Answer Type Questions-II (4 marks each)

1. Mega Ltd. holds an Annual Management Programme every year in the month of March in which the top managerial personnel formulate plans for the next year by analysing and predicting the future to meet future events effectively.

As they are responsible for providing direction to the organisation, facts are thoroughly checked through scientific calculations. Detailed plans are prepared after discussion with professional experts. Preliminary investigations are also undertaken to find out the viability of the plan. Since it is an intellectual activity requiring intelligent imagination and sound judgement, it is mainly done by the top management. Usually rest of the members just implement the plans. Middle level managers are neither allowed to deviate from the plans nor are they permitted to act on their own. The top management ensures that the expenses incurred in formulating the plans justify the benefits derived from them.

State two limitations and two features of planning discussed above. A [Delhi Set-1, 2, 3, 2019]

Ans. Two limitations of planning discussed above are :

(i) Planning reduces creativity as it is mostly done by the top management; rest of the members just carry out orders and think on the same lines as others.

(ii) Planning involves huge costs in terms of time and money. The costs incurred sometimes may not justify the benefits derived from the plans.

(If an examinee has given only the headings, ½ mark for each heading should be awarded)

Two features of planning discussed above are:

(i) Planning is futuristic as it involves looking ahead and preparing for the future to meet future events effectively to the best advantage of the organisation.

(ii) Planning is a mental exercise as it requires application of mind involving foresight, intelligent imagination and sound judgement. It is an intellectual activity of thinking rather than doing.

(If an examinee has given only the headings, ½ mark for each heading should be awarded)

2+2=4

[Marking Scheme, Delhi, 2019]

This Question is for practice and its solution is given at the end of the chapter.

2. In 2015, Naveen left his luxurious life in Mumbai, where he worked as a manager for Blue Birds Ltd. He shifted to Begampur, Chhattisgarh to fulfil his grandmother's dream of converting their 25-acre ancestral land into a fertile farm. For this, he set out specific goals along with the activities to be performed to achieve the goals.

Every activity was a challenge since he was clueless about farming. He learnt every activity from tilling the land to sowing the seeds. To aid farmers, he launched his own company 'Innovative Agriculture Solutions Pvt. Ltd'.

It was difficult initially as no one trusted an urban youth telling farmers about farming. But when everything was discussed in detail, the farmers started taking interest. He wanted to ensure that the future events meet effectively the best interests of the company. Through sales forecasting, he prepared an annual plan for production and sales.

He also found that the farmers grew only paddy, which was an activity of 3-4 months and the land remained idle for the rest 8-9 months of the year. He not only identified but evaluated various alternatives through which the farms could be utilised for the remaining months of the year. Through correct foresight and logical and systematic thinking based on analysis of all facts, all alternatives were examined and evaluated. He presented a plan to the farmers, where after harvesting paddy, vegetables could be grown.

The above case highlights the features of one of the functions of management. By quoting lines from the above identify and explain these features.

A [Delhi & Outside Delhi 2018]

Concept Applied | Features of Planning

Ans. Features of planning are:

(i) Planning focuses on achieving objectives

'He set out specific goals along with the activities to be performed to achieve the goals'

Planning focuses on achieving objectives as specific goals set out in the plans along with activities to be undertaken to achieve the goals.

(ii) Planning is futuristic

'He wanted to ensure that the future events meet effectively the best interests of the company'.

OR

'Through sales forecasting, he prepared an annual plan for production and sales'

Planning is futuristic as it involves looking ahead and preparing for the future.

(iii) Planning involves decision making

'He not only identified but evaluated various alternatives through which the farms could be utilised for the remaining months of the year'.

OR

'…. all alternatives were examined and evaluated'

Planning involves decision making as it involves a choice from among the various alternative courses of action.

(iv) Planning is a mental exercise

'Through correct foresight and logical and systematic thinking based on analysis of all facts…'.

Planning is a mental exercise as it is an intellectual activity of thinking rather than doing. **[1×4=4]**

[Marking Scheme,Delhi & OD 2018]

Long Answer Type Questions (6 marks each)

1. "Planning is worth the huge costs involved?" Do you agree? Explain any four reasons in support of your answer.

U [SQP 2020-21]

Ans. Yes.

Importance of Planning:

(i) **Planning provides direction:** Planning ensures that the goals or objectives are clearly stated so that they act as a guide for deciding what action should be taken and in which direction. If goals are well-defined, employees are aware of what the organisation has to do and what they must do to achieve those goals.

(ii) **Planning reduces the risks of uncertainty:** Planning is an activity which enables a manager to look ahead and anticipate changes. By deciding in advance the tasks to be performed, planning shows the way to deal with changes and uncertain events.

Changes or events cannot be eliminated but they can be anticipated and managerial responses to them can be developed.

(iii) **Planning reduces overlapping and wasteful activities:** Planning serves as the basis of coordinating the activities and efforts of different divisions, departments and individuals.

It helps in avoiding confusion and misunderstanding. Since planning ensures clarity in thought and action, work is carried on smoothly without interruptions. Useless and redundant activities are minimised or eliminated.

(iv) **Planning promotes innovative ideas:** Since planning is the first function of management, new ideas can take the shape of concrete plans. It is the most challenging activity for the management as it guides all future actions leading to growth and prosperity of the business.

(v) **Planning facilitates decision-making:** Planning helps the manager to look into the future and make a choice from amongst various alternative courses of action. The manager has to evaluate each alternative and select the most viable proposition. Planning involves setting targets and predicting future conditions thus helping in taking rational decisions.

(vi) **Planning establishes standards for controlling:** Planning provides the goals or standards against which actual performance is measured. By comparing actual performance with some standard, managers can know whether they have actually been able to attain the goals. If there is any deviation it can be corrected. Therefore, we can say that planning is a pre-requisite for controlling.

(Any four) 1½ × 4 = 6

[Marking Scheme SQP, 2020-21]

2. A2O Technology deals in manufacturing mobile phones. It plans for a successful year of production and sale this year. It has in advance given targets to all its departments and employees. The departments and employees are happy about this. They know that now they won't have to do unconcerned activities thus leading to more focused approach resulting in saving of resources. The company is thinking of starting two new plants in the southern portion of India. For this some concrete plan has to be made. The main core team of the company has decided to weigh all the options and then choose the best one. The road might be long but the company is geared to face all the challenges. In the above case identify and explain the importance of planning highlighted. A [OEB]

Ans. The importance of planning indicated in the above case are:

(i) Planning provides directions: By stating in advance how work is to be done planning provides direction for action. Planning ensures that the goals or objectives are clearly stated so that they act as a guide for deciding what action should be taken and in which direction. If goals are well defined, employees are aware of what the organisation has to do and what they must do to achieve those goals. Departments and individuals in the organisation are able to work in coordination. If there was no planning, employees would be working in different directions and the organisation would not be able to achieve its desired goals.

(ii) Planning reduces overlapping and wasteful activities: Planning serves as the basis of coordinating the activities and efforts of different divisions, departments and individuals. It helps in avoiding confusion and misunderstanding. Since planning ensures clarity in thought and action, work is carried on smoothly without interruptions. Useless and redundant activities are minimised or eliminated. It is easier to detect inefficiencies and take corrective measures to deal with them.

(iii) Planning facilitates decision making: Planning helps the manager to look into the future and make a choice from amongst various alternative courses of action. The manager has to evaluate each alternative and select the most viable proposition. Planning involves setting targets and predicting future conditions, thus helping in taking rational decisions

2×3=6

3. 'Planning provides clear benefits to organisations, but planning can also harm organisations if is not implemented properly.' Explain the limitations of planning. [SQP 2023-24]

Concept Applied	Limitations of Planning

Ans. Planning is an important management function that helps organisations set goals, allocate resources, and develop strategies to achieve those goals. However, planning has several limitations that can impact an organisation's ability to succeed. Here are some limitations of planning:

(i) Rigidity: Planning can lead to rigidity in an organisation, as a well-defined plan with specific goals may decide the future course of action, leaving little room for changes even in changing circumstances. This may not be in the organisation's best interest.

(ii) Inadequate in a dynamic environment: The dynamic nature of the business environment, including economic, political, physical, legal, and social dimensions, makes it difficult to accurately assess future trends. Planning cannot foresee everything, and changes in policies, competition, and natural calamities may upset the plan.

(iii) Reduction in creativity: Planning can stifle creativity as middle management and other decision-makers are not allowed to deviate from plans. This reduces initiative and creativity.

(iv) High costs: Planning involves huge costs in terms of time and money, including expenses on boardroom meetings, discussions with professional experts, and preliminary investigations. Sometimes, the costs may not justify the benefits derived from the plan.

(v) Time-consuming process: Planning involves identifying and evaluating alternatives, gathering information, analysing data, and making decisions based on the information gathered. This process can be time consuming as it requires careful consideration of all available options and possible outcomes. Managers may spend weeks or months developing a comprehensive plan that includes specific goals and objectives, timelines, and resource allocation.

(vi) No guarantee of success: The success of an enterprise depends on the proper implementation of plans, and a reliance on previously successful plans can lead to complacency and a false sense of security. This may actually lead to failure instead of success. [Marking Scheme SQP, 2023-24]

Commonly Made Error

Most of the students identify the heading correctly but write the wrong content inside the heading.

Answering Tip

Learn the content inside the headings by heart. Care should be taken while describing the content of the heading properly.

TOPIC-2 Planning Process and Types of Plans

Concepts Covered

• Steps in the process of planning; • Single use and standing plans; • **Types of plans:** Objectives, policies, strategy, procedure, method, rule, budget and programme.

Revision Notes

• **Steps in the process of planning:**

(i) **Setting objectives:** Objectives may be set for the **entire** organisation and each department or unit within the organisation.

(ii) **Developing premises: Assumptions** about future events are established.

Example-1

Forecasting is important in developing premises as it is a technique of gathering information. Forecasts can be made about the demand for a particular product, policy change, interest rates, prices of capital goods, tax rates etc. Accurate forecasts, therefore become essential for successful plans.

(iii) **Identifying alternative courses of action:** All the alternative courses of action are identified.

Example-2

The risk-return trade-off is very common. The more risky the investment, the higher the returns it is likely to give. To evaluate such proposals detailed calculations of earnings, earnings per share, interest, taxes, dividends are made and decisions taken.

(iv) **Evaluating alternative courses:** The positive and negative aspect of each alternative is evaluated.

(v) **Selecting an alternative:** The alternative which is most feasible, profitable and with least negative consequences is selected as plan.

(vi) **Implementing the plan:** The selected plan is put into action.

(vii) **Follow-up action:** In case of any deviations, changes are made in the plans.

Types of Plans:

• **Single-use and standing plans:** A single-use plan is developed for a one-time event or project. A standing plan is used for activities that occur regularly over a period of time.

• **Objectives:** Objectives are very basic to the organisation and they are defined as ends which the management seeks to achieve by its operations.

Example-3

An organisation may have an objective of increasing sales by 10% or earning a reasonable rate of return on investment, earn a 20% profit from business.

• **Strategy:** A strategy provides the broad contours of an organisation's business. [Board, 2017]

Example-4

A company's marketing strategy has to address certain questions i.e., who are the customers? what is the demand for the product? which channel of distribution to use? what is the pricing policy? and how do we advertise the product. These and many more issues need to be resolved while formulating a marketing strategy for any organisation.

• **Policy:** Policies are general statements that guide thinking or channelise energies towards a particular direction.

• The company may have a recruitment policy, pricing policy within which objectives are set and decisions are made.

• **Procedures:** Procedures are routine steps on how to carry out activities.

• **Methods:** Methods provide the prescribed ways or manner in which a task has to be performed considering the objective. [Board, 2017]

• **Rule:** Rules are specific statements that inform what is to be done.

• **Programmes:** Programmes are detailed statements about a project which outlines the objectives, policies, procedures, rules, tasks, human and physical resources required and the budget to implement any course of action. [Board, 2017]

• **Budget:** A budget is a statement of expected results expressed in numerical terms. It is a plan which quantifies future facts and figures. [Board, 2017]

AMAZING FACT

Running a business without a plan is like riding a motorcycle up a craggy cliff blindfolded. Yet, way too many firms (a whopping 67%) don't have a formal business plan in place.

MNEMONICS

Concept: Planning Process:

Mnemonic: Slow Driving Is Easy and Safe.

I Follow.

Interpretations:

S: Setting objectives
D: Developing premises
I: Identifying alternative courses of action
E: Evaluating alternative courses
S: Selecting an alternative
I: Implement the plan
F: Follow-up action

SUBJECTIVE TYPE QUESTIONS

Short Answer Type Questions-I (3 marks each)

1. Name and explain the type of plan which is in the form of general statements and channelise energies towards a particular direction. U [OEB]

Ans. Policies are general statements that guide thinking or channelise energies towards a particular direction. Policies provide a basis for interpreting strategy which is usually stated in general terms. They are guides to managerial action and decisions in the implementation of strategy. For example, the company may have a recruitment policy, pricing policy within which objectives are set and decisions are made. **[3]**

2. Name and explain the type of plan which provides the broad contours of an organisation's business. U [OEB]

Ans. Strategy: A strategy provides the broad contours of an organisation's business. It will also refer to future decisions defining the organisations direction and scope in the long run. Thus, we can say a strategy is a comprehensive plan for accomplishing an organisation's objectives. **[3]**

Short Answer Type Questions-II (4 marks each)

1. Give the meaning of 'policy' and 'strategy' as types of plans. U [Delhi Set-3, 2017]

Ans. Policy: Policy is a general guideline that guides thinking or channelises energies towards a particular direction. It defines the broad parameters within which a manager may function. It brings uniformity in decision making and action for interpretation of strategy. **2**

Strategy: A strategy is a comprehensive plan for accomplishing an organisation's objectives taking business environment into consideration. It provides broad contours of an organsiation's business and refers to future decisions defining the organisation's direction and scope in the long run. **2**

[Marking Scheme Delhi, 2017]

2. Give the meaning of 'procedure' and 'rule' as types of plans. U [Delhi Set-1, 2017]

3. Give the meaning of 'objectives' and 'budget' as types of plans. U [Delhi Set-1, 2017]

Long Answer Type Questions-I (6 marks each)

1. 'The pros and cons of each alternative need to be weighed.' Name and briefly explain the logical steps in the process of planning which are followed by a manager before performing the step highlighted in the above statement. AE [SQP 2022-23]

Ans. Steps in the process of planning to be followed by a manager before performing the step of evaluation of alternatives are:

(i) Setting Objectives: The first and foremost step is setting objectives. Every organisation must have certain objectives. Objectives may be set for the entire organisation and each department or unit within the organisation. Objectives or goals specify what the organisation wants to achieve. How all departments would contribute to the organisational goals is the plan that is to be drawn up. Objectives should be stated clearly for all departments, units and employees. They give direction to all departments. Departments / units then need to set their own objectives within the broad framework of the organisation's philosophy.

(ii) Developing Premises: The manager is required to make certain assumptions about the future. These assumptions are called premises. Assumptions are the base material upon which plans are to be drawn. The base material may be in the form of forecasts, existing plans or any past information about policies. The premises or assumptions must be the same for all and there should be total agreement on them. All managers involved in planning should be familiar with and use the same assumptions.

(3) Identifying alternative courses of action: Once objectives are set, assumptions are made. Then the next step would be to act upon them. There may be many ways to act and achieve objectives. All the alternative courses of action should be identified. The course of action which may be taken could be either routine or innovative. An innovative course may be adopted by involving more people and sharing their ideas. If the project is important, then more alternatives should be generated and thoroughly discussed amongst the members of the organisation. **2×3=6**

[Marking Scheme SQP, 2022-23]

2. Briefly explain the next three steps in the process of planning which the manager will have to have to follow after using conjecture about what might happen in the future. U [SQP 2022-23]

Ans. The next three steps are:

(i) Identifying alternative courses of action: Once objectives are set, assumptions are made. Then the next step would be to act upon them. There may be many ways to act and achieve objectives. All the alternative courses of action should be identified. The course of action which may be taken could be either routine or innovative. An innovative course may be adopted by involving more people and sharing their ideas. If the project is important, then more alternatives should be generated and thoroughly discussed amongst the members of the organisation.

(ii) Evaluating alternative courses: The next step is to weigh the pros and cons of each alternative. Each course will have many variables which have to be weighed against each other. The positive and negative aspects of each proposal need to be evaluated in the light of the objective to be achieved. In financial plans, for example, the risk-return trade-off is very common. The more risky the investment, the higher the returns it is likely to give. To evaluate such

These Questions are for practice and their solutions are given at the end of the chapter.

proposals detailed calculations of earnings, earnings per share, interest, taxes, dividends are made and decisions taken. Accurate forecasts in conditions of certainty/uncertainty then become vital assumptions for these proposals. Alternatives are evaluated in the light of their feasibility and consequences.

(3) Selecting an alternative: This is the real point of decision making. The best plan has to be adopted and implemented. The ideal plan, of course, would be the most feasible, profitable and with least negative consequences. Most plans may not always be subjected to a mathematical analysis. In such cases, subjectivity and the manager's experience, judgment and at times, intuition play an important part in selecting the most viable alternative. Sometimes, a combination of plans may be selected instead of one best course. The manager will have to apply permutations and combinations and select the best possible course of action. **2×3=6**

3. **"If the project is important then more alternatives should be generated and thoroughly discussed amongst the members of the organisation." Identify and explain the step in the process of planning being discussed above. Also explain the remaining steps which grey scale will have to be carried out to complete the process.** U [SQP 2020-21]

Concept Applied	Planning process

4. **Explain 'Objectives' and 'Budget' as type of plans.** R [SQP 2023-24]

Ans. Objectives: Objectives are defined as ends which the management seeks to achieve by its operations. All other managerial activities are also directed towards achieving these objectives. They define the future state of affairs which the organisation strives to realise. They serve as a guide for overall business planning. Objectives need to be expressed in specific terms i.e., they should be measurable in quantitative terms, in the form of a written statement of desired results to be achieved within a given time period.

Budget: A budget is a statement of expected results expressed in numerical terms. It is a plan which quantifies future facts and figures. For example, a sales budget may forecast the sales of different products in each area for a particular month. A budget may also be prepared to show the number of workers required in the factory at peak production times. Since budget represents all items in numbers, it becomes easier to compare actual figures with expected figures and take corrective action subsequently. Thus, a budget is also a control device from which deviations can be taken care of. [Marking Scheme SQP, 2023-24]

Commonly Made Error

Most of the students get confused with the aims and objectives.

Answering Tip

Care should be taken to describe the objectives and not the aim.

COMPETENCY BASED QUESTIONS

Objective Type Questions

[A] Multiple Choice Questions

1. **Radha started a home cooked food delivery Dabba service. Her mother, who is a great cook, decided to help her. They relied on friends and family for orders and then on word of mouth. As a step in the process of ensuring that activities are performed as per her plan of supplying healthy, good quality, reasonable food and earning profit, she decided to keep both qualitative and quantitative benchmarks towards which she would strive to work. A function of management is being discussed above. An important characteristic of this function of management is:**

(A) It is the first function of management.
(B) It is the last function of management.
(C) It is both forward looking and backward looking.
(D) It is required only in business organisations.

A [SQP 2022-23]

Ans. Option (C) is correct.

Explanation: Planning is said to be forward looking function because it makes assumptions and sets goals to be fulfilled. Whereas planning is said to be backward looking because planning is done about past achievements and drawbacks.

2. **"Uttam Ayurvedic Ltd." is an established Indian company manufacturing organic consumer goods like toothpastes and shampoos. It has planned to increase its market share from 30% to 40% in the current financial year. With the expanding market of organic products, other companies in the consumer goods industry have also launched these products with organic components. The competition in the market has increased and it was found that the sales of Uttam Ayurvedic Ltd. came down and its market share was reduced to 23%.**
Identify the limitation of planning highlighted in the above case:

(A) Planning may not work in dynamic environment.
(B) Planning is time consuming.
(C) Planning involves huge costs.
(D) Planning reduces overlapping and wasteful activities. A [SQP Term-1 Exam, 2021-22]

Ans. Option (A) is correct.

Explanation: The business environment is dynamic, nothing is constant. The organisation has to constantly adapt itself to changes.

3. **__________ provides a rational approach for setting objectives and developing appropriate courses of action for achieving predetermined objectives.**

This Question is for practice and its solution is given at the end of the chapter.

(A) Directing (B) Staffing
(C) Planning (D) Controlling

U [SQP 2021-22]

Ans. Option (C) is correct.

Explanation: Planning involves setting objectives and developing appropriate courses of action to achieve these objectives. Objectives provide direction for all managerial decisions and actions. Planning provides a rational approach for achieving predetermined objectives. Planning is concerned with both ends and means i.e., what is to be done and how it is to be done.

4. "Changes or events cannot be eliminated but they can be anticipated and managerial responses to them can be developed" is suggested by the following importance of planning:

(A) Planning facilitates decision making.
(B) Planning promotes innovative ideas.
(C) Planning provides direction.
(D) Planning reduces the risks of uncertainty.

U [SQP 2021-22]

Ans. Option (D) is correct.

Explanation: Planning is an activity which enables a manager to look ahead and anticipate changes. By deciding in advance, the tasks to be performed, planning shows the way to deal with changes and uncertain events. Changes or events cannot be eliminated but they can be anticipated and managerial responses to them can be developed.

5. Planning is closely connected with ____________ and ____________

(A) Responsibility and accountability
(B) Delegation and decentralisation
(C) Stability and security
(D) Creativity and innovation

R [SQP 2021-22]

6. "Following a pre-decided plan, when circumstances have changed, may not turn out to be in the organisation's interest." The limitation of planning being referred to in the above statement is ____________.

(A) Planning does not guarantee success.
(B) Planning may not work in a dynamic environment.
(C) Planning leads to rigidity.
(D) Planning is a time-consuming process.

U [SQP 2021-22]

Ans. Option (C) is correct.

Explanation: In an organisation, a well-defined plan is drawn up with specific goals to be achieved within a specific time frame. These plans then decide the future course of action and managers may not be in a position to change it. This kind of rigidity in plans may create difficulty. Managers need to be given some flexibility to be able to cope with the changed circumstances. Following a pre-decided plan, when circumstances have changed, may not turn out to be in the organisations interest.

7. Which of the following statements correctly explains the limitation of planning 'planning does not guarantee success'?

(A) Planning is required at all levels of management and in all the departments of the organisation.
(B) Planning involves thorough examination and evaluation of available alternatives.
(C) Relying on a previously tried and tested successful plan just because it had worked before and will work again.
(D) By deciding in advance the tasks to be performed, planning shows the way to deal with changes and uncertain events.

U [SQP Term-1 Exam, 2021-22]

8. Which step in the process of planning function of management involves weighing pros and cons of each alternative?

(A) Developing premises
(B) Identifying alternative courses of action
(C) Evaluating alternative courses
(D) Selecting an alternative

R [SQP Term-1 Exam, 2021-22]

Ans. Option (C) is correct.

Explanation: Each course will have many variables which have to be weighed against each other. The positive and negative aspects of each proposal need to be evaluated in the light of the objective to be achieved.

9. The step in the process of 'planning' which is concerned with putting the plan into action i.e., doing what is required is called:

(A) Implementing the plan
(B) Follow-up action
(C) Developing premises
(D) Selecting an alternative

U [SQP Term-1 Exam, 2021-22]

10. Ritu Kapoor has set up a bakery 'Bakes and Cakes' in Pune. She receives online orders for cakes from within the city and supplies them on the same day. She set a target that she would earn a revenue of ₹ 5,00,000 in the first year. She informed her employees about the target and asked them to contribute ideas to achieve the same.

Ritu Kapoor has performed the first step in the process of one of the functions of management. The next step to be performed is:

(A) Identifying alternative courses of action
(B) Setting objective
(C) Developing premises
(D) Follow-up action

A [SQP Term-1 Exam, 2021-22]

Ans. Option (C) is correct.

Explanation: Planning is concerned with the future which is uncertain and every planner is using conjecture about what might happen in future. Therefore, the manager is required to make certain assumptions about the future. These assumptions are called premises. Assumptions are the base material upon which plans are to be drawn. The base material may be in the form of forecasts, existing plans or any past information about policies. The premises or assumptions must be the same for all and there should be total agreement on them. All managers involved in planning should be familiar with and use the same assumptions.

These Questions are for practice and their solutions are given at the end of the chapter.

11. **Which step in the process of planning will precede the step in which the manager is required to make certain assumptions about the future, which are the base material upon which the plans are drawn.**
(A) Implementing the plan
(B) Identifying alternative courses of action
(C) Setting objectives
(D) Selecting an alternative. U [SQP 2021-22]

12. **If there is a plan to increase production then more labour, more machinery will be required. This step in the process of planning will involve organising for labour and purchase of machinery. Identify the step in the planning process being discussed above.**
(A) Identifying alternative courses of action
(B) Setting objectives
(C) Selecting an alternative
(D) Implementing the plan U [SQP 2021-22]

13. **A sanitiser manufacturing company wants to become a market leader. For this purpose, the manager follows an activity with certain logical steps. The first step suggested by him is to increase profits by at least 30% in the next quarter. What will be the last step of the activity being followed by the manager?**
(A) Follow-up action
(B) Identifying alternative course of action
(C) Setting objectives
(D) Evaluating alternative courses of action A [SQP 2021-22]

Ans. Option (A) is correct.

Explanation: To see whether plans are being implemented and activities are performed according to schedule is also part of the planning process. Monitoring the plans is equally important to ensure that objectives are achieved.

14. 

Identify the type of plan illustrated in the picture above.
(A) Policy (B) Method
(C) Rule (D) Procedure A [OEB]

Ans. Option (C) is correct.

Explanation: Rules are specific statements that inform what is to be done. They do not allow for any flexibility or discretion. It reflects a managerial decision that a certain action must or must not be taken. They are usually the simplest type of plans because there is no compromise or change unless a policy decision is taken.

15. **Statement-I:** Plans are made on the basis of some assumptions.
Statement-II: Changes in the strategies of competitors also leads to failure of planning many times.
Choose the correct option from the options given below:
(A) Statement I is true and II is false.
(B) Statement II is true and I is false.
(C) Both the statements are true.
(D) Both the statements are false.

Ans. Option (C) is correct.

16. **Statement-I:** Methods are routine steps on how to carry out activities.
Statement-II: Procedures provide the prescribed ways or manner in which a task has to be performed considering the objective.
Choose the correct option from the options given below:
(A) Statement I is true and II is false.
(B) Statement II is true and I is false.
(C) Both the statements are true.
(D) Both the statements are false.

Ans. Option (D) is correct.

Explanation: Procedures are routine steps on how to carry out activities. They detail the exact manner in which any work is to be performed. They are specified in a chronological order. Methods provide the prescribed ways or manner in which a task has to be performed considering the objective. It deals with a task comprising one step of a procedure and specifies how this step is to be performed.

17. **Match the column:**

Column I	Column II
(1) Specify what an organisation aspires to achieve.	(a) Developing premises
(2) Planning precedes other functions.	(b) Mental exercise
(3) Planning is an intellectual activity.	(c) Goals
(4) Assumptions about the future.	(d) Primacy of planning

(A) 1-a, 2-b, 3-c, 4-d (B) 1-b, 2-d, 3-a, 4-c
(C) 1-c, 2-d, 3-b, 4-a (D) 1-d, 2-a, 3-b, 4-c U [OEB]

Ans. Option (C) is correct

[B] Assertion & Reason

Directions: In the following questions, a statement of assertion (A) is followed by a statement of reason (R). Mark the correct choice as:

(A) **Both assertion (A) and reason (R) are true and reason (R) is the correct explanation of assertion (A).**
(B) **Both assertion (A) and reason (R) are true but reason (R) is not the correct explanation of assertion (A).**

These Questions are for practice and their solutions are given at the end of the chapter.

(C) Assertion (A) is true but reason (R) is false.
(D) Assertion (A) is false but reason (R) is true.

1. **Assertion (A):** Planning is futuristic.
Reason(R): Planning is concerned with the future which is certain and does not require forecast.
U [SQP 2021-22]

Ans. Option (C) is correct.
Explanation: Planning essentially involves looking ahead and preparing for the future. The purpose of planning is to meet future events effectively to the best advantage of an organisation. Planning is, regarded as a forward looking function based on forecasting. Planning is certainly important as it tells us where to go, it provides direction and reduces the risk of uncertainty by preparing forecasts.

2. **Assertion (A):** Planning is a primary function of management.
Reason (R): Planning is required at all levels of management as well as in all departments of the organisation. R [OEB]

3. **Assertion (A):** Monitoring of plans is very important to ensure that the plans are being implemented according to the schedule.
Reason (R): Regular checks and comparisons of the results with set standards are done to ensure that objectives are achieved. U [OEB]

Ans. Option (B) is correct.
Explanation: To see whether plans are being implemented and activities are performed according to schedule is also part of the planning process. Monitoring the plans is equally important to ensure that objectives are achieved.

4. **Assertion (A):** The manager is required to make certain assumptions about the future.
Reason (R): Planning is concerned with the future which is uncertain. U [OEB]

Ans. Option (A) is correct.
Explanation: Planning is concerned with the future which is uncertain and every planner is using conjecture about what might happen in future. Therefore, the manager is required to make certain assumptions about the future. These assumptions are called premises.

5. **Assertion (A):** Developing planning premises is the primary step.
Reason (R): Objectives are end results which the management wants to achieve by its operations.
U [OEB]

Ans. Option (D) is correct.
Explanation: Setting objectives is the primary step in the process of planning which specifies the objective of an organisation, i.e. what an organisation wants to achieve.

[C] Case Based MCQs

I. Read the following text and answer the following questions on the basis of the same:

Simplex Limited had been taken over by Mundhra Group immediately following India's independence. Since then it enjoys a rich record of industry presence and experience. In 2005, with the aim to accelerate growth the company had gone through several rounds of meetings and discussions before launching ERP system to attract large projects. The management had done effective forecast and critical thinking regarding allocation of resources to reduce wastage. For this purpose, the company had laid down multiple courses of action to meet the challenge of adverse situations. In 2008, the company suffered loss in many projects due to the great recession despite taking many cost cutting measures. The management had taken utmost care regarding the possible outcome and timely review of the plans to achieve the set target during that hard time. In 2010 the system implemented successfully which subsequently helped the company to execute numerous projects with precision and timeliness.
[OEB]

1. **"In 2005, with the aim to accelerate growth the company had gone through several rounds of meetings and discussions." What is the objective mentioned here according to the process stated here?**
(A) Developing Premises
(B) Growth and development
(C) Launching IT enabled system
(D) Cost cutting

Ans. Option (B) is correct.

2. **"The management had done effective forecast and critical thinking regarding allocation of resources to reduce wastage." Identify the function of management mentioned here.**
(A) Planning (B) Organising
(C) Controlling (D) Directing

Ans. Option (A) is correct.

3. **"In 2008, the company suffered loss in many projects due to the great recession despite taking many cost cutting measures." Which limitation of the management process is indicated here?**
(A) It fails to cope with sudden changes.
(B) It involves huge cost.
(C) It requires critical thinking.
(D) Need to construct multiple action plans.

Ans. Option (A) is correct.

4. **"The management had taken utmost care regarding the possible outcome and timely review of the plans to achieve the set target during that hard time." Which is the last step of the process mentioned here?**
(A) Implementation of plan
(B) Timely execution of projects
(C) Follow up
(D) To prepare alternative course of action

Ans. Option (C) is correct.
Explanation: To see whether plans are being implemented and activities are performed according to schedule is also part of the planning process. Monitoring the plans is equally important to ensure that objectives are achieved.

II. Read the following text and answer the questions given below:

Sana inherited a 20 acre ancestral land from her grandparents. She decided to venture into agriculture. For this purpose she set out specific goals, objectives and activities. Everything was a challenge

This Question is for practice and its solution is given at the end of the chapter.

because she was not aware about farming. She learnt every activity and in the process thought of assisting other farmers as well. She eventually launched her own company Agricultural Solutions Ltd. She wanted to be sure that the activities effectively met the best interests of the company and the farmers. Hence, she prepared an annual plan for production, sales and marketing through sales forecasting. She also realized that farmers were growing only one or two crops. On account of this; the land remained idle for the rest of the year. Thus, she identified and evaluated different alternatives through which the farms could be utilized throughout the year. She used her foresight and logical and systematic thinking based on analysis of all facts and examined and evaluated all the alternatives. She presented a plan to the farmers union, where after harvesting the primary crop, seasonal vegetables and fruits could be grown.

1. **"For this purpose she set out specific goals, objectives and activities." Which feature of planning is depicted in the statement?**
   (A) Planning focuses on achieving objectives.
   (B) Planning is a primary function of management.
   (C) Planning is pervasive.
   (D) Planning is continuous.

Ans. Option (A) is correct.

Explanation: Specific goals are set out in the plans along with the activities to be undertaken to achieve the goals. Thus, planning is purposeful. Planning has no meaning unless it contributes to the achievement of predetermined organisational goals.

2. **"Hence, she prepared an annual plan for production, sales and marketing through sales forecasting." Which feature of planning is depicted in the statement?**
   (A) Planning is continuous.
   (B) Planning is futuristic.
   (C) Planning involves decision making.
   (D) Planning is a mental exercise.

Ans. Option (B) is correct.

Explanation: Planning essentially involves looking ahead and preparing for the future. The purpose of planning is to meet future events effectively to the best advantage of an organisation. It implies peeping into the future, analysing it and predicting it.

3. **"Thus, she identified and evaluated different alternatives through which the farms could be utilized throughout the year." Which feature of planning is depicted in the statement?**
   (A) Planning is pervasive.
   (B) Planning is continuous.
   (C) Planning is futuristic.
   (D) Planning involves decision-making.

Ans. Option (D) is correct.

Explanation: Planning essentially involves choice from among various alternatives and activities. Planning involves thorough examination and evaluation of each alternative and choosing the most appropriate one.

4. **"She used her foresight and logical and systematic thinking based on analysis of all facts and examined and evaluated all the alternatives." Which feature of planning is depicted in the statement?**
   (A) Planning focuses on achieving objectives.
   (B) Planning is a primary function of management.
   (C) Planning involves decision making.
   (D) Planning is a mental exercise.

Ans. Option (D) is correct.

Explanation: Planning requires application of the mind involving foresight, intelligent imagination and sound judgement. It is basically an intellectual activity of thinking rather than doing, because planning determines the action to be taken.

SOLUTIONS FOR PRACTICE QUESTIONS (TOPIC-1)

Short Answer Type Questions-II

Ans 4. Importance of planning:
(i) Provides directions
(ii) Reduces the risk of uncertainty
(3) Facilitates decision-making
(iv) Reduces overlapping and wasteful activities
(v) Promotes innovative ideas
(vi) Establishes standards for controlling

(If an examinee has not given the headings as above but has given the correct explanation full credit be given) (Any three) 1×3=3

[Marking Scheme OD, 2019]

SOLUTIONS FOR PRACTICE QUESTIONS (TOPIC-2)

SATQs-II

Ans. 2. Procedure: It consists of sequence of routine steps performed in a chronological order to carry out activities within a broad policy framework. It details the exact manner in which any work is to be performed. 2

Rule: A rule is a statement that specifies what is to be done or not to be done. It is a guide to behaviour. A rule does not allow for any flexibility or discretion and prescribes a penalty for violation.

[Marking Scheme Delhi, 2017] 2

Ans 3. Objectives: Objectives are the end points which are numerically expressed, that the management seeks to achieve within a given time period. These are set by the top management and focus on broad general issues. They serve as a guide for overall business planning. 2

Budget: A budget is a statement of expected results for a given future period expressed in numerical terms from where deviations can be taken care of. It is a fundamental planning instrument as making a budget involves forecasting. 2

[Marking Scheme Delhi, 2017]

LATQs-I

Ans. 3. Identifying alternative courses of action: Once objectives are set, assumptions are made. Then the next step would be to act upon them. There may be many ways to act and achieve objectives. All the alternative courses of action should be identified. The course of action which may be taken could be either routine or innovative. An innovative course may be adopted by involving more people and sharing their ideas. Remaining steps to be carried out to complete the process are as follows:

(i) Evaluating alternative courses: The next step is to weigh pros and cons of each alternative. Each course will have many variables which have to be weighed against each other. The positive and negative aspects of each proposal need to be evaluated in the light of the objective to be achieved.

(ii)Selecting an alternative: This is the real point of decision-making. The best plan has to be adopted and implemented. The ideal plan, of course, would be the most feasible, profitable and with least negative consequences. Most plans may not always be subjected to a mathematical analysis.

(iii)Implementing the plan: This is the step where other managerial functions also come into the picture. The step is concerned with putting the plan into action.

(iv)Follow up action: To see whether plans are being implemented and activities are performed according to schedule is also part of the planning process. Monitoring the plans is equally important to ensure that objectives are achieved. **[2 + 4 = 6]**

[Marking Scheme SQP, 2020-21]

SOLUTIONS FOR OBJECTIVE PRACTICE QUESTIONS

[A] MCQs

Ans. 5. Option (D) is correct.

Explanation: Planning is deciding in advance what to do and how to do. It is one of the basic managerial functions. Before doing something, the manager must formulate an idea of how to work on a particular task. Thus, planning is closely connected with creativity and innovation.

Ans. 7. Option (C) is correct.

Explanation: Managers have a tendency to rely on previously tried and tested successful plans. It is not always true that just because a plan has worked before, it will work again. Besides, there are so many other unknown factors to be considered. This kind of complacency and false sense of security may actually lead to failure instead of success. However, despite its limitations, planning is not a useless exercise.

Ans. 9. Option (A) is correct.

Explanation: This is the step where other managerial functions also come into the picture. The step is concerned with putting the plan into action, i.e., doing what is required. For example, if there is a plan to increase production then more labour, more machinery will be required. This step would also involve organising for labour and purchase of machinery.

Ans. 11. Option (C) is correct.

Explanation: The step before developing premises is setting objectives. Every organisation must have certain objectives. Objectives may be set for the entire organisation and each department or unit within the organisation. Objectives should be stated clearly for all departments, units and employees. They give direction to all departments. If the end result is clear it becomes easier to work towards the goal.

Ans. 12. Option (D) is correct.

Explanation: This is the step where other managerial functions also come into the picture. The step is concerned with putting the plan into action, i.e., doing what is required. For example, if there is a plan to increase production then more labour, more machinery will be required. This step would also involve organising for labour and purchase of machinery.

[B] A & R

Ans 2. Option (B) is correct.

Explanation: Planning lays down the base for other functions of management. All other managerial functions are performed within the framework of the plans drawn. Thus, planning precedes other functions.

REFLECTION

(a) Were you able to explain the concept of planning?
(b) Were you able to describe the importance of planning?
(c) Could you identify the limitation of planning in the below mentioned line:
"When plans are drawn up huge costs are involved in their formulation."
(d) Were the steps involved in the process of planning clear to you?
(e) Were you able to distinguish between single-use plans and standing plans?
(f) Were you able to differentiate between objective and strategy as types of plan?
(g) Were you able to differentiate between method and budget as types of plan?

SELF ASSESSMENT PAPER - 4

Maximum Time: 1 hour **MM: 30**

General Instructions:

(i) All the questions are compulsory

(ii) Q.1 to Q.10 are 1 mark questions

(3) Q.11 to Q.12 are 3 mark questions

(iv) Q.13 to Q.14 are 4 marks questions

(v) Q.15 is a 6 marks question

Objective Type Questions [1 Mark]

1. Arrange the following steps of planning process in a correct sequence.

(i) Implementing the plan
(ii) Evaluating alternative courses of action
(iii) Follow up action
(iv) Selecting an alternative

(A) i, ii, iii, iv **(B)** iv, ii, i, iii
(C) ii, iv, i, iii **(D)** ii, i, iv, iii.

2. YTS, a Shipping company has been successfully carrying out its shipping business for the past five years. Last year, it rolled out a new shipping initiative during the holiday season, with the promise to deliver all packages by a particular time before the holidays. The company had an objective of increasing the profit at a consistent rate. The unexpected high demand hassled the workers and the delivery team, causing a delay in the delivery of a large number of packages. The company did not recognise the logistical difficulties in training new staff, in order to meet its delivery schedules as promised. The complacency of the company to think that a consistent rate of profit could be maintained, led to its failure. Identify the limitation of planning discussed above.

(A) Planning is a time consuming process.
(B) Planning does not guarantee success.
(C) Planning involves huge cost
(D) Planning reduces creativity.

3. Which of the following statement is true with respect to single use plan?

(A) This plan is developed for a one-time event or project.
(B) The duration of this plan may depend upon the type of the project.
(C) These plans include budgets, programmes and projects.
(D) All of the above. **[1]**

4. Mehta and Mehta Company has recently entered into the textile industry. Before setting objectives of the company and deciding what to do, the top management started recruiting the required staff and land up in recruiting more staff than what it is required in the company.

Which of the following feature of planning is ignored by Mehta and Mehta Company in the above case?

(A) Planning is pervasive.
(B) Planning focuses on achieving objectives.
(C) Planning is a primary function of management.
(D) Planning is continuous. **[1]**

5. For the following two statements, choose the correct option:

Statement I: Standing plans include policies, procedures, methods and rules.

Statement II: A standing plan is used for activities that occur regularly over a period of time.

Choose the correct option from options given below:

(A) Statement I is correct and statement II is wrong.
(B) Statement II is correct and statement I is wrong.
(C) Both the statements are correct.
(D) Both the statements are wrong. **[1]**

6. For the following two statements, choose the correct option:

Statement I: Programme provides the prescribed ways or manner in which a task has to be performed considering the objective.

Statement II: Rules are routine steps on how to carry out activities.

Choose the correct option from options given below:

(A) Statement I is correct and statement II is wrong.
(B) Statement II is correct and statement I is wrong.
(C) Both the statements are correct.
(D) Both the statements are wrong. **[1]**

Read the following text and answer the following questions on the basis of the same:

Simplex limited had been taken over by Mundhra Group immediately following India's independence. Since then it enjoys a rich record of industry presence and experience. In 2005, with the aim to accelerate growth the company had gone through several rounds of meetings and discussions before launching ERP system to attract large projects. The management had done effective forecast and critical thinking regarding allocation resources to reduce wastage. For this purpose the company had laid down multiple courses of action to meet the challenge of adverse situations. In 2008, the company suffered loss in many projects due to the great recession despite taking many cost cutting measures. The management had taken utmost care regarding the possible outcome and timely review of the plans to achieve the set target during that hard time. In 2010 the system implemented successfully which subsequently helped the company to execute numerous projects with precision and timeliness.

7. "In 2005, with the aim to accelerate growth the company had gone through several rounds of Meetings and discussions." What is the objective mentioned here according to the process stated here? **[1]**

(A) Developing Premises
(B) Growth & development
(C) Launching IT enabled system
(D) Cost cutting.

8. "In 2008, the company suffered loss in many projects due to the great recession despite taking many cost cutting measures." Which limitation of the management process is indicated here? **[1]**

(A) It fails to cope with sudden changes
(B) It involves huge cost
(C) It requires critical thinking
(D) Need to construct multiple action plans

9. State whether the given statement is true or false: "The management had done effective forecast and critical thinking regarding allocation of resources to reduce wastage." **[1]**

10. "The management had taken utmost care regarding the possible outcome and timely review of the plans to achieve the set target during that hard time." Which is the last step of the Process mentioned here? **[1]**

(A) Implementation of plan
(B) Timely execution of projects
(C) Follow up
(D) To prepare alternative course of action.

Short Answer Type Questions - I [3 Marks]

11. An established firm has twenty years of experience in FMCG industry. The company time and again proves itself as one of the dominant figures in the market. The plan for the whole year is given a lot of importance. According to the owner of the company their plans are the basic structures upon which other important functions of management rest. It is important that the plans are communicated to the employees. The top management ensures that the plans are communicated and implemented at all levels and in all departments. To learn from past mistakes is a habit of this successful company. They prepare plans for short term as well as long term where it can be seen that throughout the year the plans are prepared one after another. The industry needs such dedicated companies. The goals are specific and the activities to achieve these specific goals are undertaken. The company has planned a growth of 20% in revenue this year. Let's see how much it's possible for it to achieve it by the end of the year.

Identify and explain the type of plan indicated in the above case?

12. Vinay is a very hard working manager. After working for the implementation of his well chalked out plan he, from the start of August, decides to see in what ways and up to what accuracy has his plan been implemented. Which step of the planning process will be involved by Vinay from the starting of August?

Short Answer Type Questions - I [4 Marks]

13. Amit is working as a worker at low level in Rel Tech Ltd. He is given a target of assembling two computers per day. Due to his habit of doing things differently, an idea struck him which would not only reduce the assembling time of computers but would also reduce the cost of production of the computers. Amit's supervisor instead of appreciating him, ordered him to complete the work as per the methods and techniques decided earlier as nothing could be changed at that stage. The above para describes one of the limitations of planning function of management. Identify and explain the limitation.

14. Gautam Khanna is the CEO of a company which deals in manufacturing leather bags. He, in accordance with the other board members, decides to formulate a general statement which will be guiding the thinking of the employees. He further goes on to formulate many such statements in the next three months. These statements could be divided into two categories. Identify and explain the type of plan indicated above?

Long Answer Type Questions-II [6 Marks]

15. The CEO of a fast-growing tech company has asked the head of operations to lead a workshop for department heads on effective planning. The workshop will cover different types of plans, including strategies, policies, programme, objectives, rules and procedures. The goal is to enhance their understanding of these planning components and how they contribute to the company's success. Write six points to include in this workshop.

CHAPTER 5

ORGANISING

LEARNING OBJECTIVES

After going through this unit, the student/learner would be able to:
- Understand the concept of organizing as a structure and as a process.
- Explain the importance of organising.
- Describe the steps in the process.
- Describe functional and divisional structures of organisation.
- Explain the advantages, disadvantages and suitability of functional and divisional structure.
- Understand the concept of formal and informal organisation.
- Discuss the advantages, disadvantages of formal and informal organisation.
- Understand the concept of delegation.
- Describe the elements of delegation.
- Appreciate the importance of Delegation.
- Understand the concept of decentralisation.
- Explain the importance of decentralisation.
- Differentiate between delegation and decentralisation.

Study Plan
Maximum Time = 3.45 Hrs
Maximum Questions = 73

LIST OF TOPICS

TOPIC-1 Organising: Concept, Importance, and Process

Concepts Covered
- Concept of organising as a structure and as a process. • Importance of organising. • Steps in the process of organising.

Revision Notes

- Organising essentially implies a process which coordinates human efforts, assembles resources and integrates both into a unified whole to be utilised for achieving specified objectives.
- Organising can be defined as a process that initiates implementation of plans by clarifying jobs and working relationships and effectively deploying resources for the attainment of identified and desired results (goals). [Board, 2022]

Example-1

Suppose twelve students work for the school library in the summer vacations. One afternoon they are told to unload a shipment of new releases, stock the bookshelves, and then dispose of all waste (packaging, paper etc). If all the students decide to do it in their own way, it will result in mass confusion. However, if one student supervises the work by grouping students, dividing the work, assigning each group their quota and developing reporting relationships among them, the job will be done faster and in a better manner.

- **Steps in the Process of Organising:** [Board, 2019]

(i) **Identification and division of work:** The total work is identified and divided into various activities.

(ii) **Departmentalisation:** Work of same nature is grouped together and assigned to a particular department.

(iii) **Assignment of duties:** The responsibility of each individual or post is decided.

(iv) **Establishing reporting relationships:** Each individual should know from whom he has to take orders and to whom he is accountable. It helps in coordination among various departments.

- **Importance of Organising:** It helps in the growth and survival of an enterprise in a dynamic environment by providing the following benefits:

(i) **Benefits of specialisation:** Repetitive performance of a particular task allows a worker to gain experience in that area and leads to specialisation. [Board, 2019]

(ii) **Clarity in working relationships:** The establishment of working relationships clarifies lines of communication and specifies who is to report to whom.

(iii) **Optimum utilisation of resources:** Organising leads to proper usage of all material, financial and human resources.

(iv) **Adaptation to changes:** The process of organising allows a business enterprise to accommodate changes in the business environment.

(v) **Expansion and growth:** Organising helps in the growth and diversification of an enterprise by enabling it to deviate from existing norms and taking up new challenges.

(vi) **Development of personnel:** Organising stimulates creativity amongst the managers, which develops in the subordinate, the ability to deal effectively with challenges and helps them to realise their full potential.

(vii) **Effective administration:** Clarity in working relationships enables proper execution of work. Management of an enterprise thereby becomes easy and this brings effectiveness in administration.

Organising

- **Concept**
  - Organising is the process of defining and grouping the activities of an enterprise and establishing authority and responsibility relationships among them.
- **Importance**
  - Benefits of specialisation
  - Clarity in working relationship
  - Optimum utilisation of resources
  - Effective administration
  - Expansion and growth
- **Organising Process**
  - Identification and division of work
  - Departmentalisation
  - Assignment of duties
  - Establishing reporting relationships
- **Structure of Organisation**
  - Functional Structure
    - An organisation structure in which departments are created on the basis of different functions.
  - Divisional Structure
    - An organisation structure in which various departments are created on the basis of products, territory or region.
- **Formal Organisation**
  - Meaning
    - The organisation structure which is designed by the management to accomplish a particular task.
  - Advantages of Formal Organisation
    - Easier to fix responsibility
    - Avoids duplication of efforts
    - Effective accomplishment of goals
    - Stability of the organisation
    - Established chain of command
  - Disadvantages of Formal Organisation
    - Leads to procedural delays in decision making
    - Does not allow any deviations from rigidly laid down policies
    - Ignores psychological and social needs of the employees
- **Informal Organisation**
  - Meaning
    - Interaction among people at work gives rise to a 'network of social relationships among employees'.
  - Advantages of Informal Organisation
    - Faster speed of communication
    - Fulfils social needs of the members
    - Fills wide gaps of formal structure
  - Disadvantages of Informal organisation
    - (i) Spreads rumours
    - (ii) Resists changes
    - (iii) Peer pressure
- **Delegation**
  - Meaning
    - It refers to the downward transfer of authority from a superior to subordinate to operate within the prescribed limit.
  - Elements
    - **Authority :** It implies the right of an individual to take decisions and to command his subordinates.
    - **Responsibility :** It is an obligation of a subordinate.
    - **Accountability :** It implies being answerable for the final outcome.
  - Importance
    - Effective management
    - Employees' development
    - Motivation to employees
    - Better coordination
- **Decentralisation**
  - Meaning
    - It refers to systematic effort to delegate work to the lowest level, all authority except that which can be exercised at central point.
  - Importance
    - It facilitates growth
    - It gives relief to top management
    - It helps in quick decision making
    - It develops managerial talent for the future.

Trace the Mind Map

▸ First Level ▸ Second Level ▸ Third Level

MNEMONICS

Concept: Steps in the Process of Organizing:
I Don't Agree with Everything
Interpretations:
I : Identification and division of work
D : Departmentalisation
A : Assignment of duties
E : Establishing authority and reporting relationships

Concept: Importance of Organising:
Skip Coffee And/ Or Eat Dinner Early
Interpretations:
S : Specialisation
C : Clarity in working relationships
A : Adaptation to change
O : Optimum utilisation of resources
E : Effective administration
D : Development of personnel
E : Expansion and growth

KEY TERMS

Departmentalisation: An organisational structure which separates people into groups.

Specialisation: The process of becoming an expert in a particular area.

SUBJECTIVE TYPE QUESTIONS

Short Answer Type Questions-I (3 marks each)

1. **"Organisation is the harmonious adjustment of specialised parts for the accomplishment of some common purpose or purposes." In the light of this statement, explain the following points of importance of organising:**
   (i) Clarity in working relationships
   (ii) Benefits of specialisation R [OEB]

Ans. (i) Clarity in working relationships: Authority and responsibility are defined in a manner that every person knows whom to report to and for what. This removes confusion in transfer of information and instructions and assists in creating a hierarchical order.

(ii) Benefits of Specialisation: In organising, work is divided into manageable activities and systematically allocated. This increases productivity and efficiency of the workforce.

Consequently, on account of repetitive work, one gets experience in a particular field which results in specialisation. [1½×2 = 3]

2. **Nikhil and Sapna have decided to open a coaching centre in Pune. They have already taken the necessary steps in order to start the operations in the next 5 weeks which includes identifying and dividing the work into manageable activities as well as the process of departmentalisation. Explain the next two steps that Nikhil and Sapna have to perform as a part of their organising process.** A [OEB]

Ans. The next two steps to be performed by Nikhil and Sapna are:

(i) Assignment of Duties: This implies allocating duties to the workers as per their abilities and competencies. In order to get the best results, an appropriate match should exist between the nature of **work and ability of an individual.**

(ii) Establishing Reporting Relationships: The last step is to allocate authority and responsibility among employees so that there is no ambiguity and each person clearly knows who is reporting to whom and for what purpose. This also creates **a** hierarchical structure and improves coordination. 1½ × 2 = 3

3. **Explain the following terms in context of the Organising function of management:**
   (i) Specialisation
   (ii) Departmentalisation R [OEB]

Short Answer Type Questions-II (4 marks each)

1. **Organising involves a series of steps that need to be taken in order to achieve the desired goal. Explain the steps.** U [Delhi Set-1, 2019]

Ans. Organising as a process involves the following steps:

(i) Identification and Division of Work: The first step in the organising process is identifying and dividing the whole work into manageable activities, so that the duplication of work can be avoided and the burden of work can be reduced.

(ii) Departmentalisation: Departmentalisation refers to the process of grouping the activities of similar nature under the same department. Departmentalisation can be done on the basis of function, type of product, territory, etc. It facilitates specialisation in an organisation.

(iii) Assignment of Duties: This implies assigning duties to the workers according to their abilities and competencies. For getting best results, a proper match should exist between the nature of work and ability of the individual.

(iv) Establishing Reporting Relationships: Next step is to allocate the authority and responsibility among employees in such a way that each person knows who is reporting to whom and for what. [1×4=4]

2. **With the help of any four points, explain the crucial role of 'Organising' function in an enterprise.** [Delhi Set-1, 2019]

OR

Explain any four points of importance of 'Organising'. R [Outside Delhi Comptt. Set-1, 2017]

These Questions are for practice and their solutions are given at the end of the chapter.

Long Answer Type Questions (6 marks each)

1. JK Cyles is a cycle manufacturing company. The company was into cycle business since 1980. The company now decided to start a new branch in the Middle East. The company has recognised the amount of work to be done in number of hours. The company has found out that it will take 25,000 hours of man work and has subsequently divided the number of hours for different operations. The real challenges of the company begin here. Very methodically responsibility of the recognised amount of work has been given to different individuals according to their capabilities.

(i) Which function of management is highlighted above?

(ii) Identify the two steps of this function of management indicated above by quoting lines from the paragraph. U [OEB]

Ans. (i) The function of management which is highlighted above is 'Organising'. **[1]**

(ii) The two steps of Organising which are indicated in the above case are:

(a) Identification and division of work: The first step in the process of organising involves identifying and dividing the work that has to be done in accordance with previously determined plans. The work is divided into manageable activities so that duplication can be avoided and the burden of work can be shared among the employees.

"The Company has found out that it will take 25000 hours of man work and has subsequently divided the number of hours for different operations." **[2½]**

(b) Assignment of duties: It is necessary to define the work of different job positions and accordingly allocate work to various employees. Once departments have been formed, each of them is placed under the charge of an individual. Jobs are then allocated to the members of each department in accordance to their skills and competencies. It is essential for effective performance that a proper match is made between the nature of a job and the ability of an individual. The work must be assigned to those who are best fitted to perform it well.

"Very methodically responsibility of the recognised amount of work has been given to different individuals according to their capabilities." **[2½]**

2. Unique Style Limited has ventured into the business of ready-made garments. The following gain activities have been identified which the firm needs to undertake:

(i) Purchase of machinery and equipment

(ii) Purchase of textiles

(iii) Production of garments

(iv) Procuring finance

(v) Identification of markets for sale of garments

(vi) Sale of garments

(vii) Appointment of workers

In order to carry out the work, the company decided to appoint four managers:

(i) Production

(ii) Finance

(iii) Marketing

(iv) Human Resource

(a) Which function of management is involved in the above case? Give its meaning.

(b) Group the main activities under different departments.

(c) Enumerate the steps of the function identified in (a) above. A [OEB]

Ans. (a) The organising function of management is involved in the aforementioned case.

Meaning: The process of **identifying, defining and grouping activities** to be performed and establishing authority relationships is known as Organising. Thus, it is essentially a process which **clarifies the jobs and working relationships**. This helps to coordinate the efforts towards achieving a specific objective.

(b) (i) Production: Purchase of machinery and equipment, production of garments, purchase of textiles.

(ii) Finance: Procurement of finance.

(iii) Marketing: Identification of markets for sale of garments.

(iv) Human resource: Appointment of workers.

(c) Steps in the organising process:

(i) Identification and division of work

(ii) Departmentalisation

(iii) Assignment of duties

(iv) Establishing reporting relationships **[2+2+2=6]**

3. Fly Colours Ltd. is a profit making colour producing company. The company deals in making different types of colours used in painting. The organisation has always been systematic in its approach and due to good organising has seen a continuous increase in its revenue. Workers are given their respective jobs clearly which leads to gaining of experience since they do their respective jobs on a regular basis leading to high productivity. The organisation has many challenges and it wants to improve. There is no doubt in the lines of communication and everyone knows who has to report to whom. With the passage of time, there is more need to connect with the employees. They are the most important asset to the organisation. When managers delegate work to their subordinates they set themselves free from routine jobs and this leads to great amount of learning for the subordinates in practical situations. Identify and explain the importance of organising that have been highlighted in the above case? A [OEB]

Concept Applied: Importance of Organising

This Question is for practice and its solution is given at the end of the chapter.

TOPIC-2 Organisational Structure

Concepts Covered:

• Meaning, advantages, disadvantages and suitability of functional and divisional structure. • Meaning, advantages, disadvantages of formal and informal organisation.

Revision Notes

- An **organisation structure** provides the framework which enables the enterprise to function as an integrated unit by regulating and coordinating the responsibilities of individuals and departments.

Scan this

Functional Organisation Structure

Example-1

Smita opened her own travel agency, sometime back. She assigned work to her three employees in the following manner 'Neha, you are incharge of air plane, train and bus reservations.' 'Karan, you will take care of accommodation booking' 'Sahil, you will keep track of online queries and credit card payments'. I want regular reports from the three of you. Thus, in a few sentences an organisation structure has been created specifying lines of authority and areas of responsibility.

- The **span of management**, to a large extent gives shape to the organisational structure.
- **Functional Structure:** It is formed by grouping of activities of similar nature under one department.
- **Suitability:**

(i) Large organisations producing one line of product.
(ii) Organisations which require high degree of functional specialisation with diversified activities.

- **Advantages:**

(i) Leads to occupational specialisation.
(ii) Promotes control and coordination within a department.
(iii) Increases managerial and operational efficiency.
(iv) Leads to economies of scale which reduces cost.
(v) Makes training of employees easier.
(vi) Ensures that different functions get due attention.

- **Disadvantages:**

(i) A functional structure places less emphasis on overall enterprise objectives than the objectives pursued by a functional head.
(ii) Difficulty in inter-departmental coordination.
(iii) Leads to inter-departmental conflicts.
(iv) Leads to inflexibility in functioning of an organisation.

- **Divisional structure:** In a divisional structure, the organisation structure comprises of separate business units or divisions. [Board, 2023]
- **Suitability:**

(i) Suitable for those business enterprises where a large variety of products are manufactured using different productive resources.
(ii) When an organisation grows and needs to add more employees, more departments or introduce new levels of management.

- **Advantages**

(i) Leads to product specialisation.
(ii) Helps in fixation of responsibility for divisional performance.
(iii) Promotes flexibility, new initiatives and faster decision making.
(iv) Facilitates expansion and growth of organisation.

- **Disadvantages**

(i) Divisional conflicts over funds allocation.
(ii) Increase in cost due to duplication of work.
(iii) Ignorance of organisational interest.

- **Formal Organisation:** Formal organisation refers to the organisation structure which is designed by the management to accomplish a particular task.
- **Features:** [Board, 2019]

(i) Specifies the relationships among various job positions and the nature of their interrelationship.
(ii) It is a means to achieve the objectives specified in the plans.
(iii) Efforts of various departments are coordinated.
(iv) It is deliberately designed by the top management.
(v) It places more emphasis on work to be performed than interpersonal relationships among the employees.

- **Advantages:**

(i) It is easier to fix responsibility.
(ii) There is no ambiguity in the role that each member has to play as duties are specified.
(iii) Unity of command is maintained through an established chain of command.
(iv) It leads to effective accomplishment of goals.
(v) It provides stability to the organisation.

- **Disadvantages:**

(i) The formal communication may lead to procedural delays.
(ii) Poor organisation practices may not provide adequate recognition to creative talent.
(iii) It is difficult to understand all human relationships in an enterprise as it places more emphasis on structure and work.

- **Informal Organisation:** Interaction among people at work gives rise to a 'network of social relationships among employees' called the informal organisation.
- **Features:** [Board, 2019]

(i) An informal organisation originates from within the formal organisation.
(ii) The standards of behaviour evolve from group norms rather than officially laid down rules and regulations.
(iii) Independent channels of communication without specified direction of flow of information are developed by group members.
(iv) It emerges spontaneously and is not deliberately created by the management.
(v) It has no definite structure or form because it is a complex network of social relationships among members.

- **Advantages:**

(i) Prescribed lines of communication are not followed.

(ii) It helps to fulfill the social needs of the members and allows them to find like minded people.

(iii) It contributes towards fulfillment of organisational objectives by compensating for inadequacies in the formal organisation.

- **Disadvantages:**

(i) When an informal organisation spreads rumours, it becomes a destructive force and goes against the interest of the formal organisation.

(ii) The management may not be successful in implementing changes if the informal organisation opposes them.

(iii) It pressurises members to conform to group expectations. This can be harmful to the organisation if the norms set by the group are against organisational interests.

SUBJECTIVE TYPE QUESTIONS

Short Answer Type Questions-I (3 marks each)

1. Distinguish between Functional and Divisional structure on the basis of the following points :
(i) Coordination;
(ii) Managerial Development; and
(iii) Cost. [Outside Delhi Set-1, 2019]

Ans.

S. No.	Basis	Functional Structure	Divisional Structure
1	Coordination	Coordination is **difficult for a multiproduct company.**	Coordination is easy as all functions related to a particular product are **integrated** in one department.
2	Managerial development	Managerial development is **difficult as each functional** manager has to report to the top management. They perform similar function.	Managerial development is **easier** because a divisional manager has the autonomy as well as the chance to perform multiple functions.
3	Cost	It is **economical as the functions** are not duplicated.	It is **costly as** there is duplication of activities in various departments.

2. What is meant by functional structure of an organisation? State it's any two advantages. [3] [Delhi Set-1, 2015]

Ans. Functional structure is an organisational structure **formed by grouping of jobs of similar nature** under functions and organising these major functions as separate departments like production, finance etc.

Advantages: (Any two)

(a) It leads to **occupational specialisation** since emphasis is placed on specific functions.

(b) It **promotes control and coordination** within a department because of similarity in the tasks being performed.

(c) It **increases managerial and operational efficiency.**

(d) It **lowers cost** as it reduces duplication of effort.

(e) It makes **training of employees** easier as it focuses on a limited range of skills.

(f) It ensures that different functions get due attention.

(If an examinee has given only the heading, ½ mark for each heading should be awarded)

3. Distinguish between Formal and Informal organisation on the basis of the following:
(i) Origin;
(ii) Authority; and
(iii) Leadership. U [Outside Delhi Set-1, 2019]

Ans.

S. No.	Basis	Formal	Informal Organisation
(i)	**Origin**	It arises as a result of **company rules and polices.**	It arises as a result of **social interaction among the employees.**
(ii)	**Authority**	Authority arises on the **basis of position of management.**	Managerial development is easier because a **divisional manager has the autonomy as well as the chance to perform multiple functions.**
(iii)	**Leadership**	**Managers are leaders.**	**Leaders may or may be managers.** They are chosen by the group.

[1×3=3]

4. 'Auxy Ltd. decided to set-up its steel manufacturing factory in the backward area of UP where very less job opportunities were available. People of that area welcomed this effort of 'Auxy Ltd.' To attract people to work in its factory it also decided to provide many other facilities like school, hospital, market, etc. in

the factory premises. 'Auxy Ltd.' started earning huge profits. Another competing company asked its production manager Prakash to investigate the reasons of earning huge profits by 'Auxy Ltd.'

Prakash found that in both the companies there was systematic coordination among the various activities to achieve organisational goals. Every employee knew who was responsible and accountable to whom. The only difference was that in his organisation communication took place only through the scalar chain whereas 'Auxy Ltd.' was allowing flow of communication in all the directions as per the requirement which lead to faster spread of information as well as quick feedback. Identify and explain the type of organisation which permits 'Auxy Ltd.' the flow of communication in all the directions. **A [OEB]**

Concept Applied Concept of Informal Organisation

Ans. Informal Organisation: Informal organisation emerges from within the formal organisation when people interact beyond their officially defined roles. Informal organisation has no written rules, is fluid in form and scope and does not have fixed lines of communication. Independent channels of communication without specified direction of flow of information are developed by group members. It emerges spontaneously and is not deliberately created by the management.

Commonly Made Error

Most of the students identified the incorrect type of organisation wrong and misinterpreted the case study.

Answering Tip

Learn the different types of organisation with examples by making a flow chart.

5. What is meant by 'Divisional Structure' of an organisation ? State any two advantages. **R [OEB]**

Short Answer Type Questions-II (4 marks each)

1. Give the meaning of 'Formal Organisation'. State any three of its advantages. **R [Delhi Set-3, 2019]**

OR

State any four advantages of Formal Organisation. **R [Outside Delhi Comptt. Set-1, 2, 2017]**

OR

A.V.M Ltd. set-up its electric appliances manufacturing factory in a backward area of Himachal Pradesh where subsidies are provided by the government and labour is available at cheaper rates. A.V.M Ltd., was able to produce its products at low cost thereby generating enough profits in the first year itself. It was because of the fact that the limits of authority and responsibility of the employees were clearly defined and the activities of various departments were coordinated and integrated. The Production Manager of the company also came to know about the availability of raw material at cheaper rates from a vendor. For this, he wrote a letter to the Managing Director of the company for getting sanction. But because of procedural delays in getting this sanction and procuring funds from the Finance Manager, the order could not be placed.

(i) Identify the type of organisation that led to procedural delays and because of which the company could not get the advantage of procuring raw material at cheaper rates.

(ii) State any three advantages of the type of organisation identified in above other than those discussed in the above case.

A [Comptt. Delhi Set-1, 2, 3, 2018]

Ans. Formal Organisation refers to the organisation structure which is deliberately created by the management to **accomplish a particular task.**

It specifies the **boundaries of authority and responsibility** clearly and there is systematic co-ordination among the various activities to achieve organisational goals. (or any other correct meaning)

Advantages of Formal Organisation:

(i) It is easier to fix responsibility since mutual relationships are clearly defined.

(ii) It avoids duplication of effort since there is no ambiguity in the role that each member has to play.

(iii) It maintains unity of command through an established chain of command.

(iv) It leads to accomplishment of goals by providing a framework for the operations to be performed.

(v) It provides stability to the organisation because there are specific rules to guide behaviour of employees. **(Any three)**

(If an examinee has given only the heading, ½ mark for the heading should be awarded) **[1+3=4]**

[Marking Scheme, 2019]

2. Give the meaning of 'Informal Organisation'. State any three of its advantages.

R [Delhi Set-2, 2019]

3. State any four features of an organisation which is an aggregate of interpersonal relationships and is formed without any conscious purpose.

R [APQ Set-2, 2023-24] [4]

Ans. Features of Informal Organisation are:

(a) An informal organisation originates **from within the formal organisation** as a result of personal interaction among employees.

(b) The **standards of behaviour evolve from group norms** rather than officially laid down rules and regulations.

(c) Independent channels of communication **without specified direction of flow** of information are developed by group members.

(d) It **emerges spontaneously and** is not deliberately created by the management.

(e) It has **no definite structure** or form because it is a complex network of social relationships among members. **(Any four) [1×4=4]**

These Questions are for practice and their solutions are given at the end of the chapter.

4. Unsparked Limited started off as an electric wire manufacturer. After a few years, it also started manufacturing other electric appliances like electric bulbs, tube lights and fans. The decision-making authority rested in the hands of a few top executives. Now, Unsparked Limited is planning to diversify its operations and start the manufacture of other household appliances like food processors, washing machines and air fryers. For this, they want to change their organisational structure and introduce new levels of management which will be responsible for different functions for each of these products. It also wants to empower its middle management with the decision-making authority to help in the smooth operations of the organisation.

(i) Which organisational structure should Unsparked Limited adapt?

(ii) Write any two advantages of that organisational structure.

(iii) What should be done to empower the middle management with the decision-making authority?

[CFPQ 2023-24]

Ans. (i) Unsparked Limited should adopt a divisional organisational structure. **[1]**

(ii) The advantages of divisional organistaional structure are:

(a) Product specialisation helps in the development of varied skills in a divisional head.

(b) Divisional heads are accountable for profits.

(c) Promotes flexibility and initiative.

(d) Facilitates expansion and growth. **[Any two]**

(iii) The Organisation should move towards decentralisation. They should decentralise the decision-making authority to place it nearest to the point of action.

Long Answer Type Questions-I (6 marks each)

1. Voltage fluctuations have been common and quite high in India. They harm our electrical appliances like televisions, refrigerators and air conditioners, often leaving them in a permanently damaged condition. N-Guard Company decided to manufacture stabilisers for North India where the voltage fluctuation ranges from 220 V to 230 V. Once the demand for North India was taken care of, they decided to launch stabilisers of varying voltages from 90 V–260 V for meeting the requirements of voltage fluctuations in other regions of India also. Three engineers were appointed for South, West and East regions of India, as the voltage was different in all the three regions. Though all the engineers were appointed to manufacture stabilizers but the product differed from region to region.

(i) Identify the organisational structure of N-Guard Company.

(ii) State any two advantages and two limitations of the structure identified in the above para.

A [Delhi Set-1, 2019]

Ans. Divisional Structure

Advantages: The divisional structure offers many benefits. Prominent among these are as follows:

(a) Product specialisation helps in the development of varied skills in a divisional head and this prepares him for higher positions. This is because he gains experience in all functions related to a particular product.

(b) Divisional heads are accountable for profits, as revenues and costs related to different departments can be easily identified and assigned to them. This provides a proper basis for performance measurement. It also helps in fixation of responsibility in cases of poor performance of the division and appropriate remedial action can be taken.

(c) It promotes flexibility and initiative because each division functions as an autonomous unit which leads to faster decision making.

(d) It facilitates expansion and growth as new divisions can be added without interrupting the existing operations by merely adding another divisional head and staff for the new product line. (Any two)

Disadvantages: The divisional structure has certain disadvantages. Some of them are as follows:

(a) Conflict may arise among different divisions with reference to allocation of funds and further a particular division may seek to maximise its profits at the cost of other divisions.

(b) It may lead to increase in costs since there may be a duplication of activities across products. Providing each division with separate set of similar functions increases expenditure.

(c) It provides managers with the authority to supervise all activities related to a particular division. In course of time, such a manager may gain power and in a bid to assert his independence may ignore organisational interests. **(Any two)**

2. Diligent developers, a website design company in Bangalore is a startup initiative of Mr. Maniraj which aims at achieving a profit margin of 10% in its first year. Mr. Maniraj appointed Mr. Advait as the Digital marketing Head, Mr. Kiyansh as the head of Backend department and Mr. Nirved headed the Graphics Designing Department. Since each head was specialised in specific skills, it resulted in increased efficiency and better coordination. However, problems arose when Mr. Advait started considering group objectives superior to organisational objectives and stopped exchanging information with Mr. Kiyansh and Mr. Nirved. The company had to bear the brunt of lack of coordination and was unable to achieve its objectives.

(a) Identify and state the organisational structure adopted by the company.

(b) State two benefits and two limitations of the identified structure highlighted in the above case.

[SQP 2023-24]

Ans. (a) The organisational structure adopted by Diligent Developers is Functional structure. Functional structure is an organisational design that groups similar or related jobs together.

(b) Benefits of functional structure:

(1) It leads to occupational specialization since emphasis is placed on specific functions. This promotes efficiency in utilization of manpower as employees perform similar tasks within a department and are able to improve performance.

(2) It promotes control and coordination within a department because of similarity in the tasks being performed.

Limitations of functional structure:

(a) A functional structure places less emphasis on overall enterprise objectives than the objectives pursued by a functional head. Such practices may lead to functional empires wherein the importance of a particular function may be overemphasised. Pursuing departmental interests at the cost of organisational interests can also hinder the interaction between two or more departments.

(b) It may lead to problems in coordination as information has to be exchanged across functionally differentiated departments.

[Marking Scheme SQP 2023-24]

3. Due to spread of COVID-19 pandemic, employees of almost all the companies were working online from their homes. In 2022 when most of the companies called them back to their office and started working offline, Taty Software Ltd. still asked their employees to work from home. Because of this, employees of Taty Software Ltd.' were feeling bored. Hence for recreation they formed a cricket-club. They started meeting every Saturday and Sunday on a ground near their office building.

(i) Identify and state the type of organisation formed by the employees of Taty Software Ltd.'

(ii) Also, state any two advantages and two limitations of the type of organisation identified in (1) above.

[Delhi Set-1, 2023]

Ans. (i) The type of organization so formed is 'Informal Organization'.

Informal organization is a network of personal and social relations not established or required by the formal organization but arising spontaneously as people associate with one another.

(or any other correct meaning)

(ii) Advantages of Informal Organisation: (Any two)

(i) It leads to faster spread of information as well as a quick feedback.

(ii) It fulfills the social needs of the members.

(iii) It contributes towards fulfillment of organisational objectives by compensating for inadequacies in the formal organisation.

(If an examinee has only listed the points, ½ mark for each point should be awarded).

[CBSE Marking Scheme, 2023]

4. Aradhana and Gandharv are heads of two different departments in 'Yumco Ltd.' They are efficient managers and are able to motivate the employees of their respective departments to improve performance. However, their drive to excel in their own sphere of activity instead of giving emphasis on objectives of the enterprise has hindered the interaction between the departments that Aradhana and Gandharv are heading. Often there are inter-departmental conflicts and they have become incompatible. This has proved to be harmful in the fulfilment of the organisational objectives. The situation has deteriorated to such an extent that the CEO of 'Yumco Ltd.' has hired a consultant, Rashmi, to resolve the problem. After studying the situation closely, Rashmi found that the problem has arisen due to inflexibility and a narrow perspective on the part of both Aradhana and Gandharv. She is of the view that this situation is a result of the type of organisational structure 'Yumco Ltd.' has adopted.

From the above information, identify the organisational structure adopted by Yumco Ltd.' and state any three advantages of the structure so identified.

[Delhi Set-1, 2018]

Ans. Functional Structure is the organisational structure adopted by 'Yumco Ltd.'.

Advantages of Functional Structure: (Any three)

(a) It leads to occupational specialisation since emphasis is placed on specific functions.

(b) It promotes control and coordination within a department because of similarity in the tasks being performed.

(c) It increases managerial and operational efficiency.

(d) It lowers cost as it reduces duplication of effort.

(e) It makes training of employees easier as it focuses on a limited range of skills.

(f) It ensures that different functions get due attention.

(If an examinee has given only the heading, ½ mark for each heading should be awarded)

[Marking Scheme, Delhi 2018]

Tips & Tricks

When the division is according to functions like marketing, selling, finance etc. then it is a functional organisation and when separate departments are there, it is a divisional organisation.

5. Amit has joined a manufacturing firm as a worker. He has recently started working on the shop floor. The management is quite liberal and has allowed the workers to form a cricket fan club. The workers assemble and play cricket in the evening after the completion of their work. However, the management is a little worried about the outcomes. The management is trying to change the schedule of the workers but they are unsure about the reaction of the workers. Though majority of the workers are sincere, like Amit, yet the management is concerned about their companions in the cricket fan club.

(i) Identify and explain the type of organisation the cricket fan club is?

(ii) Also give the disadvantages of the organisation identified in the above para. A [OEB]

Ans. (i) Informal Organisation: Interaction among people at work gives rise to a 'network of social relationships among employees' called the informal organisation. Informal organisation emerges from within the formal organisation when people interact beyond their officially defined roles. When people have frequent contacts, they cannot be forced into a rigid formal structure. Rather, based on their interaction and friendship they tend to form groups which show conformity in terms of interest. Examples of such groups formed with common interest may be those who take part in cricket matches on Sundays, meet in the cafeteria for coffee, are interested in dramatics, etc. Informal organisation has no written rules, is fluid in form and scope and does not have fixed lines of communication.

(ii) Disadvantages: The informal organisation has certain disadvantages. Some of them are as follows:

(a) When an informal organisation spreads rumours, it becomes a destructive force and goes against the interest of the formal organisation.

(b) The management may not be successful in implementing changes if the informal organisation opposes them. Such resistance to change may delay or restrict growth.

(c) It pressurises members to conform to group expectations. This can be harmful to the organisation if the norms set by the group are against organisational interests. **[3 +3=6]**

6. What is meant by "Divisional Structure" of an organisation ? For which type of business enterprise is this structure most suitable ? State any four advantages of this form of organisational structure. **U [OEB]**

Concept Applied	Concept and Advantages of divisional structure

Ans. Divisional structure is an organisational structure comprising of separate business divisions or units created on the basis of category of products manufactured. Herein each division is multi-functional as each division performs its own functions.

It is suitable for those enterprises:

(i) Where two or more products are manufactured.

(ii) When an organisation grows and diversifies.

(Any one)

Advantages of Divisional Structure:

(i) Product specialisation helps in the development of varied managerial skills.

(ii) It helps in the fixation of responsibility as divisional heads become accountable for profits, revenues and costs related to their departments.

(iii) It promotes flexibility, initiative and quick decision making as each division is an autonomous unit.

(iv) It eases expansion and growth as new divisions can be added without interrupting the existing operations.

(v) It reduces the problem of coordination across departments as all activities concerning a particular product line are integrated together. **(Any four)**

[1 + 1 + 4 = 6]

TOPIC-3 Delegation and Decentralisation

Concepts Covered:

- Meaning, elements and importance of delegation. • Meaning and importance of decentralisation.

Revision Notes

- **Meaning of Delegation of Authority:**
  The delegation of authority refers to the division of labour and decision-making responsibility to an individual that reports to a manager.
- **Elements of Delegation:**

(i) Authority: It is the right of an individual to command his subordinates and to take decisions and actions within the scope of his position.

(ii) Responsibility: It is the obligation of a subordinate to properly perform the assigned duty.

(iii) Accountability: It means being answerable for the final outcome.

- **Importance of Delegation** **[Board, 2017]**

(i) Effective management: By empowering the employees, the managers are able to function more efficiently as they get more time to concentrate on important matters.

(ii) Employee development: Delegation empowers the employees by providing them with the chance to use their skills, gain experience and develop themselves for higher positions.

(iii) Motivation of employees: Superior's trust improves employee's self-esteem and confidence . When a superior entrusts a subordinate with a task, it is not merely the sharing of work but involves trust on the superior's part and commitment on the part of the subordinate.

(iv) Facilitation of growth: Delegation helps in the expansion of an organisation by providing a ready workforce to take up leading positions in new ventures.

(v) Basis of management hierarchy: Delegation of authority establishes superior-subordinate relationships, which are the basis of hierarchy of management.

(vi) Better co-ordination: Clarity in reporting relationships help in developing and maintaining effective coordination amongst the departments, levels and functions of management.

- **Decentralisation:** **[Board, 2019]**
  Decentralisation explains the manner in which decision making responsibilities are divided among hierarchical levels.
- **Centralisation:**
  An organisation is centralised when decision-making authority is retained by higher management levels whereas it is decentralised when such authority is delegated.
- **Importance of Decentralisation:** **[Board, 2019]**

(i) Develops initiative among subordinate: Decentralisation helps to promote self-reliance and confidence amongst the subordinates.

(ii) **Develops managerial talent for the future:** Formal training plays an important part in equipping subordinates with skills that help them rise in the organisation but equally important is the experience gained by handling assignments independently.

(iii) **Quick decision making:** In a decentralised organisation since decisions are taken at levels which are nearest to the points of action and there is no requirement for approval from many levels, the process is much faster.

(iv) **Relief to the top management:** Decentralisation leaves the top management with more time which they can devote to important policy decisions rather than occupying their time with both policy as well as operational decisions.

(v) **Facilitates growth:** With each department doing its best in a bid to outdo the other, the productivity levels increase and the organisation is able to generate more returns which can be used for expansion purposes.

(vi) **Better control:** Decentralisation makes it possible to evaluate performance at each level and the departments can be individually held accountable for their results.

KEY TERMS

Authority: Right to take decisions inherent in a managerial position to tell people what to do and expect them to do it.

Hierarchy: A system or organisation that has many levels from the lowest to the highest.

MNEMONICS

Concept: Elements of Delegation
Interpretations:
Act and Repeat
A : Authority A : Accountability R : Responsibility
Concept: Importance of Delegation:
Interpretations:
Caring Mom Buys Fruits to Eat and Enjoy
C: Coordination
M: Motivation of employees
B: Basis of management hierarchy
F: Facilitation of growth
E: Effective management
E: Employee development

SUBJECTIVE TYPE QUESTIONS

Short Answer Type Questions-I (3 marks each)

1. **"Delegation of authority, undoubtedly empowers an employee to act for his superior, but the superior would still be accountable for the outcome. Explain the elements of delegation of authority discussed above.** [SQP 2019-20]

Ans. **Three elements of delegation are:**

(i) **Authority:** Right of an individual to **command his subordinates** and to take action within the scope of his position. It is right to take decisions inherent in a job position.

(ii) **Responsibility:** It is the **obligation of subordinate** to properly perform the assigned duty. It arises from superior subordinate relationship. It flows upwards.

(iii) **Accountability:** It implies being **answerable** for the final outcome, i.e. subordinate will be answerable to superior for satisfactory performance of work.

[1×3=3]

2. **Shlok Mehta started a company Etech Ltd. with twenty employees to assemble economical computers for the Indian rural market. The company did very well in its initial years. As the product was good and marketed well, the demand went up. To increase production, the company decided to recruit additional employees. Shlok Mehta, who was earlier taking all the decisions for the company, had to selectively disperse the authority. He believed that people are competent, capable and resourceful and can assume responsibility for the effective implementation of their decisions. This paid off and the company was not only able to increase its production but also expanded its product range with different features. Identify and explain the concept used by Shlok Mehta through which he was able to steer his company to greater heights.** A [OEB]

Ans. The concept used by Shlok Mehta through which he is able to steer his company to greater heights is Decentralisation.

Decentralisation explains the manner in which decision-making responsibilities are divided among hierarchical levels. Decentralisation refers to delegation of authority throughout all the levels of the organisation. Decision making authority is shared with lower levels and is consequently placed nearest to the points of action. In other words, decision making authority is pushed down the chain of command. When decisions taken by the lower levels are numerous as well as important an organisation can be regarded as greatly decentralised. **[3]**

3. **Give any three points of differences between authority, responsibility and accountability.** R [OEB]

4. **Explain how delegation leads to the development of an employee.** U [OEB]

Short Answer Type Questions-II (4 marks each)

1. **What is meant by 'Delegation'? State any three points which highlight the importance of delegation in an organisation.** A I A [SQP Term-1, 2021-22]

Ans. 'Delegation is the entrustment of responsibility and authority to another and the creation of accountability for performance.' (or any other correct meaning) **[1]**

Importance of Delegation of Authority:

(i) It helps in effective management as the managers get more time to concentrate on important matters.

(ii) It helps in development of employees as the employees get more opportunities to utilise their talent.

These Questions are for practice and their solutions are given at the end of the chapter.

(iii) It helps to motivate employees as the employees feel encouraged and try to improve their performance further.

(iv) It facilitates growth by providing a ready workforce to take up leading positions in new ventures.

(v) It establishes a management hierarchy through clear superior subordinate relationships.

(vi) It helps in better co-ordination by avoiding overlapping of duties. **[(Any three) 1×3=3]**

[Marking Scheme, SQP 2019]

2. What is meant by 'Decentralisation'? State any three points that highlight the importance of decentralisation in an organization.

R [Delhi Set-3, 2019]

OR

Samir Gupta started a telecommunication company, ' Donira Ltd.' to manufacture economical mobile phones for the Indian rural market with 15 employees. The company did very well in its initial years. As the product was good and marketed well, the demand of its products went up. To increase production, the company decided to recruit additional employees. Samir Gupta, who was earlier taking all the decisions for the company had to selectively disperse the authority. He believed that subordinates are competent, capable and resourceful and can assume responsibility for effective implementation of their decisions. This paid off and the company was not only able to increase its production but also expanded its product range.

(a) Identify the concept used by Samir Gupta through which he was able to steer his company to greater heights.

(b) Also, explain any three points of importance of this concept. **U [Delhi Set-1, 2015]**

OR

Infocom has diversified itself into several product lines: Telecommunications, Engineering, financial services. Each subsidiary is self-sufficient with their-own administrative functions, propagating the belief that people can assume the responsibility for the effective implementation of their decisions and should be given autonomy. This has reduced the need for direct supervision by superiors, has promoted flexibility, initiative and faster decision making. The orders of customers are never delayed, as a result of good policy decisions of top management.

(a) Identify and explain any two points of importance of the concept being discussed above.

(b) Name and briefly explain a suitable framework for the company within which the managerial and operating task are to be performed.

U [SQP 2019-20]

Ans. Decentralisation refers to systematic delegation of authority through all the levels of management and in all the departments except that which can be exercised only at central points. (or any other correct meaning)

Importance of Decentralisation:

(i) Relief to top management: It gives relief to the top management as, when the subordinates are given the freedom to act, the top management gets more time to devote on important policy decisions rather than handling operational decisions.

(ii) Develops initiative amongst subordinates: It develops initiative amongst subordinates by promoting self-reliance and confidence among them. This is because when lower managerial levels are given freedom to take their own decisions they learn to depend on their own judgement.

(iii) Develops managerial talent for future: It develops managerial talent for the future by giving the subordinates a chance to prove themselves, thus, creating reservoir of qualified manpower to fill up challenging positions in future. Suitable framework: Divisional structure–In a divisional structure, the organisation structure comprises of separate business units or divisions. Each division is self-contained as it develops expertise in all functions related to a product line.

Commonly Made Error

⚠ Most of the students write the importance of delegation instead of decentralisation.

Answering Tip

Learn the importance of delegation and decentralisation separately under different headings as these are two different concepts of organising.

Long Answer Type Questions (6 marks each)

1. Jojo and Jojo is a company known for its consumer business of baby oil and bandages, but many people do not know that the company also runs a medical device and diagnostics business, as well as a pharmaceutical company. With more than 1,80,000 employees worldwide the company has chosen to share decision making authority with lower levels and place it nearest to the point of action. Therefore the response does not take time. This propagates the belief that people are competent, capable and resourceful who can get a chance to prove their abilities, and enables the company in identifying those executives who have the necessary potential to become dynamic leaders, so that the checking required on decisions taken by lower levels of management is the least. This makes it possible to evaluate performance at each level and each department can be individually held accountable for their results.

By quoting the lines given above identify and briefly explain the benefits of the concept discussed above.

A [SQP 2022-23]

Ans. Importance of Decentralisation:

(i) "Response does not take time".

Quick decision making: In a decentralised organisation since decisions are taken at levels which are nearest to the point of action and there is no requirement for approvals from many levels, the process is much faster.

(ii) "Who can get a chance to prove their abilities". Develops managerial talent for the future: Decentralisation gives managers a chance to prove their abilities and create a reservoir of qualified manpower that can be considered to fill up more challenging positions through promotion.

(iii) "Identifying those executives who have the necessary potential to become dynamic leaders".
Develops initiative among subordinates: Decentralisation helps to promote self-reliance and confidence amongst the subordinates. It also keeps them in a state wherein they are constantly challenged and have to develop solutions for various problems they encounter.

(iv) "This makes it possible to evaluate performance at each level and each department can be individually held accountable for their results." Better control: Feedback from levels helps to analyse variances and improve operations. **[1½×4=6]**

2. An important difference between S&M Ltd. and most other companies is that instead of operating as one large corporation it operates as 180 smaller companies each focused on a specific product and area, implying selective dispersal of authority, recognising the decision makers need for autonomy, as decision making authority is pushed down the chain of command. It enables the company to maintain short lines of communication with customers and employees, and accelerate the development of talent.

(i) Identify the philosophy that is being followed by S&M Ltd. through which it is dividing the decision-making responsibilities among the hierarchical levels.

(ii) State any five points of importance of the philosophy identified. A **[SQP 2020-21]**

OR

'E-Solutions Ltd.' started its operations in the year 2000. At the time of its inception, the company had only ten employees with two departments, a Production department and an Administration department. The products supplied and the services provided by the company started gaining popularity over the years. The management had faith in the abilities of the employees and thus they allowed them freedom of action. The management recognised that the decision-makers at different levels of the organisation need to be given more autonomy. They took a policy decision that there will be less control of superiors over subordinates. This increased the role of the subordinates in the organisation and now they were in a position to take numerous as well as important decisions. As a result, its business has diversified into many areas. Presently, it has its operations throughout the country with seven branches overseas. Its organisational structure has now changed into divisional structure and ten thousand people are working with the company.

(a) Identify the concept of management which helped the company to diversify into many areas and branches abroad.

(b) Explain five points of importance of the concept identified in (i) above.

U **[Outside Delhi Set-1, 2019] [6]**

OR

Neeraj Gupta started a company 'YoYo Ltd.' with ten employees, to assemble economical computers for the Indian rural market. The company did very well in its initial years. As the product was good and marketed well, the demand went up. To increase production the company decided to recruit additional employees. Neeraj Gupta, who was earlier taking all decisions for the company, had to selectively disperse the authority. He believed that people are competent, capable and resourceful and can assume responsibility for effective implementation of their decisions. This paid off and the company was not only able to increase its production but also expanded its product range with different features.

(a) Identify the concept used by Neeraj Gupta through which he was able to steer his company to greater heights.

(b) Also explain any three points of importance of this concept. U **[Outside Delhi Set-1, 2015]**

Ans. Decentralisation

Importance of Decentralisation **(Any five)**

1. **Develops initiative among subordinates:** Decentralisation helps to promote self-reliance and confidence amongst the subordinates.
2. **Develops managerial talent for the future:** Formal training plays an important part in equipping subordinates with skills that help them rise in the organisation but equally important is the experience gained by handling assignments independently.
3. **Quick decision making:** The management hierarchy can be looked upon as a chain of communication. In a decentralised organisation however, since decisions are taken at levels which are nearest to the points of action and there is no requirement for approval from many levels the process is much faster.
4. **Relief to top management:** Decentralisation diminishes the amount of direct supervision exercised by a superior over the activities of a subordinate because they are given the freedom to act and decide albeit within the limits set by the superior.
5. **Facilitates growth:** Decentralisation awards greater autonomy to the lower levels of management as well as divisional or departmental heads. This allows them to function in a manner best suited to their department and fosters a sense of competition amongst the departments.
6. **Better control:** Decentralisation makes it possible to evaluate performance at each level and the departments can be individually held accountable for their results. **(Any five)**

[Marking Scheme OD, 2019]

3. Aman Chadha started 'Bulls Eye' a company for providing cyber security solutions to businesses. Its objective is to prevent, detect and respond to cyber attacks and protect critical data. He was a hardworking software engineer and an expert in cyber security. His reputation grew by leaps and bounds as he was not only a person of integrity but also did his work with utmost honesty and sincerity. The business started growing day by day.

He was delighted when he was offered a big project by the Ministry of Defence. While working on the project, he found that the volume of work made it impractical for him to handle all the work by himself. He decided to expand the team. The company maintained a close liaison with a local engineering college. During a campus placement, Ishan and Vrinda were appointed to work for the new project.

He found the new employees capable, enthusiastic and trustworthy. Aman Chadha was thus, able to focus on objectives and with the help of Ishan and Vrinda, the project was completed on time. Not only this Aman Chadha was also able to extend his area of operations. On the other hand, Ishan and Vrinda also got opportunities to develop and exercise initiative.

(i) Identify and briefly explain the concept used by Aman Chadha in the above case which helped him in focusing on objectives.

(ii) Also, state any four points of importance of the concept identified in (i) above.

A [Delhi Set-1, 2017]

Ans. (i) Delegation of authority

Delegation of authority is the process of granting of authority to the subordinates to operate within prescribed limits. Delegation refers to the downward transfer of authority from a superior to a subordinate. It is a prerequisite to the efficient functioning of an organisation because it enables a manager to use his time on high priority activities. It also satisfies the subordinate's need for recognition and provides them with opportunities to develop and exercise initiative.

(ii) Importance of delegation of authority:

(a) Effective management: By empowering the employees, the managers are able to function more efficiently as they get more time to concentrate on important matters. Freedom from doing routine work provides them with opportunities to excel in new areas.

(b) Employee development: As a result of delegation, employees get more opportunities to utilise their talent and this may give rise to latent abilities in them. It allows them to develop those skills which will enable them to perform complex tasks and assume those responsibilities which will improve their career prospects. It makes them better leaders and decision makers. Thus, delegation helps by preparing better future managers. Delegation empowers the employees by providing them with the chance to use their skills, gain experience and develop themselves for higher positions.

(c) Motivation of employees: Delegation helps in developing the talents of the employees. It also has psychological benefits. When a superior entrusts a subordinate with a task, it is not merely the sharing of work but involves trust on the superior's part and commitment on the part of the subordinate. Responsibility for work builds the self-esteem of an employee and improves his confidence. He feels encouraged and tries to improve his performance further.

(d) Facilitation of growth: Delegation helps in the expansion of an organisation by providing a ready workforce to take up leading positions in new ventures. Trained and experienced employees are able to play significant roles in the launch of new projects by replicating the work ethos they have absorbed from existing units, in the newly set up branches.

(e) Basis of management hierarchy: Delegation of authority establishes superior-subordinate relationships, which are the basis of hierarchy of management. It is the degree and flow of authority which determines who has to report to whom. The extent of delegated authority also decides the power that each job position enjoys in the organisation.

(f) Better coordination: The elements of delegation, namely authority, responsibility and accountability help to define the powers, duties and answerability related to the various positions in an organisation. This helps to avoid overlapping of duties and duplication of effort as it gives a clear picture of the work being done at various levels. Such clarity in reporting relationships help in developing and maintaining effective coordination amongst the departments, levels and functions of management.

(Any four) [2+4=6]

4. The manager of a retail store has a team of ten sales associates. To improve efficiency, she decides to implement the principle of "Division of Work" and delegate specific tasks to each team member. However, one sales associate is unhappy with their assigned responsibilities and believes they should have more authority in decision-making.

(a) How can the principle of "Division of Work" help improve the store's efficiency and productivity?

(b) How can the manager balance the delegation of tasks while ensuring appropriate authority is given to each team member? Explain in three points.

A [APQ Set-1, 2023-24]

Ans. (a) The principle of "Division of Work," as proposed by Henry Fayol, advocates dividing the overall work into specialised tasks and assigning them to individuals based on their skills and expertise. Implementing this principle in the retail store can lead to several benefits that improve efficiency and productivity. **[3]**

(b) As a manager, follow these steps to achieve a balanced approach:

(i) Assess Individual Capabilities: Before task delegation, assess each team member's strengths, weaknesses, skills, and preferences. Understanding their capabilities enables the manager to allocate tasks that align with their expertise, ensuring a better fit between the individual and the assigned responsibility.

(ii) Encourage Input and Involvement: Involve team members in the decision-making process. Allow them to provide suggestions, express preferences, and contribute ideas regarding the tasks they are assigned. This involvement fosters a sense of ownership and encourages proactive engagement.

(iii) Set Clear Expectations: Clearly communicate the expectations associated with each task. Define objectives, timelines, and desired outcomes. Additionally, outline the boundaries of authority for each role to avoid confusion and ensure everyone understands their level of decision-making autonomy.

(iv) Foster a Collaborative Culture: Promote an environment where collaboration and teamwork are encouraged. Even with specialised tasks, encourage communication and cooperation among team members. This promotes knowledge sharing and support, enhancing overall efficiency.

(v) Provide Feedback and Recognition: Regularly provide constructive feedback to team members about their performance. Recognise their efforts and accomplishments, acknowledging their contributions. This feedback loop helps in continuous improvement and boosts morale.

(vi) Monitor Progress: Keep track of task progress without micromanaging. Regularly check in with team members to ensure tasks are on track and offer support or guidance when needed. Monitoring progress allows for timely intervention if any issues arise. **(Any three) [1×3=3]**

COMPETENCY BASED QUESTIONS

Objective Type Questions

[A] Multiple Choice Questions

1. Rishabh joined an entertainment company Avtaar, as a creative head. As a manager looking after the creative unit of the company, one of the functions he has to perform is the process of organising. Which step of the process will he need to perform after identifying and dividing the work that has to be done in accordance with previously determined plans?

(A) Identification and division of work
(B) Departmentalisation.
(C) Assignment of duties.
(D) Establishment of reporting relationships.

U [SQP 2022-23]

Ans. Option (B) is correct.

Explanation: Departmentalisation is an organisational structure that separates people into groups, or departments, based on a particular set of criteria. These departments have their own leadership and work together to complete tasks. With large or complicated projects, multiple departments may work together.

2. Aarohan Ltd. is a company manufacturing automobiles where division of work into key areas includes production, purchase, marketing, accounts and personnel. Which of the following is a disadvantage of the organisation structure of Aarohan Ltd.?

(A) It may lead to increase in cost
(B) Managers may gain power and assert independence and ignore organisation interests.
(C) It ensures that different functions get due attention.
(D) Heads do not get training for top management positions.

U [SQP 2022-23]

Ans. Option (D) is correct.

Explanation: Functional heads do not get training for top management positions in Arohan Ltd. because they are unable to gather experience in diverse areas.

3. Name the outcome of the function of management which includes designing of roles to be filled by suitably skilled people and defining the inter relationship between roles so that ambiguity in performance of duties can be eliminated.

(A) Organisation structure
(B) Delegation of authority
(C) Decentralisation
(D) Controlling

U [SQP 2022-23]

Ans. Option (A) is correct.

Explanation: The organisational structure determines how information flows between levels within the company. For example, in a centralised structure, decisions flow from the top down, while in a decentralised structure, decision-making power is distributed among various levels of the organisation.

4. Which of the following statements is correct with reference to 'organising' function of management?

(A) Leads to systematic allocation of jobs and facilitates specialisation.
(B) Reduces the risk of uncertainty.
(C) Helps in obtaining competent personnel.
(D) Judges accuracy of standards.

U [SQP 2021-22]

5. 'While performing the organising function, jobs are allocated to the members of each department in accordance with their skills and competencies.' Identify the step in the organising function being discussed above:

(A) Identification and division of work.
(B) Departmentalisation.
(C) Assignment of duties.
(D) Establishment of reporting relationships.

A [SQP 2021-22]

Ans. Option (C) is correct.

Explanation: Once departments have been formed, each of them is placed under the charge of an individual. Jobs are then allocated to the members of each department in accordance to their skills and competencies. It is essential for effective performance that a proper match is made between the nature of a job and the ability of an individual. The work must be assigned to those who are best fitted to perform it well.

This Question is for practice and its solution is given at the end of the chapter.

6. "Grouping similar nature jobs into larger units called departments" is the step in the process of one of the functions of management. Identify the function of management.

(A) Planning **(B)** Organising
(C) Directing **(D)** Staffing

R [SQP 2021-22]

7. Arrange the following steps in the process of organising in the correct sequence:

(A) Assignment of duties
(B) Departmentalisation
(C) Identification and division of work
(D) Establishing reporting relationship

Choose the correct option:

(A) (A) ; (B) ; (D) ; (C)
(B) (C) ; (B) ; (A) ; (D)
(C) (C) ; (B) ; (D) ; (A)
(D) (B) ; (C) ; (A) ; (D)

R [SQP 2021-22]

Concept Applied: Steps in organising process

Ans. Option (B) is correct.

Explanation: The first step in the process of organising involves identifying and dividing the work that is to be done in accordance with previously determined plans. Then the activities which are similar in nature are grouped together to define the work of different job positions. Once departments have been formed, each of them is placed under the charge of an individual. Jobs are then allocated to the members of each department in accordance to their skills and competencies. Merely allocating work is not enough. Each individual should also know who he has to take orders from and to whom he is accountable.

8. The purpose of 'departmentalisation 'in the process of 'organising' is:

(A) To adapt changes in the business environment.
(B) To facilitate specialisation.
(C) To facilitate expansion and growth of the organisation without interrupting the existing operations.
(D) To help in increasing managerial efficiency.

U [SQP 2021-22]

9. .... is the process of dividing work into manageable activities and then grouping the activities which are similar in nature.

(A) Coordination
(B) Departmentalisation
(C) Organisation structure
(D) Delegation of authority

AI U [SQP 2020-21]

10. Which type of organisational structure will you suggest for a firm which has diversified activities and operations requiring a high degree of specialisation?

(A) Centralised structure
(B) Decentralised Structure
(C) Divisional structure
(D) Functional structure

U [SQP 2021-22]

Ans. Option (D) is correct.

Explanation: Grouping of jobs of similar nature under functions and organising these major functions as separate departments creates a functional structure. All departments report to a coordinating head. For example, in a manufacturing concern division of work into key functions will include production, purchase, marketing, accounts and personnel. These departments may be further divided into sections. Thus, a functional structure is an organisational design that groups similar or related jobs together.

11. Name the concept that refers to the number of subordinates that can be effectively managed by a superior and determines the number of levels of management in the organisation.

(A) Organisation structure
(B) Span of management
(C) Hierarchy of authority
(D) Delegation of Authority

U [SQP 2021-22]

Ans. Option (B) is correct.

Explanation: The span of management, to a large extent gives shape to the organisational structure. Span of management refers to the number of subordinates that can be effectively managed by a superior. This determines the levels of management in the structure. A proper organisation structure is essential to ensure a smooth flow of communication and better control over the operations of a business enterprise.

12. ________ ensures that the heads of separate business units in the organisation are responsible for profit or loss of their unit and have authority over it.

(A) Span of management
(B) Divisional structure
(C) Functional structure
(D) Hierarchy of authority

U [SQP 2020-21]

13. ________ ensures that the subordinate performs tasks on behalf of the manager thereby reducing his workload and providing him with more time to concentrate on important matters.

(A) Decentralisation
(B) Delegation of authority
(C) Authority
(D) Accountability

U [SQP 2021-22]

Ans. Option (B) is correct.

Explanation: Delegation refers to the downward transfer of authority from a superior to a subordinate. It is a prerequisite to the efficient functioning of an organisation because it enables a manager to use his time on high priority activities. Delegation helps a manager to extend his area of operations as without it, his activities would be restricted to only what he himself can do.

14. For the following two statements choose the correct option:

Statement I: Accountability can be delegated.

Statement II: Responsibility can be delegated completely.

Choose the correct option from the options given below:

(A) Statement I is correct and II is wrong
(B) Statement II is correct and I is wrong
(C) Both the statements are correct
(D) Both the statements are incorrect

U [SQP 2021-22]

These Questions are for practice and their solutions are given at the end of the chapter.

Ans. Option (D) is correct.

Explanation: Accountability implies being answerable for the final outcome. Once authority has been delegated and responsibility accepted, one cannot deny accountability. It cannot be delegated and flows upwards, *i.e.*, a subordinate will be accountable to a superior for satisfactory performance of work. Responsibility is the obligation of a subordinate to properly perform the assigned duty. It arises from a superior-subordinate relationship because the subordinate is bound to perform the duty assigned to him by his superior. Responsibility cannot be entirely delegated. Thus, responsibility flows upwards, i.e., a subordinate will always be responsible to his superior. Thus, for effective delegation, the authority granted must be commensurate with the assigned responsibility.

15. The type of organisational structure in which jobs of similar nature are grouped together on the basis of functions to form departments is called:

(A) Functional structure **(B)** Divisional structure
(C) Informal structure **(D)** Grouped structure

R [SQP Term-1, Exam 2021-22]

Ans. Option (A) is correct.

Explanation: Grouping of jobs of similar nature under functions and organising these major functions as separate departments creates a functional structure. All departments report to a coordinating head. For example, in a manufacturing concern division of work into key functions will include production, purchase, marketing, accounts and personnel. These departments may be further divided into sections. Thus, a functional structure is an organisational design that groups similar or related jobs together.

16. 'Agile Pvt. Ltd.' manufactures athletic footwear. Owing to its popularity among sports teams across the country, it recently decided to enter into manufacturing of sports clothing and accessories. The type of organisational structure which is suitable for the company is:

(A) Functional structure **(B)** Divisional structure
(C) Horizontal structure **(D)** Informal structure

A [SQP Term-1, Exam 2021-22]

Ans. Option (B) is correct.

Explanation: Divisional structure is particularly suitable for those enterprises which have more than one category of products to offer. In a divisional structure, the organisation structure comprises of separate business units or divisions. Each unit has a divisional manager responsible for performance and who has authority over the unit.

17. The element of delegation which relates to the obligation of a subordinate to properly perform the assigned duty is known as:

(A) Authority **(B)** Responsibility
(C) Accountability **(D)** Centralisation

U [Delhi Term-1, Exam 2021-22]

Ans. Option (B) is correct.

Explanation: Responsibility is the obligation of a subordinate to properly perform the assigned duty. It arises from a superior– subordinate relationship because the subordinate is bound to perform the duty assigned to him by his superior. Thus, responsibility flows upwards, *i.e.*, a subordinate will always be responsible to his superior.

18. Name the concept which explains the manner in which decision-making responsibilities are divided among hierarchical levels:

(A) Organisational structure
(B) Span of management
(C) Delegation
(D) Decentralisation R [SQP Term-1, Exam 2021-22]

Ans. Option (D) is correct.

Explanation: Decentralisation refers to delegation of authority throughout all the levels of the organisation. Decision making authority is shared with lower levels and is consequently placed nearest to the points of action. In other words, decision making authority is pushed down the chain of command. Decentralisation explains the manner in which decision-making responsibilities are divided among hierarchical levels.

19. Which of the following statements is true?

(A) Accountability can be entirely delegated.
(B) Accountability flows downward.
(C) Accountability refers to answerability for final outcome of the assigned task.
(D) Accountability means the right of an individual to command his subordinates.

U [Term-1, Exam 2021-22]

Ans. Option (C) is correct.

Explanation: Delegation of authority, undoubtedly empowers an employee to act for his superior but the superior would still be accountable for the outcome. Accountability implies being answerable for the final outcome. Once authority has been delegated and responsibility accepted, one cannot deny accountability.

20. Match the options of Column I with their correct options given in Column II.

Column I	Column II
(1) Identification and Division of work	(a) Allocation of work
(2) Departmentalisation	(b) Creation of accountability
(3) Assignment of duties	(c) Grouping of similar tasks
(4) Establishing authority relationship	(d) Avoiding duplication of work

Choose the correct option:

(A) 1-a, 2-b, 3-c, 4-d **(B)** 1-b, 2-c, 3-d, 4-a
(C) 1-d, 2-c, 3-a, 4-b **(D)** 1-d, 2-a, 3-b, 4-c

U [OEB]

Ans. Option (C) is correct.

21. Statement-I: Sound organisation encourages initiative and relative thinking on part of the employees.

Statement-II: Planning develops the subordinates' ability and helps him to realise his full potential.

U [OEB]

Choose the correct option from the options given below:

(A) Statement I is true and II is false.
(B) Statement II is true and I is false.
(C) Both the statements are true.
(D) Both the statements are false.

Ans. Option (A) is correct.

Explanation: Delegation develops in the subordinate the ability to deal effectively with challenges and helps them to realise their full potential.

22. Which of the following is NOT an element of delegation? A [CFPQ 2023-24]

(A) Responsibility (B) Accountability
(C) Centralisation (D) Authority

Ans. Option (C) is correct.

Explanation: There are three elements of delegation- authority, responsibility and accountability. Centralisation means concentrating the decision-making authority at the top-level of management.

23.

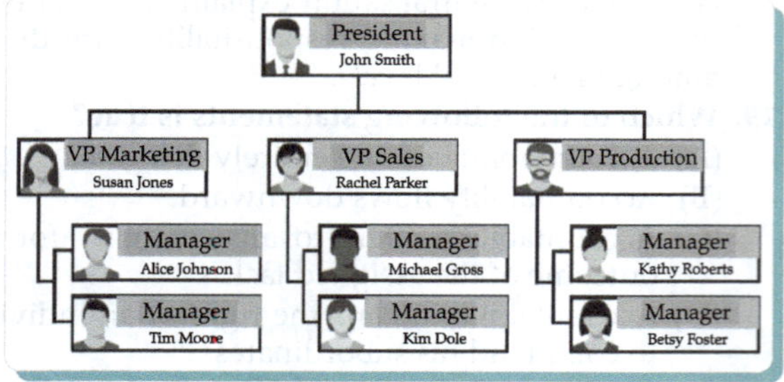

Identify the organisational structure illustrated in the above image.

(A) Functional structure (B) Divisional structure
(C) Informal structure (D) Horizontal structure

A [OEB]

Ans. Option (A) is correct.

Explanation: Functional structure is formed by grouping of activities of similar nature under one department.

24. Concentration of decision-making functions at the apex of management hierarchy is called ....

(A) Decentralisation
(B) Delegation
(C) Organisational structure
(D) Centralisation R [SQP 2023-24]

Ans. Option (D) is correct.

Explanation: Centralisation refers to concentration of authority of power in few hands at the top level.

25. The obligation of a subordinate to properly perform the assigned duty is called:

(A) Authority (B) Responsibility
(C) Accountability (D) Decentralisation

R [Delhi Set-1, 2023]

Ans. Option (B) is correct

Explanation: Responsibility is the commitment of a subordinate to perform the appointed duty appropriately. It emerges from a superior-subordinate relationship on the grounds that the subordinate will undoubtedly perform the duty doled out to him by his boss. Responsibility streams upward.

26. Identify the type of organisation structure depicted in the above diagram:

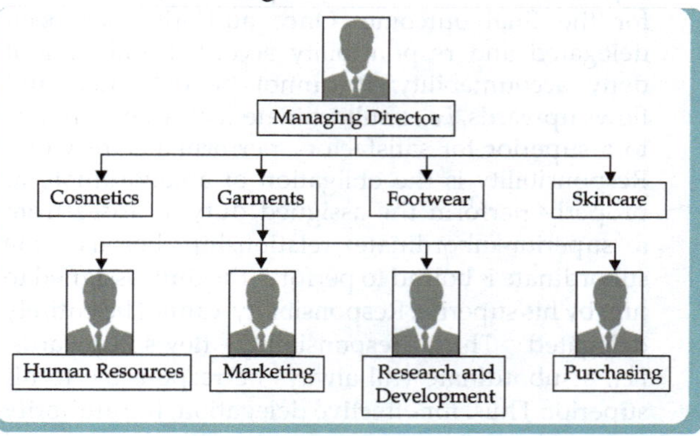

(A) Divisional structure
(B) Functional structure
(C) Informal structure
(D) Both Informal and Functional structure [1]

U [Outside Delhi Set-1, 2023]

Ans. Option (A) is correct.

Explanation: Divisional structure refers to an organisational design which consists of separate business units or divisions. All the divisions have to report to a Divisional Head. Manpower is generally grouped on the basis of different products manufactured.

27. 'An organisation structure is deliberately designed by the top management to facilitate smooth functioning of the organisation'.
Which of the following is not a feature of such a structure? U [Outside Delhi Set-1, 2023]

(A) It clarifies who has to report to whom.
(B) There is systematic coordination among the various activities to achieve organisational goals.
(C) The standards of behaviour evolve from group norms rather than officially laid down rules and regulations.
(D) It places more emphasis on work to be performed than interpersonal relationships among the employees.

Ans. Option (C) is correct.

Explanation: Standards of behaviour evolves from the group norms in case of informal organisation. Others are the features of formal organisational structure.

28. The process that initiates implementation of plans by clarifying jobs, working relationships and effectively deploying resources for attainment of identified and desired results is called:

U [Delhi Term-1, 2022]

(A) Coordination (B) Management
(C) Organising (D) Delegation

Ans. Option (C) is correct.

Explanation: Organising can be defined as a process that initiates implementation of plans by clarifying jobs and working relationships and effectively deploying resources for attainment of identified and desired results (goals).

29. _______________gives shape to the organisation structure. R

(A) Extent of delegation (B) Span of Management
(C) No of employees (D) Planning

[SQP 2019-20]

Ans. Option (B) is correct.

30. Which step of the Organising Process involves stating the job description, a document that clearly defines the contents and responsibilities related to a job ? A [APQ, 2023-24]

(A) Departmentalisation
(B) Assignment of duties
(C) Establishing reporting relationships
(D) Identification and division of work

Ans. Option (B) is correct.

Explanation: The assignment of duties step in the organising process defines job roles through job descriptions, outlining responsibilities and tasks for each position within an organisation. This process ensures clarity, efficiency, and accountability among employees regarding their roles and contributions.

31. What is the significance of delegation in the scenario where Sara, as a superior, entrusts her authority to Tiara, her subordinate, to enable her learning, skill development, and better chances of promotion?

(A) Facilitation of growth
(B) Effective management
(C) Employees' development
(D) Motivation of employees

U [APQ, 2023-24]

Ans. Option (C) is correct.

Explanation: By entrusting authority to Tiara, Sara enables her to learn and develop skills necessary for her growth and potential promotion. Delegation, in this context, fosters the professional development of employees by granting them responsibilities and opportunities to enhance their abilities and take on more significant roles within the organisation.

32. In__________, it is easier to fix responsibility for performance. R [APQ, 2023-24]

(A) Functional structure and formal organisation
(B) Divisional structure and informal organisation
(C) Functional structure and informal organisation
(D) Divisional structure and formal organisation

Ans. Option (D) is correct.

Explanation: In a divisional structure within a formal organisational framework, where different divisions or units operate with autonomy but still adhere to formal guidelines and structures, it becomes easier to fix responsibility for performance. Each division has its own defined objectives, roles, and responsibilities, allowing for clearer attribution of performance outcomes to specific divisions or units within the organisation.

33.

The above picture is highlighting the absence of a concept which is causing a delay in decision making. Identify the concept.

(A) Organising
(B) Span of management
(C) Delegation
(D) Accountability A [APQ, 2023-24]

Ans. Option (C) is correct.

Explanation: Delegation refers to the process of assigning authority and responsibility from a manager or leader to a subordinate or team member to perform specific tasks or make decisions. It involves transferring some of the decision-making powers to others while holding them accountable for the outcomes. Delays in delegation can have far-reaching implications, impacting not only individual workloads but also overall team dynamics, innovation, and organisational effectiveness. Prompt and effective delegation is essential for fostering a productive and empowered workforce.

34. Match the following concepts with their meaning:

	Column I		Column II
A	Authority	i	Increases the role of subordinates in the organisation by giving them more autonomy
B	Functional structure	ii	Flows downwards from superior to subordinate
C	Decentralisation	iii	Cannot be entirely delegated
D	Responsibility	iv	Minimum duplication of efforts and hence economical

(A) A - i, B - iii, C - ii, D - iv
(B) A - ii, B - iv, C - i, D - iii
(C) A - iii, B - iv, C - i, D - ii
(D) A - iii, B - i, C - iv, D - ii

R [APQ, 2023-24]

Ans. Option (B) is correct.

Explanation: **A.** Authority refers to the flow of power or decision-making from higher levels to lower levels in an organisation.

B. Functional structure organises departments by specific functions, reducing redundancy and promoting efficiency.

C. Decentralisation involves delegating decision-making authority to lower levels in the hierarchy, empowering subordinates.

D. While authority can be delegated, ultimate responsibility remains with the person in charge; it cannot be entirely transferred.

35. -------------- is the process of defining and grouping activities of the enterprise and establishing authority relationships among them.

(A) Decentralisation (B) Planning
(C) Staffing (D) Organising

R [APQ, 2023-24]

Ans. Option (D) is correct.

Explanation: Organising is about designing the framework of the organisation, setting up the structure that will enable the efficient accomplishment of goals and facilitate coordination among different parts of the enterprise.

36. AirIndia is a large airline company. It is already listed on the National Stock Exchange. It has grown very quickly over the past 15 years. But recently due to operational inefficiencies and lockdowns in different countries, it is finding it difficult to remain profitable, due to which it had to make 150 employees redundant. The other employees are feeling demotivated because of the recent occurrence. In order to motivate the employees, the company is considering giving different incentives. In order to improve efficiencies, AirIndia wants to transfer the authority from superior to subordinate at all levels of the management. AirIndia also wants to raise capital to expand its operations to 2 different countries.

________ refers to the downward transfer of authority from a superior to a subordinate throughout all the levels of the organisation. A [CFPQ 2023-24]

(A) Decentralisation (B) Delegation

(C) Functional structure (D) Accountability

Ans. Option (A) is correct.

Explanation: Decentralisation is the transfer of authority from a superior to subordinate at all the levels of the management. Delegation is the downward transfer of authority from a superior to a subordinate at one level of the organisation. Functional structure refers to an organisational structure where jobs of a similar nature are grouped together. Accountability is an element of delegation.

[B] Assertion & Reason

Directions: In the following questions, a statement of assertion (A) is followed by a statement of reason (R). Mark the correct choice as:

(A) Both assertion (A) and reason (R) are true and reason (R) is the correct explanation of assertion (A).

(B) Both assertion (A) and reason (R) are true but reason (R) is not the correct explanation of assertion (A).

(C) Assertion (A) is true but reason (R) is false.

(D) Assertion (A) is false but reason (R) is true.

1. **Assertion (A):** Organising leads to proper usage of all material, financial and human resources.

Reason (R): The proper assignment of jobs avoids overlapping of work and also makes possible the best use of resources. [OEB]

Ans. Option (A) is correct.

Explanation: Avoidance of duplication of work helps in preventing confusion and minimising the wastage of resources and efforts.

2. **Assertion (A):** A proper organisation structure is essential to ensure a smooth flow of communication and better control over the operations of a business enterprise.

Reason (R): An organisation structure provides the framework which enables the enterprise to function as an integrated unit by regulating and coordinating the responsibilities of individuals and departments. [OEB]

3. **Assertion (A):** Identification and division of work is the first step in the process of organising.

Reason (R): Organising involves identifying and dividing the work that has to be done in accordance with previously determined plans. [OEB]

Concept Applied	Steps in the process of organising

4. **Assertion (A):** Organising provides a clear description of jobs and related duties.

Reason (R): Organising stimulates creativity amongst the managers. [OEB]

Ans. Option (A) is correct.

Explanation: The organisation structure can be defined as the framework within which managerial and operating tasks are performed. It specifies the relationships between people, work and resources.

5. **Assertion (A):** Functional structure makes training of employees easier as the focus is only on a limited range of skills.

Reason (R): Divisional heads are accountable for profits. [OEB]

6. **Assertion (A):** The formal organisation provides a complete picture of how an organisation works.

Reason (R): An informal organisation originates from within the formal organisation as a result of personal interaction among employees. [OEB]

7. **Assertion (A):** Delegation is a prerequisite to the efficient functioning of an organisation.

Reasoning (R): It enables a manager to use his time on high priority activities. [SQP 2021-22]

Ans. Option (A) is correct.

Explanation: Delegation refers to the downward transfer of authority from a superior to a subordinate. It is a prerequisite to the efficient functioning of an organisation because it enables a manager to use his time on high priority activities. It also satisfies the subordinate's need for recognition and provides them with opportunities to develop and exercise initiative. Delegation helps a manager to extend his area of operations as without it, his activities would be restricted to only what he himself can do.

[C] Case Based MCQs

I. Read the below case and answer the questions that follow:

JS Printing Solutions Ltd. is a company manufacturing printers and scanners. The management of this company is known for speedy and prompt delivery of orders. As a result, the market share of this company is growing. The company grabbed a new project to supply 1,500 printers to Uprise Bank Ltd. for its various branches, within two weeks. The production manager, Ashok, made one of his efficient subordinates, Deepak, in charge of the project and also gave him the right to command workers in order to meet the target. Now Ashok could use his time on high priority areas. He felt that this will also give an opportunity to Deepak to gain experience and develop himself for

These Questions are for practice and their solutions are given at the end of the chapter.

higher positions. On getting the charge, Deepak was very happy, his confidence level increased and he was encouraged to do his best to fulfil the responsibility. Considering his responsibility, Ashok kept a track of the completion of work with Deepak and he provided him the needed guidance to reach the target on time.

[Delhi Term-1, 2022]

1. **Identify the concept of management used by Ashok to ensure accomplishment of the new project.**
   (A) Functional structure
   (B) Divisional structure
   (C) Delegation
   (D) Decentralisation

Ans. Option (C) is correct.

Explanation: If a manager desires to meet the organisational goals, he should focus on the objectives and ensure that all work is accomplished, he must delegate authority. Delegation is a prerequisite to the efficient functioning of an organisation because it enables a manager to use his time on high priority activities.

2. **The application of the concept used above allows Ashok to use his time on high priority areas. This will lead the organisation towards:**
   (A) Adaptation to change
   (B) Effective management
   (C) Economies of scale
   (D) Reduction in conflicts among different divisions.

Ans. Option (B) is correct.

Explanation: By empowering the employees by delegation, the managers are able to function more efficiently as they get more time to concentrate on important matters.

3. **'On getting the charge, Deepak was very happy, his confidence level increased and he was encouraged to do his best to fulfill the responsibility given to him.'**
   The concept discussed above helps in:
   (A) Departmentalisation
   (B) Reduction in conflicts among different divisions.
   (C) Motivating the employees.
   (D) Promoting control and co-ordination within a department.

Ans. Option (C) is correct.

Explanation: Delegation helps in developing the talents of the employees. It also has psychological benefits. When a superior entrusts a subordinate with a task, it is not merely the sharing of work but involves trust on the superior's part and commitment on the part of the subordinate. Responsibility for work builds the self-esteem of an employee and improves his confidence. He feels encouraged and tries to improve his performance further.

A [SQP 2021-22]

4. **The concept discussed above provides benefits to:**
   (A) Superior only
   (B) Subordinate only
   (C) Both superior and subordinate
   (D) Neither superior nor subordinate

Ans. Option (C) is correct.

Explanation: Delegation enables a manager to extend his area of operation as without it, his activities would be restricted to only what he himself can do. He can use his time on high priority activities. It also satisfies the subordinate's need for recognition and provides them with opportunities to develop and exercise initiative.

II. Read the below case and answer the questions that follow:

'Saarthi', the name has been associated with the manufacturing and sale of Fashion products since 1960, when Kapil Saarthi opened his first retail fashion clothing outlet in Ahmedabad. Sarathi Cosmetics was incorporated in India in 1940, and became a member of the S & M family of companies in 1959. Saarthi Perfumes began operations in Gujarat in an existing administrative S&M facility in 1985. An important difference between S&M and most other companies is that instead of operating as one large corporation it operates as 180 smaller companies each focused on a specific product and area, implying selective dispersal of authority, recognising the decision makers need for autonomy, as decision making authority is pushed down the chain of command. It enables the company to maintain short lines of communication with customers and employees, and accelerate the development of talent. [SQP Term-1, 2021-22]

1. **Identify the philosophy that is being followed by S&M through which it is dividing the decision-making responsibilities among hierarchical levels.**
   (A) Delegation of authority
   (B) Decentralisation of authority
   (C) Division of work
   (D) Span of management

Ans. Option (B) is correct.

Explanation: Decentralisation is much more than a mere transfer of authority to the lower levels of management hierarchy. It is a philosophy that implies selective dispersal of authority because it propagates the belief that people are competent, capable and resourceful. They can assume the responsibility for the effective implementation of their decisions. Thus, this philosophy recognises the decision maker's need for autonomy. The management,however, needs to carefully select those decisions which will be pushed down to lower levels and those that will be retained for higher levels.

2. **'Why is there, need to apply the philosophy being followed by S&M, with caution?**
   (A) As it can cause a delay in communication.
   (B) As it can cause disintegration of the organisation.
   (C) As it can increase the workload of the top management.
   (D) As it can reduce the chances of growth of the firm.

Ans. Option (B) is correct.

Explanation: Decentralisation should be applied with caution as it can lead to organisational disintegration if the departments start to operate on their own guidelines which may be contrary to the interest of the organisation. Decentralisation must always be balanced with centralisation in areas of major policy decisions.

3. **The application of the philosophy discussed above can foster a sense of competition amongst the departments, which in turn will help the firm in the following manner:**

(A) Facilitates growth
(B) Better control
(C) Relief to top management
(D) Quick decision making.

Ans. Option (A) is correct.

Explanation: Decentralisation awards greater autonomy to the lower levels of management as well as divisional or departmental heads. This allows them to function in a manner best suited to their department and fosters a sense of competition amongst the departments. Consequently, with each department doing its best in a bid to outdo the other, the productivity levels increase and the organisation is able to generate more returns which can be used for expansion purposes.

4. Quote the line from above which highlights the importance of the philosophy towards providing management education to employees.

(A) Maintain short lines of communication
(B) Accelerate the development of talent
(C) Selective dispersal of authority
(D) Recognises decision makers need for autonomy

Ans. Option (B) is correct.

Explanation: Formal training plays an important part in equipping subordinates with skills that help them rise in the organisation but equally important is the experience gained by handling assignments independently. Decentralisation gives them a chance to prove their abilities and creates a reservoir of qualified man power who can be considered to fill up more challenging positions through promotions. It also helps to identify those who may not be successful in assuming greater responsibility. Thus, it is a means of management education as well as an opportunity for trained man- power to use its talent in real life situations.

SOLUTIONS FOR PRACTICE QUESTIONS (TOPIC-1)

SATQs-I

Ans. 3. (i) Specialisation: Organising function calls for identification and division of work. Since work is divided into manageable tasks, it is allocated systematically among the workers. Thus, workload gets divided and workers perform the job on a regular basis resulting in increased efficiency and productivity. This repetitive performance of a particular task allows a worker to gain expertise in that area and is known as specialisation.

(ii) Departmentalisation: Under organising, once work has been divided into small and manageable activities, it is grouped and activities of similar nature are put together. This grouping process is known as departmentalisation and departments can be created using any basis like zones or regions *i.e.*, north, south, etc. or products *e.g.*, appliances, cosmetics, etc.

[1½×2 = 3]

SATQs-II

Ans. 2. The importance of organising can be described as follows:

(i) Benefits of Specialisation: In organising, work is divided into manageable activities and systematically allocated. This increases productivity and efficiency of the workforce. Consequently, on account of repetitive work, one gets experience in a particular field which results in specialisation.

(ii) Adaptation to changes: Organising facilitates business firms to accommodate workload changes caused due to business environment. On account of this, organisational structure can be modified and for revision of relationships at organisational levels, makes it easier to adapt to changes.

(iii) Clarity in working relationships: Authority and responsibility are defined in a manner that every person knows whom to report to and for what. This removes confusion in transfer of information and instructions and assists in creating a hierarchical order.

(iv) Optimum utilisation of resources: Proper allocation of resources helps in avoiding any duplication and overlapping of work and ensures optimum use of all available resources namely human, physical and financial resources.

(v) Effective administration: By clearly describing the job's related duties, duplication of work and confusion can be avoided in the organisation. Thus, it ensures effective administration and managing becomes easy.

(vi) Development of personnel: Delegation of authority reduces the work load of a manager and enables him to focus on and explore new areas of growth for his organisation. It enables the subordinates also to effectively deal with the challenges and to realise their full potential.

(vii) Expansion and growth: Organising enables an enterprise to take up new challenges. For example, more job positions, departments, new product lines, new geographical territories, etc. to increase sales/ profits, market share and growth of the enterprise.

(Any four) [1½ × 4 = 6]

LATQs

Ans. 3. The importance of organising highlighted in the above case are:

(i) Benefits of specialisation: Organising leads to a systematic allocation of jobs amongst the work force. This reduces the workload as well as enhances productivity because of the specific workers performing a specific job on a regular basis. Repetitive performance of a particular task allows a worker to gain experience in that area and leads to specialisation.

(ii) Clarity of working relationships: The establishment of working relationships clarifies lines of communication and specifies who is to report to whom. This removes ambiguity in transfer of information and instructions. It helps in creating a hierarchical order thereby enabling the fixation of responsibility and specification of the extent of authority to be exercised by an individual.

(iii) Development of personnel: Organising stimulates creativity amongst the managers. Effective delegation allows the managers to reduce their workload by assigning routine jobs to their subordinates. The reduction in workload allows the manager to develop new methods and ways of performing tasks. Delegation also develops in the subordinate the ability to deal effectively with challenges and helps them to realise their full potential. **[2×3=6]**

SOLUTIONS FOR PRACTICE QUESTIONS (TOPIC-2)

SATQs-I

Ans. 5. Divisional structure refers to an organisational design which consists of separate business units or divisions. All the divisions have to report to a divisional head. Manpower is generally grouped on the basis of different products manufactured.

Advantages of Divisional Structure:

(i) Product Specialisation: Divisional structure leads to product specialisation as the divisional head gains experience in all the functions related to a particular product. This also helps in preparing them for higher positions.

(ii) Greater Accountability: Divisional heads can be held accountable for the profits as the revenues and costs related to different departments can be identified without difficulty and assigned to them. This provides a proper basis for measuring their performance. **[1+2=3]**

SATQs-II

Ans. 2. Informal organisation is a network of personal and social relations which emerges spontaneously from within the formal organisation as people associate with one another beyond their officially defined roles. It has no written rules, is fluid in form and scope and does not have fixed lines of communication. **[1]**

Advantages of Informal Organisation:

(i) It leads to faster spread of information as well as towards a quick feedback. **[1]**

(ii) It fulfils the social needs of the members. **[1]**

(iii) It contributes towards fulfilment of organisational objectives by compensating for inadequacies in the formal organisation. **[1]**

[Marking Scheme, Delhi, 2019]

SOLUTIONS FOR PRACTICE QUESTIONS (TOPIC-3)

SATQs-I

Ans. 3. Differences between authority, responsibility and accountability:

Basis	Authority	Responsibility	Accountability
Meaning	Right to command.	Obligation to perform an assigned task.	Answerability for outcome of the assigned task.
Delegation	Can be delegated.	Cannot be entirely delegated.	Cannot be delegated at all.
Origin	Arises from formal position.	Arises from delegated authority.	Arises from responsibility.
Flow	Flows downward from superior to subordinate.	Flows upward from subordinate to superior.	Flows upward from subordinate to superior

(Any three) [1×3=3]

Commonly Made Error

Most of the students mix up the content of different elements of delegation and accordingly write the wrong differences.

Answering Tip

Learn the differences of different elements of delegation on the basis of meaning, delegation, origin and flow.

Ans 4. As a result of delegation, employees get more opportunities to utilise their talent and this may give rise to latent abilities in them. It allows them to develop those skills which will enable them to perform complex tasks and assume those responsibilities which will improve their career prospects. It makes them better leaders and decision makers. Thus, delegation helps by preparing better future managers. Delegation empowers the employees by providing them with the chance to use their skills, gain experience and develop themselves for higher positions. **[3]**

SOLUTIONS FOR OBJECTIVE PRACTICE QUESTIONS

[A] MCQs

Ans. 4. Option (A) is correct.

Explanation: Organising leads to a systematic allocation of jobs amongst the work force. This reduces the workload as well as enhances productivity because of the specific workers performing a specific job on a regular basis. Repetitive performance of a particular task allows a worker to gain experience in that area and leads to specialisation.

Ans. 6. Option (B) is correct.

Explanation: Organising involves identifying and dividing the work that has to be done in accordance with previously determined plans.

Once work has been divided into small and manageable activities then those activities which are similar in nature are grouped together. Such sets facilitate specialisation. This grouping process is called departmentalisation. Departments can be created using several criteria as a basis.

Ans. 8. Option (B) is correct.

Explanation: Once work has been divided into small and manageable activities then those activities which are similar in nature are grouped together. Such sets facilitate specialisation. This grouping process is called departmentalisation.

Ans. 9. Option (B) is correct.

Explanation: Once work has been divided into small and manageable activities, then those activities which are similar in nature, are grouped together. This process is called departmentalisation.

Ans. 12. Option (B) is correct.

Explanation: In a divisional structure, the organisation structure comprises of separate business units or divisions. Each unit has a divisional manager responsible for performance and who has authority over the unit.

[B] A & R

Ans. 3. Option (A) is correct.

Explanation: The organising function begins with the division of total work into smaller units. Each unit of total work is called a job. The division of work into smaller jobs leads to specialisation because jobs are assigned to individuals according to their qualifications and capabilities.

Ans. 4. Option (B) is correct.

Explanation: Organising provides a clear description of jobs and related duties. This helps to avoid confusion and duplication. Clarity in working relationships enables proper execution of work.

Ans. 5. Option (B) is correct.

Explanation: Functional structure makes training of employees easier, as the focus is only on a limited range of skills. Divisional heads are held accountable for profits since revenues and costs associated with various departments are clearly identifiable and attributed to them. This gives a solid foundation for measuring performance.

Ans. 6. Option (B) is correct.

Explanation: Divisional heads are accountable for profits, as revenues and costs related to different departments can be easily identified and assigned to them. This provides a proper basis for performance measurement. It also helps in fixation of responsibility in cases of poor performance of the division and appropriate remedial action can be taken.

REFLECTION

(a) Did you understand the importance of organising?

(b) Were you able to describe the steps in the process of organising?

(c) Were you able to explain the advantages, disadvantages and suitability of functional and divisional structure?

(d) Could you discuss the advantages and disadvantages of formal and informal organisation?

(e) Were you able to describe the elements of delegation?

(f) Could you appreciate the importance of delegation?

(g) Were you able to differentiate between delegation and decentralisation?

(h) Were you able to differentiate between authority, responsibility and accountability?

(i) Were you able to identify the importance of decentralisation in the below mentioned line: "A decentralisation policy helps to identify those executives who have the necessary potential to become dynamic leaders.

SELF ASSESSMENT PAPER - 5

Maximum Time: 1 hour **MM: 30**

General Instructions:

(i) All the questions are compulsory
(ii) Q.1 to Q.10 are 1 mark questions
(3) Q.11 to Q.12 are 3 mark questions
(iv) Q.13 to Q.14 are 4 marks questions
(v) Q.15 is a 6 marks question

Objective Type Questions [1 Mark]

1. The 'Occasion Planners' is an event management company. They organise mostly marriages as they believe that marriage is a relationship that unites two souls. The different functions of marriages are organised by the people who are specialised in their own jobs. They always appoint specialised people in their company as it leads to a systematic allocation of jobs amongst the work force and reduces the workload as well as enhances productivity.
Identify the importance of organising highlighted in the above text?
(A) Benefits of specialisation
(B) Optimum utilisation of resources
(C) Adaptation to change
(D) None of these [1]

2. Match the options of Column I with their correct options given in Column II.

Column I	Column II
(1) Authority	(a) Answerability for outcome of the assigned task.
(2) Responsibility	(b) Downward transfer of authority from a superior to a subordinate.
(3) Accountability	(c) Obligation to perform an assigned task.
(4) Delegation	(d) Right to command.

(A) 1-a, 2-b, 3-c, 4-d **(B)** 1-b, 2-c, 3-d, 4-a
(C) 1-d, 2-c, 3-a, 4-b **(D)** 1-d, 2-a, 3-b, 4-c [1]

3. Which of the following is an example of informal organisation?
(A) Member of a sports club formed by a company.
(B) Production manager is responsible for increasing the production.
(C) Both (A) and (B)
(D) None of these [1]

4.

Identify the concept of organisation illustrated in the picture above.
(A) Delegation
(B) Centralisation and Decentralisation
(C) Functional Structure
(D) None of these [1]

5. In the following question, a statement of assertion (A) is followed by a statement of reason (R). Mark the correct choice as:
Assertion (A): Delegation helps them to realise their full potential.
Reason (R): Delegation develops in the subordinate, the ability to deal effectively with challenges and
(A) Both assertion (A) and reason (R) are true and reason (R) is the correct explanation of assertion (A).
(B) Both assertion (A) and reason (R) are true but reason (R) is not the correct explanation of assertion (A).
(C) Assertion (A) is true but reason (R) is false.
(D) Assertion (A) is false but reason (R) is true.

6. For the following two statements, choose the correct option:
Statement I: Delegation helps a manager ton extend his areas of operations.
Statement II: Authority relationships help to maintain order in the organisation by giving the managers the right to exact obedience and given directions to the work force under them.
Choose the correct option from options given below:
(A) Statement I is correct and statement II is wrong.
(B) Statement II is correct and statement I is wrong.
(C) Both the statements are correct.
(D) Both the statements are wrong. [1]

Read the below text and answer the Q. 7-10 on basis of the same.

BBS International School is looking forward to celebrate his annual sports day in school in the coming month. It is an occasion where pupils, teachers, and parents come together for a day of competitive sport. The principal and the sports teachers have started planning different races, dances and events and also started assigning the duties and responsibilities to various staff members and students accordingly. Different departments and committees were formed to look into and to organise different activities of sports day such as welcoming of parents, handing out refreshments, overseeing races, blowing whistles, or awarding medals and prizes etc. All the decision-making authority is retained by the Principal. The responsibility of refreshment was given to Mr. Gopal, who was an art teacher in school. Mr. Gopal calculated the number of students, staff and parents and came to the conclusion that minimum 1,400 audience will be gathered on the sports day. Accordingly, he decided to order 1,500 snack boxes. He gave the order to the local bakery shop and made payment for 700 boxes in advance. On the day of the sports day only 500 snack boxes were delivered. The distribution and counting of medals were assigned to Ms. Ruchi. But Ms. Ruchi was ignoring her responsibilities. So, the Principal decided to appoint Ms. Salma to work with Ms. Ruchi. Ruchi did not like to work with Ms. Salma. Most of the times, Principal noticed the tension developing between the two. However, she didn't want to get involved in their personal issues as long as the work was completed effectively and efficiently by them. One day, the tension between them reached the heights and Ms. Ruchi complained to Principal stating that her duties were being largely taken over by Ms. Salma. Principal issued the order stating the clear allocation of the jobs and related duties between the two. She further clarified the working relationship between them by specifying who will take responsibility of which event as the school has planned many events for the sports day. This helped in reducing the workload, enhancing productivity and removing ambiguity.

7. Which of the following importance of organising is highlighted in the below mentioned lines: "She further clarified the working relationship between them by specifying who will take reasonability of which event as the school has planned many events for the sports day".

(A) Optimum utilisation of resources
(B) Adaptation to change
(C) Effective administration
(D) Clarity in working relationships **[1]**

8. Which of the following concept of organisation is described in the below mentioned lines:

"All the decision-making authority is retained by the Principal".

(A) Centralisation
(B) Decentralisation
(C) Informal organisation
(D) None of these **[1]**

9. Which type of organisation is being followed by BBS International School?

(A) Informal **(B)** Formal
(C) Both (A) and (B) **(D)** None of these **[1]**

10. Which of the following elements of delegation is being described in the below mentioned lines with respect to Mr. Gopal:

"He decided to order 1,500 snack boxes. He gave the order to the local bakery shop and made payment for 700 boxes in advance. On the day of the sports day only 500 snack boxes were delivered".

(A) Authority and Responsibility
(B) Accountability and Responsibility
(C) Authority and Accountability
(D) None of these **[1]**

Short Answer Type Questions - I [3 Marks]

11. Home Wood is a company dealing in making home furniture. The company chose to diversify its operations to improve its growth potential and increase market share. As the project was important, many alternatives were generated for the purpose and were thoroughly discussed amongst the members of the organisation. After evaluating the various alternatives, the Managing Director of the company, decided that they should add office Interiors and Furnishings as a new line of business activity.

Identify and explain the framework, which the diversified organisation should adopt, to enable it to cope with the emerging complexity?

12. Sakshi, an environmentalist, decided to start a campaign to create awareness among people for developing clean surroundings in their area. Her goal is to protect and preserve the environment. She promotes interacting with nature and using natural resources safely through research and lobbying. She formed a team of fifteen members to list the different ways for cleaning the surroundings. One suggested to take the help of local residents, another suggested that they may involve school-going children in their venture. One more suggestion was to take the help of the unemployed youth. On evaluation of different ways, it was decided to take the help of local residents. To achieve the desired goal, various activities are identified like purchase of necessary items like dustbins, garbage bags, brooms, etc., collection of garbage, disposal of garbage, etc. After identification of different activities, the work was allocated to different members.

Identify and explain the concept of management involved in the above situation.

Short Answer Type Questions - II [4 Marks]

13. Soapic Ltd. is a hand making domestic soap company. The company makes all kinds of soaps with natural ingredients. The company has grown in size. It was a market leader but with changes in business environment and with the entry of MNCs, its market share is declining. To cope up with the situation, the CEO starts delegating some of his authority to the General Manager, who also felt himself overburdened and with the approval of CEO disperses some of his authority to various levels throughout the organisation. Identify the concept of management discussed above.

14. An organisation is working by clubbing similar related jobs under different departments. The HR department is not in direct touch with the Marketing Department and this has created problems. The HR head feels that he only knows about the HR department and similar is the case with the Marketing department. However, the truth is both of them have limited and specific skills.

(i) Identify and explain the type of organisation structure does this organisation has?

(ii) Also, give any three disadvantages of this type of organisation structure?

Long Answer Type Questions - II [6 Marks]

15. 'Pharma Plus' is a company which is highly focused in delivering quality medicines to patients in need through excellence in innovation, development, manufacturing, and commercialisation. The company offer high-quality, cost-effective products with the highest level of customer service. Recently the company decided to go for a major shift in policy decision by handing over the decision-making authority to the lower most level of employees. For this the company went for a thorough planning. Within few months the positive results of this major policy decision were recognisable. The employees felt a lot of development in their skill of taking first step to manage things on their own. Some major newspapers also covered this development. The production of the company increased. The company's top management could now focus on new areas of innovation as the employees turned more reliable. One day it so happened that the company's manufacturing branch in one of the areas in Delhi could not fulfil even half of its production target and the operations manager was held answerable for the assigned target. He was called in the office. When he was questioned it was found that his right to command the workers was insufficient and it should have been more to create results. The management decided to listen to him and he was given more power. When he went to the shop floor, he told the workers that the standard of behaviour of the workers should come from the official rules and procedures.

(i) Identify the concept of management that has been mentioned in the above case.

(ii) Explain the two advantages of the concept has been highlighted in the above case.

(iii) Identify and explain the two elements of delegation that have been highlighted in the above case.

STAFFING

LEARNING OBJECTIVES

After going through this chapter, the student would be able to:

- Understand the concept of staffing.
- Explain the importance of staffing.
- Understand the specialized duties and activities performed by Human Resource Management.
- Describe the steps in the process of staffing.
- Understand the meaning of recruitment.
- Discuss the sources of recruitment.
- Explain the merits and demerits of internal and external sources of recruitment.
- Understand the meaning of selection.
- Describe the steps involved in the process of selection.
- Understand the concept of training and development.

Study Plan
Maximum Time = 3.45 Hrs
Maximum Questions = 80

LIST OF TOPICS

TOPIC-1 Staffing: Concept, Features, Importance, Process

Concepts Covered

- Meaning, features and importance. • Staffing as a part of Human Resource Management. • Steps in the process of staffing.

Revision Notes

Scan to know more about this topic
Staffing

- **Staffing**: Staffing is one of the functions of management which relates to filling and keeping filled the positions in the organisation structure.
- **Features of Staffing:**

(i) It is an integral part of the management.
(ii) It is a pervasive function of the management related to manpower or human resources.
(iii) It is a continuous process.
(iv) It has a wide scope.
(v) It is a multiple objective activity.

- **Importance:** [Board, 2023]

(i) Discovers and obtains competent personnel for filling in the vacancies.
(ii) Improves performance by putting right person at the right job.
(iii) Ensures continuous survival and growth of an organisation.
(iv) Ensures optimum utilisation of human resources.
(v) Improves job satisfaction and morale of the employees.

- **Staffing as a part of Human Resource Management:** In small organisations, the function of staffing is performed by all the managers but in large organisations, the function of staffing is the responsibility of a separate department called the "Human Resource Department".
- **Following are the activities to be performed by Human Resource Personnel:**

(i) Recruitment
(ii) Preparation of job descriptions
(iii) Selection
(iv) Preparation of compensation and incentive plans
(v) Placement and orientation
(vi) Training and development
(vii) Performance appraisal
(viii) Maintaining labour relations by handling complaints and grievances of employees
(ix) Providing social security and welfare of employees
(x) Handling law suits and legal complications of company

- **Process of Staffing:**

(i) **Estimating manpower requirements:** Assess number and type of employees needed by an organisation in near future through workload analysis and workforce analysis.
(ii) **Recruitment:** Search prospective employees and stimulate them to apply for the job.
(iii) **Selection:** Choose the best person out of the pool of prospective candidates.
(iv) **Placement and Orientation:** Employee occupies the post and gets familiar with the organisation.
(v) **Training and Development:** Improve the job knowledge and competence of employees.
(vi) **Performance Appraisal:** Employee's performance is evaluated for salary hike, promotion, etc.
(vii) **Promotion and Career Planning:** Opportunity for higher position with more pay, responsibility, etc.
(viii) **Compensation:** Pay plans are determined.

KEY TERMS

Staffing: Putting the right people in the right jobs.
Pervasive: Existing in every part of something spreading to all parts of something.

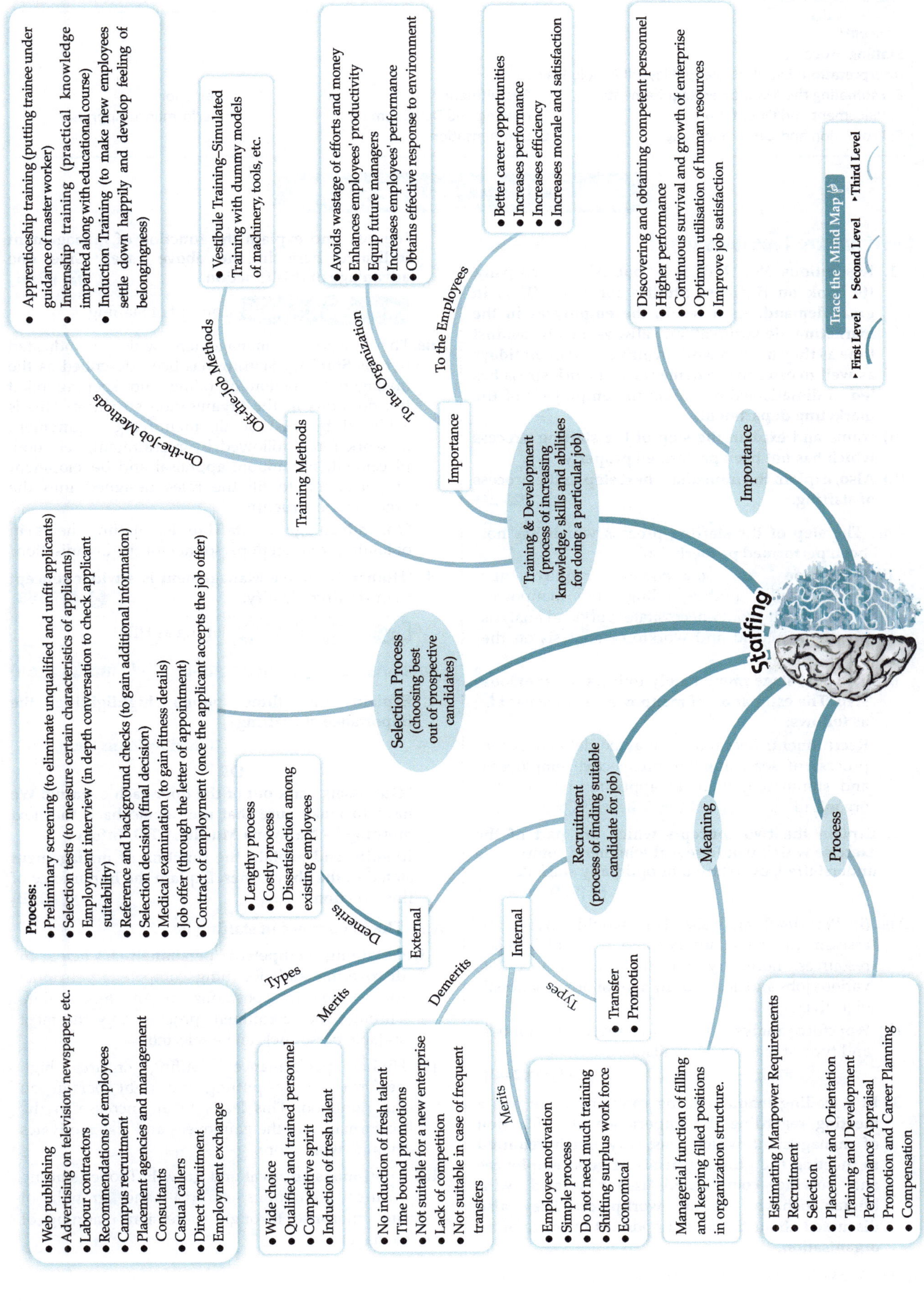

Staffing

Meaning
Managerial function of filling and keeping filled positions in organization structure.

Process
- Estimating Manpower Requirements
- Recruitment
- Selection
- Placement and Orientation
- Training and Development
- Performance Appraisal
- Promotion and Career Planning
- Compensation

Importance
- Discovering and obtaining competent personnel
- Higher performance
- Continuous survival and growth of enterprise
- Optimum utilisation of human resources
- Improve job satisfaction

Recruitment (process of finding suitable candidate for job)

Internal
Types
- Transfer
- Promotion

Merits
- Employee motivation
- Simple process
- Do not need much training
- Shifting surplus work force
- Economical

Demerits
- No induction of fresh talent
- Time bound promotions
- Not suitable for a new enterprise
- Lack of competition
- Not suitable in case of frequent transfers

External
Types
- Web publishing
- Advertising on television, newspaper, etc.
- Labour contractors
- Recommendations of employees
- Campus recruitment
- Placement agencies and management Consultants
- Casual callers
- Direct recruitment
- Employment exchange

Merits
- Wide choice
- Qualified and trained personnel
- Competitive spirit
- Induction of fresh talent

Demerits
- Lengthy process
- Costly process
- Dissatisfaction among existing employees

Selection Process (choosing best out of prospective candidates)
Process:
- Preliminary screening (to eliminate unqualified and unfit applicants)
- Selection tests (to measure certain characteristics of applicants)
- Employment interview (in depth conversation to check applicant suitability)
- Reference and background checks (to gain additional information)
- Selection decision (final decision)
- Medical examination (to gain fitness details)
- Job offer (through the letter of appointment)
- Contract of employment (once the applicant accepts the job offer)

Training & Development (process of increasing knowledge, skills and abilities for doing a particular job)

Training Methods
On-the-Job Methods
- Apprenticeship training (putting trainee under guidance of master worker)
- Internship training (practical knowledge imparted along with educational course)
- Induction Training (to make new employees settle down happily and develop feeling of belongingness)

Off-the-Job Methods
- Vestibule Training–Simulated Training with dummy models of machinery, tools, etc.

Importance
To the Organization
- Avoids wastage of efforts and money
- Enhances employees' productivity
- Equip future managers
- Increases employees' performance
- Obtains effective response to environment

To the Employees
- Better career opportunities
- Increases performance
- Increases efficiency
- Increases morale and satisfaction

Trace the Mind Map
- First Level
- Second Level
- Third Level

MNEMONICS

Concept:

Staffing Process:

Interpretation: Eat, Rest, Sleep, Play Till People Play Cards

E: Estimating the Manpower Requirements
R: Recruitment
S: Selection
P: Placement and Orientation
T: Training and Development
P: Performance Appraisal
P: Promotion and Career Planning
C: Compensation

SUBJECTIVE TYPE QUESTIONS

Short Answer Type Questions-I (3 marks each)

1. Resolutions Pvt. Ltd. is a publishing company. Its book on Business Studies for class XII is in great demand. As a result, the employees in the marketing department are always racing against time as they have to work overtime and on holidays as well to cater to the demand. The work stress has led to dissatisfaction among the employees of the marketing department.

(i) Name and explain the step of the staffing process which has not been performed properly.

(ii) Also, explain the immediate next step in the process of staffing. [SQP 2023-24]

Ans. The step of the staffing process which has not been performed properly is:

(i) Estimation of manpower requirements: Operationally, understanding the manpower requirements would necessitate workload analysis on the one hand and workforce analysis on the other.

(ii) The next stage immediately follows the previous step. The estimation of manpower requirement is as follows:

Recruitment: Recruitment may be defined as the process of searching for prospective employees and stimulating them to apply for jobs in the organisation. [Marking Scheme SQP 2023-24]

2. Explain the two concepts which are part of the exercise which would reveal whether a company is understaffed, overstaffed or optimally staffed. U [SQP 2021-22]

Ans. (i) Workload analysis: This would enable an assessment of the number and types of human resources necessary for the performance of various jobs and accomplishment of organisational objectives.

(ii) Workforce analysis: This would reveal the number and type of manpower available.

[Marking Scheme SQP 2021-22] **[1½×2=3]**

3. In a leading manufacturing company there was a meeting regarding the importance of a function of management which was very much required in meeting the growing needs of good employees and solving complicated issues related with human behavior at the workplace. They also discussed about the most important resource of an organisation.

Identify and explain the function of management indicated here in the above case? Give one advantage of this function. A [OEB]

Concept Applied: Concept of Staffing

Ans. The function of management which is indicated here is **Staffing**. Staffing has been described as the managerial function of filling and keeping filled the positions in the organisation structure. This is achieved by, first of all, identifying requirement of work force, followed by recruitment, selection, placement, promotion, appraisal and development of personnel, to fill the roles designed into the organisation structure.

One advantage of staffing is: Staffing helps in obtaining competent personnel for the organisation.

4. 'Human Resource Management is a wider concept than staffing.' Justify. A [OEB]

Concept Applied: Staffing as HRM

Short Answer Type Questions-II (4 marks each)

1. Explain any three points highlighting the importance of Staffing.

[Outside Delhi Set-3, 2023]

OR

"Our assets walk out of the door each evening. We have to make sure that they come back the next morning." - Narayana Murthy, CEO, Infosys

Identify and explain the function of management stated in the above lines. Explain the importance of this function. A [OEB]

Ans. The importance of staffing is:

(i) Obtaining competent personnel: It helps in discovering and obtaining competent personnel for various job positions in an organisation. Through the recruitment process, only the most suitable personnel can be selected.

(ii) Higher performance: Staffing ensures high performance by putting the right person on the right job. This leads to an increase in the performance of the employees and also motivates them to work more.

(iii) Continuous survival and growth: Proper staffing ensures continuous survival and growth of the enterprise through succession planning of managers.

This Question is for practice and its solution is given at the end of the chapter.

(iv) Optimum utilisation of human resources: Proper staffing ensures optimum utilisation of human resources. It avoids overstaffing and disruption of work by indicating in advance the shortages of personnel.

(v) Key to the effectiveness of other functions: Staffing is key to the effectiveness of other functions as no other function can be carried out without staffing, if there are no employees, the managers cannot modulate other functions as per the requirements. [Marking Scheme, OD, 2023]

2. 'In an interview with a leading news channel, Mr. Rakesh Kwatra, CEO of 'Get My Job' has suggested that the companies which want more and more people to apply for jobs in their organisation should make the process for applying for jobs easier and candidate friendly.' It is for this reason, he said, that most progressive companies today have a short application process. He also said that the application form filled by the candidate is very important as it is the information supplied in the application forms, which helps the manager in eliminating unqualified or unfit job seekers. The company can create a mechanism that attempts to measure certain characteristics of individuals like aptitude, manual dexterity, and intelligence to personality. The candidate may then be called for an in-depth conversation to evaluate their suitability for the job. Name the process and steps in the process of identifying and choosing the best person out of a number of prospective candidates for a job discussed above. A [SQP 2021]

3. Welcome Prints Pvt. Ltd. is a publishing company. Its book on Accountancy for class XII is very popular among the students. On account of this, the employees in the marketing department are always facing high pressure in tense situations. The employees have to devote extra time at work and on even on holidays to cater to the demand. Consequently, they cannot avail their leaves as well. Managers in the marketing department are always worried as they have to handle more than two territories. The work stress has led to discontent among the employees and managers.

(i) Which step of staffing process has not been performed properly.

(ii) Explain the next two stages immediately following the step identified in part (i). A [SQP 2016-17]

Ans. (i) Step: Estimation of manpower requirement

Meaning: It involves finding out the number and type of people that the performance of each job necessitates and the appointment of an appropriate person to the job who possesses the specific set of educational qualifications, work experience, etc. This calls for undertaking workload analysis and workforce analysis necessarily.

(ii) (a) Recruitment: It is a process where the organisation searches for its prospective employees. It stimulates them to apply for job openings in the organisation. There are two **sources of recruitment – Internal and External**. Recruitment from within the company is an internal source *e.g.*, transfers and promotions. A company has to explore the external sources as well for different positions because all the vacant positions cannot be filled through internal sources *e.g.*, direct recruitment, campus recruitment, etc.

(b) Selection: It is the process where the organisation chooses from among its pool of the potential job-seekers, which was developed by it at the recruitment stage. Thus, it helps to choose the most suitable candidate and reject the unsuitable ones. The selection procedure includes tests and interviews which help to ensure that the organisation is able to hire the best among the available talent pool. **2+2=4**

Long Answer Type Questions (6 marks each)

1. 'Big Steps' is a progressive women footwear company with a very good HR record. Recently it created a pool of prospective candidates for jobs to be given in various departments. The company is always willing to complete its HR duties properly. Various job positions exist in the company. The company makes it compulsory for the HR department to prepare job descriptions so that necessary information about the jobs could be created. For its decent HR practices the company has won several awards. It knows that the most important asset of an organisation is its image and to protect it the company should always be ready to do extra efforts. Last year when a few groups filed a complaint against the company it made great efforts to fight legally and came out victorious. It has a very good set up to promote the interests of the employees. In order to give them a familiar environment the company promotes various informal organisations and proper celebration of all festivals. It is very responsive towards its workers and always attends to their problems. There is a special cell in the HR department which is very responsive to the complaints made by the employees regardless of the level at which they work. Recently a national newspaper made a very favourite mentioning of the absence of strikes in the company as the management-labour relations are very good and a lot of importance is given to the demands of the labour unions. A very peaceful environment exists in the organisation.

Identify and explain the duties of the HR department highlighted in the above case. [OEB]

Concept Applied | Staffing in HRM

Ans. The various duties of the HR department highlighted above are:

(i) Recruitment is done in order to create the pool of candidates who can then be made to go through the process of selection. Recently it created a pool of prospective candidates for jobs to be given in various departments.

(ii) Analysing jobs and preparing job descriptions. The company makes it compulsory for the HR department to prepare job descriptions so that necessary information about the jobs could be created.

This Question is for practice and its solution is given at the end of the chapter.

(iii) Defending the company in case any law suit is filed against the company. Last year when a few groups filed a complaint against the company it made great efforts to fight legally and came out victorious.

(iv) Helps in fulfilling social needs thus providing welfare and social security. In order to give them a familiar environment the company promotes various informal organisation and proper celebration of all festivals.

(v) Handles grievances of the employees and makes timely attention to the complaints made by them. There is a special cell in the HR department which is very responsive to the complaints made by the employees regardless of the level at which they work.

(vi) Maintaining proper relations between labour and management. Recently a national newspaper made a very favourite mentioning of the lack of strikes in the company as the management labour relations are very good and a lot of importance is given to the demands of the labour unions. [1 × 6 = 6]

Commonly Made Error

⚠ Most of the students write the importance of staffing instead of writing the duties performed by Human resource department.

Answering Tip

Learners should learn the concept of human resource department well and should not mix with staffing. They should be aware of the fact that staffing is a part of human resource department.

2. AB$^+$ is a very old pharma company. Recently it was found by the management that the employees who were working in the organisation were lethargic with limited skills. The management compared its organisation with that of others and found a huge difference. When a proper analysis of job positions and their occupants was done it was found that many of them were not working at places suitable to them. This increased the worry of the management. The organisation had already spent five decades in the industry and was worried about the successful continuation of business which required capable future managers but the current employees were not much capable. The company had recently suffered huge losses. It was running out of budget. To add to its problems the number of employees was more than required so the company had to bear additional cost. It is said that one bad thing leads to another. This came true for the company when there was some negative reporting about its HR practices in a daily newspaper where it was mentioned that the employees were not satisfied and suffered with low morale. The scene forty years back was different when the company used to be the number one brand in its segment.

(i) Which function of management doesn't seem to be working well for the company in the above case?

(ii) Identify and explain any five benefits, associated with the proper utilisation of this function, the company would have enjoyed if everything had worked in its favour. A [OEB]

Concept Applied Staffing

3. The FMCG major India Unilever Ltd. is terminating the employment of its senior managers if, after evaluating their performance against pre-determined standards, which was found to be lacking. On account of these dismissals, analysts say that a large number of existing workforce may become redundant unless they learn new skills and apply the knowledge to work on new and emerging technologies. India Unilever Ltd. is ready to facilitate employee learning, through its in-house centres.

(i) Name the function of management performed by India Unilever Ltd. to maintain a satisfactory work force.

(ii) Identify and discuss the two steps in the process of the function of management discussed above.

(iii) Also state any two steps of the function of management discussed, that the firm undertook before performing the above steps. A [OEB]

Concept Applied Concept and Steps of Staffing

Ans. (i) The function of management being performed by India Unilever Ltd. to maintain a satisfactory work force is Staffing. [1]

(ii) The two steps of staffing discussed above are:

(a) Training and Development: This can be facilitated by having either internal training centres or agreements with training and educational institutes to ensure continuous learning of their employees. This proves beneficial for the organisations as well.

(b) Performance Appraisal: Organisations can use formal or informal means of appraising their employee's performance. Performance Appraisal means assessing an employee's current and/or previous performance against certain preset standards.

The performance appraisal process includes activities like defining the job, appraising performance, and providing feedback. [1½ × 2 = 3]

(iii) Given below are the two steps in the process of staffing that the management had to perform before performing the above steps:

(a) Estimating manpower requirements: It involves knowing how many persons the company needs and also of what type. This would necessitate workload analysis and workforce analysis.

(b) Recruitment: It is defined as the process of looking for suitable employees and encouraging them to apply for jobs in the organisation. The idea is to create a pool of prospective employees.

(c) Selection: It is the process of choosing from among the pool of the prospective candidates which was developed at the recruitment stage. It ensures that the organisation gets the best among the available.

(d) Orientation: It is introducing the selected employee to his peers, superiors as well as subordinates and familiarising him with the rules and policies of the organisation. Placement refers to the employee taking up the position or post on which he has been selected. **(Any two) [1 × 2 = 2]**

This Question is for practice and its solution is given at the end of the chapter.

TOPIC-2 Recruitment Process

Concepts Covered

• Concept of Recruitment • Source of recruitment • Types of various source of recruitment • Merits and Demerits of various source of recruitment

Revision Notes

- **Recruitment** has been defined as 'the process of searching for prospective employees and stimulating them to apply for jobs in an organisation.
- **Internal Sources of Recruitment:**

(i) Meaning: It refers to re-arrangement of existing staff to fill up the vacant jobs.

(ii) Types:

(a) Transfer: It involves shifting of an employee from one job to another, one department to another or from one shift to another, without a substantive change in the responsibilities and status of the employee.

(b) Promotion: Promotion leads to shifting an employee to a higher position, carrying higher responsibilities, facilities, status and pay.

(iii) Advantages: [Board, 2023]

(a) Motivates employees to improve their performance.
(b) Simplifies the process of selection and placement.
(c) No need of induction training.
(d) Maintenance of adequate workforce in an organisation.
(e) Jobs are filled economically.

(iv) Disadvantages:

(a) Scope for induction of fresh talent is reduced.
(b) Time bound promotions make employees lethargic.
(c) Not applicable to new enterprise.
(d) Spirit of competition among employees is hampered.
(e) Frequent transfers reduce employees' productivity.

- **External Sources of Recruitment:**

(i) Meaning: It refers to searching for employees from the sources outside the organisation.

(ii) Types:

(a) Direct recruitment: Under the direct recruitment, a notice is placed on the notice-board of the enterprise specifying the details of the jobs available.

(b) Casual callers: Many reputed business organisations keep a database of unsolicited applicants in their offices. Such job-seekers can be a valuable source of man power.

(c) Advertisement: Placement agencies provide a nationwide service in matching personnel demand and supply. Management consultancy firms help the organisations to recruit technical, professional and managerial personnel.

(d) Employment exchange: Employment exchanges run by the Government are regarded as a good source of recruitment for unskilled and skilled operative jobs.

(e) Placement agencies and management consultants: Placement agencies provide a nationwide service in matching personnel demand and supply. Management consultancy firms help the organisations to recruit technical, professional and managerial personnel.

Scan to know more about this topic

NEU

(f) Campus recruitment: Colleges and institutes of management and technology have become a popular source of recruitment for technical, professional and managerial jobs.

(g) Recommendation of employees: Applicants introduced by present employees, or their friends and relatives may prove to be a good source of recruitment.

(h) Labour contractors: Labour contractors maintain close contacts with labourers and they can provide the required number of unskilled workers at short notice.

(i) Web publishing: There are certain websites specifically designed and dedicated for the purpose of providing information about both job seekers and job opening.

(j) Advertising on Television: The practice of telecasting of vacant posts over Television is gaining importance these days. The detailed requirements of the job and the qualities required to do it are publicised along with the profile of the organisation where vacancy exists.

(iii) Advantages: [Board, 2023]

(a) Attracts qualified personnel to apply for the jobs
(b) Gives a wider choice to management while selection
(c) Brings fresh talent in the organisation
(d) Develops competitive spirit among the existing staff

(iv) Disadvantages:

(a) Develops dissatisfaction among existing staff
(b) Lengthy process
(c) Heavy cost on advertisement and selection process

MNEMONICS

Concept: External Sources of Recruitment
Interpretation: Child CRAWLED while Playing
C : Campus recruitment
C : Casual callers
R : Recommendation of employees
A : Advertisement
W : Web publishing
L : Labour contractors
E : Employment exchange
D : Direct recruitment
P : Placement agencies and management consultants

SUBJECTIVE TYPE QUESTIONS

Short Answer Type Questions-I (3 marks each)

1. State any three benefits of using internal sources of recruitment. [Outside Delhi Set-1, 2023]

OR

Filling vacancies for various job positions from within the organisations has many benefits. State any four such benefits. [Outside Delhi Set-1, 2023]

Ans. The benefits of Internal Sources of Recruitment are:

(i) Internal recruitment helps to motivate and improve the morale of the employees as it fills vacancies for higher jobs by promoting employees from within the organisation.

(ii) Internal recruitment builds loyalty amongst the staff, thereby reducing labour turnover and absenteeism.

(iii) It is an economical source of recruitment as money is not wasted on advertisements, tests, interviews, checking references, etc. Full information about the candidate is already available.

(iv) It does not require any induction training for employees. They are already familiar with the rules and regulations and the working environment of the organisation. [Marking Scheme, OD, 2023]

2. State any four benefits of using external sources of recruitment. [Outside Delhi Set-1, 2023]

Ans. The benefits of using external sources of recruitment are:

(i) The management can attract qualified and trained people to apply for vacant jobs in the organisation.

(ii) The management has a wider choice while selecting the right candidate.

(iii) External sources bring fresh talent to the organisation.

(iv) External sources encourage a competitive spirit among the existing staff.

[Marking Scheme, OD, 2023]

3. Mrs. Ahilya Pasi is the Principal of a prestigious school in New Delhi. The school has a vacancy of a headmistress/ headmaster of the junior wing of the school. The senior teachers of the school have the opinion that only internal candidates should be considered for this post. However, Mrs. Pasi and the management would like to invite application from external sources too. Briefly explain any three justifications the management can provide to convince the staff for inviting applications of external candidates for the vacant post.

A [SQP 2023]

OR

State any three merits of external sources of recruitment. R [Delhi Comptt. Set-1, 2017]

Ans. Merits of external sources:

(i) **Qualified personnel:** By using external sources of recruitment, the management can attract qualified and trained people to apply for vacant jobs in the organisation.

(ii) **Wider choice:** When vacancies are advertised wisely, a **large number of applicants from outside the organisation can apply**. The management has a wider choice while selecting the people for employment.

(iii) **Fresh Talent:** The present employees may be insufficient or they may not fulfil the specifications of the jobs to be filled. **External recruitment provides wider choice** and brings new blood in the organisation.

(iv) **Competitive spirit:** If a company taps external sources, the existing sources, the existing staff will have to compete with the outsiders. They will work harder to show better performance.

(Any three) [1×3 = 3]

4. Identify and explain the two sources of recruitment which cannot be used when the existing staff is either insufficient or does not fulfil the eligibility criteria of the jobs to be filled. U [SQP 2021-22]

Ans. Two sources of internal recruitment:

(i) **Promotion** refers to shifting of an employee to a higher position, carrying higher responsibilities, facilities, status and pay.

(ii) **Transfer** involves shifting of an employee from **one job to another,** one department to another, without substantive change in the responsibilities and status of the employee.

[Marking Scheme SQP 2021-22] [1½ + 1½ = 3]

5. State any three merits of internal sources of recruitment. R [Delhi Comptt. Set 2, 2017] [Outside Delhi Comptt. Set 1, 2, 3, 2017]

Ans. Merits of internal sources of recruitment:

(i) Employees are motivated as promotion at a higher level may lead to a chain of promotions at lower levels in the organisation.

(ii) Internal sources simplify the process of selection as the candidates are already known to the organisation.

(iii) People recruited from within the organisation do not need induction training as the employees are already familiar with the organisation.

(iv) These sources help in adjustment of surplus staff in those departments where there is a shortage of staff.

(v) Filling of jobs internally is economical as compared to external sources of recruitment. **(Any three)**

(If an examinee has given only the headings, ½ mark for each heading should be awarded)

[1 × 3 = 3]

[Marking Scheme, Delhi, OD 2017]

6. Nupur, a very able HR manager, is called by her boss. He tells her to judge whether there is under manning or over manning in the organisation. She takes her work sincerely and finds out that the total number of employees in the organisation

is less than required. Then she starts a process of searching potential employees for the organisation. identify and explain process is started by Nupur to meet the problem of under manning? A [OEB]

Concept Applied | Recruitment

Ans. The process started by Nupur to meet under manning is recruitment. Recruitment refers to the process of finding suitable candidates for a job or a function. It has been defined as 'the process of searching for prospective employees and stimulating them to apply for jobs in an organisation.'

7. State any three limitations of external sources of recruitment. R [Delhi Comptt. Set-3, 2017]

Short Answer Type Questions-II (4 marks each)

1. Explain briefly 'Casual Callers' and 'Labour Contractors' as an external sources of recruitment.

U [Outside Delhi Set 1, 2, 3, 2017]

Ans. Casual Callers:

(i) It is an external source of recruitment in which a list of job-seekers is prepared and screened to fill the vacancies as they arise, from the database of unsolicited applications kept in the office.

(ii) It reduces the cost of recruitment.

Labour Contractors:

(i) It is an external source of recruitment in which a labour contractor maintains close contacts with labourers and provides the required number of unskilled workers at short notice.

[Marking Scheme, OD 2017] **[2 + 2 = 4]**

2. Explain briefly 'transfers' and 'promotions' as an internal sources of recruitment.

U [Delhi Set 1, 2, 3, 2017]

Long Answer Type Questions-I (6 marks each)

1. Identify and explain the source of an external recruitment used in the following examples:

(i) Ashish introduced Prem to his company, Mahey Ltd., and he was immediately hired.

(ii) Bushra, an HR from Bhawan Ltd., found the resume of Preetika very attractive, listed on Indeed.com, and so she called her for the selection process.

(iii) Pranita went for the job interview which was held in her college.

(iv) The notice of walk-in interview was placed at the gate of Preety Enterprises. [SQP 2023-24]

Ans. (i) Recommendations by Employees: Sometimes, the existing employees of the organisation recommend applicants who can be their friends and relatives. This type of recruitment proves to be a good source of recruitment as the employee's background is sufficiently known. A type of preliminary screening takes place because the present employees know both the company and the candidates and they would try to satisfy both.

(ii) Web Publishing: There are certain websites specifically designed and dedicated to providing information about both job seekers and job openings.

(iii) Campus Recruitment: Campus Recruitment, an external source of recruitment, means a program conducted within an educational institute or in a common place to provide jobs to students pursuing education and are nearing completion of the program.

(iv) Gate Hiring or Direct Recruitment: Under direct recruitment, a notice is placed on the notice board of the enterprise specifying the details of the jobs available. Job seekers assemble outside the premises of the organisation on the specified date and selection is done on the spot.

[Marking Scheme, SQP 2023-24]

2. There were two vacancies for the post of Assistant Manager in 'Gyan Electrics Private Ltd.' Parth, the Human Resources Manager identified one suitable candidate Vishwas from within the organisation and promoted him to the post of Assistant Manager. For another post, the Manager Parth took help of a placement agency and selected Saleem. After six months, Parth observed that Vishwas's performance was much better than Saleem's performance though Vishwas was less qualified than Saleem. Hence, Parth decided that in future he will not make any appointment with the help of an outside source. Explain any four reasons on the basis of which Parth would have taken the above decision.

A [Delhi Set 1, 2, 3, 2018]

3. Harold Chemicals is looking for qualified and talented people to apply for vacant jobs in the organisation. With the passage of time the organisation has learned a lot with its experience. It knows when it goes for final selection of candidates, if will have to design different tests. They want to test the employees on the basis of their learning and decision-making ability. The company wants to ensure proper testing of the recruited candidates. After this the candidates will be judged on the basis of in-depth formal conversation. After the selection the candidates are placed and trained. Employees have to be trained on the equipment they will be using but this training will take place away from the workplace.

(i) Identify the type of recruitment should the company depend upon.

(ii) Also, state any four advantages of type of recruitment identified in part (i). A [OEB]

Concept Applied | Merits of external recruitment

Ans. (i) The company should depend upon external recruitment to meet its needs. Harold chemicals is looking for qualified and talented people to apply for vacant jobs in the organisation.

(ii) The advantages of using external sources of recruitment are as follows:

(a) Qualified Personnel: By using external sources of recruitment, the management can attract qualified and trained people to apply for vacant jobs in the organisation.

(b) Wider Choice: When vacancies are advertised widely, a large number of applicants from outside

These Questions are for practice and their solutions are given at the end of the chapter.

the organisation apply. The management has a wider choice while selecting the people for employment.

(iii) Fresh Talent: The present employees may be insufficient or they may not fulfill the specifications of the jobs to be filled. External recruitment provides wider choice and brings new blood in the organisation. However, it is expensive and time consuming.

(iv) Competitive Spirit: If a company taps external sources, the existing staff will have to compete with the outsiders. They will work harder to show better performance. [1+4=5]

4. Mohit, the Marketing Head, Rakesh, the Assistant Manager and John, the Human Resource Manager of Aural Textile Ltd. decided to leave the company. The Chief Executive Officer of the company called John, the Human Resource Manager and requested her to fill up the vacancies before leaving the organisation. Informing that her subordinate Aarti Shukla was very competent and trustworthy, John suggested that if she could be moved up in the hierarchy, she would do the needful. The Chief Executive Officer agreed for the same. Aarti Shukla contacted ABC Recruiters who advertised for the post of marketing head for Aural Textile Ltd. They were able to recruit a suitable candidate for the company. Rakesh's vacancy was filled up by screening the database of unsolicited applications lying in the office.

Identify and explain the internal/external sources of recruitment used by Aural Textile Ltd. to fill up the above stated vacancies. A [OEB]

Concept Applied: Internal and External sources of recruitment

Ans. Sources of recruitment used by Aural textile Ltd:

(i) Promotion: Business enterprises generally follow the practice of filling higher jobs by promoting employees from lower jobs. Promotion leads to shifting an employee to a higher position, carrying **higher responsibilities, facilities, status and pay.** Promotion is a vertical shifting of employees. This practice helps to improve the motivation, loyalty and satisfaction level of employees.

(ii) Placement Agencies and Management Consultants: Placement agencies provide a nationwide service in matching personnel demand and supply. These agencies compile bio-data of a large number of candidates and recommend suitable names to their clients. Such agencies charge fee for their services and they are useful where extensive screening is required. Management consultancy firms help the organisations to recruit technical, professional and managerial personnel.

(iii) Casual Callers: Many reputed business organisations keep a database of unsolicited applicants in their offices. Such job-seekers can be a valuable source of man power. A list of such job-seekers can be prepared and can be screened to fill the vacancies as they arise. The major merit of this source of recruitment is that it reduces the cost of recruiting workforce in comparison to other sources. [2×3=6]

5. Srija runs an NGO under the name 'Sarthak' in Delhi. The organisation is engaged in offering waste paper recycling services to all kinds of institutions in the Delhi NCR region. It also manufactures custom made paper stationery out of recycled paper on order for the interested institutions at a very competitive price. The website of 'Sarthak' provides a link to a Careers site wherein the people desirous of joining the NGO can use simple Job Search to find the right opportunity for themselves. The NGO also keeps a database of unsolicited applicants in its office so that job seekers may be notified of future opportunities when they arise.

By quoting lines from the paragraph, identify and explain the two sources of external recruitment being used by the NGO 'Sarthak' by quoting lines from the paragraph. A [OEB]

Ans. The two sources of external recruitment being used by the NGO 'Sarthak' are as follows:

(i) Web Publishing: Internet is becoming a common source of recruitment these days. There are certain **websites** specifically designed and dedicated for the purpose of providing information about both job seekers and job opening. In fact, websites are very commonly visited both by the prospective employees and the organisations searching for suitable people.

Lines - "The website of 'Sarthak' provides a link to a Careers site wherein the people desirous of joining the NGO can use simple Job Search to find the right opportunity for themselves"

(ii) Casual Callers: Many reputed business organisations keep a database of unsolicited applicants in their offices. Such job-seekers can be a valuable source of man power. A list of such job-seekers can be prepared and can be screened to fill the vacancies as they arise. The major merit of this source of recruitment is that it reduces the cost of recruiting workforce in comparison to other sources.

Lines - "The NGO also keeps a database of unsolicited applicants in its office so that job seekers may be notified of future opportunities when they arise."

[3 + 3 = 6]

6. Race Tech Ltd. is one of the top IT companies in India. The company does mass recruitment each year from different colleges offering fresher level job to the final year students. This helps in recruiting the brightest and the best available talent in the educational institutions.

In context of the above case:

(i) Identify and explain the source of external recruitment adopted by the company.

(ii) Explain briefly any three advantages of using the external sources of recruitment. A [OEB]

Ans: (i) Campus Recruitment is the source of external recruitment adopted by the company. **Colleges** and **institutes of management** and technology have become a popular source of recruitment for technical, professional and managerial jobs. Many big organisations maintain a close liaison with the universities, vocational schools and management institutes to recruit qualified personnel for various jobs. Recruitment from educational institutions is a well-established practice of businesses. This is referred to as campus recruitment.

(ii) The advantages of using the external sources of recruitment are stated below:

(a) **Qualified Personnel:** By using external sources of recruitment, the management can attract qualified and trained people to apply for vacant jobs in the organisation.

(b) **Wider Choice:** As the vacancies are advertised widely a large number of applicants from outside the organisation are likely to apply. This gives the organisation a wider choice while selecting the people for employment.

(c) **Fresh Talent:** The present employees may be insufficient or they may not fulfill the specifications of the jobs to be filled. External recruitment provide wider choice and brings new blood in the organisation. However, it is expensive and time consuming. [1½×4=6]

7. Ali Mohammad, the CEO of Super Ltd believes that Human Resources is the most important asset of the firm. He believes that no organisation can be successful unless it can fill and keep filled the various positions provided for in the structure with the right kind of people. Identify the function of management being discussed above and state the benefits to the organisation that its proper application in the firm will ensure. [SQP 2023-24]

Ans. Proper staffing ensures the following benefits for the organisation:

(i) Helps in discovering and obtaining competent personnel for various jobs.

(ii) Ensures higher performance by putting the right person on the right job.

(iii) Ensures the continuous survival and growth of the enterprise through succession planning for managers.

(iv) Helps to ensure optimum utilisation of the human resources. By avoiding overmanning, it prevents under-utilisation of personnel and high labour costs. At the same time, it avoids disruption of work by indicating in advance the shortages of personnel.

(v) Improves job satisfaction and morale of employees through objective assessment and fair rewarding of their contribution. [Marking Scheme, SQP 2023-24]

TOPIC-3 Selection Process

Concepts Covered

- Meaning of selection
- Steps involved in the process of selection

Revision Notes

- Selection is the process of identifying and choosing the best person out of a number of prospective candidates for a job.
- **Process of Selection** [Board, 2018]

(i) **Preliminary Screening:** Elimination of unqualified and unfit job-seekers.

(ii) **Selection Tests:** Measure certain characteristics of individuals.

(iii) **Employment Interview:** In-depth conversation to evaluate applicant's suitability.

(iv) **Reference and Background Check:** Verify and gain additional information about an applicant.

(v) **Selection Decision:** Candidates who pass tests, interviews and reference checks are finally selected.

(vi) **Medical Examination:** Candidate undergoes a medical fitness test.

Scan to know more about this topic

Selection Process

(vii) **Job Offer:** Letter of appointment is offered to the applicant for acceptance of the applicant.

(viii) **Contract of Employment:** Contract documents are exchanged between the employer and the employee.

MNEMONICS

Concept: Selection Process:

Interpretation: Please Smile Else Renowned Star Michael Jackson won't Come

P : Preliminary Screening
S : Selection Tests
E : Employment Interview
R : Reference and Background Checks
S : Selection Decision
M : Medical Examination
J : Job Offer
C : Contract of Employment

SUBJECTIVE TYPE QUESTIONS

Short Answer Type Questions-I (3 marks each)

1. Stelo Plastic makers has decided to include a team of dynamic managers in the company. For this they want to judge the pattern of interests of the potential managers. After giving this test they want to further know how much the candidate is useful for organisation. They decide to take another test which can measure the existing skills of the candidates. Rakesh, an exceptional candidate, is given certain document which contains information like job title, pay, allowances, responsibilities, etc. After the employees join they are given a very good training. The Company doesn't want to stop at 'training' which is a job related process. They want to bring a concept which is a career related process. Identify and explain the document which is given to Rakesh in the above case? U [OEB]

Concept Applied | Selection Process

Ans. The document which is given to Rakesh is contract of employment. After the job offer has been made and candidate accepts the offer, certain documents need to be executed by the employer and the candidate. One such document is the attestation form. This form contains certain vital details about the candidate, which are authenticated and attested by him or her. Attestation form will be a valid record for future reference. There is also a need for preparing a contract of employment. Basic information that should be included in a written contract of employment will vary according to the level of the job.

2. State the steps in the selection procedure, after the employment interview and before the job offer. R [Delhi & Outside Delhi, 2018]

3. Mohan runs a security service providers agency. Considering that psychological testing is a critical step for judging the potential of the prospective candidates for a career in law enforcement, he uses various types of psychological tests as part of the selection processes. This is done to ensure that potential new officers are emotionally and psychologically suited to carry out the requirements of the job.

Identify and explain the type of test that Mohan may use to assess the potential of the prospective candidates. A [OEB]

Short Answer Type Questions-II (4 marks each)

1. HRA & Co. is looking for a Sales Manager. It has posted an opening on its website post on which it received 1000 applications. The human resource manager is suggesting doing the first step filter exercise by holding a selection test. However, not everyone is convinced with this idea. Mention any three important selection tests that the human resource manager can use to convince the team. [SQP 2023-24]

Ans. Here are three important benefits of using selection tests in the hiring process that the human resource manager can use to convince the team:

(i) Objective assessment: Selection tests can provide an objective assessment of the candidate's skills and abilities, which is not influenced by personal biases or perceptions. This ensures that all candidates are evaluated based on the same criteria, providing a fair and consistent selection process.

(ii) Predictive validity: Selection tests can have high predictive validity, which means that they can accurately predict job performance based on the candidate's test scores. This can help to identify candidates who are likely to be successful in the job and can reduce the risk of hiring the wrong candidate.

(iii) Time and cost-effectiveness: Selection tests can be time and cost-effective compared to other selection methods such as interviews or assessment centres. They can be administered to a large number of candidates simultaneously, saving time and resources. This can be particularly useful when there are a large number of candidates to be evaluated, as in the case of HRA & Co. with 1000 applicants. [Marking Scheme, SQP 2023-24]

2. Name the mechanism that attempts to measure certain characteristics of individuals in the process of identifying and choosing the best person out of the number of prospective candidates for the job. Enumerate any three of its types. A [SQP 2023] [1]

Ans. Selection test

Types of tests are:

(i) Intelligence test is one of the important psychological tests used to measure the level of intelligence quotient of an individual and is an indicator of a person's ability or the ability to make decisions and judgments.

(ii) Aptitude test is a measure of an individual's potential for learning new skills and indicates the person's capacity to develop.

(iii) Personality tests provide clues to a person's emotions, her reactions, maturity, and value system and probe the overall personality.

(iv) Trade tests measure the existing skills of the individual, level of knowledge and proficiency in the area of professions or technical training.

(v) Interest tests are used to know the pattern of interests or involvement of a person. **(Any three) [1×3=3]**

3. Mr. Murthy is the Human Resource Manager of Jai Hind Hospital in Vellore. He has to appoint nurses for the hospital. Since patients in the hospital are of different types, he wants to find out the candidates' maturity and emotions in dealing with the patients. He also wants to know about the candidates' ability to make decisions.

Explain two types of tests that Mr. Murthy can use to meet his requirements.

A [Delhi Comptt. Set 1, 2, 3, 2017]

Concept Applied | Selection type

Ans. Two types of tests that Mr Murthy can use to meet his requirements are:

(i) Personality Test It provides clues to a person's emotions, reactions, maturity, value systems etc. They probe the overall personality and are difficult to design and implement.

(ii) Intelligence Test It measures the level of intelligence quotient of an individual. It is an indicator of a person's learning ability or the ability to make decisions and judgments.

4. "After the selection decision and before the job offer is made, the candidate is required to undergo a medical fitness test." Explain the next two steps in the process of selection after the step mentioned in the above lines. U [OEB]

Ans. (i) Job Offer: The next step in the selection process is job offer to those applicants who have passed all the previous hurdles. Job offer is made through a **letter of appointment/confirm** his acceptance. Such a letter generally contains a date by which the appointee must report on duty. The appointee must be given reasonable time for reporting.

(ii) Contract of Employment: After the job offer has been made and candidate accepts the offer, certain documents need to be executed by the employer and

These Questions are for practice and their solutions are given at the end of the chapter.

the candidate. One such document is the attestation form. This form contains certain vital details about the candidate, which are authenticated and attested by him or her. Attestation form will be a valid record for future reference. There is also a need for preparing a contract of employment. **[2+2=4]**

Long Answer Type Questions-I (6 marks each)

1. In an interview with a leading news channel, Mr. Rakesh Kwatra, CEO of 'Get My Job" has suggested that the companies which want more and more people to apply for jobs in their organisation should make the process of applying for jobs easier and candidate friendly. It is for this reason, he said, that most progressive companies today have a short application process. He also said that the application form filled by the candidate is very important as it is the information supplied in the application forms, which helps the manager in eliminating unqualified or unfit job seekers. The company can create a mechanism that attempts to measure certain characteristics of individuals like aptitude, manual dexterity, and intelligence to personality. The candidate may then be called for an in-depth conversation to evaluate their suitability for the job.

(i) Name the process and steps in the process of identifying and choosing the best person out of a number of prospective candidates for a job discussed above.

(ii) Also explain the next two steps in the process which can be subsequently performed by the company.

A [SQP 2021-22]

Ans. (i) Selection

Steps in the process of selection discussed:

(a) Preliminary Screening

(b) Selection Tests

(c) Employment interview **[½×4=2]**

(ii) Next two steps:

(a) **Reference and background checks:** Many employers request names, addresses and telephone numbers of references for the purpose of verifying information and gaining additional information on an applicant. Previous employers, known persons, teachers and university professors can act as references. **[2]**

(b) **Selection Decision:** The final decision has to be made from among the candidates who passed the tests, interviews and reference checks. The views of the concerned manager will be generally considered in the final selection. **[2]**

[Marking Scheme, SQP 2021-22]

2. 'Entertainment India Ltd.' has been incorporated with the objective of entertaining people by organising festivals, programmes and other similar events depicting the rich cultural heritage of the country. The company management has renowned personalities from the field of art, literature and culture. They decided to give a platform to young budding musicians, poets and artists. The company decided its organisational structure by grouping similar jobs together. Thereafter, the heads of different departments were also appointed. Nisha, one of the heads, did an analysis of the number, type and qualification necessary for people to be appointed. The information generated in the process of writing the job description and the candidate profile was used to develop 'Situations vacant' advertisement. This was published in print media and flashed in electronic media. This brought in a flood of response.

Explain the other steps which Nisha has to perform to complete the process being discussed above.

A [Delhi Set-1, 2019]

Ans.

Topper's Answer, 2019

– The other steps which Nisha has to perform to complete the process of ~~selection are~~ Staffing are–

i– Selection–' Selection refers to the process of discovering and choosing the most suitable and promising candidate to fill the vacant posts and rejecting the unsuitable ones. Selection is a negative process because at every stage many people are eliminated from the process and a few move on ~~to~~ to the next stage until the right type of person is found.

ii– Placement and Orientation– The selected employees have to be placed at the right jobs. Placement refers to occupying of position by the employees for which they had been selected. Orientation refers to the process of introducing the selected employees to other employees and familiarising them with the rules and policies of the organisation.

iii– ~~Tran~~ Training and Development–
Training is the process by which aptitudes, skills and knowledge of employees to perform specific jobs are improved. The management has to organise training programmes for employees for the purpose of enrichment of skills required to perform the job. Training can be organised through in-house training centres or forged alliances with foreign institutes to ensure continuing learning of employees. Development is the process by which employees acquire skills and competencies to handle higher jobs in future. The organisation should put in considerable efforts to organise training and development programmes for the staff.

iv- Performance Appraisal - The next step is to evaluate employee's performance through performance appraisal. Performance appraisal means evaluating an employee's current and past performances as against certain predetermined standards. It involves defining the job, appraising performance and providing feedback. Every organisation has some formal and informal means of evaluating their employee's performance.

v- Promotion & Career Planning - The next step is related with career planning which includes all activities related to promotion and transfer of employees based on their performance so as to improve their skills and satisfy their esteem needs and basic physiological needs.

vi- Compensation - The last step is to fix up the compensation of an employee to match his contribution to the organisation with his remuneration. Compensation includes all forms of pay and rewards given to employees. It may be in the form of direct financial payments like wages, salaries, bonus or indirect payments like employer's paid insurance and paid-leaves.

3. Explain briefly the various selection or employment tests used by the management for selecting the employees. A I A [OEB]

Ans. The different types of Selection Tests are:

(i) Intelligence Test: It is one of the types of psychological tests which is used to **measure the level of intelligence** quotient of an individual. The concept behind this test is to measure mental age. It is an indicator of a person's intellect.

(ii) Aptitude Test: It measures the **individual's potential for learning new skills**. It indicates how well a person would be able to perform after training. Such tests are good indices of a person's future success score.

(iii) Personality Test: Personality tests measure various **dimensions of a personality** such as person's emotions, his reactions, maturity and value system, etc. These tests are difficult to design, implement and interpret as these probe the overall personality.

(iv) Trade Test: It is developed to measure the actual skills possessed to perform a job. Trade tests **measure the level of knowledge and proficiency** in the area of profession or technical training.

(v) Interest Tests: Every individual has more interest in a particular type of job than the other. Interest tests are developed to **measure the pattern of interests** or involvement of a person for a particular job.

(Any four) [1½ × 4 = 6]

4. Amit Gupta runs a service providers agency. The services provided by her firm include all kinds of research and information gathering in fields such as financial market, medicine, animation and design, etc. He believes that the success of the company can be achieved mainly through the people it chooses to employ. Therefore, he aims to attract the best people and provides them innumerable opportunities to enhance their knowledge and skill relevant to their position.

Considering that psychological testing is a critical step for judging the potential of the prospective candidates for a career in law enforcement, he uses various types of psychological tests as part of the selection processes. This is done to ensure that potential new officers are emotionally and psychologically suited to carry out the requirements of the job. In context of the above case, identify and explain steps involved in the selection process after conducting the assessment tests. A [OEB]

Concept Applied: Steps in the selection process

Ans. The further important steps in the process of selection, after conducting assessment tests are as follows:

(i) Employment Interview: It is a formal interaction between the employer and job candidate. It is an in-depth conversation which is conducted to evaluate an applicant's suitability for the position. The interviewer seeks information and the interviewee provides the same.

(ii) Reference and Background Checks: A large number of employers ask for names, addresses and telephone numbers of references. These are people known to the job candidate and the purpose is to verify information as well as gain additional information about an applicant. For instance, previous employers, colleagues, teachers, etc. may act as references.

(iii) Selection Decision: The final candidate is chosen from among the candidates who have cleared all the stages *i.e.*, passed the tests, cleared the interviews as well as reference checks.

(iv) Medical Examination: Once selection decision is made but before the job offer is given, the candidate has to undergo a medical fitness test in order to assess his physical well-being. Thus, the job offer is given to a person who is declared fit after the medical examination.

(v) Job Offer: The next step in the selection process is job offer, given to those applicants who have passed all the previous tests.

(vi) Contract of Employment: After the job offer has been made and candidate accepts the offer, certain documents need to be executed by the employer and the candidate. One such document is the attestation form. This form contains certain vital details about the candidate, which are authenticated and attested by him or her. Attestation form will be a valid record for future reference. **[1×6=6]**

TOPIC-4 Training and Development

Concepts Covered

• Concept of training and development. • Importance of training to the organisation and to the employees. • Meaning of Induction, vestibule, apprenticeship and internship training. • Difference between training and development. • Concept of on the job and Off the job training.

Revision Notes

Scan to know more about this topic

Training and Development

• Training and Development is an attempt to improve the current or future employee's performance by increasing an employee's ability to perform through learning, usually by changing the employee's attitude or increasing his or her skills and knowledge.

• **Importance of Training and Development**

(i) **To the Organisation:** [Board, 2018]

(a) Systematic learning prevents wastage of efforts and money.

(b) Enhances employee's productivity leading to higher profits.

(c) Enables employee to become managers in future.

(d) Increases employee morale and reduces employee turnover.

(e) Obtains better response to the dynamic environment.

(ii) **To the Employee:**

(a) Leads to better career due to improved skills.

(b) Increases earning due to enhancement in performance.

(c) Reduces accidents due to careful handling of machines.

(d) Increases satisfaction and morale of the employees.

• **Training Methods:**

(i) **On-the-Job Methods:**

(a) **Apprenticeship Programmes:** Apprentice (trainee) works under the guidance of a master worker to acquire a higher level of skill, *e.g.*, plumbers, electricians, etc. [Board, 2019]

(b) **Internship Training:** It is a joint programme between an educational institution and business firm in which students work in firms to gain practical knowledge and skills.

(c) **Induction Training:** New employee is introduced to the organisation, its work culture and colleagues to make him familiar and comfortable on the job.

(ii) **Off-the-Job Methods:**

Vestibule Training: Artificial/simulated work environment is created in a class room, away from actual work floor, where training is given on dummy models of actual equipment. [Board, 2019]

KEY TERMS

Training: Any process by which the aptitudes, skills and abilities of employees to perform specific jobs are increased.

Development: Learning opportunities designed to help employees grow.

SUBJECTIVE TYPE QUESTIONS

Short Answer Type Questions-I (3 marks each)

1. The allocation of resources for employee training and development has long-term value for the organisation's growth and sustainability.

[APQ 2023-24]

Ans. (i) When we invest in training and development, we empower our employees with the skills and knowledge they need to excel in their roles. Well-trained employees are more confident, efficient, and productive.

(ii) Investing in training and development allows us to stay ahead of the competition by adapting to emerging trends, technological advancements, and changing customer needs.

(iii) Employees value organisations that prioritise their growth and development. By investing in training, we show our commitment to their professional advancement, fostering higher employee engagement and job satisfaction.

(iv) A learning culture encourages employees to think creatively, leading to innovation and process improvements. Investing in employee development, we nurture a culture that values continuous learning, enabling us to adapt swiftly to changing market conditions and customer demands.

[Marking Scheme APQ 2023-24]

2. Give any three differences between training and development. U [OEB]

3. Explain 'Vestibule Training' and 'Apprenticeship Programme' as methods of training.

U [Outside Delhi Set-1, 2019]

Concept Applied	Concept of vestibule and apprenticeship training

Ans. Vestibule Training

(i) Vestibule Training is a method of training which is conducted on the equipments and machines employees will be using, away from the actual place of work.

(ii) It is generally used where the employees are required to handle sophisticated machinery.

Apprenticeship Programme

(i) Apprenticeship Training/ Programme is a method of training in which the trainee is kept under guidance of a master worker for a prescribed period of time to acquire a higher level of skill.

(ii) People who want to enter skilled trades *e.g.*, plumbers and electricians are often required to undergo such programme. [1½ +1 ½ = 3]

[Marking Scheme, OD 2019]

This Question is for practice and its solution is given at the end of the chapter.

4. Explain the following methods of training:
(i) Vestibule Training; and
(ii) Internship Training.

U [Outside Delhi Comptt. Set 1, 2, 3, 2017]

Ans. (i) Vestibule Training:

(a) It is a method of training which is imparted with the help of equipments and machines identical to those at the place of work.

(b) The training is conducted away from actual work floor and is generally used where the employees are required to handle sophisticated machinery.

(ii) Internship Training:

(a) Internship Training is a joint programme of training between educational institutions and business firms.

(b) Besides carrying out regular studies, the trainees also work in some factory or office to acquire practical knowledge and skills. **1½ × 2 = 3**

[Marking Scheme, OD 2017]

5. Describe briefly the following methods of training:
(i) Apprenticeship Training
(ii) Internship Training.

U [Delhi Comptt. Set 1, 2, 3, 2017]

Ans. (i) Apprenticeship Training

(a) Apprenticeship Training is a method of training in which the trainee is kept under guidance of a master worker for a prescribed period of time.

(b) It is designed to acquire a higher level of skill.

(c) People who want to enter skilled trades *e.g.*, plumbers and electricians are often required to undergo such programme.

(ii) Internship Training

(a) Internship Training is a joint programme of training between educational institutions and business firms.

(b) Besides carrying out regular studies, the trainees also work in some factory or office to acquire practical knowledge and skills. **[1½ × 2 = 3]**

[Marking Scheme, Delhi 2017]

Short Answer Type Questions-II (4 marks each)

1. Explain the 'Apprenticeship Programme' as a method of training. [Outside Delhi Set-2, 2023]

Ans. In the Apprenticeship Programme type of training, theoretical instructions and practical learning are provided in training institutes to trainees. Apprenticeship training puts the trainee under the guidance of a leader. These are designed to acquire a higher level of skills. People seeking to enter skilled traits to become, for example, plumbers, electricians, or iron workers, are often required to undergo apprenticeship training.

2. After passing his secondary school examination, David left the school at the age of 15 years and started getting training under his father. His father, a renowned electrician, had worked for many companies. He everyday started accompanying his father on work and watched him carefully while working. David was a good learner and learnt the techniques of work quickly. Now his father started passing on the tricks of the trade to David. With the passage of time David acquired a high level skill and became a well-known electrician in Indore. Big business-houses started calling him for electrical-wiring.

(i) Name the method of training discussed in the above para.

(ii) State any three benefits which David could get on being trained. R [Delhi Set 1, 2, 3, 2018]

Ans. (i) Apprenticeship Training

(ii) Benefits which David could get on being trained:

(a) It may lead to his promotion and career growth due to improved skills and knowledge.

(b) It will help him to earn more due to improved performance.

(c) It will reduce accidents as he will be more efficient to handle machines.

(d) It will increase his satisfaction and morale.

(Any three)

(If an examinee has given only the heading, ½ mark for each heading should be awarded.)

[1 + 3 = 4]

[Marking Scheme, Delhi, 2018]

3. Enumerate any four benefits of the process by which the aptitudes, skills and abilities of employees to perform specific jobs are increased. U [SQP 2023-24]

OR

Explain any three benefits of training to the employees. [Outside Delhi Set-1, 2023]

OR

'Training not only improves the current or future performance of employees but also benefits the organisation in many ways.' State any four such benefits. [Outside Delhi Set-2, 2023]

Ans. The benefits of training to an organisation are as follows:

(i) Training is a systematic learning, Always better than hit and trial methods which lead to wastage of efforts and money.

(ii) It enhances employee productivity both in terms of quantity and quality, leading to higher profits.

(iii) Training equips the future manager who can take over in case of emergency.

(iv) Training increases employee morale and reduces absenteeism and employee turnover.

(v) It helps in obtaining an effective response to a fast changing environment technological and economic. **(Any four) [1×4=4]**

[Marking Scheme, SQP 2023-24]

4. The workers of 'Vyam Ltd.' are unable to work on new and hi-tech machines imported by the company to fulfil the increased demand. Therefore, the workers are seeking extra guidance from the supervisor. The supervisor is overburdened with the frequent calls of workers.

Suggest how the supervisor, by increasing the skills and knowledge of workers, can make them handle their work independently. Also state any three benefits that the workers will derive by the decision of the supervisor. C [OEB]

Ans. Training of Employees/Vestibule Training/On- the-Job Training

The benefits that workers will derive by the decision of the supervisor are:

(i) It helps in promotion and career growth due to improved skills and knowledge.

(ii) It helps them to earn more due to the improved performance.

(iii) It reduces accidents as the employees are more efficient to handle machines.

(iv) It increases the morale of the employees as the employees are more satisfied. **(Any three)**

[1 + 3 = 4]

Long Answer Type Questions (6 marks each)

1. 'Moga Industries Ltd.' approached a well-established university in the city of Madurai to recruit qualified personnel for various technical and professional jobs. They selected Tanya, Ritu, Garima and Chetan for various vacancies in the organisation. After the selection and placement, 'Moga Industries Ltd.' felt the need to increase the skills and abilities, and the development of the positive attitude of the employees to perform their specific jobs better. The company also realised that learning new skills would improve the job performance of the employees. Hence, the company decided to take actions for the same.

(i) Name the step of the staffing process regarding which the company decided to take action.

(ii) State the benefits of the action to 'Moga Industries Ltd.' A [Delhi & Outside Delhi 2018]

Ans. (i) Training and Development

(If an examinee has written 'Training' instead of 'Training and Development', ONLY ½ mark to be awarded)

(ii) Benefits of training to 'Moga Industries Ltd.':

(a) It avoids wastage of efforts and money as training is systematic learning, better than hit and trial methods.

(b) It enhances employee productivity both in terms of quantity and quality leading to higher profits.

(c) It equips the future manager to take over in an emergency.

(d) It reduces employees' turnover as it increases employee morale and reduces absenteeism.

(e) It helps in obtaining effective response in a fast changing environment.

(If an examinee has given only the headings, ½ mark for each heading should be awarded)

1+5=6

[Marking Scheme, Delhi & OD 2018]

2. Training is a life-long necessity, both for the employees as well as for the organisation. Justify the statement by giving three arguments each in favour of the employees and the organisation. AI A [OEB]

OR

"Training is beneficial both for the organisation as well as for the employees." Explain any three benefits of training towards the organisation and any three towards the employees. A [OEB]

Concept Applied: Benefits of training in employee and organisation context

Ans. Training is a life-long necessity for employees:

(i) It leads to better career of the individual.

(ii) It helps them to earn more by increased performance.

(iii) It increases the satisfaction and morale of the employees.

(iv) It makes the employees more efficient to handle machines and therefore, lesser prone to accidents.

(Any three)

Training is a life-long necessity for organisations:

(i) It avoids wastage of efforts and money by systematic learning of skills.

(ii) It enhances employee's productivity leading to higher profits in the organisation.

(iii) It equips the future manager who can take over in case of an emergency.

(iv) It reduces absenteeism and increases turnover of the organisation by increasing employees' morale.

(v) It helps in obtaining an effective response to a fast changing environment. **(Any three) [3 + 3 = 6]**

3. Mecho Ltd. purchased a new machinery from Japan for manufacturing some auto components. It was a cost-effective and quality production machine but during the production process, manager observed that the quality of the production was not as per standards. On investigation, it was found that there was lack of knowledge of using these hi-tech machines. So, frequent visits by engineers were required from Japan but this resulted in high overhead charges.

Suggest what can be done to develop the skills and abilities of employees for producing quality products by using these hi-tech machines. Also state how the employees or the organisation will be benefited by your suggestion. C [OEB]

4. The employees of 'Bells and Pepper' a restaurant, are trained through a structured programme that provides training in each area within the restaurant. The employees are put under the guidance of a master worker. Employees learn their jobs on the cooking equipment they will be using. The trainees learn the skills necessary for running each of the 12 workstations in the restaurant, from taking orders to the cooking area. This enables the employees to gain a broader understanding of all parts of the business and how the restaurant functions as a whole. The trainee gets fully involved in the department's operations and also gets a chance to test his/her own aptitude and ability. When employees are trained by this method, the organisation finds it easier at the time of promotions, replacements or transfers. Identify and explain the methods of training described in the above case. U [OEB]

This Question is for practice and its solution is given at the end of the chapter.

Ans. (i) Apprenticeship Programmes: Apprenticeship programmes put the trainee under the guidance of a master worker. These are designed to acquire a higher level of skill. People seeking to enter skilled jobs, to become, for example, plumbers, electricians or iron-workers, are often required to undergo apprenticeship training. These apprentices are trainees who spend a prescribed amount of time working with an experienced guide, or trainer. A uniform period of training is offered to trainees, in which both fast and slowly learn here, are placed together. Slow learners may require additional training.

(ii) Vestibule Training: Employees learn their jobs on the equipment they will be using, but the training is conducted away from the actual work floor. Actual work environments are created in a class room and employees use the same materials, files and equipment. This is usually done when employees are required to handle sophisticated machinery and equipment. **[3+3=6]**

COMPETENCY BASED QUESTIONS

Objective Type Questions

[A] Multiple Choice Questions

1. The next step in the 'Selection Process' after 'Selection Decision' is

(A) Job Offer
(B) Medical Examination
(C) Selection Tests
(D) Contract of Employment [Delhi Set-1, 2023]

Ans. Option (B) is correct.

Explanation : After the selection decision and before the job offer is made, the candidate is required to undergo a medical fitness test. The job offer is given to the candidate being declared fit after the medical examination. [Marking Scheme, Delhi 2023]

2. 'RP Infotech Ltd.' decided to approach 'Patel Engineering College' to recruit qualified personnel for various technical jobs in its newly opened branch in Surat. Which source of recruitment from the following has been used by 'RP Infotech Ltd.' in the above case:

(A) Direct Recruitment
(B) Placement Agencies and Management Consultants
(C) Campus Recruitment
(D) Recommendation of employees [Delhi Set-1, 2023]

Ans. Option (C) is correct.

Explanation: Campus recruitment involves companies visiting educational institutions such as colleges and universities to identify and hire potential candidates directly from the campus. This method is commonly used to hire fresh graduates and entry-level employees.

3. Identify the External Source of Recruitment illustrated by the picture given below:

(A) Direct Recruitment
(B) Casual Callers
(C) Advertisement
(D) Labour Contractor [Delhi Set-1, 2023]

Ans. Option (A) is correct.

4. Biru Nandan, Chairman of Lalit Group of Companies founded 'Biru University' for undergraduate and postgraduate courses in diverse disciplines. The Information Technology department of the Lalit Power Ltd., had few vacancies related to cyber security. The Human Resource Department of the company decided to recruit fresh engineering graduates from 'Biru University' for the same. Identify the type of source of recruitment.

(A) Advertisement
(B) Employment exchange
(C) Placement agencies and management consultants
(D) Campus recruitment A [Delhi Set-1, 2, 3, 2019]

Ans. Option (D) is correct.

Explanation: Colleges and institutes of management and technology have become a popular source of recruitment for technical, professional and managerial jobs. Many big organisations maintain a close liaison with the universities, vocational schools and management institutes to recruit qualified personnel for various jobs. Recruitment from educational institutions is a well-established practice of businesses. This is referred to as campus recruitment.

5. Which of the following step in the process of staffing involves the process of searching for prospective employee and stimulating them to apply for respective job in the organisation?

(A) Recruitment
(B) Selection
(C) Training and Development
(D) Placement and Orientation R [OEB]

6. Which of the following step in the process of staffing involves the process of streamlining the attributes of a person required for doing a job?

(A) Recruitment
(B) Selection

This Question is for practice and its solution is given at the end of the chapter.

(C) Training and Development

(D) Placement and Orientation R [OEB]

Ans. Option (C) is correct.

Explanation: Organisations have either inhouse training centers or have forged alliances with training and educational institutes to ensure continuing learning of their employees. The organisations too benefit in turn. If employee motivation is high, their competencies are strengthened, they perform better and thus, contribute more to organisational effectiveness and efficiency. By offering the opportunities for career advancement to their members, organisations are not only able to attract but also retain its talented people.

7. Which aspect of staffing is concerned with upgradation of the knowledge and skills of the employees?

(A) Placement and Orientation

(B) Training and Development

(C) Selection

(D) Estimating manpower requirement R [OEB]

Concept Applied | Training and Development

Ans. Option (B) is correct.

Explanation: Organisations have either inhouse training centers or have forged alliances with training and educational institutes to ensure continuing learning of their employees. The organisations too benefit in turn. If employee motivation is high, their competencies are strengthened, they perform better and thus, contribute more to organisational effectiveness and efficiency. By offering the opportunities for career advancement to their members, organisations are not only able to attract but also retain its talented people.

8. Which of the following are the specialised activities performed by Human Resource Management:

(A) Maintaining labour relations and union-management relations

(B) Recruitment

(C) Ensuring social security and welfare of employees

(D) All the above R [OEB]

9. For the following two statements, choose the correct option:

Statement I: Human resources are the foundation of any business.

Statement II: The right people can help you take your business to the top; the wrong people can break your business.

Choose the correct option from options given below: U [OEB]

(A) Statement I is correct and statement II is wrong.

(B) Statement II is correct and statement I is wrong

(C) Both the statements are correct.

(D) Both the statements are wrong.

Ans. Option (C) is correct.

10. Staffing is a process which involves a series of steps. Arrange the following steps in correct order.

(i) Placement and Orientation

(ii) Recruitment

(iii) Selection

(iv) Estimating manpower

(A) (iv), (ii), (iii), (i) (B) (iv), (iii), (ii), (i)

(C) (i), (ii), (iii), (iv) (D) (ii), (iv), (iii), (i)

R [OEB]

Ans. Option (A) is correct.

Explanation: Staffing has been described as the managerial function of filling and keeping filled the positions in the organisation structure. This is achieved by, first of all, identifying requirement of work force, followed by recruitment, selection, placement, promotion, appraisal and development of personnel, to fill the roles designed into the organisation structure.

11. Real Tech Builders has to deliver the flats to its buyers for possession on time. Due to this, there is a sudden increase in workload. Therefore, the company needs to arrange workers to work at the sites at a short notice. The source of recruitment which may be used by the company to tap the casual vacancy is: A [OEB]

(A) Direct recruitment

(B) Advertisement

(C) Recommendation of employees

(D) Employment exchange

Ans. Option (A) is correct.

Explanation: Under the direct recruitment, a notice is placed on the notice-board of the enterprise specifying the details of the jobs available. Job seekers assemble outside the premises of the organisation on the specified date and selection is done on the spot. The practice of direct recruitment is followed usually for casual vacancies of unskilled or semi-skilled jobs. Such workers are known as casual or 'badli' workers and they are paid remuneration on daily wage basis.

12. Which of the following is true regarding transfers:

(A) Involves shifting of an employee from one job to another

(B) Involves shifting of an employee from one department to another or from one shift to another.

(C) There is no substantive change in the responsibilities and status of the employee.

(D) All the above U [OEB]

13. For the following two statements, choose the correct option:

Statement I: Applicants introduced by present employees, or their friends and relatives may prove to be a good source of recruitment.

Statement II: Labour contractors maintain close contacts with labourers and they can provide the required number of unskilled workers at short notice.

Choose the correct option from options given below:

(A) Statement I is correct and statement II is wrong.

(B) Statement II is correct and statement I is wrong.

(C) Both the statements are correct.

(D) Both the statements are wrong. U [OEB]

Ans. Option (C) is correct.

These Questions are for practice and their solutions are given at the end of the chapter.

14. For the following two statements, choose the correct option:

Statement I: Transfers can be used for training of employees for learning different jobs.

Statement II: At the time of transfer, it should be ensured that the employee to be transferred to another job is capable of performing it.

Choose the correct option from options given below:

(A) Statement I is correct and statement II is wrong.
(B) Statement II is correct and statement I is wrong.
(C) Both the statements are correct.
(D) Both the statements are wrong. U [OEB]

Ans. Option (C) is correct.

15. Which of the following steps in the process of selection, helps the manager to eliminate unqualified or unfit job-seekers based on the information supplied in the application form:

(A) Preliminary Screening
(B) Employment Interview
(C) Reference and Background Checks
(D) Selection Decision U [OEB]

Ans. Option (A) is correct.

Explanation: Preliminary screening helps the manager eliminate unqualified or unfit job seekers based on the information supplied in the application forms. Preliminary interviews help reject misfits for reasons, which did not appear in the application forms.

16. For the following two statements, choose the correct option:

Statement I: The job offer is given to the candidate being declared fit after the medical examination.

Statement II: Job offer is made through a letter of appointment/confirm his acceptance.

Choose the correct option from options given below:

(A) Statement I is correct and statement II is wrong.
(B) Statement II is correct and statement I is wrong.
(C) Both the statements are correct.
(D) Both the statements are wrong. U [OEB]

Ans. Option (C) is correct.

Explanation: After the selection decision and before the job offer is made, the candidate is required to undergo a medical fitness test. The job offer is given to the candidate being declared fit after the medical examination. Job offer is made through a letter of appointment/confirm his acceptance. Such a letter generally contains a date by which the appointee must report on duty. The appointee must be given reasonable time for reporting.

17. For the following two statements, choose the correct option: U [OEB]

Statement I: Interview is a formal, in depth conversation conducted to evaluate the applicant's suitability for the job.

Statement II: Aptitude test is one of the important psychological tests used to measure the level of intelligence quotient of an individual.

Choose the correct option from options given below:

(A) Statement I is correct and statement II is wrong.
(B) Statement II is correct and statement I is wrong.
(C) Both the statements are correct.
(D) Both the statements are wrong.

Ans. Option (A) is correct.

Explanation: Interview is a formal, in-depth conversation conducted to evaluate the applicant's suitability for the job. The role of the interviewer is to seek information and that of the interviewee is to provide the same. Intelligence Tests is one of the important psychological tests used to measure the level of intelligence quotient of an individual. It is an indicator of a person's learning ability or the ability to make decisions and judgments.

18. Match the options of Column I with their correct options given in Column II. A [OEB]

Column I	Column II
(1) Intelligence test	**(a)** An indicator of a person's learning ability
(2) Aptitude test	**(b)** To judge the involvement of a person
(3) Trade test	**(c)** To measure the level of knowledge and proficiency in the area of professions or technical training
(4) Interest test	**(d)** Indicates the person's capacity to develop

(A) 1-a, 2-b, 3-c, 4-d **(B)** 1-b, 2-a, 3-c, 4-d
(C) 1-a, 2-b, 3-d, 4-c **(D)** 1-a, 2-d, 3-c, 4-b

Ans. Option (D) is correct.

19.

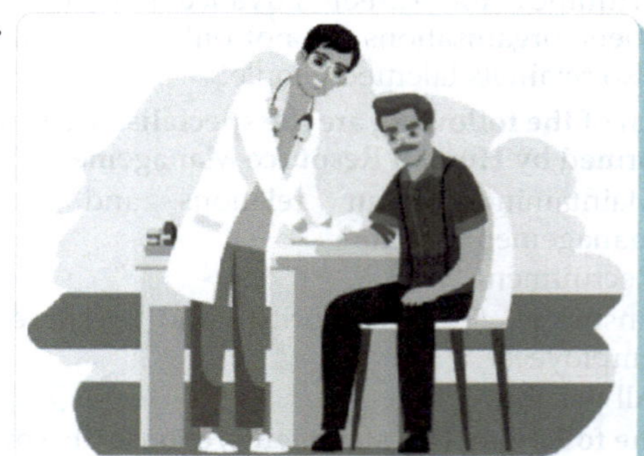

Identify the step in the process of selection illustrated in the picture above. U [OEB]

(A) Reference and Background Check
(B) Selection Decision
(C) Medical Examination
(D) Job Offer

Ans. Option (C) is correct.

Explanation: After the selection decision and before the job offer is made, the candidate is required to undergo a medical fitness test. The job offer is given to the candidate being declared fit after the medical examination.

20. Soler Horse Ltd. decided to import new hi-tech machines from Korea to decrease the cost of production and increase quality of work. It decided to give one month training to 5 supervisors and 10

workers to provide technical knowledge and skills to operate those machines. For this, dummy models of machinery were provided to them to practice on it. Identify the type of training provided by Soler Horse Ltd. A [OEB]

(A) Internship Training
(B) Apprenticeship Training
(C) Induction Training
(D) Vestibule Training

Ans. Option (D) is correct.

Explanation: Employees learn their jobs on the equipment they will be using, but the training is conducted away from the actual work floor. Actual work environments are created in a class room and employees use the same materials, files and equipment. This is usually done when employees are required to handle sophisticated machinery and equipment.

21. For the following two statements, choose the correct option:

Statement I: Training is long term process.

Statement II: Development is a short term process.

Choose the correct option from options given below:

(A) Statement I is correct and statement II is wrong.
(B) Statement II is correct and statement I is wrong.
(C) Both the statements are correct.
(D) Both the statements are wrong. U [OEB]

Ans. Option (D) is correct.

Explanation: The term training is used to indicate the process by which attitudes, skills and abilities of employees to perform specific jobs are increased. But the term development means growth of individual in all respects. Training is short term process but development is an on going process. Also, development includes training.

22. For the following two statements, choose the correct option:

Statement I: Apprenticeship programmes put the trainee under the guidance of a master worker.

Statement II: Apprenticeship programmes are designed to acquire a higher level of skill.

Choose the correct option from options given below:

(A) Statement I is correct and statement II is wrong.
(B) Statement II is correct and statement I is wrong.
(C) Both the statements are correct.
(D) Both the statements are wrong. U [OEB]

Ans. Option (C) is correct.

Explanation: Apprenticeship programmes put the trainee under the guidance of a master worker. These are designed to acquire a higher level of skill. People seeking to enter skilled jobs, to become, for example, plumbers, electricians or iron-workers, are often required to undergo apprenticeship training. These apprentices are trainees who spend a prescribed amount of time working with an experienced guide, or trainer. A uniform period of training is offered to trainees, in which both fast and slow learn here, are placed together. Slow learners may require additional training.

[B] Assertion & Reason

Directions: In the following questions, a statement of assertion (A) is followed by a statement of reason (R). Mark the correct choice as:

(A) Both assertion (A) and reason (R) are true and reason (R) is the correct explanation of assertion (A).
(B) Both assertion (A) and reason (R) are true but reason (R) is not the correct explanation of assertion (A).
(C) Assertion (A) is true but reason (R) is false.
(D) Assertion (A) is false but reason (R) is true.

1. **Assertion (A):** Human resources are the liability of an organisation.

   Reason (R): The ability of an organisation to achieve its goal depends upon the quality of its human resources. U [OEB]

Ans. Option (D) is correct.

Explanation: Human resources are the most important asset of an organisation because they are the one who make things happen.

2. **Assertion (A):** Staffing begins with workforce planning and includes different other functions like recruitment, selection, training, development, promotion, compensation and performance appraisal of work force.

   Reason (R): Staffing is putting people to jobs. [OEB]

3. **Assertion (A):** Personality tests are difficult to design and implement.

   Reason (R): The difference between aptitude test and trade test is that the former measures the potential to acquire skills and the later the actual skills possessed. [OEB]

Ans. Option (B) is correct.

Explanation: Personality tests provide clues to a person's emotions, her reactions, maturity and value system etc. These tests probe the overall personality. Hence, these are difficult to design and implement. Trade tests measure the existing skills of the individual. They measure the level of knowledge and proficiency in the area of professions or technical training. The difference between aptitude test and trade test is that the former measures the potential to acquire skills and the later the actual skills possessed.

4. **Assertion (A):** The role of the interviewer is to seek information and that of the interviewee is to provide the same.

   Reason (R): Letter of appointment generally contains a date by which the appointee must report on duty. [OEB]

Ans. Option (B) is correct.

Explanation: Interview is a formal, in-depth conversation conducted to evaluate the applicant's suitability for the job. The role of the interviewer is to seek information and that of the interviewee is to provide the same. Job offer is made through a letter of appointment/confirm his acceptance. Such a letter generally contains a date by which the appointee must report on duty. The appointee must be given reasonable time for reporting.

5. **Assertion (A):** Interest tests are used to know the pattern of interests or involvement of a person.

This Question is for practice and its solution is given at the end of the chapter.

Reason (R): Intelligence tests is one of the important psychological tests used to measure the level of intelligence quotient of an individual. [OEB]

Ans. Option (B) is correct.

Explanation: Intelligence test is one of the important psychological tests used to measure the level of intelligence quotient of an individual. It is an indicator of a person's learning ability or the ability to make decisions and judgments. Every individual has fascination for some job than the other. Interest tests are used to know the pattern of interests or involvement of a person.

6. **Assertion (A):** Through internal source of recruitment, employees work with commitment and loyalty and remain satisfied with their jobs

Reason (R): The candidates that are already working in the enterprise can be evaluated more accurately and economically. [OEB]

Ans. Option (B) is correct.

Explanation: Employees are motivated to improve their performance. A promotion at a higher level may lead to a chain of promotion at lower levels in the organisation. This motivates the employees to improve their performance through learning and practice. Employees work with commitment and loyalty and remain satisfied with their jobs

7. **Assertion (A):** On-the-Job methods are applied to the workplace, while the employee is actually working.

Reason (R): Off-the-Job methods means learning before doing. [OEB]

[C] Case Based MCQs

I. Read the below case and answer the questions that follow:

Mr. Vikas Goel is an H.R. Manager of "Sanduja Furniture Private Limited." At the beginning of the new year he anticipated that the company will need 30 new additional persons to fill up different vacancies. He gave an advertisement in the newspaper inviting applications for filling up different vacant posts. As many as 120 applications were received. The same were scrutinised. Out of these, conditions of 15 applicants were not acceptable to the company. Letters of regret, giving reasons, were sent to them. Remaining candidates were called for preliminary interview. The candidates called for were asked to fill up blank application forms. Thereafter, they were given four tests.

The objective of the first test was to find out how much interest the applicant takes in his work.

The objective of the second test was to find out 'specialisation' of the applicant in any particular area.

Third test aimed at making sure whether the applicant was capable of learning through training or not.

The purpose of the fourth test was to find out how much capability a person has to mix-up with other persons, and whether he can influence other persons and get influenced by them. [OEB]

1. **The purpose of the fourth test was too find out how much capability a person has to mix-up with other persons, and whether he can influence other persons and get influenced by them. Which tests is indicated in this situation?**

(A) Personality Test (B) Intelligent Test
(C) Aptitude Test (D) Trade Test

Ans. Option (A) is correct.

Explanation: Personality tests provide clues to a person's emotions, her reactions, maturity and value system etc. These tests probe the overall personality. Hence, these are difficult to design and implement.

2. **At the beginning of the new year he anticipated that the company will need 30 new additional persons to fill up different vacancies. Identify the first step of staffing.**

(A) Placement and Orientation
(B) Training and Development
(C) Recruitment
(D) Estimating Manpower Requirement

Ans. Option (D) is correct.

Explanation: It involves finding out the number and type of people that the performance of each job necessitates and the appointment of an appropriate person to the job who possesses the specific set of educational qualifications, work experience, etc. This calls for undertaking workload analysis and workforce analysis necessarily.

3. **From the given lines, 'Out of these, conditions of 15 applicants were not acceptable to the company.' Letters of regret, giving reasons, were sent to them. Which aspect of staffing is highlighted in the statement?**

(A) Recruitment (B) Selection
(C) Training (D) Education

Ans. Option (B) is correct.

Explanation: Selection is the process of choosing from among the pool of the prospective job candidates developed at the stage of recruitment. Even in case of highly specialised jobs where the choice space is very narrow, the rigour of the selection process serves two important purposes:

(i) it ensures that the organisation gets the best among the available, and

(ii) it enhances the self-esteem and prestige of those selected and conveys to them the seriousness with which the things are done in the organisation.

4. **The applicants were given four tests like intelligent test to interest test after filling up blank application form. Identify which step of selection process was followed by the management.**

(A) Selection Decision
(B) Selection Test
(C) Job Offer
(D) Medical Examination

Ans. Option (B) is correct.

Explanation: An employment test is a mechanism (either a paper and pencil test or an exercise) that attempts to measure certain characteristics of individuals. These characteristics range from aptitudes, such as manual dexterity, to intelligence to personality.

This Question is for practice and its solution is given at the end of the chapter.

II. Read the below case and answer the questions that follow: [OEB]

Motorcycles Rides Pvt. Ltd. decided to modernise the plant as they are going to manufacture on large scale and cater to the export market as well as the domestic market. So, it has become necessary to provide knowledge and skills to the existing workers to cope with new technology. The company believes that training will help its workers to improve their functioning and performance in many areas. Thus, the company has decided to train its workers so as to equip them with the latest production technology. But the company is in a dilemma with respect to the training method to be adopted. The HR department wants to adopt a training method which is more suitable for a manufacturing concern than a trading concern as the workers will be involved in operating many sophisticated machines, majority of which the company is planning to import from Japan. Thus, they have decided to create actual work environments in a class room and employees to use the same materials, files and equipment in order to equip themselves with the imported new technology. The company also plans to shift the trainees from one department to another or from one job to another in order to make them more versatile. This will enable the trainee to gain a broader understanding of all parts of the manufacturing and assembling unit and how the organisation as a whole functions. They also plan to recruit more people especially freshers to meet the rise in demand and train them accordingly. For this purpose they have decided to select candidates who are studying but will also work in their factory or office to acquire practical knowledge and skills.

1. Training will help the company's workers to improve which of the following areas:

(A) Aptitudes
(B) Prepare them for any intended job
(C) Improve their performance on the current job
(D) All the above

Ans. Option (D) is correct.

Explanation: Training is any process by which the aptitudes, skills and abilities of employees to perform specific jobs are increased. It is a process of learning new skills and application of knowledge. It attempts to improve their performance on the current job or prepare them for any intended job.

2. Which training method has been chosen by Motorcycles Rides Pvt. Ltd. to train its existing workers?

(A) Apprenticeship Training
(B) Internship Training
(C) Vestibule Training
(D) None of these

Ans. Option (C) is correct.

Explanation: Employees learn their jobs on the equipment they will be using, but the training is conducted away from the actual work floor. Actual work environments are created in a class room and employees use the same materials, files and equipment. This is usually done when employees are required to handle sophisticated machinery and equipment.

3. Which training method has been chosen by Motorcycles Rides Pvt. Ltd. to train its new workers?

(A) Lectures
(B) Internship Training
(C) Vestibule Training
(D) Apprenticeship Training

Ans. Option (B) is correct.

Explanation: It is a joint programme of training in which educational institutions and business firms cooperate. Selected candidates carry on regular studies for the prescribed period. They also work in some factory or office to acquire practical knowledge and skills.

4. Training enhances employee productivity in terms of ________ leading to higher profits.

(A) Quality **(B)** Quantity
(C) Both (A) and (B) **(D)** None of these

Ans. Option (C) is correct.

Explanation: Training is a systematic learning, always better than hit and trial methods which lead to wastage of efforts and money. It enhances employee productivity both in terms of quantity and quality, leading to higher profits. Training equips the future manager who can take over in case of emergency. Training increases employee morale and reduces absenteeism and employee turnover. It helps in obtaining effective response to fast changing environment – technological and economic.

SOLUTIONS FOR PRACTICE QUESTIONS (TOPIC-1)

SATQs-I

Ans. 4. Human Resource Management includes many specialised activities and duties which the human resource personnel must perform and one of them is Staffing. So, staffing is a subset of Human Resource Management or a narrow concept, including workforce and workload analysis, recruitment, selection, placement and orientation, training and development, performance appraisal, promotion and career planning and compensation. Including these, there are various other activities like, providing social security, defending the company in lawsuits and avoiding legal complications, etc. for which Human Resource Management is responsible. **[3]**

SATQs-II

Ans. 2. Selection: Selection is the process of choosing from among the pool of the prospective job candidates developed at the stage of recruitment. Even in case of highly specialised jobs where the choice space is very narrow, the rigour of the selection process serves two important purposes

(i) It ensures that the organisation gets the best among the available; and

(ii) It enhances the self-esteem and prestige of those selected and conveys to them the seriousness with which the things are done in the organisation.

Steps in the process of selection discussed:

1. Preliminary Screening.
2. Selection Tests.
3. Employment interview

LATQs

Ans. 2. (i) The function of management which doesn't seem to be working well for the organisation is 'Staffing'.

(ii) The benefits of staffing highlighted above are:

(a) Competent Personnel: Recently it was found by the management that the employees who were working in the organisation were lethargic with limited skills.

(b) Right person for right job: When a proper analysis of job positions and their occupants was done it was found that many of them were not working at places suitable to them.

(c) Succession Planning: The organisation had already spent five decades in the industry and was worried about the successful continuation of business which required able future managers but the current employees were not much capable.

(d) Optimum utilisation of human resources: To add to its problems the number of employees were more than required, so the company had to bear additional cost.

(e) Improves job satisfaction and morale of the employees: This came true for the company when there was some negative reporting about its HR practices in a daily newspaper where it was mentioned that the employees were not satisfied and suffered with low morale. **[1 + 5 = 6]**

SOLUTIONS FOR PRACTICE QUESTIONS (TOPIC-2)

SATQs-I

Ans. 7. Limitations of external sources of recruitment :

(i) It may lead to dissatisfaction among existing employees as they may feel that their chances of promotion are reduced.

(ii) It is a lengthy process as the vacancies have to be notified and applications received before selection.

(iii) It is a costly process as a lot of money is spent on advertisement and processing of applications.

(If an examinee has given only the heading, ½ mark for each heading should be awarded)

[1 × 3 = 3]

[Marking Scheme, Delhi, 2017]

Commonly Made Error

⚠ Generally, students get confused and write for internal sources when asked for external sources.

Answering Tip

⚠ Learn the differences between internal and external sources of recruitment.

SATQs-II

Ans. 2. Transfers:

(i) Transfers involve shifting of an employee from one job to another, one department to another or from one shift to another, without a substantive change in the responsibilities and status of the employee.

(ii) It may lead to changes in duties and responsibilities, working condition, etc., but not necessarily salary.

Promotions:

(i) Promotions involve shifting an employee to a higher position, carrying higher responsibilities, facilities, status and pay.

(ii) This practice helps to improve the motivation and increases loyalty and satisfaction level of employees.

[Marking Scheme, Delhi, 2017] [2+2=4]

LATQs

Ans. 2. Reasons on the basis of which 'Parth' would have taken the decision not to make appointment with the help of an outside source are:

(i) Internal sources are more reliable way of recruitment since the candidates are already known to the organisation.

(ii) If internal source are used, there is no need for induction training as the employees are already familiar with the organisation.

(iii) Internal sources help to improve the motivation, loyalty and satisfaction level of existing employees.

(iv) Promotion at a higher level may lead to a chain of promotions at lower levels in the organisation.

(v) They simplify the process of selection as the candidates are already known to the organisation.

(vi) They help in adjustment of surplus staff in those departments where there is a shortage of staff.

(vii) Filling of jobs internally is cheaper as compared to getting candidates from external sources.

(Any four) [1½ × 4 = 6]

[Marking Scheme, Delhi, 2018]

SOLUTIONS FOR PRACTICE QUESTIONS (TOPIC-3)

SATQs-I

Ans. 2. Steps in the selection procedure, after the employment interview and before the job offer are:

(i) Reference and background checks for the purpose of verifying the information and gaining additional information.

(ii) Selection decision from among the candidates who pass the tests, interviews and reference checks.

(iii) Medical examination which includes a medical fitness test which the candidate is required to undergo.

[Marking Scheme, Delhi & OD 2018] **[1 × 3 = 3]**

Ans. 3. Interest Tests: Every individual has fascination for some job than the other. Interest tests are used to know the pattern of interests or involvement of a person. **[3]**

SOLUTIONS FOR PRACTICE QUESTIONS (TOPIC-4)

SATQs-I

Ans. 2.

Training	Development
It is a process of increasing knowledge and skills.	It is a process of learning and growth.
It is to enable the employee to do the job better.	It is to enable the overall growth of the employee.
It is a job oriented process.	It is a career oriented process.

[1 × 3 = 3]

LATQs

Ans. 3. Training should be provided to the employees to develop their skills and abilities for producing quality products by using these hi-tech machines. The benefits of imparting training to the employee are as follows:

(i) Better career: Training leads to better career opportunities for the employees as it helps to improve their skills and knowledge of doing the job.

(ii) Increased earnings: Training leads to increased performance by the employees thereby helping them to earn more.

(iii) Increased efficiency: Training makes the employees more efficient in handling machines and less prone to accidents.

(iv) Improved motivation: Training increases the satisfaction and morale of employees thereby motivating them to work with greater enthusiasm.

[2+4=6]

Commonly Made Error

Generally, students write the benefits of training to organisation instead of training to employees.

Answering Tip

Learn the benefits of training to organisation and to employees separately under different heads.

SOLUTIONS FOR OBJECTIVE PRACTICE QUESTIONS

[A] MCQs

Ans. 5. Option (A) is correct.

Explanation: **Recruitment** may be defined as the **process of searching** for prospective employees and stimulating them to **apply for jobs** in the organisation. The information generated in the process of writing the job description and the candidate profile may be used for developing the 'situations vacant' advertisement. The advertisement may be displayed on the factory/ office gate or else it may be got published in print media or flashed in electronic media. This step involves locating the potential candidate or determining the sources of potential candidates.

Ans. 8. Option (D) is correct.

Explanation: Human Resource Management includes many specialised activities and duties which the human resource personnel must perform. These duties are recruitment, *i.e.*, search for qualified people, maintaining labour relations and union management relations, providing for social security and welfare of employees etc.

Ans. 12. Option (D) is correct.

Explanation: It involves shifting of an employee from one job to another, one department to another or from one shift to another, without a substantive change in the responsibilities and status of the employee. It may lead to changes in duties and responsibilities, working condition etc., but not necessarily salary. Transfer is a good source of filling the vacancies with employees from over-staffed departments. It is practically a horizontal movement of employees.

[B] A & R

Ans. 2. Option (A) is correct.

Explanation: After planning and selection of the organisation structure, the next step in the management process is to fill the various posts provided in the organisation. This is termed as the management of staffing function. In the simplest terms, staffing is 'putting people to jobs. It begins with workforce planning and includes different other functions like recruitment, selection, training, development, promotion, compensation and performance appraisal of work force. In other words, staffing is that part of the process of management which is concerned with obtaining, utilising and maintaining a satisfactory and satisfied work force. Today, staffing may involve any combination of employees including daily wagers, consultants and contract employees.

Ans. 7. Option (B) is correct.

Explanation: On-the-Job methods refer to the methods that are applied to the workplace, while the employee is actually working. Off-the-Job methods are used away from the work place. The former means learning while doing, while the latter means learning before doing.

REFLECTION

(a) Were you be able to explain the importance of staffing?
(b) Have you understand the specialised duties and activities performed by Human Resource Management
(c) Were you be able to describe the steps in the process of staffing?
(d) Were you able to discuss the sources of recruitment?
(e) Could you describe the steps involved in the process of selection?
(f) Will you be able to appreciate the importance of training to the organisation and to the employees?
(g) Were you able to discuss on the job and off the job methods of training?
(h) Were you able to differentiate between training and development?
(i) Were you able to identify the method of training in the below mentioned line:
'Employees learn their jobs on the equipment they will be using, but the training is conducted away from the actual work floor.'
(j) Were you be able to explain different types of selection tests?
(k) Were you able to identify the source of recruitment in the below mentioned line:
'A notice is placed on the notice-board of the enterprise specifying the details of the jobs available.'

SELF ASSESSMENT PAPER - 6

Maximum Time: 1 hour **MM: 30**

General Instructions:

(i) All the questions are compulsory
(ii) Q.1 to Q.10 are 1 mark questions
(3) Q.11 to Q.12 are 3 mark questions
(iv) Q.13 to Q.14 are 4 marks questions
(v) Q.15 is a 6 marks question

Objective Type Questions [1 Mark]

1. The ____________ function follows the planning and organising functions.

(A) Staffing **(B)** Controlling
(C) Directing **(D)** None of these **[1]**

2. Match the options of Column I with their correct options given in Column II.

Column I	Column II
(1) Development	**(a)** Process of learning new skills
(2) Training	**(b)** Learning opportunities designed to help employees grow
(3) Selection	**(c)** Searching for prospective employees
(4) Recruitment	**(d)** Choosing the best person out of a number of prospective candidates

(A) 1-a, 2-b, 3-c, 4-d **(B)** 1-b, 2-a, 3-c, 4-d
(C) 1-a, 2-b, 3-d, 4-c **(D)** 1-b, 2-a, 3-d, 4-c **[1]**

3. __________ means evaluating an employee's current and/or past performance as against certain predetermined standards.

(A) Training
(B) Development
(C) Performance appraisal
(D) Promotion **[1]**

4.

Identify the step in the process of staffing illustrated in the picture above.

(A) Recruitment
(B) Placement and Orientation
(C) Estimating the Manpower Requirements
(D) Training and Development **[1]**

5. For the following two statements, choose the correct option:

Statement I: Recruitment seeks to attract suitable applicants to apply for available jobs.

Statement II: Promotion is a tool of training the employees to prepare them for higher jobs.

Choose the correct option from options given below:

(A) Statement I is correct and statement II is wrong.
(B) Statement II is correct and statement I is wrong.
(C) Both the statements are correct.
(D) Both the statements are wrong. **[1]**

6. In the following questions, a statement of assertion (A) is followed by a statement of reason (R). Mark the correct choice as:

Assertion (A): Training makes the employee more efficient to handle machines.

Reason (R): Training indicates the process by which attitudes, skills and abilities of employees to perform specific jobs are increased.

(A) Both assertion (A) and reason (R) are true and reason (R) is the correct explanation of assertion (A).
(B) Both assertion (A) and reason (R) are true but reason (R) is not the correct explanation of assertion (A).
(C) Assertion (A) is true but reason (R) is false.
(D) Assertion (A) is false but reason (R) is true.

Read the following text and answer the following questions on the basis of the same:

XYZ Corporation, a leading technology company, is in the midst of expansion and has initiated a strategic staffing process to ensure it has the right talent in place to support its growth objectives. The company is known for its innovative products and services and is looking to attract, develop, and retain top talent. XYZ Corporation has identified key areas for growth and innovation in the technology sector. To support these initiatives, the company recognises the importance of strategic staffing to bring in individuals with the right skills and expertise. Sara, the HR manager at XYZ Corporation, is tasked with developing and implementing a strategic staffing plan. The plan involves a combination of internal promotions, external hires, and training programs to meet the organisation's current and future needs.

Based on the above case answer the following question:

7. What is the primary objective of XYZ Corporation's strategic staffing plan? **[1]**

(A) Reducing Costs
(B) Retaining Existing Employees

(C) Supporting Growth Objectives
(D) Minimising Workload

8. How does XYZ Corporation plan to achieve internal staffing needs? **[1]**
(A) Hiring external candidates
(B) Implementing training programs
(C) Promoting employees from within
(D) Reducing the workforce

9. In the context of staffing, what does the term "strategic" imply for XYZ Corporation? **[1]**
(A) Short term hiring goals
(B) Aligning staffing with business objectives
(C) Random recruitment processes
(D) Limited focus on employee development

10. What role does Sara, the HR manager, play in the staffing process at XYZ Corporation? **[1]**
(A) Overseeing financial operations
(B) Developing marketing strategies
(C) Implementing the strategic staffing plan
(D) Managing IT infrastructure

Short Answer Type Questions - I [3 Marks]

11. Rahul Agarwal is working with 'High Security Ltd'. He is also recruiting security guards for the company. The company provides security services in nearby places at short notice to various companies. The guards are recruited on a temporary basis. The guards provided by this company are known for their honesty and punctuality. Rahul Agarwal is well-known in his village for providing employment to unskilled people. Identify and explain the source of recruitment used by company here.

12. Notebooks Ltd. is a publishing company. Its book on commerce subjects is in great demand. As a result, the employees in the marketing department are always racing against time. The employees have to work overtime and on holidays to cater to the demand. Managers in the marketing department are under stress as they have to handle more than two territories. The work stress has led to dissatisfaction among the employees and managers. Identify and explain the step of staffing process which has not been performed properly.

Short Answer Type Questions - II [4 Marks]

13. 'Lingo' is a highly reputed potato chips making company and many people wanted to join this company. The employees of this organisation are very glad and happy. One fine day, some of the employees met in canteen in Lunch time and started discussing how they came in contact with this organisation.
Geeta said that she was introduced by the present Sales Manager, Sonakshi said that she had applied through the newspaper and was appointed as the H.R. Manager. Mohit said that he was neither related to any employee of the organisation nor was there any advertisement in the newspaper, even then, he was directly called from IIM Ahmedabad from where he was about to complete his MBA. Identify and explain the step in the process of staffing that has been discussed in the above paragraph.

14. Frills and Frocks Ltd. is the company which manufacturers clothes and accessories for children and infants. Initially, the company employed twenty senior technicians to work on machines imported from Germany for manufacturing of children clothes. The technicians were employed on a probation of one year and were put on their respective jobs after fifteen days of on-the-job training. Because of the faulty selection process, they could not perform well. Five of them left the job on their own and remaining had to be removed by the company during the probation period. Now the company is in the process of selecting new technicians. Advice the company about any four types of selection tests that may be used for selecting the desired technicians.

Long Answer Type Questions - II [6 Marks]

15. 'Yellow Light' is a firm manufacturing jute lampshade. It uses leftover jute pieces from various jute factories to manufacture economical lampshades which are supplied to various hotels in nearby towns. It employs men and women from nearby villages as workers for creating good lampshade designs. The firm is not able to meet its targets. Vinayak, the supervisor of the company, was told to analyse the reasons for the poor performance. He found the following problems and suggested certain solutions in the working of the business. The number of workers employed was less than what was required for the work. As a result, the existing workers were overburdened. The firm decided to search for new workers and it asked the present employees to introduce candidates or recommend their friends and relatives to the firm. This enabled the firm to 'put people to jobs' and assured the attainment of objectives according to plans.
(i) Identify and explain the concept and its source used by the firm to attract more workers for the firm.
(ii) Also, explain any other three sources of the concept identified in part (i).

DIRECTING

Scan this topic

Directing

LEARNING OUTCOMES

After going through this chapter, the student would be able to:
- Describe the concept of directing.
- Discuss the importance of directing.
- Describe the various elements of directing.
- Understand the concept of motivation.
- Develop an understanding of Maslow's Hierarchy of needs.
- Discuss the various financial and non-financial incentives.
- Understand the concept of leadership.
- Understand the various styles of leadership.
- Understand the concept of communication.
- Understand the elements of the communication process.
- Discuss the concept of formal and informal communication.
- Discuss the various barriers to effective communication.
- Suggest measures to overcome barriers to communicate.

Study Plan
Maximum Time = 2.30 Hrs
Maximum Questions = 48

LIST OF TOPICS

TOPIC-1 Concept, Importance and Elements

Concepts Covered
- Meaning of Directing. • Features of Directing. • Importance of Directing. • Meaning of various elements of Directing.

Revision Notes

- **Directing**: Means giving instructions and guiding people in doing work.
- **Importance of Directing:** [Board 2017]

(i) Helps to initiate action: Directing helps to initiate action by people in the organisation towards attainment of desired objectives.

Example-1

If a supervisor guides his subordinates and clarifies their doubts in performing a task, it will help the worker to achieve work targets given to him.

(ii) Integrates employees' efforts: Directing **integrates** employees efforts in the organisation in such a way that every individual effort contributes to the organisational performance.

(iii) Guides employees to fully realise their potential: Directing **guides** employees to fully realise their potential and capabilities by motivating and providing effective leadership.

(iv) Facilitates changes in the organisation: Effective directing through motivation, communication and leadership helps to reduce resistance and develop required cooperation in introducing changes in the organisation.

Example-1

If a manager wants to introduce new system of accounting, there may be initial resistance from accounting staff. But, if manager explains the purpose, provides training and motivates with additional rewards, the employees may accept change and cooperate with manager.

(v) Brings stability and balance in the organisation: Effective directing helps to bring **stability** and balance in the organisation since it fosters cooperation and commitment among the people and helps to achieve balance among various groups, activities and the departments.

Scan this

Importance of Directing

Elements of Directing:
- **Motivation:** It means incitement or inducement to act or move. In the context of an organisation, it means the process of making subordinates to act in a desired manner to achieve certain organisational goals.
- **Leadership:** It is the process of influencing the behaviour of people by making them strive voluntarily towards achievement of organisational goals.
- **Communication:** It is a process of exchange of ideas, views, facts, feelings, etc., between or among people to create common understanding.

KEY TERMS

Directing: The process of instructing, guiding, counselling, motivating and leading people in the organisation to achieve its objectives.
Stability: A situation in which something such as an economy, company, or system can continue in a regular and successful way without unexpected changes.

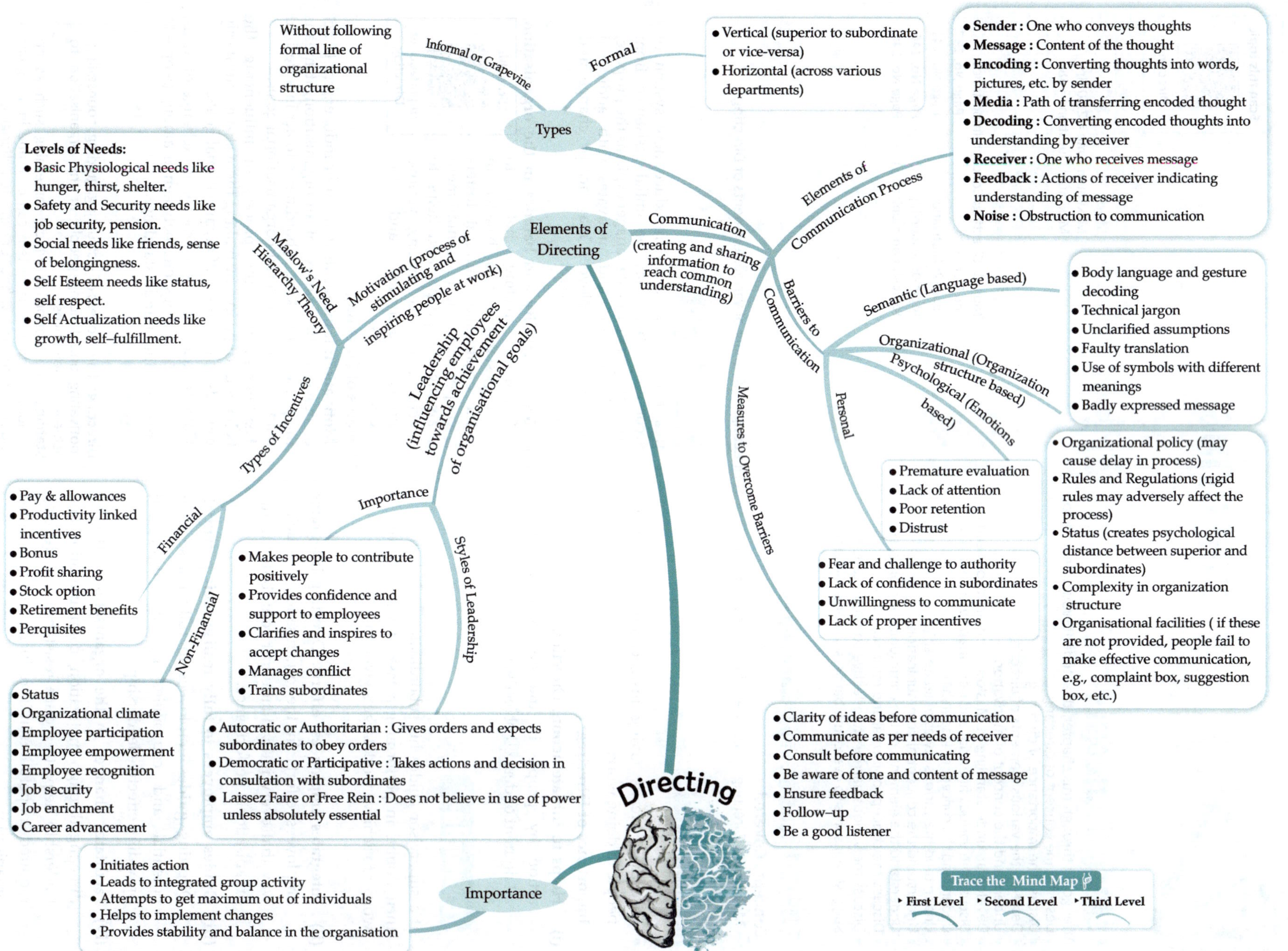
Directing
Elements of Directing
Communication (creating and sharing information to reach common understanding)
Types
Formal
• Vertical (superior to subordinate or vice-versa)
• Horizontal (across various departments)
Informal or Grapevine
Without following formal line of organizational structure
Elements of Communication Process
• Sender : One who conveys thoughts
• Message : Content of the thought
• Encoding : Converting thoughts into words, pictures, etc. by sender
• Media : Path of transferring encoded thought
• Decoding : Converting encoded thoughts into understanding by receiver
• Receiver : One who receives message
• Feedback : Actions of receiver indicating understanding of message
• Noise : Obstruction to communication
Barriers to Communication
Semantic (Language based)
• Body language and gesture decoding
• Technical jargon
• Unclarified assumptions
• Faulty translation
• Use of symbols with different meanings
• Badly expressed message
Organizational (Organization structure based)
• Organizational policy (may cause delay in process)
• Rules and Regulations (rigid rules may adversely affect the process)
• Status (creates psychological distance between superior and subordinates)
• Complexity in organization structure
• Organisational facilities (if these are not provided, people fail to make effective communication, e.g., complaint box, suggestion box, etc.)
Psychological (Emotions based)
• Premature evaluation
• Lack of attention
• Poor retention
• Distrust
Personal
• Fear and challenge to authority
• Lack of confidence in subordinates
• Unwillingness to communicate
• Lack of proper incentives
Measures to Overcome Barriers
• Clarity of ideas before communication
• Communicate as per needs of receiver
• Consult before communicating
• Be aware of tone and content of message
• Ensure feedback
• Follow–up
• Be a good listener
Motivation (process of stimulating and inspiring people at work)
Maslow's Need Hierarchy Theory
Levels of Needs:
• Basic Physiological needs like hunger, thirst, shelter.
• Safety and Security needs like job security, pension.
• Social needs like friends, sense of belongingness.
• Self Esteem needs like status, self respect.
• Self Actualization needs like growth, self–fulfillment.
Types of Incentives
Financial
• Pay & allowances
• Productivity linked incentives
• Bonus
• Profit sharing
• Stock option
• Retirement benefits
• Perquisites
Non-Financial
• Status
• Organizational climate
• Employee participation
• Employee empowerment
• Employee recognition
• Job security
• Job enrichment
• Career advancement
Leadership (influencing employees towards achievement of organisational goals)
Importance
• Makes people to contribute positively
• Provides confidence and support to employees
• Clarifies and inspires to accept changes
• Manages conflict
• Trains subordinates
Styles of Leadership
• Autocratic or Authoritarian : Gives orders and expects subordinates to obey orders
• Democratic or Participative : Takes actions and decision in consultation with subordinates
• Laissez Faire or Free Rein : Does not believe in use of power unless absolutely essential
Importance
• Initiates action
• Leads to integrated group activity
• Attempts to get maximum out of individuals
• Helps to implement changes
• Provides stability and balance in the organisation
Trace the Mind Map
First Level
Second Level
Third Level

SUBJECTIVE TYPE QUESTIONS

Short Answer Type Questions-I (3 marks each)

1. Mukta had been working as an assistant manager with Jelly & Jelly Enterprises for the last fifteen years. She was very popular amongst her colleagues because of her commitment and dedication towards work. When the manager senior to her retired, all her colleagues thought that now Mukta would be promoted. But to everyone's surprise, the vacant post was filled by an outsider, Neelam. Mukta felt demoralised and her performance started declining. She would absent herself often and could not meet her targets.

Neelam was a good leader, who would not only instruct her subordinates but would also guide and inspire them. She noticed Mukta's behaviour and felt that her performance could be improved. She started involving Mukta in the decision-making issues related to the organisation and made her a part of a high-level joint-management committee. Mukta was now punctual in office and her performance started improving. Identify and explain the function of management being performed by Neelam. A [OEB]

Concept Applied | Concept of Directing

Ans. Neelam has performed the directing function of management.

Directing refers to the process of instructing, guiding, counselling, motivating and leading people in the organisation to achieve its objectives. Directing guides towards achievement of common objectives. Through directing, managers not only tell the people in the organisation as to what they should do, when they should do and how they should do but also see that their instructions are implemented in proper perspective.

Commonly Made Error

 Generally, students misinterpret the case-based questions and identify the function of management wrong.

Answering Tip

 Learn the different functions of management with their appropriate content and examples by heart by making a diagram or flow chart.

2. State any three points of importance of directing. U [SQP 2021-22]

OR

Explain any three points that highlight the importance of directing function of management. U [Delhi Set-2, 2017]

Ans. Importance of Directing:

(i) Integrates employee efforts: The organisational goals are achievable only when individual efforts are integrated. Directing integrates employee's endeavours in such a manner that independent individual efforts add to the organisational performance.

(ii) Facilitates changes: An enterprise operates in a constantly changing environment. In case an appropriate system of direction exists in an organisation then it helps in motivating the workers to take up challenges of unfamiliar situations. Thus, directing helps a firm to become dynamic and responsive to new developmental changes.

(iii) Initiates action: Directing helps an organisation to progress. With the help of directing, other managerial functions get initiated and operational. It helps the management to supervise, exchange information, guide and encourage people at work to perform in the desired way for achieving organisational aims and objectives.

(iv) Directing guides employees to realise their potential: Every employee is capable and has potential and capacity to generate results and this needs to be harnessed by his seniors. The elements of direction, *i.e.*, Supervision, Motivation, Leadership and Communication, can be used to raise the efficiency of employees through willing cooperation.

(v) Brings stability and balance in the organisation: Directing promotes cooperation and commitment among the employees and helps to achieve stability and balance among various internal stakeholders, activities and departments. **(Any three) [1 × 3 = 3]**

[Marking Scheme SQP, 2021-22]

Short Answer Type Questions-II (4 marks each)

1. Identity and explain the elements of directing mentioned below:

(i) Astha, a manager, has the ability to influence others to bring about a change in their behaviour.

(ii) Neeraj, a managing director, declares share in the profits to the manager for their contribution to increase profits of the company.

Concept Applied | Concept of leadership and motivation.

A [SQP 2020-21]

Ans. (i) Leadership: Leadership is the process of influencing the behaviour of people by making them strive voluntarily towards the achievement of organisational goals. Leadership indicates the ability of an individual to maintain good interpersonal relations with followers and motivate them to contribute for achieving organisational objectives.

(ii) Motivation: Motivation means incitement or inducement to act or move. In the context of an organisation it means the process of making subordinates to act in a desired manner to achieve certain organisational goals.

[Marking Scheme, SQP 2020-21]

[2 + 2 = 4]

2. Give any four reasons to justify that directing is essential for efficient and effective functioning of the organisation. C [APQ 2023-24]

Ans. Directing is essential for effective and efficient functioning of the organisation due to the following reasons:

(i) Directing helps to initiate action by people in the organisation towards attainment of desired objectives.

(ii) Directing integrates employees' efforts in the organisation in such a way that every individual effort contributes to the organisational performance. Thus, it ensures that the individuals work for organisational goals.

(iii) Directing guide's employees to fully realise their potential and capabilities by motivating and providing effective leadership.

(iv) Directing facilitates introduction of needed changes in the organisation. Effective directing through motivation, communication and leadership helps to reduce such resistance and develop required cooperation in introducing changes in the organisation.

(v) Effective directing helps to bring stability and balance in the organisation since it fosters cooperation and commitment. [Marking Scheme, APQ 2023-24]

Long Answer Type Questions (6 marks each)

1. Clave is a pioneering advertisement making company. Mr. Gopal is a dynamic manager who has recently joined the organisation. He receives complete support from the management. There is proper infrastructure, planning mechanism and subordinate support. He gives orders and starts the actual working of a new unit from the 1st of May. His schedule becomes very hectic. The demanding work involves him almost throughout the day. He is busy giving messages, talking to his subordinates or seniors, etc. throughout the day. One day he meets his friend Tarun who is working at the lower level management though he himself is a part of middle level management. He finds that even Tarun, is involved in communicating and supervising his employees throughout the year though he works at the lower level management. Similar is the case with his seniors working at the higher level management. He feels relaxed after knowing this and continues his work with even more dedication.

(i) Which function of management is highlighted in the above case? Explain.

(ii) By quoting lines from the paragraph, identify the features of this function of management highlighted in the above case. A [OEB]

Ans. (i) The function of management which is highlighted in the above case is directing.

Directing refers to the process of instructing, guiding, counselling, motivating and leading people in the organisation to achieve its objectives. Directing is a key managerial function. A manager has to perform this function along with planning, organising, staffing and controlling while discharging his duties in the organisation. While other functions prepare a setting for action, directing initiates action in the organisation.

(ii) The features of directing highlighted in the above case are:

(a) Directing initiates action: He gives orders and starts the actual working of a new unit from the 1st of May.

(b) Directing takes place at every level of management: He finds that even Tarun is involved in communicating and supervising his employees throughout the year though he works at the lower level management. Similar is the case with his seniors working at the higher level of management.

(c) Directing is a continuous process: He is busy giving messages, talking to his subordinates or seniors, etc. throughout the day. **[3 + 3 = 6]**

2. Gelaxo Ltd. is an FMCG company which deals in consumer goods. Mr. Parth, who works in the company, influences the behaviour of people and makes them to positively contribute their energies for the benefit of the organisation. The company has a policy of granting leave as per the requirement of the workers. Workers are generally granted leave on festivals and special occasions. Recently on Puja festival, it received a big order. Workers are keen to take Puja holidays while management is pressing hard for overtime. This matter was placed before Mr. Parth who called the meeting of operative managers and workers to inform them about the changes in the incentive plan which states payment of double wages for working overtime and triple wages for working on holidays. Workers without any pressure voluntarily took limited holidays and were able to increase their earning by working overtime and on holidays. During Board of Directors meeting, Mr. Parth was asked to update the management for achieving higher output, meeting timely supplies without any confrontation with workers. By quoting the lines from above paragraph explain any two elements of directing. A [OEB]

Ans. (i) Motivation: Motivation is the process of stimulating people to action to accomplish desired goals. Motivation is an internal feeling. The urge, drives, desires, aspirations, striving or needs of human being, which are internal, influence human behaviour.

Lines: "To pay double wages for working overtime and triple wages for working on holidays".

(ii) Leadership: Leadership is the process of influencing the behaviour of people by making them strive voluntarily towards achievement of organisational goals. Leadership indicates the ability of an individual to maintain good interpersonal relations with followers and motivate them to contribute for achieving organisational objectives.

Lines: "Mr. Parth, who works in the company, influences the behaviour of people and makes them to positively contribute their energies for the benefit of the organisation." **[3 + 3 = 6]**

TOPIC-2 Motivation

Concepts Covered:
- Meaning and features of motivation • Maslow's Need Hierarchy-Theory of Motivation • Financial and non-financial incentives.

Revision Notes

- **Motivation** means the process of making subordinates to act in a desired manner to achieve certain organisational goals.
- **Features of Motivation:** [Board, 2019]

(i) Internal feeling

Example-1

People may have the urge or desire for possessing a motorbike, comfortable house, reputation in the society. These urges are internal to an individual.

(ii) Produces goal-directed behaviour

Example-2

The promotion in the job may be given to employee with the objective of improving his performance. If the employee is interested in promotion, it helps to produce a behaviour to improve performance.

(iii) Can be either **positive or negative**
(iv) Complex process

- **Maslow's Need Hierarchy Theory of Motivation:**
- **Abraham Maslow categorised human needs into five types:** [Board, 2019]

(i) **Basic physiological needs:** Also known as survival needs, *e.g.*, food, shelter, clothing, etc.

(ii) **Safety or security needs:** Protection from physical dangers and economic security, *e.g.*, pension plans, job security, etc.
(iii) **Affiliation/Belonging needs:** Also known as social needs, *e.g.*, affection, acceptance, etc.
(iv) **Esteem needs:** Self-respect, status, etc.
(v) **Self actualisation needs:** Desire of becoming what one is capable of becoming, *e.g.*, growth, self-fulfillment, etc.

- It helps managers to realise that the unsatisfied needs of employees should be identified so as to provide motivation to them.
- **Financial Incentive:** It refers to the incentives which are measurable in monetary terms such as: [Board, 2022]

(i) Pay and allowances
(ii) Productivity linked wage incentives
(iii) Bonus
(iv) Profit sharing
(v) Co-partnership/stock option
(vi) Retirement benefits
(vii) Perquisites

- **Non-Financial Incentives:** It refers to the **incentives** which are related to psychological, social and emotional factors: [Board, 2022]

(i) Status
(ii) Organisational climate
(iii) Career advancement opportunity
(iv) Job enrichment
(v) Employee recognition programmes
(vi) Job security
(vii) Employee participation
(viii) Employee empowerment

MNEMONICS

Concept: Maslow's Need Hierarchy Theory of Motivation
Interpretation: Play Some Act for entertainment or Sleep
P: Physiological needs
S: Safety or security needs
A: Affiliation/ Belonging needs
E: Esteem needs
S: Self-actualisation needs

KEY DIAGRAM

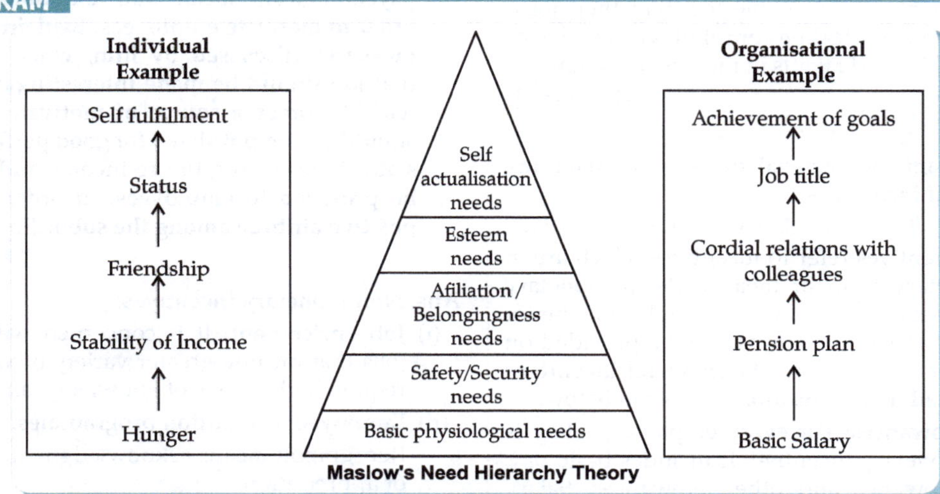

Maslow's Need Hierarchy Theory

SUBJECTIVE TYPE QUESTIONS

Short Answer Type Questions-I (3 marks each)

1. Agrima, Arunima and Avika are pursuing MBA from a reputed institution. Now it is the time of their placement.

Agrima wants to work in a company which would provide her more authority for fulfilling her duties and will give recognition, rewards, perquisites and prestige of job.

Arunima wants to work in an organisation in which behaviour of individuals is influenced by its characteristics like autonomy, reward orientation, consideration to employees, risk taking, etc.

Avika wants to join the organisation which has appropriate skill development programmes and sound promotion policy that encourages employees to exhibit improved performance.

Identify and state the incentives about which Agrima, Arunima and Avika are talking about.

A [Delhi Set-1, 2022]

Ans. Agrima is talking about the incentive employee recognition. Most people have a need for evaluation of their work and due recognition. They feel that what they do should be recognised by others concerned. Recognition means **acknowledgment** with a show of appreciation. When such appreciation is given to the work performed by employees, they feel motivated to perform/work at higher level.

Arunima is talking about the incentive job enrichment. Job enrichment is concerned with designing jobs that include greater variety of work content, require higher level of knowledge and skill; give workers more autonomy and responsibility; and provide the opportunity for personal growth and a meaningful work experience. If jobs are enriched and made interesting, the job itself becomes a source of motivation to the individual.

Avika is talking about the incentive employee empowerment. Empowerment means giving more autonomy and powers to subordinates. Empowerment makes people feel that their jobs are important. This feeling contributes positively to the use of skills and talents in the job performance.

[1 × 3 = 3]

[Marking Scheme Delhi, 2022]

2. What is meant by financial incentives? State any two financial incentives.

U [Term-2, Outside Delhi Set-1, 2022]

Ans. Financial incentives refer to incentives which are in direct monetary form or measurable in monetary term and serve to motivate people for better performance. These incentives may be provided on individual or group basis. **The financial incentives generally used in organisations are listed below:**

(i) Pay and allowances: For every employee, salary is the basic monetary incentive. It includes basic pay, dearness allowance and other allowances. Salary system consists of regular increments in the pay every year and enhancement of allowances from time-to-time. In some business organisations, pay hike and increments may be linked to performance.

(ii) Productivity linked wage incentives: Several wage incentive plans aim at linking payment of wages to increase in productivity at individual or group level.

(iii) Bonus: Bonus is an incentive offered over and above the wages/ salary to the employees.

(iv) Profit Sharing: Profit sharing is meant to provide a share to employees in the profits of the organisation. This serves to motivate the employees to improve their performance and contribute to increase in profits.

(v) Co-partnership/Stock option: Under these incentive schemes, employees are offered company shares at a set price which is lower than market's price. Sometimes, management may allot shares in line of various incentives payable in cash. The allotment of shares creates a feeling of ownership to the employees and makes them to contribute for the growth of the organisation. In Infosys the scheme of stock option has been implemented as a part of managerial compensation.

(vi) Retirement Benefits: Several retirement benefits such as provident fund, pension, and gratuity provide financial security to employees after their retirement. This acts as an incentive when they are in service in the organisation.

(vii) Perquisites: In many companies, perquisites and fringe benefits are offered such as car allowance, housing, medical aid, and education to the children etc., over and above the salary. These measures help to provide motivation to the employees/ managers.

(Any two) [1+2=3]

3. Mr. Pawan Kumar, the CEO of an E-Commerce start up, which was facing the problem of huge employee turnover, decided to hold a meeting with the managers to discuss the issue. While addressing the managers in the meeting, he advised them to take certain measures which focus on psychological, social and emotional factors, in order to motivate employees. Explain any two such measures discussed by him, when he suggested that job should be made interesting so that the job itself becomes a source of motivation, employees should be congratulated for good performance, also, stability regarding future income and work should be provided to employees, in order to develop a positive attitude among the subordinates.

A [SQP 2021-22]

Ans. Non-monetary incentives:

(i) Job enrichment: It is concerned with designing jobs that include greater variety of work content, require higher level of knowledge and skill, etc,.

(ii) Employee recognition programmes:

Recognition means acknowledgment with a show of appreciation.

(iii) **Job security:** Employees want their job to be secure. They want certain stability about income and work so that they do not feel worried about these aspects and work with greater zeal.

(Any two) [1½ × 2 = 3]

[Marking Scheme, SQP 2021-22]

4. **State 'Job Enrichment' and 'Employee Participation' as non-financial incentives. How do they motivate employees?** A I U [Delhi Set-1,2,3, 2019]

Ans. Job Enrichment

(i) Job Enrichment means designing jobs that include greater variety of work content, require higher level of knowledge and skill, give workers more autonomy and responsibility and provide the opportunity for personal growth and a meaningful work experience.

(ii) If jobs are enriched and made more interesting, the job itself becomes a source of motivation to the individual.

Employee Participation

(i) Employee Participation means giving more autonomy and powers to the employees.

(ii) It makes them feel that their jobs are important and this feeling makes them contribute positively to the use of their skills and talents in the job performance.

[1 ½ + 1 ½ =3]

[Marking Scheme, Delhi 2019]

5. **Neha was a regional sales manager in 'Good Look Garments Ltd.' for ten years. On the retirement of the marketing manager, Neha applied for the same post as she was extremely ambitious and had dedicated all her energies to obtain the post of marketing manager. However, the top management of the company decided to fill this post by selecting a better person from outside the company. Because of this, Neha was heart-broken and her performance declined. When the new marketing manager joined, one of her major problems was how to motivate and inspire Neha to her former level of performance.**

Suggest any three non-financial incentives that the new marketing manager may use to motivate Neha. A I C [Delhi Comptt. Set 1, 2015]

Ans. The non-financial incentives that the new marketing manager may use to motivate Neha are:

(i) **Job Enrichment,** which is concerned with designing jobs that include a greater variety of work content, which require higher level of knowledge and skill, and which give more autonomy and opportunity for personal growth.

(ii) **Employee Recognition,** which means acknowledgement with a show of appreciation.

(iii) **Employee Participation,** which means involving employees in decision making of issues related to them.

(iv) **Employee Empowerment,** which means giving more autonomy and powers to subordinates.

(v) **Job Security,** refers to providing stability to the employees about future income and work so that they do not feel worried on these aspects and work with a greater zeal. **(Any three) [1 × 3 = 3]**

[Marking Scheme, Delhi 2015]

Short Answer Type Questions-II (4 marks each)

1. **In Saarthak Steel, several initiatives have been taken to further improve the motivation levels of employees through designing jobs that include greater variety of work content, providing certain stability about future income and work, providing fringe benefits like housing, medical aid, etc., allotment of shares in line with various incentives. Identify and briefly explain the incentives being given by the organisation to the employees.**

A [SQP 2022-23]

Ans. Incentives being given by the organisation to the employees are:

(i) **Job enrichment**: Job enrichment is concerned with designing jobs that include greater variety of work content, require higher level of knowledge and skill; give workers more autonomy and responsibility; and provide opportunity for personal growth and a meaningful work experience.

(ii) **Job security:** Employees want their jobs to be secure. They want certain stability about future income and work so that they do not feel worried about these aspects and work with greater zeal.

(iii) **Perquisites:** In many companies perquisites and fringe benefits are offered such as car allowance, housing, medical aid and education to the children, etc., over and above the salary.

(iv) **Co-partnership/stock option:** Under these incentive schemes, employees are offered company shares at a set price which is lower than market price. Sometimes, management may allot shares in line of various incentives payable in cash. **[1×4=4]**

[Marking Scheme SQP, 2022-23]

2. **Kunal joined as a shop level manager in the Production department of a textile company in the year 2005. Because of his good work, he became the Deputy Production Manager of the company in the year 2010. He had status and prestige and was well respected by all in the company. On 1st March, 2019, he was promoted as the General Manager of the company. Kunal was very happy on his promotion as now he had become what he was capable of becoming. As a good manager, Kunal decided to motivate his subordinates, after understanding the Need Hierarchy theory which is based on various assumptions. He realised that people's behaviour is based on their needs and the manager can influence the behaviour of his employees by satisfying their needs.**

(i) **One of the assumptions of Need Hierarchy theory is stated in the above paragraph. State the other three assumptions of this theory.**

(ii) **State the needs of Kunal which are being satisfied through promotion.** A [Delhi Set-1,2,3, 2019]

Ans. (i) The following are the assumptions of Maslow's Need Hierarchy theory other than the one discussed above:

(a) People's needs are in hierarchical order, starting from basic needs to other higher level needs.

(b) A satisfied need can no longer motivate a person; only next higher level need can motivate him.

(c) A person moves to the next higher level of the hierarchy only when the lower need is satisfied.

(ii) Needs of Kunal which are being satisfied through promotion are:

(a) Esteem Needs which refer to the need for self respect, autonomy status, recognition and attention.

(b) Self actualisation needs which refer to the drive to become what one is capable of becoming. These needs include growth, self- fulfillment and achievement of goals. **[3 + 1 = 4]**

[Marking Scheme, Delhi 2019]

3. The HR manager of Starflight Ltd., has to develop an employee motivation and engagement strategy that focuses on non-financial incentives. Highlight and explain the various types of non-financial incentives she can introduce to foster a positive work environment. [APQ 2023-24]

Ans. (i) Employee Recognition Program: Introduce an employee recognition program to acknowledge and appreciate outstanding performance and achievements. Employees can be recognised through a "Employee of the Month" program or regular shout-outs in team meetings. Recognition helps boost self-esteem and encourages a sense of belonging within the organisation.

(ii) Opportunities for Employee Involvement: Involve employees in decision-making processes, such as project planning or policy development. Providing opportunities for employee involvement fosters a sense of ownership and commitment to the organisation's success.

(iii) Autonomy: Empowering employees with a sense of autonomy and involvement in decision-making increases their job satisfaction and commitment to the organisation.

(iv) Employee Development and Growth Opportunities: Providing opportunities for skill enhancement and career growth demonstrates the organisation's commitment to employee development, encouraging a sense of loyalty and dedication among employees.

[Marking Scheme, APQ 2023-24]

4. Ram Murthy, the CEO of 'Goodcare Hospitals', a leading chain of hospitals, decided to reward the good work of the doctors of this organisation. For this he instituted two running trophies. A 'Healthcare Achievers Trophy' to acknowledge and appreciate the tireless efforts of the doctors who rendered selfless services to the patients and another 'Beti Bachao Trophy' to recognise the outstanding work done by the doctors in saving the girl child.

The CEO also wanted to improve the health services in rural areas all over the country. He decided that all doctors must work in rural areas for at least six months. He also decided that the paramedical staff should be employed locally.

(i) Identify the incentive provided by 'Goodcare Hospitals' to its doctors through running trophies.

(ii) Which need of the doctors will be satisfied through the incentive identified in part (i)?

A [Delhi & Outside Delhi 2018]

Topper's Answer, 2018

i) The incentive provided is Non Financial Incentive - Employee recognition programmes.

ii) The need satisfied is Esteem Needs.

These needs help the employee to satisfy his need for recognition, autonomy, self-respect, job title, job status etc.

5. State the assumptions of Maslow's Need Hierarchy Theory of motivation. [SQP 2023-24]

Ans. The assumptions of Maslow's Need Hierarchy Theory are:

(i) Man is a wanting being, i.e., his wants are growing continuously even when some wants are satisfied. Human needs are of varied and diversified nature. They can be arranged in a hierarchy of importance progressing from a lower to a higher order of needs.

(ii) People's behaviour is based on their needs. Satisfaction of such needs influences their behaviour.

(iii) People's needs are in a hierarchical order, starting from basic needs to other higher level needs.

(iv) A satisfied need can no longer motivate a person; only next higher level need can motivate him.

(v) A person moves to the next higher level of the hierarchy only when the lower need is satisfied

[Marking Scheme SQP 2023-24]

Long Answer Type Questions (6 marks each)

1. Pratap Singh is the Chief Executive Officer of Nissar Enterprises. It is an automobile parts manufacturing company. The enterprise has a functional structure in which jobs of similar nature have been grouped together as Production, Finance, Marketing and Human Resource. Nissar Enterprises has its manufacturing unit at Manesar. The factory has been plagued with many problems for a long time which was in the knowledge of the Production Manager, Varun Sharma. The workers had internal differences. Time and again, there were misunderstandings between the management and the workers. Keeping the problems in mind, Varun Sharma appointed Siyaram Singh who had 14 years of experience of working with the actual work force and passing on instructions of the middle management to the workers. Siyaram Singh met Varun Sharma to understand what the management

wanted. Thereafter, he met the workers and conveyed the ideas of management to them. He also promised the workers to convey their problems to the management. In this way, he cleared the misunderstanding between the management and the workers. He also sorted out internal differences and was able to unite the workers within a month of his joining. His work was acknowledged and he was given a certificate of good performance along with 10% increase in salary.

(i) Siyaram Singh performed some of the functions which are required to be performed at the position he is working at. State any five other functions Siyaram Singh is expected to perform.

(ii) Name the incentives provided to Siyaram Singh.

A [Delhi Set-1, 2, 3, 2019]

Ans. (i) Five other functions Siyaram Singh is expected to perform are:

(a) Maintaining day to day contact and friendly relations with the workers. He should act as a friend, philosopher and a guide to the workers.

(b) Providing good on-the-job training to the workers to build an efficient team.

(c) Building up high morale among workers through good leadership.

(d) Giving feedback to the workers after analysing their work and suggesting ways of developing their work skills.

(e) Ensuring performance of work according to the targets set.

(f) To oversee the efforts of the workforce.

(g) To ensure that the quality of output is maintained and wastage of material is minimised.

(h) To ensure safety standards are maintained.

(Any five)

(ii) Incentives provided to Siyaram Singh are:

(a) Pay and allowances/ Financial Incentive

(b) Employee Recognition Programmes/ Non- Financial Incentive. **[5+1=6]**

[Marking Scheme, Delhi 2019]

2. Leeva Ltd. is a garment making company. It has recently decided to make the job environment better by redefining the workplace for the employees by designing jobs having greater variety of content. This has definitely increased the interest of employees in their work. This step of the company has earned a favourite mentioning in a national newspaper. The promotion policy of the company has now been made more effective by allowing employees to grow to the higher levels. Many of the employees had earlier complained of fear of getting fired. The company has clarified its stance on this and told them not to worry by assuring them permanency after crossing the ad hoc period of six months. With everything going right for the organisation the top management has started devoting a lot of time on special features of the internal environment which will distinguish the organisation from other companies in the industry. The employees know that working in this organisation will only add to their good track record. The company assures the employees a higher ranking in the organisational set up, provided one works hard, with authority, rewards, recognition and better perquisites. With such an effort, the organisation is geared to touch new heights. Identify and explain any four non-financial incentives that have been highlighted in the above case. A [OEB]

Concept Applied	Different types of non-financial incentives.

Ans. The various non-financial incentives highlighted in the above case are:

(i) Job Enrichment: Job enrichment is concerned with designing jobs that include greater variety of work content, require higher level of knowledge and skill; give workers more autonomy and responsibility; and provide the opportunity for personal growth and a meaningful work experience. If jobs are enriched and made interesting, the job itself becomes a source of motivation to the individual.

(ii) Career Advancement Opportunity: Every individual wants to grow to the higher level in the organisation. Managers should provide opportunity to employees to improve their skills and be promoted to the higher-level jobs. Appropriate skill development programmes, and sound promotion policy will help employees to achieve promotions. Promotion works as a tonic and encourages employees to exhibit improved performance.

(iii) Job security: Employees want their job to be secure. They want certain stability about future income and work so that they do not feel worried on these aspects and work with greater zeal. However, there is one negative aspect of job security. When people feel that they are not likely to lose their jobs, they may become complacent.

(iv) Organisational Climate: Organisational climate indicates the characteristics which describe an organisation and distinguish one organisation from the other. These characteristics influence the behaviour of individuals in the organisation. Some of these characteristics are individual autonomy, reward orientation, consideration to employees, risk-tasking, etc., If managers take positive measures regarding these aspects, it helps to develop better organisational climate.

(v) Status: In the organisational context, status means ranking of positions in the organisation. The authority, responsibility, rewards, recognition, perquisites and prestige of job indicate the status given to a person holding a managerial position. Psychological, social and esteem needs of an individual are satisfied by status given to their job.

(Any four) (1½ × 4 = 6)

TOPIC-3 Leadership

Concepts Covered:

- Meaning and Features of Leadership • Various styles of leadership - authoritative, democratic and laissez faire.

Revision Notes

- **Leadership** is the process of influencing the behaviour of people by making them strive voluntarily towards achievement of organisational goals.

Scan this
Leadership Styles

- **Features of Leadership**

(i) Process of influencing people
(ii) Brings behavioural changes
(iii) Inter-personal relationship between a leader and a follower
(iv) Continuous process
(v) Exercised to achieve common goals

- **Leadership styles**

(i) **Authoritative/Autocratic Leadership:** A style in which the leader centralises all decision making powers and exercises complete control over his subordinates. **[2022]**

(ii) **Democratic/Participative Leadership:** A style in which the leader consults the subordinates in the decision making process and encourages them to give suggestions. **[2018]**

(iii) **Free Rein/Laissez Faire Leadership:** A style in which the leader gives complete freedom to the subordinates in setting the goals and delegates the entire authority of decision making to them.

SUBJECTIVE TYPE QUESTIONS

Short Answer Type Questions-I (3 marks each)

1. Give the meaning of 'Autocratic' style of Leadership. U **[Outside Delhi Set-1, 2022]**

Ans. Autocratic or Authoritarian leader: An autocratic leader gives orders and expects his subordinates to obey those orders. If a manager is following this style, then communication is only one-way with the subordinate only acting according to the command given by the manager. This leader is dogmatic i.e., does not change or wish to be contradicted. His following is based on the assumption that reward or punishment both can be given depending upon the result. This leadership style is effective in getting productivity in many situations like in a factory where the supervisor is responsible for production on time and has to ensure labour productivity. **[3]**

[Marking Scheme, OD 2022]

2. Define leadership as an element of directing? Enumerate any two styles of leadership. U **[SQP 2021-22]**

Ans. Leadership indicates the ability of an individual to maintain good interpersonal relations with followers and motivate them to contribute for achieving organisational objectives.

Styles of leadership:

(i) Autocratic or Authoritarian leader gives orders and expects his subordinates to obey those orders.

(ii) Democratic or Participative leaders will develop action plans and make decisions in consultation with their subordinates.

(iii) Laissez faire or Free-rein leader does not believe in the use of power unless it is absolutely essential.

(Any two) [1 × 3 = 3]

[Marking Scheme, SQP 2021-22]

3. Sandhya is a successful manager at Manisons Enterprises. She has a team of twelve people working under her. She encourages them to set their own objectives and take decisions. She respects their opinions and supports them, so that they can perform their duties and accomplish organisational objectives. To manage and exercise effective control, she uses forces within the group. As an intelligent manager, at times, she also makes use of positive aspects of informal communication. This way, she is able to unify diverse interests and ensure that targets are met.

(i) There are many theories and styles of influencing people's behaviour. Identify the style used by Sandhya which is based on the use of authority.

(ii) State two positive aspects of the communication discussed above, which Sandhya is using as an intelligent manager. A **[Delhi, Outside Delhi 2018]**

Concept Applied Concept of Democratic style of leadership.

Ans. (i) Democratic Style

(ii) Two positive aspects of communication which Sandhya is using as an intelligent manager are:

(a) It carries information rapidly and therefore may be useful to the manager at times.

(b) It is used by the manager to transmit information so as to know the reaction of his/ her subordinates.

[Marking Scheme, Delhi 2018] [1 + 2 = 3]

Short Answer Type Questions-II (4 marks each)

1. Explain the following leadership styles:

(a) Autocratic leadership

(b) Laissez Faire leadership **[SQP 2023-24]**

Ans. (a) Autocratic Authoritarian leadership style: An autocratic leader gives orders and expects his subordinates to obey those orders. This leadership style is effective in getting productivity in many situations like in a factory where the supervisor is responsible for production on time and has to ensure labour productivity. Quick decision making is also facilitated.

(b) Laissez fair or Free-rein leader: Such a leader does not believe in the use of power unless it is absolutely essential. The followers are given high degree of independence to formulate their own objectives or ways to achieve them. The manager is only there to support them and supply them the required information to complete the task assigned.

[Marking Scheme, SQP 2023-24]

2. Pramod is a supervisor at `Shyam Breads and Biscuits Factory'. The factory produces 20,000 packets of bread and biscuits every day. As a supervisor, Pramod ensures that work goes on smoothly and there is no interruption in production. He is a good leader who gives orders only after consulting his subordinates, working out the policies with the acceptance of the group. Identify and explain the leadership style being adopted by Pramod.

A [SQP 2020-21]

Long Answer Type Questions (6 marks each)

1. "The leaders always play a key role for the success and excellence of any organisation". Justify the statement. A [OEB]

Ans. The leaders always play a key role for the success and excellence of any organisation. Leadership is the process of influencing the behaviour of people by making them strive voluntarily towards achievement of organisational goals. Leadership indicates the ability of an individual to maintain good interpersonal relations with followers and motivate them to contribute for achieving organisational objectives.

An examination of the above definition reveals the following important features of leadership:

(i) Leadership indicates ability of an individual to influence others.

(ii) Leadership tries to bring change in the behaviour of others.

(iii) Leadership indicates interpersonal relations between leaders and followers.

(iv) Leadership is exercised to achieve common goals of the organisation.

(v) Leadership is a continuous process. **[1 + 5 = 5]**

2. Make a comparative study between Authoritative, Democratic and Laissez faire styles of leadership. U [OEB]

Ans.

S.No.	Basis	Authoritative	Democratic	Laissez faire
(i)	Degree of freedom to the subordinates	Little freedom given to the subordinates.	Moderate freedom as they participate in decision making process.	Much freedom. They are free to take decisions themselves.
(ii)	Degree of control by the leader	The leader exercises strict control over subordinates.	Moderate control over the subordinates.	No control of the leader
(iii)	Decision making authority	The leader alone takes decision. The Subordinates are passive listeners only.	The leaders and the followers mutually take decisions.	The leaders give full authority and freedom to followers to take decisions.
(iv)	Leader's guidance	Maximum guidance	Moderate	Minimum only
(v)	Extent of responsibility	Only leader is responsible.	Shared responsibility between the leader and the followers.	Minimal responsibility of the leader.
(vi)	Output of the group	Order and discipline maintained so high productivity and output.	Productivity less than the Authoritative.	Very low as compared to other two.
(vii)	Efficiency	Increases leader's efficiency.	Combined efficiency of the leader and the followers.	Only follower's efficiency to take actions and decisions used.
(viii)	Suitability	Group projects which requires unskilled and inexperienced works, where quick decisions are taken by the head only.	For those group projects where experienced, creative persons can take complex decisions under flexible situations and decisions require lot of discussion and deliberation.	For those organisations where followers are qualified, motivated, requiring no supervision or control over themselves and where direct reward is paid for their efforts.

(Any six) [1 × 6 = 6]

This Question is for practice and its solution is given at the end of the chapter.

TOPIC-4 Communication

Concepts Covered

- Meaning of communication. • Elements of the communication process. • Concept of formal and informal communication. • Barriers to effective communication. • Measures to overcome barriers to communication.

Revision Notes

- Communication is a process of exchange of ideas, views, facts, feelings, etc., between or among people to create common understanding.
- **Elements of Communication:**

(i) Sender: Conveyor.
(ii) Message: Subject matter of communication.
(iii) Encoding: Converting message into symbols.
(iv) Media: Path or medium to transmit message.
(v) Decoding: Translating encoded message into language.
(vi) Receiver: Receiving the message.
(vii) Feedback: Reaction to the sender.
(viii) Noise: Hindrance in effective communication process.

- **Channels of Communication:**

(i) Formal Communication: Official communication taking place in the organisation through official channels.
(ii) Informal Communication: Unofficial communication that arises from the **social** interaction of people.

Example-1

Workers chit chating in a canteen about the behaviour of the superior, discussing about rumours that some employees are likely to be transferred are some examples of informal communication.

- **Barriers to the Communication:** [Board, 2018]

(i) Semantic Barriers: Related to encoding and decoding of message:
(a) Badly expressed message
(b) Symbols with different meanings
(c) Faulty translation
(d) Unclarified assumptions

Example-2

A boss may instruct his subordinate, "Take care of our guest". Boss may mean that subordinate should take care of transport, food, accommodation of the guest until he leaves the place. The subordinate may interpret that guest should be taken to hotel with care. Actually, the guest suffers due to these unclarified assumptions.

(e) Technical Jargon
(f) Body language and Gesture decoding

(ii) Psychological Barriers: Related to the state of mind of both the sender and the receiver.
(a) Premature evaluation
(b) Lack of attention
(c) Loss by transmission and poor retention
(d) Distrust

(iii) Organisational Barriers: Related to organisation structure, authority relationships, rules and regulations etc.

(a) Organisational policy

Example-3

In an organisation with highly centralised pattern, people may not be encouraged to have free communication.

(b) Rules and regulations
(c) Status
(d) Complexity in Organisation Structure
(e) Organisational facilities

(iv) Personal Barriers: Related to the personal attitudes of both the sender and the receiver.
(a) Fear of challenge to the authority
(b) Lack of confidence of superior on his subordinates
(c) Unwillingness to communicate
(d) Lack of proper incentive

Example-4

There is no reward or appreciation for a good suggestion, the subordinates may not be willing to offer useful suggestions.

- **Measures to improve communication effectiveness:**

(i) Clarify the ideas before communication
(ii) Communicate according to the need of the receiver
(iii) Consult others before communicating
(iv) Be aware of the language, tone and content of the message
(v) Convey things of help and value to listeners
(vi) Ensure proper feedback
(vii) Communicate for the present as well as for the future
(viii) Follow up communications
(ix) Be a good listener

MNEMONICS

(i) Concept: Communication Barriers:
Mnemonics: SO Pray Please

S: Semantic	O: Organisational
P: Personal	P: Physiological needs

(ii) Concept: Elements of Communication
Mnemonics: Some Make Easy Money but you Do Right For Nothing

S: Sender	M: Message
E: Encoding	M: Media
D: Decoding	R: Receiver
F: Feedback	N: Noise

SUBJECTIVE TYPE QUESTIONS

Short Answer Type Questions-I (3 marks each)

1. Lakhan, an expert in the area of Financial Management, sent an e-mail to his subordinate, Thomas about a new project for a client in France. Though, the e-mail was in English, a language known to Thomas, he was not able to understand the actual meaning of many words used in the e-mail. He was also not a specialist in the field of Financial Management. Not only this, some portions of the e-mail were translated from French to English in such a manner that many mistakes crept in, causing different meaning to the message.

(i) Identify two specific barriers to communication in Lakhan's e-mail.

(ii) State any two measures which can be taken by Lakhan to overcome the barriers identified in part (i) above to improve in future the effectiveness of his communication.

A [Comptt. Delhi Set-1, 2, 3, 2018]

Ans. (i) Two specific barriers to Communication in Lakhan's e-mail were:

(a) Faulty translations

(b) Technical jargon

(ii) Measures to overcome communication barriers:

(a) Lakhan should communicate according to the needs, education and understanding levels of subordinates.

(b) He should take a proper feedback to improve the communication process and make it more responsive.

(c) He should regularly follow up communication and review the instructions given to subordinates.

(d) He should be aware of languages, tone and content of the message to make it understandable to the receiver. **(Any two)**

(If an examinee has given only the heading, ½ mark for each heading should be awarded.) **[1 + 2 = 3]**

[Marking Scheme, Delhi 2018]

2. Explain briefly any three semantic barriers to communication. R [Outside & Delhi, Set-1, 2017]

Topper's Answer, 2017

SEMANTIC BARRIERS
- Badly expressed message
- Technical Jargon
- Faulty translations.

1. BADLY EXPRESSED MESSAGES

· Sometimes, intended meaning may not be conveyed by manager to subordinates.

· These badly expressed messages arise on account of
  · inadequate vocabulary
  · usage of wrong words
  · omission of needed words etc.

Boss: We have to reach six sigma level
Worker: ??

Technical Jargon

2. TECHNICAL JARGON :

· It is usually found that specialists use technical jargon while explaining to persons who are not specialists in the concerned field.

· Therefore, they may not understand the actual meaning of many such words.
  · inadequate vocabulary
  · usage of wrong words
  · omission of needed words etc.

3. FAULTY TRANSLATIONS :

· Sometimes communications originally drafted in one language (English) need to be translated into a language understandable to workers (Hindi).

· If translator is not proficient in both the languages, mistakes may creep in causing different meanings to communications.

[1 + 2 = 3]

Short Answer Type Questions-II (4 marks each)

1. State any four barriers to communication which are concerned with problems and obstructions in the process of encoding and decoding the message into words or impressions. U [SQP 2022-23]

Ans. Semantic barriers:

(i) Sometimes intended meaning may not be conveyed by a manager to his subordinates due to badly expressed messages which may be on account of inadequate vocabulary, usage of wrong works, omission of needed words, etc.

(ii) A word may have different meanings and the receiver has to perceive one such meaning for the word used by the communicator.

(iii) If the translator is not proficient with both the languages, mistakes may creep in causing different meanings to communication.

(iv) Some communications may have certain assumptions which are subject to different interpretations.

(v) It is usually found that specialists use technical jargon while explaining to persons who are not specialists in the concerned field and therefore they may not understand the actual meaning of many words.

(vi) If there is no match between what is said and what is expressed in body movements, communications may be wrongly perceived. **(Any four) [1×4=4]**

[Marking Scheme, SQP 2022-23]

2. State any four barriers to communication which are related to authority relationships, rules and regulations of the company. U [SQP 2022-23]

Ans. Organisational barriers:

(i) If organisational policy either explicit or implicit is not supportive to free flow of communication it may hamper effectiveness of communications.

(ii) Rigid rules and regulations, cumbersome procedures may be a hurdle to communication, as communications through prescribed channels may result in delays.

(iii) Status of superior may create psychological distance between him and his subordinates.

(iv) Complexity in the organisation caused by the number of managerial levels may delay and distort the communication as the number of filtering points is more.

(v) If facilities like frequent meetings, suggestion box, and complaint box, social and cultural gathering, transparency in operations, etc, for smooth, clear and timely communications are not provided, communications may be hampered.

(Any four) [1×4=4]

3. **Briefly explain the positive and negative aspects of the type of communication which arises out of the need of employees to exchange their views.**

U [SQP 2020-21]

4. **State any four elements involved in the communication process.**

Ans. The elements involved in communication process are explained below:

(i) **Sender:** Sender means the person who conveys his thoughts or ideas to the receiver.

(ii) **Message:** It is the content of ideas, feelings, suggestions, order, etc., intended to be communicated.

(iii) **Encoding:** It is the process of converting the message into communication symbols such as words, pictures, gestures, etc.

(iv) **Media:** It is the path/channel through which encoded message is transmitted to the receiver, e.g., face to face, phone call, internet, etc.

(v) **Decoding:** It is the process of converting encoded symbols of the sender.

(vi) **Receiver:** The person who receives communication of the sender.

(vii) **Feedback:** Feedback is the response or reaction of the receiver. Without feedback the sender will not be able to judge the effectiveness of his message and the communication process will remain incomplete.

5. **State any four semantic barriers of communication.**

[SQP, 2023-24]

Ans. Semantic Barriers:

(a) **Badly expressed message:** Sometimes intended meaning may not be conveyed by a manager to his subordinates. These badly expressed messages may be on account of inadequate vocabulary, usage of wrong words, omission of needed words, etc.

(b) **Symbols with different meanings:** A word may have several meanings. Receiver has to perceive one such meaning for the word used by communicator.

(c) **Faulty translations:** Sometimes the message originally drafted in one language (e.g., English) needs to be translated to the language understandable by workers (e.g., Hindi). If the translator is not proficient with both the languages, mistakes may creep in causing different meanings to the communication.

(d) **Unclarified assumptions:** Some communications may have certain assumptions which are subject to different interpretations. For example, a boss may instruct his subordinate, "Take care of our guest". Boss may mean that sub-ordinate should take care of transport, food, accommodation of the guest until he leaves the place. The subordinate may interpret that guest should be taken to hotel with care. Actually, the guest suffers due to these unclarified assumptions.

(e) **Technical jargon:** It is usually found that specialists use technical jargon while explaining to persons, who are not specialists in the concerned field. Therefore, they may not understand the actual meaning of many such words.

(f) **Body language and gesture decoding:** Every movement of body communicates some meaning. The body movement and gestures of communicator matters while conveying the message. If there is no match between what is said and what is expressed in body movements, message may be wrongly perceived. [Marking Scheme, SQP 2023-24]

Long Answer Type Questions-I (6 marks each)

1. **Telpro India Ltd. is an IT company having 1,500 employees. All its employees take things easy and are easily approachable for minor queries and problems. Due to this, the operations of the company are disturbed and its revenue has fallen. Everyone is seen talking to each other resulting in inefficiency at work. It has also resulted in loss of secrecy and confidential information being easily available. Explain the measures that the manager should adopt to improve communication system of Telpro India Ltd.'.** C [OEB]

OR

'The organisations which are keen on developing effective communication, should adopt suitable measures to overcome the barriers to communication and improve communication effectiveness.' Suggest and explain any such five measures. AE [OEB]

OR

The barriers to effective communication exist in all organisations to a greater or less degree. State any six measures to overcome these barriers. AE [OEB]

Concept Applied	Measures to overcome communication barriers.

Ans. Measures to overcome communication barriers are:

(i) **Simple language:** The sender of the message should use uncomplicated language and familiar words. It is beneficial for sender to use that language which is already known to the receiver.

(ii) **Clarify the idea before communication:** The entire problem or message to be communicated by sender should be studied in detail and expressed in such a manner that there is no scope of doubt when the message is conveyed to subordinate or receiver.

(iii) **Consult others before communication:** It is always advantageous to involve subordinates *i.e.,* the

This Question is for practice and its solution is given at the end of the chapter.

receiver to get their acceptance or willing co-operation easily available, before communicating the message to them.

(iv) Ensure proper feedback: Communication is said to be effective when the desired feedback is received by the sender after it is understood by the receiver. So, the receiver should be encouraged to give his feedback and to be more responsive regarding the message sent.

(v) Communicate for present as well as future: Generally communication is done to meet the present needs and commitment. But in order to maintain consistency, communication should be aimed at future goals of the organisation as well.

(vi) Follow up communication: There should be regular follow-up and review of the information and instructions given to the subordinate *i.e.*, the receiver. Such follow up helps in maintaining ongoing clarity and in removing hurdles in implementing the instructions.

(vii) Communicate according to the needs of the receiver: Manager should adjust his communication message as per the education and understanding level of the subordinates.

(viii) Be careful about language and content of message: The content of the message, tone, language and manner in which the message is to be imparted are some important aspects of effective communication that need to be paid attention to. The language should be easily and clearly understandable to the receiver.

(ix) Convey things of help and value to the listeners: While conveying any message to others, it is beneficial to know the interest and needs of the people with whom one is communicating as the likelihood of the message being understood by them increases. **(Any six) [1×6=6]**

Commonly Made Error

Sometimes students write about barriers instead of measures to overcome them. At times, points also overlap.

Answering Tip

Avoid repetition of points with different language and learn various barriers along with the measure to overcome that particular barrier.

2. Managers, at times face several problems due to communication breakdowns or barriers. In the light of this statement describe the psychological barriers to effective communication. A I U [OEB]

Ans. Some of the psychological barriers are as follows:

(i) Premature evaluation: When some people form a judgment before listening the entire message then it is known as premature evaluation. This type of an early evaluation distorts the proper understanding of the message and acts as a barrier to the effective communication.

(ii) Lack of attention: Communication becomes less effective on account of inadequate attention to the message and the message is likely to be misunderstood. Lack of attention may be on account of the preoccupied mind of receiver or may be the result of not listening the message properly.

(iii) Loss by transmission and poor retention: Loss by transmission happens when the message passes through various levels in the organisation, then the result is inaccurate information and happens more often in case of oral communication. Poor retention is another issue when people cannot retain the information for a long period of time in case they have been if inattentive or disinterested.

(iv) Distrust: Lack of mutual trust between the message sender and its receiver acts as a barrier to effective communication. When the parties do not believe each other due to any reason then they cannot understand each other's message as it is meant to be.

COMPETENCY BASED QUESTIONS

Objective Type Questions

[A] Multiple Choice Questions

1. At support.com, there is no reward or appreciation for a good suggestion. Thus, the subordinates are not willing to offer any useful suggestions to their superiors. Identify the type of barrier to communication that has been created in the firm due to this.

(A) Semantic barrier
(B) Personal barrier
(C) Organisational barrier
(D) Psychological barrier A [SQP 2019-20]

Ans. Option (B) is correct.

Explanation: The personal factors of both sender and receiver may exert influence on effective communication. If there is no motivation or incentive for communication, subordinates may not take initiative to communicate. For example, if there is no reward or appreciation for a good suggestion, the subordinates may not be willing to offer useful suggestions.

2. Rama, the Marketing Manager of Weaver Garments Ltd., does not allow the salesmen working under her to freely express their frank opinion and feelings regarding work related matters. Identify the organisational barrier to communication that has been created by Rama.

(A) Status
(B) Rules and regulations
(C) Organisational policy
(D) Organisational facilities A [SQP 2019-20]

Concept Applied: Communication barrier

Ans. Option (A) is correct.

Explanation: Status of superior may create psychological distance between him and his subordinates. A status conscious manager also may not allow his subordinates to express their feelings freely.

3. For the following two statements, choose the correct option:

Statement I: Directing ensures that the individuals work for organisational goals.

Statement II: Directing guides employees to fully realise their potential and capabilities by motivating and providing effective leadership.

Choose the correct option from options given below:

(A) Statement I is correct and statement II is wrong.
(B) Statement II is correct and statement I is wrong.
(C) Both the statements are correct.
(D) Both the statements are wrong. U [OEB]

Ans. Option (C) is correct.

4. Which of the following statements is true about Directing:

(A) Directing is necessary at planning stage.
(B) Directing is needed at every level of management in each department.
(C) Directing is initiated at lower level of management.
(D) Directing is the least important function of management. U [OEB]

Ans. Option (B) is correct.

Explanation: Directing takes place at every level of management. Every manager, from top executive to supervisor performs the function of directing. The directing takes place wherever superior – subordinate relations exist.

6. For the following two statements, choose the correct option:

Statement I: Motivation can only be positive.

Statement II: Motivation produces goal directed behaviour. [OEB]

Choose the correct option from options given below:

(A) Statement I is correct and statement II is wrong.
(B) Statement II is correct and statement I is wrong.
(C) Both the statements are correct.
(D) Both the statements are wrong.

Ans. Option (B) is correct.

Explanation: Motivation can either be positive or negative. Positive motivation provides positive rewards like increase in pay, promotion, recognition etc. Negative motivation uses negative means like punishment, stopping increments, threatening etc. which also may induce a person to act in the desired way. Motivation produces goal directed behaviour. For example, the promotion in the job may be given to employee with the objective of improving his performance. If the employee is interested in promotion, it helps to produce a behaviour to improve performance.

7. Match the NEEDS as per Maslow's Need Hierarchy Theory of Motivation in Column I with their correct Examples in Column II

	Column I	Column II
(i)	Security Needs	Friendship
(ii)	Self Actualisation Needs	Recognition
(iii)	Esteem Needs	Achievement of goals
(iv)	Belonging Needs	Stability of income

(A) (i), (iii), (iv), (ii) (B) (iv), (iii), (ii), (i)
(C) (iv), (ii), (i), (iii) (D) (ii), (i), (iii), (iv)

R [OEB]

Ans. Option (B) is correct.

8. Mr. Prateek Goyal, the Ex-chairman of India Original Ltd., built up his successor before retiring. Following the norms set up by himself, he handed over the reins of the company to the co-founder Mr. Arvind Mishra, who had the potential to bring about change in the behaviour of others. Name the concept of management which was the reason, why Mr. Prateek Goyal choose Mr. Arvind Mishra to be his successor.

(A) Motivation (B) Leadership
(C) Communication (D) Staffing A [OEB]

Concept Applied: Concept of leadership.

Ans. Option (B) is correct.

Explanation: Leadership is the process of influencing the behaviour of people by making them strive voluntarily owards achievement of organisational goals. Leadership indicates the ability of an individual to maintain good interpersonal relations with followers and motivate them to contribute for achieving organisational objectives.

9. Which of the following statement is not true regarding Democratic Style of Leadership?

(A) The leader exercises more control by using forces within the group.
(B) The leader encourages subordinates to participate in decision making.
(C) The leader gives orders and insists that they are obeyed.
(D) The leader supports and respects the subordinate's opinion. U [OEB]

10. Which of the following statement is true regarding Laissez Faire Style of Leadership?

(A) The leader gives complete freedom to the subordinates.
(B) The leader gives orders and insists that they are obeyed.
(C) The leader does not change or wish to be contradicted.
(D) Communication is only one-way. U [OEB]

11. Mr. Saxam, production manager of Creative Concepts, discusses with his staff about the new export order. All the staff members unanimously agree that they all will work together to do overtime to complete the order and meet the deadline. Mr. Saxam is following .... leadership style.

(A) Democratic (B) Autocratic
(C) Authoritative (D) Laissez Faire

A [OEB]

These Questions are for practice and their solutions are given at the end of the chapter.

Ans. Option (A) is correct.

Explanation: A democratic leader will develop action plans and makes decisions in consultation with his subordinates. He will encourage them to participate in decision-making. This kind of leadership style is more common now-a-days, since leaders also recognise that people perform best if they have set their own objectives. They also need to respect the other's opinion and support subordinates to perform their duties and accomplish organisational objectives. They exercise more control by using forces within the group.

12. For the following two statements, choose the correct option:

Statement I: Leadership indicates ability of an individual to influence others.

Statement II: Leadership tries to bring change in the behaviour of others. U [OEB]

Choose the correct option from options given below:

(A) Statement I is correct and statement II is wrong.
(B) Statement II is correct and statement I is wrong.
(C) Both the statements are correct.
(D) Both the statements are wrong.

Ans. Option (C) is correct.

Explanation: Leadership is the process of influencing the behaviour of people by making them strive voluntarily towards achievement of organisational goals. Leadership indicates the ability of an individual to maintain good interpersonal relations with followers and motivate them to contribute for achieving organisational objectives.

13. For the following two statements, choose the correct option:

Statement I: Democratic leader is dogmatic.

Statement II: Autocratic leadership style is effective in getting productivity in many situations. U [OEB]

Choose the correct option from options given below:

(A) Statement I is correct and statement II is wrong.
(B) Statement II is correct and statement I is wrong.
(C) Both the statements are correct.
(D) Both the statements are wrong.

Ans. Option (B) is correct.

Explanation: An autocratic leader gives orders and expects his subordinates to obey those orders. If a manager is following this style, then communication is only one-way with the subordinate only acting according to the command given by the manager. This leader is dogmatic, i.e., does not change or wish to be contradicted. His following is based on the assumption that reward or punishment both can be given depending upon the result. This leadership style is effective in getting productivity in many situations like in a factory where the supervisor is responsible for production on time and has to ensure labour productivity. Quick decision-making is also facilitated.

14.

Identify the style of leadership shown in the above image.

(A) Autocratic leadership
(B) Democratic leadership
(C) Free rein leadership
(D) None of these A [OEB]

Ans. Option (A) is correct.

Explanation: Autocratic leadership is a leadership style in which the leader centralises all decision making powers and exercises complete control over his subordinates.

[B] Assertion & Reason

Directions: In the following questions, a statement of assertion (A) is followed by a statement of reason (R). Mark the correct choice as:

(A) Both assertion (A) and reason (R) are true and reason (R) is the correct explanation of assertion (A).
(B) Both assertion (A) and reason (R) are true but reason (R) is not the correct explanation of assertion (A).
(C) Assertion (A) is true but reason (R) is false.
(D) Assertion (A) is false but reason (R) is true.

1. **Assertion (A):** Directing helps to bring stability and balance in the organisation.
   Reason (R): Directing fosters cooperation and commitment among the people and helps to achieve balance among various groups, activities and the departments. [OEB]

Ans. Option (A) is correct.

2. **Assertion (A):** Directing is a key managerial function.
   Reason (R): Directing is a managerial process which takes place throughout the life of an organisation. [OEB]

Ans. Option (B) is correct.

Explanation: Directing is not a mere issue of communication but encompasses many elements like motivation and leadership. It is one of the key managerial functions performed by every manager. Directing is a managerial process which takes place throughout the life of an organisation. A manager has to perform this function along with planning, organising, staffing and controlling while discharging his duties in the organisation. While other functions prepare a setting for action, directing initiates action in the organisation.

3. **Assertion (A):** Directing is a continuous process.
   Reason (R): Every manager can direct his immediate subordinate and take instructions from his immediate boss. [OEB]

Ans. Option (B) is correct.

Explanation: Directing is a continuous activity. It takes place throughout the life of the organisation irrespective of people occupying managerial positions. Organisations like Infosys, Tata, BHEL, HLL and the managers may change but the directing process continues because without direction the organisational activities cannot continue further. Directing is first initiated at top level and flows to the bottom through organisational hierarchy. It means that every manager can direct his immediate subordinate and take instructions from his immediate boss.

4. **Assertion (A):** The leaders always play a key role for the success and excellence of any organization.

   Reason (R): Leadership is exercised to achieve common goals of the organization.

Ans. Option (A) is correct.

Explanation: The leaders always play a key role for the success and excellence of any organisation. Leadership is the process of influencing the behaviour of people by making them strive voluntarily towards achievement of organisational goals. Leadership indicates the ability of an individual to maintain good interpersonal relations with followers and motivate them to contribute for achieving organisational objectives.

5. **Assertion (A):** Non-financial incentives are measurable in monetary term.

   Reason (R): Non-financial incentives mainly focus on social and emotion needs.

Ans. Option (D) is correct.

Explanation: Financial incentives refer to incentives which are in direct monetary form or measurable in monetary term and serve to motivate people for better performance. These incentives may be provided on individual or group basis. All the needs of individuals are not satisfied by money alone. Psychological, social and emotional factors also play important role in providing motivation. Non-financial incentives mainly focus on these needs. Sometimes, monetary aspect may be involved in non-financial incentives as well. However, the emphasis is to provide psychological and emotional satisfaction rather than money driven satisfaction.

[C] Case Based MCQs

I. Read the following text and answer the following questions on the basis of the same:

Mr. Sunil Diali is a safety officer in a reputed PSU sector ECL. He supervises the workers towards the predetermined goals of the organisation and directs how to eradicate unsafe practices of inundation, fire breakouts, existence of inflammable gases etc. On one such instances there was huge fire breakout in the underground mines and the workers morale was down and demotivated because of several risk hazards. Mr. Diali observed the whole situation and consulted with all his workers and constantly monitored, guided and inspired them to integrate their efforts and accept the situation as a challenge and take adequate safety measures for fire extinguish and subsidizing its effects. Thereby, production turnover was outstanding and outperformed other subsidiaries. Mr. Diali was recognized with Bravery Award from CIL. **[OEB]**

1. **Mr. Diali worked towards predetermined goals of the organisation. Which important function of directing is addressed here?**
   (A) Means of motivation
   (B) Initiates action
   (C) Facilitate change
   (D) Brings stability

Ans. Option (B) is correct.

Explanation: Directing is a key managerial function. A manager has to perform this function along with planning, organising, staffing and controlling while discharging his duties in the organisation. While other functions prepare a setting for action, directing initiates action in the organisation.

2. **Mr. Diali consulted with all his workers, he listened to their opinions. Which form of leadership is identified here?**
   (A) Laissez-faire (B) Autocratic
   (C) Democratic (D) Free-rein

Ans. Option (C) is correct.

Explanation: A democratic leader will develop action plans and makes decisions in consultation with his subordinates. He will encourage them to participate in decision-making. This kind of leadership style is more common now-a-days, since leaders also recognise that people perform best if they have set their own objectives. They also need to respect the other's opinion and support subordinates to perform their duties and accomplish organisational objectives. They exercise more control by using forces within the group.

3. **Bravery award is ______________ form of non-financial incentive.**
   (A) Status
   (B) Job security
   (C) Career advancement
   (D) Employee recognition

Ans. Option (D) is correct.

Explanation: Most people have a need for evaluation of their work and due recognition. They feel that what they do should be recognised by others concerned. Recognition means acknowledgment with a show of appreciation. When such appreciation is given to the work performed by employees, they feel motivated to perform/work at higher level.

4. **Under Maslow's hierarchy need theory which need of Mr. Diali has been met through respect and recognition among other employees?**
   (A) Self - actualisation need
   (B) Safety and security needs
   (C) Esteem needs
   (D) Physiological needs

Ans. Option (C) is correct.

Explanation: Esteem needs include factors such as self-respect, autonomy status, recognition and attention.

II. Read the following text and answer the questions given below:

Hema is a permanent employee of a very large company called Global Pvt. Ltd. She has been working with the company for the last 5 years and is now eligible for retirement benefits as well. She likes her work and performs her responsibilities with due diligence. She has always displayed utmost dedication while being at work. As per the job agreement, she had to work for 40 hours per week and was free to work overtime. Hema worked overtime during the weekdays and on some occasions, she also used to work on weekends for 8 to 10 hours. On account of which she fell sick and had to take leave from her work as she got hospitalized for a fairly long period of time. The company did not show any concern and neither did it enquire about her health. She realised that On one hand, she was able to fulfill only some of her needs as she only had the stability of income and pension plans since she had completed 5 years already with the organization. On the other hand some other needs still remained unfulfilled which she realized on account of the indifferent attitude of the company during her sickness. Thus, Hema felt that though her most basic needs are being met as per Maslow's need hierarchy theory, she has a long way to go before her highest level needs are met.

1. Which of the following need of Hema is being fulfilled:

(A) Security needs **(B)** Belongingness needs
(C) Esteem needs **(D)** All the above

Ans. Option (A) is correct.

Explanation: Safety/Security needs provide security and protection from physical and emotional harm. Examples: job security, stability of income, Pension plans etc.

2. Which need of Hema is not being fulfilled?

(A) Belongingness needs **(B)** Esteem needs
(C) Both (A) and (B) **(D)** Neither (A) nor (B)

Ans. Option (C) is correct.

Explanation: Affiliation/Belonging needs refer to affection, sense of belongingness, acceptance and friendship. Esteem needs include factors such as self-respect, auto nomy status, recognition and attention.

3. In the light of the above case, what are the most basic needs of Hema known as?

(A) Safety needs
(B) Affiliation needs
(C) Physiological needs
(D) Self-actualization Needs

Ans. Option (C) is correct.

Explanation: Basic physiological needs are most basic in the hierarchy and corresponds to primary needs. Hunger, thirst, shelter, sleep and sex are some examples of these needs. In the organisational context, basic salary helps to satisfy these needs.

4. In the light of the above case, which is the highest level of needs of Hema which she believes will take a fairly long time to fulfil?

(A) Security needs
(B) Belongingness needs
(C) Esteem needs
(D) Self-actualization needs

Ans. Option (D) is correct.

Explanation: Self actualisation needs is the highest level of need in the hierarchy. It refers to the drive to become what one is capable of becoming. These needs include growth, self-fulfillment and achievement of goals.

SOLUTIONS FOR PRACTICE QUESTIONS (TOPIC-3)

SATQs-II

Ans 2. Democratic or participative leader: A democratic leader will develop action plans and make decisions in consultation with his subordinates. He will encourage them to participate in decision-making. This kind of leadership style is more common now-a-days, since leaders also recognise that people perform best if they have set their own objectives. They also need to respect others opinion and support subordinates to perform their duties and accomplish organisational objectives. They exercise more control by using forces within the group. [1 + 3 = 4]

[Marking Scheme, SQP 2020-21]

SOLUTIONS FOR PRACTICE QUESTIONS (TOPIC-4)

SATQs-II

Ans. 3. Positive aspects of informal communication:

(i) Sometimes, grapevine channels may be helpful as they carry information rapidly and therefore, may be useful to the manager at times.

(ii) Informal channels are used by the managers to transmit information so as to know the reactions of his/her subordinates.

Negative aspects of informal communication:

(i) The grapevine/informal communication some times gets distorted. It also leads to generating rumours and informal discussions and sometimes may hamper the work environment.

(ii) It is very difficult to detect the source of such communication. **[1 × 4 = 4]**

[Marking Scheme, SQP 2020-2021]

SOLUTIONS FOR OBJECTIVE PRACTICE QUESTIONS

[A] MCQs

Ans 9. Option (C) is correct.

Explanation: A democratic leader will develop action plans and makes decisions in consultation with his subordinates. He will encourage them to participate in decision-making. This kind of leadership style is more common now-a-days, since leaders also recognise that people perform best if they have set their own objectives. They also need to respect the other's opinion and support subordinates to perform their duties and accomplish organisational objectives. They exercise more control by using forces within the group.

Ans 10. Option (A) is correct.

Explanation: Such a leader does not believe in the use of power unless it is absolutely essential. The followers are given a high degree of independence to formulate their own objectives and ways to achieve them. The group members work on their own tasks resolving issues themselves. The manager is there only to support them and supply them the required information to complete the task assigned. At the same time, the subordinate assumes responsibility for the work to be performed.

REFLECTION

(a) Were you able to explain the features and importance of directing?
(b) Were you able to describe the various elements of directing?
(c) Could you develop an understanding of Maslow's Need Hierarchy Theory of Motivation?
(d) Did you understand the various financial and non-financial incentives?
(e) Were you able to explain the various styles of leadership?
(f) Were you able to understand the elements of the communication process?
(g) Have you understood the concept of formal and informal communication?
(h) Were you able to discuss the various barriers to effective communication?
(i) Could you suggest some measures to overcome barriers to communication?
(j) Were you able to identify the style of leadership in the below mentioned line:
"Such a leader does not believe in the use of power unless it is absolutely essential."
(k) Were you able to identify the type of incentive in the below mentioned line:
"These incentives are in direct monetary form or measurable in monetary term and serve to motivate people for better performance."

SELF ASSESSMENT PAPER - 7

Maximum Time: 1 hour **MM: 30**

General Instructions:

(i) *All the questions are compulsory*
(ii) *Q.1 to Q.10 are 1 mark questions*
(3) *Q.11 to Q.12 are 3 mark questions*
(iv) *Q.13 to Q.14 are 4 marks questions*
(v) *Q.15 is a 6 marks question*

Objective Type Questions [1 Mark]

1. ________ is the most popular grapevine communication network in organisations.
(A) Gossip (B) Cluster (C) Probability (D) None of these [1]

2. Match the options of Column I with their correct options given in Column II.

	Column I		Column II
(1)	Motivation	(a)	Process of exchange of ideas
(2)	Leadership	(b)	Incitement or inducement to act or move
(3)	Communication	(c)	Process of influencing the behaviour of people

(A) 1-b, 2-c, 3-a (B) 1-c, 2-a, 3-b (C) 1-a, 2-b, 3-c (D) None of these [1]

3. Which of the following non-financial incentive is concerned with designing jobs?
(A) Job Enrichment
(B) Employee Recognition programmes
(C) Job security
(D) Career Advancement Opportunity [1]

4. ____________ is the process of converting encoded symbols of the sender.
(A) Encoding **(B)** Decoding
(C) Media **(D)** All of these [1]

5. For the following two statements, choose the correct option:
Statement I: Downward communication refers to flow of communication from subordinate to superior.
Statement II: The pattern through which communication flows within the organisation is generally indicated through communication network.
Choose the correct option from options given below:
(A) Statement I is correct and statement II is wrong.
(B) Statement II is correct and statement I is wrong.
(C) Both the statements are correct.
(D) Both the statements are wrong. [1]

6. For the following two statements, choose the correct option:
Statement I: Semantic barriers are concerned with problems and obstructions in the process of encoding and decoding of message.
Statement II: The barriers may prevent communication or filter part of it or carry incorrect meaning due to which misunderstandings may be created.
Choose the correct option from options given below:
(A) Statement I is correct and statement II is wrong.
(B) Statement II is correct and statement I is wrong.
(C) Both the statements are correct.
(D) Both the statements are wrong. [1]

Read the text given below and answer Q. 7-10 based on it.
Mr. Saxena is an exceptional team leader. He knows that for a team to achieve its goals and progress nicely communicative effectiveness is required. He always maintains what he says, focuses on future goals of the organisation and never goes against his commitments. You can find him most of the times busy communicating with his superiors or subordinates. When he once delivers the message, he always checks whether his team is able to understand the concept he is trying to communicate and he does it through proper questioning. He has a very pleasing personality. Whenever he delivers a speech he focuses on his language, his voice and the sentiments of his listeners. He is a real team leader. He gives members of his team opportunities to express themselves. Whenever he is about to make a speech, he consults his team members for developing a plan of communication by their participation and involvement. He always says that whatever is useless should be rejected and whatever is useful should be accepted. His purpose of speaking is to help others. He believes that a speech should be such which takes into consideration interests and needs of the listeners. There is a lot one can learn from Mr. Saxena's personality.

7. Which measure of communicative effectiveness has been adopted by Mr. Saxena in the following lines:
"He always maintains what he says, focuses on future goals of the organisation and never goes against his commitments."
(A) Communicate for present as well as future
(B) Follow up communications
(C) Convey things of help and value to listeners
(D) Ensure proper feedback [1]

8. Which measure of communicative effectiveness has been adopted by Mr. Saxena in the following lines:
"Whenever he is about to make a speech, he consults his team members for developing a plan of communication by their participation and involvement."

(A) Consult others before communicating
(B) Clarify the ideas before communication
(C) Communicate according to the needs of receiver
(D) Be aware of languages, tone and content of message [1]

9. Identify the element of directing illustrated in the picture above.

(A) Motivation (B) Leadership
(C) Communication (D) None of these [1]

10. Which measure of communicative effectiveness has been adopted by Mr. Saxena in the following lines:
"He believes that a speech should be such which takes into consideration interests and needs of the listeners."
(A) Consult others before communicating
(B) Clarify the ideas before communication
(C) Communicate according to the needs of receiver
(D) Be aware of languages, tone and content of message [1]

Short Answer Type Questions - I [3 Marks]

11. What is meant by 'directing' function of management? State any three points highlighting the importance of 'directing' function.

12. "This leader is dogmatic, i.e., does not change or wish to be contradicted".
Identify and explain the style of leadership highlighted in the above-mentioned line.

Short Answer Type Questions - II [4 Marks]

13. Identity and explain the elements of directing mentioned below:
(i) Tina, the manager, sends an e-mail to all the employees asking them to come to a meeting at 4:00 pm.
(ii) Rahul sees that his employee Astha is not working efficiently. He promises her incentives if she improves her work.
(iii) Anita directs her employee Hemant to work on the new project.
(iv) Manju tells her employee Harshita to start working properly or else she will be fired from her job.

14. After pursuing a course in MBA from a reputed university from Europe, Rohit started a workshop in Mumbai to support his father's business. He is used to speaking in English but the local skilled workers understand only Hindi and Marathi. Hence, he started facing problems in the work due to miscommunications between him and the workers. As a result, he is not able to get the business done in the desired manner.
(i) Identify the type of communication barrier being referred to in the above paragraph.
(ii) Explain any three types of barriers identified in part (i).

Long Answer Type Questions [6 Marks]

15. Abheet has been working as a sewing machine operator in an export house for the past ten years. His basic work is to seam the parts of a garment together, and attach buttons, hooks, zippers, and accessories to produce clothing. Considering the fact that Abheet is an experienced operator, he is well versed with the fundamentals of industrial production and possesses good communication skills. The plant superintendent in the factory recommends Abheet's name to the production manager for the post of supervisor which will fall vacant after a month on the retirement of the present supervisor. Consequently, Abheet is assigned the post of supervisor and his salary is increased accordingly. Moreover, as per the policy of the export house, he is offered free medical aid and education to his two children. Now his responsibility also increases. He knows that the duties and responsibilities of him are challenging. He knows in order to make his team work with a positive frame of mind, he will have to set a personal example as a role model and influence their behaviour and working style to increase the output of his team. For this he organised a series of meetings to know the suggestions of his team members on various issues. His subordinates appreciate his habit of consulting his team before he takes any major decisions. In context of the above case:
(i) Identify and explain the style of leadership mentioned in the above passage quoting lines from the paragraph.
(ii) Identify and explain the types of financial incentives offered to Abheet by quoting lines from the paragraph.

CONTROLLING

LEARNING OBJECTIVES

After going through this chapter, the student would be able to:

- Understand the concept of controlling.
- Explain the importance of controlling.
- Describe the relationship between planning and controlling.
- Discuss the steps in the process of controlling.

Study Plan
Maximum Time = 2.00 Hrs
Maximum Questions = 28

Revision Notes

Scan to know more about this topic
Importance of Controlling

- Controlling means ensuring that activities in an organisation are performed as per the plans.
- **Nature/Features of Controlling:**

(i) Goal-Oriented: Ensures resources are used effectively.

(ii) Pervasive Function: Performed at all levels and in all types of organisations.

(iii) Continuous: Brings management cycle back to planning.

Scan to know more about this topic
Relationship between Planning and Controlling

- **Importance of Controlling:** [Board, 2022]

(i) Helps in accomplishing the organisational goals.

(ii) Helps in judging accuracy of standards.

(iii) Helps in making the efficient use of resources.

(iv) Helps in improving employee motivation.

(v) Helps in ensuring order and discipline.

(vi) Helps in facilitating coordination in action.

- **Relationship between Planning and Controlling:** [Board, 2017]

(i) Both are interrelated and interdependent

(a) Planning based on facts makes controlling easier and effective.

(b) Controlling improves future planning by providing information derived from past experience.

(ii) Planning is prescriptive and controlling is evaluative:

(a) Planning prescribes appropriate action.

(b) Controlling evaluates performance.

(iii) Both are backward looking as well as forward looking:

(a) Planning is based on the past experiences and done for future.

Scan to know more about this topic
Process of Controlling

(b) Controlling evaluates past activities and improves the future performance.

- **Controlling Process:** [2019]

(i) Setting performance standards: Against which actual performance will be measured.

Example-1

Standards set in terms of cost to be incurred, revenue to be earned, product units to be produced and sold, time to be spent in performing a task, all represents quantitative standards.

(ii) Measurement of actual performance: Through personal observation, sample checking, performance reports, etc.

(iii) Comparing actual performance with standards: To reveal the **deviations** between actual and desired results.

Example-2

Performance of a worker in terms of units produced in a week can be easily measured against the standard output for the week.

(iv) Analysing deviations: By using **critical point control** and **management by exception** techniques.

(v) Taking corrective action: Involves **training** of employees, replacement of machinery, etc.

MNEMONICS

Concept: Controlling Process

Interpretations: Such a Mischievous CAT

S : Setting performance standards

M : Measurement of actual performance

C : Comparison of actual performance with standards

A : Analysis of deviations

T : Taking corrective action

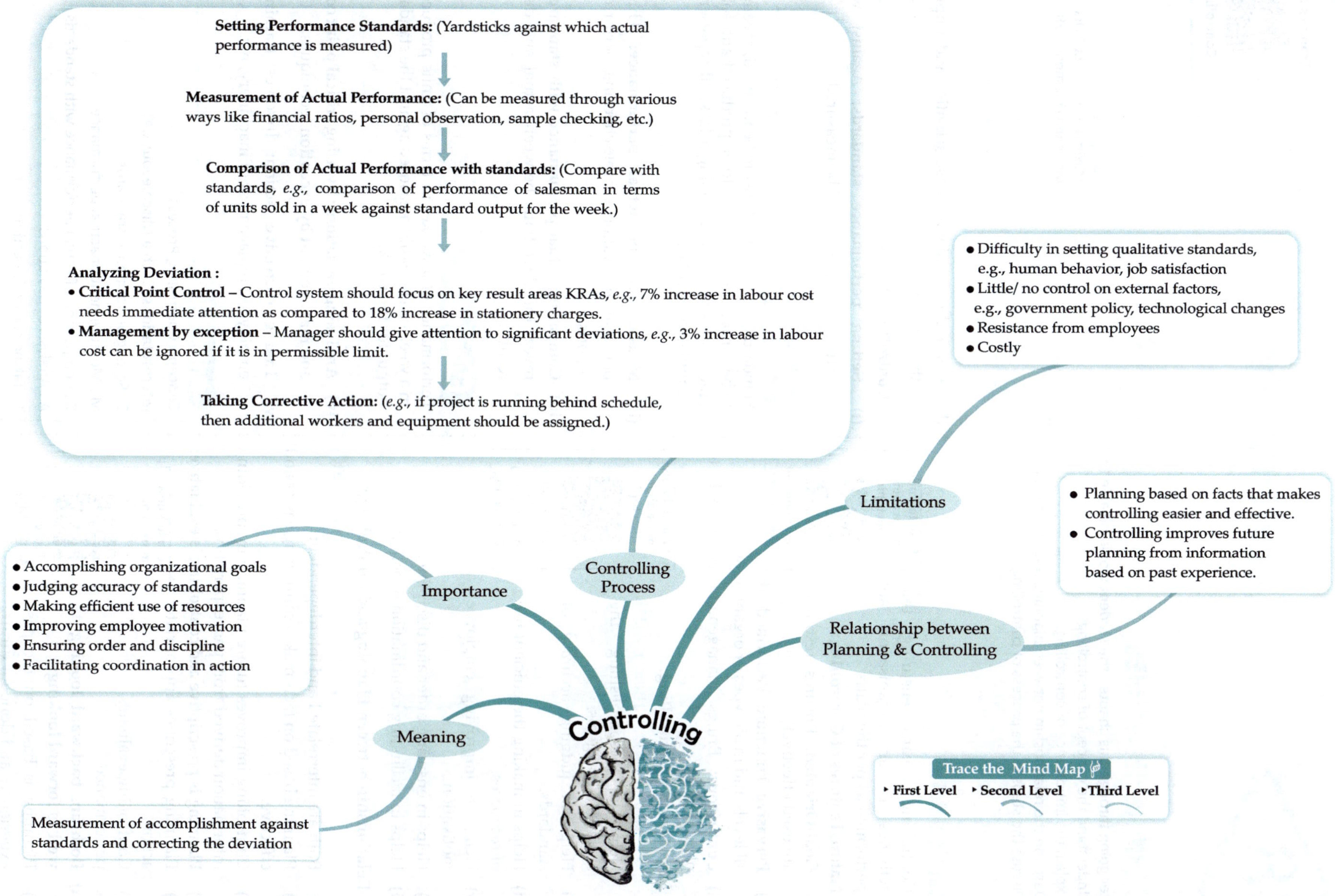

Controlling

Meaning

Measurement of accomplishment against standards and correcting the deviation

Importance

- Accomplishing organizational goals
- Judging accuracy of standards
- Making efficient use of resources
- Improving employee motivation
- Ensuring order and discipline
- Facilitating coordination in action

Controlling Process

Setting Performance Standards: (Yardsticks against which actual performance is measured)

↓

Measurement of Actual Performance: (Can be measured through various ways like financial ratios, personal observation, sample checking, etc.)

↓

Comparison of Actual Performance with standards: (Compare with standards, *e.g.,* comparison of performance of salesman in terms of units sold in a week against standard output for the week.)

↓

Analyzing Deviation :

- **Critical Point Control** – Control system should focus on key result areas KRAs, *e.g.,* 7% increase in labour cost needs immediate attention as compared to 18% increase in stationery charges.
- **Management by exception** – Manager should give attention to significant deviations, *e.g.,* 3% increase in labour cost can be ignored if it is in permissible limit.

↓

Taking Corrective Action: (*e.g.,* if project is running behind schedule, then additional workers and equipment should be assigned.)

Limitations

- Difficulty in setting qualitative standards, e.g., human behavior, job satisfaction
- Little/ no control on external factors, e.g., government policy, technological changes
- Resistance from employees
- Costly

Relationship between Planning & Controlling

- Planning based on facts that makes controlling easier and effective.
- Controlling improves future planning from information based on past experience.

Trace the Mind Map

First Level · Second Level · Third Level

SUBJECTIVE TYPE QUESTIONS

Short Answer Type Questions-I (3 marks each)

1. Explain "Critical point control" with respect to analysing deviations, a step in the process of controlling. Give a suitable example.
U [SQP 2022-23]

Ans. Critical point control: It is neither economical nor easy to keep a check on each and every activity in an organisation. Control should therefore focus on key result areas which are critical to the success of an organisation. These KRAs are set as the critical points. If anything goes wrong at the critical points, the entire organisation suffers. For instance, in a manufacturing organisation, an increase of 5% in the labour cost may be more troublesome than a 15% increase in postal charges. **[2+1=3]**
[Marking Scheme, SQP 2022-23]

2. Explain "Management by exception" with respect to analysing deviations, a step in the process of controlling. Give a suitable example.
U [SQP 2022-23]

Ans. Management by Exception: Management by exception, which is often referred to as control by exception, is an important principle of management control based on the belief that an attempt to control everything results in controlling nothing. Thus, only significant deviations which go beyond the permissible limit should be brought to the notice of the management. For instance, if the plans lay down 2% increase in labour cost as an acceptable range of deviation in a manufacturing organisation, only an increase in labour cost beyond 2% should be brought to the notice of the management. However, in case of major deviation from the standard (say, 5%), the matter has to receive immediate action of management on a priority basis. **[3]**
[Marking Scheme, SQP 2022-23]

3. 'The final step in the controlling process is taking corrective action, but when deviations are within acceptable limits no corrective action is required.' When and why corrective action is required? State.
U [Delhi Set-1, 2022]

Ans. The final step in the controlling process is taking corrective action. No corrective action is required when the deviations are within acceptable limits.

When: However, when the deviations go beyond the acceptable range, especially in the important areas, it demands immediate managerial attention so that deviations do not occur again and standards are accomplished.

Why: A corrective action plan outlines what is needed to solve a problem and helps a company to meet its goal. **[3]**
[Marking Scheme, Delhi, 2022]

4. Explain the following as steps in the process of controlling:
(i) Setting performance standards
(ii) Measurement of actual performance. [SQP, 2023-24]

Ans. (i) Setting Performance Standards: The first step in the controlling process is setting up of performance standards. Standards are the criteria against which actual performance would be measured. Thus, standards serve as benchmarks towards which an organisation strives to work. Standards can be set in both quantitative as well as qualitative terms. **[1½]**

(ii) Measurement of actual performance: This step involves comparison of actual performance with the standard. Such comparison will reveal the deviation between actual and desired results. Comparison becomes easier when standards are set in quantitative terms. **[1½]**
[Marking Scheme, SQP, 2023-24]

5. State any three points of importance of controlling function of management. U [Delhi Set-1, 2022]

OR

State any three reasons as to why controlling is regarded as an indispensable function of management. [SQP, 2023-24]

Ans. Importance of controlling function of management:

(i) Accomplishing organisational goals: The controlling function measures progress towards the organisational goals and brings to light the deviations, if any, and indicates corrective action. It, thus, guides the organisation and keeps it on the right track so that organisational goals might be achieved.

(ii) Judging accuracy of standards: A good control system enables management to verify whether the standards set are accurate and objective. An efficient control system keeps a careful check on the changes taking place in the organisation and in the environment and helps to review and revise the standards in light of such changes.

(iii) Making efficient use of resources: By exercising control, a manager seeks to reduce wastage and spoilage of resources. Each activity is performed in accordance with predetermined standards and norms. This ensures that resources are used in the most effective and efficient manner.

(iv) Improving employee motivation: A good control system ensures that employees know well in advance what they are expected to do and what are the standards of performance on the basis of which they will be appraised. It, thus, motivates them and helps them to give better performance.

(v) Ensuring order and discipline: Controlling creates an atmosphere of order and discipline in the organisation. It helps to minimise dishonest behaviour on the part of the employees by keeping a close check on their activities.

(vi) Facilitating coordination in action: Controlling provides direction to all activities and efforts for achieving organisational goals. Each department and employee are governed by predetermined standards which are well coordinated with one another. This ensures that overall organisational objectives are accomplished. **(Any three) [1×3=3]**

[Marking Scheme, Delhi, 2022]

6. **Priya is a regional manager of XYZ. Ltd. She is a hardworking employee and is trying to reduce wastage of resources in her company. She has set standards for performance of different activities and is ensuring that targets are met according to these standards with minimal wastage of resources. She has set up CCTV cameras which helps her to keep a close check on the activities of the subordinates and know how the employees are performing. She also rewards the employees with a bonus when these standards are met. She is trying her best to ensure a good performance of her team this year through the application of an important function of management. Explain any two benefits of the function of management highlighted above.**

A [SQP 2021-22]

Ans. Importance of controlling (Any two):

1. **Accomplishing organisational goals:** The controlling function measures progress towards the organisational goals and brings to light the deviations, if any, and indicates corrective action.
2. **Ensuring Order and discipline:** Controlling creates an atmosphere of order and discipline in the organisation. It helps to minimise dishonest behaviour by keeping a close check on their activities.
3. **Making efficient use of resources:** Each activity is performed in accordance with predetermined standards and norms. This ensures that resources are used in the most effective and efficient manner.
4. **Improving employee motivation:** A good control system ensures that employees know well in advance what they are expected to do and what are the standards of performance on the basis of which they will be appraised. It, thus, motivates them and helps them to give better performance.

[1½ × 2 = 3]

7. **'Analysing deviations' is an important step in the process of controlling. It is therefore important to focus on key result areas which are critical to the success of an organisation. Identify and give the meaning of the concept discussed above.**

U [Delhi Set-2, 3, 2022]

Ans: Some deviations in performance can be expected in all activities. It is, therefore, important to determine the acceptable range of deviations. Also, deviations in key areas of business need to be attended more urgently as compared to deviations in certain insignificant areas. Critical point control should be used by a manager in this regard.

Critical Point Control: It is neither economical nor easy to keep a check on each and every activity in an organisation. Control should, therefore, focus on key result areas (KRAs) which are critical to the success of an organisation. These KRAs are set as the critical points. If anything goes wrong at the critical points, the entire organisation suffers. **[3]**

[Marking Scheme, Delhi, 2022]

8. **One of the functions of management completes one cycle of management process and improves planning in the next cycle in the light of the problems that were identified in the existing plans. Identify and state the function of management discussed above.** U [Outside Delhi Set-1, 2022]

Ans. Controlling function brings back the management cycle back to the planning function. The controlling function finds out how far actual performance deviates from standards, analyses the causes of such deviations and attempts to take corrective actions based on the same. This process helps in formulation of future plans in the light of the problems that were identified and, thus, helps in better planning in the future periods. Thus, controlling only completes one cycle of management process and improves planning in the next cycle. **[3]** [Marking Scheme, OD, 2022]

9. **"Controlling is an indispensable function of management. Without controlling the best of plans can go awry ". Do you agree? Explain any two reasons in support of your answer.**

AE [SQP 2020-21]

10. **"It is generally believed that measurement of performance should be done after the task is completed." Identify and explain the step in the process of the function of management being discussed above and the step followed by the same in the process.** A [SQP 2020-21]

Ans. Measurement of Actual performance: Performance should be measured in an objective and reliable manner. There are several techniques for measurement of performance wherever possible measurement of work should be done during the performance.

Comparing actual performance with standards: This step involves comparison of actual performance with the standard. Such comparison will reveal the deviation between actual and desired results. Standards become easier when standards are set in quantitative terms. **[1½ × 2 = 3]**

[Marking Scheme, SQP 2020-21]

Short Answer Type Questions-II (4 marks each)

1. **Vinber Ltd. set up a manufacturing unit at Bhiwadi at Himachal Pradesh to manufacture electric geysers and supply them to dealers all over the country. Their production target was 500 geysers per week. It was decided by the management that variation in production upto 10 units would be acceptable.**

   At the end of the first week, the production was 450 geysers. The next week, production increased to 470 geysers. A week later, production was 460 geysers.

   On investigation, it was found out that fluctuation in production was due to irregular supply of electricity.

   (i) The above para discusses some of the steps of one of the functions of management. Explain the steps.

   (ii) Also, state the step(s) not discussed in the above para. AE [Delhi Set-1, 2, 3, 2019]

This Question is for practice and its solution is given at the end of the chapter.

Concept Applied Steps in the process of controlling.

Ans. (i) Steps in the process of controlling discussed in the above para:

(a) Setting performance standards: Standards should be set in precise quantitative terms. These are set at the stage of planning. They should be flexible in nature so that they can be altered as per need.

(b) Measuring actual performance: Performance should be measured in an objective and reliable manner. There are several techniques for measurement of performance wherever possible measurement of work should be done during the performance.

(c) Analysing deviations: Some deviation in performance can be expected in all activities. It is, therefore, important to determine the acceptable range of deviations. Also, deviations in key areas of business need to be attended more urgently as compared to deviations in certain insignificant areas. Critical point control and management by exception should be used by a manager in this regard.

(ii) Steps not discussed in the above para:

(a) Comparing actual performance with standards to find out the deviations.

(b) Taking corrective action if deviations go beyond the acceptable limits.

(In case the examinee has not written the steps in the right sequence, ½ mark may be deducted)

[Marking Scheme, Delhi 2019] **[3+1=4]**

2. Explain any four points of importance of the controlling function of management.

A I R [Delhi/OD, 2018]

Long Answer Type Questions (6 marks each)

1. John after completing his degree in MBA joins as a production manager in a Tyre manufacturing company. Recently he noticed that his team could not achieve the target production of 100 units per day. Instead on an average the production touched the target of only 70 units. On thorough analysis he found out that the deviation between standard production and actual production is far beyond acceptable range, on overall analysis he also found out that there has been a marginal increase in office stationery expenses. Moreover, he detected that the machine installed for the purpose of manufacturing was not able to perform at its best. Identify and explain the step that should be followed by John in the above case. A [OEB]

Ans. The step that should follow by the John in the above case is analysing deviations.

Some deviation in performance can be expected in all activities. It is, therefore, important to determine the acceptable range of deviations. Also, deviations in key areas of business need to be attended more urgently as compared to deviations in certain insignificant areas. Critical point control and management by exception should be used by a manager in this regard.

(i) Critical Point Control: It is neither economical nor easy to keep a check on each and every activity in an organisation. Control should, therefore, focus on key result areas (KRAs) which are critical to the success of an organisation. These KRAs are set as the critical points. If anything goes wrong at the critical points, the entire organisation suffers. For instance, in a manufacturing organisation, an increase of 5 per cent in the labour cost may be more troublesome than a 15 per cent increase in postal charges.

(ii) Management by Exception: Management by exception, which is often referred to as control by exception, is an important principle of management control based on the belief that an attempt to control everything results in controlling nothing. Thus, only significant deviations which go beyond the permissible limit should be brought to the notice of management. Thus, if the plans lay down 2 per cent increase in labour cost as an acceptable range of deviation in a manufacturing organisation, only increase in labour cost beyond 2 per cent should be brought to the notice of the management. However, in case of major deviation from the standard (say, 5 per cent), the matter has to receive immediate action of management on a priority basis. **[2 + 4 = 6]**

2. Describe briefly the relationship between controlling and planning. U [Delhi 2017]

3. Kapil and Kamal & Co. is a large manufacturing unit. Recently the company had conducted time and motion studies and concluded that on an average, a worker could produce 300 units per day. However, it has been noticed that the average daily production of a worker is in the range of 200-225 units.

(i) Name the function of management and identify and explain the step in the process of this function which helped in finding out that the actual production of worker is less than the set target.

(ii) To complete the process of the function identified in (i) and to ensure the performance as per time and motion studies, identify and explain what further step a manager has to take. A [OEB]

Ans. (i) The function of management is 'Controlling':

This is the third step of controlling process i.e., comparison of actual performance with established standards. This step involves finding deviations and their extent and in identifying the causes of such deviations.

(ii) Taking corrective actions: This is the last step of Controlling process. By comparing actual performance with established standards, deviations are revealed. The remedial or corrective action is to be taken to remove deficiencies. Here, it involves change in working methods, material, machines, policies and procedures. It may also require improvement in the motivation, supervision and modifications in the business plans.

These Questions are for practice and their solutions are given at the end of the chapter.

COMPETENCY BASED QUESTIONS

Objective Type Questions

[A] Multiple Choice Questions

1. Identify an important principle of management control in which only significant deviations which go beyond the permissible limit should be brought to the notice of management.

(A) Management by control
(B) Control by exception
(C) Critical point control
(D) Both (A) & (B) U [SQP 2020-21]

Ans. Option (B) is correct.

Explanation: Management by exception, which is often referred to as control by exception, is an important principle of management control based on the belief that an attempt to control everything results in controlling nothing. Thus, only significant deviations which go beyond the permissible limit should be brought to the notice of management.

2. Name the function of management which helps in the formulation of future plans, in the light of the problems that were identified and thus, helps in better planning in the future period.

(A) Planning (B) Organising
(C) Directing (D) Controlling

U [SQP 2020-21]

3. Which of the following statements establishes a relationship between planning and controlling:

(A) Planning and controlling are inseparable twins of management.
(B) Planning is clearly a prerequisite for controlling.
(C) Planning is looking ahead while controlling is looking backward.
(D) All of the above U [OEB]

Concept Applied: Relationship between planning and controlling.

Ans. Option (D) is correct.

4. Which of the following steps in the controlling process state that comparison becomes easier when standards are set in quantitative terms?

AI U [OEB]

(A) Analysing deviations
(B) Measurement of actual performance
(C) Comparing actual performance with standards
(D) Setting performance standards

Ans. Option (C) is correct.

Explanation: This step involves comparison of actual performance with the standard. Such comparison will reveal the deviation between actual and desired results. Comparison becomes easier when standards are set in quantitative terms. For instance, performance of a worker in terms of units produced in a week can be easily measured against the standard output for the week.

5. An important project at AMB Consultants is running behind schedule by a month. This has upset their clients and might affect the reputation of the company in the long run. No managerial action like assigning more workers, equipment or giving overtime has been able to solve the problem. What managerial action may now be taken by the company to avoid such a situation from arising in future? A [OEB]

(A) Revise the schedule
(B) Assigning additional workers and equipment to the project
(C) Get permission for further overtime work
(D) Both (B) and (C)

Ans. Option (A) is correct.

Explanation: A good control system enables management to verify whether the standards set are accurate and objective. An efficient control system keeps a careful check on the changes taking place in the organisation and in the environment and helps to review and revise the standards in light of such changes.

6. Controlling means ensuring that activities in an organisation are performed as per the __________.

(A) Plans (B) Goals
(C) Resources (D) None of these

7.

Identify the step in the process of controlling illustrated in the picture above.

(A) Setting performance standards
(B) Measurement of actual performance
(C) Analysing deviations
(D) Taking corrective action [OEB]

Ans. Option (D) is correct.

[B] Assertion & Reason

Directions: In the following questions, a statement of assertion (A) is followed by a statement of reason (R). Mark the correct choice as: [OEB]

(A) Both assertion (A) and reason (R) are true and reason (R) is the correct explanation of assertion (A).
(B) Both assertion (A) and reason (R) are true but reason (R) is not the correct explanation of assertion (A).

These Questions are for practice and their solutions are given at the end of the chapter.

(C) Assertion (A) is true but reason (R) is false.

(D) Assertion (A) is false but reason (R) is true.

1. **Assertion (A):** Standards can be set in both quantitative as well as qualitative terms.

   Reason (R): Standards are the criteria against which actual performance would be measured. [OEB]

Ans. Option (B) is correct.

Explanation: Standards are the criteria against which actual performance would be measured. Thus, standards serve as benchmarks towards which an organisation strives to work. Standards can be set in both quantitative as well as qualitative terms. For instance, standards set in terms of cost to be incurred, revenue to be earned, product units to be produced and sold, time to be spent in performing a task, all represents quantitative standards. Sometimes standards may also be set in qualitative terms. Improving goodwill and motivation level of employees are examples of qualitative standards.

2. **Assertion (A):** Controlling creates an atmosphere of order and discipline in the organisation.

   Reason (R): By exercising control, a manager seeks to reduce wastage and spoilage of resources.

   U [OEB]

Ans. 2. Option (B) is correct.

Explanation: Controlling creates an atmosphere of order and discipline in the organisation. It helps to minimise dishonest behaviour on the part of the employees by keeping a close check on their activities. By exercising control, a manager seeks to reduce wastage and spoilage of resources. Each activity is performed in accordance with predetermined standards and norms. This ensures that resources are used in the most effective and efficient manner.

3. **Assertion (A):** Managers of only top level need to perform controlling function of management.

   Reason (R): Controlling is a function that brings back the management cycle back to the planning function. U [OEB]

4. **Assertion (A):** Controlling is like a postmortem of past activities to find out deviations from the standards.

   Reason (R): Plans are prepared for future and are based on forecasts about future conditions.

   U [OEB]

Ans. 4. Option (B) is correct.

Explanation: Plans are prepared for future and are based on forecasts about future conditions. Therefore, planning involves looking ahead and is called a forward-looking function. On the contrary, controlling is like a postmortem of past activities to find out deviations from the standards. In that sense, controlling is a backward looking function. However, it should be understood that planning is guided by past experiences and the corrective action initiated by control function aims to improve future performance. Thus, planning and controlling are both backward-looking as well as a forward-looking function.

[C] Case Based MCQs

I. Read the below case and answer the questions that follow:

Vinay was the Chief Operating Officer of 'Easy Solutions Ltd.', a company providing advanced software solutions to Indian Defence Services. They had been carrying on business successfully for the last twelve years and earning enough profits. But from the last one year, they realised that though the business is getting big orders which are being fulfilled on time, even then the revenues kept on decreasing. Vinay was not able to find out where the problem was. He started keeping a close check on the progress of activities as he could sense that something was wrong. He wanted to take some action before any major damage could be done to the business. Vinay appointed a cyber security expert who monitored the company's processes and found out that the computer operator was deleting the entries from the computers and pocketing the revenues. He was caught and handed over to the police. This created an atmosphere of order and discipline in the organisation and helped in minimising dishonest behaviour on the part of the employees. [OEB]

1. **Which management function proved helpful in creating an atmosphere of order and discipline in the organisation and helped in minimising dishonest behaviour on the part of the employees?**

   (A) Planning (B) Organising

   (C) Directing (D) Controlling

Ans. Option (D) is correct.

Explanation: Controlling creates an atmosphere of order and discipline in the organisation. It helps to minimise dishonest behaviour on the part of the employees by keeping a close check on their activities.

2. **What did the measurement of performance reveal?**

   (A) The company was earning enough profits.

   (B) Declining revenues despite getting big orders which were being fulfilled on time.

   (C) The company was running successfully.

   (D) All of the above.

Ans. Option (B) is correct.

Explanation: Performance should be measured in an objective and reliable manner. There are several techniques for measurement of performance. These include personal observation, sample checking, performance reports, etc. As far as possible, performance should be measured in the same units in which standards are set as this would make their comparison easier.

3. **What did the analysis by Vinay reveal?**

   (A) Nothing was wrong.

   (B) The computer operator was deleting the entries from the computers and pocketing the revenues.

This Question is for practice and its solution is given at the end of the chapter.

(C) Vinay was not able to find out where the problem was.
(D) None of the above.

Ans. Option (B) is correct.

Explanation: Some deviation in performance can be expected in all activities. It is, therefore, important to determine the acceptable range of deviations. Also, deviations in key areas of business need to be attended more urgently as compared to deviations in certain insignificant areas.

4. What corrective action did Vinay take?

(A) He did not take any action as no major damage was done.
(B) Computer operator was caught and handed over to the police.
(C) Computer operator was warned with dire consequences.
(D) None of the above.

Ans. Option (B) is correct.

Explanation: No corrective action is required when the deviations are within acceptable limits. However, when the deviations go beyond the acceptable range, especially in the important areas, it demands immediate managerial attention so that deviations do not occur again and standards are accomplished.

II. Read the below case and answer the questions that follow:

Sameer Sweets, a renowned name for quality sweets since 1950 had maintained its standards ever since then. It is an ancestral sweet shop and Sana, the present owner of Sameer Sweets, is the third generation entrepreneur who has taken the charge of the sweet shop from her father. Sana has been handling her responsibilities exceptionally well except that she was worried as the sales had declined during the last three months despite her best efforts and involvement in business. When she enquired from the Sales Manager, Ajay, he reported that there were some complaints about the quality of sweets from many customers recently. Therefore, Sana ordered for sample checking of sweets by her quality control team. The team investigated and reported to Sana. She realised that during peak demand, quality was being compromised by her team to satisfy the customers. She decided to invest more capital in order to increase production to be able to meet the increasing demand especially during peak seasons like festivals and marriage catering. [OEB]

1. '______ a renowned name for quality sweets since 1950 had maintained its standards ever since then.' Which step does this represent in the controlling process?

(A) Setting performance standards
(B) Measurement of actual performance
(C) Comparison of actual performance with standards.
(D) Analysis of deviations

Ans. Option (A) is correct.

Explanation: Standards are the criteria against which actual performance would be measured. Thus, standards serve as benchmarks towards which an organisation strives to work.

2. '______ sales had declined during the last three months.' Which step does this represent in the controlling process?

(A) Measurement of actual performance
(B) Comparison of actual performance with standards
(C) Analysis of deviations
(D) Taking corrective action

Ans. Option (A) is correct.

Explanation: Performance should be measured in an objective and reliable manner. There are several techniques for measurement of performance. These include personal observation, sample checking, performance reports, etc. As far as possible, performance should be measured in the same units in which standards are set as this would make their comparison easier.

3. '_____ Sana ordered for sample checking of sweets by her quality control team.' Which step does this represent in the controlling process?

(A) Measurement of actual performance
(B) Comparison of actual performance with standards
(C) Analysis of deviations
(D) Taking corrective action

Ans. Option (C) is correct.

Explanation: Some deviation in performance can be expected in all activities. It is, therefore, important to determine the acceptable range of deviations. Also, deviations in key areas of business need to be attended more urgently as compared to deviations in certain insignificant areas. Critical point control and management by exception should be used by a manager in this regard.

4. 'She decided to invest more money in order to increase production to be able to meet the increasing demand ____' Which step does this represent in the controlling process?

(A) Measurement of actual performance
(B) Comparison of actual performance with standards
(C) Analysis of deviations
(D) Taking corrective action

Ans. Option (D) is correct.

Explanation: When the deviations go beyond the acceptable range, especially in the important areas, it demands immediate managerial attention so that deviations do not occur again and standards are accomplished. In case the deviation cannot be corrected through managerial action, the standards may have to be revised.

SOLUTIONS FOR PRACTICE QUESTIONS

SATQs-I

Ans. 9. Yes.

Importance of controlling:

(i) Accomplishing organisational goals: The controlling function measures progress towards the organisational goals and brings to light the deviations, if any, and indicates corrective action.

(ii) Judging accuracy of standards: A good control system enables management to verify whether the standards set are accurate and objective.

(iii) Making efficient use of resources: By exercising control, a manager seeks to reduce wastage and spoilage of resources. Each activity is performed in accordance with predetermined standards and norms.

(iv) Improving employee motivation: A good control system ensures that employees know well in advance what they are expected to do and what are the standards of performance on the basis of which they are appraised.

(v) Ensuring order and discipline: Controlling creates an atmosphere of order and discipline in the organisation.

(vi) Facilitating coordination in action: Controlling provides direction to all activities and efforts for achieving organisational goals.

(Any two) [1½ × 2 = 3]

[Marking Scheme, 2021]

SATQs-II

Topper's Answer, 2018

Ans. 2.

A.16 Importance of controlling function

Increases employee motivation

Judging the accuracy of ~~facts~~ standard ← Importance of Controlling → ensures order and discipline

Ensures coordination in action

1. Judging accuracy of ~~facts~~ standards

- Controlling function ensures that the objectives set are accurate and objective
- A good control system keeps a check on activities taking place outside the organisation and inside the organisation and helps in reviewing the standards.

2. Ensures order and discipline

- Controlling reduces the dishonest behaviour of employees by keeping close check on the activities of employees.
- This way it ensures order and discipline.

3. Ensures coordination in action

- Controlling ensures that all the activities in an organisation move in the same direction.
- As all the activities are performed according to predetermined objectives, it ensures coordination and reduces overlapping of activities.

4. Increases Employee Motivation

- Controlling sets up some standards of employees and employees know the standards against which their performance will be measured.
- It thus increases employee motivation.

Commonly Made Error

Students write the importance of management or steps of controlling instead of importance of controlling.

Answering Tip

Thoroughly study the importance/objectives/steps of every function of management.

LATQs

Ans. 2. The relationship between controlling and planning is described below:

(a) Planning and controlling are inseparable twins of management. Planning provides the basis for controlling. The desired standards are set in the process of planning in clear, specific and terms. In the process of controlling the actual performance is measured and compared with these standards and the deviations if any are identified and appropriate corrective action is taken. However, in the absence of any standards it would not be possible to gauge the actual performance. Thus, planning without controlling is meaningless and controlling without planning is blind.

(b) Planning is prescriptive whereas controlling is evaluative. Planning is an intellectual activity which is concerned with thinking, articulating and analysing various alternative course of actions and prescribing the best possible alternative in order to achieve the desired goals efficiently and effectively. Controlling on the other hand is concerned with ensuring that events conform to plans. Thus, it involves monitoring and measuring the extent to which the desired goals have been realised.

(c) Planning is looking ahead while controlling is looking back. Plans are prepared for future and are based on forecasts about future conditions. Therefore, planning involves looking ahead and is called a forward-looking function. On the contrary, controlling is like a postmortem of past activities to find.

SOLUTIONS FOR OBJECTIVE PRACTICE QUESTIONS

[A] MCQs

Ans. 2. Option (D) is correct.

Explanation: Controlling function finds out how far actual performance deviates from standards, analyses the causes of such deviations and attempts to take corrective actions based on the same. This process helps in formulation of future plans in the light of the problems that were identified and, thus, helps in better planning in the future periods. Thus, controlling only completes one cycle of management process and improves planning in the next cycle.

Ans. 6. Option (A) is correct.

Explanation: Controlling is one of the important functions of a manager. In order to seek planned results from the subordinates, a manager needs to exercise effective control over the activities of the subordinates. In other words, controlling means ensuring that activities in an organisation are performed as per the plans.

[B] A & R

Ans. 3. Option (D) is correct.

Explanation: Controlling function of a manager is a pervasive function. Managers at all levels of management— top, middle and lower-need to perform controlling functions to keep a control over activities in their areas.

The controlling function finds out how far actual performance deviates from standards, analyses the causes of such deviations and attempts to take corrective actions based on the same. This process helps in formulation of future plans in the light of the problems that were identified and, thus, helps in better planning in the future periods. Thus, it is a function that brings back the management cycle back to the planning function.

REFLECTION

(a) Were you able to explain the importance of controlling?

(b) Could you describe the relationship between planning and controlling?

(c) Were you able to discuss the steps in the process of controlling?

(d) Were you able to identify the step in the process of controlling in the below mentioned line:
"Such comparison will reveal the deviation between actual and desired results."

(e) Were you able to identify the importance of controlling in the below mentioned line:
"Each department and employee is governed by predetermined standards which are well coordinated with one another."

(f) Were you able to explain the statement: "Planning is prescriptive whereas, controlling is evaluative."

SELF ASSESSMENT PAPER - 8

Maximum Time: 1 hour **MM: 30**

General Instructions:

(i) All the questions are compulsory
(ii) Q.1 to Q.10 are 1 mark questions
(3) Q.11 to Q.12 are 3 mark questions
(iv) Q.13 to Q.14 are 4 marks questions
(v) Q.15 is a 6 marks question

Objective Type Questions **[1 Mark]**

1. Once a plan becomes operational, ____________ is necessary to monitor the progress.

(A) Controlling **(B)** Organising **(C)** Directing **(D)** Staffing **[1]**

2. Match the options of Column I with their correct options given in Column II.

	Column I		Column II
(1)	Accomplishing organisational goals	**(a)**	Minimise dishonest behaviour on the part of the employees
(2)	Judging accuracy of standards	**(b)**	Guides the organisation so that goals might be achieved.
(3)	Ensuring order and discipline	**(c)**	Careful check on the changes taking place in the organisation

(A) 1-a, 2-b, 3-c **(B)** 1-c, 2-b, 3-a **(C)** 1-c, 2-a, 3-b **(D)** 1-b, 2-c, 3-a **[1]**

3. Standards can be set in __________ .

(A) Quantitative terms **(B)** Qualitative terms
(C) Both (A) and (B) **(D)** None of these **[1]**

4. For the following two statements, choose the correct option:

Statement I: Standards should be flexible enough to be modified whenever required.

Statement II: Comparison becomes easier when standards are set in quantitative terms.

Choose the correct option from options given below:

(A) Statement I is correct and statement II is wrong.
(B) Statement II is correct and statement I is wrong.
(C) Both the statements are correct.
(D) Both the statements are wrong. **[1]**

5. For the following two statements, choose the correct option:

Statement I: Controlling helps in facilitating coordination in action.

Statement II: Controlling helps in accomplishing organisational goals.

Choose the correct option from options given below:

(A) Statement I is correct and statement II is wrong.
(B) Statement II is correct and statement I is wrong.
(C) Both the statements are correct.
(D) Both the statements are wrong. **[1]**

Read the text given below and answer the Q. 7-10 based on it.

Rahul started a take away eating joint in a nearby market. He ensured that the food was properly cooked, a standard taste was maintained, packing of food was done effectively and the orders were executed on time. But unfortunately, his business suffered losses and he have to shut down his business. A few months later, he joined popular food joint "Burger Point". A critical point control (CPC) approach is followed by him in"Burger Point"in the cooking and handling process so that any food safety threat can be prevented, eliminated, or reduced to an acceptable level. Hence, continuous monitoring of activities is undertaken to ensure that the process is right at each critical point control. It is, therefore, important to determine the acceptable range of deviations. The main principle followed by him for cooking at "Burger Point" is "less amount many time" which can ensure the high quality and high fresh level of the food. Here, workers should be given training if the production target could not be met. For instance, if four hamburgers have to be made, a worker cannot cook all the four hamburgers at one time. The time figured out for making one hamburger is one hundred and forty-five seconds. Moreover, nearly all foods in the "Burger Point" have the specific holding time, the holding time for hamburgers is ten minutes and for French fries is seven minutes. If it is not sold within that time it is thrown away. Also, the temperature of the milk sent by the supplier must be under 5° C, otherwise, it will be returned. He has also set standards in terms of cost to be incurred and revenue to be earned. Time to time, he has to verify whether the standards set are accurate and objective. He also ensures that the resources should be used in the most effective and efficient manner so that there is no wastage.

6. Which of the following step in the controlling process is described in the below mentioned line?

"It is, therefore, important to determine the acceptable range of deviations."

(A) Analysing Deviations
(B) Comparing Actual Performance with Standards
(C) Measurement of Actual Performance
(D) Setting Performance Standards **[1]**

7. Which of the following importance of controlling is described in the below mentioned line?

"He also ensures that the resources should be used in the most effective and efficient manner so that there is no wastage."

(A) Improving employee motivation
(B) Facilitating coordination in action
(C) Making efficient use of resources
(D) Ensuring order and discipline **[1]**

8. Which of the following importance of controlling is described in the below mentioned line?

"Time to time, he has to verify whether the standards set are accurate and objective."

(A) Judging accuracy of standards
(B) Facilitating coordination in action
(C) Making efficient use of resources
(D) Ensuring order and discipline **[1]**

9. Which of the following step in the controlling process is described in the below mentioned line?

"He has also set standards in terms of cost to be incurred and revenue to be earned."

(A) Analysing Deviations
(B) Comparing Actual Performance with Standards
(C) Measurement of Actual Performance
(D) Setting Performance Standards **[1]**

Short Answer Type Questions - I [3 Marks]

10. Some employees have been assigned the job of judging the output of production in a neutral and reliable way. They are applying different techniques for achieving this aim. Some of these are personal observation, sample checking, etc. They are also keeping the units of measurement same to that of the units of set standards. Identify and explain the step in the controlling process highlighted in the above case.

11. "Planning is clearly a prerequisite for controlling." Explain the statement.

Short Answer Type Questions - II [4 Marks]

12. Jeetendra is a good performer. He works in a company which manufactures school books and stationery items. He tries his best to reduce wastage of resources in his company. He is trying to do it in the best possible manner. He has set standards for performance of different types of activities and is doing his level best to perform according to these set standards to minimise wastage of resources. Things are not going to be over for him as he will have to look into other aspects too. He has set up a good monitoring system which helps him know how to employees ate performing according to set standards as when the employees meet these standards, they will be given incentives. He is hoping to pull out a good performance from his team this year.

(a) Identify the function of management that has been referred to in the above case?

(b) Explain the benefits of this function of management have been highlighted in the above case by quoting lines from the passage?.

13. Atul works as an interior designer. He gets a contract to redesign a play school. He employs three painters on the site assuming that an average painter will be able to paint 10 desks in a day. At the end of the first day of their work, he finds that the painter *A*, painter *B* and painter *C* have painted 12, 14 and 15 desks respectively. On comparing the actual performance with the planned performance, he realises that the standard set by him is too low. Consequently, he decides to review and revise the standard and raise it.

Explain the following statement with reference to the above paragraph:

"Planning and controlling are both backward looking as well as forward looking functions."

Long Answer Type Questions [4 Marks]

14. Malti is always a topper in her exams. She loves to take challenges in every area of her life. After completing her graduation, she has been assigned the job of quantity controller. She knows this is a tough and a challenging job but she also realises the importance of it. Her daily routine is to send alarm to the manufacturing department about the deviations in the number of units produced so that the target of the day could be achieved. This helps the whole department to focus towards its main plan of action. However, one day she realises that the number of units which are to be produced is 400 which is very high and creates chaos at the shop floor. She discusses it with the management and the target is reduced to 350. This has helped the manufacturing department in maintaining quality of the work done. There are 15 workers at the shop floor where Malti does inspection. She divided the task into 30 units for each worker so that by the end of the day the target of the department is completed. Identify and explain the importance of controlling that have been highlighted in the above case by quoting lines from the passage?

FINANCIAL MANAGEMENT

Scan this topic
Financial Management

LEARNING OBJECTIVES

After going through this chapter, the student would be able to:
- Understand the concept of financial management.
- Explain the role of financial management in an organisation.
- Discuss the objectives of financial management.
- Discuss the three financial decisions and the factors affecting them.
- Describe the concept of financial planning and its objectives.
- Explain the importance of financial planning.
- Describe the factors determining the choice of an appropriate capital structure of a company
- Understand the concept of fixed and working capital.
- Describe the factors determining the requirements of fixed and working capital.

Study Plan
Maximum Time = 3.00 Hrs
Maximum Questions = 71

LIST OF TOPICS

TOPIC-1 Financial Management: Concept, Objective, Role and Financial Decisions

Concepts Covered
- Meaning, Importance and Objectives of Financial Management. • Meaning and Factors affecting the three financial decisions: investment, financing and dividend.

Revision Notes

- **Financial Management:** Financial Management is concerned with optimal procurement as well as the usage of finance.
- **Objectives of Financial Management:** The primary objective of financial management is to maximise shareholders' wealth.
- **Role of Financial Management:** The importance of financial management can be judged by the fact that almost all items in the financial statements of a business are affected directly or indirectly through some financial management decisions. Some of the examples are:

(i) Size and composition of fixed assets of the business for example a capital budgeting decision of investing an amount of ₹100 crores in fixed assets would raise the size of fixed assets block.
(ii) Quantum of current assets and its break-up into cash, inventory and receivables.
(iii) Amount of long term and short term funds to be used.
(iv) Breakup of long-term financing into debt, equity, etc.
(v) All items in the Profit and Loss Account e.g. interest, expenses, depreciation etc..

- **Types of Financial Decisions:**

(i) Investment Decision: It is concerned with investment of firm's funds in different assets. [Board, 2023]

(a) A long-term investment decision in fixed assets is called a capital budgeting decision.
(b) A short-term investment decision in cash, inventory, and debtors is called as working capital decision.

Factors affecting capital budgeting decision are:
(a) Cash flows of the project
(b) Rate of return
(c) Investment criteria

(ii) Financing Decision: It deals with the quantum of finance to be raised from various long-term sources *viz.* debt and equity. It involves identification of various available sources. The main sources of funds for a firm are **shareholders' funds** and **borrowed funds.**

Factors affecting financing decision are:
(a) Cost
(b) Floatation Costs
(c) Cash flow position of business
(d) Control consideration
(e) Capital market
(f) State of fixed operating cost
(g) Risk

(iii) Dividend Decision: It determines how much of the profits are to be distributed as dividends and how much to be retained for the investment requirement. [Board, 2023]

Factors affecting dividend decisions are:
(a) Amount of earnings
(b) Stability of earnings
(c) Stability of dividends
(d) Growth opportunities
(e) Cash flow position
(f) Shareholders' preference
(g) Taxation policy
(h) Stock market reaction
(i) Access to capital market
(j) Legal constraints
(k) Contractual constraints

Scan to know more about this topic

Financial Decisions

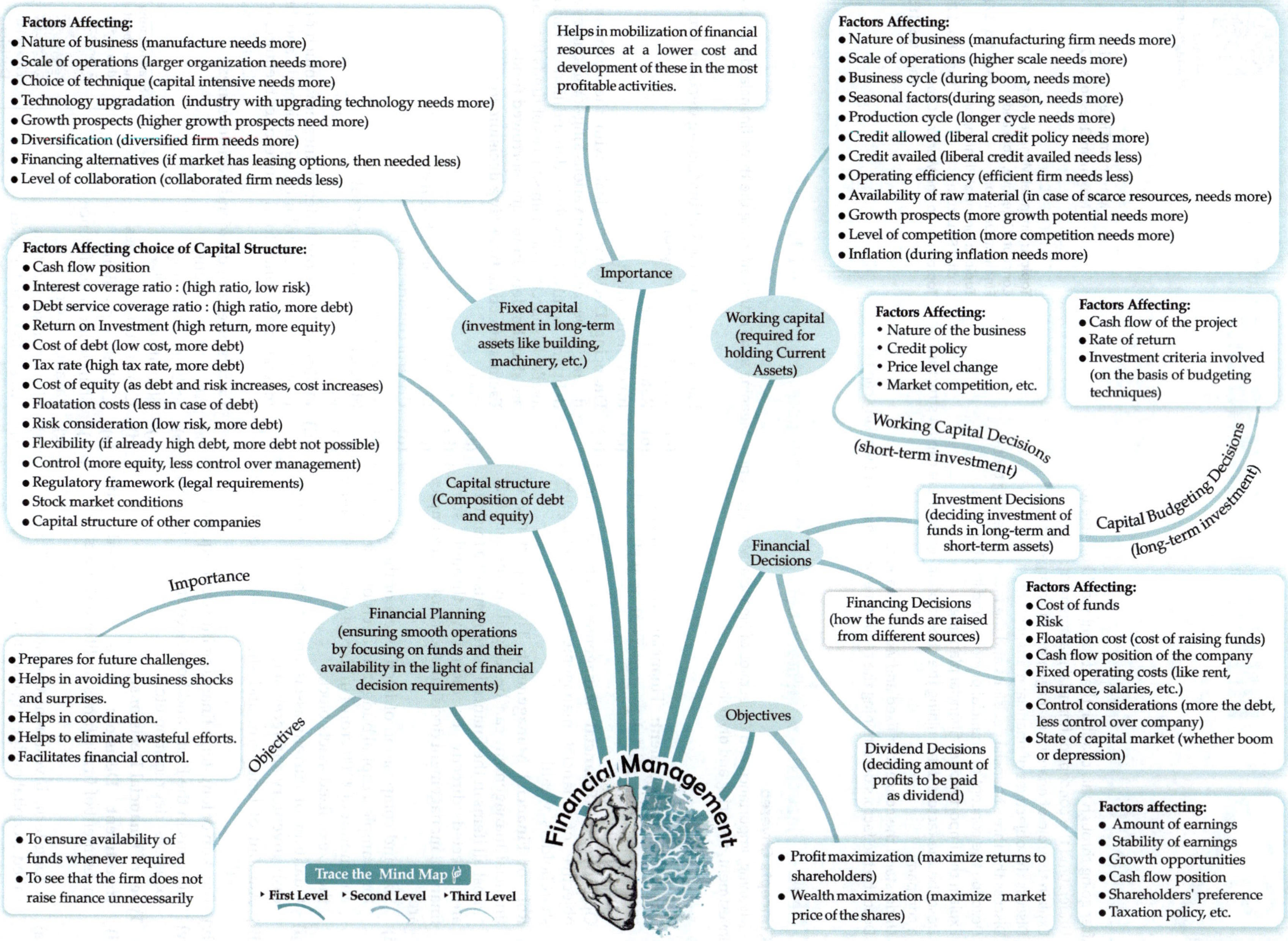

Financial Management

Trace the Mind Map: First Level, Second Level, Third Level

Importance

Helps in mobilization of financial resources at a lower cost and development of these in the most profitable activities.

Fixed capital (investment in long-term assets like building, machinery, etc.)

Factors Affecting:
- Nature of business (manufacture needs more)
- Scale of operations (larger organization needs more)
- Choice of technique (capital intensive needs more)
- Technology upgradation (industry with upgrading technology needs more)
- Growth prospects (higher growth prospects need more)
- Diversification (diversified firm needs more)
- Financing alternatives (if market has leasing options, then needed less)
- Level of collaboration (collaborated firm needs less)

Capital structure (Composition of debt and equity)

Factors Affecting choice of Capital Structure:
- Cash flow position
- Interest coverage ratio : (high ratio, low risk)
- Debt service coverage ratio : (high ratio, more debt)
- Return on Investment (high return, more equity)
- Cost of debt (low cost, more debt)
- Tax rate (high tax rate, more debt)
- Cost of equity (as debt and risk increases, cost increases)
- Floatation costs (less in case of debt)
- Risk consideration (low risk, more debt)
- Flexibility (if already high debt, more debt not possible)
- Control (more equity, less control over management)
- Regulatory framework (legal requirements)
- Stock market conditions
- Capital structure of other companies

Financial Planning (ensuring smooth operations by focusing on funds and their availability in the light of financial decision requirements)

Importance
- Prepares for future challenges.
- Helps in avoiding business shocks and surprises.
- Helps in coordination.
- Helps to eliminate wasteful efforts.
- Facilitates financial control.

Objectives
- To ensure availability of funds whenever required
- To see that the firm does not raise finance unnecessarily

Working capital (required for holding Current Assets)

Factors Affecting:
- Nature of business (manufacturing firm needs more)
- Scale of operations (higher scale needs more)
- Business cycle (during boom, needs more)
- Seasonal factors(during season, needs more)
- Production cycle (longer cycle needs more)
- Credit allowed (liberal credit policy needs more)
- Credit availed (liberal credit availed needs less)
- Operating efficiency (efficient firm needs less)
- Availability of raw material (in case of scarce resources, needs more)
- Growth prospects (more growth potential needs more)
- Level of competition (more competition needs more)
- Inflation (during inflation needs more)

Financial Decisions

Investment Decisions (deciding investment of funds in long-term and short-term assets)

Working Capital Decisions (short-term investment)

Factors Affecting:
- Nature of the business
- Credit policy
- Price level change
- Market competition, etc.

Capital Budgeting Decisions (long-term investment)

Factors Affecting:
- Cash flow of the project
- Rate of return
- Investment criteria involved (on the basis of budgeting techniques)

Financing Decisions (how the funds are raised from different sources)

Factors Affecting:
- Cost of funds
- Risk
- Floatation cost (cost of raising funds)
- Cash flow position of the company
- Fixed operating costs (like rent, insurance, salaries, etc.)
- Control considerations (more the debt, less control over company)
- State of capital market (whether boom or depression)

Dividend Decisions (deciding amount of profits to be paid as dividend)

Factors affecting:
- Amount of earnings
- Stability of earnings
- Growth opportunities
- Cash flow position
- Shareholders' preference
- Taxation policy, etc.

Objectives

- Profit maximization (maximize returns to shareholders)
- Wealth maximization (maximize market price of the shares)

KEY TERMS

Financial decision: These are the decisions which are concerned with three aspects - viz. investment, financing and dividend.
Fixed Operating Costs: Costs like building rent, insurance premium, salaries, etc. which have to be incurred irrespective of the production level.
Dividend: It is that portion of profit which is distributed to shareholders.
Shareholders' funds: Refers to the equity capital and the retained earnings.
Borrowed funds: Refers to the finance raised through debentures or other forms of debt.

SUBJECTIVE TYPE QUESTIONS

Short Answer Type Questions-I (3 marks each)

1. Explain the three major decisions every manager has take to while performing the finance function. AI U [Delhi Set-2, 2019]

Ans. Three major decisions every manager has to take while performing the finance function are:

(i) Investment Decision: It relates to how the firm's funds are invested **in different assets** in the **long-term and the short-term.**

(ii) Financing Decision: It relates to the quantum of finance to be raised from various long-term sources. It determines the overall cost of capital and financial risk of the enterprise.

(iii) Dividend Decision: It relates to how much of the profit earned by the company (after paying tax) is to be distributed to the shareholders and how much of it should be retained in the business. **[3]**

Commonly Made Error

The students don't understand the question properly and explain one of the financial decisions.

Answering Tip

Read and understand the question properly and identify and explain the three types of financial decisions.

2. State any three factors affecting dividend decision of a company. R [OEB]

3. What is meant by 'Financial Management'? State the primary objective of Financial Management. R [Delhi Set-1, 2019]

4. Atul after completing his MBA wants to open a restaurant and is looking for a proper place to open it. He is also thinking of the amount of funds which will be required for some of the set ups like food making and storing machineries. Identify and explain the type of decision mentioned in the above case. U [OEB]

Ans. Investment decisions are mentioned in the above case.

Investment decisions relate to how the firm's funds are invested in different assets. Investment decision can be long term or short-term. A long-term investment decision is also called a Capital Budgeting decision. It involves committing the finance on a long-term basis. For example, making investment in a new machine to replace an existing one or acquiring a new fixed asset or opening a new branch, etc. Short-term investment decisions (also called working capital decisions) are concerned with the decisions about the levels of cash, inventory and receivables. These decisions affect the day-to-day working of a business. **[1+2=3]**

Commonly Made Error

Most of the students were not able to interpret case-based question correctly and have written the wrong financial decision.

Answering Tip

Students should be perfect in the concepts of three different financial decisions – investment, financing and dividend.

5. 'G. Motors' is the manufacturer of sophisticated cranes. The Production manager of the company, reported to the Chief Executive Officer, Ashish Jain that one of the machines used in manufacturing sophisticated cranes had to be replaced to compete in the market, as other competitors were using automatic machines for manufacturing cranes. After a detailed analysis, it was decided to purchase a new automatic machine having the latest technology. It was also decided to finance this machine through long-term sources of finance. Ashish Jain compared various machines and decided to invest in the machine which would yield the maximum returns to its investors.

(i) Identify the financial decision taken by Ashish Jain.

(ii) Explain any three factors affecting the decision identified in (i) above.

A [Outside Delhi Set-1, 2019]

Ans. **(i)** The financial decision taken by Ashish Jain is **long–term investment or capital budgeting decision.**

(ii) The factors affecting long-term investment decisions are:

(a) Cash Flows of the Project: The cash flows in the form of cash receipts and cash payments from each investment proposal should be carefully analysed before considering capital budgeting decision.

(b) The Rate of Return: The expected rate of return over the investment proposal and the risk involved should be analysed and that proposal should be accepted which contains least risk and cost but maximum ROI.

(c) The Investment Criteria Involved: The amount of investment, cash flows, interest rate, tax benefits, rate of returns, cost of financing should be kept in

These Questions are for practice and their solutions are given at the end of the chapter.

mind as the criteria for selecting best decision after their evaluation on these points. **(3)**

6. Explain how the following will impact the dividend decision of a business.

(i) Taxation policy

(ii) Growth opportunities

(iii) Contractual constraints U [CFPQ]

Ans. (i) Taxation policy: If the dividend distribution tax on the dividend is high, it is better to pay less by way of dividends. As compared to this, **higher dividends** may be declared if **tax rates are relatively lower.**

(ii) Growth opportunities: Companies having good growth opportunities retain more money out of their earnings so as to finance the required investment. The dividend in growth companies is, therefore, **smaller than that in the non– growth companies.**

(iii) Contractual constraints: While granting loans to a company, sometimes the lender may impose **certain restrictions** on the payment of dividends in future. The companies are required to ensure that the dividend does not violate the terms of the loan agreement in this regard. **(3)**

Commonly Made Error

- The students don't write specific answer and they discuss these concepts in the context of financing or investing decision.

Answering Tip

- Be specific while writing the answer. Explain in context of dividend decision only.

Short Answer Type Questions-II (4 marks each)

1. State any four factors affecting the decision that determines the overall cost of capital and the financial risk of the enterprise. [Delhi Set-1, 2023]

Ans. The following are four factors affecting the decision that determines the overall cost of capital and the financial risk of the enterprise:

(i) Interest Rates: Interest rates are the **cost of borrowing** money and play a significant role in determining the **cost of capital**. Higher interest rates result in a higher cost of capital.

(ii) Market Conditions: Market conditions such as the availability of funds, investor preferences, and economic conditions can also affect the cost of capital.

(iii) Financial Policies: The **financial policies of the company** such as the dividend payout ratio, the use of debt, and the level of retained earnings can also affect the cost of capital.

(iv) Business Risk: The business risk of the company can also impact the cost of capital. **Higher business risk** is generally associated with a higher cost of capital. Factors that can increase business risk include market competition, technological changes, and regulatory changes.

2. State any four factors that affect the decision related to how much profit is to be distributed and how much profits are to be retained in the business. U [Delhi Set-2, 2023]

OR

Identify the financial decision that is concerned with deciding how much of the profit earned by a company is to be distributed to shareholders and how much should be retained in the business. Also state any three factors affecting the identified decision. U [Outside Delhi Set-1, 2023]

Ans. Dividend decision is concerned with deciding how much of the profit earned by a company is to be distributed to shareholders and how much should be retained in the business.

The factors affecting the decision are:

(i) Earnings: Earnings are a major determinant of dividend decision as dividends are paid out of current and past earnings. If the earning of the company is high it means that the higher dividends could be declared by the company to its shareholders along with maintaining a good amount of retained profit for future contingencies.

(ii) Growth Opportunities: If a company has **good growth opportunities**, it pays out less dividend. This is because, the extra profit will be used to help the company in the growth and expansion. This in any way is beneficial for the shareholders in the long-run as due to growth prospects the earnings of the company will increase in the near future and in the long run the dividend will increase.

(iii) Shareholder's preference: It is kept in mind by the management before declaring dividends. If the shareholders want to have more dividend the management will declare higher dividend in order to attract more investment in the form of new share capital to be issued.

(iv) Stability in Earnings: A company having higher and stable earnings can declare higher dividends than a company with lower and unstable earnings.

(v) Stability of Dividends: Generally, companies try to **stabilise dividends** per share. A steady dividend is given each year. A change is only made if the company's earning potential has gone up and not just the earnings of the current year. **[Any three]**

3. 'Zenith Mall' is a famous shopping mall in Mumbai, owned by 'Pinnacle Group'. It is very popular for its international and national brands of fashionable clothes, restaurants, cinema halls and food courts.

The management of Pinnacle Group has decided to open a new branch of the mall in Pune. This decision was very crucial for the management as it involves huge amounts.

(i) Identify and state the financial decision involved in the above case.

(ii) State any two factors affecting the decision identified in (i) above.

A [Outside Delhi Set-1, 2023]

Ans. (i) Investment Decision is stated in the above case.

It relates to how the firm's funds are invested in different assets in the long-term and the short-term.

- A long-term investment decision in fixed assets is called as Capital Budgeting Decision.
- A short-term investment decision in cash, inventory and debtors is called as working capital decisions. **(2)**

(ii) The factors affecting investment decision are:

(a) Cash Flow of the Project: The cash flow in the form of cash receipts and cash payments from each investment proposal should be carefully analysed before considering **capital budgeting decision**.

(b) Rate of Return: The expected rate of return over the investment proposal and the risk involved should be analysed and that proposal should be accepted which contains least risk and cost but maximum ROI.

(c) Investment Criteria Involved: The amount of investment, cash flow, interest rate, tax benefits, rate of return, cost of financing should be kept in mind as the criteria for selecting best decision after their evaluation on these points. **(Any two)**

4. Dhaval Acharya, after acquiring a bachelor's degree in Hotel Management joined his father's chain of vegetarian restaurants in Ahmednagar. Being young and enterprising, he suggested his father to add a new section of vegetarian bakery items which required an investment of ₹5 crores. His father Mr. Aariketh Acharya suggested him to take the decision with caution and understood everything comprehensively as bad decision may damage the financial fortune of business.

Identify the decision suggested by Mr. Aariketh Acharya. State by giving any three reasons as to why he must have advised his son to take decision with caution. AI A [SQP 2023-24]

Ans. Mr Aariketh Acharya has suggested **capital budgeting decision**.

Reasons why he must have advised this decision are:

(i) These decisions have bearing on the long-term growth. They affect the future prospects of the business.

(ii) These decisions result in large portion of funds being blocked in **long-term projects**, these investments are planned after a detailed analysis.

(iii) These decisions affect the returns of the firm, therefore influence the overall business risk complexion of the firm.

(iv) These decisions once taken, are not reversible without incurring heavy losses. Abandoning a project after heavy investment is costly in terms of waste of funds.

5. Saksham Ltd., a firm manufacturing textile, wished to diversify its business. They were considering two options, either to diversify into manufacturing tooth-paste or switches. They wanted to invest in the purchase of land, to set up a manufacturing unit in the backward areas of Gujarat, which would also lead to the generation of employment opportunities in the area, but only after fulfilling all legal requirements and taking appropriate steps to ensure that the environment was not polluted. The finance manager of the company, Mr. Ramakant was asked by the management to prepare a report on the factors which should be considered while making the above investment decision.

(i) State any two factors that Mr. Ramakant would give in his report.

(ii) Also state any two reasons which makes it important for the above decision to be made carefully.

A [OEB]

Ans. (i) Factors that should be kept in mind by the company while making the investment decision:

(a) The amount of cash flows should be carefully analysed before considering the decision.

(b) The rate of return of the project based on expected return and assessment of the risk involved from each proposal should be analysed.

(c) The decision to invest in a particular project involves a number of calculations regarding the amount of investment, interest rate, cash flows and rate of return. **(Any two)**

(ii) The following are the reasons that make the above decision to be made carefully:

(a) These decisions have a bearing on the long-term growth.

(b) These decisions result in a substantial portion of capital funds being blocked in long-term project.

(c) These decisions influence the overall business risk complexion of the firm.

(d) These decisions once taken, are not reversible without incurring heavy losses. **(Any two) [2+2=4]**

Long Answer Type Questions (6 marks each)

1. Ananta Ltd. is a company dealing in ready-made garments from last many years. Recently the profit of the company have started increasing. The finance manager decided to retain the profit instead of distributing it among shareholders.

(i) Identify and state the financial decision taken by finance manager in the above case.

(ii) State any four factors affecting the decision identified in (i) above. A [Delhi Set-1, 2022]

OR

Vansh Limited is a large and reputed company which manufactures ventilators. After the outbreak of 'COVID-19' in 2020 the company witnessed an increase in revenue by 40%. It has plans to further increase its production capacity and also start production of PPE kits, sanitisers and masks in 2022. The finance manager of the company Mr. Rajiv feels confident about the future of the company and its liquidity position. Discuss the meaning of dividend decision and in the light of the above statement explain any two factors which should be considered by 'Vansh Limited' while formulating the dividend policy of the company. A [SQP 2021-22]

Ans. (i) Dividend Decision: Dividend is that portion of profit which is distributed to shareholders. The decision involved here is how much of the profit earned by company (after paying tax) is to be distributed to the shareholders and how much of it should be retained in the business. The dividend constitutes the **current income reinvestment as retained earnings** increase the firm's future earning capacity.

(ii) Factors affecting dividend decision are as follows:

(a) Amount of Earnings: Dividends are paid out of current and past earnings. Therefore, earnings are a major determinant of the decision about dividend.

(b) Stability of Earnings: Other things remaining the same, a company having stable earning is in a better position to declare higher dividends. As against this, a company having unstable earnings is likely to pay smaller dividend.

(c) Stability of Dividends: Companies generally follow a policy of stabilising dividend per share. The increase in dividends is generally made when there is confidence that their earning potential has gone up and not just the earnings of the current year. In other words, dividend per share is not altered if the change in earnings is small or seen to be temporary in nature.

(d) Growth Opportunities: Companies having **good growth opportunities retain more money out** of their earnings so as to finance the required investment. The dividend in growth companies is, therefore, smaller, than that in the non– growth companies.

(e) Cash Flow Position: The payment of dividend involves an **outflow of cash**. A company may be earning profit but may be short on cash. Availability of enough cash in the company is necessary for declaration of dividend.

(f) Shareholders' Preference: While declaring dividends, management must keep in mind the **preferences of the shareholders** in this regard. If the shareholders in general desire that at least a certain amount is paid as dividend, the companies are likely to declare the same. There are always some shareholders who depend upon a regular income on their investments.

(g) Taxation Policy: The choice between the payment of dividend and retaining the earnings is, to some extent, affected by the difference in the tax treatment of dividends and **capital gains**. If tax on dividend is **higher**, it is better to **pay less by way of dividends**. As compared to this, higher dividends may be declared if tax rates are relatively lower. Though the dividends are free of tax in the hands of shareholders, a dividend distribution tax is levied on companies. Thus, under the present tax policy, shareholders are likely to prefer higher dividends.

(h) Stock Market Reaction: Investors, in general, view an increase in dividend as good news and stock prices react positively to it. Similarly, a decrease in dividend may have a negative impact on the share prices in the stock market. Thus, the possible impact of dividend policy on the equity share price is one of the important factors considered by the management while taking a decision about it.

(i) Access to Capital Market: Large and reputed companies generally have **easy access to the capital market** and, therefore, may depend less on retained earnings to finance their growth. These companies tend to pay higher dividends than the smaller companies which have relatively low access to the market.

(j) Legal Constraints: Certain provisions of the **Companies Act place restrictions on payouts as dividend**. Such provisions must be adhered to while declaring the dividend.

(k) Contractual Constraints: While granting loans to a company, sometimes the lender may impose certain restrictions on the payment of dividends in future. The companies are required to ensure that the dividend does not violate the terms of the loan agreement in this regard. **(Any four) [2+4=6]**

Commonly Made Error

Students made the wrong identification. They wrote investment or financial decision instead of dividend decision.

Answering Tip

Understand the details of the three financial decisions properly wit examples.

2. Ravi has joined as a finance manager in MTA Ltd. He had to arrange funds of rupees one crore for the company. The Chief Executive Officer of the company wants to arrange the funds by a public issue whereas the finance manager wants to have a mix of debt and equity as this will determine the overall cost of capital and the financial risk of the enterprise.

(i) Identify and give the meaning of the financial decision suggested by the finance manager in the above case.

(ii) State any four factors affecting the decision identified in (i) above. **A [Delhi Set-1, 2022]**

OR

NB Ltd. is India's largest manufacturer of cement. Its operations are spread throughout the country with 17 modern cement factories. It has a work force of 9,000 persons. Since its inception, the company has been a trend setter for the cement industry. The company is planning to grow in the long-run and wants to double its capacity in the next 3 years. For this the Finance Manager has to decide about the quantum of finance to be raised from various long-term sources. For this he needs to identify various available sources of funds and the proportion of funds from each source.

(i) Identify the financial decision to be taken by the Finance Manager.

(ii) State any four factors which would affect the decision identified in (i) above.

A [Outside Delhi Set-1, 2022]

Tips & Tricks

For the correct identification of financial management decision, always remember that investment decision is about the long-term or short-term assets, financing decision is about the proportion of debt and equity and dividend decision is about retained earnings and the dividend to be distributed.

Ans. (i) Financing Decision: This decision is about the **quantum of finance** to be raised from various long-term sources. Short term sources are studied under the 'working capital management'. A firm has to decide the proportion of funds to be raised from either from shareholder's funds or borrowed funds, based on their basic characteristics.

(ii) Factors affecting financing decision are as follows:

(a) Cost: The cost of raising funds through different sources is different. A prudent financial manager would normally opt for a source which is the cheapest.

(b) Risk: The risk associated with each of the sources is different.

(c) Flotation Costs: Higher the flotation cost, less attractive the source.

(d) Cash Flow Position of the Company: A stronger cash flow position may make debt financing more viable than funding through equity.

(e) Fixed Operating Costs: If a business has high fixed operating costs (e.g., building rent, insurance premium, salaries, etc.), it must reduce fixed financing costs. Hence, lower debt financing is better. Similarly, if fixed operating cost is less, more of debt financing may be preferred.

(f) Control Considerations: Issues of more equity may lead to dilution of management's control over the business. Debt financing has no such implication. Companies afraid of a takeover bid would prefer debt to equity.

(g) State of Capital Market: Health of the capital market may also affect the choice of source of fund. During the period when stock market is rising, more people invest in equity. However, depressed capital market may make issue of equity shares difficult for any company. **[2+4=6]**

3. Alpha Ltd. is a renowned multiplex operator in India. Presently, it owns 234 screens in 45 properties at 20 locations in the country. Considering the fact that the there is a growing trend among the people to spend more of their disposable income on entertainment, two years back the company had decided to add more screens to its existing set up and increase facilities to enhance leisure, food chains, etc. It had then floated an initial public offer of equity shares in order to raise the desired capital. The issue was fully subscribed and paid. Over the years, the sales and profits of the company have increased tremendously and it has been declaring higher dividend and the market price of its shares has increased manifolds. Identify and explain the different kinds of financial decisions taken by the company by quoting lines from the paragraph.

A [OEB]

Ans. The different kinds of financial decisions taken by the company are as follows:

(i) Investment decision: Investment decision relates to how the firm's funds are invested in different assets. Investment decision can be **long term or short-term**. A long-term investment decision is also called a **Capital Budgeting decision**. It involves committing the finance on a long-term basis. For example, making investment in a new machine to replace an existing one or acquiring a new fixed asset or opening a new branch, etc. **Short-term investment decisions (also called working capital decisions)** are concerned with the decisions about the levels of cash, inventory and receivables. These decisions affect the day-to-day working of a business.

Lines: "Two years back the company had decided to add more screens to its existing set up and increase facilities to enhance leisure, food chains etc."

(ii) Financing decision: This decision is about the quantum of finance to be raised from various **long-term sources**. It involves identification of various available sources. The main sources of funds for a firm are shareholders' funds and borrowed funds. The shareholders' funds refer to the **equity capital and the retained earnings. Borrowed funds refer to the finance raised through debentures or other forms of debt**. A firm has to decide the proportion of funds to be raised from either source, based on their basic characteristics. Interest on borrowed funds have to be paid regardless of whether or not a firm has earned a profit. Likewise, the borrowed funds have to be repaid at a fixed time.

Lines: "It had then floated an initial public offer of equity shares in order to raise the desired capital."

(iii) Dividend decision: Dividend decision is related with **how much of the profit earned by company (after paying tax) is to be distributed to the shareholders** and how much of it should be **retained in the business**. While the dividend constitutes the current income, re-investment as retained earnings increases the firm's future earning capacity. The extent of retained earnings also influences the financing decision of the firm. Since the firm does not require funds to the extent of re-invested retained earnings, the decision regarding dividend should be taken keeping in view the overall objective of maximising shareholder's wealth.

Lines: "Over the years, the sales and profits of the company have increased tremendously and it has been declaring higher dividend. **[2×3=6]**

4. "The role of financial management cannot be overemphasised, since it has a direct bearing on the financial health of a business." In the light of this statement, with the help of any four points explain the importance of financial management. U [OEB]

Ans. The importance of financial management can be understood with the help of the following points:

(i) The size and the composition of fixed assets of the business: Capital Budgeting decision involves committing the finance on a **long-term basis**. For example, a capital budgeting decision to invest a sum of ₹ 100 crores in fixed assets would raise the size of fixed assets block by this amount.

(ii) The quantum of current assets and its break-up into cash, inventory and receivables: With an increase in the investment in fixed assets, there is a **commensurate increase in the working capital requirement**. The quantum of current assets is also influenced by financial management decisions. In addition, decisions about credit and inventory management affect the number of debtors and inventory which in turn affect the total current assets as well as their composition.

(iii) The amount of long-term and short-term funds to be used: Financial management, among others, involves decision about the **proportion of long-term and short-term funds**. An organisation wanting to have more liquid assets would raise relatively more amount on a long-term basis. There is a choice between liquidity and profitability. The underlying assumption here is that current liabilities cost less than long term liabilities.

(iv) Break-up of long-term financing into debt, equity etc.: Of the total long-term finance, the proportions to be raised by way of debt and/or equity is also a financial management decision. The amounts of debt, equity share capital, preference share capital is affected by the financing decision, which is a part of financing management.

(v) All items in the Profit and Loss Account, e.g., interest, expense, depreciation, etc.: Higher amount of debt means higher interest expense in future. Similarly, use of higher equity may entail higher payment of dividends. Similarly, an expansion of business which is a result of capital budgeting decision is likely to affect virtually all items in the profit and loss account of the business. **(Any four) [1½ × 4 = 6]**

5. Myra Ltd. manufacturing televisions, is planning to expand its business and requires ₹250 crore for the same. A number of projects are available to the company to invest in and each project has to be evaluated carefully. The Finance Manager of the company, has assessed the projects in terms of the rate of return from each project and wanted to select the one with the higher rate of return. But before selecting the project he has to take into consideration other factors also.

(i) Identify and explain the financial decision discussed in the above paragraph.

(ii) Explain the other factors that the Finance Manager should consider before selecting the project.

AI A [Outside Delhi Set-1, 2022]

Ans. Investment Decision: The investment decision, relates to how the firm's funds are invested in different assets. Investment decision can be long term or short-term. A long-term investment decision is also called a Capital Budgeting decision. It involves committing the finance on a long-term basis. Short-term investment decisions (also called working capital decisions) are concerned with the decisions about the levels of cash, inventory and receivables.

Factors affecting investment decision are as follows:

(a) Cash flows of the project: When a company takes an investment decision involving **huge amount** it expects to generate some **cash flows** over a period. These cash flows are in the form of a series of cash receipts and payments over the life of an investment. The amount of these cash flows should be carefully analysed before considering a capital budgeting decision.

(b) The rate of return: The most important criterion is the **rate of return** of the project. These calculations are based on the **expected returns from each proposal** and the assessment of the risk involved. Suppose, there are two projects, A and B (with the same risk involved), with a rate of return of 10 per cent and 12 per cent, respectively, then under normal circumstance, project B should be selected.

(c) The investment criteria involved: The decision to invest in a particular project involves a number of calculations regarding the amount of investment, interest rate, cash flows and rate of return. There are different techniques to evaluate investment proposals which are known as capital budgeting techniques. These techniques are applied to each proposal before selecting a particular project.

(Any two)

6. What is meant by 'Investment Decision'? State how 'Long term Investment Decision' and 'Short term Investment Decision' affect the business.

R [Delhi Set-3, 2023]

Ans. Investment decision refers to selecting and acquiring the long-term and short-term assets in which funds will be invested by the business.

Long-term investment decision is referred to as the capital budgeting decision. It relates to the investment in fixed assets e.g. buying a new machine. Before taking the final decision, the finance manager makes a comparative study of various alternatives available in the market on the basis of their cost and profitability.

Short term investment decisions are also called **working capital decisions**. These are concerned with the decisions about the inventories, debtors, bills receivable and level of cash etc. It affects the day to day working of the business.

7. Analyse the following scenarios and identify the specific factors that may affect the financial decisions of the company.

Scenario 1: The company is considering expanding its production capacity by investing in new machinery and technology. This expansion will require a significant upfront investment, but it is expected to increase production efficiency and potentially open new market opportunities.

Scenario 2: The company is contemplating taking on debt to fund its expansion plans. By leveraging debt financing, the company can accelerate its growth and take advantage of current market opportunities.

Scenario 3: The company's management is evaluating a cost-cutting initiative to improve profitability and reduce operating expenses. They are considering workforce restructuring and optimising the supply chain to achieve higher cost efficiency.

Scenario 4: The company is exploring the option of entering new international markets to diversify its revenue sources and reduce dependence on the domestic market. AI A [APQ Set-1, 2023-24]

Ans. As an evaluator of the financial decisions of a manufacturing company, the following scenarios have been presented for analysis:

Scenario 1

Market Demand: Assessing current and projected market demand is essential to ensure that the expanded production capacity aligns with potential sales and revenue growth.

Scenario 2

Risk Assessment: The management should conduct a risk assessment to understand the potential consequences of increased debt, such as interest rate fluctuations and refinancing risks.

Scenario 3

Cost Analysis: A comprehensive cost analysis is necessary to identify areas where cost-cutting measures can be implemented without compromising product quality or customer satisfaction.

Scenario 4

Market Entry Costs: Assessing the expenses associated with market entry, such as marketing, distribution, and infrastructure setup, is essential for financial decision-making. **[1×4=4]**

TOPIC-2 Financial Planning and Capital Structure

Concepts Covered

• Meaning and objectives of financial planning • Importance of financial planning. • Meaning of capital structure • Factors determining the choice of an appropriate capital structure of a company.

Revision Notes

- **Financial Planning:** It is the process of estimating the fund requirement of a business and specifying the sources of funds.

  Example: A growth of 20% in sales is predicted. However, it may happen that the growth rate eventually turns out to be 10% or 30%. Many items of expenses shall be different in these three situations. By preparing a blueprint of these three situations the management may decide what must be done in each of these situations. This preparation of alternative financial plans to meet different situations is clearly of immense help in running the business smoothly.
- **Objectives of Financial Planning:** [Board, 2019]

(i) To ensure the availability of funds whenever required.

(ii) To ensure that the firm does not raise resources unnecessarily.

- **Importance of Financial Planning:** [Board, 2023]

(i) Prepares for future challenges.

(ii) Avoids business shocks and surprises.

(iii) Co-ordinates various business functions.

(iv) Eliminates wasteful efforts.

(v) Links present with future.

(vi) Links investment with financing decision.

(vii) Facilitates financial control.

Scan this
Capital Structure

- **Capital Structure:** It refers to the mix between owner's funds i.e., equity and borrowed funds raised by a company i.e., Debt. It can be calculated as debt-equity ratio i.e., Debt/Equity or as the proportion of debt out of the total capital i.e., Debt/Debt + Equity. The proportion of debt in the overall capital is also called financial leverage.
- **Trading on Equity:** It refers to an increase in profit earned by the equity shareholders due to the presence of fixed financial charges like interest.
- **Factors determining the capital structure:**

(i) Cash flow position

(ii) Interest Coverage Ratio (ICR)

(iii) Debt Service Coverage Ratio (DSCR)

(iv) Return on Investment (ROI)

(v) Cost of debt

(vi) Tax rate

(vii) Cost of equity

(viii) Floatation costs

(ix) Risk consideration

(x) Flexibility

(xi) Control

(xii) Regulatory framework

(xiii) Stock market condition

(xiv) Capital structure of other companies

Scan this
Financial Management

SUBJECTIVE TYPE QUESTIONS

Short Answer Type Questions-I (3 marks each)

1. Explain the objectives of financial planning.

U [Delhi Set-1, 2019]

OR

Explain the twin objectives of financial planning.

U [Outside Delhi Set-2, 2023]

OR

Somnath Ltd. is engaged in the business of export of garments. In the past, the performance of the company had been upto the expectations. In line with the latest technology, the company decided to upgrade its machinery. For this the Finance Manager, Dalmia estimated the amount of funds required and the timings. This will help the company in linking the investment and the financial decisions on a continuous basis. Dalmia therefore, began with the preparation of a sales forecast for the next four years. He also collected the relevant data about the profit estimates in the coming years. By doing this he wanted to be sure about the availability of funds from the internal sources of the business. For the remaining funds he is trying to find out alternative sources from outside. Identify the financial concept discussed in the above para. Also state the objectives to be achieved by the use of financial concept, so identified. AI A [Delhi Set-1, 2017]

Ans. The concept discussed over here is financial planning.

Objectives of Financial Planning:

(i) To ensure availability of funds whenever required which involves estimation of the funds required, the time at which these funds are to be made available and the sources of these funds.

(ii) To see that the firm does not raise resources unnecessarily as excess funding is almost as bad as inadequate funding. Financial planning ensures that enough funds are available at right time.

[1½ × 2 = 3]

[Marking Scheme, Delhi 2019]

Commonly Made Error

The students are not able to identify the concept being discussed here.

Answering Tip

Understand the concept of financial planning properly. Differentiate it from planning process and write the objectives correctly.

2. State any three points of importance of financial planning.

R [Delhi Set-3, 2019] [Outside Delhi Set-1, 2023]

Ans. Importance of Financial Planning:

(i) It helps in avoiding business shocks and surprises and helps the company to prepare for the future.

(ii) It helps in coordinating various business functions by providing clear policies and procedures.

(iii) Detailed plans of action prepared under financial planning helps in **reducing waste, duplication of efforts and gaps in planning**.

(iv) It tries to **link the** present with the future.

(v) It provides a link between investment and financing decisions on a continuous basis.

(vi) It makes the evaluation of actual performance easier by spelling out detailed objectives for various business segments. (Any three)

(If an examinee has given only the headings, ½ mark for each heading should be awarded).

[1 × 3 = 3]

[Marking Scheme, Delhi, 2019]

3. Ramnath Ltd. is dealing in import of organic food items in bulk. The company sells the items in smaller quantities in attractive packages. Performance of the company has been up to the expectations in the past. Keeping up with the latest packaging technology, the company decided to upgrade its machinery. For this, the Finance Manager of the company, Mr. Vikrant Dhull, estimated the amount of funds required and the timings. This will help the company in linking the investment and the financing decisions on a continuous basis. Therefore, Mr. Vikrant Dhull began with the preparation of a sales forecast for the next four years. He also collected the relevant data about the profit estimates in the coming years. By doing this, he wanted to be sure about the availability of funds from the internal sources. For the remaining funds, he is trying to find out alternative sources. Identify the financial concept discussed in the above paragraph. Also, state any two points of importance of the financial concept so identified. A [Outside Delhi Set-1, 2017]

Concept Applied	Concept and importance of financial planning.

Topper's Answer, 2017

FINANCIAL PLANNING:
Importance:
① It helps in avoiding business shocks & surprises and helps company in preparing for future.
② It provides a link between investment & financing decisions on a continuous basis.

4. Stelo Steel Ltd. is thinking of raising finance to further its projects overseas. For this the company is observing the other companies' raising of finance. Their debt and equity ratios are being thoroughly studied by the financial experts of the company. Identify and explain the factor affecting the choice of capital structure. A [OEB] [3]

Ans. The factor affecting the choice of capital structure is capital structure of other companies. A useful guideline in the capital structure planning is the debt equity ratios of other companies in the same industry. There are usually some industry norms which may help. Care however must be taken that the company does not follow the industry norms blindly. For example, if the business risk of a firm is higher, it cannot afford the same financial risk. It should go in for low debt. Thus, the management must know what the industry norms are, whether they are following them or deviating from them and adequate justification must be there in both cases.

Commonly Made Error

Students often start explaining all the factors affecting the capital structure instead of the one discussed over here.

Answering Tip

Identify the factor properly only after reading the complete question. Learn and understand the factors properly.

5. The Return on Investment (ROI) of a company ranges between 10-12% for the past three years. To finance its future fixed capital needs, it has the following options for borrowing debt:

Option 'A': Rate of interest 9%

Option 'B': Rate of interest 13%

Which source of debt, 'Option A' or 'Option B', is better? Give reason in support of your answer. Also state the concept being used in taking the decision.

C [Delhi & Outside Delhi, 2018]

Ans. Option 'A' is better. This is because in this option, Return on Investment (10-12%) is higher than the Rate of Interest (9%). The concept being used in taking the decision is Trading on Equity. Trading on equity refers to the use of fixed cost sources of finance such as preference shares, debentures and long-term loans in the capital structure so as to increase the return on equity shares. **[3]**

[Marking Scheme, Delhi & OD 2018]

Commonly Made Error

Students don't read the question properly and make assumptions for the correct answer instead of doing the logical calculation.

Answering Tip

Read and understand the question properly. Analyse both the options to get correct answer.

6. Harish is working as a finance manager in 'Kozee Softwares Ltd.' He has been awarded 'Best employee of the year Award' because of his foresightedness. Hez always aims at smooth operations of all the financial activities by focusing on fund requirements and their availability in the light of financial decisions. He takes into consideration the growth. Performance, investments and requirement of funds for a given period so that financial resources are not left idle and don't unnecessarily add to the cost.

By doing all this Harish strives to achieve the two main objectives of an important concept of financial management. Identify the concept and explain its two objectives. [Delhi Set-1, 2023]

Ans. The important concept of financial management discussed is Financial Planning.

Two objectives are:

(i) To ensure availability of funds whenever required:

- This includes a proper estimation of the funds required for different purposes such as for the purchase of long-term assets or to meet day-to- day expenses of business etc.
- To estimate the time at which these funds are to be made available and to specify possible sources of these funds.

(ii) To see that the firm does not raise resources unnecessarily:

- Financial planning ensures that enough funds are available at right time.
- If adequate funds are not available the firm will not be able to honour its commitments and carry out its plans.
- On the other hand, if excess funds are available, it will unnecessarily add to the cost. [1 + 1 + 1 = 3]

Short Answer Type Questions-II (4 marks each)

1. Explain how does financial planning ensure availability of adequate funds at the right time and check excess funding? A I U [OEB]

Ans. (i) Ensures availability of adequate funds at the right time: This includes a proper estimation of funds required for different purposes such as for the purchase of long-term assets or to meet day-to-day expenses of business. It estimates the time at which the funds are to be made available. Based on these facts, funds could be raised from short-term and long-term sources.

(ii) Ensures that the firm does not raise resources unnecessarily: Excess funding is almost as bad as inadequate funding. So, the financial manager must see to it that the company **does not raise more capital than the requirement** of the business. In case, there is surplus cash or liquidity, the excess funds should be utilised judiciously. [2 + 2 = 4]

2. A company was expecting a sale increase of 20% in comparison to the last year. However, due to poor support from the economic situations around the world, the increase turned out to be only 10%. The company however, had prepared itself for this situation. It knew how to change its expenses in case the sales increase goes down in comparison to the expectations. Identify the concept of financial management which is highlighted in the above case. What should have been the action taken by the company if the situation had been different like increase in revenue by 30%. A [OEB]

Ans. The concept of financial management highlighted in the above case is 'financial planning'. The company would keep different items of expenditure in the case of 30% as it would be having more cash in hand. It could start new projects and involve more man power in its new projects. High revenue may help streamline operations in a better manner. The company definitely is going to have **more freedom in deciding future courses of action.**

3. Sameer has been given a task of evaluating the financial performance of two companies, Alfa Ltd. and Beltex Ltd., in the same industry. Both companies have been trading on equity as part of their financial strategy. Given is the information that Sameer received. Which company is using trading on equity more effectively?

Alfa Ltd.:

Total Assets: ₹500,000

Equity Capital: ₹300,000

Debt Capital: ₹200,000

Net Income: ₹50,000

Beltex Ltd.:

Total Assets: ₹800,000

Equity Capital: ₹400,000

Debt Capital: ₹400,000

Net Income: ₹60,000.

A I Ap [APQ Set-1, 2023-24]

Ans. To determine which company is using trading on equity more effectively, compare their Return on Equity (ROE) ratios. ROE is a key financial ratio that measures how efficiently a company is using its shareholders' equity to generate profits.

ROE is calculated as follows:

ROE = (Net Income / Shareholders' Equity) × 100

Calculate the ROE for both companies:

For Alfa Ltd.:

ROE = (50,000 / 3,00,000) × 100

ROE = 0.1667 × 100

ROE = 16.67%

For Beltex Ltd.:

ROE = (60,000 / 4,00,000) × 100

ROE = 0.15 × 100

ROE = 15.00%

Now, let's compare the ROE ratios for both companies:

Alfa Ltd. has an ROE of 16.67%, and Beltex Ltd. has an ROE of 15.00%. Based on the provided financial data, Alfa is using trading on equity more effectively than Beltex. Alfa's higher ROE of 16.67% indicates that it is generating a better return on its shareholders' equity compared to Beltex, which has an ROE of 15.00%. This suggests that Alfa is utilising its equity more efficiently to generate profits, making its trading on equity strategy more effective. **[2+2=4]**

Commonly Made Error

Students make calculation errors while calculating the answer due to which they lose marks.

Answering Tip

Calculate the answer with utmost care. The questions are easy but require due diligence and concentration while making the calculations.

4. Explain any four factors that affect the choice of capital structure of a company.

U [SQP 2020-2021]

OR

Determining the relative proportion of various types of funds depends upon various factors. Explain any six such factors.

U [Delhi Set-1, 2019]

OR

"Determining the overall cost of capital and the financial risk of the enterprise depends upon various factors". Explain any six such factors.

U [Delhi Set-3, 2019]

OR

Explain briefly any four factors that affect the choice of capital structure of a company.

U [Delhi Set-1, 2017, OD Set-3, 2017]

Ans. Following are the factors affecting capital structure of the company:

(i) Cash Flow Position: Size of projected cash flows must be considered before borrowing. Cash flows must not only cover fixed cash payment obligations but there must be sufficient buffers also.

(ii) Interest Coverage Ratio (ICR): The interest coverage ratio refers to the number of times earnings before interest and taxes of a company covers the interest obligation.

(iii) Debt Service Coverage Ratio (DSCR): Debt Service Coverage Ratio takes care of the **deficiencies** referred to in the Interest Coverage Ratio (ICR). The cash profits generated by the operations are compared with the total cash required for the service of the debt and the preference share capital.

(iv) Cost of debt: A firm's ability to **borrow at a lower rate increases** its capacity to employ higher debt. Thus, more debt can be used if debt can be raised at a lower rate.

(v) Tax Rate: A **higher tax rate makes** debt relatively cheaper vis-a-vis equity.

(vi) Floatation cost: Process of raising funds involves some costs, these considerations may affect the choice between debt and equity, hence the capital structure.

(vii) Risk Consideration: Business risk depends upon fixed operating cost. Fixed operating costs result in higher business risk and vice-versa. Total risk depends upon business risk and financial risk.

(viii) Flexibility: To maintain flexibility it must maintain some borrowing powers to take care of unforeseen circumstances.

(ix) Capital Structure of Other Companies: It has been observed that the capital structure of competing companies also affects the capital structure of the company in question.

(x) Stock Market Conditions: Stock market conditions often affect the choice between equity and debt.

(Any four) [1 × 4 = 4]

[SQP Marking Scheme 2020-21]

5. 'Smart Stationery Ltd.' wants to raise funds of ₹40,00,000 for its new project. The management is considering the following mix of debt and equity to raise this amount:

Capital Structure	Alternatives		
	I (₹)	II (₹)	III (₹)
Equity	40,00,000	30,00,000	10,00,000
Debt	0	10,00,000	30,00,000

Other details are as follows:

Interest Rate on Debt 9%

Face Value of Equity Shares ₹100 each

Tax Rate 30%

Earnings before Interest and Tax (EBIT) ₹8,00,000

(i) Under which of the three alternatives will the company be able to take advantage of Trading on Equity ?

(ii) Does Earning Per Share always rise with increase in debt ? Ap **[Outside Delhi Set-1, 2019]**

Ans. (i)

	Alternative I	Alternative II	Alternative III
Equity 9% Debt	40,00,000 -	30,00,000 10,00,000	10,00,000 30,00,000
Capital Employed	40,00,000	40,00,000	40,00,000
Earning before Interest and Tax Less: Interest @ 9%	8,00,000 -	8,00,000 (90,000)	8,00,000 (2,70,000)
Earning before Tax Less: Tax @30%	8,00,000 (2,40,000)	7,10,000 (2,13,000)	5,30,000 (1,59,000)

	Alternative I	Alternative II	Alternative III
Earnings After Tax/Profit Available to Shareholders	5,60,000	4,97,000	3,71,000
Earning Per Share	5,60,000/ 40,000 = ₹ 14	4,97,000/ 30,000 = ₹ 16.57	3,71,000/ 10,000 = ₹ 37.1

Thus, under Alternative III, the company will be able to take advantage of Trading on Equity.

(Note: Calculation for Earning Per Share may be shown in any way)

(ii) No, earning per share does not always rise with increase in debt. **[3+1=4]**

[Marking Scheme, OD 2019]

6. Krish limited is in the business of manufacturing and exporting carpets and other home décor products. It has a share capital of ₹ 70 lacs at the face value of ₹ 100 each. Company is considering a major expansion of its production facilities and wants to raise ₹ 50 lacs. The finance manager of the company Mr. Prabhakar has recommended that the company can raise funds of the same amount by issuing 7% debentures. Given that earning per share of the company after expansion is ₹ 35 and tax rate is 30%, did Mr. Prabhakar give a justified recommendation? Show the working. [SQP 2022-23]

Ans. Earnings per share = ₹ 35

EPS = Earning after tax / No. of equity shares

35 = Earning after tax / 70,000

Earning after tax = ₹ 24,50,000

Interest = 50,00,000 × 7/100 = ₹ 3,50,0000

Let the Earning before tax (EBT) = x

EBT – Tax = EAT

$x - 0.30\,x = 24{,}50{,}000$

$0.70\,x = 24{,}50{,}000$

$x = 24{,}50{,}000/0.70$

$x = 35{,}00{,}000$

Earning before tax = ₹ 35,00,000

EBIT = Earning before tax + Interest

= 35,00,000 + 3,50,000

= ₹ 38,50,000

ROI = EBIT/Total Investment × 100

= 38,50,000 / 1,20,00,000 × 100 = 32.08%

As ROI (32.08%) > Rate of interest (7%). The company can choose to use trading on equity to increase its EPS. The finance manager was justified in making this recommendation.

[Marking Scheme SQP 2022-23]

Long Answer Type Questions (6 marks each)

1. "Sound Financial Planning is essential for the success of any enterprise." Explain this statement by giving any six reasons. [Delhi Set-2, 2019]

Ans. Financial planning is important because:

(a) It helps in **avoiding business shocks** and surprises and helps the company to prepare for the future.

(b) It helps in **coordinating various business functions** by providing clear policies and procedures.

(c) Detailed plans of action prepared under financial planning helps in **reducing waste**, duplication of efforts and gaps in planning.

(d) It tries to **link the present with the future.**

(e) It provides a link between **investment and financing decisions** on a continuous basis.

(f) It makes the evaluation of actual performance easier by spelling out detailed objectives for various business segments.

(If an examinee has given only the headings, 1/2 mark for each heading should be awarded).

[Marking Scheme, Delhi 2019] **[6]**

2. Gasex Fertilisers Ltd. expected a growth of 10% in the sales in the previous quarter. However, due to the prevailing economic situation around the world, the actual growth in sales was only 5%. The company's Finance Manager was called for an urgent meeting, by the senior management of the company, in which he clarified that he was already prepared for the situation, as he had made a financial blueprint for the future operations. He also reassured the management that he knew how to control the expenses, in case the sales were lower than the expectation.

(a) Identify the concept that enabled the Finance manager to tackle the situation discussed above.

(b) State any five points highlighting how the concept discussed above can help in smooth functioning of the organisation. Ap [APQ, 2023-24]

Ans. (a) Concept identified is Financial Planning. **[1]**

(b) Significance of Financial Planning:

(i) It helps in forecasting what may happen in future under different business situations. By doing so, it helps the firms to face the eventual situation in a better way. In other words, it makes the firm better prepared to face the future.

(ii) It helps in avoiding business shocks and surprises and helps the company in preparing for the future.

(iii) If helps in coordinating various business functions, e.g., sales and production functions, by providing clear policies and procedures.

(iv) Detailed plans of action prepared under financial planning reduce waste, duplication of efforts, and gaps in planning.

(v) It tries to link the present with the future.

(vi) It provides a link between investment and financing decisions on a continuous basis.

(vii) By spelling out detailed objectives for various business segments, it makes the evaluation of actual performance easier. **(Any five) [1×5=5]**

3. 'Viyo Ltd.' is a company manufacturing textile. It has a share capital of ₹ 60 lakh. The earning per share in the previous year was ₹ 0.50. For diversification, the company requires additional capital of ₹ 40 lakh. The company raised funds by issuing 10% debentures for the same. During the current year the company earned profit of ₹ 8 lakh on capital employed. It paid tax @ 40%.

(a) State whether the shareholders gained or lost, in respect of earning per share on diversification. Show your calculations clearly.

(b) Also, state any three factors that favour the issue of debentures by the company as part of its capital structure. Ap [Delhi Set-1, 2016]

Ans. Calculation of Earnings per share after issue of Debentures: (assuming face value of ₹ 10 per share)

Particulars	
Share capital	60,00,000
10% Debentures	40,00,000
Total	1,00,00,000
Profit before interest and tax	8,00,000
Less: Interest	4,00,000
Profit before tax	4,00,000
Less: Tax @ 40%	1,60,000
Profit available to shareholders	2,40,000
Earnings per share = 2,40,000/6,00,000	= ₹ 0.40

This clearly shows that the shareholders have lost after the issue of debentures since the Earning per share has decreased from ₹0.50 to ₹0.40.

[Note: In case, a student has calculated Return on Investment as 8% (8,00,000 / ₹1,00,00,000) and compared it with the rate of interest which is 10% and concluded that the shareholders have lost after the issue of Debentures since the interest rate is greater than the Return of Investment.]

[In case the examinee has assumed any other face value and has shown correct calculations and given the correct conclusion, full credit be given.]

[Marking Scheme 2016]

4. Brick India Limited is a brick manufacturer. Due to rapid urbanisation, it is experiencing excessive demand for its product. It is planning to set up a new brick kiln to cash on the increased demand. Finance Manager prepared a detailed plan to estimate the financial needs of the upcoming firm. It is estimated that it will require about ₹500 crores to set up and about ₹50 crores of working capital to start the new plant.

(i) What is such a plan called?

(ii) Explain the importance of having such a plan for this company.

(iii) Give an imaginary plan to support your answer. A I C [OEB]

Ans. (i) Such a plan is known as a financial plan.

(ii) Importance of Financial Plan:

(a) It helps the company to be prepared for the future by estimating and forecasting what may happen in the future under different business scenarios.

(b) It helps in avoiding business shocks and surprises which if not taken care of, may jeopardise business operations.

(c) It helps in co-ordinating various business functions by providing clear policies and procedures which ensure smooth operations.

(d) It makes performance measurement easier as standards are predetermined.

(iii) Financial Plan for this company:

Total Finance Required:

Fixed Capital: ₹ 5,000

Working Capital: ₹ 50

Source of finance: 1:1 Ratio i.e., 50% finance collected by issue of shares and 50% through borrowed capital.

[1 + 4 + 1 = 6]

5. Vedansh Limited has a share capital of ₹ 10,00,000 divided into shares of ₹ 100. For expansion company requires additional funds of ₹ 5,00,000. The management is considering the following alternatives for raising funds:

Alternative 1: Issue of 5000 Equity shares of ₹ 100 each.

Alternative 2: Issue of 10% Debentures of ₹ 5,00,000.

The company's present Earnings Before Interest and Tax (EBIT) is ₹ 4,00,000 p.a. Assuming that the Rate of Return of Investment remains the same after expansion, which alternative should be used by the company in order to maximise the returns to the equity shareholders. The Tax rate is 50%. Show the working. AE [SQP 2021-22]

Ans. Rate of Return of Investment is

$$= \frac{₹ 4,00,000}{₹ 10,00,000} \times ₹ 100 = 40\%$$

EBIT after expansion = 40% × ₹ 15,00,000
= ₹ 6,00,000

Calculation of EPS		
	Plan 1	Plan 2
EBIT	₹ 6,00,000	₹ 6,00,000
(–) Interest	–	₹ 50,000
EBT	₹ 6,00,000	₹ 5,50,000
(–) Tax(50%)	₹ 3,00,000	₹ 2,75,000
EAT	₹ 3,00,000	₹ 2,75,000
No. of shares	₹ 15,000	₹ 10,000
EPS	₹ 20	₹ 27.5

The company should use Plan 2 in order to increase the return to the equity shareholders. **[6]**

6. **Agrotech Fertilisers Limited has planned to set up a plant for manufacturing urea fertiliser which has very high market potential as there is excess demand as compared to supply. It is a capital-intensive project involving an investment of ₹ 2,000 crores. Major portion of this investment will be in fixed capital. Financial institutions prefer to finance such a project because it is in the core sector. Since market for urea fertiliser is quite high, it is sold mostly on a cash basis.**
   (i) What is the most desirable debt/equity ratio for the company?
   (ii) On what basis should investment in working capital be determined? A [OEB]

Ans. (i) Since the project is **capital intensive, proportion of debt should be** much higher than equity. Since financial institutions prefer advancing loans for such a project, raising loans from them should not be a problem for the company.

(ii) The company should determine investment in **working capital** on the basis of meeting the following requirements:

(a) To purchase and maintain required level of inventory of raw materials.

(b) To pay wages/salaries to employee.

(c) To meet overhead expenses for power, fuel, stationery and other items.

(d) To pay taxes, insurance premium, etc.

(e) To meet marketing and general expenses.

(f) To maintain required level of inventory of finished goods.

(g) To have cash in hand and at bank to meet recurring expenses and meet contingencies.

(Any four) [2 + 4 = 6]

TOPIC-3 Fixed and Working Capital

Concepts Covered

- Meaning of fixed and working capital, • Factors determining the requirements of fixed and working capital.

Revision Notes

- Fixed capital refers to investment in long-term assets. **Examples:** Land, buildings, manufacturing machinery, equipment, and other assets.
- **Features of Fixed capital/Investment decision/Capital budgeting decision:**

(i) Long-term growth and impact
(ii) Large amount of funds involved
(iii) Risk involved
(iv) Irreversible decision

Scan this
Fixed and Working Capital

- **Factors affecting the requirement of fixed capital:** [Board, 2023]

(i) Nature of business
(ii) Scale of operations
(iii) Choice of technique
(iv) Technology upgradation
(v) Growth prospects
(vi) Diversification
(vii) Financing alternatives
(viii) Level of collaboration

- Working capital represents the amount of funds invested in current assets like debtors, stock-in-trade and cash required for meeting day-to-day expenses, paying wages/ salaries to its work-force and clearing dues of its creditors.
- Working Capital = Current Assets – Current Liabilities
- **Factors affecting the working capital requirements:**

(i) Nature of business
(ii) Scale of operations
(iii) Business cycle
(iv) Seasonal factors
(v) Production cycle
(vi) Credit availed
(vii) Credit allowed
(viii) Operating efficiency
(ix) Availability of raw material
(x) Growth prospects
(xi) Level of competition
(xii) Inflation

SUBJECTIVE TYPE QUESTIONS

Short Answer Type Questions-I (3 marks each)

1. **Pinnacle Ltd. deals in the sale of stationery and office furniture. They source the finished products from reputed brands that give them four to six months credit. Seeing the demand for electronic items, they are also planning to market these items by opening outlets throughout India. For this, they have decided to join hands with a Japanese electronic goods manufacturer.**
   Identify and state any two factors that would affect the fixed capital requirement of Pinnacle Ltd. as discussed above. C [Delhi Comptt. Set 1, 2, 3, 2017]

Ans. Two factors that would affect the fixed capital requirement of Pinnacle Ltd. are:

(i) Diversification: It will increase the fixed capital requirements as the investment in fixed capital will increase.

(ii) Level of Collaboration: Collaboration reduces the level of investment in fixed assets. [1½ × 2 = 3]

2. State any three factors that determine the requirement of fixed capital of a company.

U [Outside Delhi Set-1, 2023]

Ans. The factors that determine the requirement of fixed capital of a company are:

(i) **Nature of the business:** Fixed capital requirement varies according to the **nature of the business**. Manufacturing companies require heavy investment in fixed capital such as land, building and plant and machinery while trading enterprises require less fixed capital.

(ii) **Size of the business:** A large scale enterprise generally requires **more fixed capital than a small-scale enterprise** because of the increased scale of operations. For example: Public utility concern like railways and electric supply companies require huge investment in fixed assets.

(iii) **Types of technique:** Type of technique affects the fixed capital requirement. A **capital-intensive company requires more investment in fixed capital** as large investment is required in plants and machinery. However, the firms using labour intensive technique requires less fixed capital.

(iv) **Growth Prospects:** Where a company wants to take growth opportunities, it would require more investment in plant and machinery to increase the productive capacity of the firm which increases the fixed capital requirement.

(v) **Diversification:** Diversification involves **increasing the product line of the business**. If a company diversifies it operations, it requires higher amount of fixed capital.

(vi) **Level of Collaboration:** If the companies are preferring collaborations or joint ventures, then, companies will need less fixed capital as they can share plant and machinery with their add full stop after collaborators. But if company prefers to operate independently then there is more requirement of fixed capital. **(Any three) 1 × 3 = 3**

3. 'Win Step Ltd.' is a high turnover shoe manufacturing company. It has made a lot of success in the past. But recently the company has not been doing so well in the business. The company is trying to diversify in the car business. The newspapers are flooded with this news. People are also considering this as a smart move by the company. What do you think will happen to the fixed capital requirement of the company because of this move? Also, explain the factor affecting the fixed capital requirement over here

U [OEB]

4. Miracle Ltd. deals in the sale of stationery and office furniture. They source the finished products from reputed brands who give them four to six months credit. Because of increase in the demand for electronic items, they are planning to sell these items also. For this, they have decided to join hands with a Japanese electronic goods manufacturer, to open sales outlets throughout India.

State any three factors affecting working capital requirement of Miracle Ltd., other than the factors discussed above.

A [Outside Delhi Comptt. Set 1, 2, 3, 2017]

OR

Explain any four factors that can affect the working capital requirement of a company.

U [Delhi Set-1, 2023], [Outside Delhi Set-2, 2023]

Concept Applied	Factors affecting working capital requirements

Ans. Factors which affect the requirements of working capital are:

(i) **Business cycle** as in case of boom, larger working capital is required as the sales and production are more.

(ii) **Seasonal factors** as peak season requires higher working capital than lean season due to higher level of activity.

(iii) **Production cycle** as working capital requirement is higher in firms with longer processing cycle.

(iv) **Credit allowed** to customers results in higher amount of debtors, increasing the working capital requirement.

(v) **Operating efficiency** as firms managing their raw materials efficiently require lesser working capital.

(vi) **Free and continuous availability of raw materials** enables the firms to keep lesser stock and hence work with smaller working capital.

(vii) **Higher growth prospects** will require larger amounts of working capital so that the firm is able to meet higher production and sales targets.

(viii) **Level of competition** as higher competition requires larger stocks to meet urgent orders from customers and thus higher working capital.

(ix) **Inflation** increases the working capital requirements as larger amount of money is required to maintain a constant volume of production and sales. **(Any three)**

(If an examinee has given only the heading, ½ mark for each heading should be awarded)

[1 × 3 = 3]

[Marking Scheme OD, 2017]

Short Answer Type Questions-II (4 marks each)

1. Dheeraj wants to start a business of selling N-95 masks after the outbreak of the global pandemic of COVID-19. Due to the uncertain market conditions he wants to make a low investment in fixed capital. Suggest how the decisions related to the choice of technique and financing alternatives can help Dheeraj in ensuring a low investment in fixed capital requirements.

A [SQP 2020-21]

Ans. Choice of Technique: As he wishes to stick to a low investment model, we may suggest him to go with the labour-intensive approach to manufacture N-95 masks. Since better technology would cost him much and his risk appetite is not conducive for capital intensive techniques of production.

Financial Alternatives: As he wishes to stick to a low investment model, we may suggest him to go with the lease option for fixed assets like building, heavy machinery, etc. as this may reduce his investments requirement in the business.

[SQP Marking Scheme, 2020-21] **[2 + 2 = 4]**

This Question is for practice and its solution is given at the end of the chapter.

2. **A businessman who wants to start a manufacturing concern approaches you to suggest him whether following manufacturing concerns would require large or small working capital:**
   (i) Bread
   (ii) Coolers
   (iii) Furniture manufacturing against specific orders
   (iv) Motor car
   Give your view point with reasons in each of the above cases. A [OEB]

Ans. (i) Bread: A small amount of working capital is needed as the product is sold for cash or at very short credit and has a quick cash turnover.

(ii) Coolers: It is a seasonal product. Therefore, it requires large amount of working capital to store the output during the non-seasonal period.

(iii) Furniture manufacturing against specific order: It requires small working capital as it is quickly converted into cash sales and many times advance from customers is also available.

(iv) Motor car: A large amount of working capital is required because the gestation period is long.

[1×4=4]

3. **Ashutosh Savarkar has recently opened a Tortilla base manufacturing unit in Pune. Processing time being short, as soon as the product is ready, it is dispatched to various outlets and restaurants, in order to keep it fresh. The restaurants are required to give their orders 24 hours in advance as there is no fixed consumption pattern in the city.**
   (a) Determine whether the working capital requirement of Ashutosh Savarkar's business is high/low? State the reason in support of your answer.
   (b) State any two other factors, apart from the one identified above, that should be considered, while determining the working capital requirement of a business. AI A [APQ, 2023-24]

Ans. (a) The working capital requirement of Ashutosh Savarkar **is low** as the **production cycle is shorter. [1]**

(b) Factors that should be considered before determining the working capital requirement are:

1. **Nature of Business:** A trading organisation usually needs a smaller amount of working capital compared to a manufacturing organisation. This is because there is usually no processing. Similarly, service industries which usually do not have to maintain inventory require less working capital.
2. **Scale of Operations:** For organisations which operate on a higher scale of operation, the quantum of inventory and debtors required is generally high. Such organisations, therefore, require large amount of working capital.

Long Answer Type Questions (6 marks each)

1. **Car Tech Ltd. is manufacturing small cars at its manufacturing unit in Gujarat. The demand of its cars is increasing at the rate of 20% annually. It is planning to set up a new car manufacturing unit at Delhi. For this the company will require approximately ₹ 1,500 crores as fixed capital and ₹ 400 crores as working capital. The company has already arranged for its working capital.**
   There is another company 'Furni Tech Ltd.' manufactures furniture at its manufacturing unit that in Maharashtra. The demand of its furniture is high. The company has estimated a 20% increase in the demand of its furniture. It is planning to set up a new manufacturing unit. For this the company will require approximately ₹ 2,000 crores as fixed capital and ₹ 500 crores as working capital. The company has already arranged for its fixed capital.
   (i) Identify and explain any three factors that the finance manager of Car Tech Ltd. should keep in mind while arranging its fixed capital.
   (ii) Identify and explain any three factors that the finance manager of the Furni Tech Ltd. should keep in mind while arranging its working capital. A [OEB]

OR

Naresh, a businessman, is engaged in purchasing and selling of ice creams. Identify the working capital requirements giving reasons in support of your answer. Further, he is willing to start his own ice cream factory. Explain any four factors that will affect his fixed capital requirements. AE [OEB]

Ans. (i) Factors affecting the requirements of fixed capital:

(a) Nature of business: The type of business has a bearing upon the **fixed capital requirements**. For example, a trading concern needs lower investment in fixed assets compared with a manufacturing organisation; since it does not require to purchase plant and machinery, etc.

(b) Scale of operations: A larger organisation operating at a higher scale needs bigger plant, more space, etc. and therefore, requires **higher investment** in fixed assets when compared with the small organisation.

(c) Choice of technique: Some organisations are **capital intensive** whereas others are **labour intensive**. A capital-intensive organisation requires higher investment in plant and machinery as it relies less on manual labour. The requirement of fixed capital for such organisations would be higher. Labour intensive organisations on the other hand, require less investment in fixed assets. Hence, their fixed capital requirement is lower.

(d) Technology upgradation: In certain industries, assets become obsolete sooner. Consequently, their replacements become due faster. Higher investment in fixed assets may, therefore, be required in such cases. For example, computers become obsolete faster and are replaced much sooner than say, furniture. Thus, such organisations which use assets which are prone to obsolescence require higher fixed capital to purchase such assets. **(Any three) [1 × 3 = 3]**

(ii) Factors affecting the requirement of working capital:

(a) Nature of business: The basic nature of a business influences the amount of working capital required. A **trading organisation usually needs a smaller amount of working capital** compared to a manufacturing organisation. This is because there is usually no processing. Similarly, service industries which usually do not have to maintain inventory require less working capital.

(b) Scale of operation: For organisations which operate on a higher scale of operation, the **quantum of inventory** and **debtors** required is generally high. Such organisations, therefore, require large amount of working capital as compared to the organisations which operate on a lower scale.

(c) Business cycle: Different phases of business cycles affect the requirement of working capital by a firm. In case of **boom**, sales as well as production are likely to be **larger** and, therefore, **larger amount of working capital is required**. As against this, the requirement for working capital will be lower during the period of depression as the sales as well as production will be small.

(d) Seasonal factors: Most business have some seasonality in their operations. In **peak season, because of higher level of activity,** larger amount of working capital is required. As against this, the level of activity as well as the requirement for working capital will be lower during the lean season.

(Any three) [1 × 3 = 3]

2. Vinay has started a pizza base manufacturing business. The early morning schedule is very busy as the product is dispatched as soon as it is made to keep it fresh and is sent to the various pizza making restaurants or hotels. Daily fresh pizza base has to be delivered on the basis of estimated orders as there is no sure about consumption pattern in the city. What do you think is going to be the working capital requirement of this business? Explain the factor that has affected the working capital of the business over here. A [OEB]

COMPETENCY BASED QUESTIONS

Objective Type Questions

[A] Multiple Choice Questions

1. Vedant Ltd. is a company with a decreasing EBIT. The company has a significant amount of debt in the form of debentures, and further borrowing through debentures could exacerbate the situation. Which factor determining the Capital Structure is the CFO of Vedant Ltd. primarily concerned about ? AI U [APQ, 2023-24]

(A) Cost of debt
(B) Return on investment
(C) Interest coverage ratio
(D) Debt service coverage ratio

Ans. Option (C) is correct.

Explanation: The interest coverage ratio (ICR) is a financial metric used to assess a company's ability to cover its interest expenses with its earnings before interest and taxes (EBIT). It reflects how easily a company can pay interest on outstanding debt.

2. Aarti Steel limited is a large creditworthy company manufacturing Steel. The company seeks to enter the Asian market and therefore wants to raise additional funds of ₹1 crore from the primary market. The finance manager of the company Mr. Sundaram has suggested raising funds by issuing debentures, in order to take advantage of 'Trading on Equity'. Identify the factor which is an important determinant of the company's ability to use the 'Trading on Equity' and thus the capital structure.

(A) Return on investment
(B) Cost of debt
(C) Cost of equity
(D) Risk consideration

AI U [APQ Set-2, 2023-24]

Ans. Option (A) is correct.

Explanation: The return on investment is a crucial factor that influences a company's ability to effectively utilise 'Trading on Equity.' A higher return on investment allows the company to generate more earnings from the assets financed by debt, thus magnifying returns for equity shareholders. A higher return on investment enhances the company's capacity to leverage debt and subsequently impact its capital structure decisions. **[1]**

3. Match the factors affecting fixed capital requirements given in the Column-I with their explanations given in Column-II:

	Column I		Column II
(a)	Nature of Business	(i)	A trading organisation needs lower investments in fixed assets as compared to a manufacturing organisation.
(b)	Technology Up gradation	(ii)	A textile manufacturing company is installing a cement manufacturing plant and thus its investments in fixed assets is increasing.
(c)	Diversification	(iii)	A capital-intensive organisation requires higher investments in fixed assets as compared to labour intensive organisation.
(d)	Choice of Technique	(iv)	Mobile phones became obsolete faster and are replaced much sooner than furniture or many other assets. Hence these types of businesses require more fixed capital.

R [Delhi, 2023-24]

This Question is for practice and its solution is given at the end of the chapter.

Options:

	a	b	c	d
(A)	i	iv	ii	iii
(B)	ii	iii	iv	i
(C)	iii	ii	i	iv
(D)	iv	i	iii	ii

Ans. Option (A) is correct

4. _______ refers to the increase in profit earned by the equity shareholders due to the presence of fixed financial charges like interest.

U [Delhi Set-1, 2023]

(A) Capital structure
(B) Earnings per share
(C) Trading on equity
(D) Return on investment

Ans. Option (C) is correct

Explanation: Investors and borrowers use borrowed funds to increase their potential returns on investments with the presence of fixed financial charges like interests. This is called Trading on Equity

5. Which of the following is NOT a factor affecting capital structure of a company?

R [Delhi Set-1, 2023]

(A) Cost of Debt
(B) Growth Opportunities
(C) Cash Flow Position
(D) Interest Coverage Ratio

Ans. Option (B) is correct

Explanation: The growth opportunity definition can be described as the chance to grow significantly. Whether that growth be in your career, personal life, or hobbies. Opportunities to grow are key to overall satisfaction and success.

6. When the proportion of debt and equity is such that it results in an increase in the value of equity share the_______ is/are said to be optimal.

R [Outside Delhi Set-1, 2023]

(A) working capital
(B) fixed capital
(C) capital structure
(D) Both (A) and (B)

Ans. Option (C) is correct.

7. The Board of directors of Medex Pharma Ltd. decided to issue debentures worth ₹40 lakhs in order to finance a major Research and Development project. This would increase the Debt Equity ratio from 1:1 to 2:1. However, at the same time it would increase the Earnings per share.

AI [SQP 2023-24] U

The reason that will justify the above situation is:

(A) Unfavourable financial leverage, as the financial risk will be higher.
(B) Unfavourable financial leverage, as return on investment is lower than the cost of debt.
(C) Favourable financial leverage as debt is easily available
(D) Favourable financial leverage, as return on investment is higher than cost of debt

Ans. Option (D) is Correct.

Explanation: The financial leverage is favourable in the above given case as EPS is increased when debt in increase. More the earning per share, more it is favourable.

8. In which of the following situations will the EPS of a company rise with an increased use of debt?

AI U [CFPQ 2023-24]

(A) When the rate of interest is more than the return on investment
(B) When the rate of interest is equal to the return on investment
(C) Can't say from the given information
(D) When the rate of interest is less than the return on investment

Ans. Option (D) is correct.

Explanation: When the rate of interest is less than the return on investment, then this will result in favourable financial leverage. When the rate of interest is more than the ROI, there will be unfavourable financial leverage. When rate of interest is equal to ROI, the EPS will remain constant.

9. A decision to acquire a new & modern plant to upgrade an old one is known as __________ decision.

R [SQP 2019-20]

(A) Financing decision
(B) Working capital decision
(C) Investment decision
(D) Dividend decision

Ans. Option (C) is correct.

Explanation: It is an investing decision—a capital budgeting decision as long-term investment in assets has to be made.

10. ABC Ltd. has Debt Equity ratio of 3:1 whereas XYZ Ltd. has Debt Equity ratio of 1:1. Name the advantage ABC Ltd. will have over XYZ Ltd., when the rate of interest is lower than the rate of return on investment of the company. Ap [SQP 2019-20]

(A) Trading on equity
(B) Low risk
(C) Low cost of equity
(D) Greater flexibility

Ans. Option (A) is correct.

Explanation: Trading on Equity refers to the increase in profit earned by the equity shareholders due to the presence of fixed financial charges like interest.

11. Vikrant joins his father's business of Organic masalas, near Kotgarh in Himachal after completing his MBA. In order to capture a major share of the market, he decided to sell the product in small attractive packages by using the latest packaging technology. His father suggested that they hire financial consultants to estimate the amount of funds that would be required for the purpose & timings when it would be required. The concept being discussed by Vikrant's father, links which financial decision with the investment decision?

AI U [SQP 2019-20]

(A) Dividend decision
(B) Financial Planning
(C) Capital structure decision
(D) Financing decision.

Ans. Option (B) is correct.

Explanation: The financial statements are prepared keeping in mind the requirement of funds for investment in the fixed capital and working capital. Then the expected profits during the period are estimated so that an idea can be made of how much of the fund requirements can be met internally.

12. For the following two statements, choose the correct option:

Statement I: The market price of equity share increases, if the benefit from a decision exceeds the cost involved.

Statement II: All financial decisions aim at ensuring that each decision is efficient and adds some value.

Choose the correct option from options given below:

(A) Statement I is correct and statement II is wrong.
(B) Statement II is correct and statement I is wrong.
(C) Both the statements are correct.
(D) Both the statements are wrong. U [OEB]

Ans. Option (C) is correct.

Explanation: The market price of equity share increases, if the benefit from a decision exceeds the cost involved. All financial decisions aim at ensuring that each decision is efficient and adds some value.

Such value additions tend to increase the market price of shares. Therefore, those financial decisions are taken which will ultimately prove gainful from the point of view of the shareholders. The shareholders gain if the value of shares in the market increases. Those decisions which result in decline in the share price are poor financial decisions.

13. For the following two statements, choose the correct option:

Statement I: A proper matching of funds requirements and their availability is sought to be achieved by financial planning.

Statement II: Financial planning takes into consideration the growth, performance, investments and requirement of funds.

Choose the correct option from options given below:

(A) Statement I is correct and statement II is wrong.
(B) Statement II is correct and statement I is wrong.
(C) Both the statements are correct.
(D) Both the statements are wrong. U [OEB]

Ans. Option (C) is correct.

Explanation: A proper matching of funds requirements and their availability is sought to be achieved by financial planning. This process of estimating the fund requirement of a business and specifying the sources of funds is called financial planning. Financial planning takes into consideration the growth, performance, investments and requirement of funds for a given period.

14. For the following two statements, choose the correct option:

Statement I: Higher fixed operating costs result in higher business risk.

Statement II: If a firm's business risk is higher, its capacity to use debt is higher.

Choose the correct option from options given below:

(A) Statement I is correct and statement II is wrong.
(B) Statement II is correct and statement I is wrong.
(C) Both the statements are correct.
(D) Both the statements are wrong. R [OEB]

Ans. Option (A) is correct.

Explanation: Business risk depends upon fixed operating costs. Higher fixed operating costs result in higher business risk and vice-versa. The total risk depends upon both the business risk and the financial risk. If a firm's business risk is lower, its capacity to use debt is higher and vice-versa.

[B] Assertion & Reason

Directions: In the following questions, a statement of assertion (A) is followed by a statement of reason (R). Mark the correct choice as:

(A) Both assertion (A) and reason (R) are true and reason (R) is the correct explanation of assertion (A).
(B) Both assertion (A) and reason (R) are true but reason (R) is not the correct explanation of assertion (A).
(C) Assertion (A) is true but reason (R) is false.
(D) Assertion (A) is false but reason (R) is true.

1. Assertion (A): Financial Management is concerned with optimal procurement as well as the usage of finance.

Reason (R): For optimal procurement, different available sources of finance are identified and compared in terms of their costs and associated risks. U [OEB]

Ans. Option (B) is correct.

Explanation: Financial Management is concerned with optimal procurement as well as the usage of finance. Similarly, the finance so procured needs to be invested in a manner that the returns from the investment exceed the cost at which procurement has taken place.

2. Assertion (A): Financial management involves decision about the proportion of long-term and short-term funds.

Reason (R): Good financial management aims at mobilisation of financial resources at a lower cost and deployment of these in most lucrative activities. U [OEB]

3. Assertion (A): A labour intensive organisation requires higher investment in plant and machinery.

Reason (R): Those manufacturing enterprises which make use of modern and automatic machines need large amount of fixed capital. U [OEB]

Ans. Option (D) is correct.

Explanation: Some organisations are capital intensive whereas others are labour intensive. A capital-intensive organisation requires higher investment in plant and machinery as it relies less on manual labour. The requirement of fixed capital for such organisations would be higher. Labour intensive organisations on the other hand require less investment in fixed assets. Hence, their fixed capital requirement is lower.

4. Assertion (A): Financial planning tries to link the present with the future.

Reason (R): Financial planning is essentially the preparation of a financial blueprint of an organisation's future operations. U [OEB]

5. Assertion (A): Financial planning ensures that the firm does not raise resources unnecessarily.

Reason (R): Excess funding is almost as bad as inadequate funding. R [OEB]

These Questions are for practice and their solutions are given at the end of the chapter.

Ans. Option (B) is correct.

Explanation: Excess funding is almost as bad as inadequate funding. Even if there is some surplus money, good financial planning would put it to the best possible use so that the financial resources are not left idle and don't unnecessarily add to the cost.

6. **Assertion (A):** Financial planning includes determining the objectives, policies, procedures and programmes to deal with financial activities.

   Reason (R): Financial planning facilitates in developing a sound capital structure which gives maximum returns to shareholders. U [OEB]

Ans. Option (B) is correct.

Explanation: Financial planning involves estimating the amount of capital to be raised; determining the pattern of financing *i.e.*, deciding on the form and proportion of capital to be raised; and formulating the financial policies and procedures for procurement, allocation and effective utilisation of funds.

7. **Assertion (A):** Debt and equity differ significantly in their cost and riskiness for the firm.

   Reasoning (R): Debt is cheaper but is riskier for a business because the payment of interest and the return of principal is obligatory for the business. R [OEB]

Ans. Option (A) is correct.

Explanation: The cost of debt is lower than the cost of equity for a firm because the lender's risk is lower than the equity shareholder's risk, since the lender earns an assured return and repayment of capital and, therefore, they should require a lower rate of return. There is no such compulsion in case of equity, which is therefore, considered risk less for the business.

8. **Assertion (A):** A higher DSCR indicates better ability to meet cash commitments.

   Reasoning (R): If a firm uses its debt potential to the full, it loses flexibility to issue further debt. U [OEB]

Ans. Option (B) is correct.

Explanation: A higher DSCR indicates better ability to meet cash commitments and consequently, the company's potential to increase debt component in its capital structure. If a firm uses its debt potential to the full, it loses flexibility to issue further debt. To maintain flexibility, it must maintain some borrowing power to take care of unforeseen circumstances.

9. **Assertion (A):** A trading organisation usually needs a smaller amount of working capital compared to a manufacturing organisation.

   Reason (R): The basic nature of a business influences the amount of working capital required. R [OEB]

Ans. Option (A) is correct.

Explanation: The basic nature of a business influences the amount of working capital required. A trading organisation usually needs a smaller amount of working capital compared to a manufacturing organisation. This is because there is usually no processing.

10. **Assertion (A):** In peak season, larger amount of working capital is required.

    Reason (R): Most business have some seasonality in their operations. In peak reason business have higher level of activity due to increased demand. R [OEB]

Ans. Option (A) is correct.

Explanation: Most business have some seasonality in their operations. In peak season, because of higher level of activity, larger amount of working capital is required. As against this, the level of activity as well as the requirement for working capital will be lower during the lean season.

[C] Case Based MCQs

I. Read the following text and answer the following questions on the basis of the same:

Mr. A. Bose is running a successful business. Mr. Bose is the owner of R. K. Cement Ltd. Mr. Bose decided to expand his business by acquiring a steel factory. This required an investment of ₹ 60 crores. To seek advice in this matter, he called his financial advisor Mr. T. Ghosh who advised him about the judicious mix of equity (40%) and debt (60%). Employ more of cheaper debt may enhance the EPS. Mr. Ghosh also suggested him to take loan from a financial institution as the cost of raising funds from financial institutions is low. Though this will increase the financial risk but will also raise the return to equity shareholders. He also apprised him that issue of debt will not dilute the control of equity shareholders. At the same time, the interest on loan is a tax-deductible expense for computation of tax liability. After due deliberations with Mr. Ghosh, Mr. Bose decided to raise funds from a financial institution. [OEB]

(i) Identify the concept of Financial Management as advised by Mr. Ghosh in the above situation.

(A) Capital Budgeting
(B) Capital Structure
(C) Dividend Decision
(D) Working Capital Decision

Ans. Option (B) is correct.

Explanation: Capital structure refers to the mix between owners and borrowed funds. Capital structure of a company affects both the profitability and the financial risk. A capital structure will be said to be optimal when the proportion of debt and equity is such that it results in an increase in the value of the equity share.

(ii) In the above case Mr. Ghosh suggested to raise more funds from debt. Higher debt-equity ratio results in:

(A) Lower financial risk
(B) Higher degree of operating risk
(C) Higher degree of financial risk
(D) Higher earning of profit

Ans. Option (C) is correct.

Explanation: Deciding about the capital structure of a firm involves determining the relative proportion of various types of funds. This depends on various factors. For example, debt requires regular servicing. Interest payment and repayment of principal are obligatory on a business. In addition a company planning to raise debt must have sufficient cash to meet the increased outflows because of higher debt.

(iii) "Mr. T. Ghosh who advised him about the judicious mix of equity (40%) and debt (60%)" The proportion of debt in the overall capital is called__________.

(A) Working Capital (B) Financial Leverage
(C) Total Assets (D) None of these

Ans. Option (B) is correct.

Explanation: The proportion of debt in the overall capital is also called financial leverage. As the financial leverage increases, the cost of funds declines because of increased use of cheaper debt but the financial risk increases.

(iv) Employ more of cheaper debt may enhance the EPS. Such practice is called:

(A) Equity Trading **(B)** Financial Leverage
(C) Investment Decision (D) Trading on Equity

Ans. Option (D) is correct.

Explanation: Trading on Equity refers to the increase in profit earned by the equity shareholders due to the presence of fixed financial charges like interest. With higher use of debt, the difference between RoI and cost of debt increases the EPS. This is a situation of favourable financial leverage. In such cases, companies often employ more of cheaper debt to enhance the EPS. Such practice is called Trading on Equity.

II. Read the following text and answer the following questions on the basis of the same:

Sunrises Ltd. dealing in ready-made garments, is planning to expand its business operations in order to cater to international market. For this purpose, the company needs additional ₹ 80,00,000 for replacing machines with modern machinery of higher production capacity. It involves committing the finance on a long-term basis. These decisions are very crucial for any business since they affect its earning capacity in the long run. The company wishes to raise the required funds by issuing debentures. The debt can be issued at an estimated cost of 10%. The EBIT for the previous year of the company was ₹8,00,000 and total capital investment was ₹1,00,00,000. Instead of issuing 10% debentures the company can issue equity Shares for raising the fund. The financial manager of the company would normally opt for a source which is the cheapest. **[OEB]**

(i) What is the other name of long-term decision ?

(A) Capital budgeting
(B) Gross working capital
(C) Financial management
(D) Working capital

Ans. Option (A) is correct.

Explanation: A long-term investment decision is also called a capital budgeting decision. It involves committing the finance on a long-term basis. For example, making investment in a new machine to replace an existing one or acquiring a new fixed asset or opening a new branch, etc. These decisions are very crucial for any business since they affect its earning capacity in the long run. The size of assets, profitability and competitiveness are all affected by capital budgeting decisions. Moreover, these decisions normally involve huge amounts of investment and are irreversible except at a huge cost.

(ii) A decision for replacing machines with modern machinery of higher production capacity is an:

(A) Financing decision
(B) Working capital decision
(C) Investment decision
(D) None of the above

Ans. Option (C) is correct.

Explanation: The investment decision relates to how the firm's funds are invested in different assets. Investment decision can be long term or short-term. A long-term investment decision is also called a capital Budgeting decision. It involves committing the finance on a long-term basis. For example, making investment in a new machine to replace an existing one or acquiring a new fixed asset or opening a new branch, etc.

(iii) A decision for raising fund of ₹80,00,000 either from 10% debenture or equity shares is a:

(A) Financing decision **(B)** Dividend decision
(C) Investment decision **(D)** None of the above

Ans. Option (A) is correct.

Explanation: This decision is about the quantum of finance to be raised from various long-term sources. Short-term sources are studied under the 'working capital management'. It involves identification of various available sources. The main sources of funds for a firm are shareholders' funds and borrowed funds. The shareholders' funds refer to the equity capital and the retained earnings. Borrowed funds refer to the finance raised through debentures or other forms of debt. A firm has to decide the proportion of funds to be raised from either sources, based on their basic characteristics.

(iv) The financing decisions are affected by various factors. Which one of the following factor is discussed in the above case? Choose the correct option.

(A) Cash flow position of the company
(B) Cost
(C) Amount of earnings
(D) Taxation policy

Ans. Option (B) is correct.

Explanation: The cost of raising funds through different sources are different. A prudent financial manager would normally opt for a source which is the cheapest.

SOLUTIONS FOR PRACTICE QUESTIONS (TOPIC-1)

SATQs-I

Ans 2. Factors affecting dividend decision are:

(i) Earnings: Earnings are a major determinant of **dividend decision** as dividends are paid out of current and past earnings.

(ii) Stability of earnings: It is another factor affecting dividend decision as a company having stable earnings is in a position to **declare higher dividends**.

(iii) Stability of dividends: Companies generally prefer to maintain **stability of dividends** while taking dividend decision.

(iv) Growth opportunities: If a company has good growth opportunities, it pays out fewer dividends.

(v) Cash flow position: A good cash flow position is necessary for declaration of dividend.

(vi) Shareholders' preference: It is kept in mind by the management before declaring dividends.

(vii) Taxation policy: It affects the dividend decision as a **higher dividend distribution tax** will lead to lesser dividend payout.

(viii) Stock market reaction: The possible stock market reaction on the share price to dividend policy is one of the important factors affecting dividend decision. The stock market reacts positively to an increase in the dividend and negatively to a decrease in the dividend.

(ix) Access to capital market: While taking dividend decision, companies take into consideration their access to capital market.

(x) Legal constraints: Certain provisions of the Companies Act *i.e.*, legal constraints place restrictions on payout of dividend.

(xi) Contractual constraints: While taking dividend decision, companies keep in mind the restrictions imposed by the lenders *i.e.*, contractual constraints.

(Any three) [1 × 3 = 3]

Commonly Made Error

⚠ The students often get confused between the factors affecting different types of decisions and mix the factors of dividend decision with financing or investment decision.

Answering Tip

Understand the difference between the different types of decisions and learn the factors affecting them properly.

Ans 3. Financial Management is concerned with management of flow of funds and involves decisions relating to procurement of funds, investment of funds and distribution of earnings.

OR

Financial Management may be defined as planning, organising, directing and controlling the financial activities of an organisation.

Objective of Financial Management: The objective of financial management is to maximise shareholders wealth *i.e.*, to maximise the market price of equity shares of the company. This is because a company's funds belong to the shareholders and the manner in which these are invested and the return earned on them determines the market value or price of shares. **[1 ½ +1 ½ = 3]**

[Marking Scheme, Delhi 2019]

Commonly Made Error

⚠ The students leave the keywords of the answer 'Maximise the shareholder's wealth'. Some mention the objective as increasing the profit, increasing the share price etc.

Answering Tip

Focus on the keywords and write the answer properly.

SOLUTIONS FOR PRACTICE QUESTIONS (TOPIC-3)

SATQs-I

Ans 3. The fixed capital requirement of the company will increase because of this decision.

The factor affecting the fixed capital requirement over here is diversification. A firm may choose to diversify its operations for various reasons. With diversification, fixed capital requirements increase e.g., a textile company is diversifying and starting a cement manufacturing plant. Obviously, its investment in fixed capital will increase. **[3]**

LATQs

Ans. 2 The working capital requirement of this business will be low. The reason for this low requirement is that the production cycle for pizza base is short and as the production is made on estimated order no inventory is required which will further prevent inventory costs.

Production cycle is the time span between the receipt of raw material and their conversion into finished goods. Some businesses have a longer production cycle while some have a shorter one. Duration and the length of production cycle, affects the amount of funds required for raw materials and expenses. Consequently, working capital requirement is higher in firms with longer processing cycle and lower in firms with shorter processing cycle. **[3 + 3 = 6]**

Commonly Made Error

⚠ Most of the students were not able to interpret correctly about the requirement of the working capital.

Answering Tip

The concept of working capital and the factors affecting its requirement should be understood thoroughly with examples.

SOLUTIONS FOR OBJECTIVE PRACTICE QUESTIONS

[B] A & R

Ans 2. Option (B) is correct.

Explanation: Financial management involves decision about the proportion of long-term and short-term funds. An organisation wanting to have more liquid assets would raise relatively more amount on a long-term basis. There is a choice between liquidity and profitability. The underlying assumption here is that current liabilities cost less than long term liabilities.

Ans. 4. Option (A) is correct.

Explanation: Financial planning means deciding in advance how much to spend, on what to spend according to the funds at your disposal. It enables the management to foresee the fund requirements both the quantum as well as the timing.

REFLECTION

(a) Were you able to explain the role and objectives of financial management in an organisation?
(b) Were you able to explain the three financial decisions and the factors affecting them?
(c) Have you understood the concept and objectives of financial planning?
(d) Were you able to describe the factors determining the choice of an appropriate capital structure of a company?
(e) Have you Understood the concept of fixed and working capital?
(f) Were you able to describe the factors determining the requirements of fixed and working capital?
(g) Could you identify the factor affecting the fixed capital requirement in the below mentioned line: "Higher growth of an organisation generally requires higher investment in fixed assets."
(h) Could you identify the factor affecting the working capital requirement in the below mentioned line: "Duration and the length of production cycle, affects the amount of funds required for raw materials and expenses."

SELF ASSESSMENT PAPER - 9

Maximum Time: 1 hour **MM: 30**

General Instructions:

(i) All the questions are compulsory
(ii) Q.1 to Q.10 are 1 mark questions
(3) Q.11 to Q.12 are 3 mark questions
(iv) Q.13 to Q.14 are 4 marks questions
(v) Q.15 is a 6 marks question

Objective Type Questions [1 Mark]

1. ________ is concerned with optimal procurement as well as the usage of finance.

(A) Financial Management
(B) Financial Planning
(C) Financial Decisions
(D) None of these [1]

2. Match the options of Column I with their correct options given in Column II.

	Column I		Column II
(1)	Investment Decision	**(i)**	Capital budgeting decision
(2)	Financing Decision	**(ii)**	Quantum of finance to be raised from various long-term sources
(3)	Dividend Decision	**(iii)**	Distribution of dividend.

(A) a – i, b – ii, c – iii **(B)** a – ii, b – iii, c – i **(C)** a – iii, b – i, c – ii **(D)** None of these [1]

3. The objective of ________is to ensure that enough funds are available at right time.

(A) Financial planning
(B) Financial management
(C) Investment decisions
(D) None of these [1]

4. Long-term financial planning focuses on:

(A) Budget **(B)** Capital expenditure
(C) Fixed expenditure **(D)** None of these [1]

5. For the following two statements, choose the correct option:

Statement I: Labour intensive organisations require more investment in fixed assets.

Statement II: A capital intensive organisation requires higher investment in plant and machinery.

Choose the correct option from options given below:

(A) Statement I is correct and statement II is wrong.
(B) Statement II is correct and statement I is wrong.
(C) Both the statements are correct.
(D) Both the statements are wrong. [1]

6. In the following questions, a statement of assertion (A) is followed by a statement of reason (R). Mark the correct choice as:

Assertion (A): In peak season, larger amount of working capital is required.

Reason (R): Most business have some seasonality in their operations. In peak reason business have higher level of activity due to increased demand.

(A) Both assertion (A) and reason (R) are true and reason (R) is the correct explanation of assertion (A). e4
(B) Both assertion (A) and reason (R) are true but reason (R) is not the correct explanation of assertion (A).
(C) Assertion (A) is true but reason (R) is false.
(D) Assertion (A) is false but reason (R) is true.

Read the text given below and answer Q. 7-10 based on it.

Rahul and Rohit were two brothers. Rahul wanted to start a big trading business of toys. His idea is to take his business to great heights. Though he doesn't have experience in this business yet he wants to give this business a try. He feels that if he gives the best quality services then his business will reach great heights. He has to make investments in plant and machinery, furniture and fixture, land and building, vehicles, etc. He needs bigger plant and more space and therefore, requires higher investment in fixed assets. To deal with different trading businessmen quickly and to make his business online, he decided to make use of good and advanced speedy computers.

Rohit starts a thermometer manufacturing business. He too like his brother wants to take his business towards great success. He is new to this business and is busy getting to know about the technical side of the business as much as possible. He wants to make the best quality thermometers which are ultrasensitive to temperature changes and can resist shocks. For making thermometers, he ordered raw materials which were taking some time to be delivered due to which he faced some difficulty in making thermometers on time. However, he decided to follow a liberal credit policy to sell thermometers.

Despite all these good ambitions in mind a sudden shock takes place for both the brothers. The economy shows sign of depression and within a few months is totally engulfed by it.

7. Which concept of financial management is highlighted in the below mentioned line:

"He has to make investments in plant and machinery, furniture and fixture, land and building, vehicles, etc."

(A) Fixed Assets **(B)** Current Assets
(C) Financial planning **(D)** Financial decisions [1]

8. Which of the following factor affecting the fixed capital requirement of a business is described in the below mentioned line:

"To deal with different trading businessmen quickly and to make his business online, he decided to make use of good and advanced speedy computers."

(A) Technology upgradation
(B) Financing alternatives
(C) Scale of operations
(D) Choice of technique **[1]**

9. Which of the following factor affecting the working capital requirement of a business is described in the below mentioned line:

"The economy shows sign of depression and within a few months is totally engulfed by it."

(A) Seasonal Factors **(B)** Production Cycle
(C) Business Cycle **(D)** Scale of Operations **[1]**

10. Which of the following factor affecting the working capital requirement of a business is described in the below mentioned line:

"For making thermometers, he ordered raw materials which were taking some time to be delivered due to which he faced some difficulty in making thermometers on time."

(A) Credit allowed **(B)** Production Cycle
(C) Inventory **(D)** Scale of Operations **[1]**

Short Answer Type Questions - I [3 Marks]

11. 'White Express' specialises in Courier Services. Its 'wide range of express package and parcel service' help business firms to make sure that the goods are made available to the customers at the right place and at the right time.

State with reason, whether the working capital requirements of 'White Express' will be high or low. Also, explain the factor affecting the working capital requirement of White Express.

12. Explain the following factors affecting dividend decision:

(i) Stability of Dividends
(ii) Growth Opportunities

Short Answer Type Questions - II [4 Marks]

13. Alex completed his Business Administration from Australia. He is a multitasking. He tries to evaluate two projects. The projects have equal level of risk. According to this parameter he finds both projects at par. However, when it comes to knowing the rate of return of the two projects, he finds that Project A will yield a rate of return of 10% and Project B will yield a rate of return of 12%. So, he decides to go ahead with the project B. Identify the type of financial decision mentioned in the above case and explain the factor affecting the decision.

14. Shimmer Ltd. is engaged in the business of export of garments. In the past, the performance of the company had been up to the expectations. In line with the latest technology, the company decided to upgrade its machinery. For this, the Finance Manager, Rakesh estimated the amount of funds required and the timings. This will help the company in linking the investment and the financing decisions on a continuous basis. Rakesh therefore, began with the preparation of a sales forecast for the next four years. He also collected the relevant data about the profit estimates in the coming years. By doing this, he wanted to be sure about the availability of funds from the internal sources of the business. For the remaining funds he is trying to find out alternative sources from outside.

(i) Identify the financial concept discussed in the above para.
(ii) Also explain the objectives to be achieved by the use of financial concept, so identified.

Long Answer Type Questions [6 Marks]

15. BonBon Limited is engaged in the business of manufacturing various kinds of biscuits. They produce 4 million packets of biscuits in a day. The company has a share capital of ₹ 20,00,000 divided into shares of ₹ 100 each. For expansion purpose, the company requires additional funds of ₹ 15,00,000. The management is considering the following alternatives for raising funds:

Alternative 1: Issue of 10,000 Equity shares of ₹ 100 each
Alternative 2: Issue of 20% Debentures of ₹ 20,00,000

The company's present Earnings Before Interest and Tax (EBIT) is ₹ 10,00,000 p.a. Assuming that the rate of return on investment remains the same after expansion, which alternative should be used by the company in order to maximise the returns to the equity shareholders. The tax rate is 50%. Show the working.

FINANCIAL MARKET

LEARNING OBJECTIVES

After going through this chapter, the student would be able to:

- Understand the concept of financial market.
- Understand the concept of money market.
- Discuss the concept of capital market.
- Explain primary and secondary markets as types of capital market.
- Differentiate between capital market and money market.
- Distinguish between primary and secondary markets.
- Give the meaning of a stock exchange.
- Explain the functions of a stock exchange.
- Discuss the trading procedure in a stock exchange.
- Give the meaning of depository services and demat account as used in the trading procedure of securities.
- State the objectives of SEBI.
- Explain the functions of SEBI.

Study Plan
Maximum Time = 2.30 Hrs
Maximum Questions = 52

LIST OF TOPICS

TOPIC-1 Financial Market: Concept and Types

Concepts Covered

- Concept of financial market, • Concept of money market, • Concept of capital market. • Primary and secondary markets as types of capital market.

Revision Notes

Scan this
Financial markets

- **Financial market:** A business is a part of an economic system that consists of two main sectors – households which save funds and business firms which invest these funds.
- A financial market helps to link the savers and the investors by mobilising funds between them. In doing so it performs what is known as an allocative function.
- It allocates or directs funds available for investment into their most productive investment opportunity.
- **Money Market:** The money market is a market for short-term funds which deals in **monetary assets** whose period of maturity is up to one year.
- **Capital Market:** Capital market includes all those organisations, institutions and instruments that provide long-term and medium-term funds through shares, bonds, debentures, etc.
- **Types of Capital Market:** [Board, 2022]

(i) **Primary Market:** It refers to the market wherein securities (shares, debentures) are sold for the first time. It is also known as new issue market.

(ii) **Secondary Market:** It is a market for the purchase and sale of existing securities.

KEY TERMS

Financial Market: Market for the creation and exchange of financial assets.
Monetary Assets: Those short-term assets that can be liquidated easily and quickly like cash and cash equivalents, short-term investments etc.
Capital Market: Refers to facilities and institutional arrangements through which long-term funds, both debt and equity are raised and invested.

SUBJECTIVE TYPE QUESTIONS

Short Answer Type Questions-I (3 marks each)

1. 'Gujarat Textiles Ltd.' needs to raise a fund of ₹80 crore. It cannot afford the cost of a public issue, so it was decided to allot its equity shares to institutional investors like LIC and some selected investors. Identify and explain the method of floating new issues used by 'Gujarat Textiles Ltd.'

A [Outside Delhi Set-1, 2022]

Ans. Private Placement: Private placement is the allotment of securities by a company to institutional investors and some selected individuals. It helps to raise capital more quickly than a public issue. Access to the primary market can be expensive on account of various mandatory and non-mandatory expenses. Some companies, therefore, cannot afford a public issue and choose to use private placement.

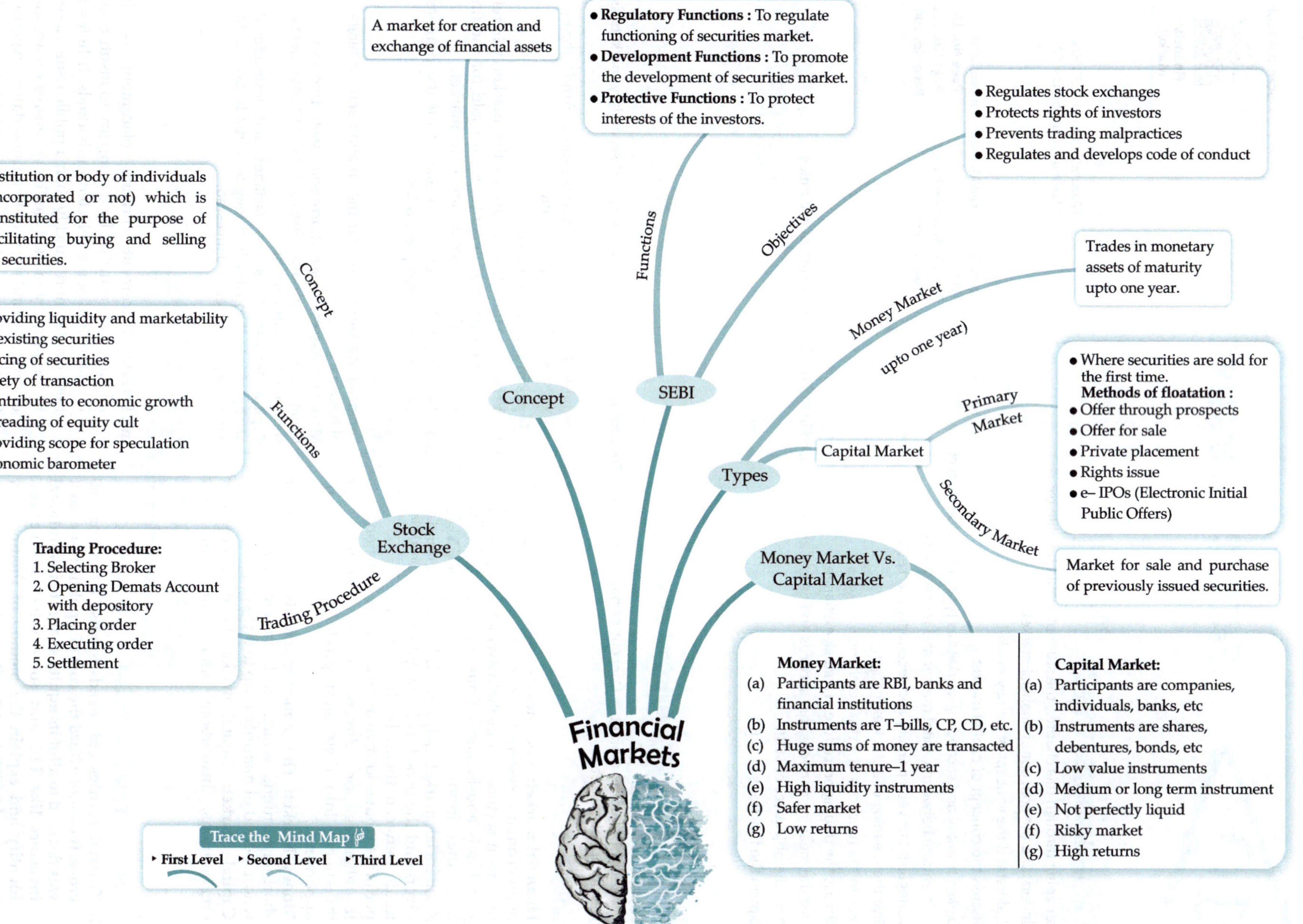
Financial Markets
Concept
A market for creation and exchange of financial assets
SEBI
Functions
Regulatory Functions : To regulate functioning of securities market.
Development Functions : To promote the development of securities market.
Protective Functions : To protect interests of the investors.
Objectives
Regulates stock exchanges
Protects rights of investors
Prevents trading malpractices
Regulates and develops code of conduct
Types
Money Market
upto one year)
Trades in monetary assets of maturity upto one year.
Capital Market
Primary Market
Where securities are sold for the first time.
Methods of floatation :
Offer through prospects
Offer for sale
Private placement
Rights issue
e– IPOs (Electronic Initial Public Offers)
Secondary Market
Market for sale and purchase of previously issued securities.
Money Market Vs. Capital Market
Money Market:
(a) Participants are RBI, banks and financial institutions
(b) Instruments are T–bills, CP, CD, etc.
(c) Huge sums of money are transacted
(d) Maximum tenure–1 year
(e) High liquidity instruments
(f) Safer market
(g) Low returns
Capital Market:
(a) Participants are companies, individuals, banks, etc
(b) Instruments are shares, debentures, bonds, etc
(c) Low value instruments
(d) Medium or long term instrument
(e) Not perfectly liquid
(f) Risky market
(g) High returns
Stock Exchange
Concept
Institution or body of individuals (incorporated or not) which is constituted for the purpose of facilitating buying and selling of securities.
Functions
Providing liquidity and marketability to existing securities
Pricing of securities
Safety of transaction
Contributes to economic growth
Spreading of equity cult
Providing scope for speculation
Economic barometer
Trading Procedure
Trading Procedure:
1. Selecting Broker
2. Opening Demats Account with depository
3. Placing order
4. Executing order
5. Settlement
Trace the Mind Map
First Level
Second Level
Third Level

Commonly Made Error

⚠ Students fail to identify the right floating method.

Answering Tip

Learn and understand the methods of floatation properly to identify the correct one. Always read the question twice for better understanding.

2. Explain 'Private Placement' and 'Rights Issue' as methods of flotation of new issues in the primary market. R [Delhi Set-1, Term-2, 2022]

Ans. Private Placement: Private placement is the **allotment of securities** by a company to institutional investors and some selected individuals. It helps to raise capital more quickly than a public issue. Access to the primary market can be expensive on account of various mandatory and non-monetary expenses. Some companies, therefore, cannot afford a public issue and choose to use private placement.

Rights Issue: This is a **privilege given to existing shareholders** to subscribe to a new issue of shares according to the terms and conditions of the company. The shareholders are offered the 'right' to buy new shares in proportion to the number of shares they already possess.

3. Celery Plus is a pharmaceutical company which deals in manufacturing herbal medicines. The value of securities issued by a company is low. It has not set up a huge financial outlay. Mr. Amit Goyal has purchased 200 units of shares with the value of ₹ 10 each. Though he has small savings yet he is able to invest money in this financial market. Identify and explain the type of financial market described in the above case. U [OEB]

Concept Applied	Concept and types of capital market

Ans. The type of financial market described in the above case is **capital market.**

The term capital market refers to facilities and institutional arrangements through which **long-term funds, both debt and equity** are raised and invested. It consists of a series of channels through which savings of the community are made available for industrial and commercial enterprises and for the public in general. Investment in the capital market i.e., securities does not necessarily require a huge financial outlay. The value of units of securities is generally low i.e., ₹ 10, ₹ 100 and so is the case with minimum trading lot of shares which is kept small i.e., 5, 50, 100 or so. This helps individuals with small savings to subscribe to these securities. **[3]**

Short Answer Type Questions-II (4 marks each)

1. These days, the development of a country is also judged by its system of transferring finance from the sector where it is in surplus to the sector where it is needed the most. To give strength to the economy, SEBI is undertaking measures to develop the capital market. In addition to this, there is another market in which unsecured and short-term debt instruments are actively traded every day. These markets together help the savers and investors in directing the available funds into their most productive investment opportunity.

(i) Name the function being performed by the market in the above case.

(ii) Name the market segment other than the capital market segment in which unsecured and short-term debt instruments are traded. Also, give any three points of difference between the two.

AI A [Outside Delhi Set-1, 2019]

Topper's Answer, 2019

Ans.

(a) ALLOCATIVE FUNCTION

(b) MONEY MARKET trades in unsecured & short term debt instruments.

	Basis	Money Market	Capital Market
①	Participants	Participants in money market are: • commercial banks • non banking finance companies • RBI • State Governments • Large Corporate Houses • Mutual funds	Participants in capital market are • banks • financial institutions • corporate entities • foreign investors • Ordinary retail investors from members of public.
②	Duration	~~Capital~~ Money market deals with Short term debt instruments which have maximum tenure upto one year & may be issued for single day.	Capital market deals in both medium & long term securities like equity shares & debentures.
③	liquidity	Capital market securities are liquid. However share may not be actively traded as it may not easily find a buyer. Money market instruments enjoy higher degree of liquidity because there is	~~Money~~ Capital market securities are considered liquid. However, share may not be actively traded as it may not easily find a buyer

2. Ketan won a cash prize of ₹20,000 in the National Level Robotics Competition. On the advise of his father, he visits a nearby bank to open a fixed deposit account in his name with the prize money. His sister Suhasini accompanied him to the bank. On reaching the bank, he notices big banners which are placed within the premises containing information about the various arrangements through which corporates may raise their capital through the bank. Being a finance graduate, Suhasini explains to Ketan that banks play the role of financial intermediary by helping in the process of channelising the savings of the households into the most profitable business ventures.

In context of the above case:

(i) Name another financial intermediary that helps in the process of channelising the savings of the households into the most productive use.

(ii) Also, outline any two functions of another financial intermediary as identified in part (i). U [OEB]

Ans. (i) Financial markets is the other **financial intermediary** that helps in the process of channelising the savings of the households into the most productive use.

(ii) The two functions of financial market are as follows:

(a) It helps to **determine the price** for the financial asset in a particular financial market through the market forces of demand and supply.

(b) It provides **liquidity to the financial assets** by providing ready markets wherein the securities can be converted into cash or vice versa easily. **[2+2=4]**

3. Distinguish between 'Capital Market' and 'Money Market' on the basis of following:

[Outside Delhi Set-2, 2022] **[4]**

(i) Participants
(ii) Safety
(iii) Investment Outlay
(iv) Expected Return

OR

Distinguish between 'Capital Market' and 'Money Market' on the basis of following:

[Outside Delhi Set-2, 2022] [Outside Delhi Set-3, 2023] **[4]**

(i) Duration
(ii) Safety
(iii) Liquidity
(iv) Investment Outlay

OR

Distinguish between 'Capital Market' and 'Money Market'. [CFPQ]

Ans. The difference between Capital Market and Money Market are:

Basis of Distinction	Capital Market	Money Market
Participants	Stock brokers, Insurance companies, Commercial banks, Underwriters are among the various participants in the capital market.	Commercial banks, Non-financial institutions, Central banks, Bill brokers, Acceptance houses, Chit funds are among the various participants in the money market.
Safety	The risk involved in investment is comparatively high.	The risk involved in investment is comparatively low.
Investment Outlay	The investment outlay is comparatively lower.	The investment outlay is comparatively higher.
Expected Return	The return on the investment is expected to be high.	The return on investment is expected to be low.
Duration	Maturity period is much longer.	Maturity takes place within the year.
Liquidity	The liquidity is low in case of Capital Market.	The liquidity is high in case of Money Market.

Tips and Tricks

For scoring full marks in this question, remember to write in tabular form only while mentioning the basis and proper explanation of each point.

Long Answer Type Questions-I (6 marks each)

1. What is meant by financial market? State any four functions of financial market?

U [Delhi Set-1, Outside Delhi Set-1, 3, 2022]

Ans. A financial market is a market for the **creation and exchange of financial assets**. Financial markets exist wherever a financial transaction occurs. Financial transactions could be in the form of creation of financial assets such as the initial issue of shares and debentures by a firm or the purchase and sale of existing financial assets like equity shares, debentures and bonds.

Functions performed by a Stock Exchange (any four):

(i) Stock Exchanges provide liquidity and marketability to existing securities by giving investors the chance to disinvest and reinvest.

(ii) They help in determining the prices of securities through the forces of demand and supply.

(iii) Stock exchanges ensure the investors safety of transactions and fair deal on the market as they are well-regulated and their dealings are well-defined according to the existing legal framework.

(iv) Stock exchanges contribute to economic growth through the process of disinvestment and reinvestment and channelising the savings into most productive investment avenues.

(v) Stock exchanges spread equity cult by regulating new issues, better trading practices and taking effective steps in educating the public about investments.

(vi) Stock exchanges provide sufficient scope for speculation within the provisions of law in a restricted and controlled manner. **[2 + 4 = 6]**

2. **State any six points of difference between 'Primary Market' and 'Secondary Market'.** [Delhi Set-2, 2022] U

Ans. Difference between Primary Market and Secondary Market:

S.No.	Basis	Primary Market (New Issue Market)	Secondary Market (Stock Exhange)
(i)	**Securities traded**	There is sale of securities by **new companies** for further (new) issues of securities by existing companies to investors.	There is trading of **existing securities** only.
(ii)	**Instruments**	Securities are sold by the company to the **investor directly** (or through an intermediary)	Ownership of existing securities is **exchanged between investors**. The company is not involved at all.
(iii)	**Capital formation**	The flow of funds is from **savers to investors**, i.e., the primary market directly promotes capital formation.	Enhances **encashability (liquidity) of securities**, i.e., the secondary market indirectly promotes capital formation.
(iv)	**Buying/Selling**	**Only buying** of securities takes place in the primary market. Securities cannot be sold by the investors.	**Both the buying and the selling** of securities can take place on the stock exchange.
(v)	**Price determination**	Prices are determined and decided by the **management** of the company.	Prices are determined by **demand and supply** of the securities.
(vi)	**Location**	There is **no fixed geographical location.**	Located at **specified places.**

[1 × 6 = 6]

3. **State the difference between 'Capital Market' and 'Money Market' on any six basis.** U [Delhi Set-3, 2022]

OR

Differentiate between 'Capital Market' and 'Money Market' on the basis of following:
(i) Participants (ii) Instruments (iii) Expected Return (iv) Safety

U [Outside Delhi Set-2, 2022]

Ans.

S.No.	Basis	Capital Market	Money Market
(i)	**Meaning**	It refers to the facilities and institutional arrangements through which funds; both debt and equity are **invested and raised.**	It is the market where **low risk, unsecured, highly liquid short term debt instruments** are issued and traded.
(ii)	**Participants**	The participants are financial institutions, banks, corporates, foreign investors and retail investors.	The participants are RBI, financial institutions, banks and corporates.
(iii)	**Instruments**	Instruments traded are shares, debentures and bonds.	Instruments traded are treasury bill, commercial paper, certificates of deposit, call money and commercial bill.
(iv)	**Investment**	Investment outlay is **small.**	Investment outlay is **large.**
(v)	**Duration**	It deals in **medium term and long term securities.**	It deals in **short term securities.**
(vi)	**Liquidity**	Capital market securities are comparatively less liquid.	Money market securities are comparatively **more liquid.**
(vii)	**Expected Return**	The investment in capital markets generally **yields a higher return.**	The expected rate of return of the money market is **less.**
(viii)	**Security/Safety**	Capital market instruments are **risky** with respect to returns and principal repayment.	Money market instruments are generally **much safer** with a minimum risk of default.
(ix)	**Location**	There is **no fixed geographical area.** All the institutions, banks, foreign investors, etc. constitute primary market.	There is a **fixed geographical area and working hours.**

[1 × 6 = 6]

4. Kynaa, a beauty products e-commerce company, is diversifying into men's grooming. It is also tapping the demand for beauty products in the fashion industry and amid professionals such as make-up artists. As it diversifies its online presence, Kynaa is also expanding its physical presence. They have 41 outlets across 18 cities presently and plan to expand to 180 outlets. Each store requires a capital expenditure of 60–80 lakh rupees. The company has decided to raise funds by issuing equity shares but not directly to the public, rather by offering them for sale through brokers. Identify and briefly explain the method of floatation followed by the company. Also name and explain the other methods of floatation that can be used by the company for raising funds from the public, in the primary market.

U [SQP 2019-20]

Ans. Method of floatation used is **offer for sale:** In this method securities are not offered directly to the public but are offered for **sale through intermediaries** like **stock brokers.** (1 mark for identification and 1½ mark for explanation)

Other methods are:

1. **Offer through prospectus:** This method involves inviting **subscription** from public through prospectus. The issue may be underwritten and has to be listed with one stock exchange.
2. **E-IPO:** A company proposing to **issue capital to the public through online** system of stock exchange.

[Marking Scheme, 2019]

TOPIC-2 Stock Exchange

Concepts Covered

• Meaning of a stock exchange. • Functions of a stock exchange. • Trading procedure in a stock exchange.

Revision Notes

- **Meaning of Stock Exchange:** According to Securities Contracts (Regulation) Act 1956, stock exchange means any body of individuals, whether incorporated or not, constituted for the purpose of assisting, regulating or controlling the business of buying and selling or dealing in securities.

- **Functions of a Stock Exchange:** [2019]

(i) Provides liquidity and marketability to existing securities

(ii) Ensures safety of transactions

(iii) Contributes to economic growth

(iv) Spreads out equity cult

(v) Determines price of securities

(vi) Provides scope for speculation

- **Trading Procedure on a Stock Exchange:** [2019]

(i) Selecting a broker

(ii) Opening a demat account

(iii) Placing an order

(iv) Executing the order

(v) Settlement of transaction

MNEMONICS

Concept: Trading Procedure on a Stock Exchange:

Interpretations: SO Parrots Eat Strawberries

S: Selecting a broker O: Opening a demat account P: Placing an order E: Executing the order S: Settlement of transaction

Concept: Players in the depository system:

Interpretations: DID your Breakfast?

D: Depository I: Issuer D: Depository participant B: Beneficial owner

SUBJECTIVE TYPE QUESTIONS

Short Answer Type Questions-I (3 marks each)

1. State any three functions performed by stock exchange. U [SQP 2022-23]

Ans. Following are the functions of stock exchange:

(i) Providing liquidity and marketability to existing securities.

(ii) Pricing of securities on the stock exchange is determined by the forces of demand and supply.

(iii) Safety of transaction is ensured as membership of a stock exchange is well regulated and its dealings are well defined.

(iv) Contributes to economic growth through the process of **disinvestment and reinvestment**.

(v) Spreading of equity cult by ensuring wider ownership by way of regulating new issues.

(vi) Providing scope for speculation by ensuring speculative activity within the provisions of law for speculative activity in a restricted and controlled manner.

(Any three) [1 × 3 = 3]

2. State the first three steps involved in the screen-based trading for buying and selling of securities

[SQP 2023-24] **[3]**

Ans. The first three steps in screen-based trading in securities are as follows:

(i) Investor has to first approach a **registered broker** and enter into agreement. He has to open a **broker-client agreement** and a client registration form before placing the order. He has to provide few details like PAN number, date of birth and address, educational qualification and occupation, Residential status, Bank account details, Depository account details, name of any other broker with whom registered, client code number in the client registration form. The broker opens a trading account in the name of investor.

(ii) The investor has to open a **demat account** or beneficial owner account with a depository participant for holding and transferring securities in the demat form.

(iii) The investor places an order with the broker to buy or sell shares. Clear instructions have to be given about the number of shares and price at which shares can be bought or sold. The broker will go ahead with the deal to mention the best price available. **Order confirmation** slip is issued to the investor by the broker. [1 × 3 = 3]

3. Explain how stock exchange provides safety of transaction and contributes to economic growth?

U [OEB]

Ans. (i) Safety of Transaction: The membership of a stock exchange is **well- regulated** and its dealings are **well defined** according to the existing legal framework. This ensures that the investing public gets a safe and fair deal on the market.

(ii) Contributes to Economic Growth: Stock exchange is a market in which existing securities are resold or traded. Through this process of disinvestment and reinvestment savings get channelised into their most productive investment avenues. This leads to capital formation and economic growth. [1½×2=3]

4. Explain how a stock exchange provides liquidity and marketability to existing securities?

U [OEB]

Short Answer Type Questions-II (4 marks each)

1. Stock exchange acts as a regulator of the securities market. It creates a continuous market where the securities are bought and sold. It gives investors the chance to disinvest and reinvest. Through this process of disinvestment and reinvestment, savings get channelised into their most productive investment avenues. To ensure that the investing public gets a safe and fair deal in the market, the membership of the stock exchange is well regulated and its dealings are well defined according to the existing legal framework. It also ensures wider share ownership by regulating new issues, better trading practices and taking effective steps in educating the public about investments.

Various functions performed by the Stock Exchange are discussed in the above para.

AI A [Delhi Set-1, 2, 3, 2019]

Ans. Various functions performed by the stock exchange are:

(i) Providing liquidity and marketability to existing securities as the stock exchange creates a continuous market where the securities are bought and sold. It gives investors the chance to disinvest and reinvest. It creates a continuous market where the securities are bought and sold.

(ii) Contributes to economic growth as through the process of disinvestment and reinvestment, savings get channelised into their most productive investment avenues.

(iii) Safety of transactions as the membership of the stock exchange is well regulated and its dealings are well defined according to the existing legal framework. This ensures that the investing public gets a safe and fair deal on the market.

(iv) Spreading of equity cult as the stock exchange ensures wider shared ownership by regulating new issues, better trading practices and taking effective steps in educating the public about investments.

2. The trading and settlement procedure involves a series of steps. Discuss the first four steps which an investor has to go through during the screenbased trading for buying and selling of securities.

[OEB]

Concept Applied | Functions of a stock exchange

Long Answer Type Questions (6 marks each)

1. Akash who is a broker in a stock exchange has to face challenging questions from society. His own family sometimes asks him to think about his decision to become a broker. He however, has full faith in the stock exchange. He knows that the membership of a stock exchange is properly regulated abiding the legal system and the public doing investment is safe in making deals. His children one day asked him the reason behind the ups and downs in the stock market. He clarified their doubt by telling them that forces of supply and demand decide the prices of securities in the secondary market. Off late he has decided to write a book on the functioning of stock exchange and its significance in the Indian economy. He is trying to highlight in his book how through the process of investment and disinvestment existing securities are sold and resold and savings are channelised into the most productive opportunities. Definitely Akash is justifying his presence in his job. Identify and explain the functions of stock exchange discussed in the above case by quoting lines from the paragraph.

A [OEB]

Ans. **The different functions of stock exchange highlighted in the above case are:**

(i) Ensures safety of transaction: The membership of a stock exchange is well regulated and its dealings are well defined according to the existing legal framework. This ensures that the investing public gets a safe and fair deal on the market.

Lines: "He knows that the membership of a stock exchange is properly regulated abiding the legal system and the public doing investment is safe in making deals."

(ii) Helps in deciding pricing of securities: Share prices on a stock exchange are determined by the forces of demand and supply. A stock exchange is a mechanism of constant valuation through which the

These Questions are for practice and their solutions are given at the end of the chapter.

prices of securities are determined. Such a valuation provides important instant information to both buyers and sellers in the market.

Lines: "He clarified their doubt by telling them that forces of supply and demand decide the prices of securities in the secondary market."

(iii) Helps in contributing to the economic growth: A stock exchange is a market in which existing securities are **resold or traded**. Through this process of disinvestment and reinvestment savings get **channelised into their most productive investment** avenues. This leads to capital formation and economic growth.

Lines: "He is trying to highlight in his book how through the process of investment and disinvestment existing securities are sold and resold and savings are channelised into the most productive opportunities." **[2×3=6]**

2. Arpita got ₹20,00,000 after selling her parental property and jewellery which she had got as a gift from her grandmother. Her friend advised her to invest in securities in the stock market. Arpita was a novice and was unaware of the procedure for the same. Her friend introduced her to a stock broker, who was registered with NSE. Arpita approached the broker who guided her to open a demat account with a depository, as well as a bank account. Arpita opened a bank account and demat account with Exim Bank.

(i) Identify the steps in the trading procedure for buying and selling of securities which have been discussed above.

(ii) State the next four steps of the trading procedure.

A [OEB]

Ans. (i) The steps discussed in above para are:

(a) Selection of broker: The buying and selling can be through a **SEBI broker**. For this purpose, a broker is to be selected and the investor has to sign a client-broker agreement with him which will enable the broker to buy/sell securities on behalf of the investor.

(b) Opening demat account with a depository participant.

(ii) The next four steps of the trading procedure are:

(a) Placing an order: Investor places an order with the broker to buy or sell shares. He can communicate the same via email or telephone or personally. Brokers go ahead with the deal and order confirmation slip is issued to the investor by the broker.

(b) Match the order: The broker goes online and matches the share and the **best price** available.

(c) Executing the order: When the shares can be bought and sold at the price mentioned, it is updated to the broker terminal and order is **executed electronically. The broker then issues trade confirmation** slip to the investor.

(d) Issue of contract note: After the trade has been executed, within 24 hours the broker issues **contract note** which contains details regarding number and price of shares. **[2 + 4 = 6]**

Commonly Made Error

Generally, students do not write the procedure in sequence.

Answering Tip

Stress should be laid upon the sequence of steps while learning.

TOPIC-3 SEBI

Concepts Covered

- Objectives of SEBI • Functions of SEBI

Revision Notes

- **Securities and Exchange Board of India (SEBI):** It was established by the Indian Government in 1988 under the administrative control of the Ministry of Finance, Government of India. Later, it became a statutory body under the SEBI Act, 1992.

- **Objectives of SEBI:** [2022]

(i) To regulate stock exchanges

(ii) To protect investor's rights and interests

(iii) To prevent trading **malpractices**

(iv) To regulate and develop the **code of conduct**

- **Functions of the SEBI:**

(i) Regulatory Functions: [2016]

(a) Registration of players in the market

(b) Registration of investment schemes

(c) Regulation of intermediaries

(d) Regulation of takeover bids

(e) Calling for information

(f) Levying fees

(g) Others as delegated by the Government of India

(ii) Developmental Functions:

(a) Training of intermediaries

(b) Conducting research

(c) Developing capital markets

(iii) Protective Functions:

(a) Prohibition of unfair trade practices

(b) Controlling insider trading

(c) Investors' protection

MNEMONICS

Concept: Objectives of SEBI
Mnemonics: Paris and Rome are Dream Places
Interpretations:
P: Prevent trading malpractices
R: Regulate stock exchanges and the securities industry
D: Develop a code of conduct and fair practices
P: Protect the rights and interests of investors
Concept: Functions of SEBI
Mnemonics: Pretty Red Dress
Interpretations:
P: Protective Functions
R: Regulatory Functions
D: Developmental Functions

SUBJECTIVE TYPE QUESTIONS

Short Answer Type Questions-I (3 marks each)

1. **'Due to various malpractices and multiplied investors grievances the government of India decided to set-up a separate regulatory body to protect the interest of investors and to regulate the securities market.'**
   (i) Identify the regulatory body set-up by government of India for the above stated purpose.
   (ii) State any two objectives of the regulatory body identified in (i) above. U [Delhi Set-1, 2022]

OR

State any three objectives of the Securities Exchange Board of India. R [SQP 2022-23]

Ans. (i) SEBI (Securities and exchange board of India) **[1]**

(ii) **Objectives of SEBI:** The overall objective of SEBI is to protect the interests of investors and to promote the development of and regulate the securities market. **This may be elaborated as follows:**

(a) To **regulate stock exchanges and the securities** industry to promote their orderly functioning.

(b) To protect the rights and interests of investors, particularly individual investors and to guide and educate them.

(c) To prevent trading malpractices and achieve a balance between self regulation by the securities industry and its statutory regulation.

(d) To regulate and develop a code of conduct and fair practices by intermediaries like brokers, merchant bankers, etc., with a view to making them competitive and professional. **(Any two) [1 × 2 = 2]**

2. **State the development functions of the Securities and Exchange Board of India.** U [SQP 2020-21]

OR

Keeping in mind the emerging nature of the securities market in India, Securities and Exchange Board of India (SEBI) was entrusted with the twin task of regulation and development of securities market. Out of this, state the developmental functions of Securities and Exchange Board of India (SEBI). A [Outside Delhi Comptt. Set-1, 2015]

OR

A business magazine, 'Btimes' has published a report on how SEBI is serious about training of the intermediaries and deciding their code of conduct. A lot of research has been going on in various related areas and the information of use is being published so that various participants can get useful results from it. Identify and explain the type of function of SEBI mentioned in the above case. U [OEB]

Concept Applied	Development functions of SEBI

3. **One of the functions of Securities and Exchange Board of India is 'promotion of fair practices and code of conduct in securities market'. State the category to which this function belongs and state any two other functions of this category.** A [Outside Delhi Set-1, 2, 3, 2019]

Ans. Protective Function

Other functions of this category are:

(i) It prohibits fraudulent and unfair trade practices like misleading statements, manipulations, price rigging, etc.

(ii) It controls insider trading and imposes penalties for such practices.

(iii) It undertakes steps for investor protection.

(Any two)

[Marking Scheme, 2019] **[1+2=3]**

4. **Demonstrate your understanding of SEBI's regulatory functions by designing the steps SEBI should take to investigate and resolve a suspected case of fraudulent activities by a listed company.** U [APQ Set-1, 2023-24]

Ans. Step 1: Preliminary Investigation: SEBI should initiate a preliminary investigation based on the information received about the **suspected fraudulent** activities by the listed company. This involves gathering initial evidence, identifying potential violations, and assessing the gravity of the situation.

Step 2: Formal Investigation: Upon finding substantial evidence during the preliminary investigation, SEBI should launch a **formal investigation**. This involves a deeper examination of the company's activities, including financial records, transactions, and management practices. The investigation may involve summoning company officials, scrutinising books, and seeking expert opinions.

Step 3: Inspection of Books and Records: As part of its **regulatory function**, SEBI has the authority to inspect the books and records of listed companies

These Questions are for practice and their solutions are given at the end of the chapter.

to ensure compliance with securities laws. This step involves a detailed examination of the company's financial records and transactions. **[1×3=3]**

Commonly Made Error

Students are not able to understand the question and they get confused between different functions of SEBI.

Answering Tip

Read the question properly and underline the important part of the question to understand what exactly you are supposed to write in the answer.

Short Answer Type Questions-II (4 marks each)

1. Mr. Sanjay Nehra was the Chairman of 'Taran Bank.' The bank was earning good profits. Shareholders were happy as the bank was paying regular dividends. The market price of their shares was also steadily rising. The bank was about to announce taking over of 'Vena Bank.' Mr. Sanjay Nehra knew that the share price of 'Taran Bank' would rise on this announcement. Being a part of the bank, he was not allowed to buy shares of the bank. He called one of his rich friends Sudhir and asked him to invest ₹ 5 crores in the shares of his bank promising him the capital gains. As expected the share prices went up by 40% and the market price of Sudhir's shares was now ₹ 7 crores. He earned a profit of ₹ 2 crores. He gave ₹ 1 crore to Mr. Sanjay Nehra and kept ₹ 1 crore with himself. On regular inspection and by conducting enquiries of the brokers involved, Securities and Exchange Board of India (SEBI) was able to detect this irregularity. The SEBI imposed a heavy penalty on Mr. Sanjay Nehra. By quoting the lines from the above paragraph, identify and state any two functions that were performed by SEBI in the above case. AI A [Delhi Set-1, 2016]

Concept Applied: Functions of SEBI

Ans. Functions that were performed by SEBI in the above case were:

(i) **Regulatory function: Line**: 'On regular inspection and by conducting enquiries of the brokers involved, Securities and Exchange Board of India (SEBI) was able to detect this irregularity.

'SEBI can call for information by undertaking inspection, conducting enquiries and audits of stock exchanges and intermediaries.

(ii) **Protective function: Line**: 'The SEBI imposed a heavy penalty on Sanjay Nehra.

SEBI controls insider trading and imposes penalties for such practices. **[2+2=4]**

Commonly Made Error

Generally, students are not able to identify the category of functions, i.e., regulatory and protective.

This Question is for practice and its solution is given at the end of the chapter.

Answering Tip

Learn the various function of SEBI under different categories, e.g., Protective, Regulatory and Development.

2. State the protective functions of Securities and Exchange Board of India. AI R [Delhi/Outside Delhi 2018]

Long Answer Type Questions-I (6 marks each)

1. State any six regulatory functions of the Securities and Exchange Board of India. R [SQP 2021-22]

Ans. Regulatory functions of Securities and Exchange Board of India are :

(i) Registration of brokers and sub-brokers and other players in the market.

(ii) Registration of collective investment schemes and Mutual Funds.

(iii) Regulation of stock brokers, portfolio exchanges, underwriters and merchant bankers and the business in stock exchanges and any other securities market.

(iv) Regulation of takeover bids by companies.

(v) Calling for information by under- taking inspection, conducting enquiries and audits of stock exchanges and intermediaries.

(vi) Levying fee or other charges for carrying out the purposes of the Act.

(vii) Performing and exercising such power under Securities Contracts (Regulation) Act 1956, as may be delegated by the Government of India.

(Any five) [Marking Scheme, SQP 2021-22]

2. The car company, TEXO TECH Ltd. is run by the four directors namely, Mohit Gupta, Amit Gupta, Vinayak Gupta and Aryan Gupta. The SEBI has imposed a penalty of ₹500 crores on the company who had mobilised funds from the general public through illegal collective investment schemes in the name of purchase and development of agriculture land. While imposing the penalty, the biggest in its history, Securities and Exchange Board of India (SEBI) said the company deserved "maximum penalty" for duping the common man. Its Prevention of Fraudulent and Unfair Trade Practices Regulations provides for "severe to severe penalties" for dealing with such violations. As per SEBI norms, it can impose a penalty of ₹25 crores or three times of the profit made by indulging in fraudulent and unfair trade practices and in the present case, the regulator has imposed a fine equivalent to three times of the illicit gains.

In the context of the above case:

(i) State the objectives of setting up SEBI.

(ii) Identify and explain the type of function performed by SEBI by quoting lines from the paragraph. A [OEB]

Ans. (i) The objectives of SEBI are stated below:

(a) To prevent trading malpractice in the securities markets.

(b) To protect the rights and interest of investors, and to guide and educate them.

(c) To regulate and develop a code of conduct and fair practices by intermediaries like brokers, merchant bankers, etc. with a view to making them competitive and professional.

(d) To regulate stock exchanges and the securities market to promote their orderly functioning. **(Any three) [3]**

(ii) Protective function is performed by SEBI: The Protective Functions of SEBI include prohibition of fraudulent and unfair trade practices like making misleading statements, manipulations, price rigging etc., controlling insider trading and imposing penalties for such practices, undertaking steps for investor protection and promotion of fair practices and code of conduct in securities market.

Lines: "The SEBI has imposed a penalty of ₹500 crores on the company who had mobilised funds from the general public through illegal collective investment schemes in the name of purchase and development of agriculture land." **[3]**

3. "To promote orderly and healthy growth of the securities market and protection of the investors, Securities and Exchange Board of India was set up." With reference to this statement, explain the objectives of Securities and Exchange Board of India.

AI U [OEB]

COMPETENCY BASED QUESTIONS

Objective Type Questions

[A] Multiple Choice Questions

1. ___________ is a number assigned to each transaction by the stock exchange and is printed on the contract note.

(A) Client code number
(B) Unique order code
(C) Permanent account number
(D) Depository participant number

U [SQP 2022-23]

Ans. Option (B) is correct.

Explanation: Unique order code is a number assigned to each transaction by the stock exchange and is printed on the contract note.

2. Arrange the steps involved in trading procedure at the stock exchange in correct sequence:

(i) Settlement of order
(ii) Opening of demat account
(iii) Placing of order
(iv) Execution of order

(A) (ii); (iv); (iii); (i) **(B)** (ii); (i); (iii); (ii)
(C) (iii); (ii); (ii); (i) **(D)** (ii); (iii); (iv); (i)

U [SQP 2022-23]

Ans. Option (D) is correct.

Explanation: The trading procedure involves the following steps:

(i) Selection of a broker
(ii) Opening a demat account with depository
(iii) Placing the order
(iv) Executing the order
(v) Settlement

3. Match the various terms of Financial Markets Column-I with their respective Statements in Column-II

	Column-I		Column-II
a.	Financial market	(i)	It is also known as the stock market.
b.	Primary market	(ii)	It is a market for creation and exchange of financial assets.
c.	Secondary market	(iii)	It is also known as new issue market.

(A) (ii), (iii), (i) **(B)** (i), (iii), (ii)
(C) (iii), (ii), (i) **(D)** (i), (ii), (iii)

U [SQP 2022-23]

Ans. Option (A) is correct.

Explanation: Financial markets include any place or system that provides buyers and sellers the means to trade financial instruments. A primary market is a source of new securities. The secondary market is where investors buy and sell securities, they already own.

4. Which of the following statements is incorrect?

(A) Providing liquidity to securities is one of the functions of stock exchange.
(B) Process of holding shares in electronic form is known as dematerialisation.
(C) Securities Exchange Board of India performs the regulatory function of controlling insider trading and imposing penalties for such practices.
(D) Capital market consists of commercial banks, development banks and stock exchanges.

U [SQP 2022-23]

Ans. Option (C) is correct.

Explanation: Prevent insider trading is one of the protective functions of SEBI. By this SEBI protects the interest of investors and other financial participants.

5. Aman had 55 shares of Vani Ltd. He wanted to sell 30 shares, so he went for a specific market to sell them through online portal. He went for which of following markets?

(A) Money Market
(B) Secondary Market
(C) Primary Market
(D) None of these

AI A [OEB]

Concept Applied: Concept of Secondary market

Ans. Option (B) is correct.

Explanation: The secondary market is also known as the stock market or stock exchange. It is a market for the purchase and sale of existing securities. It helps existing investors to disinvest and fresh investors to enter the market.

This Question is for practice and its solution is given at the end of the chapter.

6. Rishu's friend Devina works as a finance manager in Perfect Solutions Ltd. Devina in a meeting with the directors of the company came to know that the firm would soon be declaring a bonus issue which would lead to an increase in the price of shares. On this basis, Devina advised Rishu to purchase the shares of Perfect Solutions Ltd., who thus bought the shares. SEBI can control malpractices like these through which of the following functions:

(A) Protective functions
(B) Regulatory functions
(C) Development functions
(D) All the above

AI A [OEB]

Concept Applied	Concept of protective functions of SEBI

Ans. Option (A) is correct.

Explanation: The protective function implies the role that SEBI plays in protecting the investor interest and also that of other financial participants. Prohibition of fraudulent and unfair trade practices like making misleading statements, manipulations, price rigging etc. is the function of SEBI.

7. Zebronics Technology Solutions, a leading tech company, recently announced its plan to raise additional funds to fuel its expansion and research initiatives. The company's board of directors approved an offer to the existing shareholders to purchase additional shares at a discounted price. This offer will be available for a specific period. How is Zebronics Technology Solutions planning to raise additional funds in the primary market, while offering its existing shareholders the opportunity to purchase more shares?

(A) Conducting an e-IPO to reach a wider digital audience
(B) Privately placing shares with select institutional investors
(C) Launching an Initial Public Offering to enter the stock market
(D) Issuing right shares for existing shareholders at a discounted price.

AI U [APQ Set-1, 2023-24]

Ans. Option (D) is correct.

Explanation: Right shares are a type of offering where existing shareholders are given the right but not the obligation to purchase additional shares at a predetermined price and within a specified time frame. This allows the company to raise additional capital by offering shares to its existing shareholders in proportion to their current holdings.

8. Which of the following statements accurately represents one of the protective functions of SEBI in real-life scenarios?

AI U [APQ Set-1, 2023-24]

(A) It is responsible for managing government budgets and allocating funds for various developmental projects.
(B) It ensures the safety and security of data transmitted during online trading transactions.
(C) It promotes and regulates the insurance industry to safeguard policyholders' interests.
(D) It monitors and regulates the securities market to protect investors and maintain market integrity.

Ans. Option (D) is correct.

Explanation: SEBI primarily functions as the regulator for the securities market in India. Its role includes overseeing and regulating various entities and activities within the securities market to safeguard the interests of investors, ensure fair practices, prevent fraudulent activities, and maintain the integrity of the market. SEBI's regulations aim to promote transparency, protect investors from market manipulation, and create a fair and level playing field for all participants in the securities market.

9. Given below are two statements marked as I and II respectively. Read both statements and choose the correct option.

I. Demutualisation refers to the legal structure of an exchange whereby the ownership, the management and the trading rights at the exchange are segregated from one another.

II. Demutualisation refers to the process by which a public share company converts into a mutual company.

Choose the correct option from the following:

(A) I is true and II is false.
(B) II is true and I is false.
(C) Both I and II are true.
(D) Both I and II are false.

AI U [APQ Set-1, 2023-24]

Ans. Option (A) is correct.

Explanation: Demutualisation refers to the process where a mutual company (owned by its members) converts into a shareholder-owned company, segregating ownership, management, and trading rights.

10. Which of the following statements is incorrect?

R [Delhi Set-1, 2023]

(A) Capital market refers to facilities and institutional arrangements through which long-term funds, both debt and equity are raised and invested.
(B) Secondary market is the market where securities are sold by the company to the investor directly or through an intermediary.
(C) Primary market is the market where only buying of securities takes place. Securities cannot be sold there.
(D) Money market is a market for short term funds which deals in monetary assets whose period of maturity is up to one year.

Ans. Option (B) is correct

Explanation: Secondary market refers to a market where securities are traded after being initially offered to the public in the primary market and/or listed on the Stock Exchange.

11. Statement-I: Capital market instruments are considered riskier both with respect to returns and principal repayment.

Statement-II: Capital market investment generally yields a higher return for investors.

Choose the correct option from the options given below: R [Outside Delhi Set-1, 2023]

(A) Statement - I is true and II is false.
(B) Statement-II is true and I is false.
(C) Both the statements are true.
(D) Both the statements are false.

Ans. Option (C) is correct.

Explanation: Capital market securities are riskier as compared with money market instruments. The investment in capital market yields higher return due to longer duration and is therefore more stable.

12. Which of the following statements is Not true for primary market? U [Outside Delhi Set-1, 2023]

(A) There is no fixed Geographical location.
(B) Only buying of securities takes place, securities cannot be sold there.
(C) Prices are determined by demand and supply of the security.
(D) It directly promotes capital formation.

Ans. Option (C) is correct.

Explanation: Prices are determined and decided by the management of the company after giving consideration to a lot of factors.

13. Which of the following is not a function of Securities and Exchange Board of India (SEBI)? U [Outside Delhi Set-1, 2023]

(A) Training of intermediaries of the securities market
(B) Controlling insider trading
(C) Registration of brokers and sub-brokers and other players in the market
(D) Pricing of securities

Ans. Option (D) is correct.

14. SEBI calls for information and issues a show cause notice to stock exchange and its officials seeking explanation and conducting audit and enquiry. Which function is SEBI performing? R [SQP 2023-24]

(A) Regulatory function
(B) Development function
(C) Protective function
(D) Both (A) and (C)

Ans. Option (A) is Correct.

Explanation: SEBI plays the role of conducting enquiries and audits of stock exchanges. It regulates the activities of stock brokers and merchant bankers.

15. Statement I: Electronic holdings can be converted into physical certificates with the process of dematerialisation.

Statement II: There is no danger of theft, loss or forgery of share certificates in dematerialisation.

Choose the correct option from the following:

(A) Statement I is true and II is false
(B) Statement II is true and I is false
(C) Both the statements are true
(D) Both the statements are false U [SQP 2023-24]

Ans. Option (B) is correct.

Explanation: Dematerialisation is about converting physical share certificates into electronic holding so the first statement in incorrect.

16. Through which of the following methods of floatation can a company raise capital through an issuing house? R [CFPQ]

(A) Offer for sale (B) Private placement
(C) Right issue (D) E-IPOs

Ans. Option (A) is correct.

Explanation: Under offer for sale, securities are not issued directly to the public but are offered for sale through intermediaries like issuing houses or stock brokers. Private placement is the allotment of securities by a company to institutional investors and some selected individuals. Right Issue is a privilege given to existing shareholders to subscribe to a new issue of shares according to the terms and conditions of the company. A company proposing to issue capital to the public through the online system of the stock exchange has to enter into an agreement with the stock exchange. This is called an Initial Public Offer (IPO).

[B] Assertion & Reason

Directions: In the following questions, a statement of assertion (A) is followed by a statement of reason (R). Mark the correct choice as:

(A) Both assertion (A) and reason (R) are true and reason (R) is the correct explanation of assertion (A).
(B) Both assertion (A) and reason (R) are true but reason (R) is not the correct explanation of assertion (A).
(C) Assertion (A) is true but reason (R) is false.
(D) Assertion (A) is false but reason (R) is true.

1. Assertion (A): Activities in the money market are conducted over the telephone and through the internet.

Reason (R): The major participants in the market are the Reserve Bank of India (RBI), commercial banks, etc. [OEB]

Ans 1. Option (B) is correct.

Explanation: Money market has no physical location, but is an activity conducted over the telephone and through the internet. It enables the raising of short-term funds for meeting the temporary shortages of cash and obligations and the temporary deployment of excess funds for earning returns. The major participants in the market are the Reserve Bank of India (RBI), Commercial Banks, Non-Banking Finance Companies, State Governments, Large Corporate Houses and Mutual Funds.

2. Assertion (A): Secondary market helps existing investors to disinvest and fresh investors to enter the market.

Reason (R): Secondary market is a market for the purchase and sale of existing securities. [OEB]

3. Assertion (A): Stock exchange contributes to economic growth.

Reason (R): Through the process of disinvestment and reinvestment savings get channelised into their most productive investment avenues. [OEB]

These Questions are for practice and their solutions are given at the end of the chapter.

4. **Assertion (A):** Stock exchange is an unorganised market.

Reason (R): Stock exchange makes complete information available to public in regard to prices and volume of transactions taking place every day. [OEB]

Ans. Option (D) is correct.

Explanation: A stock exchange is organised as an association, a society or a company with a limited number of members. It is open only to these members who act as brokers for the buyers and sellers. The Securities Contract (Regulation) Act has defined stock exchange as an "association, organisation or body of individuals, whether incorporated or not, established for the purpose of assisting, regulating and controlling business of buying, selling and dealing in securities".

5. **Assertion (A):** Stock exchange provides safety to dealings and investment.

Reason (R): Transactions on the stock exchange are conducted only amongst its members with adequate transparency. [OEB]

6. **Assertion (A):** Government of India decided to set-up a separate regulatory body known as Securities and Exchange Board of India.

Reasoning (R): SEBI was set up to prevent trading malpractices and achieve a balance between self-regulation by the securities industry and its statutory regulation. [OEB]

7. **Assertion (A):** Controlling insider trading and imposing penalties for such practices is a protective function of a SEBI.

Reasoning (R): Registration of collective investment schemes and Mutual Funds is a development function of SEBI. [OEB]

Ans. Option (C) is correct.

Explanation: Registration of collective investment schemes and Mutual Funds are a regulatory function of SEBI. Regulatory functions involve establishment of rules and regulations for the financial intermediaries along with corporates that helps in efficient management of the market.

[C] Case Based MCQs

I. Read the following text and answer the questions given below:

"Unicon Securities Pvt. Ltd." was established to deal in securities. It was registered as a stockbroker with National Stock Exchange (NSE) and Bombay Stock Exchange (BSE) to trade in securities listed at these exchanges. It is also a depository participant with CDSL and NSDL. In the first three years, it developed its business successfully. After that, the composition of Board of Directors changed. Some customers complained to the customer care centre of the company that shares purchased by them and for which the payment has been duly made, were not transferred to their Demat Accounts by "Unicon Securities Pvt. Ltd.". The executive of customer care centre promised the aggrieved customers that their shares will be transferred to their respective Demat Accounts very soon. But the company delayed the matter and didn't transfer the shares of the customers to their Demat Accounts. This eroded investors' confidence and multiplied their grievances. On regular inspection and by conducting enquiries of the brokers involved, the Securities and Exchange Board of India (SEBI) was able to detect this irregularity. [OEB]

(i) Identify the step of trading procedure in a stock exchange which has not been followed by "Unicon Securities Pvt. Ltd.".

(A) Opening a Demat Account
(B) Placing the order
(C) Executing the order
(D) Settlement

Ans. Option (D) is correct.

Explanation: A T+2 rolling settlement cycle is followed in Indian stock market which means that transactions in securities are to be settled within 2 days after the trade date. Delivery of shares is made in dematerialised form and each exchange has its own clearing house which assumes all settlement risk.

(ii) Which apex statutory body of capital market inspected and conducted enquiries in order to detect irregularities?

(A) Stock exchange (B) Primary market
(C) Secondary market (D) SEBI

Ans. Option (D) is correct.

Explanation: SEBI was developed to create an environment to facilitate efficient mobilisation and allocation of resources through the securities markets. It also aims to stimulate competition and encourage innovation. This environment includes rules and regulations, institutions and their interrelationships, instruments, practices, infrastructure and policy framework.

(iii) By not converting and transferring the shares to the investors' Demat Account, i.e., electronic form, which process was not followed?

(A) Dematerialisation (B) Settlement
(C) Registration (D) Rematerialisation

Ans. Option (A) is correct.

Explanation: The process where securities held by the investor in the physical form are cancelled and the investor is given an electronic entry or number so that she/he can hold it as an electronic balance in an account. This process of holding securities in an electronic form is called dematerialisation. For this, the investor has to open a demat account with an organisation called a depository

(iv) Identify the function of SEBI being stated in paragraph.

(A) Development (B) Protective
(C) Regulatory (D) None of these

Ans. Option (C) is correct.

Explanation: Regulatory functions of SEBI include Registration of brokers and sub brokers and other players in the market, Registration of collective investment schemes and Mutual Funds, Regulation of stock brokers, portfolio exchanges, underwriters and merchant bankers and the business in stock exchanges and any other securities market,

These Questions are for practice and their solutions are given at the end of the chapter.

Regulation of takeover bids by companies, Calling for information by undertaking inspection, conducting enquiries and audits of stock exchanges and intermediaries etc.

II. Read the following text and answer questions on the basis of the same:

ISQAA SOLAR limited is searching options to raise ₹20,000 crores from the primary market for diversification and modernisation of existing projects. It hired the services of a renowned financial consultancy firm, DHAN LAXMI PVT. LTD. for suggesting options for the same. DHAN LAXMI PVT. LTD. suggested a list of options to the Board of Directors of the company. It was decided that for the immediate requirement of ₹1500 crores the company will give a privilege to existing shareholders to subscribe to a new issue of shares according to the terms and conditions of the company. ₹4500 crores would be raised by allotment of securities to a consortium of financial institutions, instead of inviting subscription from the public by making a direct appeal to investors to raise capital. It was further decided to raise capital to the tune of ₹6000 crores through an issuing house. All these options were accepted by the Board of Directors. The Board further decided to raise ₹8,000 crores through the on-line system of the stock exchange by entering into an agreement with the exchange. U [SQP 2020-21]

(i) Identify the method of floatation of new issues in the primary market, not taken up by ISQAA SOLAR LTD.

(A) Offer for sale
(B) Rights issue
(C) E-IPO
(D) Offer through prospectus

Ans. Option (D) is correct

(ii) "₹4500 crores would be raised by allotment of securities to a consortium of financial institutions, instead of inviting subscription from the public by making a direct appeal to investors to raise capital." Identify the method of floatation of new issues in the primary market being discussed above, which the company has decided to use.

(A) Offer for sale
(B) Private placement
(C) Right issue
(D) Offer through prospectus

Ans. Option (B) is correct.

(iii) Identify the reason which has made the firm raise funds from the institutional investors.

(A) It helps to raise funds quickly
(B) It is not expensive
(C) Both A & B
(D) None of the above.

Ans. Option (C) is correct.

(iv) How much money was raised by the company through E-IPO's

(A) ₹8000 crores (B) ₹4500 crores
(C) ₹20,000 crores (D) ₹6000 crores

Ans. Option (A) is correct.

SOLUTIONS FOR PRACTICE QUESTIONS (TOPIC-2)

SATQs-I

Ans 4. The basic function of a stock exchange is the creation of a continuous market where securities are bought and sold. It gives investors the chance to disinvest and reinvest. This provides both liquidity and easy marketability to already existing securities in the market.

SATQs-II

Ans 2. First four steps:

(i) Selecting the Broker: Investors choose a brokerage firm based on factors such as reputation, services offered, and fees.

(ii) Opening the Demat Account: Investors establish a Demat account with a Depository Participant (DP) to hold securities electronically, replacing the traditional paper-based share certificates.

(iii) Placing the Order: Investors instruct their chosen broker to buy or sell securities, specifying details such as quantity, price, and type of order (e.g., market order or limit order).

(iv) Connecting to the Stock Exchange: The broker connects to the stock exchange electronically, where the order is matched with potential buyers or sellers in the market.

SOLUTIONS FOR PRACTICE QUESTIONS (TOPIC-3)

SATQs-I

Ans 2. Development Functions of Securities and Exchange Board of India:

(i) Training of intermediaries of the securities market.

(ii) Conducting research and publishing information useful to all market participants.

(iii) Undertaking measures to develop the capital markets by adapting a flexible approach.

[SQP Marking Scheme, 2021] **[1 × 3 = 3]**

SATQs-II

Ans 2. Protective functions of SEBI:

(i) It prohibits fraudulent and unfair trade practices like misleading statements, manipulations, price rigging, etc.

(ii) It controls insider trading and imposes penalties for such practices.

(iii) It undertakes steps for investor protection.

(iv) It promotes fair practices and code of conduct in securities market.

(If an examinee has given only the headings, ½ mark for each heading should be awarded)

[Marking Scheme, 2018] **[1×4=4]**

Commonly Made Error

 Students write the functions of SEBI but overlook the term, 'protective'.

Answering Tip

 Learn SEBI's functions with the help of chart or diagram under headings of: 'Protective, Regulatory and Development'.

LATQs

Ans 3. Objectives of SEBI are:

(i) To **regulate stock exchanges and the securities** industry to promote their orderly functioning.

(ii) To **protect the rights and interests** of the investors, particularly individual investors and to guide and educate them.

(iii) To **prevent trading malpractices** and achieve a balance between self-regulation and statutory regulation.

(iv) To **regulate and develop a code of conduct and** fair practices by intermediaries like brokers, merchant bankers, etc. with a view to making them competitive and professional.

(v) To provide a market place in which the issuers can raise finances in an easy, fair and efficient manner.

(vi) To **create an environment to facilitate efficient** mobilisation and allocation of resources. **[1 × 6 = 6]**

SOLUTIONS FOR OBJECTIVE PRACTICE QUESTIONS

[A] MCQs

Ans. 14. Option (C) is correct.

Explanation: SEBI prevents trading malpractices and achieve a balance between self regulation by the securities industry and its statutory regulation. SEBI regulates and develops a code of conduct and fair practices by intermediaries like brokers, merchant bankers etc., with a view to making them competitive and professional.

[B] A & R

Ans 2. Option (A) is correct.

Explanation: The secondary market is also known as the stock market or stock exchange. It is a market for the purchase and sale of existing securities. It helps existing investors to disinvest and fresh investors to enter the market. It also provides liquidity and marketability to existing securities. It also contributes to economic growth by channelising funds towards the most productive investments through the process of disinvestment and reinvestment.

Ans 3. Option (A) is correct.

Explanation: Stock exchange offers a platform for trading of securities of the various companies. This process of trading involves continuous disinvestment and reinvestment, which offers opportunities for capital formation and subsequently, growth of the economy. A stock exchange is a market in which existing securities are resold or traded. Through this process of disinvestment and reinvestment savings get channelised into their most productive investment avenues. This leads to capital formation and economic growth.

Ans 5. Option (A) is correct.

Explanation: Transactions on the stock exchange are conducted only amongst its members with adequate transparency and in strict conformity to its rules and regulations which include the procedure and timings of delivery and payment to be followed. This provides a high degree of safety to dealings at the stock exchange. There is little risk of loss on account of non-payment or non-delivery.

Ans 6. Option (A) is correct.

Explanation: Many malpractices started taking place such as rigging of prices, non-adherence of provisions of the Companies Act, violation of rules and regulations of stock exchanges, etc. Due to these malpractices, people started losing confidence in the stock market. The government felt a sudden need to set up an authority to regulate the working and reduce these malpractices. As a result, the Government came up with the establishment of SEBI.

REFLECTION

(a) Were you able to explain the concept of financial market?

(b) Were you able to explain the concept of money market?

(c) Could you differentiate between capital market and money market?

(d) Were you able to explain the meaning of primary and secondary markets as types of capital market.

(e) Could you distinguish between primary and secondary markets?

(f) Could you identify the function of a stock exchange in the below mentioned line:
"Through this process of disinvestment and reinvestment savings get channelised into their most productive investment avenues"

(g) Could you identify the function of a SEBI in the below mentioned line:
"Undertaking measures to develop the capital markets by adapting a flexible approach.

SELF ASSESSMENT PAPER - 10

Maximum Time: 1 hour **MM: 30**

General Instructions:

(i) All the questions are compulsory

(ii) Q.1 to Q.10 are 1 mark questions

(3) Q.11 to Q.12 are 3 mark questions

(iv) Q.13 to Q.14 are 4 marks questions

(v) Q.15 is a 6 marks question

Objective Type Questions [1 Mark]

1. A financial market helps to link the savers and the investors by mobilising funds between them. In doing so it performs what is known as a/an:

(A) Allocative function **(B)** Production function **(C)** Speculative function **(D)** None of these [1]

2. Match the options of Column I with their correct options given in Column II.

	Column I		Column II
(1)	Regulatory Function	(a)	Regulation of takeover bids by companies.
(2)	Development Function	(b)	Training of intermediaries of the securities market
(3)	Protective Function	(c)	Undertaking steps for investor protection.

(A) a – i, b – ii, c – iii **(B)** a – ii, b – iii, c – i **(C)** a – iii, b – i, c – ii **(D)** None of these [1]

3.

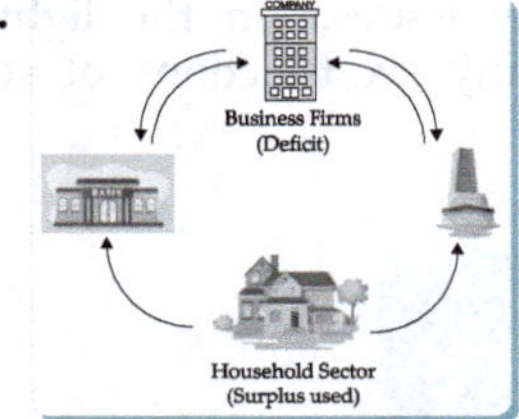

Identify the mechanism illustrated in the picture above.

(A) Financial market **(B)** Money market

(C) Capital market **(D)** None of these

4. Advances in information technology have made trading through ____________ accessible from anywhere in the country through trading terminals.

(A) SEBI **(B)** Stock exchanges

(C) Primary market **(D)** None of these [1]

5. For the following two statements, choose the correct option:

Statement I: Stock exchange ensures safety of transaction.

Statement II: The efficient functioning of a stock exchange creates a conducive climate for the primary market.

Choose the correct option from options given below:

(A) Statement I is correct and statement II is wrong.

(B) Statement II is correct and statement I is wrong.

(C) Both the statements are correct.

(D) Both the statements are wrong. [1]

6. For the following two statements, choose the correct option:

Statement I: A stock exchange has its main computer system with many terminals spread across the country.

Statement II: Trading in securities is done through brokers who are members of the stock exchange.

Choose the correct option from options given below:

(A) Statement I is correct and statement II is wrong.

(B) Statement II is correct and statement I is wrong.

(C) Both the statements are correct.

(D) Both the statements are wrong. [1]

Read the text given below and answer Q. 7–10 based on it.

Atul Agarwal is one of the directors of Malto Ltd. The company is engaged in the real estate sector, which has recently witnessed a steady fall in its revenue and the value of its assets due to a downward trend persisting in the market in specific and the economy in general. The periodical financial results of the company were to be declared in a fortnight time. Atul Agarwal, being an insider, had access to unpublished price sensitive information related to it. Consequently, he sells a major portion of his holdings in an anticipation of a fall in the market price of the shares of the Company subsequent to the announcement of periodical financial results of the company. Moreover, he doesn't inform the Securities and Exchange Commission (SEC) about the dealings.

On conducting a probe, Securities and Exchange Board of India (SEBI) finds Atul Agarwal guilty of insider trading. As per law, company directors, officials or any individual with a stake of 10% or more in the company are considered to be insiders and they are required to report their insider transactions within two business days of the date the transaction occurred.

7. The Securities and Exchange Board of India was established by the Government of India on 12 April, 1988 as an _______________.

(A) Administrative body **(B)** Statutory body

(C) Regulatory body **(D)** None of these [1]

8. Identify the type of function performed by SEBI in the below mentioned line:

"On conducting a probe Securities and Exchange Board of India (SEBI) finds Atul Agarwal guilty of insider trading." **[1]**

(A) Development **(B)** Regulatory
(C) Protective **(D)** None of these

9. Which of the following is the development function of SEBI?

(A) Training of intermediaries of the securities market.
(B) Conducting research and publishing information
(C) Undertaking measures to develop the capital markets
(D) All of the above **[1]**

10. The overall objective of SEBI is to protect the interests of:

(A) Suppliers **(B)** Investors
(C) Debtors **(D)** Creditors **[1]**

Short Answer Type Questions - I [3 Marks]

11. 'White Milk' owned by the Vikas Goel, is one of the leading manufacturers and marketers of dairy-based branded foods in India. In the initial years, its operations were restricted only to collection and distribution of milk. But, over the years it has gained a reasonable market share by offering a diverse range of dairy based products including fresh milk, flavoured yogurt, ice creams, butter milk, cheese, ghee, milk powders, etc. In order to raise capital to finance its expansion plans, the company has decided to approach capital market. The company has also decided to raise capital through the primary market in the form of equity shares, preference shares, debentures, loans and deposits.

Identify and explain the segment of capital market being approached by the company.

12. 'To promote orderly and healthy growth of securities market and protection of investors, SEBI was set up'. With reference to this statement, explain the objectives of SEBI.

Short Answer Type Questions - II [4 Marks]

13. A company wanted to raise funds so it reached out to facilities an institutional arrangement through which long term funds (debt + equity) were raised and invested. A lot of thinking was done whether the company should have gone for debt or equity. Finally, it decided to go for equity. The owner of the company decided to follow the guidelines of SEBI. Identify and explain the concept of financial market is highlighted in the starting of the case?

14. "A financial market helps to link the savers and the investors by mobilising funds between them." In the light of this statement explain the concept of financial market.

Long Answer Type Questions [6 Marks]

15. "The efficient functioning of a stock exchange creates a conducive climate for an active and growing primary market for new issues." In the light of this statement explain any six functions of stock exchange.

MARKETING

Scan this topic

Marketing

LEARNING OUTCOMES

After going through this chapter, the student would be able to:

- Understand the concept of marketing.
- Explain the features of marketing.
- Discuss the functions of marketing.
- Explain the marketing philosophies.
  Understand the concept of marketing mix.
- Describe the elements of marketing mix.
- Understand the concept of product as an element of marketing mix.
- Understand the concept of branding, labelling and packaging.
- Understand the concept of price as an element of marketing mix.
- Describe the factors determining price of a product.
- Understand the concept of physical distribution.
- Explain the components of physical distribution.
- Describe the various channels of distribution.
- Understand the concept of promotion as an element of marketing mix.
- Describe the elements of promotion mix.
- Understand the concept of advertising.
- Understand the concept of sales promotion.
- Discuss the concept of public relations.

Study Plan

Maximum Time = 3.45 Hrs

Maximum Questions = 82

LIST OF TOPICS

TOPIC-1 Marketing Concept, Functions and Philosophies

Concepts Covered

- Meaning, Features and Functions of marketing, • **Marketing philosophies:** The Production concept, The Product concept, The Selling concept, The Marketing concept, The Societal marketing concept.

Revision Notes

Scan this

Marketing

- **Marketing:** It refers to identifying a group of potential customers and finding out ways to convince them to buy the company's product.
- **Marketing Management:** It refers to planning, organising, directing and controlling the activities which facilitate exchange of goods and services to achieve the organisational objectives.
- **Features of Marketing**

(i) Identifying needs and wants of customers
(ii) Creating market offering
(iii) Developing customer value
(iv) Providing exchange mechanism

- **Functions of Marketing** [Board, 2023]

(i) Gathering and analysing market information
(ii) Market planning
(iii) Product designing and development
(iv) Standardisation and grading
(v) Packaging and labelling
(vi) Branding
(vii) Customer support services
(viii) Pricing of products
(ix) Promotion
(x) Physical distribution
(xi) Transportation
(xii) Storage or Warehousing

Marketing Management Philosophies:

Scan this

Marketing Management Philosophies

- **The Production Concept:** Production concept lays emphasis on availability and affordability of products.
- **The Product Concept:** Product concept lays emphasis on 'quality of production' rather than 'quantity of production'.
- **The Selling Concept:** This concept stresses on attracting and persuading customers to buy the product by making aggressive selling and promotional efforts.
- **The Marketing Concept:** According to this concept, customer satisfaction is the key to organisational success.
- **The Societal Marketing Concept:** The societal marketing concept is the extension of the marketing concept as supplemented by the concern for the long-term welfare of the society.

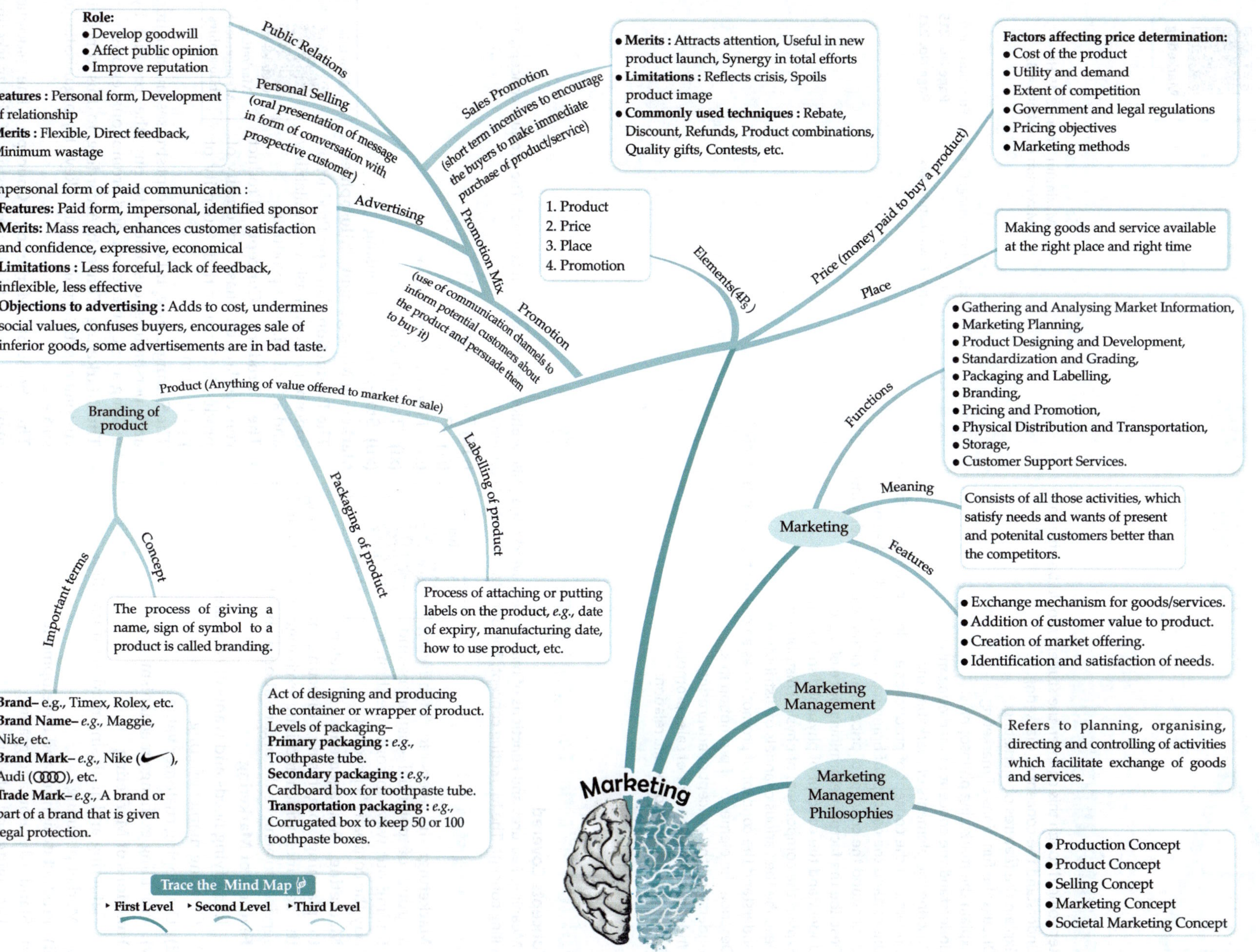
Marketing
Marketing
Meaning
Consists of all those activities, which satisfy needs and wants of present and potenital customers better than the competitors.
Features
• Exchange mechanism for goods/services.
• Addition of customer value to product.
• Creation of market offering.
• Identification and satisfaction of needs.
Functions
• Gathering and Analysing Market Information,
• Marketing Planning,
• Product Designing and Development,
• Standardization and Grading,
• Packaging and Labelling,
• Branding,
• Pricing and Promotion,
• Physical Distribution and Transportation,
• Storage,
• Customer Support Services.
Marketing Management
Refers to planning, organising, directing and controlling of activities which facilitate exchange of goods and services.
Marketing Management Philosophies
• Production Concept
• Product Concept
• Selling Concept
• Marketing Concept
• Societal Marketing Concept
Elements(4Ps)
1. Product
2. Price
3. Place
4. Promotion
Price (money paid to buy a product)
Factors affecting price determination:
• Cost of the product
• Utility and demand
• Extent of competition
• Government and legal regulations
• Pricing objectives
• Marketing methods
Place
Making goods and service available at the right place and right time
Promotion
(use of communication channels to inform potential customers about the product and persuade them to buy it)
Promotion Mix
Sales Promotion
(short term incentives to encourage the buyers to make immediate purchase of product/service)
• Merits : Attracts attention, Useful in new product launch, Synergy in total efforts
• Limitations : Reflects crisis, Spoils product image
• Commonly used techniques : Rebate, Discount, Refunds, Product combinations, Quality gifts, Contests, etc.
Public Relations
Role:
• Develop goodwill
• Affect public opinion
• Improve reputation
Personal Selling
(oral presentation of message in form of conversation with prospective customer)
• Features : Personal form, Development of relationship
• Merits : Flexible, Direct feedback, Minimum wastage
Advertising
Impersonal form of paid communication :
• Features: Paid form, impersonal, identified sponsor
• Merits: Mass reach, enhances customer satisfaction and confidence, expressive, economical
• Limitations : Less forceful, lack of feedback, inflexible, less effective
• Objections to advertising : Adds to cost, undermines social values, confuses buyers, encourages sale of inferior goods, some advertisements are in bad taste.
Product (Anything of value offered to market for sale)
Labelling of product
Process of attaching or putting labels on the product, e.g., date of expiry, manufacturing date, how to use product, etc.
Packaging of product
Act of designing and producing the container or wrapper of product.
Levels of packaging–
Primary packaging : e.g., Toothpaste tube.
Secondary packaging : e.g., Cardboard box for toothpaste tube.
Transportation packaging : e.g., Corrugated box to keep 50 or 100 toothpaste boxes.
Branding of product
Concept
The process of giving a name, sign of symbol to a product is called branding.
Important terms
Brand– e.g., Timex, Rolex, etc.
Brand Name– e.g., Maggie, Nike, etc.
Brand Mark– e.g., Nike ( ), Audi ( ), etc.
Trade Mark– e.g., A brand or part of a brand that is given legal protection.
Trace the Mind Map
First Level
Second Level
Third Level

KEY TERMS

Marketing Management Philosophy: Thinking that should guide the marketing efforts of an organisation.
Product: An article or substance offered for sale.

MNEMONICS

Concept: Features of Marketing:
Mnemonics: DIP in Cream
Interpretations:
D: Developing customer value
I: Identifying needs and wants of customers
P: Providing exchange mechanism
C: Creating market offering
Concept: Functions of Marketing
Mnemonics: Go to Market When Brother Comes from school and Party 5 times
Interpretations:
G: Gathering and analysing market information
T: Transportation
M: Market planning
W: Warehousing
B: Branding
C: Customer support services
S: Standardisation and grading
P: Product designing and development
P: Packaging and labelling
P: Pricing of products
P: Promotion
P: Physical distribution
Concept: Marketing Management Philosophies:
Mnemonics: Please Pay Money soon Son
Interpretations:
P: Product concept
P: Production concept
M: Marketing concept
S: Societal Marketing concept
S: Selling concept

SUBJECTIVE TYPE QUESTIONS

Short Answer Type Questions-I (3 marks each)

1. Ginika, Tanish and Rohit were friends from college days and now they are doing different kinds of business. They regularly meet and discuss their business ideas and exchange notes on customer satisfaction, marketing efforts, product designing, selling techniques, social concerns etc. In one of such meetings, Ginika drew the attention of Tanish and Rohit towards the exploitation of consumers. She said that most of the sellers were exploiting the consumers in various ways and were not paying attention towards the social, ethical and ecological aspects of marketing, whereas she was not doing so. Tanish said that they were under pressure to satisfy the consumers, but stated that the consumers would not buy or not buy enough unless they were adequately convinced and motivated for the same. Rohit stressed that a company cannot achieve its objectives without understanding the needs of the customers. It was the duty of the businessmen to keep consumer satisfaction in mind because business is run by the resources made available to them by the society. He further stated that he himself was taking into consideration the needs of the customers.

Identify the various types of thinking that guided Ginika, Tanish and Rohit in the marketing efforts of business. Also, state one more feature of the various types of thinking identified that is not given in the above para. AI A [Delhi Set-1, 2017]

Ans. Various types of thinking that guided the marketing efforts were :

Ginika

Societal Marketing concept

Feature of Societal marketing concept :

(i) It takes care of long-term well-being of the consumers as well as the society.

(ii) It uses integrated marketing as a means to achieve the objective.

(iii) Its objective is to earn profits through customer satisfaction and social welfare.

(iv) The marketing efforts start from the identification of needs of the target market and the society. **[1]**

Tanish:

Selling concept

Feature of Selling concept:

(i) It uses aggressive selling and promotional techniques like advertising, personal selling and sales promotion to achieve the objective.

(ii) It involves pushing the sale of existing products.

(iii) Its objective is to earn profits through increased volume of sales.

(iv) The marketing efforts start after the product is produced in the factory. **(Any one) [1]**

Rohit

Marketing concept

Feature of Marketing concept:

(i) It involves development of products for satisfying needs of the target market better than the competitors.

(ii) Its focus is on satisfaction of customer's needs.

(iii) It uses integrated marketing as a means to achieve the objective.

(iv) The marketing efforts start from the identification of needs of the target market. **(Any one) [1]**

[Marking Scheme, Delhi 2017]

(Any one)

2. Mohit was a pen manufacturer. He used to make ball point pens in a small factory in the basement of his house. Daily he would go to the market place and distribute pens to the retailers. Some of the pens were sold by him of his own by meeting persons on road. He had not kept any name for his pens. They were just blue, black and red pens. One of his friends suggested him to keep a good name of his pens. He kept Roloxo as a name and started selling pens. Gradually his business started to pick up even more and he made good revenue. Identify and explain the function of marketing highlighted in the above case. A [OEB]

Concept Applied | Concept of Branding

Ans. The function of marketing highlighted in the above case is **Branding**. Selection of the brand name plays an important role in the success of a product. Brand name helps in creating product differentiation, i.e., providing basis for distinguishing the product of a firm with that of the competitor, which in turn, helps in building **customer's loyalty** and in **promoting its sale**. The important decision areas in respect of branding include deciding the branding strategy, say whether each product will be given a separate brand name or the same brand name will be extended to all products of the company. **[3]**

Commonly Made Error

Most of students identify the function 'Branding' correctly. However, students do not write the explanation of branding correctly. They mix up the content with brand name, brand mark and trade mark.

Answering Tip

Emphasis should be laid upon the terms branding, brand name, brand mark and trade mark while learning the content.

3. W10 planet are the leading manufacturers of scooty and scooters in the industry. They have the first mover advantage in the industry. When they started manufacturing scooty and scooters, no other company was doing it. They manufacture scooters and the middle class purchases them in a high number. With each passing year the number of scooters sold is increasing. The company's main concern usually is to produce maximum number of scooty and scooters. Company's profit is governed by the maximum number of scooty and scooters they produce. Identify and explain the marketing management philosophy mentioned in the above case. U [OEB]

Ans. Marketing management philosophy mentioned in the above case is **production concept**. Production concept lays emphasis on **availability and affordability of products**. Under this concept, the focus of business activities was on the production of goods. It was believed that profits could be maximised by producing at large scale, thereby reducing the average cost of production. It was also assumed that consumers would favour those products which were **widely available at an affordable price**. Thus, availability and affordability of the product were considered to be the key to the success of a firm. Therefore, greater emphasis was placed on improving the production and distribution efficiency of the firms.

Commonly Made Error

Most students write the 'product marketing philosophy' instead of 'production marketing philosophy'.

Answering Tip

Learn the different marketing philosophies using key words with proper examples.

Short Answer Type Questions-II (4 marks each)

1. What is meant by 'Production Concept' of marketing? U [OEB]

Ans. Production Concept: Production concept of marketing philosophy believes that customers are interested only in the **low-priced products**, easily and **extensively available goods** and finer points of the product are not very important to them. Hence, producers believe that they must concentrate only on efficient and extensive production. The idea is to maximise profits by producing on a large scale, thereby reducing the average cost of production. Availability and affordability of the product were considered to be the key to the success of a firm. A company which believes in this approach, concentrates and achieves high production efficiency and wide distribution coverage, resulting in lower cost of production.

2. Explain the following functions of marketing:
(i) Product designing and development;
(ii) Standardisation and Grading

U **[Delhi Set-1, 2019]**

3. Explain the following functions of marketing:
(i) Marketing planning;
(ii) Customer support services. U **[Delhi Set-2, 2019]**

Ans. (i) Marketing planning

(a) Marketing planning involves **development of marketing plans** to achieve the marketing objectives of the organisation.

(b) A complete marketing plan will include important aspects like increasing the level of production, promotion of the products, etc.

This Question is for practice and its solution is given at the end of the chapter.

(ii) Customer support services

(a) Customer support services include services like after sales services, handling customer complaints and adjustments, maintenance services, technical services, etc.

(b) These services are **very effective in bringing repeat sales** from the customers and developing brand loyalty for a product. **[2+2=4]**

[Marking Scheme, Delhi 2019]

4. 'Time Line' watch manufacturing company is a renowned company marketing watches. It performs various activities like, market analysis, product designing or merchandising, packaging, warehousing, branding, pricing, promotion and selling. The company maintains good customer relations through various follow up activities. This helps the company in procuring repeat sales orders.

(i) Name and explain the concept related to the activities mentioned in the above paragraph.

(ii) Explain any two features of the concept identified in part (i). A [SQP 2016-17]

Concept Applied	Concept and features of marketing

Ans. (i) Marketing: Marketing is a social process wherein people interact with others, in order to persuade them to act in a particular way, say to purchase a product or a service, rather than forcing them to do so.

(ii) Features of marketing:

(a) Need and wants: Marketing is a customer-oriented process. So, marketing activities should be oriented towards identification of needs and wants of the present and potential customers and develop products and services that satisfy such needs and wants. The process of marketing helps individuals and groups in obtaining what they need and want. Thus, the primary reason or motivation for people to engage in the process of marketing is to **satisfy some of their needs or wants.** In other words, the focus of the marketing process is on satisfaction of the needs and wants of individuals and organisations.

(b) Creating market offering: Market offering refers to a complete offer for a product or service, having given features like size, quality, taste, etc; at a certain price; available at a given outlet or location and so on. A good "market offer" is one which is developed after **analysing the needs and preferences** of the potential buyers.

(c) Customer value: The process of marketing facilitates exchange of products and services between the buyers and the sellers. The buyers, however, make buying decisions on their **perceptions of the value** of the product or service in satisfying their need, in relation to its cost. A product will be purchased only if it is perceived to be giving greatest benefit or value for the money. The job of a marketer, therefore, is to **add to the value of the product** so that the customers prefer it in relation to the competing products and decide to purchase it.

(d) Exchange mechanism: The process of marketing works through the **exchange mechanism.** The individuals (buyers and sellers) obtain what they need and want through the process of exchange. In other words, the process of marketing involves exchange of products and services for money or something considered valuable by the people. Exchange refers to the process through which two or more parties come together to obtain the desired product or service from someone, offering the same by giving something in return. **(Any two) [1+3=4]**

Long Answer Type Questions (6 marks each)

1. 'Maharana' is a famous take-away food outlet in Meerut. It is quite popular among local people and travellers on the national highway.

It offers a wide variety of 'paranthas' and 'sandwiches' packed in special containers which are designed and developed by them to keep the food hot and fresh. Considering the tough competition in the nearby area, the prices have been set reasonably low. The owner Nirmal Singh spends huge sums of money to put large hoardings and kiosks in the vicinity, to inform the people about the outlet's location and the special items on its menu.

The firm is performing various marketing functions to achieve its marketing objectives.

On the basis of the information given in the above case identify and explain any three marketing functions. [Outside Delhi Set-1, 2023]

Ans. Marketing Functions (any three):

(i) Branding– Branding is the process of giving a name or sign or a symbol to a product which helps in identifying and distinguishing it from the competitor's products.

(ii) Packaging– Packaging refers to designing and developing the package for the products. It is important not only for protection of the products but also serves as a promotional tool.

(iii) Pricing of Product– Price of product refers to the amount of money customers have to pay to obtain a product. Generally, lower the price, higher would be demand for the product and vice versa.

(iv) Promotion – Promotion of products involves informing the customers about the firm's product, its features, etc. and persuading them to purchase these products. The methods of promotion include advertising, personal selling, public relations and sales promotion. **(Any three) 2 × 3 = 6**

2. Choco Ltd. offers a wide variety of chocolate products. It has an action program of not selling its

products by their generic name but under different names like Choco-silk bar, Choco-Munchy and Choco-crunchy etc. for different customer segments. All these names have great popularity and acceptability in the markets. As the company policy the products were offered at reasonable and affordable prices for targeting a mass customer base. During the festive season the company launched a massive promotional campaign to increase its revenue and achieve its communication objectives. The company introduced free gifts for the customers. Their on-ground sales team delivers the product not only to the departmental stores but also to small shops, so that all segments of customers can easily get the products. They also provide information and support services to customers to ensure repeat sales. From the viewpoint of the management function, briefly explain any four activities of marketing which the firm will be involved in, apart from the above-mentioned ones it's already performing.

[SQP 2022-23]

Ans. Functions of marketing, apart from the ones Choco Ltd is already performing:

1. **Gathering and analysing market information:** This is necessary to identify the **needs of the customers** and make various decisions for the successful marketing of the products and services. This is important for making an analysis of the available opportunities and threats as well as strengths and weaknesses of the organisation and help in deciding what opportunities can best be pursued by it.
2. **Product designing and development:** The design of the product contributes to **making the product attractive to the target customers**. A good design can improve performance of a product and give it a competitive advantage in the market.
3. **Standardisation:** Standardisation refers to producing goods of **predetermined specifications** which help in achieving uniformity and consistency in the output
4. **Packaging and labelling:** Packaging refers to **designing and developing the package** for the products. Labelling refers to **designing and developing the label** to be put on the product.
5. **Transportation:** Transportation involves physical movement of goods from one place to another. As generally the users of products particularly consumer products are **wide spread and geographically separated** from the place where they are produced.
6. **Storage and warehousing:** In order to maintain smooth flow of products in the market, there is a need for proper storage of the products. Further there is need for storage of **adequate stock of goods to protect against unavoidable delays** in delivery or to meet out contingencies in the demand. Ram Kumar the CEO of Sabarmati Enterprises in a meeting with the middle management of the company advised that the personal goals of the people should be reconciled with the organisational objectives for harmony in the organisation. Briefly explain the objective of management that he was referring to.

(Any four)

3. Read the statements given in point 1 and 2, answer the questions that follow: **[SQP 2023-24]**

(i) Tea is produced in Assam but is carried to customers not only in this state but also in other parts of the country.

(a) Identify and explain the function of marketing that enables the marketer to achieve its goals.

(b) Enumerate any two factors that marketer should take into consideration in order to analyse the identified needs.

(ii) Paddy is grown during summer season but its demand and sale takes place throughout the year.

(a) Name and state the function of marketing which should be undertaken to reduce the gap between production and consumption of Paddy.

(b) State by giving two reasons as to why proper discharge of this function is important.

Ans. Concept Applied- Functions of Marketing

(i) (a) The function of marketing that enables the marketer to achieve its goals is **Transportation**.

It involves physical movement of goods from one place to another. Since the user of products are wide spread and geographically separated from the place where they are produced it is necessary to move them to the place where they are needed for consumption.

(b) The factors that should be taken into consideration to analyse the marketing needs are nature of the product, and cost and location of target market.

(ii) (a) The function of marketing that reduces the gap between production and consumption of paddy is Storage or **Warehousing**.

Due to irregular demand or supply, there may be time gap between production of goods and their sale. Storage helps in reducing the time gap between production and consumption and provides time utility.

(b) Importance of warehousing:

(i) To ensure smooth flow of products in the market

(ii) To protect against any unavoidable delays in delivery or meet contingencies in demand.

4. Atul is a manager in a company which deals in manufacturing chocolate and chocolate products. The company sells chocolates by the brand 'Milky White'. His main area of focus is to generate revenue for the company through repeated sales. He decides to develop a product for the company which can generate revenue in the long run. For this he meets a team of R&D (Research & Development) of his company. After a long meeting they decide to do survey. Based on the survey a product is made to fulfil needs of the customers. The product later produces a lot of revenue through repeated sales in the long run. To generate more revenue, the company wants to go global and has entered a foreign country. It has found that the youth is going to be the appropriate section of society to be targeted. Atul has a vision for the company for another 10 years to make its mark in the market. The major challenge would be to beat the existing chocolates selling companies by giving chocolates of better taste so that the existing young buyers

could make 'Milky White' as their favourite brand. The company is quite clear about its objectives. It has decided to make a net profit of at least ₹100 crores in its first year and later on it would like to increase this profit with passing years. Definitely the vision of the company is quite clear.

(i) Identify and explain the marketing philosophy described in the above case.

(ii) Also state any four pillars of the marketing philosophy concept discussed in the above case.

A [OEB]

Ans. (i) The marketing philosophy described in the above case is **marketing concept.** **[1]**

Marketing orientation implies that focus on **satisfaction of customer's needs** is the key to the success of any organisation in the market. It assumes that in the long run an organisation can achieve its objective of **maximisation of profit** by identifying the **needs of its present and prospective buyers** and satisfying them in an effective way. All the decisions in a firm are taken from the point of view of the customers. In other words, **customer's satisfaction** become the focal point of all decision making in the organisation. **[1]**

(ii) The marketing concept is based on the following pillars:

(a) Identification of market or customer who are chosen as the target of marketing effort.

(b) Understanding needs and wants of customers in the target market.

(c) Development of products or services for satisfying needs of the target market.

(d) Satisfying needs of target market better than the competitors.

(e) Doing all this at a profit. **(Any four) [4]**

TOPIC-2 Marketing Mix

Concepts Covered:

- Meaning of marketing mix.
- Elements (4P's) of marketing mix - Product, Price, Physical Distribution, and Promotion.
- Concept of branding, labelling and packaging.
- Factors determining price of a product.
- Components of physical distribution.
- Various channels of physical distribution.
- Elements of promotion mix - Advertising, Personal Selling, Sales Promotion and Public Relations.

Revision Notes

- The Marketing manager concentrates on four major decision areas while planning the marketing activities, namely, (i) product, (ii) price, (iii) place (distribution), and (iv) promotion. These 4 'P's are called elements of marketing and together they constitute the **marketing mix**.
- **Product:** Product means goods or services or 'anything of value', which is offered to the market for sale.
- The explanation for price, promotion and place is mentioned below after the explanation of product is done.

Example: Hindustan lever offers number of consumer products like toiletries (Close-Up toothpaste, Lifebuoy soap, etc.), detergent powder (Surf, Wheel), food products (Refined Vegetable Oil); Tata offers Tata Steel, Trucks, Salt and a large number of other products; LG Electronics offers televisions, refrigerators, colour monitors for computers, etc; Amul offers a number of food products (Amul milk, ghee, butter, cheese, chocolates, etc.).

Important decisions related to a Product

- Brand: It is a name, term, sign, symbol, design or any combination used to differentiate product from its competitors. Its components are:

I. Branding: It is a process of giving a name or a sign or a symbol to a product.

(i) Brand name: Verbal component of a brand.

Example: Asian Paints, Safola, Maggie, Lifebuoy, Dunlop, and Uncle Chips are the brand names.

(ii) Brand mark: Recognised in the form of symbol, colour, etc. but non-utterable.

Example: swoosh of Nike or Devil of Onida or symbol of Yogkshma of LIC or Yellow smile of Amazon

(iii) Trade mark: A brand or part of a brand that is given legal protection is called trademark.

A good brand name should be easy to pronounce, suggestive, distinctive, flexible, versatile, legally registered and permanent.

II. Packaging: It is the art of designing and producing the container or the wrapper of a product.

Levels of Packaging

(i) Primary package: It refers to product's immediate container.

(ii) Secondary package: It refers to an additional layer of protection, kept till the product is ready to use.

(iii) Transportation package: It refers to further packaging components necessary for storage and transportation of the product.

- **Functions of Packaging**

(i) Product identification

(ii) Product protection

(iii) Facilitating use of the product

(iv) Product promotion

III. Labelling: Labelling refers to designing and developing the label to be put on the package.

Label: Labels are useful in providing detailed information about the product, its contents, method of use, etc.

- **Functions of Labelling**

(i) Describe the product and specify its contents.

(ii) Identify the product or the brand.

(iii) Helps in grading of the products.

(iv) Helps in promotion of the products.

(v) Provides information required by law.

- **Price:** It is the amount paid by a buyer or received by a seller in consideration of the purchase/sale of a product.

- **Factors affecting Price determination**

(i) Product cost
(ii) Utility and demand
(iii) Extent of competition in the market
(iv) Government and legal regulations
(v) Pricing objectives
(vi) Marketing methods used

- **Physical Distribution:** It is concerned with making the goods and services available at the right place, so that people can purchase the same.
- **Components of Physical Distribution:** (i) Order Processing (ii) Transportation (iii) Warehousing (iv) Inventory Control **[2023]**
- **Channels of physical Distribution:**

(i) **Direct Channel (Zero Level):** Goods are made directly available by the manufacturers to customers, without involving any intermediary.

(ii) Manufacturer-Retailer–Consumer **(One Level Channel):** In this form of arrangement one intermediary *i.e.*, retailers is used between the manufacturers and the customers.

(iii) Manufacturer-Wholesaler-Retailer-Consumer **(Two Level Channel):** Here the wholesaler and retailer function as connecting links between the manufacturer and consumer.

(iv) Manufacturer-Agent-Wholesaler-Retailer-Consumer **(Three Level Channel):** In this case, manufacturers use their own selling agents or brokers who connect them with wholesalers and then the retailers.

- **Promotion mix:** It refers to a combination of tools used to communicate with potential customers to inform them about a product and persuade them to buy it.
- **Elements of a Promotion Mix**

I. **Advertising:** It is an impersonal form of communication which is paid by the marketers to promote goods or services.

II. **Personal Selling:** It involves face-to-face contact between seller and the prospective customer for effecting a sale.

III. **Sales Promotion:** It refers to short-term incentives, offered to encourage immediate sale of the product.

IV. **Public Relations:** It involves activities required to promote and protect the image of a company or its product.

MNEMONICS

Concept: Elements of Promotion Mix:
Mnemonics: Special People Act Smartly
Interpretations:
A: Advertising
P: Personal Selling
S: Sales Promotion
P: Public Relations

SUBJECTIVE TYPE QUESTIONS

Short Answer Type Questions-I (3 marks each)

1. A chocolate manufacturing company has started a campaign where it will be going to different schools during the class timings. During this time free samples of chocolate will be distributed to the students and the teachers. The idea is to make them aware about the taste and the quality of the product in advance. The company is taking this initiative as it has in the past given very good results to its other products. Through free samples it will develop first contact of its chocolates and its goodness with the potential customers. Identify and explain the element of marketing mix described in the above case. **A [OEB]**

Concept Applied: Concept of Promotion

Ans. **Promotion** is the element of marketing mix described in the above case.

Promotion of products and services include activities that communicate availability, features, merits, etc. of the products to the target customers and persuade them to buy it. Most marketing organisations, undertake various **promotional activities and spend substantial amount of money** on the promotion of their goods through using number of tools such as advertising, personal selling and sales promotion techniques (like price discounts, free samples, etc.). A large number of decisions are to be taken in each of the area specified above.

2. The R&D department of Organic Beverages Ltd. has decided to diversify from manufacturing organic health drinks to cereals made from Ragi. The company will have to communicate to the people the benefits of eating Ragi so as to aid the sales of its product. Thus, they plan to sponsor various events like book launch, marathon, etc. and persuade people to switch to healthy eating and drinking through newsletters.

(i) Identify and explain the promotional tool being discussed in the case.

(ii) Explain two other promotional tools that can be used by the company, apart from the one discussed above. **A [OEB]**

Ans. (i) Public relations: It involves variety of activities designed in order to maintain the company's relation with the public which **promote or protect** the image of the company or its product in the eyes of general public.

(ii) Other Promotional Tools are:

(a) Advertising: Any paid form of non-personal promotion of goods and services by an identified sponsor with the objective of making people aware about the goods and services is known as advertising.

(b) Personal Selling: Personal selling involves face-to-face interaction or conversation with one or more potential customers for the purpose of convincing customer to make a purchase. A sales person, appointed by the company, gives oral presentation to the perspective consumers to create awareness about the product.

(c) **Sales Promotion:** Sales promotion includes short-term incentives, designed to encourage the prospective customers to make an immediate purchase of a product or service, *e.g.*, discounts, rebate, etc. **(Any two) [1+2=3]**

3. Fast Runners has become one of the most recognised athletic brands in India. It deals in a wide variety of sportswear. However, of late it has been facing difficulty in keeping its inventory under control. In 2022, the company adopted an inventory management software which helped it to predict items that could sell best and prepare the company to meet their demand. This has helped the company in providing better customer satisfaction by making the goods physically available to them. State the three activities Fast Runners should undertake other than the one discussed above, in order to ensure the availability of its products at the right place, at right time and in right quantity. A [APQ, 2023-24]

Ans. Three other activities that will ensure availability of products at the right time, at the right place and in right quantity are:

1. **Order Processing:** A good physical distribution system should provide for an accurate and speedy processing of orders, in the absence of which, goods would reach the customers late or in wrong quantity or specifications. This would result in customer dissatisfaction, with the danger of loss of business and goodwill.
2. **Transportation:** Transportation is the means of carrying goods and raw materials from the point of production to the point of sale. It is important because unless the goods are physically made available, the sale cannot be completed.
3. **Warehousing:** Warehousing refers to the act of storing and assorting products in order to create time utility. Generally larger the number of warehouses a firm has, lesser would be the time taken in serving customers at different locations but greater would be the cost of warehousing and vice-versa. Thus, the firm has to strike a balance between the cost of warehousing and the level of customer service.

[1 × 3 = 3]

Short Answer Type Questions-II (4 marks each)

1. Differentiate between 'Advertising' and 'Personal selling' on any four basis. U [Delhi Set-2, 2019]

OR

'Advertising' and 'Personal selling' both are communication tools used by the marketers to promote their products, yet they differ in their approach. Differentiate between the two by giving any six points. U [SQP 2020-21]

Ans. Difference between Advertising and Personal Selling:

Basis	Advertising	Personal Selling
Nature	It is an **impersonal form** of communication.	It is a **personal form** of communication.
Message	It involves **transmission of standardised** messages.	It **adjusts the sales** talk keeping in view customer's background and needs.
Flexibility	It is **inflexible** as the message can't be adjusted to the needs of the buyer.	It is **highly flexible** as the message can be adjusted.
Reach	It reaches **masses.**	Only a **limited number** of people can be contacted.
Cost	The cost per person is very **low.**	The cost per person is **quite high.**
Coverage	It can cover the market in a **short time.**	It takes a **lot of time** to cover the **entire market.**
Media used	It makes use of **mass media** such as television, radio, newspaper, and magazines.	It makes use of **sales staff,** which has limited reach.
Feedback	It **lacks direct feedback.** Marketing research efforts are needed to judge customers' reactions.	It **provides direct** and immediate feedback.
Role	It is more useful in creating and building **interest of the consumers** in the firm's products.	It plays an important role at the **awareness stage** of decision making.
Suitability	It is more useful in **marketing to the ultimate consumers** who are large in number.	It is more helpful in selling products to the **industrial buyers or to intermediaries** who are relatively few in number.

[Marking Scheme, Delhi 2019] **(Any four) [1×4=4]**

2. Price of a product is influenced by many factors. Explain any four such factors. AI U [Delhi Set-3, 2019]

OR

Explain any four factors which affect the fixation of price of a product. U [Outside Delhi Set-1,2,3, 2019]

This Question is for practice and its solution is given at the end of the chapter.

3. Sara was pursuing her graduation. Everyday she saw her mother working tirelessly at home after coming back from her work-place. She decided to start a tiffin service to increase her family income. To begin with, she started supplying tiffin only in the neighbourhood. Everyday she detailed out the menu after consulting her mother. For informing the people about her service, she designed a beautiful informative pamphlet, got it printed and started distributing it through the daily newspapers. She also appointed two delivery boys to deliver tiffins. The business was slow to begin with but picked-up well afterwards. She was able to earn a profit of 20% of the revenue in the first month.

(i) Identify the promotional tool used by Sara to communicate to the customers about her tiffin service.

(ii) State any three roles of the promotional tool identified in (i) above in marketing of goods and services. A [Delhi. Comptt. Set 1, 2, 3, 2018]

Ans. (i) Advertising

(ii) Role of advertising in marketing:

(a) It helps to create demand by informing the prospective customers about the product.

(b) It provides economies of scale as increased demand leads to higher production.

(c) It educates consumers by informing about the availability of different products in the market.

(d) It generates employment by creating various kinds of jobs to artists, script writers, etc.

(e) It improves standard of living by giving information regarding new products and increasing income levels of people.

(f) It sustains the media by acting as a source of revenue. **(Any four)**

(If an examinee has given only the heading, ½ mark for the heading should be awarded.)

[Marking Scheme, Delhi 2018] **[1+3=4]**

4. A company was marketing 'water purifiers' which were very popular due to their quality and after sales services provided to the customers. The company was a leading company in the market and earning huge profits. Because of huge profits, the company ignored the after sales services. As a result, its relations with the customers got spoiled and the image of the company was damaged in the public. Top management became concerned when the profits for the current quarter fell steeply. On analysis it was revealed that ignoring the after sales services was its reason. Therefore, the company took all possible measures to protect and promote its favourable image in the eyes of the public. As a result, the goodwill of the company improved in the society.

(a) Name and state the communication tool used by the marketer in the above case to improve its image.

(b) Also explain role of the tool as identified in part (a).

[Delhi Set-1, 2016]

Ans. (a) Public Relations: Public Relations refer to a variety of programmes to promote and protect a company's image or its products in the eyes of the public. **[1]**

(b) Role of Public Relations:

(i) Building corporate image: To build image or goodwill, companies can contribute **money and time to social problems**. For example, upkeep of parks in the city or sponsoring will promote their products.

(ii) Smooth functioning of the business: Co-operation of public is essential for any company to achieve its objectives and smooth functioning. Therefore, companies involved in public relation have to **satisfy different public groups** so that no obstacles are imposed on the smooth functioning of business.

(iii) Supplement to advertising: As a supplement to advertising, public relations are usually undertaken by marketing managers to **spread awareness and knowledge** about new and established products. Its cost is less than media advertising as there is no need to pay for media sale and time.

(iv) Launching a new product: An effective public relations programme conveys information about the new products of company to customers before they are launched. Before launching the new brand, a **good publicity increases the demand** of it during the advertised period.

(v) Building interests in the established products: To **attract and motivate the customers to buy** the products, an effective public relation campaign is essential. Public relation professionals collect information about **public opinion** for product and company from various media channels. It helps the company to chalk out its actions which are relevant to the public. **(Any three) [1×3=3]**

Long Answer Type Questions (6 marks each)

1. Best Electronics started manufacturing washing machines under the brand name 'Amaze'. Once the washing machines were manufactured, packaged, branded, priced and promoted, they had to be made available to the customers at the right place, in the right quantity and at the right time.

'Best Electronics' provided for accurate and speedy processing of orders so that the washing machines reach the customers in time, in the right quantity and specifications. They also ensured that the washing machines are physically made available to the customers. Further, 'Best Electronics' arranged for facilities to store the washing machines at different locations near the market to minimise the charges on transportation. Explain any three components of physical distribution discussed in the above case.

[Delhi Set-1, 2023]

Ans. The components of physical distribution being discussed here are as follows:

(i) Order Processing: Order processing is the first point or in other words, the starting point of the distribution activity. The functions involved in order processing are receiving order, handling the received order, granting of credit for the item ordered, generating invoice, dispatching of order and collecting the bills. the order cycle time which is the time between placing an order by the customer and delivery of the goods at the customer's place.

(ii) Storage and Warehousing: Storage deals with the storing of goods in proper condition till the time it is ordered by the customer. Goods that cannot be generally made available throughout the year need to be stored.

Warehouses act as **centres of storage** and by providing the functionality it helps businesses meet the demands of customers. Apart from being a source of storage, a warehouse also acts as centres for assembling the goods.

(iii) Inventory Control: Inventory control refers to the process of efficient control of goods that are stored in the warehouses. Businesses need to maintain adequate levels of inventory in order to ensure uninterrupted fulfilment of orders.

The level of inventory needs to be **optimal**, it should not be too less or too more, as less inventory results in out-of-stock goods, lost business and unhappy customers, while a high level of inventory requires huge investment.

2. Define the three primary levels of packaging in the context of product distribution, and provide a real-life example for each level. [APQ, 2023-24]

Ans. (i) Primary Packaging: It is the layer of packaging that **directly encloses the product**. It is the first level of packaging that comes into direct contact with the product and is often the most visible to the consumer.

Real-Life Example: For a consumer electronics company, the primary packaging for a smartphone would be the box that holds the phone itself, along with any accessories such as charging cables and earphones.

(ii) Secondary Packaging: It refers to the packaging **used to group and protect multiple units** of the primary package during distribution. It is designed to facilitate handling and transportation of the product.

Real-Life Example: Continuing with the smartphone example, the secondary packaging would be the larger carton that holds multiple individual phone boxes for shipment to retailers.

(iii) Tertiary Packaging: It is the **outermost layer of** packaging used for bulk transportation and storage of products. It is designed to protect products during long-distance transportation and warehousing.

Real-Life Example: In the context of the consumer electronics company, the tertiary packaging would be the large pallets or crates used to hold and transport numerous secondary packages filled with smartphones to distribution centres or retail stores

Award 1 mark to each level of packaging and 1 mark for each example given. **[2×3=6]**

3. Drug price watchdog 'National Pharmaceutical Pricing Authority'(NPPA) has decided to cap the prices of the medicines, for which the prices rise by more than 20% in a year. This has been done in pursuance of the 'public interest 'clause in the drugs law.

(a) Identify the consideration that is being kept in mind by the NPPA while fixing the price of medicines.

(b) State any five other considerations affecting the fixation of price of the product, apart from the one identified above. [APQ, 2023-24] **[6]**

Ans. (a) Government and other regulations **[1]**

(b) Other factors affecting price of a product are:

1. **Product cost:** One of the most important factors affecting price of a product or service is its **cost**. This includes the **cost of producing, distributing and selling the product**. The cost sets the minimum level or the floor price at which the product may be sold.
2. **The Utility and Demand:** While the product costs set the lower limits of the price, the utility provided by the product and the intensity of demand of the buyer sets the **upper limit of price**, which a buyer would be prepared to pay. The buyer may be ready to pay up to the point where the utility from the product is at **least equal to the sacrifice made in terms of the price** paid. According to the law of demand, consumers usually purchase more units at a low price than at a high price.
3. **Extent of Competition in the Market:** The price will tend to reach the upper limit in case there is **lesser degree of competition** while under conditions of free competition, the price will tend to be set at the **lowest level**.
4. **Pricing Objectives:** If the firm decides to maximise profits in the short run, it would tend to **charge maximum price for its products**. But if it is to maximise its total profit in the long run, it would opt for a lower per unit price so that it can capture larger share of the market.
5. **Marketing Methods Used:** Price fixation process is also affected by other elements of marketing such as distribution system, quality of salesmen employed, quality and amount of advertising, sales promotion efforts, the type of packaging, product differentiation, credit facility and customer services provided. **[1×5=5]**

4. "The elements of marketing mix are popularly known as 4 P's of marketing." Briefly explain these elements. U [SQP 2021-22]

5. Ashima purchased a bottle of tomato sauce from a local grocery shop. The information provided on the bottle was not clear. She fell sick on consuming it. She filed a case in the District Forum under Consumer Protection Act and got the relief.

(i) Identify the important aspect neglected by the marketer in the above case.

(ii) Explain briefly the functions of the aspect identified in (i) above. A [OEB]

Ans. (i) Labelling

(ii) Functions of labelling:

(i) Describes the product and specifies its contents: Label describes the product, its **usage, cautions in its use, and specifies its contents, etc.**, e.g., a popular brand of Prickly Heat Powder, describes how the product provides relief from prickly heat and controls bacterial growth and infection.

(ii) Product or Brand identification: The label **identifies the product or the brand**. For example, the name stamped on a cold drink identifies it as Pepsi, Coke, Thumbs Up, Fanta, etc.

(iii) Grading of products: The label might also grade the product into different categories, where the differentiation tends to be marginal.

(iv) Providing information required by the law: It is a carrier of information, which is to be provided to the customer. The label describes the product, the manufacturer, date of manufacture, its contents, directions for use, price, etc.

(v) Product promotion: A carefully designed label can facilitate **product promotion**. It attracts attention, describes the product and gives the reason to purchase. Particularly in case of fast moving consumer goods sector (FMCGs), label has become a patent tool of sales promotion. **[1+5=6]**

6. Tasty Drinks Ltd. has scanned a profitable opportunity for marketing of soft drinks with Indian Traditional Flavour. The company wants to market its products in India and in neighbouring countries. A board meeting of the company was held wherein the marketing manager was asked to give a presentation to develop this market offering. For this it was also decided to set-up its manufacturing unit in a village of Bihar. This will not only help in the development of the village but will also provide employment to the youth of the village. The marketing manager chooses a combination of variables to prepare its market offering. He used a set of marketing tools that firm will use to pursue its marketing objectives in the target market.

(i) Name and explain the concept of marketing used by the marketing manager for creating its market offering.

(ii) Also, explain briefly the various elements of this concept. A [OEB]

Ans. (i) The concept of marketing used by the marketing manager for creating its market offering is marketing mix. The combination of variables chosen by a firm to prepare its market offering is also called marketing mix. Thus, marketing mix is described as the set of marketing tools that a firm uses to pursue its marketing objectives in a target market. **[2]**

(ii) The elements of marketing mix are discussed below:

(a) Product: Product means goods or services or '**anything of value**', which is offered to the market for sale. The concept of product relates to not only the physical product but also the benefits offered by it from customer's view point. The concept of product also includes the extended product or what is offered to the customers by way of after sales services, handling complaints, availability of spare parts, etc. The important product decisions include deciding about the features, quality, packaging, labelling and branding of the products.

(b) Price: Price is the amount of money customers have to pay to obtain the product. In case of most of the products, level of **price affects the level of their demand**. The marketers have not only to decide about the objectives of price setting but to analyse the factors determining the price and fix a price for the firm's products. Decisions have also to be taken in respect of discounts to customers, traders and credit terms, etc. so that customers perceive the price to be in line with the value of the product.

(c) Place: Place or Physical Distribution include activities that make firm's products available to the target customers. **Important** decision areas in this respect include selection of dealers or intermediaries to reach the customers, providing support to the intermediaries. The intermediaries in turn keep inventory of the firm's products, demonstrate them to potential buyers, negotiate price with buyers, close sales and also service the products after the sale. The other decision areas relate to managing inventory, storage and warehousing and transportation of goods from the place it is produced to the place it is required by the buyers.

(d) Promotion: Promotion of products and services include activities that **communicate availability, features, merits,** etc. of the products to the target customers and persuade them to buy it. Most marketing organisations, undertake various promotional activities and spend substantial amount of money on the promotion of their goods through using number of tools such as advertising, personal selling and sales promotion techniques. **[1×4=4]**

COMPETENCY BASED QUESTIONS

Objective Type Questions

[A] Multiple Choice Questions

1. For the following two statements, choose the correct option:

Statement-I: Transportation helps in creating time utility and warehousing helps in creating place utility.

Statement-II: The process of classification of products into different groups on the basis of their important characteristics is known as standardisation.

Choose the correct option from the options given below:

(A) Statement I is true and II is false.

(B) Statement II is true and I is false.

(C) Both the statements are true.

(D) Both the statements are false. [SQP 2022-23]

Ans. Option (D) is correct.

Explanation: Transportation helps in creating place utility and warehousing helps in creating time utility. Grading is a process of classification of products into different groups on the basis of some important characteristics such as quality, size, etc.

2. One of the following is considered to be an extension of the marketing concept, which apart

from customer satisfaction pays attention to ethical and ecological aspects of marketing. Identify the concept.

(A) Selling concept
(B) Product concept
(C) Production concept
(D) Societal marketing concept U [SQP 2022-23]

Ans. Option (D) is correct.

Explanation: The societal marketing concept holds that the task of any organisation is to identify the needs and wants of the target market and deliver the desired satisfaction in an effective and efficient manner so that the long-term well-being of the consumers and the society is taken care of. Thus, the societal marketing concept is the extension of the marketing concept as supplemented by the concern for the long-term welfare of the society.

3. While the product costs set the lower limits of the price for a product, the upper limit of price which a buyer would be prepared to pay is decided by:

(A) Utility and demand of the product
(B) The marketing manager of the firm
(C) The government
(D) The competitors of the firm AE [SQP 2022-23]

Ans. Option (A) is correct.

Explanation: According to the law of demand, consumers usually purchase more units at a low price than at a high price. The price of a product is affected by the elasticity of demand of the product. The demand is said to be elastic if a relatively small change in price results in large change in the quantity demanded. Here numerically, the price elasticity is greater than one. In the case of inelastic demand, the total revenue increases when the price is increased and goes down when the price is reduced. If the demand of a product is inelastic, the firm is in abetter position to fix higher prices.

4. Which of the following statements about advertising is incorrect?

(A) It is a personal form of communication.
(B) It is a paid form of communication.
(C) It is a mass selling technique.
(D) It is inflexible as the message can't be adjusted to the needs of the buyer. U [SQP 2022-23]

Ans. Option (A) is correct.

Explanation: Advertising is the non-personal communication of information usually paid for and usually persuasive in nature about products, services or ideas by identified sponsors through the various media.

5. One of the important decision areas under the marketing function of .... is managing inventory.

(A) Branding **(B)** Pricing
(C) Promotion **(D)** Physical distribution U [SQP 2022-23]

Ans. Option (D) is correct.

Explanation: The two major decision areas under physical distribution function include (i) decision regarding channels of distribution or the marketing intermediaries (like wholesalers, retailers) to be used and (ii) physical movement of the product from where it is produced to a place where it is required by the customers for their consumption or use. The important decision areas under physical distribution include managing inventory (levels of stock of goods), storage and warehousing and transportation of goods from one place to the other.

6. Which of the following options explains the 'standardisation and grading' function of marketing?

(A) It affects the success or failure of a product in the market.
(B) It refers to designing and developing the package for the products.
(C) It helps in achieving uniformity and consistency in the output and classifies products into different groups based on their size.
(D) It reduces the need for inspection of products. U [Delhi Term-1, 2021-22]

Ans. Option (C) is correct.

Explanation: Standardisation refers to producing goods of predetermined specifications, which helps in achieving uniformity and consistency in the output. Grading is the process of classification of products into different groups, on the basis of some of its important characteristics such as quality, size, etc.

7. Which of the following functions of marketing can improve performance of the product and also give it a competitive advantage in the market by attracting the target customers?

(A) Marketing planning
(B) Product designing and development
(C) Promotion
(D) Branding U [Delhi Term-1, 2021-22]

8. The function of marketing, which involves taking decisions regarding channels of distribution or marketing intermediaries, is called:

(A) Physical distribution
(B) Promotion
(C) Warehousing
(D) Marketing planning R [Delhi Term-1, 2021-22]

Ans. Option (A) is correct.

Explanation: The important decision areas under physical distribution include managing inventory (levels of stock of goods), storage and warehousing and transportation of goods from one place to the other.

9. Which of the following statements is incorrect?

(A) Marketing is a social process.
(B) Focus of the marketing activities is on customer needs.
(C) Marketing is merely a post-production activity.
(D) Marketing mix is a wider term than product mix. U [SQP 2021-22]

Ans. Option (C) is correct.

Explanation: Marketing includes many activities that are performed even before goods are actually produced, and continue even after the goods have been sold. For example, activities such as identification of customer needs, collection of information for developing the product, designing suitable product package and giving it a brand name are performed before commencement of the actual

These Questions are for practice and their solutions are given at the end of the chapter.

production. Similarly, many follow up activities are required for maintaining good customer relations for procuring repeat sales.

10. ____________ is an important function of marketing which is important not only for protection of the product but also serves as a promotional tool.

(A) Grading (B) Labeling
(C) Packaging (D) Branding

U [SQP 2021-22]

11. __________ is a process of classification of products into different groups on the basis of some important characteristics such as quality, size, etc.

(A) Standardisation
(B) Grading
(C) Product development
(D) Selling R [SQP 2021-22]

Ans. Option (B) is correct.

Explanation: Grading is particularly necessary for products which are not produced according to predetermined specifications, such as in the case of agricultural products, say wheat, oranges, etc. Grading ensures that goods belong to a particular quality and helps in realising higher prices for high quality output.

12. A person feeling hungry may get food by offering to give money or some other product or service in return to someone who is willing to accept the same for food. The important feature of marketing illustrated above is:

(A) Exchange mechanism
(B) Customer value
(C) Creating a market offering
(D) Needs and wants A [SQP 2021-22]

Concept Applied	Exchange mechanism as a feature of marketing

Ans. Option (A) is correct.

Explanation: The process of marketing works through the exchange mechanism. The individuals (buyers and sellers) obtain what they need and want through the process of exchange. In other words, the process of marketing involves exchange of products and services for money or something considered valuable by the people.

13. Zolo, a marketer of cars having 40 % of the current market share of the country aims at increasing the market share to 70% in next few years. For achieving this objective, the manager of the company specified the action programme covering various aspects. Identify the function of marketing discussed above:

(A) Customer support services
(B) Gathering and analysing market information
(C) Product designing and development
(D) Marketing planning A [SQP 2021-22]

Ans. Option (D) is correct.

Explanation: A marketer is to develop appropriate marketing plans so that the marketing objectives of the organisation can be achieved.

14. The function of marketing that involves physical movement of goods from one place to another is called:

(A) Promotion
(B) Transportation
(C) Storage and warehousing
(D) Customer support services

U [Delhi Term-1, 2021-22]

Ans. Option (B) is correct.

Explanation: Transportation involves physical movement of goods from one place to the other. As generally the users of products, particularly consumer products are wide spread and geographically separated from the place these are produced, it is necessary to move them to the place where it is needed for consumption or use.

15. "Availability and affordability of the product were considered to be the key to the success of a firm." Identify the concept of marketing management highlighted by this statement.

(A) Production concept (B) Product concept
(C) Societal concept (D) Marketing concept

U [SQP 2021-22]

Ans. Option (A) is correct.

Explanation: Production concept lays emphasis on availability and affordability of products. It was believed that profits could be maximised by producing at large scale, thereby reducing the average cost of production. It was also assumed that consumers would favour those products which were widely available at an affordable price. Thus, availability and affordability of the product were considered to be the key to the success of a firm. Therefore, greater emphasis was placed on improving the production and distribution efficiency of the firms.

16. The marketing management philosophy which is based on the premise that any activity which satisfies human needs but does not pay attention to the ethical and ecological aspects of marketing cannot be justified is known as:

(A) Marketing concept
(B) Societal marketing concept
(C) Production concept
(D) Product concept U [SQP 2021-22]

17. Which marketing management philosophy lays emphasis on bringing continuous improvement in the quality of the product?

(A) Production concept
(B) Product concept
(C) Marketing concept
(D) Social marketing concept U [SQP 2021-22]

Ans. Option (B) is correct.

Explanation: Product concept lays emphasis on 'quality of production' rather than 'quantity of production'. Mere availability and low price of the product could not ensure increased sale and as such the survival and growth of the firm. Thus, with the increase in the supply of the products, customers started looking for products which were superior in quality, performance and features. Therefore, the emphasis of the firms shifted from quantity of

These Questions are for practice and their solutions are given at the end of the chapter.

production to quality of products.

18. The element of marketing mix by which marketers make use of various tools of communication to encourage exchange of goods and services in the market is called:

(A) Branding (B) Promotion
(C) Physical distribution (D) Price

U [SQP Term-1, Exam 2021-22]

19. The tool of promotion which involves making use of short-term incentives designed to encourage the buyers to make immediate purchase of a product or a service is called:

(A) Advertising (B) Personal selling
(C) Sales promotion (D) Public relations

U [Delhi Term-1, Exam 2021-22]

Concept Applied | Concept of Sales promotion

Ans. Option (C) is correct.

Explanation: Sales promotion Sales promotion activities include offering cash discounts, sales contests, free gift offers, and free sample distribution. Sales promotion is usually undertaken to supplement other promotional efforts such as advertising and personal selling.

20. Harshita Verma has set up a factory to manufacture herbal hand sanitizers in Meerut. The size and shape of the bottles in which the products are packed are specially designed so that it should be convenient to handle and use by the consumers. The bottles in which the sanitizers are packed is a part of:

(A) Primary packaging
(B) Secondary packaging
(C) Tertiary packaging
(D) Both secondary and tertiary packaging

A [Delhi Term-1, Exam 2021-22]

Ans. Option (A) is correct.

Explanation: It refers to the product's immediate container. In some cases, the primary package is kept till the consumer is ready to use the product (e.g., plastic packet for socks); whereas in other cases, it is kept throughout the entire life of the product (e.g., a toothpaste tube, a match box, etc.).

21. Priya Seth, a fashion designer, has launched a new range of dresses by the name, 'Sukriti'. To give her dresses a distinct image and to distinguish them from the competitor's products, she has designed a unique symbol with a distinct colour scheme. This symbol is available on all the labels, packaging and advertising campaigns of this new range of dresses. She has also registered this symbol to give it a legal protection against its use by other firms.

From the following, name the term used to denote the symbol designed by Priya Seth in the above case:

(A) Brand mark (B) Trade mark
(C) Brand name (D) Brand icon

A [Delhi Term-1, Exam 2021-22]

Ans. Option (B) is correct.

Explanation: A brand or part of a brand that is given legal protection is called trademark. The protection is given against its use by other firms. Thus, the firm, which got its brand registered, gets the exclusive right for its use. In that case, no other firm can use such name or mark in the country.

22. 'Safe Life Technologies Private Ltd.' is a renowned pharmaceutical company in India. It has launched a new medicine to treat high blood pressure. To create awareness about the new medicine and to build a positive image about it, the company organised a seminar, which was attended by doctors from various hospitals and dealers in medicines. During the seminar, the representatives of company discussed about the chemical composition and the functioning of the medicine.

Identify the tool of promotion used by 'Safe Life Technologies Private Ltd.' in the above case:

(A) Advertising (B) Sales promotion
(C) Personal selling (D) Public relations

A [Delhi Term-1, 2021-22]

Ans. Option (D) is correct.

Explanation: Public relations involve a variety of programmes designed to promote or protect a company's image and its individual products in the eyes of the public.

23. For the following two statements, choose the correct option:

Statement I: If the demand of a product is inelastic, the firm is in a position to fix higher prices.

Statement II: In case the degree of competition is high, the firm is in a position to set high prices.

(A) Statement I is correct and statement II is wrong.
(B) Statement II is correct and statement I is wrong.
(C) Both the statements are correct.
(D) Both the statements are wrong.

U [SQP Term-1, 2021-22]

Ans. Option (A) is correct.

Explanation: In a highly competitive market, firms often have limited pricing power. High competition typically drives prices down as firms compete for market share. Therefore, firms may not be able to set high prices in such a scenario.

24. Marketing mix is a set of __________ that the firm uses to pursue its marketing objectives in the target market.

(A) Production tools
(B) Capital tools
(C) Marketing tools
(D) Selling tools

R [SQP 2021-22]

25. A brand or part of the brand that is given legal protection is called __________

(A) Brand mark (B) Trademark
(C) Brand (D) Brand name

R [SQP 2021-22]

Ans. Option (B) is correct.

Explanation: A brand or part of a brand that is given legal protection is called trademark. The protection is given against its use by other firms. Thus, the firm, which got its brand registered, gets the exclusive right for its use. In that case, no other firm can use such name or mark in the country.

26. Which product-related decision is concerned with providing detailed information about the product on its package?

(A) Branding (B) Packaging
(C) Labeling
(D) Both branding and packaging

These Questions are for practice and their solutions are given at the end of the chapter.

U [Delhi Term-1, Exam 2021-22]

Ans. Option (C) is correct.

Explanation: Labelling refers to designing and developing the label to be put on the package. One of the most important functions of labels is to give detailed information about the product i.e., describe the product, its usage, cautions in use, etc. and specify its contents.

27.

What will come at the place of B in the above image.

(A) Product (B) Price

(C) Place (D) Promotion [OEB]

Ans. Option (C) is correct.

Explanation: Place mix or distribution mix is an arrangement of channels, both physical and non-physical, through which the product is made available to customers for purchase.

28.

'Maharaja' of Air India shown in the above image is an example of:

(A) Brand name (B) Brand mark

(C) Brand (D) Trademark [OEB]

Ans. Option (B) is correct.

Explanation: That part of a brand which can be recognised but which is not utterable is called brand mark.

29.

Identify the element of marketing mix stated in the above image.

(A) Product (B) Price

(C) Place (D) Promotion [OEB]

Ans. Option (D) is correct.

Explanation: Promotion mix refers to a combination of tools used to communicate with potential customers to inform them about a product and persuading them to buy it.

30.

Wheatgerm Bread Medium Sliced 800g

Ingredients: **Wheat Flour,** Water, **Wheatgerm** (11%), Yeast, Salt, **Wheat Protein,** Vinegar, **Fermented Wheat Flour, Barley Flour, Soya Flour,** Emulsifier: E4722 (made from Vegetable oils), Vegetable Fat, **Barley Fibre, Flour Treatment Agent:** Ascorbic Acid (Vitamin C).

Price $ 1.35

Use By: 19.10.13

Nutrition	Per 100g	Per Slice 25g
Energy	947kJ 224 kcal	237kJ 56 kcal
Carbohydrate	38.6g	9.7g
of which sugars	3.1g	0.8g
Fat	2.2g	0.5g
of which saturates	0.4g	0.1g
Fibre	5.3g	1.3g
Sodium	0.39g	0.10g
Equivalent as salt	0.96g	0.24

UNIT 56, TOOTSWWOOD INDUSTRIAL ESTATE, TOOTSWOOD, BR6 9JK

Identify the product related decision illustrated by the picture given above, concerned with providing detailed information about the product on its package?

(A) Branding

(B) Packaging

(C) Labeling

(D) Both branding and packaging [OEB]

Ans. Option (C) is correct.

Explanation: Labelling means designing and developing a label to be put on the package.

31. Which of the following activities is not considered to be part of customer support services?

(A) After sales services

(B) Handling customer complaints and adjustments

(C) Procuring credit services

(D) Identifying the needs of the customers and taking various marketing decisions

U [Delhi Term-1, 2021-22]

Ans. Option (D) is correct.

Explanation: Customer support services includes services such as after sales services, handling customer complaints and adjustments, procuring credit services, maintenance services, technical services and consumer information.

32.

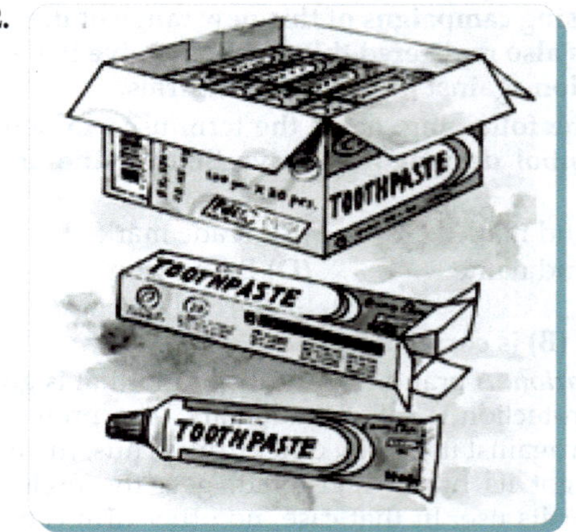

Identify the concept of marketing illustrated in the picture above.

(A) Levels of packaging **(B)** Labelling
(C) Branding **(D)** None of these [OEB]

Ans. Option (A) is correct.

Explanation: There can be three different levels of packaging. Primary package refers to the product's immediate container. In some cases, the primary package is kept till the consumer is ready to use the product; whereas in other cases, it is kept throughout the entire life of the product. Secondary packaging refers to additional layers of protection that are kept till the product is ready for use, Transportation packaging refers to further packaging components necessary for storage, identification or transportation.

33. Statement-I: The concept of product relates to not only the physical product but also the benefits offered by it from customer's point of View.

Statement-II: The concept of product does not include the extended product by way of after sale services, availability of spare parts, handling complaints etc. Choose the correct option from the following: U [Delhi Set-1, 2023]

(A) Both Statement-I and Statement-II are correct.
(B) Both Statement-I and Statement-II are incorrect.
(C) Statement-I is correct and Statement-II is incorrect.
(D) Statement-I is incorrect and Statement-II is correct.

Ans. Option (A) is correct

34. The most commonly used tool of promotion which is a paid form of communication and in which the sponsor bears the cost of communicating with the prospects is: R [Delhi Set-1, 2023]

(A) Advertising. **(B)** Personal selling.
(C) Sales promotion. **(D)** Public relations.

Ans. Option (A) is correct

Explanation : Advertising is a form of communication used to persuade an audience to take some action, usually with respect to a commercial offering, such as an item for sale or a service. Examples of advertising include television and print advertisements, product placements, and infomercials.

35. A name, term, sign, symbol, design or some combination of them used to identify the products - goods or services of one seller or group of sellers and to differentiate them from those of the competitors is known as R [Delhi Set-1, 2023]

(A) brand **(B)** brand mark
(C) brand name **(D)** trade mark

Ans. Option (A) is correct

Explanation: A brand is a product, service or concept that is publicly distinguished from other products, services or concepts so that it can be easily communicated and usually marketed. Branding is the process of creating and disseminating the brand name, its qualities and personality.

36. From the following, identify the channel of distribution in which goods pass from the manufacturer to the retailers who, in turn, sell them to the final users. R [Delhi Set-1, 2023]

(A) One level channel **(B)** Two level channel
(C) Three level channel **(D)** Zero level channel

Ans. Option (a) is correct

Explanation: A marketing channel in which there is only one intermediary (for example, a retailer) between manufacturer and end-user.

37. Which of the following statements is incorrect about Personal Selling? U [Delhi Set-1, 2023]

(A) It is a direct face to face dialogue that involves an interactive relationship between the seller and buyer.
(B) It refers to short-term incentives designed to encourage the buyers to make immediate purchase of a product or service.
(C) It allows a sales-person to develop personal relationship with the prospective customers.
(D) In this it is possible to take direct feedback from the customer and to adopt the presentation according to the needs of the prospects.

Ans. Option (B) is correct.

Explanation: Personal selling is an integral part of a promotional mix because it allows the salesperson to build a personal relationship with the customers for promoting their products but it does not allow the salesperson to give any short-term incentives to encourage the customers to purchase their product.

38. Match the various items of Column - I with the respective statements in Column - II: Ap [OD Set-1, 2023]

	Column-I		Column-II
a	Advertising	(i)	Creates a positive image about the company and its products.
b	Personal selling	(ii)	Paid form of impersonal communication.
c	Public relations	(iii)	Develop personal relationship with the prospective buyer.

Options:

	a	b	c
(a)	(ii)	(iii)	(i)
(b)	(i)	(iii)	(ii)
(c)	(iii)	(ii)	(i)
(d)	(ii)	(i)	(iii)

Ans. Option (A) is correct.

39. The________ function of marketing ensures the buyers that goods confirm to predetermined standards of quality and reduces the need for inspection.

It also ensures that goods belong to a particular quality and helps in realising higher prices for high quality output. U [Outside Delhi Set-1, 2023]

(A) Product Designing and Development
(B) Standardisation and Grading
(C) Marketing Planning
(D) Branding

Ans. Option (B) is correct.

Explanation: Standardisation is the function involving setting standards to which all products of a similar type should confirm. It brings about uniformity in size, colour, ingredients etc. of the products. Grading means sorting out the products on the basis of their quality. It helps in the fixation of prices and also on the targeted customers on the basis of quality.

40. A bottle of Anti-dandruff shampoo mentions 'Clean your hair and get rid of dandruff in one squeeze'. The product related decision involved is:

Ap [SQP 2023-24]

(A) Branding (B) Product quality
(C) Packaging (D) Labelling

Ans. Option (D) is correct.

Explanation: Labelling implies providing all the essential information about the product on its package. It includes information regarding size, weight, ingredients, date of manufacture expiry, price, etc. of the product.

41. Name the function of marketing which is effective in bringing repeat sales from the customers and developing brand loyalty for a product.

R [SQP 2023-24]

(A) Standardisation and grading
(B) Promotion
(C) Customer support services
(D) Packaging and labelling

Ans. Option (C) is correct.

Explanation: Effective services to customers after the sales helps in bringing repeat sales as it makes effective impression on the customers.

42. Statement I: For products requiring long term storage like agricultural products, the warehouses are located near to the market.

Statement II: Higher the level of inventory, higher will be the level of service to customers but the cost of carrying the inventory will also be high.

Choose the correct option from the following:

(A) Statement I is true and II is false
(B) Statement II is true and I is false
(C) Both the statements are true
(D) Both the statements are false U [SQP 2023-24]

Ans. Option (B) is Correct.

Explanation: For long term storage, the warehouse need not to be near the market.

43. Under which of the following marketing management philosophies did the focus of business activity change to bringing continuous improvement in the quality and incorporating new features?

(A) The product concept
(B) The marketing concept
(C) The selling concept
(D) The production concept R [CFPQ]

Ans. Option (A) is correct.

Explanation: The product concept includes improving the quality of the product to persuade customers to purchase it. The marketing concept includes meeting the customers' needs and expectations. The selling concept includes undertaking aggressive selling and promotional efforts to make customers buy their products. The production concept includes producing goods in large quantities to bring down their costs and make them easily accessible.

44. In which of the following situations, a company will fix high price for its product?

U [Outside Delhi Set-1, 2023]

(A) When firm's objective is to obtain larger share of the market.
(B) When the firm is facing difficulties in surviving in the market because of intense competition.
(C) When the firm wants to cover high cost of Research and Development to attain product quality leadership.
(D) When the firm wants to maximise its total profit in the long run.

Ans. Option (C) is correct.

Explanation: To attain product quality leadership, the firm charges higher prices for providing high quality products because it incurs heavy expenditure on research and development.

45. What is the primary strategic focus of the company, considering its "The Complete Man" tagline, top position in the menswear industry, and longstanding collection that has enriched a modern gentleman's wardrobe for decades?

(A) Ensuring ethical sourcing
(B) Reinforcing cultural heritage
(C) Establishing a unique identity
(D) Maximising production efficiency

A [APQ, 2023-24]

Ans. Option (C) is correct.

Explanation: The tagline "The Complete Man" suggests a focus on offering a comprehensive range of products or services that cater to various aspects of a modern man's lifestyle. This indicates a unique positioning in the market, not merely as a clothing provider but as a brand representing a complete lifestyle or persona.

46. Daniel and Andrew are two friends engaged in their respective businesses. Daniel concentrates on producing products that meet the needs of producers and sells whatever is produced by any means necessary. Andrew believes in achieving the firm's goals through understanding the needs of consumers and delivering the right products to them and constantly monitoring competitors.

Which Marketing Management Philosophies do Daniel and Andrew adhere to in their businesses?

(A) Product and Selling
(B) Selling and Marketing
(C) Marketing and Product
(D) Production and Product U [APQ, 2023-24]

Ans. Option (B) is correct.

Explanation: Daniel's focus on selling whatever is produced by any means necessary aligns with a Selling orientation, emphasising aggressive sales tactics to move products regardless of consumer needs. Andrew's approach better aligns with a marketing philosophy. His focus on understanding consumer needs, delivering suitable products, and monitoring competitors indicates a prioritisation of marketing-oriented principles.

47. Ms. Arundhati, the CEO of Sunlife Ltd., is delivering a speech to a group of investors. She is emphasising the significance of the company's success and achievement, which relies on the support of customers, shareholders, suppliers, and intermediaries. She also discusses how establishing a positive association with these parties contributes to enhancing the company's public image in the market.

What is the primary goal of Ms. Arundhati's speech?

(A) to increase sales
(B) to generate positive publicity
(C) to improve the company's image
(D) to build relationships with stakeholders

U [APQ, 2023-24]

Ans. Option (D) is correct.

Explanation: Her emphasis on the significance of customers, shareholders, suppliers, and intermediaries and how their support contributes to the company's success indicates a focus on nurturing and strengthening relationships with these stakeholders. Additionally, highlighting how establishing positive associations contributes to enhancing the company's public image implies a strategic effort to build rapport and trust among these stakeholders, ultimately aiming to foster lasting relationships for the company's benefit.

48. Statement I: Channel of distribution is important as goods are produced at one place and customers are scattered all over in the nook and corner of the country, so the producer needs to distribute the goods through middlemen.

Statement II: Physical movement of goods is transportation of goods from place of production to place of ultimate consumption.

Choose the correct option from the following:

(A) Statement I is true and II is false.
(B) Statement II is true and I is false.
(C) Both the statements are true.
(D) Both the statements are false.

A [APQ, 2023-24]

Ans. Option (C) is correct.

[B] Assertion & Reason

Directions: In the following questions, a statement of assertion (A) is followed by a statement of reason (R). Mark the correct choice as:

(A) Both assertion (A) and reason (R) are true and reason (R) is the correct explanation of assertion (A).
(B) Both assertion (A) and reason (R) are true but reason (R) is not the correct explanation of assertion (A).
(C) Assertion (A) is true but reason (R) is false.
(D) Assertion (A) is false but reason (R) is true.

1. **Assertion (A):** The design of the product contributes to making the product attractive to the target customers.

   Reason (R): Customer support services are very effective in bringing repeat sales from the customers and developing brand loyalty for a product. U [OEB]

Ans. Option (B) is correct.

Explanation: The design of the product contributes to making the product attractive to the target customers. A good design can improve performance of a product and also give it a competitive advantage in the market.

2. **Assertion (A):** A marketer has to take several crucial decisions in respect of promotion of the products and services.

   Reason (R): Promotion of products and services involves informing the customers about the firm's product, its features, etc. and persuading them to purchase these products. [OEB]

3. **Assertion (A):** Gathering and analysing market information is necessary to identify the needs of the customers.

   Reason (R): Marketing is concerned with exchange of goods and services from producers to consumers. [OEB]

4. **Assertion (A):** Marketing includes many activities that are performed even before goods are actually produced, and continue even after the goods have been sold.

   Reason (R): In modern times, emphasis is placed on describing marketing as an economical process. [OEB]

Ans. Option (C) is correct.

Explanation: Marketing includes many activities that are performed even before goods are actually produced, and continue even after the goods have been sold. For example, activities such as identification of customer needs, collection of information for developing the product, designing suitable product package and giving it a brand name are performed before commencement of the actual production. Similarly, many follow up activities are required for maintaining good customer relations for procuring repeat sales. In modern times, emphasis is placed on describing marketing as a social process. It is a process whereby people exchange goods and services for money or for something of value to them.

5. **Assertion (A):** Under the production concept, greater emphasis was placed on improving the production and distribution efficiency of the firms.

   Reason (R): Product improvement became the key to profit maximisation of a firm, under the concept of product orientation. U [OEB]

6. **Assertion (A):** Marketing orientation implies that focus on satisfaction of customer's needs is the key to the success of any organisation in the market.

   Reason (R): The marketing concept is based on the identification of market or customer who are chosen as the target of marketing effort. U [OEB]

Ans. Option (B) is correct.

Explanation: The focus of the marketing concept is on customer needs and the customer satisfaction becomes the means to achieving the firms' objective of maximising profit. The purpose of marketing is to generate customer value at a profit. The marketing concept is based on the identification of market or customer who are chosen as the target of marketing

These Questions are for practice and their solutions are given at the end of the chapter.

effort, understanding needs and wants of customers in the target market, development of products or services for satisfying needs of the target market and satisfying needs of target market better than the competitors.

7. Assertion (A): The purpose of societal marketing philosophy is to generate customer value at a profit.

Reason (R): A prerequisite for the success of any organisation is to understand and respond to customer needs. U [OEB]

8. Assertion (A): Personal selling plays a very important role in the introduction stage of a new product.

Reason (R): Personal selling helps in persuading customers about the merits of the product. U [OEB]

9. Assertion (A): Advertising is a medium through which a large number of people can be reached.

Reason (R): Advertising is less flexible. U [OEB]

Ans. Option (B) is correct.

Explanation: Advertising is a medium through which a large number of people can be reached over a vast geographical area. For example, an advertisement message placed in a national daily reaches lakhs of its subscribers. Advertising is less flexible as the message is standardised and is not tailor made to the requirements of the different customer groups.

10. Assertion (A): The Supervisory Level performs the activities according to the plans of Top and Middle level management.

Reason (R): The Supervisory Level motivates the employees and boosts their morale.

(A) Both (A) and (R) are true and (R) is the correct explanation of (A).

(B) Both (A) and (R) are true but (R) is not the correct explanation of (A).

(C) (A) is true but (R) is false.

(D) (A) is false but (R) is true. [APQ, 2023-24]

Ans. Option (B) is correct.

Explanation: Supervisory level ensures that day-to-day operations align with the broader goals and guidelines established by top and middle management. This level often involves overseeing teams, ensuring tasks are completed, and managing resources to achieve the objectives laid out by higher management tiers.

[C] Case Based MCQs

I. Read the following text and answer the questions given below:

Yamuna Prasad, a small shopkeeper in Bikaner, Rajasthan used to sell the famous 'Bhujia-Sev'. It was a quick-selling product for locals and foreign tourists. His second generation expanded the business and got 'Yamuna Ki Bhujia' registered with concerned authorities. Gradually the brand offered a wide range of products to its customers like namkeen, sweets, bakery items, etc. However, 'Bhujia-Sev' remained the most popular product of the brand creating maximum revenue.

'Yamuna Ki Bhujia' offered its products at competitive prices even while offering customer services like gift packaging and free home delivery to become a household name. Now it has virtually become a synonym for bhujia-sev in the market, so much so, that people ask for 'Yamuna Ki Bhujia' instead of bhujia-sev. 'Yamuna Ki Bhujia' has developed a strong distribution network in India and abroad by setting up retail outlets and reaching out to the customers through internet selling.

Promotion of the brand had always been low profile, till the increase in competition pushed it to hire the services of a professional advertising agency, Vigyapan Pvt. Ltd. for promoting the product.

On the advice of Vigyapan Pvt. Ltd., 'Yamuna Ki Bhujia' has also worked upon managing public opinion by developing relations with the masses through sponsoring cultural and sporting events, maintenance of public parks, etc. [SQP 2021-22]

1. 'His second generation expanded the business and got 'Yamuna Ki Bhujia' registered with concerned authorities.' With reference to the given text 'Yamuna ki Bhujia' is a ________ giving it a legal protection against its use by anyone else.

(A) Brand value	**(B)** Trademark
(C) Trait mark	**(D)** Brand mark

Ans. Option (B) is correct.

Explanation: A brand or part of a brand that is given legal protection is called trademark. The protection is given against its use by other firms. Thus, the firm, which got its brand registered, gets the exclusive right for its use. In that case, no other firm can use such name or mark in the country.

2. 'Yamuna Ki Bhujia' offered its products at competitive prices even while offering customer services like gift packaging and free home delivery to become a household name.

Identify the factor affecting the element of marketing mix being discussed above.

(A) Marketing methods used

(B) Objectives

(C) Extent of competition in the market

(D) Product cost

Ans. Option (A) is correct.

Explanation: Price fixation process is also affected by other elements of marketing such as distribution system, quality of salesmen employed, quality and amount of advertising, sales promotion efforts, the type of packaging, product differentiation, credit facility and customer services provided.

3. 'Yamuna Ki Bhujia' has developed a strong distribution network in India and abroad by setting up retail outlets and reaching out to the customer through internet selling. Identify the decision related to the element of marketing mix being discussed above.

(A) Storing and assorting products in order to create time utility.

(B) Regarding the channels or using intermediaries.

(C) Both (A) and (B)

(D) Regarding branding, packaging and labelling.

Ans. Option (B) is correct.

Explanation: Physical distribution of products and services is concerned with making the goods and

These Questions are for practice and their solutions are given at the end of the chapter.

services available at the right place, so that people can purchase the same. There are two important decisions relating to this aspect—one regarding physical movement of goods from producers to consumers or users and two, regarding the channels or using intermediaries in the distribution process.

4. On the advice of Vigyapan Pvt. Ltd., 'Yamuna Ki Bhujia' has also worked upon managing public opinion by developing better relations with the masses through sponsoring cultural and sporting events, maintenance of public parks, etc. Name the department in the organisation which is generally responsible for performing the above important task of managing public opinion.

(A) Marketing department
(B) A separate department created in the firm for the purpose
(C) An outside agency
(D) Any of the above

Ans. Option (D) is correct.

Explanation: Managing public opinion of an organisation is an important task which can be performed by the marketing department. The business needs to communicate effectively to customers, suppliers, and dealers, since they are instrumental in increasing the sales and profit. Most organisations, business or otherwise nowadays, have a separate department to manage public relations. They may also utilise the services of any outside public relations agency.

II. Read the following text and answer the questions given below: [OEB]

'Hayaram' is a famous chain selling a large variety of products in the Indian market. Their products include chips, biscuits, sweets and squashes. It charges a comparatively higher price than its competitors as it sells quality products. Besides, it offers regular discounts to its customers and easy credit terms to its retailers. It has five of its own retail shops. It also sells its products through various grocery stores so that the products are made available to customers at the right place, in the right quantity and at the right time. It regularly uses different communication tools to increase its sales. But it is also concerned about the impact as the potential customers or the prospects can't be delivered the message compulsively. So there is one scheme the company has decided to launch where chips will be provided with an additional cold drink for a particular time period. It not only satisfies its customers but also provides employment to handicapped people.

1. The above para describes the combination of variables used by Hayaram to prepare its market offering. The combination of variables used by 'Hayaram' to prepare its market offering is termed as ___________.

(A) Promotion mix　　**(B)** Sales mix
(C) Price mix　　**(D)** Marketing mix

Ans. Option (D) is correct.

Explanation: Marketing mix is described as the set of marketing tools that a firm uses to pursue its marketing objectives in a target market.

2. "It also sells its products through various grocery stores so that the products are made available to customers at the right place, in the right quantity and at the right time."

Identify the element of marketing mix stated above.

(A) Product　　**(B)** Price
(C) Place　　**(D)** Promotion

Ans. Option (C) is correct.

Explanation: Place or Physical Distribution include activities that make firm's products available to the target customers.

3. Identify the sales promotion technique decided to be used by 'Hayaram'.

(A) Product combination　　**(B)** Rebate
(C) Quantity plus　　**(D)** Usable benefits

Ans. Option (A) is correct.

Explanation: Offering another product as gift along with the purchase of a product, say offer of a pack of ½ kg of rice with the purchase of a bag of Aatta (wheat flour), or 'Get 128 KB Memory Card Free with a Digicam' or Buy a TV of 25+ and Get a Vacuum Cleaner Free' or '100 Gm Bottle of Sauce Free with 1 kg Detergent.'

4. "It charges a comparatively higher price than its competitors as it sells quality products." Identify the element of marketing mix stated above.

(A) Product　　**(B)** Price
(C) Place　　**(D)** Promotion

Ans. Option (B) is correct.

Explanation: Pricing is considered to be an effective competitive weapon. In the conditions of perfect competition, most of the firms compete with each other on the basis of this factor. It is also the single most important factor affecting the revenue and profits of a firm. Thus, most marketing firms give high importance to the fixation of price for their products and services.

SATQs-II

Ans 1. (i) Product designing and development

(a) Product designing and development helps to make the product attractive to the target customers.

(b) A good design can improve performance of a product and also give it a competitive advantage in the market.

(ii) Standardisation and Grading

(a) Standardisation ensures uniformity and consistency in output and reduces the need for inspection and testing of the products.

(b) Grading ensures that the goods belong to a particular quality and helps in realising higher prices for better quality products.

[Marking Scheme, Delhi 2019] **[2 + 2 = 4]**

SOLUTIONS FOR PRACTICE QUESTIONS (TOPIC-2)

SATQs-II

Ans 2. (i) Product cost: One of the most important factors affecting the price is its **cost**. It includes cost of producing, distributing and selling the product.

(ii) Utility and demand: The product cost sets the lower limit of price; the **utility** provided by the product and **intensity of demand** of product sets the **highest price** of the product.

(iii) Extent of competition in the market: When a firm does not face any competition, it has **complete freedom in fixing up the price**. But when competition is more, the price of the product is fixed keeping in mind the competitor's price.

(iv) Government regulations: In order to protect the interests of the consumers, government has all rights to **control prices of important commodities** and services.

(v) Marketing methods used: The price of product is also affected by the **methods and techniques** used to promote the product.

(vi) Pricing objectives: Apart from profit maximisation, other objectives are:

(a) Obtaining market share leadership: If a firm wants to **capture big share of market**, it has to keep its **price low**.

(b) Surviving in competitive market: To **survive in a competitive market** the firm has to **offer discounts**.

(c) Attaining product quality leadership: Generally high prices are charged to cover cost of R&D.

(Any four) [1 × 4 = 4]

LATQs

Ans 4. The marketing mix consists of various variables, which have broadly been classified into four categories, popularly known as **4 Ps of marketing.** These are:

(i) Product
(ii) Price
(iii) Place
(iv) Promotion

(i) Product: Product means **goods or services or 'anything of value'**, which is offered to the market for exchange. The concept of product relates to not only the physical product but also the benefits offered by it from the customer's viewpoint (for example toothpaste is bought for whitening teeth, strengthening gums, etc.). The concept of product also includes the **extended product or what is offered to the customers** by way of after-sales services, handling complaints, availability of spare parts, etc. These aspects are very important, particularly in the marketing of consumer durable products (like Automobiles, Refrigerators, etc.).

The important product decisions include deciding about the features, quality, packaging, labelling and branding of the products.

(ii) Price: Price is the **amount of money customers have to pay** to obtain the product. In the case of most of the products, the level of price affects the level of their demand. The marketers have not only to decide about the objectives of price setting but to analyse the factors determining the price and fix a price for the firm's products.

(iii) Place: Place or Physical Distribution include activities that make firm's products available to the **target customers**. Important decision areas in this respect include selection of dealers or intermediaries to reach the customers, providing support to the intermediaries (by way of discounts, promotional campaigns, etc.).

(iv) Promotion: Promotion of products and services include activities that **communicate availability, features, merits**, etc. of the products to the target customers and **persuade them to buy it.**

Most marketing organisations undertake various promotional activities and spend a substantial amount of money on the promotion of their goods through using a number of tools such as advertising, personal selling and sales promotion techniques (like price discounts, free samples, etc.).

[Marking Scheme, Delhi 2021-22]

[1½×4 = 6]

SOLUTIONS FOR OBJECTIVE PRACTICE QUESTIONS

[A] MCQs

Ans. 7. Option (B) is correct.

Explanation: One of the important marketing activity or decision area relates to product designing and development. The design of the product contributes to making the product attractive to the target customers. A good design can improve performance of a product and also give it a competitive advantage in the market.

Ans. 10. Option (C) is correct.

Explanation: Packaging refers to designing and developing the package for the products. Packaging is important not only for protection of the products but also serves as a promotional tool. Sometimes, the quality of the product is assessed by the buyers form packaging. In the success of many of the consumer brands such as Lays or Uncle Chips potato wafers Clinic Plus shampoos, and Colgate Toothpaste, etc., packaging has played an important role.

Ans. 16. Option (B) is correct.

Explanation: The societal marketing concept holds that the task of any organisation is to identify the needs and wants of the target market and deliver the desired satisfaction in an effective and efficient manner so that the long-term well-being of the consumers and the society is taken care of. Apart from the customer satisfaction, it pays attention to the social, ethical and ecological aspects of marketing. There are large number of such issues that need to be attended.

Ans 18. Option (B) is correct.

Explanation: Promotion refers to the use of communication with the twin objective of informing potential customers about a product and persuading them to buy it. Promotion is an important element of marketing mix by which marketers make use of various tools of communication to encourage exchange of goods and services in the market. Various tools of communication are used by the marketers to inform and persuade customers about their firm's products. These include: **(i)** Advertising, **(ii)** Personal Selling, **(iii)** Sales Promotion, and **(iv)** Publicity. These tools are also called elements of promotion mix and can be used in different combinations to achieve the goals of promotion.

Ans 24. Option (C) is correct.

Explanation: Marketing mix is described as the set of marketing tools that a firm uses to pursue its marketing objectives in a target market. Marketing manager concentrates on four major decision areas while planning the marketing activities, namely, **(i)** products, **(ii)** price, **(iii)** place (distribution) and **(iv)** promotion. These 4 'P's are called as elements of marketing and together they constitute the marketing mix. All these are inter-related because a decision in one area affects decisions in other areas.

[B] A & R

Ans 2. Option (B) is correct.

Explanation: Promotion of products and services involves informing the customers about the firm's product, its features, etc. and persuading them to purchase these products. The four important methods of promotion include advertising, personal selling, publicity and sales promotion. A marketer has to take several crucial decisions in respect of promotion of the products and services such as deciding the promotion budget, the promotion mix, i.e., the combination of the promotional tools that will be used, the promotion budget, etc.

Ans 3. Option (B) is correct.

Explanation: One of the important functions of a marketer is to gather and analyse market information. This is necessary to identify the needs of the customers and take various decisions for the successful marketing of the products and services. This is important for making an analysis of the available opportunities and threats as well as strengths and weaknesses of the organisation and help in deciding what opportunities can best be pursued by it. Marketing is concerned with exchange of goods and services from producers to consumers or users in such a way that maximises the satisfaction of customers' needs.

Ans 5. Option (B) is correct.

Explanation: Production concept states that the highly affordable and available products are preferred by the consumers. This means that the success of the company is based upon the effective production and distribution of the products. The focus of business activities was, therefore, on production of goods. Thus, availability and affordability of the product were considered to be the key to the success of a firm. The focus of business activity changed to bringing continuous improvement in the quality, incorporating new features, etc. Thus, product improvement became the key to profit maximisation of a firm, under the concept of product orientation.

Ans 7. Option (D) is correct.

Explanation: Marketing orientation implies that focus on satisfaction of customer's needs is the key to the success of any organisation in the market. The purpose of marketing is to generate customer value at a profit.

Ans 8. Option (A) is correct.

Explanation: Personal selling is a very effective promotional tool, which helps in influencing the prospects about the merits of a product and thereby increasing its sale.

REFLECTION

(a) Were you able to explain the meaning, features and functions of marketing?
(b) Could you identify the marketing philosophy in the below mentioned line:
"The focus of business firms shifted to pushing the sale of products through aggressive selling techniques."
(c) Were you able to describe the elements of marketing mix?
(d) Have you understood the concept of branding, labelling and packaging?
(e) Were you able to describe the factors determining price of a product?
(f) Were you able to explain the components of physical distribution?
(g) Have you understood the various channels of physical distribution?
(h) Have you understood the concept of advertising, personal selling, sales promotion and public relations?
(i) Could you identify the element of promotion mix in the below mentioned line:
"A direct face-to-face dialogue takes place that involves an interactive relationship between the seller and the buyer."

SELF ASSESSMENT PAPER - 11

Maximum Time: 1 hour **MM: 30**

General Instructions:

(i) All the questions are compulsory
(ii) Q.1 to Q.10 are 1 mark questions
(iii) Q.11 to Q.12 are 3 mark questions
(iv) Q.13 to Q.14 are 4 marks questions
(v) Q.15 is a 6 marks question

Objective Type Questions **[1 Mark]**

1. Traditionally, marketing has been described in terms of its:

(A) Functions **(B)** Activities **(C)** Both (A) and (B) **(D)** None of these **[1]**

2. Match the options of Column I with their correct options given in Column II.

	Column I		Column II
(a)	Product	(i)	Anything of value which is offered to the market for sale.
(b)	Place	(ii)	Activities that make firm's products available to the target customers.
(c)	Promotion	(iii)	Activities that communicate availability, features, merits, etc. of the products to the target customers and persuade them to buy it.

(A) a – i, b – ii, c – iii **(B)** a – ii, b – iii, c – i **(C)** a – iii, b – i, c – ii **(D)** None of these **[1]**

3. Manisha found dust and small stones in the newly opened red chili powder spice pack manufactured by a reputed company, Masala Mantra Ltd. She went back to the shopkeeper from whom the pack was purchased who directed her to call up the customer care centre. When all her efforts go in vain, she went to a consumer activist, group to seek advice. The group decided to help her and take measures to impose restrictions on the sales of the firm's products of the particular batch and urge customers to refrain from buying the products of the company. Masala Mantra lost its image in the market. The Board of directors gave the responsibility of bringing back the lost image of the company to the General Manager.

Which of the following concept of marketing management which will help the General Manager to get the firm out of the above crisis?

(A) Advertising **(B)** Sales promotion
(C) Public relations **(D)** Personal selling **[1]**

4.

Identify the element of promotion mix illustrated in the picture above.

(A) Advertising **(B)** Personal Selling
(C) Sales Promotion **(D)** Publicity **[1]**

5. For the following two statements, choose the correct option:

Statement I: The basic purpose of warehousing activities is to arrange placement of goods and provide facilities to store them.

Statement II: Larger the number of warehouses a firm has, lesser would be the time taken in serving customers.

Choose the correct option from options given below:

(A) Statement I is correct and statement II is wrong.
(B) Statement II is correct and statement I is wrong.
(C) Both the statements are correct.
(D) Both the statements are wrong. **[1]**

6. In the following questions, a statement of Assertion (A) is followed by a statement of Reason (R). Mark the correct choice as:

Assertion (A): Personal selling involves written presentation of message.

Reason (R): Personal selling allows a salesperson to develop personal relationships with the prospective customers.

(A) Both Assertion (A) and Reason (R) are true and Reason (R) is the correct explanation of Assertion (A).
(B) Both Assertion (A) and Reason (R) are true but Reason (R) is not the correct explanation of Assertion (A).
(C) Assertion (A) is true but Reason (R) is false.
(D) Assertion (A) is false but Reason (R) is true.

Read the text given below and answer Q. 7–10 based on it.

Harsh is planning to start his own bakery business named 'The Cake Shop' after doing a diploma in entrepreneurship. He estimates an investment of ₹ 10 crores to set up the business. He started doing a lot of hard work and used to learn the recipes in various preparations. He also learnt many recipes to bake different types of cakes and pastries from online sites. He decided to keep the price of the products low initially to attract customers and also informed his customers about the goodness of the items sold by them. He also decided to make the packaging of the cakes attractive and unique so that customers are persuaded to buy his cakes. However, he didn't mention on the packets of cakes weather it is veg or non-veg. As a result, vegetarian people became hesitant in buying things from his shop as they had to verbally inquire from him about the inclusion of eggs in the preparation of various items.

7. Which of the following aspect related to the marketing of products has been ignored by Harsh?
   - **(A)** Labelling
   - **(B)** Packaging
   - **(C)** Transportation
   - **(D)** None of these **[1]**
8. Which of the following component of marketing is highlighted in the below mentioned lines:
   "He decided to keep the price of the products low initially to attract customers"
   - **(A)** Promotion
   - **(B)** Price
   - **(C)** Place
   - **(D)** Product **[1]**
9. "The Cake Shop" mentioned in the above text is a:
   - **(A)** Brand
   - **(B)** Brand name
   - **(C)** Brand mark
   - **(D)** Trade mark **[1]**
10. Which of the following function of packaging is highlighted in the below mentioned lines:
    "He also decided to make the packaging of the cakes attractive and unique so that customers are persuaded to buy his cakes".
    - **(A)** Product Identification
    - **(B)** Product Protection
    - **(C)** Facilitating Use of the Product
    - **(D)** All of the above **[1]**

Short Answer Type Questions - I [3 Marks]

11. The owner of Spicy Burgers has many branches throughout the country. The company believes in hiring places and giving rent to the owners of the places at highly busy places of the cities. However, the company deals with its customers on its own thus providing them freshly prepared burgers by its own staff. The company has a wide base of customers. The company has kept the nature of its channel so because of one main characteristic or nature of the product it serves. It has always tried to please its customers and for this reason the services are fast. The company has decided to launch an advertising campaign for creating awareness about its new product. It has even contacted the number one advertisement making company for this purpose. However, the top management is concerned about the impact as the potential customers or the prospects can't be delivered the message compulsively. So, there is one scheme the company has decided to launch where a burger will be provided with an additional cold drink on all days of the first week of the month. Identify and explain channel of distribution highlighted in the above case.
12. Aroma Tea is a company which manufactures all kinds of tea. Amit is a distributor of tea and sells tea to far off places. He has categorised his tea to be sold into three categories: Green, Yellow and Red. His brother Somesh, on the other hand, is running a mobile manufacturing company. His company strictly produces mobile according to the predetermined specifications. The mobiles of each variety are of same size, looks and performance. Identify and explain the function of marketing which has been highlighted in the above case.

Short Answer Type Questions - II [4 Marks]

13. White Herbal is an FMCG company which only deals in manufacturing herbal products. The company runs by the CEO, Mr. Amit Gupta. The company has its own farms where pure herbal food products are grown. The packaging is also environmentally friendly with no use of synthetic materials like plastic. The company has decided to take the benefits of consuming herbal food products to the masses. It has decided to arrange for talk shows, newspaper advertisements, TV advertisements, Celebrity involvement etc. All these efforts will be able to bring the benefits of herbal products of this company to the potential customers. Identify and explain the element of marketing mix highlighted in the above case?
14. A rice manufacturing company has put labels on its packets stating the variety of rice it is selling. Currently it has three varieties— basmati rice, brown rice, and long grain rice. The rice of the company comes from Maharashtra. So, the price of the rice is high but recently in order to stay in the market it has lowered down its prices by 10%. The company sells its rice in different markets of the world. Next year the company is thinking of selling its rice in the market of a nation having a very high population. The top management hasn't yet decided the type of channel it should choose. Two years back the company started selling its rice online, the decision brought an indirect change in one of the elements of the marketing mix and of course one element saw change directly.
    - **(i)** Identify and explain the factor of price determination which has affected the pricing of rice by the company?
    - **(ii)** Identify and explain the type of channel do you think the company should choose for the new country?

Long Answer Type Questions [6 Marks]

15. Crispy Veg are the manufacturer of vegetarian food products made with fresh vegetables. The founders

of the company originally developed this food to meet their own needs but found that their friends and families around were also keen to use the products. It was not only the vegetarians, but also those who could not get enough environment friendly sustainable food, that appreciated the product. It did not take long for the founders to recognise the potential of their little venture. In the beginning they started from their home with the product being sold through local family parties that enable guests to personally meet the owner. This helped to establish strong connections with the prospective buyers and the company could put the product on shelves of natural food store. The company used all marketing activities to grow and expand. The company began sponsoring booths at festivals, drawing attention to its newly created vegetarian products. It also disseminated relevant information to media about its products and the people who helped in building the company's reputation. The founders were invited for an interview with one of the leading TV channels in which they talked about their environment friendly vegetarian products.

(i) Identify and explain the communication tool used by Crispy Veg.

(ii) Briefly explain the role of the tool identified in (i) above.

CONSUMER PROTECTION

LEARNING OUTCOMES

After going through this chapter, the student would be able to:

- Understand the concept of consumer protection.
- Describe the importance of consumer protection.
- Discuss the scope of Consumer Protection Act, 2019.
- Understand the concept of a consumer according to the Consumer Protection Act, 2019.
- Explain the consumer rights.
- Understand the responsibilities of consumers.
- Understand who can file a complaint and against whom?
- Discuss the legal redressal machinery under Consumer Protection Act, 2019.
- Examine the remedies available to the consumer under Consumer Protection Act, 2019.
- Describe the role of consumer organisations and NGOs in protecting consumers' interests.

Study Plan
Maximum Time = 3.45 Hrs
Maximum Questions = 75

Revision Notes

- As per the Consumer Protection Act, 2019, a consumer is defined as a person who buys any good or avails a service for a consideration. It does not include a person who obtains a good for resale or a good or service for commercial purposes. It covers transactions through all modes including offline, and online through electronic means, teleshopping, multi-level marketing or direct selling.
- **Importance/Need of Consumer Protection:**

(i) From the point of view of Consumer:

Scan this
Meaning and Importance of Consumer Protection

(a) Educate consumers to avoid consumer ignorance.

(b) Protect and promote interests of unorganised consumers.

(c) Safeguard from widespread exploitation of consumers.

(ii) From the point of view of Business:

(a) Long-term interest of business

(b) Business uses society's resources

(c) Fulfils social responsibility

(d) Moral justification

(e) Avoids government intervention

- **Scope of The Consumer Protection Act, 2019:**

The scope of the Act is very wide.

(i) Extends to the whole of India except the State of Jammu and Kashmir.

(ii) Applicable to all types of undertakings, big and small, whether in the private or public sector, or in the co-operative sector, whether a manufacturer or a trader.

(iii) Applicable to all goods and services.

(iv) Provides for protection of the interests of consumers by establishing authorities for timely and effective administration and settlement of consumers' disputes.

- **Consumer Protection Act, 2019:** [Board, 2019]

(i) Who can file a complaint?

(a) A consumer; or

(b) Any voluntary consumer association registered under any law for the time being in force; or

(c) The Central Government or any State Government; or

(d) The Central Authority; or

(e) One or more consumers, where there are numerous consumers having the same interest; or

(f) In case of the death of a consumer, his legal heir or legal representative; or

(g) In the case of a consumer being a minor, his parent or legal guardian.

(ii) Consumer Rights: [Board, 2022]

(a) **Right to be Protected:** Be protected against marketing of goods and services which are hazardous to life and property.

Example: Electrical appliances which are manufactured with substandard products or do not conform to the safety norms might cause serious injury. Thus, consumers are educated that they should use electrical appliances which are ISI marked as this would be an assurance of such products meeting quality specifications.

(b) **Right to be Informed:** Be informed of the quality, quantity, potency, purity, standard and price of goods or services.

(c) **Right to be assured:** Be assured of access to a variety of goods or services at competitive prices.

(d) **Right to seek redressal:** Seek redressal against unfair or restrictive trade practices.

(e) **Right to be heard:** File a complaint and be heard in case of dissatisfaction with a good or service.

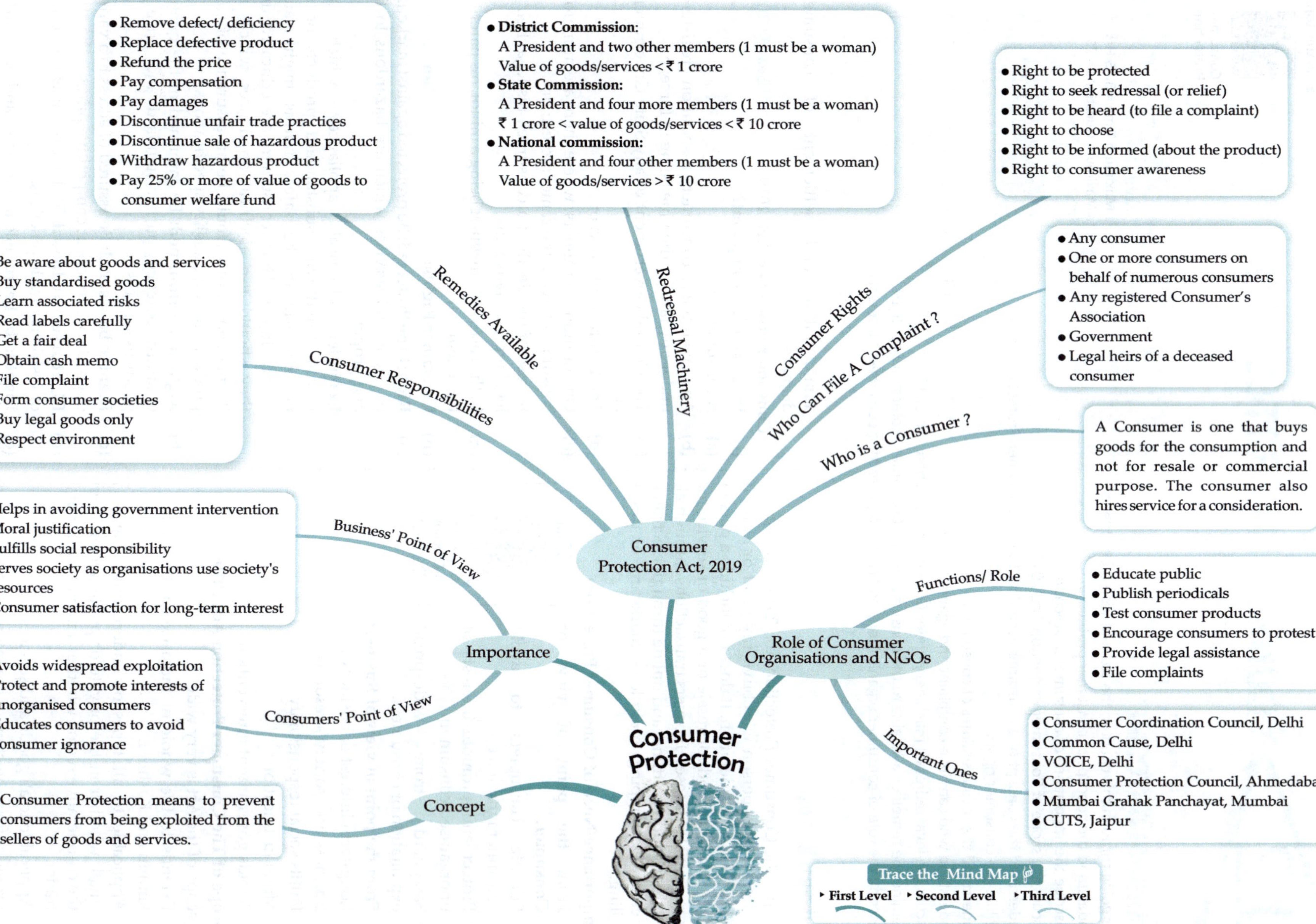
Consumer Protection
Consumer Protection Act, 2019
Remedies Available
• Remove defect/ deficiency
• Replace defective product
• Refund the price
• Pay compensation
• Pay damages
• Discontinue unfair trade practices
• Discontinue sale of hazardous product
• Withdraw hazardous product
• Pay 25% or more of value of goods to consumer welfare fund
Redressal Machinery
• District Commission:
A President and two other members (1 must be a woman)
Value of goods/services < ₹ 1 crore
• State Commission:
A President and four more members (1 must be a woman)
₹ 1 crore < value of goods/services < ₹ 10 crore
• National commission:
A President and four other members (1 must be a woman)
Value of goods/services > ₹ 10 crore
Consumer Rights
• Right to be protected
• Right to seek redressal (or relief)
• Right to be heard (to file a complaint)
• Right to choose
• Right to be informed (about the product)
• Right to consumer awareness
Who Can File A Complaint ?
• Any consumer
• One or more consumers on behalf of numerous consumers
• Any registered Consumer's Association
• Government
• Legal heirs of a deceased consumer
Who is a Consumer ?
A Consumer is one that buys goods for the consumption and not for resale or commercial purpose. The consumer also hires service for a consideration.
Consumer Responsibilities
• Be aware about goods and services
• Buy standardised goods
• Learn associated risks
• Read labels carefully
• Get a fair deal
• Obtain cash memo
• File complaint
• Form consumer societies
• Buy legal goods only
• Respect environment
Importance
Business' Point of View
• Helps in avoiding government intervention
• Moral justification
• Fulfills social responsibility
• Serves society as organisations use society's resources
• Consumer satisfaction for long-term interest
Consumers' Point of View
• Avoids widespread exploitation
• Protect and promote interests of unorganised consumers
• Educates consumers to avoid consumer ignorance
Concept
Consumer Protection means to prevent consumers from being exploited from the sellers of goods and services.
Role of Consumer Organisations and NGOs
Functions/ Role
• Educate public
• Publish periodicals
• Test consumer products
• Encourage consumers to protest
• Provide legal assistance
• File complaints
Important Ones
• Consumer Coordination Council, Delhi
• Common Cause, Delhi
• VOICE, Delhi
• Consumer Protection Council, Ahmedabad
• Mumbai Grahak Panchayat, Mumbai
• CUTS, Jaipur
Trace the Mind Map
First Level
Second Level
Third Level

(f) **Right to consumer education:** Acquire knowledge and be well informed.

(iii) **Consumer Responsibilities:** [Board, 2022]

(a) Be aware of the variety of goods and services available

(b) Ensure quality certification marks

(c) Use products safely

(d) Read labels carefully

(e) Obtain cash memo

(f) Form consumer organisations

(g) File a complaint when required

(h) Save the environment

(i) Get a fair deal

(iv) **Reliefs available:**

(a) Removal of defects

(b) Replacement of goods

(c) Compensation for loss or injury suffered

(d) Refund of prices and punitive damages

(e) Issue corrective advertisement

(f) Withdrawal of hazardous goods from sale

(g) Cease manufacturing of hazardous goods

(h) Contribution to consumer welfare fund

(i) Discontinue unfair trade practices

- **Redressal Agencies Under the Consumer Protection Act, 2019:**

(i) **District Commission:**

(a) Consists of one President and two other members (1 must be a woman).

(b) Appointed by the concerned State Government.

(c) For disputes up to ₹ 1 crore.

(d) If unsatisfied by the decision of the District Commission, a consumer can approach the State Commission within 45 days of passing of the order.

(ii) **State Commission:**

(a) Consists of one President and minimum four other members (1 must be a woman).

(b) For disputes from ₹ 1 crore to ₹ 10 crores.

(c) Appointed by the concerned State Government.

(d) If unsatisfied, appeal to the National Commission within 30 days of passing of the order.

(iii) **National Commission:**

(a) Consists of one President and four other members (1 must be a woman).

(b) For disputes exceeding ₹ 10 crores.

(c) Appointed by the Central Government.

(d) If unsatisfied by the decision of the National Commission, the consumer can appeal in the Supreme Court about a matter falling in its original jurisdiction within 30 days of passing of the order.

(e) In all other cases, the order of National Commission is final and cannot be challenged further.

- **Role of Consumer Organisations and NGOs:** These are non-profit organisations which aim at protection and promotion of the interest of the consumers.

- **Several functions are as follows:**

(i) Educating the general public about consumer rights by organising training programmes, seminars and workshops.

(ii) Publishing periodicals and other publications to impart knowledge about the consumer problems.

(iii) Carrying out comparative testing of consumer products in the accredited laboratories.

(iv) Encouraging consumers to strongly protest and take action against unfair trade practices.

(v) Providing legal assistance to the consumers.

(vi) Filing complaints in appropriate consumer courts on behalf of the consumers.

(vii) Taking an initiative in filing cases in the interest of general public.

Scan this

Remedies and Relief to a consumer

- **Important Consumer Organisations and NGOs:**

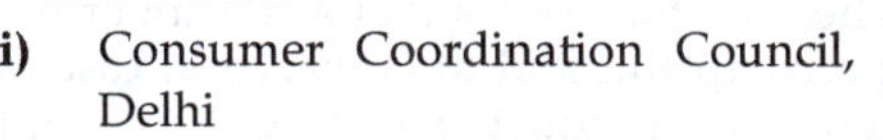

(i) Consumer Coordination Council, Delhi

(ii) Common Causes, Delhi

(iii) Voluntary Organisation in Interest of Consumer Education (VOICE), Delhi

(iv) Consumer Education and Research Centre (CERC), Ahmedabad

(v) Consumer Protection Council (CPC), Ahmedabad

(vi) Consumer Guidance Society of India (CGSI), Mumbai

(vii) Mumbai Grahak Panchayat, Mumbai

(viii) Karnataka Consumer Service Society, Bangalore

(ix) Consumers Association, Kolkata

(x) Consumer Unity and Trust Society (CUTS), Jaipur

KEY TERMS

Unfair trade practice: A trade practice used for promoting sale, use or supply of any goods or service which falsely represents its quality, standard, quantity,composition, style or model.

Consumer Protection: To protect consumers from being exploited.

Consumer redressal: Right to fair settlement of grievances of the consumers.

Complaint: Any allegation in writing made by the complainant for obtaining relief

MNEMONICS

Concept: Consumer Rights as per the Consumer Protection Act, 2019:

Mnemonics: Hey Champ, Remain Punctual In Class.

Interpretations:

H: Heard
C: Choose
R: Redressal
P: Protected
I: Informed
C: Consumer Awareness

Concept: Redressal agencies under the Consumer Protection Act, 2019:

Mnemonics: No Singing and Dancing!

Interpretations:

N: National Commission
S: State Commission
D: District Commission

SUBJECTIVE TYPE QUESTIONS

Short Answer Type Questions-I (3 marks each)

1. Ranjana bought a packet of spices from a local shopkeeper and found that the ingredients given on the label were not legible. She complained about it to the company. The company sent a written apology stating that they will make sure that existing packets are withdrawn from the market and new packets with legible labels are soon made available. State the consumer right which Ranjana exercised. U [OEB]

Ans. Right to be informed which states that a consumer has a right to have complete information about the product he intends to buy such as, ingredients, date of manufacture, price, quantity etc.

OR

Right to be heard which states that a consumer has right to file a complaint and to be heard in case of dissatisfaction with a product or a service. [3]

Commonly Made Error

⚠ The students get confused while identifying the correct right. Students consider it as the Right to seek redressal.

Answering Tip

Understand the Consumer Rights clearly with the help of suitable examples. Practice case study based questions to have a better understanding of the concepts.

2. Christmas was approaching and on the eve of Christmas, Erica purchased two kilograms of plum cake from 'The Cake Shop'. On consumption of cake her two children and husband fell sick and were to be hospitalised. Erica wanted to file a case in the consumer forum but could not do so because she did not have any proof of buying cake from 'The Cake Shop'. What proof could Erica have obtained for filing the claim in the consumer court? AI A [OEB]

Ans. Erica could have **obtained cash memo** for filing the claim in consumer court. The consumer should insist on cash memo or invoice relating to purchase of goods or availing of any services and preserve it carefully. Such proof of purchase is required for filing a complaint. In case of durable goods, the manufacturers generally provide the warranty or guarantee card along with the product. It is the duty of consumers to obtain these documents and ensure that these are duly signed, stamped and dated. The consumer must preserve them till the warranty or guarantee period is over. 3

3. Explain briefly any two points of importance of consumer protection from the point of view of business. R [OEB]

4. State any three functions performed by non-governmental organisations for consumer protection. R [Delhi Set-1, 2016]

Ans. Functions performed by non-governmental organisations for consumer protection are:

(i) Educating the general public about consumer rights. 1

(ii) Publishing periodicals and other publications.

(iii) Carrying out comparative testing of consumer products. 1

(iv) Encouraging consumers to strongly protest and take action against unscrupulous, exploitive and unfair trade practices of sellers.

(v) Providing legal assistance to consumers. 1

(vi) Filing complaints in appropriate consumer courts on behalf of the consumers. 1

(vii) Taking initiative in filing cases in consumer courts in the interest of the general public. 1 (Any three)

(If an examinee has given only the headings, ½ mark for each heading should be awarded)

[Marking Scheme, Delhi 2016]

Commonly Made Error

⚠ Students generalise the answers and write the role of NGOs in the society.

Answering Tip

Be specific while writing the answer and always focus on what is asked. Write the role of NGOs in protecting the consumers.

Short Answer Type Questions-II (4 marks each)

1. Mr. Akshay, a 20-year-old college student purchased a book online from XYZ Pvt Ltd. and when it was delivered, he noticed that there was no MRP mentioned on it. He browsed the internet and found that the book was sold at different prices in different places. He filed a case in District forum against the publisher. The court held in favour of Akshay and awarded a compensation of ₹10,000.

(a) Identify and state the consumer right violated in the above case.

(b) Name and explain the right exercised by Mr. Akshay. Ap [SQP 2023-24]

Concept Applied	Consumer Protection Act, 2019

Ans. (a) Right to be informed: Every consumer has a right to have complete information about the product he intends to buy including its ingredients, date of manufacture, price, quantity, directions for use, etc.

By hiding the MRP, the publisher has violated the right of Akshay to have complete information about the book he is buying.

(b) Right to seek redressal: This states that every consumer has the right to get relief in case the product or service falls short of expectations.

Akshay filed a case in the district forum and got a relief so he exercised his right to get relief in case of violation of the rights.

This Question is for practice and its solution is given at the end of the chapter.

Commonly Made Error

⚠ Students interchange the Right to be informed and the Right to seek redressal. They write the Right to seek redressal as the one violated.

Answering Tip

⚠ Read the case study properly and identify the correct Right exercised and violated.

2. Rajneesh purchased a 500 ml bottle of fruit juice for ₹60 in Ahmedabad from a local store. While consuming it, he found an insect floating in it. He sent a legal notice to the company immediately and decided to approach a Consumer Dispute Redressal Agency for a relief of ₹2 lakh.

(i) Which Consumer Dispute Redressal Agency did Rajneesh approach, out of the three-tier machinery set up under the Consumer Protection Act, 2019 for redressal?

(ii) If Rajneesh is not satisfied by the order of the above Agency, where can he appeal against such order and within how many days?

(iii) State any two reliefs that can be granted to Rajneesh in the above case. R [Outside Delhi Set-1, 2019]

Ans.

Topper's Answer, 2019

i) Rajneesh would have approached the District forum.

ii) If Rajneesh is not satisfied by the decision, he can appeal to the State commission within 45 days

iii) Relief that can be granted to Rajneesh in the above case are→

a) Compensation for health issues or injury suffered

b) Refund of prices & punitive damages.

Tip and Tricks

⚠ Remember that for complaints below ₹1 crore, the consumers can approach the district court. The students can write any two reliefs out of the several reliefs mentioned.

3. Sameeksha is a class XII student having Business Studies as one of her subjects. After studying Consumer Protection' as one of the chapters in Business Studies, she tried to apply the acquired knowledge while purchasing and using the goods. She is very fond of cooking and always tries new recipes. This time she wants to purchase a 'Bread Maker' to prepare homemade bread. She checked online about the various brands of Bread Makers available in the market and compared their prices so that an intelligent and wise choice could be made. Then she went to a nearby market to buy it. Being an informed consumer, she looked for the Standardisation Mark, negotiated the price printed on the label, checked the date of manufacturing and asked for guarantee or warranty of the product. After being satisfied with all the concerned information she purchased the 'Bread Maker' and as a responsible consumer asked for the cash-memo. After coming back home she opened the packaging of the 'Bread Maker' and found an instruction booklet inside. She carefully read all the instructions and operated the Bread Maker step-by-step and succeeded in making nice 'Atta Bread' for her family. Sameeksha has fulfilled many responsibilities of a consumer while purchasing and using the 'Bread Maker'.

State any four responsibilities fulfilled by Sameeksha besides asking for a cash-memo.

A I U [Delhi Set-1]

Ans. Sameeksha has fulfilled the following responsibilities of a consumer:

(i) Information: Sameeksha checked online about the various brands of bread makers available in the market and compared their prices before purchasing. She also checked for the Standardisation Mark, negotiated the price printed on the label, checked for guarantee or warranty of the product, and asked about the date of manufacturing. This shows that she was concerned about the quality and authenticity of the product she was buying.

(ii) Safety: Sameeksha asked for a guarantee or warranty of the product, which ensures that she can get the product replaced or repaired if it is defective or malfunctions. This shows that she was concerned about the safety of the product and the potential risks associated with using it.

(iii) Environmental responsibility: Sameeksha checked for the Standardisation Mark, which ensures that the product meets the necessary quality standards and is safe for use. This shows that she was concerned about the environmental impact of the product and wanted to ensure that it was safe for use.

(iv) Ethical responsibility: Sameeksha asked for the cash memo, which is a proof of purchase and helps in case of any disputes or legal issues. This shows that she was concerned about the ethical responsibility of buying a product and wanted to ensure that she was doing it legally and ethically.

4. What is meant by 'Consumer Protection'? State any three points of importance of consumer protection from the point of view of business.

[Outside Delhi Set-2, 2019]

Ans. Meaning of Consumer Protection: Consumer protection means the act of providing **adequate protection to consumers** against the unscrupulous, exploitative and **unfair trade practices** of manufacturers and service providers.

Importance of consumer protection from business point of view:

(i) Long-term interest of the business: In the competitive environment, the businessman can win and **capture a big share of the market** only through consumer satisfaction. Those who ignore the interest and satisfaction of consumers may lose their goodwill and clients.

(ii) Social Responsibility: Just like other stakeholders, towards consumers also, businessmen have got social responsibility to provide quality goods at reasonable price. Consumer protection guides businessmen to fulfil social responsibility towards consumers.

(iii) Government Intervention: If businessmen want to avoid intervention of the government, then they should **not involve in unfair trade practices** and exploitative practices towards consumers.

5. Sumit purchased an ISI marked washing machine of a famous brand 'MG' from TG Electronics Ltd. The shopkeeper asked him to wait for two days for installation of the machine. His friend, Vivek, was very fond of experimenting with new electronic products. He told Sumit that there was no need to wait for the company's representative to install the machine and that he could do it. So, both of them installed the machine without following the manufacturer's instructions. Initially, the machine worked effectively and the wash was good. But after two days, the machine started stopping in between the wash cycle, Sumit and Vivek tried their best to start the machine but failed in their efforts. Sumit, therefore, approached TG Electronics Ltd., which refused to provide any service on the plea that the installation of the machine was not done by the company.

(i) State the responsibility which Sumit had to fulfil as an aware consumer to get the services of the company,

(ii) Explain briefly any two rights which Sumit could have exercised "had he fulfilled his responsibility identified in part (i)". [Delhi Set-1, 2018]

Ans. (i) Responsibility which Sumit has to fulfil as an aware consumer to get the services of the company: Learn about the risks associated with products and services, follow manufacturer's instructions and use the products safely.

(ii) Two rights which Sumit could have exercised had he fulfilled his responsibility:

(a) Right to be heard:

The consumer has right to **file a complaint** and to be heard in case of dissatisfaction with a product or a service. It is because of this reason many firms have set up their own consumer service and grievance cells.

(b) Right to seek redressal:

The consumer has a right to **get relief in case the product or service falls short of his expectations.** The Consumer Protection Act, 1986 provides reliefs to consumers such as replacement of product, removal of defect in the product, compensation for any loss or injury suffered by the consumer.

[Marking Scheme Delhi, 2018] **[1+3=4]**

6. State any eight reliefs available to the consumer, if the court is satisfied about the genuineness of the complaint. A I R [Outside Delhi Set-1, 2019]

Ans. If the Consumer Court is satisfied with the genuineness of the complaint, it can issue one or more of the following directions to the aggrieved party as a relief:

(i) To **remove the defect** in goods or the deficiency in service.

(ii) To **replace the defective product** with a new one, free from any defect.

(iii) To **refund the price** paid for the product, or the charges paid for the service.

(iv) To **pay a reasonable amount** of compensation for any loss or injury suffered by the consumer due to negligence of the opposite party.

(v) To **pay punitive damages** in appropriate circumstances.

(vi) To **discontinue the unfair/ restrictive trade practices** and not to repeat the same in future.

(vii) Not to offer hazardous goods for sale.

(viii) To **withdraw hazardous goods** from sale.

(ix) To **cease manufacture** of hazardous goods and to desist from offering hazardous services.

(x) To pay any amount (not less than 25% of the value of the defective goods or deficient services provided), to be credited to the **Consumer Welfare Fund** or any other organisation/person, to be utilised in the prescribed manner.

(xi) To **issue corrective advertisement** to neutralise the effect of a misleading advertisement.

(xii) To **pay adequate costs** to the appropriate party.

(Any eight) [½ × 8 = 4]

Long Answer Type Questions (6 marks each)

1. Enumerate any six rights of a consumer under the Consumer Protection Act, 2019. U [SQP 2021-22]

OR

Explain the following rights of a consumer as per the provisions of Consumer Protection Act, 2019:

(i) Right to Safety

(ii) Right to be Informed R [Delhi Set-1, 2022]

OR

Explain the following rights of a consumer as provided by Consumer Protection Act, 2019:

(i) Right to Seek Redressal

(ii) Right to Consumer Education R [Delhi Set-2, 2022]

OR

Explain the following rights of a consumer as per the Consumer Protection Act, 2019:

(i) Right to Safety

(ii) Right to Consumer Education.

R [Outside Delhi Set-1, 3, 2022]

OR

Explain the following rights of a consumer as per the Consumer Protection Act, 2019:

(i) Right to be Heard

(ii) Right to be Informed R [Outside Delhi, Set-2, 2022]

Ans. Rights of a consumer under the Consumer Protection Act, 2019:

(i) Right to Safety: The consumer has a right to be **protected against goods and services** which are hazardous to life and health. For instance, electrical appliances which are manufactured with substandard products or do not conform to the safety norms might cause serious injury. Thus, consumers are educated that they should use electrical appliances which are ISI marked as this would be an assurance of such products meeting quality specifications.

(ii) Right to be Informed: The consumer has a right to have **complete information** about the product he intends to buy including its ingredients, date of manufacture, price, quantity, directions for use, etc. It is because of this reason that the legal framework in India requires the manufacturers to provide such information on the package and label of the product.

(iii) Right to be Assured: The consumer has the freedom **to choose** from a variety of products at **competitive prices**. This implies that the marketers should offer a wide variety of products in terms of quality, brand, prices, size, etc. and allow the consumer to make a choice from amongst these. According to this right, every consumer has the right to choose the goods or services of his or her likings. The right to choose means an assurance of availability, ability and access to a variety of products and services at competitive price and competitive price means just or fair price. The producer or supplier or retailer should not force the customer to buy a particular brand only. The consumer should be free to choose the most suitable product from his point of view.

(iv) Right to be Heard: The consumer has a right to **file a complaint** and to be heard in case of dissatisfaction with a good or a service. It is because of this reason that many enlightened business firms have set up their own consumer service and grievance cells. Many consumer organisations are also working towards this direction and helping consumers in redressal of their grievances.

(v) Right to Seek Redressal: The consumer has a right to get **relief** in case the product or service falls short of his expectations. The **Consumer Protection Act** provides a number of reliefs to the consumers including replacement of the product, removal of defect in the product, compensation paid for any loss or injury suffered by the consumer, etc.

(vi) Right to Consumer Education: The consumer has a right to **acquire knowledge** and to be a **well-informed** consumer throughout life. He should be aware about his rights and the reliefs available to him in case of a product or service falling short of his expectations. Many consumer organisations and some enlightened businesses are taking an active part in educating consumers in this respect. **[6]**

2. Enumerate any six responsibilities of a consumer under consumer Protection Act, 2019.

R [SQP 2021-22]

OR

Any five responsibilities of a consumer under consumer protection Act, 2019. R [Delhi Set-2022]

OR

What are the key responsibilities that consumers must fulfill to ensure they are protected under Consumer Protection Act? [AQP 2023, Set-1]

OR

(a) Enumerate the purpose of Consumer Protection Act, 2019.

(b) State any five responsibilities that should be kept in mind by a Consumer while purchasing, using and consuming goods and services, according to the Consumer Protection Act, 2019. [AQP 2023 Set-2]

Ans. Responsibilities of a Consumer under the Consumer Protection Act, 2019:

(i) Be aware of various goods and services available in the market so that an intelligent and wise choice can be made.

(ii) Buy only **standardised goods** as they provide quality assurance.

(iii) Learn about the risks associated with products and services, follow manufacturer's instructions and use the products safely.

(iv) **Read labels** carefully so as to have information about prices, net weight, manufacturing and expiry dates, etc.

(v) Assert yourself to ensure that you get a **fair deal**.

(vi) Be **honest** in your dealings. Choose only from legal goods and services and discourage unscrupulous practices.

(vii) Ask for a **cash memo** on purchase of goods or services.

(viii) **File a complaint** in an appropriate consumer forum in case of a shortcoming in the quality of goods purchased or services availed.

(ix) Form **consumer societies** which would play an active part in educating consumers and safeguarding their interests.

(x) Respect the environment.

[Marking Scheme, APQ 2021-22] **[1×6=6]**

Commonly Made Error

Students write about the rights or reliefs available instead of responsibilities.

Answering Tip

Learn rights, reliefs and responsibilities separately.

3. 'VOICE' is an important consumer organisation. It organised workshops in the months of December in Delhi/NCR for consumers. The theme was 'Organic Food – From Farm to Plate', to spread awareness on the importance of organic farming and to encourage consumers to switch from conventional food, that contains chemicals and pesticides to organic food. Expert speakers from farmers' community explained the harmful effects of usage of pesticides in farming and the importance of organic food. People were informed that the organisation regularly tests samples to detect adulteration like presence of heavy metals or pesticides. The results of the tests are published in their monthly magazine 'Consumer Voice' to make people aware of quality of different products. It also provides aid and legal advice to the consumers in seeking a remedy.

State the functions performed by the Consumer Voice for the protection and promotion of consumer interest by quoting lines from the above para.

A [Delhi Set-1, 2019]

Ans. Functions performed by the Consumer Voice for the protection and promotion of consumer interest:

(i) Educating the **general public** about consumer rights by organising training programmes, seminars and workshops.

'organised consumer workshops in the months of December in Delhi/ NCR on the theme of 'Organic Food -From Farm to Plate', as a part of its initiative to spread awareness on the importance of organic farming'

(ii) Publishing periodicals and other publications to impart knowledge about consumer problems, legal reporting, reliefs available and other matters of interest.

'The results of the tests are published in their monthly magazine. 'Consumer Voice' to make people aware of quality of different products'

(iii) Carrying out comparative testing of consumer products in accredited laboratories to test relative qualities of competing brands and publishing the test results for the benefit of consumers.

('People were informed that the organisation regularly tests samples to detect adulteration like presence of heavy metals or pesticides')

(iv) Providing legal assistance to consumers by the way of providing aid, legal advice, etc. in seeking legal remedy.

'It also provides aid and legal advice to the consumers in seeking a remedy' **[1½×4=6]**

4. State any two reliefs that the Consumer Court can grant to consumers in case of genuine complaints in each of the following situations:

(i) Divya was charged more than the printed maximum retail price (MRP) for a bottle of water.

(ii) Clara was sold a car with a defective engine.

(iii) Antony suffered injury while using newly bought defective electric heater. A [OEB]

Ans. (i) Reliefs that the Consumer Court can grant to the customer are:

(a) To **refund the price paid**.

(b) To pay **punitive damages**.

(c) To **discontinue the unfair/ restrictive trade practice** and not to repeat the same in future.

(d) To pay any amount (not less than 25% of the value of the bottle of water) to be credited to the **Consumer Welfare Fund** or any other organisation/person, to be utilised in the prescribed manner.

(e) To pay adequate costs to the appropriate party.

(Any two)

(ii) Reliefs that the Consumer Court can grant to the customer are:

(a) To **remove the defect** in engine.

(b) To **replace the defective engine** with a new one, free from any defect.

(c) To **refund** the price paid.

(d) To **pay punitive damages**.

(e) To pay any amount (not less than 25% of the value of the defective engine) to be credited to the **Consumer Welfare Fund** or any other organisation/person, to be utilised in the prescribed manner.

(f) To pay adequate costs to the appropriate party.

(Any two)

(iii) Reliefs that the Consumer Court can grant to the customers are:

(a) To **remove** the defect in electrical heater.

(b) To **replace** the defective electrical heater with a new one, free from any defect.

(c) To **refund** the price paid.

(d) To **pay a reasonable amount** of compensation for any loss or injury suffered by the consumer due to negligence of the opposite party.

(e) To pay **punitive damages**.

(f) To **discontinue** the unfair/ restrictive trade practice and not to repeat the same in future.

(g) Not to offer hazardous goods like defective electrical heater for sale.

(h) To **withdraw hazardous goods** like defective electrical heater from sale.

(i) To **cease manufacture of hazardous goods** like defective electrical heater.

(j) To pay any amount (not less than 5% of the value of the defective goods) to be credited to the Consumer Welfare Fund or any other organisation/person, to be utilised in the prescribed manner.

(k) To **pay adequate costs** to the appropriate party.

(Any two) [2+2+2=6]

5. Explain the three tier machinery under 'The Consumer Protection Act' for redressal of consumers' grievances. AI U [OEB]

6. (a) Define the scope of Consumer Protection Act, 2019.

(b) State any five functions of non-governmental organisations which aim at promoting the welfare of consumers. AI R [APQ 2023-24] [6]

Ans. (a) Scope of Consumer Protection Act, 2019

It extends to the whole of India. It is applicable to all types of businesses whether a manufacturer or a trader and whether supplying goods or providing services including e-commerce firms. **[1]**

(b) Role of Non-Governmental Organisations are:

(i) Educating the general public about consumer rights by organising training programmes, seminars and workshops.

(ii) Publishing periodicals and other publications to impart knowledge about consumer problems, legal reporting, reliefs available and other matters of interest.

(iii) Carrying out comparative testing of consumer products in accredited laboratories to test relative qualities of competing brands and publishing the test results for the benefit of consumers.

(iv) Encouraging consumers to strongly protest and take action against unscrupulous, exploitative and unfair trade practices of sellers.

(v) Providing legal assistance to consumers by way of providing aid, legal advice etc. in seeking legal remedy.

This Question is for practice and its solution is given at the end of the chapter.

(vi) Filing complaints in appropriate consumer courts on behalf of the consumers.

(vii) Taking an initiative in filing cases in consumer courts in the interest of the general public, not for any individual. (Any five) **[1×5=5]**

[Marking Scheme, APQ 2023-24]

Commonly Made Errors

- Students often define the Consumer Protection Act instead of discussing the scope of the act.
- Students tend to write the role of NGOs in a paragraph form.

Answering Tips

- Write the scope which means the area of applicability of the Consumer Protection Act, 2019.
- Always write the answers in pointers for better understanding and to score better marks in the examination.

7. Indian Youth Organisation (IYO) organised a visit of its members to an old age home to inculcate the habit of social work among them. The visit revealed that the living conditions of the inmates of the old age home were not hygienic. So, the IYO members decided to clean the premises. During their cleanliness drive, they realised that the old age home also required pest control. But some of the inmates of old age home were reluctant for it because they believed that the pest control may create health problems for them. IYO, therefore decided to provide ethical, safe and odourless pest control. They showed to the inmates of old age home a pamphlet of the proposed pest control product which promised easy, inexpensive and long lasting pest control. The inmates happily agreed and the pest control was carried out. It worked for a fortnight but to their dismay the effect started wearing off. IYO contacted the pest control company which kept on postponing their visit. After waiting for a month, IYO filed a case in the consumer court.

The consumer court was satisfied with the genuineness of the complaint and issued necessary directions to the pest control company.

State any six directions that might have been issued by the court. **[Delhi Set-1, 2017]**

Ans. (a) Directions that might have been issued by the court:

(i) To remove the deficiency in service. ½

(ii) To refund the price paid for the service provided. ½

(iii) To pay a reasonable amount of compensation for any loss suffered by the inmates of old age home. ½

(iv) To pay punitive damages. ½

(v) To discontinue the unfair/restrictive trade practice and not to repeat the same in future. ½

(vi) To pay any amount (not less than 5% of the value of the service provided) to be credited to the Consumer Welfare Fund or any other organisation/ person, to be utilised in the prescribed manner. ½

(vii) To issue corrective advertisement to neutralise the effect of misleading pamphlet. ½

(viii) To pay adequate costs to IYO. ½ **(Any six)**

[Marking Scheme, Delhi 2017]

COMPETENCY BASED QUESTIONS

Objective Type Questions

[A] Multiple Choice Questions

1. 'The consumer has the right to acquire knowledge and to be a well-informed consumer throughout life.' State what type of knowledge is required by the consumer in the above stated 'Right'.

(A) Right to Seek Redressal
(B) Right to be Heard
(C) Right of Consumer Education
(D) Right to Choose U **[OEB]**

Concept Applied	Rights of a Consumer as per COPRA, 2019

Ans. Option (C) is correct.

Explanation: A consumer, who is well informed about his rights and the reliefs available to him, would be in a position to raise his voice against any unfair trade practices or unscrupulous exploitation. In addition to this, an understanding of his responsibilities would also enable a consumer to safeguard his interests.

2. Pragya bought an iron of reputed brand for ₹ 1,500 but it caused an electric shock while it was being used. Pragya wants to exercise her 'Right'. Identify the right under which she can be protected.

(A) Right to Choose
(B) Right to be Informed
(C) Right to be Heard
(D) Right to be Protected A **[OEB]**

3. "Bhuvan, who was a vegetarian went to a snack bar for having french fries and later found out that it had non-vegetarian content. Neither the advertisement nor the packing of the product displayed that the product has non-vegetarian content." Which right of consumer is violated?

(A) Right to Choose
(B) Right to be Informed
(C) Right to be Heard
(D) Right to Seek Redressal A **[OEB]**

4. Your mother purchased a washing machine for ₹10,000 from an authorised dealer of the manufacturer with a verbal guarantee that the machine will be replaced with a new one if any of its parts becomes defective within 3 months from the date of purchase. The motor of the machine was burnt within 15 days of its purchase. On complaining, the seller refused to replace the machine. Name the redressal agency under Consumer Protection Act where your mother can file the complaint.

These Questions are for practice and their solutions are given at the end of the chapter.

Concept Applied Redressal Agencies Under the Consumer Protection Act, 201

(A) District Commission
(B) State Commission
(C) National Commission
(D) None of above A [OEB]

Ans. Option (A) is correct.

Explanation: District Commission consists of one President and two other members appointed by the concerned State Government for disputes up to ₹ 1 crore. If unsatisfied by the decision of the District Commission, a consumer can approach the State Commission within 45 days of passing of the order.

5. Under the Consumer Protection Act, 2019, ... can be approached to file a complaint by the legal heir of a deceased consumer if compensation claimed is ₹ 3 crores?

(A) District Commission
(B) State Commission
(C) National Commission
(D) All of the above A [OEB]

Ans. Option (B) is correct.

Explanation: Under the Consumer Protection Act, 2019 the State CDRC will hear complaints when the value is more than ₹ 1 crore but less than ₹ 10 crores.

6. Match the functions of marketing in column I with the appropriate activities in column II. U [OEB]

(a) Relief available	(i) To remove the defect in goods or deficiency in service.
(b) Consumer Responsibility	(ii) Assert yourself to ensure that you get a fair deal.
(c) Consumer Right	(iii) The consumer has a right to have complete information about the product.

(A) a – i, b – ii, c – iii (B) a – ii, b – iii, c – i
(C) a – iii, b – i, c – ii (D) None of these

Ans. Option (A) is correct.

7.

Identify the concept stated in the above image.

(A) Consumer awareness
(B) Consumer relief
(C) Consumer responsibilities
(D) None of these [OEB]

Ans. Option (A) is correct.

Explanation: Consumer awareness is an act of ensuring that the buyer or consumers are aware of the information about products, goods, services, and consumer's rights. It is important so that buyers can make the right decision and make the right choice at the right time.

8.

Identify the consumer right illustrated in the above image.

(A) Right to be assured (B) Right to be protected
(C) Right to safety (D) Right to be heard Ap [OEB]

Ans. Option (A) is correct.

Explanation: The consumer has the freedom to assess a variety of products at competitive prices.

9.

Identify the consumer right illustrated by the picture given above. Ap [OEB]

(A) Right to seek redressal
(B) Right to consumer education
(C) Right to be protected
(D) Right to be informed

Ans. Option (A) is correct.

Explanation: The consumer has a right to get relief against unfair trade practices or restrictive trade practices or unscrupulous exploitation in case the product or a service falls short of his expectation.

10. Which of the following will not be considered as consumers as per Consumer Protection Act, 2019? U [Outside Delhi Set-1, 2023]

(A) A person, who avails any service for a consideration which has been partly paid.
(B) Any user of goods if such use is made with the approval of the buyer.

(C) A person who purchases goods through online means.

(D) A person who obtains goods for resale purposes.

Ans. Option (D) is correct.

Explanation: As per the provisions of the Consumer Protection Act, 2019, the person who obtains goods for resale is not considered as a consumer.

11. As per Consumer Protection Act, 2019, the consumer has a right to get relief in case the product or service falls short of his expectations. Which consumer right is discussed in the above statement?

(A) Right to be heard

(B) Right to be assured

(C) Right to seek redressal

(D) Right to safety U [Outside Delhi Set-1, 2023]

Ans. Option (C) is correct.

Explanation: The consumer has the right to get relief and seek compensation if the product falls short of his expectations.

12. Which of the following is/are the role(s) of Consumer Organisations and NGOs?

(A) Filing cases in consumer courts in the interest of the general public.

(B) Encouraging consumers to strongly protest and take action against unscrupulous, exploitative and unfair trade practices of sellers.

(C) Publications to impart knowledge about consumer problems.

(D) All of the above. [CFPQ 2023-24]

Ans. Option (D) is correct.

[B] Assertion & Reason

Directions: In the following questions, a statement of assertion (A) is followed by a statement of reason (R). Mark the correct choice as:

(A) Both assertion (A) and reason (R) are true and reason (R) is the correct explanation of assertion (A).

(B) Both assertion (A) and reason (R) are true but reason (R) is not the correct explanation of assertion (A).

(C) Assertion (A) is true but reason (R) is false.

(D) Assertion (A) is false but reason (R) is true.

1. **Assertion (A):** Many enlightened business firms have set up their own consumer service and grievance cells.

Reason (R): The consumer has a right to file a complaint and to be heard in case of dissatisfaction with a good or a service. [OEB]

2. **Assertion (A):** Consumer organisations play an important role in educating consumers about their rights and providing protection to them.

Reason (R): A consumer should not ask for a cash memo on purchase of goods or services. [OEB]

Ans. Option (C) is correct.

Explanation: The consumer should insist on a valid documentary evidence (cash memo/invoice) relating to purchase of goods or availing of any services and preserve it carefully. Such proof of purchase is required for filing a complaint.

3. **Assertion (A):** The Consumer Protection Act, 2019 has not defined the criteria of Consumer Disputes Redressal Commission (CDRCs).

Reason (R): Under the Consumer Protection Act, 2019, the National CDRC will hear complaints worth more than ₹ 10 crores. [OEB]

Concept Applied Redressal Agencies under the Consumer Protection Act, 2019

Ans. Option (D) is correct.

Explanation: The act has defined the criteria of Consumer Disputes Redressal Commission (CDRCs). The National CDRC will hear complaints worth more than ₹ 10 crores. The State CDRC will hear complaints when the value is more than ₹ 1 crore but less than ₹ 10 crore. While the District CDRC will entertain complaints when the value of goods or service is up to ₹ 1 crore.

4. **Assertion (A):** It is the responsibility of the consumer to buy only standardised goods as they provide quality assurance.

Reason (R): The consumers have certain responsibilities to follow and should keep a few things in mind while purchasing goods and services. [OEB]

[C] Case Based MCQs

1. Read the following text and answer the following questions on the basis of the same:

Piyal purchased an ISI marked heater from Bharti Appliances. She made cash payment but failed to get a cash memo. While making use of the heater she observed that it was not working properly. She contacted the shopkeeper immediately and told him the problem. Shopkeeper paid no heed to her complaint. Rather he marked that the good in question was not bought from his shop. Piyali had no evidence of proving that the heater was purchased from his shop only. She discussed the problem with her friend Sohini who advised her to approach Consumer Forum and lodge the complaint. Piyali was convinced with the idea of lodging the complaint against the shopkeeper but due to lack of cash memo it was difficult for her to proceed. [OEB]

1. Identify the right of the consumer as referred to in the above paragraph.

(A) Right to be Informed

(B) Right to be Protected

(C) Right to be Heard

(D) Right to Choose

Ans. Option (B) is correct.

Explanation: The consumer has a right to be protected against goods and services which are hazardous to life and health. For instance, electrical appliances which are manufactured with substandard products or do not conform to the safety norms might cause serious injury. Thus, consumers are educated that they should use electrical appliances which are ISI marked as this would be an assurance of such products meeting quality specifications.

2. Identify the responsibility of the consumer referred in the above case.

(A) Quality conscious

(B) Must obtain cash memo

(C) Cautious consumer

(D) Ready to lodge complaint

These Questions are for practice and their solutions are given at the end of the chapter.

Ans. Option (B) is correct.

Explanation: The consumer should insist on a cash memo/invoice relating to the purchase of goods or availing of any services and preserve it carefully. Such proof of purchase is required for filing a complaint. In case of durable goods the manufacturers generally provide the warranty/guarantee card along with the product. It is the duty of consumers to obtain these documents and ensure that they are duly signed, stamped and dated. The consumer must preserve them till the warranty/guarantee period is over.

3. Piyali cannot lodge a complaint against the shopkeeper. Why?

(A) She does not have the right.
(B) She was aware of the fact.
(C) She does not have the cash memo.
(D) She was happy with the product.

Ans. Option (C) is correct.

Explanation: The consumer should insist on a cash memo/invoice relating to purchase of goods or availing of any services and preserve it carefully. Such proof of purchase is required for filing a complaint.

4. Under which Act Piyali can seek to protect her rights being a consumer?

(A) Consumer Protection Act, 2019
(B) Consumer Protection Act, 1986
(C) The Indian Contract Act, 1872
(D) The Competition Act, 2002

Ans. Option (A) is correct.

Explanation: Consumer Protection Act, 2019 is a law to protect the interests of the consumers. This Act provides safety to consumers regarding defective products, dissatisfactory services, and unfair trade practices. The basic aim of the Consumer Protection Act, 2019 is to save the rights of the consumers by establishing authorities for timely and effective administration and settlement of consumers' disputes.

II. Read the following text and answer the following questions on the basis of the same:

Suresh has opened an NGO for the welfare of the consumers. He has got a degree in law. In order to utilise his education, he quite often helps people in their legal affairs. Now that he has started an NGO he assures that whenever a consumer in his knowledge is deprived of his consumer rights he should file a complaint on his behalf in the consumer court and fight for his cause. His organisation has some of the people with journalist background. The three of them along with Suresh from the side of their NGO have launched a monthly magazine which creates awareness about the rights, reliefs and responsibilities of the consumers. All the members of this NGO work with a lot of enthusiasm. Recently in the central part of the city they organized a training program in which all the information related to the exploitation of consumers, consumer ignorance, consumer rights and reliefs available to the consumers were the key highlights. The government has also provided support to their organisation. The government laboratories are easily in touch with them and are ready for any type of confirmation of results related to the purity of products. More and more members are getting attached with the organisation. The membership is increasing. The organisation recently helped few ladies stage a demonstration outside the showroom of a company responsible for selling a fake electrical appliance responsible for the death of one man. In totality, the NGO is doing a great job. **[OEB]**

1. Which of the following function of NGO is highlighted in the below mentioned lines: "Now that he has started an NGO he assures that whenever a consumer in his knowledge is deprived of his consumer rights he should file a complaint on his behalf in the consumer court and fight for his cause."

(A) Helps the consumer to file their complaints in the concerned consumer courts.
(B) Publishes periodicals to impart knowledge.
(C) Educates the general public about the issues related with consumer interests.
(D) Carries out comparative tests of consumer products in the certified laboratories.

Ans. Option (A) is correct.

Explanation: The function of NGO is to help the consumers to file a complaint in appropriate consumer courts on behalf of the consumers.

2. Which of the following function of NGO is highlighted in the below mentioned lines: "The three of them along with Suresh from the side of their NGO have launched a monthly magazine which creates awareness about the rights, reliefs and responsibilities of the consumers."

(A) Helps the consumer to file their complaints in the concerned consumer courts.
(B) Publishes periodicals to impart knowledge.
(C) Educates the general public about the issues related with consumer interests.
(D) Carries out comparative tests of consumer products in the certified laboratories.

Ans. Option (B) is correct.

Explanation: Publishing periodicals and other publications to impart knowledge about consumer problems, legal reporting, reliefs available and other matters of interest is a function of NGO.

3. Which of the following function of NGO is highlighted in the below mentioned lines: "Recently in the central part of the city they organised a training program in which all the information related to the exploitation of consumers, consumer ignorance, consumer rights and reliefs available to the consumers were the key highlights."

(A) Helps the consumer to file their complaints in the concerned consumer courts.
(B) Publishes periodicals to impart knowledge
(C) Educates the general public about the issues related with consumer interests.
(D) Carries out comparative tests of consumer products in the certified laboratories.

Ans. Option (C) is correct.

Explanation: Educating the general public about consumer rights by organising training programmes, seminars and workshops is a function of NGO.

4. Which of the following function of NGO is highlighted in the below mentioned lines: "The government laboratories are easily in touch with them and are ready for any type of confirmation of results related to the purity of products."

(A) Helps the consumer to file their complaints in the concerned consumer courts.

(B) Publishes periodicals to impart knowledge.

(C) Educates the general public about the issues related with consumer interests.

(D) Carries out comparative tests of consumer products in the certified laboratories.

Ans. Option (D) is correct.

Explanation: Carrying out comparative testing of consumer products in accredited laboratories to test relative qualities of competing brands and publishing the test results for the benefit of consumers is a function of NGO.

SOLUTIONS FOR PRACTICE QUESTIONS

SATQs-I

Ans 3. Importance of Consumer Protection from the point of view of business:

(i) Long-term interest of the business: In the competitive environment, the businessman can win and capture a **big share of the market** only through consumer satisfaction. Those who ignore the interest and satisfaction of consumers may loose their goodwill and clients.

(ii) Business uses society's resources: As a business uses social resources, it is bound to **serve the society** by using its resources through **adoption of fair trade practices** which ensures consumer protection.

(iii) Social responsibility: Just like other stakeholders, towards consumers also, businessmen have got **social responsibility to provide quality goods at reasonable prices.** Consumer protection guides businessmen to fulfil social responsibility towards consumers.

(iv) Government intervention: If businessmen want to avoid intervention of Government, then they should **not involve in unfair trade practices** and exploitative practices towards consumers.

(v) Moral justification: Business ethics advocates adoption of moral principles in **conducting business affairs.** A business is required to adopt consumer protection as its moral duty. **(Any two) [1½ × 2 = 3]**

Commonly Made Error

⚠ The students write the importance from the point of view of consumers instead of that of a business.

Answering Tip

Read the question properly and keep the perspective in mind while answering the question correctly.

LATQs

Ans 5. The three tier machinery under the Consumer Protection Act for redressal of consumers grievances consists of:

(i) District Commission: The District Commission consists of a **President and two other members, one of whom should be a woman.** They all are appointed by the State Government concerned. A complaint can be made to the appropriate District Commission when the value of the goods or services in question, along with the compensation claimed, does not exceed **₹ 1 crore.** On receiving the complaint, the District Commission shall refer the complaint to the party against whom the complaint is filed. If required, the goods or a sample thereof, shall be sent for testing in a laboratory. The District Commission shall pass an order after considering the test report from the laboratory and hearing the party against whom the complaint is filed. In case the aggrieved party is not satisfied with the order of the District Commission, he can appeal before the State Commission within 45 days of the passing of the order.

(ii) State Commission: Each State Commission consists of a **President and not less than four other members,** one of whom should be a woman. They are appointed by the State Government concerned. A complaint can be made to the appropriate State Commission when the value of the goods or services in question, along with the compensation claimed, exceeds **₹ 1 crore but does not exceed ₹ 10 crores.** The appeals against the orders of a District Commission can also be filed before the State Commission. On receiving the complaint, the State Commission shall refer the complaint to the party against whom the complaint is filed. If required, the goods or a sample thereof, shall be sent for testing in a laboratory. The State Commission shall pass an order after considering the test report from the laboratory and hearing the party against whom the complaint is filed. In case the aggrieved party is not satisfied with the order of the State Commission, he can appeal before the National Commission within 30 days of the passing of the order.

(iii) National Commission: The National Commission consists of a **President and at least four other members, one of whom should be a woman.** They are appointed by the Central Government. A complaint can be made to the National Commission when the value of the goods or services in question, along with the **compensation claimed, exceeds ₹ 10 crores.** The appeals against the orders of a State Commission can also be filed before the National Commission. On receiving the complaint, the National Commission shall refer the complaint to the party against whom the complaint is filed. If required, the goods or a sample thereof, shall be sent for testing in a laboratory. The National Commission shall pass an order after considering the test report from the laboratory and hearing the party against whom the complaint is filed. **[2 × 3 = 6]**

These Questions are for practice and their solutions are given at the end of the chapter.

SOLUTIONS FOR OBJECTIVE PRACTICE QUESTIONS

[A] MCQs

Ans 2. Option (D) is correct.

Explanation: It is the right of the consumers to be protected against goods and services which are hazardous to health or life. For example, defective vehicles could lead to serious accidents. The same is true of electrical appliances with sub-standard material.

Ans 3. Option (B) is correct.

Explanation: The right to be informed is an important component of consumer protection. The consumer must be provided with adequate and accurate information about quality, quantity, purity, standard and the price of the goods and services. Such information helps the consumers in their buying decision and use of the product.

[B] A & R

Ans 1. Option (A) is correct.

Explanation: According to this right, the consumer has the right to represent him or to be heard or right to advocate his interest. In case a consumer has been exploited or has any complaint against the product or service then he has the right to be heard and be assured that his/her interest would receive due consideration. Under this right the companies must have complaint cells to attend the complaints of customers.

Ans 4. Option (A) is correct.

Explanation: To put a stop to adulteration and corrupt practices of the manufacturers and traders, it is the duty of every consumer to be conscious of the quality of product they buy. They should look for the standard quality certification marks like ISI, Agmark, FPO, Woolmark, Eco-mark, Hallmark, etc. while making the purchases.

REFLECTION

(a) Were you able to give the meaning of consumer as per Consumer Protection Act, 2019?
(b) Have you understood the concept of consumer protection?
(c) Could you describe the importance of consumer protection from consumer's and business point of view?
(d) Could you discuss the scope of Consumer Protection Act, 2019?
(e) Could you identify the right of consumer in the below mentioned line:
"The consumer must be provided with adequate and accurate information about quality, quantity, purity, standard and the price of the goods and services."
(f) Have you understood the rights of consumers granted by Consumer Protection Act, 2019.
(g) Are you aware about the responsibilities of a consumers?
(h) Are you aware about the reliefs and remedies available to consumer under Consumer Protection Act, 2019?
(i) Do you know who can file a complaint and against whom?
(j) Were you able to discuss the legal redressal machinery under Consumer Protection Act, 2019?
(k) Could you describe the role of Consumer Organisations and NGOs in protecting the interests of consumers?

SELF ASSESSMENT PAPER - 12

Maximum Time: 1 hour **MM: 30**

General Instructions:

(i) All the questions are compulsory
(ii) Q.1 to Q.10 are 1 mark questions
(iii) Q.11 to Q.12 are 3 mark questions
(iv) Q.13 to Q.14 are 4 marks questions
(v) Q.15 is a 6 marks question

Objective Type Questions [1 Mark]

1. Which of the following is an importance of consumer protection from business point of view?
   (A) Social Responsibility
   (B) Moral Justification
   (C) Government Intervention
   (D) All of these **[1]**

2. Under district commission, complaints can be filed if value of goods and services:
   (A) Exceed ₹1 crore. **(B)** Up to ₹1 crore.
   (C) Exceed ₹10 crores. **(D)** None of these **[1]**

3. The Consumer Protection Act, 2019 replaces the:
   (A) Consumer Protection Act, 1968
   (B) Consumer Protection Act, 1986
   (C) Consumer Protection Act, 1989
   (D) Consumer Protection Act, 1998 **[1]**

4. Which of the following is the role of consumer organisation and NGO to protect the interest of consumers?
   (A) Publishing periodicals and other publications to impart knowledge about consumer problems.
   (B) Providing legal assistance to consumers.
   (C) To protest against unscrupulous sellers.
   (D) All of the above. **[1]**

5. For the following two statements, choose the correct option:
   Statement I: Under National Commission complaints can be filed if value of goods and services is more than ₹ 10 crores.
   Statement II: Aggrieved party if unsatisfied with the jurisdiction of State Commission can file an appeal against the judgement in National Commission.
   Choose the correct option from options given below:
   (A) Statement I is correct and statement II is wrong.
   (B) Statement II is correct and statement I is wrong.
   (C) Both the statements are correct.
   (D) Both the statements are wrong. **[1]**

6. For the following two statements, choose the correct option:
   Statement I: Buy only standardised goods is a responsibility of a consumer.
   Statement II: The consumers must be aware of their rights and exercise them while buying goods and services.
   Choose the correct option from options given below:
   (A) Statement I is correct and statement II is wrong.
   (B) Statement II is correct and statement I is wrong.
   (C) Both the statements are correct.
   (D) Both the statements are wrong. **[1]**

Read the text given below and answer Q. 7-10 based on it.

Atul after his marriage, booked a flat through a private builder in Mumbai at the cost of ₹ 2 crores. As per the terms of the contract, the builder promised to provide him with all the basic and modern amenities such as continuous electric supply, CCTV camera, club facility, good quality of water, good security, etc. Although he was given the possession of the flat in time, the builder did not provide all the basic and common facilities which also included security having CCTV camera coverage for each floor. Atul kept complaining to the builder after possession of the flat for non-installation of CCTV camera and other common and basic amenities as promised at the time of agreement, but the builder kept assuring him that he will do the needful and he need not worry. After a month, Atul had to travel abroad, so he left his home to Airport with his flat duly locked. On Airport, he saw a cake shop. The cakes were packed in beautiful packaging. He bought some of them and ate it. After eating it, he realised something different in the smell of the cake and went on to enquire about the content of the cake. Then he came to know that the company produces both eggs and eggless cakes. It so happened that 500 cakes containing egg were packed in packaging having green signs. Atul who is a strict vegetarian ate it. On his questioning, one staff member agreed to the fault committed. After travelling, Atul has to return back home. But on his return, he found that his flat has been robbed and theft of ₹ 15,000 and Jewellery worth ₹ 20 Lakhs had taken place. He complained to the builder that had CCTV cameras been installed, it would have been a deterrent and the theft would not have been taken place. Also, CCTV would have ensured that no unwanted person would have entered the building. When Atul discussed this incident with his friend Vinay, who runs a consumer association, he advised him to file a case against the builder.

7. Which of the following right of consumer has Vinay advised Atul to exercise?
   (A) Right to be heard **(B)** Right to be protected
   (C) Right to be informed **(D)** None of these **[1]**

8. Which of the following right is violated by the cake company?
   (A) Right to be heard **(B)** Right to be protected
   (C) Right to be informed **(D)** None of these **[1]**

9. Which of the following is the role performed by consumer organisation?
   (A) To take an initiative in filing cases in consumer courts.
   (B) To carry out comparative testing of consumer products.

(C) To educate the general public about consumer rights.
(D) All of the above [1]

10. Under which of the following right of consumers, the consumer has a right to get relief in case the product or service falls short of his expectations.
(A) Right to be informed
(B) Right to be heard
(C) Right to seek redressal
(D) Right to be protected [1]

Short Answer Type Questions - I [3 Marks]

11. Loma is a popular electronic showroom which sells all kinds of electronic appliances. Reshma went to Loma showroom to purchase a washing machine which cost her for ₹ 20,000. However, when she confirmed the price of the washing machine form his friends and searched on the net, she found that the price of the washing machine it was ₹ 19,500. When she contacted the showroom owner, she was told that the prices of the washing machine model have come down and that the cash memo handed over to her also had the billing of ₹ 20,000. But at the time the model was introduced and the price of the model was ₹ 20,000 only.
(i) Which responsibility was fulfilled by the Reshma in the above case?
(ii) Which consumer right has been violated here?

12. Aryan is running an organisation which is beyond the control of government and the motive of the organisation is welfare of the consumers. One day Rita comes to his office and tells that her mother purchased a refrigerator two years back. She is no more and the refrigerator was purchased in her name. However, the warranty period of the refrigerator is still active. But the company is denying her the services. Aryan encouraged Rita to protest against the company and to file a complaint in appropriate consumer courts.
(i) Which type of organisation is being ran by Aryan? State two roles performed by Aryan mentioned in the above case.
(ii) Which consumer right of Rita has been violated here?

Short Answer Type Questions - II [4 Marks]

13. On her sister's wedding, Ramya decided to gift her gold earrings. When she shared her plan with her husband, he showed her an article in the daily national newspaper under the heading "Jago Grahak Jago." The campaign included details about the various aspects that people must consider before buying any gold jewellery. State any four responsibilities that Ramya must discharge as an aware consumer while buying her sister's wedding gift. U

14. Old Service Club organised a visit of its members to an Old Age Home to inculcate the habit of social work among them. The visit revealed that the living conditions of the inmates of the Old Age Home were not hygienic. So, the Club members decided to clean the premises. During their cleanliness drive, they realised that the Old Age Home also required pest control. But some of the inmates of the Old Age Home were reluctant for it because they believed that the pest control may create health problems for them. The Club, therefore, decided to provide ethical, safe and odourless pest control. They showed to the inmates of the Old Age Home a pamphlet of the proposed pest control product which promised easy, inexpensive and long-lasting pest control. The inmates happily agreed and the pest control was carried out. The effect of the pest control started wearing off after a fortnight. The Club contacted the pest control company which kept on postponing their visit. After waiting for a month, the Club filed a case in the consumer court. The consumer court was satisfied about the genuineness of the complaint and issued necessary directions to the pest control company. State any eight reliefs that might have been issued by the court.

Long Answer Type Questions [6 Marks]

15. Vipul after obtaining a degree in Business Administration, came to know about a small village located in Gujarat, where an initiative was started in the year 2000 to plant a tea tree every month. Till 2020, villagers have planted 3 million tea tree plants. This has turned the village into a harbour, as the planting of trees led to higher water levels. Vipul decided to visit the village to start a business unit, for the processing and marketing of tea tree into face gels, face mask, face oil, toners and other products. However, on visiting the village Vipul found that the villagers were suffering exploitation at the hands of local merchants who were engaged in unscrupulous, exploitative trade practices like hoarding and black marketing of food products and also selling unsafe and adulterated products to the villagers. After looking at their plight, instead of a business organisation, he decided to set up an organisation for the protection and promotion of the consumer interest of the villagers. State any five functions that the organisation established by Vipul will be performing.

ART INTEGRATION

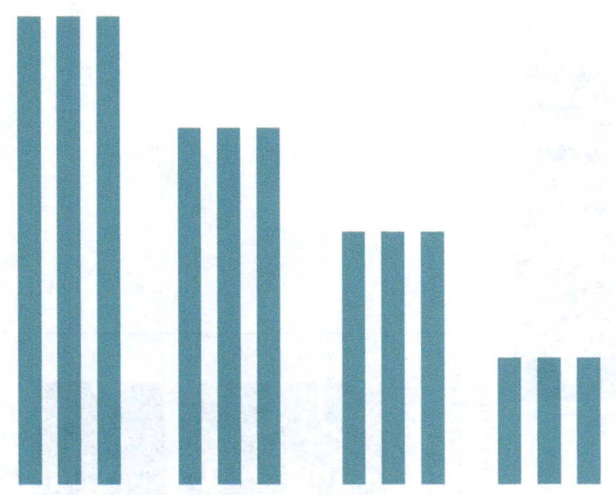

Chapter Covered	Staffing
Art Integrated	**Collage making**
Objective	1. Understand the concept of staffing 2. Relate concepts of staffing with our real world 3. Analyze real life situations to apply these concepts 4. Develop skills to relate different concepts of staffing with each other
Material Required	Chart Paper, Pictures/Newspaper cutting/Magazine cutting, Pencil, Sketch pens, and Glue stick
Methodology of activity	1. Collect Pictures/Images/Newspaper cutting/Magazine cutting or use Internet to browse scenes of movies like, Harry Porter or Avengers. 2. Relate these images with the different concepts of the chapter covered, like, manpower estimation, sources of recruitment, selection, importance of staffing, etc. 3. Paste different images on a chart paper in a collage form. 4. Write the concepts used in the form of conversation among different characters. 5. Place that on soft board and explain concepts used to the class. 6. Questions and answers will be discussed using real life situations.
Learning Outcomes	1. Students learn to develop the ability to connect different aspects with the real world. 2. Students improve their communication skills. 3. Students develop the skills of collage making.
Follow up activity	Student will be asked to prepare collage on other topics, like; process of controlling, concepts of planning, etc.

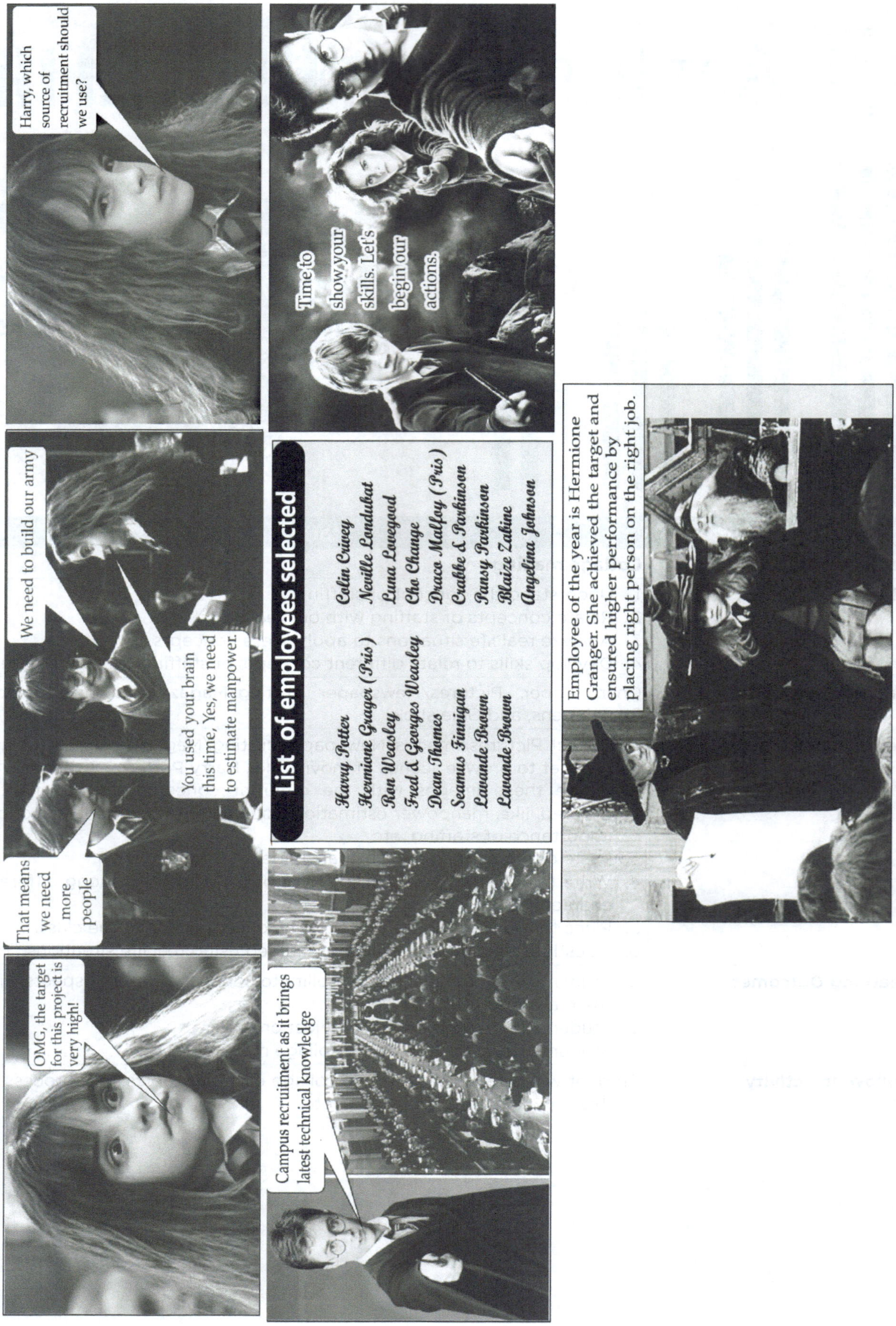

OMG, the target for this project is very high!

That means we need more people

We need to build our army

You used your brain this time, Yes, we need to estimate manpower.

Harry, which source of recruitment should we use?

Campus recruitment as it brings latest technical knowledge

List of employees selected

Harry Potter	*Colin Crivey*
Hermione Grager (Pris)	*Neville Londubat*
Ron Weasley	*Luna Lovegood*
Fred & Georges Weasley	*Cho Change*
Dean Thomes	*Draco Malfoy (Pris)*
Seamus Finnigan	*Crabbe & Parkinson*
Lavande Brown	*Pansy Parkinson*
Lavande Brown	*Blaize Zabine*
	Angelina Johnson

Time to show your skills. Let's begin our actions.

ART INTEGRATION

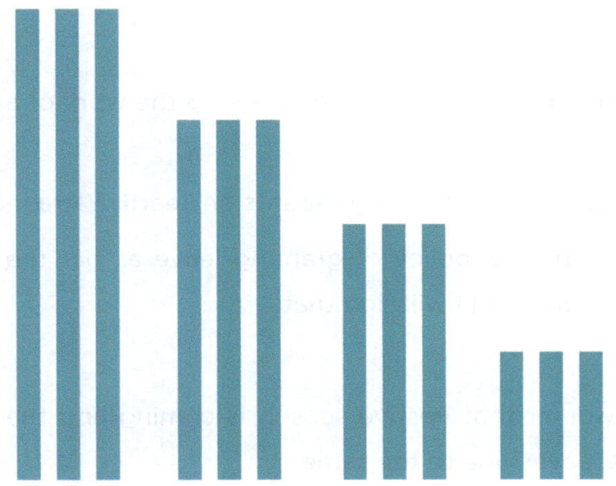

Chapter Covered	Directing
Topic covered	**Supervision and Motivation**
Art Integrated	**Role-play**
Objective	1. Understand the concept of directing 2. Understand the concept of elements of directing, viz., supervision and motivation 3. Understand the role of elements of directing 4. Understand the concept of role of financial incentives 5. Relate elements of directing with our real world 6. Have an idea about real work environment
Material Required	Stage, Costumes, Desks, Sewing Machine, Thread, Needle, Button, Patches, Pieces of Clothes. Some stitched clothes, Chairs, Desks, Items for manager's table, Audio and video aids.
Methodology of activity	1. Students will write a script including dialogue for all group Members. 3. Roles will be divided. 2. The students will perform different roles according to the script.
Learning Outcomes	1. Students learns to develop the ability to connect different aspects with the real world. 2. Students improve their communication skills. 3. Coordination and team-work will be improved. 4. Creativity will be enhanced.
Follow up activity	During the role-play, students will be closely observed by the teacher. Later, teacher will discuss the area of improvement with the students and measures to overcome them.

Role-play

The scene is a company. Few students will play the role of workers, manufacturing garments. Two students will play the role of Operative Managers. One student will play the role of Personnel Manager. 3-4 students will play the role of Board of Directors.

Company Name: XYZ Ltd.

Scene 1

Workers are manufacturing garments. One operating manager is on round and checking the work of a worker and another one is guiding how to paste a patch.

Ramesh (Worker): Sir, I want to take leave for five days as I want to take my Parents on Teerth Yatra.

Prashant (Operative Manager): Yes, you can take as we have a policy of granting leave as per the requirement of the workers. Just fill the leave application form and I will sign that.

Scene 2

After few days, Operative Manager is informing to all worker that Festive season is coming and the company received a big order. But workers want to take leaves due to the same.

Rahul (Operative Manager): Listen, there is a good news for us that due to ongoing festive season mainly Durga Puja, our company received a big order, which we need to complete by the end of this month.

Rashi (Worker): Sir, I want to take leave for 5 days as I want to go to my maternal home.

Rahul (Operative Manager): This time, we all have a pressure of work. How can I grant a leave?

Jeevan (Worker): Sir, I want to take leave for two days for festival preparation.

Brij (Worker): Sir, I also want to take leave for three days to get my house repaired and white-washed.

Prashant (Operative Manager): No, no leaves will be granted and we all have to do overtime to complete this order.

Scene 3

Meeting with Personnel Manager

Prashant and Rahul (Operative Managers): Sir, we have an issue to discuss. As you know that we recently got a new order and we don't have much time. But most of workers wants to take leaves due to Durga Puja.

Raghav (Personnel Manager): Due to festival, workers will definitely take leaves but we can motivate them to do overtime and complete their work before time. Also, we need to make sure that workers take limited leaves.

Raghav (Personnel Manager): I have an idea. We need to modify our incentive plan to motivate them. You both inform your team of workers about the changes in the incentive plan which states payment of double wages for working overtime and triple wages for working on holidays.

Scene 4

Informing workers about new incentive plan which makes workers to work overtime and even on holidays.

Scene 5

Board Meeting

Ritesh (one of the members of Board): Mr. Raghav, you completed the project very well. Our company has achieved higher output, met timely supplies without any confrontation with workers. What was the reason behind this?

Raghav (Personnel Manager): I just used a carrot with no sticks approach, i.e., I just motivate or stimulate them stimulating people to act to accomplish desired goals with the help of financial incentives.

ART INTEGRATION

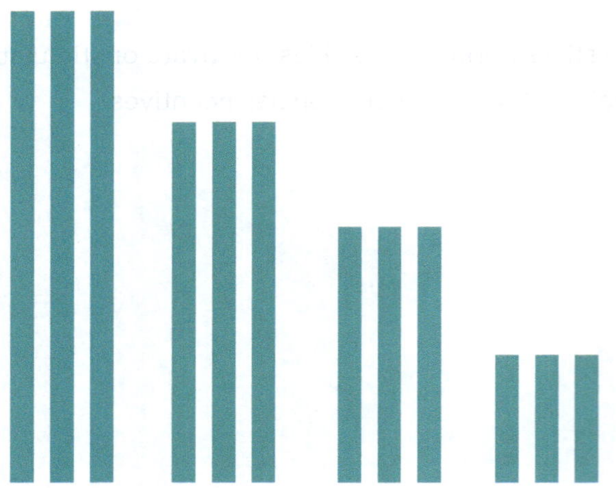

Chapter Covered	Consumer Protection
Topic covered	**Consumer Rights (Violation of rights)**
Art Integrated	**Sketching**
Objective	1. Understand the concept of consumer protection 2. Understand the importance of consumer protection 3. Relate the need of consumer protection with our real world
Material Required	Chart paper, pencil, eraser, etc.
Methodology of activity	1. Recap of consumer rights taught in the class. 2. Draw a sketch on violation of any of the consumer rights or implementation of consumer rights by a consumer or a consumer asking for bill as per consumer responsibility, etc.
Learning Outcomes	Students will become aware of consumer rights and be able to implement them in real life.

PRACTICE PAPER - 1

Maximum Time: 3 hour **MM: 80**

General Instructions:

(i) This question paper contains 34 questions.
(ii) Marks are indicated against each question.
(iii) Answers should be brief and to the point.
(iv) Answers to the questions carrying 3 marks may be from 50 to 75 words.
(v) Answers to the questions carrying 4 marks may be about 150 words.
(vi) Answers to the questions carrying 6 marks may be about 200 words.
(vii) Attempt all parts of the questions together.

SECTION – A

1. Cars Udyog Ltd. plans to manufacture solar cars in its new plant. It has an offer from Toyota for collaboration. What impact will the collaboration have on the requirement of fixed capital for Cars Udyog Ltd.? **[1]**

(A) Increase the requirement for fixed capital
(B) Decrease the requirement for fixed capital
(C) No change in fixed capital needed
(D) None of the above

2. Which product-related decision is concerned with providing detailed information about the product on its package?

(A) Branding
(B) Packaging
(C) Labelling
(D) Both branding and packaging **[1]**

3. Even though the political conditions vary from country to country, they impact the sentiment of an investor in the business, if the instability of the political conditions cause uncertainty and make it difficult for him to predict the future. Which feature of the business environment is being highlighted in the above statement? **[1]**

(A) Specific and general forces
(B) Dynamic nature
(C) Relativity
(D) All the above

4. Which of the following statement is incorrect about Personal Selling: **[1]**

(A) It is a direct face–to–face dialogue that involves an interactive relationship between the seller and the buyer.
(B) It refers to short-term incentives designed to encourage the buyers to make immediate purchase of a product or service.
(C) It allows a sales-person to develop personal relationship with the prospective customers.
(D) In this it is possible to take direct feedback from the customer and to adopt the presentation according to the needs of the prospects.

5. 'Rajni Auto Manufacturers have decided to give a special privilege to the existing shareholders to subscribe to the new issue of shares where they will be given shares according to the proportion of shares held by them. The company always gives special treatment to loyal stakeholders. Last year, the company was dealing through the capital market where both the buying and selling of securities were taking place. The owner of the company is a man of ethical business. He recently wrote an article about the watchdog of stock market. The article gained a lot of popularity and now is part of the curriculum of MBA students.

Which method of floatation was used by Rajni Auto Manufacturers? **[1]**

(A) Right issue **(B)** Private placement
(C) Offer for sale **(D)** E-IPOs

6.

Identify the function of management stated above. **[1]**

(A) Planning **(B)** Organising
(C) Staffing **(D)** Directing

7. .... is an institution or organisation, which holds securities in electronic form, in which trading is done. **[1]**

(A) Stock Exchange **(B)** SEBI
(C) Depository **(D)** None of these

8. The festive season was about to come. Mrs. Rubi, Head of Production department, called for a meeting of all the subordinates and communicated the objectives. Now she is establishing authority-responsibility relationship between superior and subordinates to avoid any delay.

.... function of management is stated in the above case. **[1]**

(A) Organising **(B)** Controlling
(C) Directing **(D)** Planning

9. Which of the following statement about Advertising is incorrect? **[1]**

(A) It is a personal form of communication.
(B) It is a paid form of communication.

(C) It is a mass selling technique.
(D) It is inflexible as the message can't be adjusted to the needs of the buyer.

10. Assertion (A): Management is responsible for setting and achieving objectives for the organisation.
Reason (R): The basic objective of any business is survival. **[1]**
(A) Both Assertion (A) and Reason (R) are true and Reason (R) is the correct explanation of Assertion (A).
(B) Both Assertion (A) and Reason (R) are true but Reason (R) is not the correct explanation of Assertion (A).
(C) Assertion (A) is true but Reason (R) is false.
(D) Assertion (A) is false but Reason (R) is true.

11. .... is the process of dividing work into manageable activities and then grouping the activities which are similar in nature. **[1]**
(A) Coordination
(B) Departmentalisation
(C) Organisation structure
(D) Delegation of authority

12. Identify an important principle of management control in which only significant deviations which go beyond the permissible limit should be brought to the notice of management. **[1]**
(A) Management by control
(B) Control by exception
(C) Critical point control
(D) Both (A) & (B)

13. For the following two statements, choose the correct option: **[1]**
Statement I: The production concept of marketing philosophy is applicable with convenience products.
Statement II: The product concept of marketing philosophy is applicable with speciality products.
(A) Statement I is correct and statement II is wrong.
(B) Statement II is correct and statement I is wrong.
(C) Both the statements are correct.
(D) Both the statements are wrong.

14. The name and taste of Coca-Cola is known to almost each and every individual in India as well as throughout the world. This carbonated soft drink holds the most market share in the soft drink market and got itself a special seat in each and every gathering. The Coca-Cola Company has on occasion introduced other cola drinks under the Coke name. The most common of these are Diet Coke, along with others including Caffeine free Coca-Cola, Diet Coke Caffeine free, Coca-Cola Zero Sugar, Coca-Cola Cherry, Coca-Cola Vanilla and the list goes on. It has capitalised on each and every opportunity to market itself effectively and place itself in the middle of every gathering. The main reason for such an outstanding placement of product goes to the way they have established the connection between every occasion and the need for Coke to be present there, product design and creative advertising.
Identify the feature of Business Environment which the Coca-Cola Company managed to get in their favour.
(A) Complex
(B) Specific and general forces
(C) Futuristic
(D) Mental exercise **[1]**

15. ____________________ organisation helps to fulfil the social needs of the members and allows them to find like-minded people. **[1]**
(A) Formal
(B) Informal
(C) Both (A) and (B)
(D) None of these

16. For the following two statements, choose the correct option: **[1]**
Statement I: Banks and financial markets are competing intermediaries in the financial system.
Statement II: Financial transactions could be in the form of creation of financial assets.
Choose the correct option from options given below:
(A) Statement I is correct and statement II is wrong.
(B) Statement II is correct and statement I is wrong.
(C) Both the statements are correct.
(D) Both the statements are wrong.

17. "Global stock indices have fallen on account of the pandemic."
The above statement DIRECTLY falls under which dimension of business environment? **[1]**
(A) Legal environment
(B) Social environment
(C) Economic environment
(D) Technological environment

18. Match the FUNCTIONS of Marketing in Column I with the appropriate ACTIVITIES in Column II. **[1]**

	Column I		Column II
(i)	Marketing Planning	**a**	Providing basis for distinguishing the product of a firm with that of the competitor.
(ii)	Product Designing and Development	**b**	Specifying the action programmes to achieve different objectives.
(iii)	Branding	**c**	Making the product attractive to the target customers.

(A) (i)-b, (ii)-a, (iii)-c **(B)** (i)-c, (ii)-a, (iii)-b
(C) (i)-a, (ii)-b, (iii)-c **(D)** (i)-b, (ii)-c, (iii)-a

19. Fredrick Winslow Taylor proposed which of the following style of management as opposed to rule of thumb:
(A) Planned management
(B) Scientific management
(C) Organised management
(D) Systematic management **[1]**

20. The sum total of all individuals, institutions and other forces that are outside the control of a business enterprise but that may affect its performance is known as _________ .

(A) Business environment
(B) Social environment
(C) Political environment
(D) Economic environment [1]

21. Monika, Rashmi and Garima are school friends. After completing their education Monika joined a school as a teacher. Rashmi joined a firm as a Chartered Accountant and Garima as a General Manager in a Multinational Company. After a long time in a re-union function of the school, they met each other. Rashmi said that they were all professionals now. Garima told Rashmi that she can say this about Monika and herself, but not about her since being a manager is not considered a full-fledged professional. Why did Garima say that she is not a professional? State any three points in support of your answer. **[3]**

22. Explain –
(i) Ensuring order and discipline, and
(ii) Facilitating co-ordination in action, as importance of controlling function of management. **[3]**

OR

Explain:
(i) Critical point control, and
(ii) Management by exception, as an important part of 'Analysing Deviations' **[3]**

23. Explain the two concepts which are a part of the exercise which would reveal whether a company is understaffed, overstaffed or optimally staffed. **[3]**

24. What is meant by 'Capital Market'? Name the two segments of Capital Market. **[3]**

OR

State any three protective functions of Securities and Exchange Board of India. **[3]**

25. Explain briefly how directing: **[4]**
(i) Attempts to get maximum out of the individuals
(ii) Brings stability and balance in the organisation.

OR

Explain the following characteristics of Directing: **[4]**
(i) Directing initiates action
(ii) Directing is pervasive

26. Explain the following methods of training. **[4]**
(a) Vestibule Training
(b) Apprenticeship Programme

OR

Explain the following as internal sources of recruitment. **[4]**
(a) Transfers
(b) Promotion

27. Mayank purchased a pack of chocolates of a renowned brand for his daughter from a shop in the nearby market. After consuming the chocolates, his daughter fell sick. He filed a case with the district forum against the renowned brand. He lost the case because of a mistake that he could not provide proof of purchase. What should be kept in mind by a consumer while purchasing, using and consuming goods and services apart from avoiding the mistake committed by Mayank, in order to enable him/her to achieve the objective of consumer protection? Enumerate any four points. **[4]**

28. Explain the following Factors affecting the requirement of working capital
(a) Business cycle
(b) Seasonal factors **[4]**

29. Identify and state the non-financial incentives used in the following cases:
(i) Fiza Ltd. try to keep the employees even after retirement as an advisor to the company.
(ii) The employees of Tina Ltd. get promotions easily or there is an increase in their status if they work well.
(iii) The management of Lokesh Enterprises is very friendly and take care of their employees very well.
(iv) Sana Housing does not only give promotions to their best employees but also help in developing new skills in them. **[4]**

30. A company was expecting a sale increase of 20% in comparison to the last year. However, due to poor support from the economic situations around the increase turned out to be only 10%. The company however had prepared itself for this situation. It knew how to change its expenses in financial case the sales increase goes down in comparison to the expectations. Identify the concept of financial management which is highlighted in the above case. What should have been the action taken by the company if the situation had been different like increase in revenue by 30%. **[4]**

31. (a) Explain the following techniques of scientific management: **[6]**
(i) Time study;
(ii) Motion study;
(iii) Functional foremanship.
(b) Difference between Scalar Chain and Order.

OR

(a) Explain the following principles of general management: **[6]**
(i) Division of work
(ii) Authority and responsibility
(iii) Discipline
(b) Explain briefly 'Initiative' and 'Esprit de Corps' as principles of general management.

32. 'Planning provides clear benefits to organizations, but planning can also harm organizations if is not implemented properly.' Explain the limitations of planning. **[6]**

OR

(a) Name and explain the type of plan which provides the broad contours of an organisation's business.
(b) Name and explain the type of plan which is in the form of general statements and channelise energies towards a particular direction. **[6]**

33. Read the statement given in point (i) and (ii) and answer the questions that follows:
(i) Sona has built a very big brand and now every customer needs the brand as created by Sona.

(a) Identify and explain the function of marketing that enables Sona to build a brand.

(b) State any two benefits that the marketer gets from the function.

(ii) The design of the product of Anupama Ltd. is very attractive and the consumer buys their product because of that.

(a) Identify and explain the function of marketing that enables to achieve the goal.

(b) Why do you think this function is important?

[3+3=6]

34. 'E-Solutions Ltd.' started its operations in the year 2000. At the time of its inception, the company had only 10 employees with two departments, a Production Department and an Administration Department. The products supplied and the services provided by the company started gaining popularity over the years. The management had faith in the abilities of the employees and thus they allowed them freedom of action. The management recognised that the decision-makers at different levels of the organisation need to be given more autonomy. They took a policy decision that there will be less control of superiors over subordinates. This increased the role of the subordinates in the organisation and now they were in a position to take numerous as well as important decisions. As a result, its business has diversified into many areas. Presently, it has its operations throughout the country with seven branches overseas. Its organisational structure has now changed into divisional structure and ten thousand people are working with the company.

(i) Identify the concept of management which helped the company to diversify into many areas and branches abroad.

(ii) Explain any five points of importance of the concept identified in (i) above. **[6]**

PRACTICE PAPER - 2

Maximum Time: 3 hour **MM: 80**

General Instructions:

(i) This question paper contains 34 questions.
(ii) Marks are indicated against each question.
(iii) Answers should be brief and to the point.
(iv) Answers to the questions carrying 3 marks may be from 50 to 75 words.
(v) Answers to the questions carrying 4 marks may be about 150 words.
(vi) Answers to the questions carrying 6 marks may be about 200 words.
(vii) Attempt all parts of the questions together.

SECTION – A

1. Mr. Raghav, finance manager of Manav Infra Tech Pvt. Ltd., prepared a detailed plan of financial needs of the firm in coming six months and the sources from where funds will be acquired to meet out these needs as company is planning to open a new branch in other states of India. Identify the financial concept discussed here:

(A) Business cycle
(B) Financial planning
(C) Capital structure
(D) Working capital **[1]**

2. Which of the following philosophy of marketing assumes that in the long run, an organisation can achieve its objective of maximisation of profit by identifying the needs of its buyers ?

(A) Selling **(B)** Marketing
(C) Product **(D)** Societal Marketing **[1]**

3. "It is very difficult to predict the changes of Business environment. As environment is changing very fast for example in IT, fashion industry frequent and fast changes are taking place."

Identify the feature of business environment being described above. **[1]**

(A) Complex **(B)** Inter-related
(C) Relative **(D)** Uncertain

4. If the company has enough funds and the management also wants to have greater control on the channel members, which channel of distribution should the company adopt? **[1]**

(A) Direct Level Channel
(B) Zero Level Channel
(C) Short channel of distribution
(D) All of these

5. Aman had 55 shares of Vani Ltd. He wanted to sell 30 shares, so he went for a specific market to sell them through online portal. He went for which of following markets? **[1]**

(A) Money market **(B)** Secondary market
(C) Primary market **(D)** None of these

6.

Identify the function of management stated above. **[1]**

(A) Planning **(B)** Organising
(C) Staffing **(D)** Directing

7. One of the functions of Securities and Exchange Board of India is 'promotion of fair practices and code of conduct in securities market'. Identify the category to which this function belongs. **[1]**

(A) Protective function
(B) Regulatory function
(C) Development function
(D) None of these

8. An important project at AMB consultants is running behind schedule by a month. This has upset their clients and might affect the reputation of the company in the long run. No managerial action like assigning more workers, equipment or giving overtime has been able to solve the problem. What managerial action may now be taken by the company to avoid such a situation from arising in the future? **[1]**

(A) Revise the schedule

(B) Assigning additional workers and equipment to the project

(C) Get permission for further overtime work

(D) Both (B) and (C)

9. "It also sells its products through various grocery stores so that the products are made available to customers at the right place, in the right quantity and at the right time."

Identify the element of marketing mix stated above.

(A) Product **(B)** Price

(C) Place **(D)** Promotion **[1]**

10. Read the following statements: Assertion (A) and Reason (R). Choose the correct alternative from those given below:

Assertion (A): Coordination begins at the planning stage and continues till controlling.

Reason (R): Coordination is a one-time process.

(A) Both Assertion (A) and Reason (R) are true and Reason (R) is the correct explanation of Assertion (A).

(B) Both Assertion (A) and Reason (R) are true but Reason (R) is not the correct explanation of Assertion (A).

(C) Assertion (A) is true but Reason (R) is false.

(D) Assertion (A) is false but Reason (R) is true. **[1]**

11. __________ explains the manner in which the decision-making responsibilities are divided among hierarchical levels.

(A) Organisational structure

(B) Span of Management

(C) Decentralisation

(D) Delegation **[1]**

12. Ram is the manager of a leading FMCG company. He is a very dedicated manager and looks after every deviation from the plan. Despite of being so vigilant, he was not appreciated by his seniors as he couldn't complete his goals on time. His senior explained him that instead of looking at each and every deviation, he should just focus on the important issues which would save his time.

What should be the 'focus point' for a manager while controlling, as controlling at each and every step is not possible?

(A) Special area **(B)** Key result area

(C) Normal area **(D)** None of these **[1]**

13. For the following two statements, choose the correct option:

Statement I: In selling, product's title is transferred from seller to buyer.

Statement II: The primary goal of marketing is to turn a product into cash.

(A) Statement I is correct and statement II is wrong.

(B) Statement II is correct and statement I is wrong.

(C) Both the statements are correct.

(D) Both the statements are wrong. **[1]**

14. KG Electrical Appliances, a company manufacturing bulb incurred heavy expenditure on scientific research and development and invented a technology that made it possible to produce an energy efficient bulb that can last at least 15 times longer than a standard LED bulb. This technology helped the company to increase its profitability and growth. Identify the significance of the business environment highlighted above.

(A) It helps in assisting and policy formulation.

(B) It helps in tapping useful resources.

(C) It helps in improving performance.

(D) It helps the firm to identify threats and early warning signals. **[1]**

15. The Purchase, Production and Sales Managers at Sharda Ltd., a firm manufacturing ready-made garments are generally at a conflict, as they have their own objectives. Usually, each think that only they are qualified to evaluate, judge and decide on any matter, according to their professional criteria. Identify the concept which will be required by the CEO Mr. Raman, to reconcile the differences in approach, interest or opinion in the organisation. **[1]**

(A) Delegation **(B)** Decentralisation

(C) Coordination **(D)** Controlling

16. For the following two statements, choose the correct option:

Statement I: Money market is a market where low risk, unsecured and long-term debt instruments that are highly liquid are traded.

Statement II: Money market has no physical location.

Choose the correct option from options given below:

(A) Statement I is correct and statement II is wrong.

(B) Statement II is correct and statement I is wrong.

(C) Both the statements are correct.

(D) Both the statements are wrong. **[1]**

17. Which of the following is a result of globalisation that has contributed to the rationalisation of tariff structures? **[1]**

(A) the formation of trade blocs

(B) increased competition among businesses

(C) enhanced ease of international business transactions

(D) governments facing pressure to reduce barriers to attract foreign investment

18. Match the tools of promotion mix in Column I with their respective examples in Column II. **[1]**

Column I	Column II
(a) Advertising	(i) Corporate giveaway items
(b) Sales Promotion	(ii) Charitable contributions
(c) Public Relations	(iii) In-store displays

(A) (iii), (i), (ii) **(B)** (ii), (i), (iii)

(C) (i), (ii), (iii) **(D)** (iii), (ii), (i)

19. The principles of management are significant because of : **[1]**

(A) Providing managers with useful insights into reality

(B) Optimum utilisation of resources and effective administration

(C) Meeting changing environment requirements

(D) All of the above **[1]**

20. "As the government has opened up its economy to Multinational Corporations, it has encouraged foreign companies to invest in some sectors of retailing." Identify which dimension of business environment is depicted here.

(A) Political environment

(B) Legal environment

(C) Technological environment

(D) Economic environment **[1]**

21. "Directing facilitates introduction of needed changes in the organization." Explain the statement. **[3]**

22. "Similar to being a system of motivation, a good control mechanism also allows for the maintenance of discipline within a business." In the light of this statement, explain how controlling helps in maintaining discipline. **[3]**

OR

"Controlling, like most other processes, is composed of a number of steps followed in sequential order. The first step is establishment of standards." Explain next two step of controlling process. **[3]**

23. Ali Mohammad the CEO of Super Ltd. believes that Human Resource is the most important asset of the firm. He believes that no organisation can be successful unless it can fill and keep filled the various positions provided for in the structure with the right kind of people. Identify the function of management being discussed above and state the benefits to the organisation that its proper application in the firm will ensure. **[3]**

24. 'Money Market is essentially a market for short term funds'. In the light of this statement, state any three features of Money Market. **[3]**

OR

Auxo Steels Ltd. has already issued shares in the stock market and is a well-known name among the people. Recently it issued shares but had to go through the proper audition process and thorough inspection about the various requirements to be fulfilled as an issuer. Identify and explain the type of function of SEBI mentioned in the above case. **[3]**

25. Explain briefly how directing:

(a) Facilitates change in the organisation

(b) Integrates the efforts of employees **[4]**

OR

Explain the following elements of directing:

(a) Motivation

(b) Leadership **[4]**

26. "External sources of recruitment are likely to strain the relations between management and the employees." Do you agree? Explain reason in support of your answer. **[4]**

OR

Name and define the process in which candidates are eliminated at every stage and few move on to the next stage till the right type of candidate is found. **[4]**

27. Grahak Shakti, an N.G.O. organised a workshop to discuss various issues relating to consumers. During the discussion, one of the members drew attention towards exploitation of consumers due to defective and unsafe products, adulteration, black marketing, hoarding etc. To this another member argued that consumers themselves are responsible as they do not raise collective voice against the exploitation. The Chairperson of the organisation was of the opinion that it was also the duty of the businessman to take care of the interests of various stakeholders. Business organisations earn money by selling goods and services to consumers. So, the interests of the stakeholders have to be well taken care of. State four points that highlight the need for consumer protection as discussed in Grahak Shakti's workshop **[4]**

28. Explain the following factors of affecting capital structure:

(i) Interest Coverage Ratio

(ii) Return on Investment **[4]**

29. Analyse the following scenarios and identify the specific barriers to effective communication in each case:

Scenario 1: During a team meeting, two team members from different status have different interpretations of a project's deadline. As a result, they end up working on different timelines, causing confusion and delays.

Scenario 2: In an email exchange between team members, one team member uses technical jargon and industry-specific terms that others may not fully understand. As a result, some team members misinterpret the message, leading to misunderstandings and misaligned tasks.

Scenario 3: A team member consistently interrupts others during team discussions, not allowing them to express their ideas fully. This behaviour leads to frustration among team members and limits open and constructive communication.

Scenario 4: During a virtual team meeting, poor internet connectivity causes frequent disruptions and audio glitches. As a result, some team members miss crucial information, and the overall meeting efficiency is reduced. **[4]**

30. Somnath Ltd. is engaged in the business of export of garments. In the past, the performance of the company had been up to the expectations. In line with the latest technology, the company decided to upgrade its machinery. For this the Finance Manager, Dalmia estimated the amount of funds required and the timings. This will help the company in linking the investment and the financial decisions on a continuous basis. Dalmia therefore, began with the preparation of a sales forecast for the next four years. He also collected the relevant data about the profit estimates in the coming years. By doing this he wanted to be sure about the availability of funds from the internal sources of the business. For the remaining funds he is trying to find out alternative sources from outside.

Identify the financial concept discussed in the above para. Also, state the objectives to be achieved by the use of financial concept, so identified. **[4]**

31. **(i)** Explain any two techniques out of the following:

(a) Functional foremanship

(b) Standardisation

(c) Piece wage system

(ii) How is the principles of equity different from the principle of Remuneration? **[6]**

OR

(i) Explain any two principles:

(a) Order

(b) Initiative

(c) Espirit De corps

(ii) Differentiate between time study and motion study. **[6]**

32. Why is planning considered an important activity for a business enterprise? **[6]**

OR

Explain the following types of plans:

(i) Objective (ii) Programme (iii) Procedure **[6]**

33. Read the statements given in point 1 and 2, answer the questions that follow:

1. Ashima purchased a bottle of tomato sauce from a local grocery shop. The information provided on the bottle was not clear. She fell sick on consuming it. She filed a case in the District Forum under Consumer Protection Act and got the relief.

(i) Identify the important aspect neglected by the marketer in the above case.

(ii) Explain briefly any two functions of the aspect identified in (i) above.

2. Shivam bought a pain-relieving ointment after seeing it being displayed in the chemist's shop. The ointment tube was packed in a cardboard box. The tubes were received by the chemist from the wholesaler in corrugated boxes containing 20 units.

(i) Identify the function of marketing stated above.

(ii) Identify and explain the different levels of the functions identified in (i) above. **[3+3=6]**

34. Atul joins as a Head Librarian of a newly constructed MBA college in Delhi. A team of four librarians is placed under him for the smooth functioning of the library. Besides, he has been assigned eight people as support service staff. On the second day of his joining, he is told to get a shipment of new books unloaded, stock the bookshelves, and then get all waste (packaging, paper etc.) disposed of within a weeks' time. In order to ensure orderliness and speed in the process of setting up of the library, he makes each of the four librarians in charge of five different subjects. Keeping in mind their competence and experience he decides to give them more authority so that they can make autonomous plans and assume the responsibility for the effective implementation of their decisions.

In context of the above case:

(i) Identify and explain the concept used by Atul keeping in mind the competence and experience of the other librarians.

(ii) Describe briefly any four points of importance of using the concept as identified in part (i) of the question. **[6]**

WRITING YOUR NOTES

Just in case you have forgotten today, takedown your notes!
But why is it so important?

Tools for the hands are tools for the brain writes Hetty Roessingh.
Handwritten notes are a powerful tool for encrypting embodied cognition and in turn supporting the brain's capacity for recuperation of information. If that sounds so scientific then in simple words: Writing notes by hand help you in:

◆ Increasing your comprehension ◆◆ Strengthening your memory Igniting your creativity
◆ Engaging your mind ◆ Increasing your attention span

Are these reasons enough to get you started?

1. ....
2. ....
3. ....
4. ....
5. ....
6. ....
7. ....
8. ....
9. ....
10. ....
11. ....
12. ....
13. ....
14. ....
15. ....
16. ....
17. ....
18. ....
19. ....
20. ....